Handbook of Self-Concept

Handbook of Self-Concept

Developmental, Social, and Clinical Considerations

Edited by
Bruce A. Bracken, PhD

JOHN WILEY & SONS, INC.

New York • Chichester • Brisbane • Toronto • Singapore

Copyright © 1996 by John Wiley & Sons, Inc.

Library of Congress Cataloging-in-Publication Data:

Handbook of self-concept : developmental, social, and clinical
    considerations / Bruce A. Bracken, editor.
        p.   cm.
    Includes index.
    ISBN 0-471-59939-5 (cloth : alk. paper)
    1. Self-perception.   I. Bracken, Bruce A.   II. Series.
    BF697.5.S43H363   1996
    155.2—dc20   95-15681

Printed in the United States of America

10 9 8 7 6 5 4 3 2 1

To Mary Jo Bracken, my loving wife

and

To my son, Bruce A. Bracken, Jr., of whom I am most proud

Contributors

Thomas J. Berndt, PhD
Professor, Department of
   Psychological Sciences
Purdue University
West Lafayette, Indiana

Bruce A. Bracken, PhD
Professor, Department of Psychology
The University of Memphis
Memphis, Tennessee

Leah Burgy, MS
Doctoral Candidate
Purdue University
Department of Psychological
   Sciences
West Lafayette, Indiana

Barbara M. Byrne, PhD
Professor
School of Psychology
University of Ottawa
Ottawa, Ontario, Canada

Ana Mari Cauce, PhD
Director, Clinical Training
Department of Psychology
University of Washington
Seattle, Washington

R. Michelle Crain, MA
Doctoral Candidate
Department of Psychology
The University of Memphis
Memphis, Tennessee

Candice Feiring, PhD
Professor of Pediatrics
Institute for the Study of Child
   Development
Robert Wood Johnson Medical School
New Brunswick, New Jersey

Kwai Grove, MS
Doctoral Candidate
Department of Psychology
University of Washington
Seattle, Washington

Susan Harter, PhD
Professor, Department of Psychology
University of Denver
Denver, Colorado

John Hattie, PhD
Professor, Department of Educational
   Research Methodology
School of Education
The University of North Carolina
Greensboro, North Carolina

Lori K. Keith, MS
Doctoral Candidate
Department of Psychology
The University of Memphis
Memphis, Tennessee

Herbert W. Marsh, PhD
Professor
School of Education
University of Western Sydney
Campbelltown, New South Wales
Australia

Natalie Novick, PhD
Postdoctoral Fellow
Department of Psychiatry &
  Behavioral Science
University of Washington
Seattle, Washington

H. Thompson Prout, PhD
Professor, Department of Human
  Services & Studies
Florida State University
Tallahassee, Florida

Susan M. Prout, MA
School Psychologist
Leon County Schools
Tallahassee, Florida

Risa J. Stein, PhD
Private Practitioner
Wilford Hall Medical Center
Lackland Air Force Base, Texas

Lynn S. Taska, PhD
Assistant Professor of Pediatrics
Institute for the Study of Child
  Development
Robert Wood Johnson Medical
  School
New Brunswick, New Jersey

Preface

During the 100 years since William James first began expressing his thoughts about the "self" in the 1890s, an incredible amount of information has been written about self-concept as an important psychological construct. In just the past 15 years, more than 11,000 articles have been identified in the PsychINFO database that cite self-concept or self-esteem as key descriptors.

Regularly, throughout this volume the reader will see historical references to William James's thoughts on self-concept and the self, as well as references to the ideas of others who have left their indelible marks on the field (e.g., Cooley's "looking-glass self"). Another important person in the field is Ruth Wylie, who contributed diligently to the self-concept literature during the 1970s and 1980s, especially in her perceptive critiques of the self-concept research and instrumentation.

Despite the hundreds of "project-developed" self-concept scales that flourished between the 1950s and 1980s, a relatively small number of individual test authors (e.g., Rosenberg, Coopersmith, Piers, Fitts) have made long-lasting contributions of significance. The principal accomplishment by each of these early psychometrists was the development of a standardized protocol for measuring self-concept. These instruments served as dependent and independent measures in self-concept research in thousands of studies and as clinical measures in thousands of schools, clinics, and hospitals. Because of measurement and theoretical problems, however, these first-generation instruments often fell short in clinical practice and yielded conflicting findings in research. Second-generation self-concept scales have improved the quality of instrumentation immeasurably for research and clinical applications.

Once the first-generation self-concept instruments were available for public consumption, the theoretical treatment of self-concept as a psychological construct began to stagnate. Lifting self-concept out of its lassitude, Richard Shavelson and his colleagues (Shavelson, Hubner, & Stanton, 1976) published their seminal article lamenting the inconsistencies in self-concept definitions, instrumentation, and research findings. In an effort to unify self-concept treatment and instrument development, Shavelson et al. suggested seven definitional characteristics of the construct: (a) theoretical organization, (b) multifaceted nature, (c) hierarchical structure, (d) stability, (e) developmental nature, (f) evaluative underpinnings, and (g) differentiality from other constructs. From this theoretical treatment of self-concept, consensus began to emerge about the nature of the construct. For example, the early conceptualization of self-concept as a unitary construct gave way to its current multidimensional representation. Also, the development of second-generation instruments and the revision of existing first-generation self-concept scales began to reflect more consistently the theoretical influences of the Shavelson et al. definitional characteristics. Since the Shavelson et al. article was published, researchers have focused additional attention and placed greater value on the psychometric properties of self-concept scales. The field has grudgingly accepted that it can no longer tolerate the use of project-developed self-concept scales or of scales that have not been normed or were normed on nonrepresentative samples from single communities, states, or regions of the United States. Shavelson and his colleagues brought the field to a point where real advances in construct refinement could be made.

Although there is agreement about many important definitional characteristics of self-concept, a number of issues related to the construct have not yet been resolved. What is the self, for example? Is self-concept part of a larger cognitive "self-system," or is the self better defined in behavioral terms? How useful is self-concept in clinical practice? What future research questions should be asked about self-concept? Are there meaningful age, race, or gender differences in self-concept? These and many other questions will be more easily addressed now that there is more consensus on what self-concept is and what it is not. These issues and many more are discussed throughout the chapters in this book.

A reasonable treatment of a topic will not provide all the answers to important questions; it should, however, answer some questions and identify even more questions to be taken up in future research. So it is with the *Handbook of Self-Concept*. This volume provides some fairly definitive answers about self-concept; it proposes additional positions for which there is little dispute; it presents many hypotheses that are still very much being debated; and, importantly, it poses several questions that will guide research and thought well into the future.

The 12 chapters in this book have been organized to facilitate the reader's understanding of the construct. Chapter 1 (Harter) develops a thorough historical perspective on self-concept, from the earliest writings to present thoughts on the subject. Chapter 2 (Marsh and Hattie) leads the reader to a clear understanding that current thoughts on self-concept are of a multidimensional nature. Chapter 3 (Keith and Bracken) recognizes the need for sound instrumentation and provides the reader with a comprehensive evaluation of existing self-concept scales. Chapters 4 through 9 address six important and primary self-concept domains that contribute to multidimensional self-concept (social, Berndt and Burgy; competence, Novick, Cauce, and Grove; affect, Prout and Prout; academic, Byrne; family, Feiring and Taska; and, physical, Stein). These chapters explore what makes individual context-domains distinct, and why each domain is important for consideration and measurement. In Chapter 10, Crain discusses the influences of age, race, and gender on the development of children's self-concepts. Hattie and Marsh present pressing issues for future self-concept research in Chapter 11. Finally, Chapter 12 (Bracken) discusses the value of self-concept in clinical practice and describes a process for synthesizing information across instruments and informants according to a multidimensional, context-dependent model of self-concept.

This book provides a thorough and diverse treatment of self-concept as a theoretical and applied construct. As editor, I sought to minimize the overlap among chapters, facilitate the transition between chapters, and maximize the content within chapters. The authors in this endeavor were all selected because of their individual contributions to the field. They have approached the topic from a variety of professional affiliations (e.g., developmental, school, clinical, educational psychology) and theoretical orientations (e.g., cognitive, behavioral, systems approach). As a result of the authors' knowledge and diverse orientations, the reader will be exposed to a comprehensive, yet integrated body of knowledge about a historically important topic. I hope this book will encourage the pursuit of self-concept as an area of study and will serve as a catalyst for continued refinement of self-concept as one of psychology's most important constructs.

BRUCE A. BRACKEN

Memphis, Tennessee
October, 1995

Acknowledgments

I would like to express my appreciation for the contributions made by several others toward the completion and quality of this book. I would like to thank Herb Reich, Senior Editor at Wiley, for his helpful suggestions and assistance throughout this project. Also, I would like to commend and thank Nancy Marcus Land, of Publications Development Company, for her diligent attention to details, great and small, during the production phase of the book. My personal thanks are extended to my doctoral student, Janet Panter, for her careful indexing of the book's many subjects and authors. Finally, I am very grateful to the University of Memphis Department of Psychology, a Tennessee designated Center of Excellence, which has allowed me the time, resources, and support to pursue my scholarly works.

Contents

Handbook of Self-Concept

CHAPTER 1

Historical Roots of Contemporary Issues Involving Self-Concept

SUSAN HARTER

Although the history of the study of the self can be traced back to ancient Greek philosophy, as revealed in the injunction "know thyself," contemporary scholars of the self-concept typically pay major intellectual homage to James (1890, 1892) and to such symbolic interactionists as Cooley (1903) and Mead (1934). The reader interested in the history of the self prior to the turn of the century is referred to excellent treatments by Baumeister (1987), Broughton (1987), and Logan (1987). The present chapter first presents the historical contributions of James and the symbolic interactionists as a general conceptual backdrop for the consideration of more contemporary issues including (a) the viability of the distinction between the I-self and the Me-self, (b) global versus multidimensional models of self, (c) discrepancies between the real and ideal self-concepts, (d) social sources of self-evaluation, (e) multiple selves versus a unified self, (f) true versus false selves, and (g) cognitive, affective, and behavioral components of the self-concept. The specific historical roots of each issue will be traced.

THE LEGACY OF WILLIAM JAMES

The contributions of James (1890, 1892) were legion. Of paramount importance was the distinction he first articulated between two fundamental aspects of the self, the "I" and the "Me," the self as subject and the self as object. For James, the I was the knower, in contrast to the Me, which represented an empirical aggregate of things objectively known about the self. It is the Me that came to be labeled the self-concept and that has received major attention in the field of self psychology. For James, however, it was essential to posit an I-self, the knower, the active agent responsible for constructing the Me-self. The self as knower was viewed as the *subjective* self because it organized and interpreted one's experiences. The Me was

1

viewed as the objective or empirical self to the extent that it was the *object* of the I-self's creation. For James, the I-self also demonstrated more specific types of awareness, for example, a concern with one's personal continuity through time, and an awareness of the uniqueness of one's life experiences leading to the distinctness of oneself as a person.

James (1890) further developed the concept of the Me-self, which he defined as the sum total of all a person can call his or her own. This total could be subdivided into what he termed the "constituents" of the self-as-known. The three major constituents were the *material* self, the *social* self, and the *spiritual* self. Under the material self, James subsumed both the bodily self as well as one's possessions, all that one can call "mine." The social self consisted of those characteristics of the self recognized by others. Given the potential diversity of others' opinions, James wisely concluded, "A man has as many social selves as there are individuals who recognize him and carry an image of him in their mind" (p. 190). The spiritual self was defined quite broadly, as an inner self comprising the individual's thoughts, dispositions, moral judgments, and so on, which he considered to be the more enduring aspects of the self.

James sought not only to dimensionalize the self but to impose a hierarchical structure onto its constituents that he felt was common across individuals. At the bottom of the hierarchy is the material self, which is required as a basis for all other selves. The social self occupies the next position, given his assumption that we should care more about friends, human ties, and honor among others than about our bodies or wealth. The spiritual self occupies the highest tier. James (1890) noted that the spiritual self is "so supremely precious that, rather than lose it, a man ought to be willing to give up friends and good fame, and property, and life itself" (p. 203). In so doing, James paved the way for future models in which the self is viewed as multidimensional and hierarchical.

In differentiating various aspects of the self, and in observing that there exists a multiplicity of views concerning the social self, James (1890) introduced the notion that these multiple selves may not all speak with the same voice. In documenting this multiplicity, James observed, "Many a youth who is demure enough before his parents and teachers, swears and swaggers like a pirate among his tough young friends" (p. 169). James further noted that this multiplicity can be harmonious, as in the case where a man who is tender to his children is also stern to the soldiers under his command. Alternatively, there may be a "discordant splitting" if the individual is afraid to let one group of acquaintances witness his or her behavior in a different setting.

For James (1890), what he termed the "conflict of the different Me's" could also be observed in the incompatibility of potential roles a person might wish to adopt in adulthood. James, himself, had fantasized about his own desires to be handsome, athletic, rich, witty, a bon vivant, lady-killer, philosopher, philanthropist, statesman, warrior, African explorer, as well as a tone-poet and a saint! He knowingly concluded that since all these roles could not possibly coexist in the same person, it was necessary to choose selectively, suppressing the alternatives. Thus, "The seeker of his truest, strongest, deepest self must review the list carefully, and pick out the one on which to stake his salvation" (p. 174).

The repudiation of particular attributes or roles was not, for James, necessarily damaging to a person's overall sense of worth, the "average tone of self-feeling which each one of us carries about" (p. 171). His own deficiency at Greek led to no sense of humiliation since he had no *pretensions* to be proficient at Greek. The role of pretensions became paramount in James' formulation of the causes of a person's level of self-esteem. Self-esteem could not simply be reduced to the aggregate of perceived successes in life. Rather, self-esteem represented a ratio of successes to *pretensions.* Thus, if the individual's perceived successes were equal to or greater than his or her pretensions or aspirations for success, high self-esteem would result. Conversely, if pretensions exceeded successes, that is, if the person were unsuccessful in domains in which there were aspirations, he or she would experience low self-esteem. Critical to this formulation is the assumption that lack of success in an area in which the person does *not* have pretensions (e.g., Greek for James) will not erode self-esteem, because it is deemed unimportant and can therefore be discounted. Thus, both the presence and absence of pretensions figured heavily in James' theorizing. He argued that abandoning certain pretensions can be as much a relief as striving to meet such goals: "How pleasant is the day when we give up striving to be young" (1890, p. 201).

In James, therefore, we find many themes that anticipate contemporary concerns and issues about the self. These include the distinction between I- and Me-selves, a multidimensional, hierarchical view of the Me-self, the potential conflict between different Me-selves, and a formulation concerning the causes of the individual's level of self-esteem, based on the ratio of successes to pretensions. Each of these issues is alive and well today, as we shall come to observe.

THE CONTRIBUTION OF THE
SYMBOLIC INTERACTIONISTS

In contrast to James, the symbolic interactionists placed heavy emphasis on how the individual's social interactions with others profoundly shaped the self. Thus, for scholars such as Cooley (1902) and Mead (1925, 1934), the self is considered to be primarily a *social construction,* crafted through linguistic exchanges (symbolic interactions) with others.

Cooley's postulation of the "looking-glass self," was perhaps the most metaphorical. In his now-famous couplet, he observed:

> Each to each a looking glass
> Reflects the other that doth pass.

For Cooley, significant others constituted a social mirror into which the individual would gaze to detect their opinions toward the self. These opinions, in turn, were incorporated into the sense of self. Cooley contended, therefore, that what becomes the self is what we imagine that others think of our appearance, motives, deeds, character, and so on. One comes to own these reflected appraisals. Such a "self-idea," in Cooley's terminology, comprised three components: (a) the imagination of our appearance to the other person; (b) the imagination of that person's judgment of that appearance; and (c) some sort of self-feeling, such as pride or shame.

Cooley noted, "The thing that moves us to pride and shame is not the mere mechanical reflection of ourselves, but an imputed sentiment, the imagined effect of this reflection upon another's mind" (1902, p. 153). Cooley was clear that this sentiment is initially social in nature, based on social custom and opinion, although it gradually becomes somewhat removed from these sources through an implied internalization process. Cooley wrote that the adult is

> not immediately dependent upon what others think; he has worked over his reflected self in his mind until it is a steadfast portion of his thought, an idea and conviction apart, in some measure, from its external origin. Here this sentiment requires time for its development and flourishes in mature age rather than in the open and growing period of youth. (p. 199)

Thus, the internalization of others' opinions about the self was a critical element in Cooley's thinking and paved the way for a more developmental perspective on how the attitudes of others are incorporated into the self. For Cooley, therefore, the more mature sense of self is not buffeted about by potentially transient or disparate views of significant others. As he observed, the person with ". . . balanced self-respect has stable ways of thinking about the image of self that cannot be upset by passing phases of praise or blame" (p. 201).

In Mead, we find an elaboration of the themes identified by Cooley, with an even greater insistence on the role of social interaction, particularly through the use of language. For Mead, "We appear as selves in our conduct insofar as we ourselves take the attitude that others take toward us. We take the role of what may be called the 'generalized' other. And in doing this we appear as social objects, as selves" (p. 270).

Mead (1925) also spoke to the issue of the origins of these attitudes in childhood. He postulated a two-stage developmental process through which the child adopted the attitudes of others toward the self, labeling these stages as the "play" and the "game." The play for Mead was the imitation of adult roles, which he documented in his description of the young child "continually acting as a parent, a teacher, a preacher, a grocery man, a policeman, a pirate, or an Indian" (p. 270). In the subsequent stage, characterized by games, there are proscribed procedures and rules:

The child must not only take the role of the other, as he does in the play, but he must assume the various roles of all the participants in the game and govern his actions accordingly. If he plays first base, it is as the one to whom the ball will be thrown from the field or from the catcher. Their organized reaction becomes what I have called the "generalized other" that accompanies and controls his conduct. And it is this generalized other in his experience which provides him with a self. (p. 271)

The concept of the generalized other, therefore, implies that the individual is reacting to more than a set of specific others with whom he or she is interacting in given situation. Rather, the person comes to adopt the perspective of a more generalized group of significant others who share a particular societal perspective on the self.

Mead's focus was primarily on the Me-self, defined more socially than the Me-self put forth by James; however, Mead also invoked the concept of an I-self. His I-self shares with the Jamesian "I" an emphasis on agency: "The I gives the sense of freedom, of initiative. . . ." (1934, p. 177) although it must act in consort with the Me-self.

In Cooley and Mead, therefore, we can identify a number of themes that find their way into contemporary treatments of the self. Paramount is the role of the opinions of others in shaping the self-concept, through social interaction. Here, the individual needs to consider not only feedback from specific significant others, but the process through which more generalized attitudes toward the self are adopted. Moreover, Cooley hints at a developmental internalization process whereby the reflected appraisals of others become incorporated in the form of relatively *enduring* attitudes about the self, a process that has implications for the stability of the self-concept. Finally, Cooley's contention that self-judgments are accompanied by self-*feelings,* ushers in a critical consideration of the role of affective processes in self-concept development. We next turn to an examination of the specific contemporary issues that have emerged from these and other historical roots.

IS THE DISTINCTION BETWEEN AN I-SELF AND A ME-SELF MEANINGFUL?

Historical scholars of the self, notably James and Mead, came to a similar conclusion, namely that two conceptually distinct but experientially intertwined aspects of the self can be meaningfully identified, the self as subject and the self as object. However, it behooves us to ask whether this distinction is still viable, and whether it enhances our understanding of the self-concept and its development.

More contemporary researchers have continued to make this distinction. Dickstein (1977), for example, has contrasted the "dynamic" self, that possesses a sense of personal agency, control, and power with the self as an object of knowledge and evaluation. For Dickstein, this distinction was applicable to children as well as adults. Lewis and Brooks-Gunn (1979), in setting the stage for their studies on the infant's acquisition of self, define this duality of selves in terms of its relevance for infancy. Thus, they make the distinction between the *existential* and the *categorical* self.

For Lewis and Brooks-Gunn, the task of the infant self as *subject* is to develop the realization that it is "existential" in the sense that it *exists* as separate from others. Self as *object* is referred to as the categorical self in that the infant must develop categories by which to define the self vis-à-vis the outside world. Thus the female infant must learn, for example, that she belongs to the category of baby or child, not adult, and that she is a girl, not a boy.

Wylie (1974, 1979) summarized the essence of these distinctions, contrasting the self as active agent or process with the self as the object of the individual's knowledge and evaluation. The I therefore, continues to be defined as the active observer, whereas the Me is the observed, the product of the process whereby attention is focused on the self. This distinction, therefore, has proved amazingly viable and appears as a recurrent theme in many theoretical treatments of the self. Empirically, however, major attention has been devoted to the study of the self as an object of the individual's knowledge and evaluation, as witnessed by the myriad number of studies on self-concept and self-esteem (see Wylie, 1961, 1974, 1979, as well as the current volume). Until recently, the self as subject, process, as active agent, has received far less attention (see also Damon & Hart, 1988).

The Me as a Theory about Self

There has been increasing focus on the view that the Me-self can be likened to a theory, which is constructed to organize the individual's thinking about his or her relationship to the social world (Brim, 1976; Epstein, 1973, 1983, 1991; Kelly, 1955; Sarbin, 1962). Kelly's (1955) theory of personal constructs represents one of the earliest such formulations. For Kelly, the self-system is hierarchically organized into core constructs— those by which a person maintains his or her identity and existence—and peripheral constructs that can be altered without serious modifications of the core structure. Self-constructs function as postulates in a theory that serves to organize and guide behavior. Brim (1976) took the analogy further. "What humans learn during life are axioms, concepts, and hypotheses about themselves in relation to the worlds around them. We can think of the sense of self as a personal epistemology, similar to theories in science in its components and its operations, but dealing with a specific person" (p. 242).

Among those initial proponents of the self as a theory, Epstein (1973) provided an even more elaborate analysis:

I submit that the self-concept is a self-theory. It is a theory that the individual has unwittingly constructed about himself as an experiencing, functioning individual, and is part of a broader theory which he holds with response to his entire range of significant experience. (p. 407)

Self-theory, in Epstein's view, possesses all the formal characteristics of a hypothetico-deductive system. It can be evaluated, therefore, by the degree to which it is extensive, parsimonious, empirically valid, internally consistent, testable, and useful. Epstein also viewed the self-theory as obeying an inherent growth principle because one characteristic of a good theory is to increase in scope with exposure to new data.

The Role of the I-Self

The view that the self is a theory that is constructed by the individual makes it critical, therefore, that we attend to characteristics of the I-self, since it is the I-self that creates or constructs the Me-self. For investigators to merely *describe* the self-theory or the self-concept, as a function of age, gender, ethnicity, social group, and so on is to miss the very processes through which it comes to be constructed. These issues are particularly critical when considering the emergence of the self-concept, during childhood and adolescence, from a cognitive-developmental perspective (see Harter, 1983).

From a Piagetian perspective, the self is an *epistemic subject,* the epitome of James's I-self (Beth & Piaget, 1966; Broughton, 1979). That is, Piaget equates the self with universalized cognitive activity, which, in turn, places emphasis on the I-self as knower. Thus, the I-self cognitively constructs the Me-self. However, a thoughtful application of the cognitive-developmental capabilities at each of Piaget's stages will make it apparent that the construction of a self-theory that would meet the criteria of Epstein and others would not be possible until well into late adolescence (see Harter, 1983, for a complete analysis). For example, the young preoperational child would not possess the cognitive capacity to logically order or hierarchically arrange the emerging categories that define the self. Nor could the young child empirically validate the rudimentary postulates of his or her self theory. Although older children may show some ability to develop limited hierarchies (e.g., I'm smart—a higher-order trait—because I am good at reading, math, and spelling—lower-order behavioral characteristics), they do not possess the ability to test more formal hypotheses in a systematic, deductive manner. Nor do these children have the cognitive capability to assess whether the postulates in their self-theory are internally consistent.

Thus, a careful consideration of the abilities as well as the *limitations* at each stage of cognitive development will reveal how the particular features of the I-self at each period necessarily dictate the very nature of the Me-self, the self-theory, that can be constructed. As a result, the self-theory will look very different at different developmental stages. Differences will be observed across numerous dimensions including complexity, differentiation, organization, coherence, abstractness, internal consistency, stability, empirical validation, and valence (see Harter, 1983, in press, for a specification of these changes). This type of developmental analysis appears promising, particularly when we consider the self as subject, as knower and theorist, to be a legitimate domain of psychological inquiry.

Such an analysis also has implications for the types of measuring instruments we construct to assess the self-concept. For the most part, self-concept questionnaires have not been terribly sensitive to developmental concerns. In our own life-span battery of self-concept instruments (see Harter, 1990b), we have taken into account that the number of domains which can be meaningfully differentiated increases with development. However, neither our measures nor the instruments of others in the field have yet captured the range of complexities with regard to how the self is constructed and organized at different developmental levels.

Information-Processing Models within the Adult Literature

We find a more cognitively oriented process approach among those psychologists who have adopted information-processing models of the self. Markus is a key figure in this literature (Markus, 1977, 1980; Markus & Herzog, 1991; Markus & Wurf, 1987; Oyserman & Markus, 1993). Markus has explicitly proposed that the individual's attempts to organize, summarize, or explain his or her own behavior will result in the formation of cognitive structures about the self that she terms *self-schemata:* "Self-schemata are cognitive generalizations about the self, derived from past experience, that organize and guide the processing of self-related information contained in the individual's social experience" (Markus, 1980, p. 64). She traces the historical roots of this particular term to the work of Barlett (1932), Kelly (1955), and Piaget (1965).

The self-schemata that Markus has focused on include traits such as independent versus dependent, sex-role schemata, and self-schemata involving creativity as well as body weight. Her experimental paradigm allows her to distinguish between adults with strong self-schemata and those she labels as "aschematics," people for whom a given dimension is not particularly relevant to their self-concept. She has demonstrated that those with well-articulated self-schemata for a particular trait or dimension can more readily process information about the self, retrieve behavioral evidence, predict their future behavior, resist counterschematic information about the self, and evaluate the relevance of new information, all with regard to that dimension.

Markus's self-schemata, which represent domain-specific knowledge structures, are similar to what Stryker (1987) has called salient identities, and what Russell, Cahill, and Spain (1992) have termed core conceptions.

Oyserman and Markus (1993) observe, "They form the coordinates of the individual's experiential world and the set of an individual's self-schemas represent the core of the self-concept" (p. 191). They go on to note that the individual plays an important agentic role in designing the self, and authoring a coherent self-narrative, consistent with a focus on the more specific functions of the Jamesian I-self.

A number of the functions articulated by James for establishing and preserving the distinctiveness of the self and the sense of agency, coherence, and continuity of the self over time have also been studied in infants (Stern, 1985) as well as children and adolescents (Damon & Hart, 1988; see also discussion by Oosterwegel & Oppenheimer, 1993). In these more recent efforts, therefore, increasing attention is being paid to the potential role of the self as knower, constructor, and agent at different points in the life span.

GLOBAL VERSUS DIFFERENTIATED MODELS OF SELF

As discussed earlier, James distinguished between three constituents of the self-system—material, social, and spiritual selves—which would seem to set the stage for a *multidimensional* model of the self. However, James also ushered in the concept of *global self-esteem,* in postulating that we possess a certain average tone of self-feeling. Cooley voiced a similar sentiment in postulating an overall sense of self-respect. Although the global and dimensional perspectives are not necessarily antithetical, theorists and researchers initially embraced the concept of global self-esteem. Coopersmith (1967) was a major proponent of the view that self-esteem is global in nature and that children, at least, do not differentiate among the domains of their life. Inadequacies in his methodology led to this erroneous conclusion (see Harter, 1983). Other investigators (e.g., Piers & Harris; Piers, 1977) began with the assumption that self-esteem was relatively undimensional. Their own empirical work, however, revealed that children do make different evaluative judgments across various domains, thereby leading them to later conclude that the self-concept is multifaceted.

There has been a dramatic shift away from global or unidimensional models of self, and prevailing models, supported by extensive data, reveal that a multidimensional model of self far more adequately describes the phenomenology of self-evaluations (see Bracken, 1992, this volume; Damon & Hart, 1980; Harter, 1982, 1985, 1990b; Hattie, 1992; Marsh, 1986, 1987, 1993; Marsh & Hattie, this volume; Mullener & Laird, 1971; Oosterwegel & Oppenheimer, 1993; Shavelson & Marsh, 1986).

However, the shift to a multidimensional focus should not preclude the existence and meaningfulness of global self-esteem or self-worth. Rosenberg (1979) was one of the first to offer a compelling argument for why we should both retain the notion of global self-esteem and focus on the constituent parts of this whole. "Both exist within the individual's phenomenal field as separate and distinguishable entities, and each can and should be studied in its own right" (p. 20). Our own findings reveal that such an assertion rings true beginning in middle childhood, in that individuals can make global judgments of their worth as a person as well as provide specific self-evaluations across a variety of domains. Younger children, however, do not possess a conscious, verbalizable concept of their overall self-esteem, nor are domains as clearly differentiated (Harter & Pike, 1984).

Our own work also reveals that the number of domains that can be differentiated increases with development across the periods of early childhood, middle and late childhood, adolescence, and adulthood (see Harter, 1990b, for a listing of the specific domains at each developmental period). For the most part, evidence for the multidimensional nature of self-evaluations has come from factor-analytic studies of self-concept measures (see Bracken, 1992; Harter, 1985, 1990b; Hattie, 1992; Marsh, 1986, 1987, 1990, 1993; Marsh & Hattie, this volume; Shavelson & Marsh, 1986). A detailed account of these issues and empirical findings will be reviewed in Chapters 2 and 3, in this volume, and therefore will not be presented here.

The Shift to Hierarchical Models

An appreciation for both global and domain-specific self-evaluations (rather than an adherence to one model versus the other) naturally led theorists to speculate on the links between the two types of self-judgments. This, in turn, produced a number of *hierarchical* models in which global self-esteem or self-concept is placed at the apex and particular domains and subdomains are nested underneath. The original models to appear were more conceptually than empirically derived. For example, Epstein (1973) suggested that the postulates the individual has about the self are hierarchically arranged where self-esteem represents the superordinate construct under which other subcategories are organized. Epstein's second-order postulates include general competence, moral self-approval, power, and love-worthiness. Lower-order postulates organized under competence include assessments of general mental and physical ability. The lowest-order postulates under competence include assessments of specific abilities. (There are similar subcategories under the other three second-order postulates.) Epstein suggests that postulates, become increasingly important to the maintenance of the individual's self-theory as they move from lower to higher order.

Of particular interest is the convergence between Epstein's second-order postulates and the four dimensions of self-evaluation proposed by Coopersmith (1967). Corresponding to competence, moral self-approval, power and love-worthiness in Epstein's scheme are the following for Coopersmith: (a) *competence* (success in meeting achievement demands), (b) *virtue* (adherence to moral and ethnical standards), (c) *power* (the ability to control and influence others), and (d) *significance* (the acceptance, attention, and affection of others).

A somewhat different hierarchical model can be found in the theorizing of Shavelson, Hubner, and Stanton (1976) who have identified two broad classes, academic and nonacademic self-concepts. The nonacademic self-concept is subdivided into social, emotional, and physical self-concepts. Physical self-concept is further differentiated into physical ability and physical appearance. The academic self-concept is subdivided into particular school subjects, namely English, history, mathematics, and science. Since this initial formulation, Marsh and Shavelson (1985) have proposed an even more differentiated model in which academic self-concept is further subdivided (Marsh, 1993; Marsh & Hattie, this volume). There has been some, though not unequivocal, empirical support for the model initially proposed by Shavelson and colleagues (see Chapter 2, this volume; also detailed review by Hattie, 1992).

One concern with such models is that certain domains may be considered more important to the individual's overall sense of self than others; yet domains are not differentially weighted in terms of their importance to the self. As James first argued, a person's global sense of self-esteem may be best explained in terms of perceived successes in domains of aspirations (or pretensions, to use James's more arcane language), where success is deemed important. The value of such an approach hinges on the differential importance of various domains to global judgments of self-worth or self-esteem.

There is certainly historical precedent for such an assumption. James made such an argument in his treatment of pretensions. Kelly (1955), as noted earlier, argued that the self was hierarchically organized into core constructs that were more critical to the maintainance of identity than were more peripheral constructs. Our own recent findings reveal that adolescents can construct a self-portrait of their attributes clearly differentiating the most central or important self-descriptions from those that are less, and least important (Harter & Monsour, 1992). Interestingly, the vast majority of the core attributes are positive in valence whereas negative attributes are relegated to the periphery of the self-portrait. Our findings with children as young as 8 years also reveal that there are clear differences in the importance they attach to various domains. Markus and Wurf (1987) have also argued that self-descriptions differ in their importance. Their findings reveal that some descriptions possess high personal relevance and function as central or core characteristics of the individual, whereas other descriptions are less personally relevant and more peripheral.

Thus, there is clear evidence that the postulates of the individual's self-theory vary in importance. However, the critical question is whether the determination of the importance of given domains adds to the predictability of global self-esteem. Several lines of work suggest the value of such an approach. Rosenberg (1979) was one of the first to take James's conceptualization seriously, arguing that the various elements of the self are weighted, hierarchized, and combined according to an extremely complex equation of which the individual is probably unaware.

There is some empirical support for James's notion that successes in domains of importance are most predictive of self-esteem. Tesser and his colleagues have demonstrated, with adult subjects, that if a dimension is highly relevant to the person's self-definition, performance judged to be inferior will threaten his or her sense of self-esteem (Tesser, 1980; Tesser & Campbell, 1983). Our own findings across numerous studies (see Harter, 1985, 1986, 1990) have consistently demonstrated that competence in domains that the individual deems important is more highly correlated with global self-esteem ($r = .70$) than competence in domains judged unimportant ($r = .30$).

Marsh (1993) has been less successful in predicting global self-esteem from weighted scores which take into account importance, although he suggests that common sense and a variety of theoretical hypotheses suggest that the effect of a specific component of self-concept on self-esteem *should* vary as a function of the individual importance of each component. He suggests a number of reasons that might enhance predictability. In our own work, we initially took James's ratio notion to heart and created *discrepancy* scores by subtracting the individual's perceptions of competence in a given domain from the rated importance of that domain. More recently, we have been even more successful in predicting global self-esteem by correlating the actual *levels* of perceived competence with global self-esteem, for just those domains judged to be important. This procedure is also faithful to James's assertion that competence in only those domains where there are aspirations should best predict self-esteem. It represents an improvement over the discrepancy procedure because the actual level of perceived competence is preserved in the correlation.

However, merely correlating levels of competence with self-esteem (not considering the importance of any domain) will yield correlations that approach in magnitude those that only include levels of competence for those domains judged important. As Marsh also argues, this is because the particular domains that investigators have included were initially selected because of their salience or importance to most individuals. However, the more appropriate test of the value of the Jamesian formulation lies in the comparison of the correlations with self-esteem of domains rated important with those rated as *unimportant.* As noted earlier, the magnitude of the differences between these two correlations is striking (.70 compared to .30), lending strong support to the formulation.

The various domain-specific, self-concept instruments, which also include a global self-esteem subscale, allow one to also address the issue of whether some domains (deemed important) are better predictors of self-esteem than others. In our own work, we have demonstrated that across the age range that we have now tested, ages 4 to 55, perceived physical appearance consistently heads the list as the number one predictor of self-esteem. Correlations range from .65 to .82, across different samples (Harter, 1990b, 1993; Harter, Marold, & Whitesell, 1991). Interpretations for this rather distressing finding are beyond the scope of this chapter; however, they can be found in the references cited. Typically, social acceptance results in the next highest correlation with self-esteem, with other domains (academic competence, behavioral conduct, athletic competence) yielding slightly lower correlations (.30 to .50). For educational and clinical purposes, however, it is critical to examine individual profiles because often the hierarchies of competence and importance are idiosyncratic, in very meaningful ways.

DISCREPANCIES BETWEEN REAL AND IDEAL SELF-CONCEPTS

Closely linked to James's distinction between the individual's perceived successes and aspirations or pretensions is the contrast between that person's *real* self (how he or she perceives the self to be, in actuality) and the *ideal* self (how he or she would like to be). The latter terminology found its way into the clinical literature through the efforts of Rogers and his colleagues (Rogers & Dymond, 1954). In their view, the magnitude of disparity between the real and ideal self was a primary index of maladjustment. This construct was operationalized in a number of measures for adults, the most popular instrument being a *Q*-sort task designed by Butler and Haigh (1954).

Zigler and his colleagues (Achenbach & Zigler, 1963; Glick & Zigler, 1986; Katz & Zigler, 1967; Katz, Zigler, & Zalk, 1975; Zigler, Balla, & Watson, 1972) challenged Rogers' assumptions that self-image disparity necessarily indicates maladjustment, suggesting an alternative developmental framework. Their findings reveal that in children and adolescents the discrepancies between real and ideal self-images increase with age. Their interpretation hinges heavily on the increasing cognitive differentiation with development. They observe that individuals at higher developmental levels should employ a greater number of categories and should make finer distinctions within each category than an individual at a lower developmental level. They reason that the use of a larger number of categories should increase the probability of a greater disparity between any two complex judgments, including those regarding real and ideal self-images.

In addition, Zigler and colleagues postulate a parallel process in the capacity to experience guilt. With increasing maturity, the individual becomes better able to incorporate social demands, morals, and values.

Because the person at a high level of development makes greater self-demands and is more often unable to fulfill them, he or she consequently will experience more guilt than someone at a lower developmental level.

These investigators have generally obtained support for the hypothesis that self-disparity increases with development. However, more recent findings reveal that the difference between the real and the ideal self-concepts was larger in middle adolescence then in early and late adolescence (Strachan & Jones, 1982). A possible explanation for this pattern is that after an initial period of differentiation, there is a subsequent period of integration in which the different self-concepts are consolidated into a more coherent whole (see Harter, 1983, 1986a; Oosterwegel & Oppenheimer, 1993).

Since the time that the earlier positions were put forth, there has been considerable advancement in theorists' thinking about real and ideal self-image discrepancies. Noteworthy are the greater number of distinctions that have been made between different facets of the real and ideal self. Rosenberg (1979) notes that the distinction between the idealized self-image and what he terms the "committed" self-image is frequently overlooked. The committed image is the one that we take seriously; it is not merely a pleasant fantasy. Thus an academic may have a fantasized image of winning a Nobel prize, whereas his or her committed image is to obtain tenure. Rosenberg suggests that in earlier work, where adult subjects were asked what they would "ideally" like to be, we have no idea whether they responded in terms of a fantasied ideal or a self that the person was earnestly committed to become.

Further distinctions have been put forth by Higgins (1987, 1989). He distinguishes between (a) the *actual* self, which is the representation of the attributes that someone (yourself or another) believes you actually possess; (b) the *ideal* self, which is the representation of the attributes that someone (yourself or another) would *like* you, ideally, to possess (the hopes, wishes, or aspirations for how you might be); and (c) the *ought* self, which is a representation of the attributes that someone (yourself or another) believes you should or *ought* to possess (given expectations about your duties, obligations, or responsibilities). The "yourself or another" distinction further points up that these three selves can be judged from a personal standpoint or from the standpoint of a significant other (e.g., parent, spouse, friend).

Higgins considers the ability to construct such discrepancies from a cognitive-developmental perspective, specifying the particular cognitive structures necessary for their emergence (Higgins, 1991). However, he also considers the magnitude of these discrepancies to represent one index of potential maladjustment. Moreover, he predicts that different types of discrepancies will produce different forms of psychological distress. Thus, discrepancies between the actual and *ideal* self—what the person would like to be—produce dejection-related emotions (feeling dissatisfied, disappointed, discouraged, sad). In contrast, discrepancies between the actual self and the self the person *ought* to become produce agitation-related emotions such as feeling worried, threatened, or on edge. Thus the field has moved away from views that emphasize either implications for malad-justment *or* the development underpinnings of self-discrepancies to a thoughtful consideration of both.

Closely related to the concepts of real and ideal selves is another dis-tinction between real and *possible* selves (Markus & Nurius, 1986; Oyser-man & Markus, 1990). Here, we can also appreciate James's (1890) legacy in his characterization of "immediate and actual" selves as well as "re-mote and potential" selves. Although much of the literature has suggested that the discrepancy between the actual and ideal self is debilitating, Markus and her colleagues have argued that such discrepancies may also have an important *motivational* function (see also Epstein, 1973; Van der Werff, 1985). Possible selves represent both the hoped-for, as well as dreaded, selves, and function as incentives that clarify those selves that are to be approached as well as avoided. From this perspective, it is most de-sirable to have a balance between both positive expected selves and nega-tive feared selves so that positive possible selves (e.g., obtaining a well-paying job, wanting to be loved by family, hoping to be recognized and admired by others) can give direction to desired future states, whereas negative possible selves (e.g., being unemployed, feeling lonely, being so-cially ignored) can clarify what is to be avoided. Markus and her col-leagues report on a variety of findings supporting these motivational functions.

Recent investigators have built on the concept of possible selves. Higgins (1990) has introduced the notion of a "can-self" which refers to a person's perceptions that he or she can achieve the image of a positive, possible self. Integrating the "can-self" into his earlier framework, Higgins reports that discrepancies between real and ideal-self concepts only predict dejection-related emotions if the can-self equals the ideal self. That is, adults did *not* report being bothered by real/ideal discrepancies if they felt that they had or could fulfill their potential (the "can-self") but that their ideal was be-yond their potential.

Oosterwegel and Oppenheimer (1993) have examined a number of dis-crepancies within a framework emphasizing real and possible selves, in subjects between the ages of 6 and 18 years. In addition to the distinction between real and possible selves, they addressed how subjects evaluate themselves, how they *think* others (e.g., parents and peers) evaluate them, and how others actually evaluate them. A complete description of their findings is beyond the scope of this chapter. However, they find that the distance between real and possible selves increases from age 6 to about age 12, especially when the perspectives of the parents are considered. They note, in keeping with Markus' orientation, that the possible self-concepts function as standards for the real self-concept. However, their findings also reveal that certain discrepancies cause more distress than others. Subjects were most bothered by the discrepancy between how they felt their parents evaluated them and what they felt the parents ideally wanted them to be (the parents' perceptions of the child's possible self).

This newer work alerts us to the complexity of self-discrepancies, including the many forms they may assume. The proliferating combinations of self-concepts and discrepancies that have now been identified may make researchers feel a bit bewildered about which to incorporate into their own work. On a more sanguine note, this complexity alerts us to the need to be extremely clear about our research goals as well as the outcomes we intend to predict. These frameworks force us to consider the *functional* role of the self, which in turn will dictate the particular self-concept constructs we select. Filling our journal pages are now hundreds of studies in which self-concept is related to group membership (e.g., age, gender, ethnicity, social class) or to other psychological variables (e.g., achievement, anxiety, depression). Such approaches will not advance our understanding of human behavior unless we take a more process-oriented perspective on the function that self-concepts, in various forms, play in the people's lives. The newer approaches are promising in their identification of the impact that self-concepts have on motivation, affect, and actual behavior. Thus, a clear specification of outcomes should, in turn, serve as a guide to which self-concepts and discrepancies warrant our attention.

SOCIAL SOURCES OF SELF-EVALUATION

In the earlier treatment of the contribution of such symbolic interactionists as Cooley (1902) and Mead (1925, 1934), it was observed that these scholars considered the self to be primarily a *social* construction. Thus, we attend to the appraisals of significant others and our perceptions of their opinions come to be incorporated into our self-concept. For Cooley, the process through which these *reflected* appraisals are constructed, which involves our imagination of how others perceive us, led him to refer metaphorically to the looking-glass self. Mead placed more emphasis on the role of language in the communication of such opinions (symbolic interactions) as well as the internalization of these opinions in the form of the "generalized other."

These themes persist as contemporary issues, although much more differentiated questions such as the following are currently being posed:

1. When does such a process commence, developmentally, and how does it overlap with the claims of attachment theorists concerning the emergence of "working models"?
2. What evidence is there that parental support forms an initial basis for children's self-esteem?
3. At different periods across the life span, are some sources of support (e.g., parent vs. peer) more critical to self-esteem than others?

4. Are some *types* of support (approval vs. emotional support) more predictive of self-esteem than others?
5. To what extent are the opinions of others communicated *directly* through the use of language?
6. What do we know about the process through which the appraisals of others are *internalized*? Moreover, which is more likely to be internalized, others' *actual* evaluations of the self or one's *perceptions* of others' appraisals of the self?
7. How can we best think about the *directionality* of the link between reflected appraisals and self-esteem?

Developmental Origins

With regard to the developmental origins of the impact of the opinions of others, attachment theorists would argue that this process begins in infancy, in the formation of "internal working models." According to Bowlby (1969), internal working models of self and of attachment figures emerge out of patterns of infant-caregiver interactions sometime around the end of the first year when the infant has attained object permanence (Piaget, 1954) and is beginning to acquire language. Thus, as Bretherton (1991) notes, a child who experiences parental figures as emotionally available and supportive will construct a working model of the self as competent and loved. In contrast, a child who experiences attachment figures as primarily rejecting may form a complementary internal working model of the self as unworthy (a precursor of low self-esteem). Bretherton goes on to observe that Epstein's (1973, 1980, 1991) model of the self-concept, as an individual's theory of reality, is strikingly close to Bowlby's notion of complementary working models of self and of attachment figures. Epstein (1980) contends that a person with high self-esteem "in effect carries within him a loving parent, one who is proud of his successes and acceptant of his failures" whereas the person with low self-esteem "carries within him a disapproving parent who is harshly critical of his failures" (p. 106). There is increasing evidence (see Bretherton, 1991) that such a model may well explain the early origins of attitudes about the self.

Parental Support

Beyond the period of infancy, findings also reveal that parental support is highly related to self-esteem. Nikkari and Harter (1994), in a study with young children, aged 4 to 7, revealed that perceived parental support was highly predictive of behavioral indexes of self-esteem (see Haltiwanger & Harter, 1993), more so than was perceived peer support.

Coopersmith's (1967) study was one of the first to describe a constellation of parent variables that impacted self-esteem in 10- to 12-year-old boys (girls were not studied). Parents of boys with high self-esteem more often had the following attitudes and behavioral practices:

1. They were accepting, approving, affectionate, and involved, treating the child's interests and problems as meaningful, showing genuine concern.
2. They were strict in the sense that they enforced rules carefully and consistently, and sought to encourage children to uphold high standards of behavior.
3. They preferred *noncoercive* forms of discipline, for example, denial of privileges and time-out, and typically discussed the reasons why the child's behavior was inappropriate.
4. They were democratic in the sense that the child's opinions were considered in decisions such as the hour for bedtime, and the child participated in making family plans (see also Maccoby, 1980).

The association of approval, acceptance, and affection with high self-esteem would be predicted from the symbolic interactionist perspective. Coopersmith speculates on why some of the other disciplinary practices might also be linked to self-esteem. For example, he suggests that well-defined limits assist the child in evaluating performance, since they facilitate comparisons and help to clarify many of the ambiguities in the realm of social behavior. For Coopersmith, limits enhance the child's self-definition by highlighting the restrictions and demands imposed by the real world, thereby clarifying his or her role in the social environment. Presumably, this would then serve to allow the child to engage in behaviors that would garner more support from parents and possibly peers, which would in turn contribute to high self-esteem.

Parent versus Peer Support

With regard to the influence of parental versus peer support, there is increasing convergence on the impact of these two sources, from a developmental perspective. Rosenberg's (1979) work has revealed that not all significant others are equally significant at every age. He observes that the younger child's conclusion about what he or she is like rests heavily on the perceived judgments of external authority, particularly parental authority. Knowledge of the self is regarded as absolute and resides in those with superior wisdom, a conclusion consistent with Piaget's (1932) observations of children's understanding of rules and sources of moral judgment. With development, respect for parental knowledge declines, and peer evaluations rise in importance (see also McGuire & McGuire, 1982).

Our own findings are partially consistent with Rosenberg's contentions. As noted previously, among 4- to 7-year-old children, parental support, in the form of approval, is a more powerful predictor of behaviorally manifest self-esteem than is peer support. The correlation between peer support, in the form of classmate approval, and global self-esteem increases with development, such that by early adolescence it equals the impact of parent support (Harter, 1990b). However, the correlations between parental approval and self-esteem do *not* decline with development. Rather, it is the increase in the relationship between peer approval and global self-esteem that represents the major change. This pattern is consistent with the recent conclusions of Oosterwegel and Oppenheimer (1993) who emphasize the importance of the parents' opinions of the self, well into adolescence.

Our own findings reveal a shift during the transition to college (Harter & Johnson, 1993). For high school seniors, both mother and father approval correlates highly with self-esteem. However, 6 months into their freshman year, the pattern changes. The correlations between both maternal and paternal approval and self-esteem drop rather dramatically, whereas peer approval, in the form of acceptance by classmates and peers in campus organizations, is a strong predictor of self-esteem. Support from college instructors/professors also correlates moderately highly.

Among adults in the world of work and family, ages 25 to 50 years, the evidence indicates that approval from one's coworkers as well as from adults within one's church or civic group was the highest predictor of self-worth (Harter, 1990b). Next came support from adults within the family, namely one's parents and one's spouse or significant other. Least critical to self-esteem was support from one's close friends and one's children.

At every developmental level we have investigated, namely middle to late childhood, adolescence, the college years, and early to middle-age adulthood, we have consistently and repeatedly found that approval from peers in the more "public domain" (e.g., classmates, peers in organizations, work settings) is far more predictive of self-esteem than is approval from close friends. We interpret this finding to suggest that support from others in the more public domain may better represent acceptance from the "generalized other," approval that may be perceived as more "objective" or from more credible sources, than the support from one's close friends. This is not to negate the importance of close friend support, which would appear to be critical as a source of acceptance, feedback, and clarification of values vis-à-vis the outside world. Such close friend support would seem to function as a secure psychological base from which the individual can reemerge to meet the challenges of the generalized other, whose acceptance appears critical to maintaining high self-esteem.

Types of Support

Are some types of support more critical to self-esteem than others? A number of investigators have begun to differentiate between a variety of types of social support (Berndt & Perry, 1986; Blyth, Hill, & Thiel, 1982;

Furman & Buhrmester, 1985; Reid, Landeman, Treder, & Jaccard, 1989). This differentiation has allowed us to address the issue of whether self-esteem might be more highly related to particular forms of support. We have addressed this question directly in our own laboratory, distinguishing between support in the form of approval (others like one as a person), emotional support (others understand and care about one's feelings) and instrumental support (others instruct, teach, or guide one in the solution of developmental tasks or problems). Our findings (see Robinson, in press) reveal that approval support is most highly related to self-esteem. Instrumental support is the least highly related, with emotional support falling in between. The greater impact of approval on self-esteem was predicted to the extent that others' approval of a person should be most readily incorporated as self-approval, or high self-esteem. Whereas emotional and instrumental support is welcome from significant others, if not necessary to the individual's functioning, it may serve as a signal of that person's weaknesses rather than strengths. Although such support reveals the caring of others, it is understandable why these forms might not translate as readily into feelings of self-esteem, as compared with approval.

For Rogers (Rogers, 1951; Rogers & Dymond, 1954), it was not only approval but acceptance, in the form of unconditional positive regard, that was an essential prerequisite to high self-esteem. We have examined this issue, distinguishing between conditional and unconditional positive regard among adolescents (Harter, Marold, & Whitesell, 1991; Marold, 1987). Conditionality is defined as the extent to which the adolescent feels that support is only forthcoming if he or she meets high, and seemingly unrealistic, parental standards or expectations. It is contrasted with unconditional positive regard in which parents accept their child even if he or she doesn't meet all their expectations. Our findings reveal that conditionality is actually not perceived as supportive, and as a result, it undermines self-esteem. Rather than communicating acceptance of the adolescent, it specifies the psychological hoops through which he or she must jump to please parents. Unconditional positive regard, in contrast, promotes high self-esteem. Thus, this represents another interesting avenue in the identification of which particular forms of support best serve as precursors to high or low self-esteem.

Communication of Approval

To what extent are perceptions of approval from significant others communicated *directly* to the self? Symbolic interactionists, particularly Mead, placed heavy emphasis on communication in the form of language. That is, the model assumed that the opinions of sifnificant others were directly expressed to the individual, who in turn interpreted and incorporated such feedback. Recent theorists, notably Felson (1993), have questioned this assumption.

Felson first notes that the reflected appraisal process consists of three elements: (a) self-appraisals; (b) the *actual* appraisals of significant others; and (c) the individual's *perceptions* of the appraisals of others, referred to as *reflected* appraisals (see also Kinch, 1963). Felson's research reveals that there is a stronger relationship between reflected appraisals and self-appraisals than between the actual appraisals of significant others and self-appraisals. His argument parallels that of Rosenberg whose own research indicated the need to qualify Mead's original expression of the principle of reflected appraisals: "We are more or less unconsciously seeing ourselves as others see us" (1934, p. 68). For Rosenberg, it is our perceptions—what we *think* others think of us that will determine our self-attitudes. Thus, he amends Mead's original statement to include this qualification: "We are more or less unconsciously seeing ourselves as we think others who are important to us and whose opinion we trust see us" (1979, p. 97).

Felson's work pursues this theme in addressing the mechanisms through which the opinions of others might be divined, suggesting that these routes may not involve direct communication from those persons whose opinions matter. Felson's findings reveal that negative feedback, in particular, is much less likely to be communicated directly to individuals. There are several other channels of communication. Negative evaluations may be inferred from the absence of positive evaluations. Third parties may provide another source of information about others' appraisals. Shared standards and social comparison processes represent another route for inferring the opinions of others. That is, shared *standards* are communicated directly by others. Individuals then engage in social comparison to determine whether their performance measures up to these standards. If they feel it does not, they conclude that those others whose standards they share must think poorly of them. Conversely, if they meet these standards, then they infer that others must be evaluating them positively.

The Internalization Process

What do we know about the process through which the appraisals of others, communicated directly or indirectly, are *internalized*? As noted in the initial treatment of Cooley's looking-glass self formulation, there was an implied internalization process. For Cooley, the individual is more sensitive to the opinions of others during youth. Such opinions are incorporated gradually, and then become increasingly distanced from their external origins, as the person comes to own these evaluations as the self. Developmental psychologists have begun to articulate some of the more specific processes and stages underlying the internalization of the opinions of others.

Harter (1983) has offered one such analysis elaborating on Selman's (1980) stage-theory of interpersonal relations, which identifies different levels of self-awareness. Thus, in the earliest stages, the I-self cannot directly evaluate or be critical of the Me-self, in part due to lack of perspective-taking skills. At the   . .evel, the I-self observes *others* evaluating the self, but cannot yet evaluate the Me-self critically. This level seems to portray the beginning of the looking-glass process during which others serve as the reflective surface providing appraisals that will eventually be incorporated into the person's definition of the Me-self. At the next level, the standards and opinions of others begin to become incorporated, and through the additional advance of social comparison skills, the I-self can determine whether the Me-self is meeting these standards. At the final level in this particular sequence, the I-self comes to directly evaluate the Me-self, having internalized both opinions and standards.

Higgins (1991) has proposed a more detailed analysis of these processes, based on cognitive-developmental principles. He describes an interesting shift from *identification* to *internalization* that occurs between the ages of 9 and 11 years. In the stage of identification, children recognize that the standards and opinions are those of others whom they want to please. However, with internalization, these standards become self-guides and children try to match their attributes to these self-guides to be the right kind of person (see Grusec, 1983; Kohlberg, 1976). Higgins notes that from a self-regulatory point of view, children's ability to make self-attributions and to respond negatively to their own actions independent of others' opinions of them is the essence of what has been termed the child's new capacity for "internal control."

Damon and Hart's (1988) developmental analysis converges with Higgins' observations. They note that in childhood and early adolescence, self-judgments depend more heavily on social comparison, normative standards, social similarities, and behaviors that enhance interpersonal interactions and social appeal. However, during adolescence, there is a normative shift toward self-attributes defined in terms of personal beliefs and internalized standards. Their analysis implies that adolescenets who do not move into this stage, but who continue to rely primarily on social standards and social comparison, may well be at risk in that they will not have developed an internalized, relatively stable sense of self that will form the basis for subsequent identity development.

In our own work, we have identified just such subgroups of adolescents (Harter, Stocker, & Robinson, in press). We became intrigued with the issue of whether adolescents consciously endorse a looking-glass self metatheory, meaning that they acknowledge that they need to have other people evaluate them positively to like themselves as a person (our definition of self-esteem). The competing metatheory is that if one likes oneself as a person, then others will necessarily like or support the self, as well. Thus, with regard to the directionality of effects, in the first case, approval precedes self-esteem whereas in the second, self-esteem precedes approval.

We first demonstrated that there are adolescents who endorse each of these metatheories about the directionality of the causal links between approval and self-esteem. Consistent with the analysis by Damon and Hart, we inferred that those still requiring the approval of others as the basis for their self-esteem represented individuals who had not yet internalized these standards and opinions. We found that such individuals reported a greater preoccupation with others' opinions, lower support, and more fluctuating support, as well as lower and more fluctuating self-esteem, compared with the group who felt that their self-esteem would impact the opinions of others. The first group was also judged, by teachers, to be more socially distracted from schoolwork.

Developmentally, a looking-glass self model represents the mechanism through which opinions of others come to impact the self. However, the healthiest developmental course would appear to be one in which the standards and opinions of others are eventually internalized, such that truly *self*-evaluations become the standards that guide behavior. A person who reaches this stage endorses a directionality orientation in which how he or she evaluates the self will impact others' opinions of the self.

Our pattern of results reveals that in the development of sequential or causal models, we need to be sensitive to the directionality of effects and not merely assume that construct A (e.g., approval) necessarily precedes construct B (e.g., self-esteem). Rather, we need to consider the developmental level of the individual as well as individual differences within a given developmental level. Felson (1993) addresses the very same issue of the directionality of approval and self-esteem, albeit from a somewhat different perspective. He observes that it may well be that, in contrast to the looking-glass formulation in which the opinions of others are internalized and therefore dictate the individual's level of self-esteem, the level of self-esteem may be driving what the person perceives to be the opinions of others. He reports a series of studies revealing that children who like themselves assume that their parents' and peers' reactions to them are favorable, leading to an alternative interpretation that he terms the "false consensus effect."

Although the label "false" seems a bit pejorative, it is highly likely that both effects, internalization of others' opinions as well as assumptions that self-approval means, others in turn will manifest their approval, are operative. These are likely to be reciprocal, transactional, influences. Our own findings suggest the fruitfulness of examining which perspective is dominant, from the *individual's* own point of view, because there are powerful correlates of adhering to one metatheory versus its opposite.

MULTIPLE SELVES VERSUS THE UNIFIED SELF

As noted earlier, James set the stage for the consideration of the multiple selves that may be manifest in different interpersonal roles or relationships. He observed that there may be incompatibility between certain role-related selves leading to the "conflict of the different Me's." Other historical scholars of the self, in contrast, placed major emphasis on the integrated, unified self (Allport, 1955, 1961; Horney, 1950; Jung, 1928; Lecky, 1945; Maslow, 1954, 1961, 1971; Rogers, 1950). For Allport, the "proprium," his term for the self, ". . . includes all aspects of personality that make for a sense of inward unity" (1955, p. 38). Allport identified a particular motive, "propriate striving," that seeks such a unification.

Those emphasizing the importance of unity have typically based their claims on clinical accounts of adults who seem unable to integrate their various self-definitions into a unified sense of self. Allport (1955), for example, noted that many mental patients seem to suffer from what he terms the proliferation of unrelated subsystems that define the self. Rogers (1950) also described patients who experience inconsistencies and partial disorganization of the self. For Maslow (1971), multiple personalities could best be described in terms of a failure of communication with the self-system.

Lecky (1945) fashioned an entire theory around the theme of self-consistency, emphasizing how behavior expresses the effort to maintain the integrity and unity of the self. More recently, Epstein (1973, 1981) argued that among the criteria that self-theories must meet is *internal consistency*. Thus, a person's self-theory will be threatened by evidence that is inconsistent with the portrait he or she has constructed of the self, or by apparently contradictory postulates within the theory. Epstein (1981) has formalized these observations under the rubric of the unity principle, emphasizing that one of the most basic needs of the individual is to maintain the unity and coherence of the conceptual system that defines the self.

In contrast to the emphasis on unity, several social psychologists (Gergen, 1968; Mischel, 1968, 1973; Vallacher, 1980) have argued that the most fruitful theory of self must take into account the multiple roles that people adopt. Gergen cites historical resistance to such a stance in the form of a "consistency ethic." Gergen contends that the "popular notion of the self-concept as a unified, consistent, or perceptually whole psychological structure is possibly ill-conceived" (1968, p. 306). As an alternative, he suggests that people adjust their behavior in accord with the specific nature of the interpersonal relationship and its situational context. In a close relationship, founded on mutual trust, personal consistency should be expected *within* that relationship. However, consistency would not necessarily be expected or desirable *across* relationships; in fact, it would most likely be damaging. Vallacher's conclusion is similar. He asserts that the association of different self-views with different roles represents *differentiation* rather than inconsistency. It is only when there are differing self-definitions *within* a role, such as when a person feels he or she has been insensitive to a close friend, that inconsistency is experienced.

There is considerable evidence that with development the self becomes increasingly differentiated. As noted earlier, self-concept inventories now reflect that, beginning in middle childhood, individuals report that they evaluate themselves differently across a variety of domains (Bracken,

1992, this volume; Harter, 1985, 1989; Marsh, 1987, 1990). Moreover, findings reveal that during adolescence there is an increasing proliferation of selves that vary as a function of different social roles or contexts. These include self with father, mother, close friend, romantic partner, and peers, as well as the self in the role of student, on the job, and as athlete (Gecas, 1972; Griffin, Chassin, & Young, 1981; Hart, 1988; Harter, 1986a; Harter & Monsour, 1992; Smollar & Youniss, 1985).

A developmental perspective can show us how problematic or distressing the existence of multiple selves might be. Our own work (Harter & Monsour, 1992) reveals that beginning in mid-adolescence, opposing attributes within the self-portrait (e.g., outgoing with peers but shy on a date, or depressed with parents but cheerful with close friends) are a source of conflict. At this cognitive-developmental stage (see Fischer, 1980), adolescents have developed the conceptual tools to *detect* inconsistencies in the self across roles but do not have the ability to *integrate* such apparent contradictions. Conflict diminishes, however, during late adolescence with the emergence of the ability to integrate seemingly opposing self-attributes into compatible higher-order abstractions about the self. For example, cheerful and depressed can be integrated into the higher-order abstraction of "moody." Older adolescents can also resolve potentially contradictory attributes by asserting that they are flexible or adaptive, thereby subsuming apparent inconsistencies under more generalized abstractions about the self. Thus, more advanced cognitive skills allow the individual to coordinate and interpret diverse self-attributes across roles or context.

A related strategy to reduce the potential conflict between opposing self-attributes is to adopt a more abstract generalization with regard to the desirability or normalcy of behaving differently in different roles (Harter & Monsour, 1992). For example, older adolescents assert, "It wouldn't be normal to act the same way with everyone; you act one way with your friends and a different way with your parents, that's the way it should be." "It's good to be able to be different with different people in your life; you'd be pretty strange and also pretty boring if you weren't."

Such a framework allows us to resolve the earlier conceptual tension between those who espoused a unified self and those who argued that differentiation across roles more aptly describes the self-system. That is, beginning in late adolescence, potentially opposing attributes that differ across social roles and context can coexist as well as be integrated into a self-theory with the emergence of the ability to create more abstract postulates that erase the contradictions and give meaning to the seeming disparities (see Harter, 1990a). Within the field of self psychology, there has been increasing zeal for models that specify how the self is *differentiated*. In future self-concept research, however, we need to give more thoughtful attention to the processes through which differentiated self-conceptualizations are organized and integrated.

TRUE VERSUS FALSE SELVES

In our own research, we became alerted to the emergence of the false self within the context of the previously described studies on the proliferation of multiple selves during adolescence. In describing their contradictory role-related attributes, many adolescents spontaneously agonized about "Which is the real me?" From a developmental perspective, the distinction between the true and the false self appears to emerge in early adolescence (Broughton, 1981; Harter, Marold, Whitesell, & Cobbs, in press; Selman, 1980).

From a *historical* perspective, an interest in the distinction between true and false self behaviors would appear to date from the 16th century (Baumeister, 1987; Trilling, 1971). Trilling describes the obsession with deception and pretense that found its way into politics, philosophy, and literature (e.g., Shakespeare) in England. Emerging from this era was a concern with the fact that a person's real self could be concealed from others. Baumeister notes, however, that people were particularly concerned with the idea that *others* (not themselves) might be hiding their true selves. With the advent of Puritanism, the difficulty of determining the underlying psychological realities was extended to self-knowledge. People became concerned about whether they were deceiving themselves with regard to their piety, faith, and virtue, attributes that were necessary for them to enter into the kingdom of heaven (Baumeister, 1987; Weintraub, 1978).

Baumeister notes that an emphasis on the hidden parts of the self was exacerbated by Victorian repressiveness, as well as the emergence of Freudianism. Self-scrutiny, coupled with impossibly high moral standards, forced Victorians to become self-deceptive. Moreover, Freud's revelations concerning the unconscious led to the conclusion that certain parts of the true self might be inaccessible to even the person him- or herself. However, it was necessary to be on guard lest these attributes be revealed to others, involuntarily, through behaviors, slips of the tongue, and so on.

The theme of true versus false self behavior emerged more explicitly in the writings of later psychoanalytically oriented theorists. Horney (1950) described the person's alienation from the real self. Self-alienation could involve active movement *away* from the real self, active movement *against* the real self, depersonalization, and depletion of energy. Bleiberg (1984) and Winnicott (1958, 1965) focused more on the developmental precursors of false self-behavior. For Bleiberg, false self-behavior resulted from caregivers who did not validate the child's true self, thus leading the infant to become alienated from his or her core self. For Winnicott, mothers who are intrusively overinvolved with their infant cause the child to develop a false self based on compliance. The infant becomes prematurely attuned to the demands of the parent and, as a result, loses touch with his or her own needs. Thus, the true self goes into hiding, as the child comes to suppress its expression. These clinical formulations emphasize the more pathological avenues to the development of a false self.

A somewhat different perspective is offered with the *social* psychological literature, in that false self-behaviors are considered to be motivated by attempts to present the self in a manner that will impress or win the acceptance of others (Snyder, 1987). High self-monitors, for example, are presumed to adjust their behavior, and thereby suppress their true self, to gain the approval of others.

Finally, within the *developmental* literature, false self-behaviors are considered to be a dimension of normative role experimentation (Broughton, 1981; Selman, 1980). Broughton describes the preoccupation with real and false or phony selves that emerges during adolescence. Selman discusses a similar theme noting that the adolescent comes to distinguish between the true self, which consists of inner thoughts and feelings, and the outer self, which comprises manifest feelings or behaviors.

In our own work (Harter, Marold, Whitesell, & Cobbs, in press), we have encountered a similar distinction, employing open-ended procedures in which adolescents describe their true and false selves. Adolescents' descriptions of their true selves include "the real me inside," "my true feelings," "what I really think and feel," and "behaving the way *I* want to behave and not how someone else wants me to be." False selves are described as the opposite: "being phony," "putting on an act," "expressing things you don't really believe or feel," and "changing yourself to be something that someone *else* wants you to be."

We have found considerable variability in the level of false self-behaviors that adolescents display, leading to the exploration of a model that would account for these individual differences. We looked to features of adolescents' parent and peer support systems. We identified two variables, *level* of support and *conditionality* of support as initial predictors. Thus, we hypothesized that adolescents who were not receiving high levels of approval and who felt that approval would only be forthcoming if they met high parental or peer expectations, would be motivated to suppress their true selves and alter their behavior in the hopes of obtaining approval from others. The best-fitting model reveals that the effect of level and conditionality of support on false self-behavior is mediated by *hopelessness* about obtaining support. Thus, the highest levels of false self-behavior are reported by those adolescents who receive conditional support, and at relatively low levels, are leading them to feel hopeless about pleasing others, which in turn causes them to suppress their true self as a potential means of garnering the desired support.

Our results also reveal that adolescents can spontaneously generate their reasons for engaging in false self behavior. Moreover, these reasons parallel the three motive categories identified in the different literatures (described earlier). Some cite reasons paralleling the motives identified in the *clinical* literature involving the devaluation of the self (e.g., parents or peers do not like them and/or they do not like themselves). Motives more consonant with the *social* psychological literature include wanting to please, impress, or gain the acceptance of others. Finally, some adolescents suggest the normative *developmental* motive of experimenting with different selves, trying different ways of acting around other people to see what it feels like.

There are powerful correlates of these three motive choices. Those citing the more clinical motives report the worst outcomes in terms of (a) engaging in the highest levels of false self-behavior, (b) not knowing who the true self really is, and (c) having lower self-esteem coupled with depressed affect. Those reporting the more *developmental* motives of role experimentation report the most positive outcomes, with those reporting approval-seeking falling in between.

These findings are interesting, in and of themselves. However, they also have implications for the responses that subjects give to self-concept instruments. To what extent do self-reports of competence or adequacy across various domains reflect the person's perceptions of the true self in those domains? Might certain responses reflect false self-behavior, either because of concealing true feelings or because of being unaware of the real self? In previous treatments within the self-concept literature, these issues have been raised as problems of socially desirable responding (Crandall, 1965; Marlowe & Crowne, 1964). Presumably, certain subjects distort or inflate their self-evaluations to look good in the eyes of those who will have access to their scores. From this perspective, subjects are viewed as inaccurate judges of their behavior, at best; lying, at worst. Such inferences are typically drawn from discrepancies between self-ratings and "more objective" ratings by others, for example, teachers, parents, or observers.

A more frutiful approach would invlove an examination of the potential processes underlying such discrepancies. The findings on the motives for false self-behavior represent a possible approach to the mechanisms underlying self-reported evaluations. The primary motive for adolescents involves the need to please or impress others. This motive can be addressed directly, which may in turn illuminate our interpretation of self-evaluations. Information on the individual's perceptions of what significant others view as the ideal for him- or herself represents another approach that both Higgins (1987, 1989) and Oosterwegel and Oppenheimer (1993) have successfully pursued. An assessment of individuals' own judgment as to how confident *they* feel about their ratings, how well they feel they know their true selves, may also be useful.

Self-report measures have come under increasing attack in recent years, particualrly when scores are discrepant with those from presumably more objective sources. Too often, such a pattern renders the sunject to be an invalid reporter of his or her behavior. Such discrepancies may be of interest in and of themselves, however, and may bear on issues having little to do with validity or the psychometric properties of a given instrument. The particular, underlying reasons for such discrepancies may be far more interesting and may ultimately tell us more about the self.

COGNITIVE, AFFECTIVE, AND BEHAVIORAL COMPONENTS OF THE SELF

Much of the content of this chapter has focused on the self as a *cognitive* construction. Historically, from a Jamesian perspective, the self was viewed as a cognitive/evaluative system in which the individual cognitively compared his or her successes or failures in various domains to the importance attached to such successes or failures. The outcome of this equation determined the global level of self-esteem. From a developmental perspective, the self has also been considered a cognitive construction, subject to changes with age as emerging capacities lead to changes in the structure and content of the self. Those who view the self as a theory also rely heavily on cognitive constructs, (e.g., schemata), in explaining self-processes.

There has, until recently, been much less emphasis on the *affective* dimensions of the self, despite the historical precedent for such a consideration in Cooley's formulation. For Cooley, an important component of the self was some sort of self-feeling, such as pride or shame. Increasingly, however, theorists and investigators have turned their attention to the affective implications of self-esteem. One notable area has involved the link between self-esteem and depressed affect.

There is clear historical precedent for including negative self-evaluations as one of a constellation of symptoms experienced in depression, beginning with Freud's (1968) observations of the low self-esteem displayed by adults suffering from depressive disorders. Those within the psychoanalytic tradition have continued to afford low self-esteem a central role in depression (Bibring, 1953; Blatt, 1974). There is now a growing body of evidence that individuals with low self-esteem will invariably report depressed affect (Abramson, Metalsky, & Alloy, 1989; Battle, 1987; Baumeister, 1990; Beck, 1975; Hammen & Goodman-Brown, 1990; Harter, 1986, 1993; Kovacs & Beck, 1977, 1978, 1986; Renouf & Harter, 1990). In a number of models, there would appear to be a pathway from not living up to personal standards to low self-esteem to depressed affect (Baumeister, 1990; Harter, 1986b, 1990b; Higgins, 1987, 1989).

Such models are critical in that they point to the functional or mediational role of self-esteem. As has been argued elsewhere (Harter, 1993), the field should be concerned only about self-esteem if we can demonstrate that it plays a critical role in people's everyday lives. The hundreds of efforts to study self-esteem may well be misguided if we cannot demonstrate that self-esteem has notable affective as well as behavioral consequences.

Historically, it is of interest to ask why the self was for so long an un-welcome guest at the behaviorist's table. Among the many reasons (see Harter, 1990c), self-constructs were not satisfying to the behaviorist's palate because their function was not clearly specified. However, there has been increasing emphasis on the *functional* role of self-representations among theorists of the self (Bandura, 1977, 1978, 1981; Epstein, 1973, 1981, 1991; Harter, 1986b, 1993; Kanfer, 1980; Weiner, 1985; Wicklund & Frey, 1980). Within this newer tradition, models typically treat self-esteem as both a dependent and an independent variable. Thus, an examination of the determinants of self-esteem render it a dependent variable. However, in its mediational role, it functions as an independent variable.

Bandura's concept of self-efficacy infuses constructs about the self with just such a functional perspective. Self-efficacy is to be differentiated from mere perceptions of competence captured on our self-concept inventories, although they will undoubtedly be related. Perceptions of competence or adequacy make reference to self-evaluations about the past or present. Self-efficacy is a motivational construct that refers to the individual's belief that he or she can act effectively in the future.

A functional perspective alerts us to a range of potential behavioral outcomes that self-constructs might mediate. As such, it creates another challenge to our model-building attempts. As previously noted, self-esteem would appear to be a powerful mediator of depression and suicidal behaviors. However, self-esteem has also been invoked as a causal factor in numerous other problem behaviors (e.g., eating disorders, delinquency including gang membership, antisocial behavior, and teen pregnancy). Among individuals with low self-esteem, what is it that leads some to terminate their own lives, others to terminate the lives of strangers, family, or acquantainces, and still others, through pregnancy, to create a new life?

Constructs such as self-concept and self-esteem, therefore, have little explanatory power, in and of themselves, to the extent that they are predictive of such diverse outcomes. Thus, the challenge to self-concept researchers will be to develop models that capture the complex antecedents of an array of behavioral outcomes that represent potential mental health concerns for the individual as well as for society.

REFERENCES

Abramson, L. Y., Metalsky, G. I., & Alloy, L. B. (1989). Hopelessness depression: A theory-based subtype of depression. *Psychological Review, 96,* 358–372.

Achenbach, T., & Zigler, E. (1963). Social competence and self-image disparity in psychiatric and non-psychiatric patients. *Journal of Abnormal and Social Psychology, 67,* 197–205.

Allport, G. W. (1961). *Pattern and growth in personality.* New York: Holt, Rinehart, & Winston.

Bandura, A. (1977). Self-efficacy: Toward a unifying theory of behavioral change. *Psychological Review, 84,* 191–215.

Bandura, A. (1978). The self system in reciprocal determinism. *American Psychologist, 33,* 344–358.

Bartlett, F. C. (1932). *Remembering.* Cambridge, MA: Cambridge University Press.

Battle, J. (1987). Relationship between self-esteem and depression among children. *Psychological Reports, 60,* 1187–1190.

Baumeister, R. F. (1987). How the self became a problem: A psychological review of historical research. *Journal of Personality and Social Psychology, 52,* 163–176.

Baumeister, R. F. (1990). Suicide as escape from self. *Psychological Review, 97,* 90–113.

Beck, A. T. (1975). *Depression: Causes and treatments.* Philadelphia: University of Pennsylvania Press.

Beth, E., & Piaget, J. (1966). *Mathematical epistemology and psychology.* Dordrecht, Holland: D. Reidel.

Bibring, E. (1953). The mechanism of depression. In P. Greenacre (Ed.), *Affective disorders: Psychoanalytic contribution to their study.* New York: International Universities Press.

Berndt, T. J., & Perry, T. B. (1986). Children's perceptions of friendships as supportive relationships. *Developmental Psychology, 22*(5), 640–648.

Blatt, S. J. (1974). Levels of object representation in anaclitic and introjective depression. *Psychoanalytic Study of the Child, 29,* 107–157.

Bleiberg, E. (1984). Narcissistic disorders in children. *Bulletin of the Menninger Clinic, 48,* 501–517.

Blyth, D. A., Hill, J. P., & Thiel, K. S. (1982). Early adolescents' significant others: Grade and gender differences in perceived relationships with familial and nonfamilial adults and young people. *Journal of Youth and Adolescence, 11*(6), 425–450.

Bowlby, J. (1969). *Attachment and loss: Vol. 1. Attachment.* New York: Basic Books.

Bracken, B. A. (1992). *Multidimensional Self Concept Scale.* Austin, TX: Pro-Ed.

Bretherton, I. (1991). Pouring new wine into old bottles: The social self as internal working model. In M. R. Gunnar & L. A. Sroufe (Eds.), *Self processes and development: The Minnesota Symposia on Child Development* (Vol. 23). Hillsdale, NJ: Erlbaum.

Brim, O. G. (1976). Theories of the male mid-life crises [Special issue]. *Counseling Psychologist: Counseling Adults.*

Broughton, J. (1978). The development of the concepts of self, mind, reality, and knowledge. In W. Damon (Ed.), *Social cognition* (pp. 75–100). San Francisco, CA: Jossey-Bass.

Broughton, J. (1981). The divided self in adolescence. *Human Development, 24,* 13–32.

Broughton, J. M. (1987). The psychology, history, and ideology of the self. In K. S. Larsen (Ed.), *Dialectics and ideology in psychology.* Norwood, NJ: Ablex.

Butler, J. M., & Haigh, G. V. (1954). Changes in the relation between self-concepts and ideal concepts consequent upon client-centered counseling. In C. R. Rogers & R. F. Dymond (Eds.), *Psychotherapy and personality change.* Chicago: University of Chicago Press.

Cooley, C. H. (1902). *Human nature and the social order.* New York: Scribner's.

Coopersmith, S. (1967). The antecedents of self-esteem. San Francisco, CA: Freeman.

Crandall, V. C., Crandall, V. J., & Katkovsky, W. (1965). A children's social desirability questionnaire. *Journal of Counseling Psychology 29,* 27–36.

Crowne, D., & Marlowe, D. (1964). *The approval motive.* New York: Wiley.

Damon, W., & Hart, D. (1988). *Self understanding in childhood and adolescence.* New York: Cambridge University Press.

Dickstein, E. (1977). Self and self-esteem: Theoretical foundations and their implications for research. *Human Development, 20,* 129–140.

Epstein, S. (1973). The self-concept revisited or a theory of a theory. *American Psychologist, 28,* 405–416.

Epstein, S. (1980). The stability of behavior: II. Implications for psychological research. *American Psychologist, 35,* 790–806.

Epstein, S. (1983). The unconscious, the preconscious and the self-concept. In J. Suls & A. Greenwald (Eds.), *Psychological perspectives on the self* (Vol. 2). Hillsdale, NJ: Erlbaum.

Epstein, S. (1991). Cognitive-experiential self theory: Implications for developmental psychology. In M. R. Gunnar & L. A. Sroufe (Eds.), *Self processes and development: The Minnesota Symposium on Child Development* (Vol. 23). Hillsdale, NJ: Erlbaum.

Felson, R. B. (1993). The (somewhat) social self: How others affect self-appraisals. In J. Suls (Ed.), *Psychological perspectives on the self* (Vol. 4). Hillsdale, NJ: Erlbaum.

Fischer, K. W. (1980). A theory of cognitive development: The control and construction of hierarchies of skills. *Psychological Review, 87,* 477–531.

Freud, S. (1968). Mourning and melancholia. In J. Strachey (Ed.), *The standard edition of the complete works of Sigmund Freud* (Vol. 14). London: Hogarth Press. (Original work published 1917)

Furman, W., & Buhrmester, D. (1985). Children's perceptions of personal relationships in their social networks. *Developmental Psychology, 21,* 1016–1024.

Gecas, V. (1972). Parental behavior and contextual variations in adolescent self-esteem. *Sociometry, 36,* 332–345.

Gergen, K. J. (1968). Personal consistency and the presentation of self. In C. Gordon & J. Gergen (Eds.), *The self in social interaction* (pp. 299–308). New York: Wiley.

Glick, M., & Zigler, E. (1985). Self-image: A cognitive-developmental approach. In R. Leahy (Ed.), *The development of the self.* New York: Academic Press.

Griffin, N., Chassin, L., & Young, R. D. (1981). Measurement of global self-concept versus multiple role-specific self-concepts in adolescents. *Adolescence, 16,* 49–56.

Grusec, J. E. (1983). The internalization of altruistic dispositions: A cognitive analysis. In E. T. Higgins, D. N. Ruble, & W. W. Hartup (Eds.), *Social cognition and social development: A sociocultural perspective.* New York: Cambridge University Press.

Hammen, C., & Goodman-Brown, T. (1990). Self-schemas and vulnerability to specific life stress in children at risk for depression. *Cognitive Therapy and Research, 14,* 215–227.

Hart, D. (1988). The adolescent self-concept in social context. In D. K. Lapsley & F. C. Power (Eds.), *Self, ego, and identity* (pp. 71–90). New York: Springer Verlag.

Harter, S. (1983). Developmental perspectives on the self-system. In E. M. Hetherington (Ed.), *Handbook of child psychology: Vol. 4. Socialization, personality, and social development* (pp. 275–386). New York: Wiley.

Harter, S. (1985). *The Self-Perception Profile for Children.* Denver, CO: University of Denver.

Harter, S. (1986a). Cognitive-developmental processes in the integration of concepts about emotions and the self. *Social Cognition, 4*(2), 119–151.

Harter, S. (1986b). Processes underlying the construction, maintenance, and enhancement of the self-concept in children. In J. Suls & A. G. Greenwald (Eds.), *Psychological perspectives on the self* (Vol. 3, pp. 137–181). Hillsdale, NJ: Erlbaum.

Harter, S. (1990a). Adolescent self and identity development. In S. S. Feldman & G. R. Elliot (Eds.), *At the threshold: The developing adolescent* (pp. 352–387). Cambridge, MA: Harvard University Press.

Harter, S. (1990b). Causes, correlates and the functional role of global self-worth: A life-span perspective. In J. Kolligian & R. Sternberg (Eds.), *Perceptions of competence and incompetence across the life-span* (pp. 67–98). New Haven, CT: Yale University Press.

Harter, S. (1993). Causes and consequences of low self-esteem in children and adolescents. In R. F. Baumeister (Ed.), *Self-esteem: The puzzle of low self-regard.* New York: Plenum.

Harter, S. (in press). Developmental changes in self-understanding across the 5 to 7 year shift. In A. Sameroff & M. Haith (Eds.), *Reason and responsibility: The passage through childhood.* Chicago: University of Chicago Press.

Harter, S., & Johnson, C. (1993). *Changes in self-esteem during the transition to college.* Unpublished manuscript, University of Denver.

Harter, S., Marold, D. B., & Whitesell, N. R. (1991). A model of psychosocial risk factors leading to suicidal ideation in young adolescents. *Development and Psychopathology, 4,* 167–188.

Harter, S., Marold, D. B., Whitesell, N. R., & Cobbs, G. (in press). A model of the effects of parent and peer support on adolescent false self behavior. *Child Development.*

Harter, S., & Monsour, A. (1992). Developmental analysis of opposing self-attributes in the adolescent self-portrait. *Developmental Psychology, 28,* 251–260.

Harter, S., & Pike, R. (1984). The pictorial scale of perceived competence and social acceptance for young children. *Child Development, 55,* 1969–1982.

Harter, S., Stocker, C., & Robinson, N. (in press). The perceived directionality of the link between approval and self-worth: The liabilities of a looking glass self orientation among young adolescents. *Journal of Adolescence,*

Hattie, J. (1992). *Self-concept.* Hillsdale, NJ: Erlbaum.

Higgins, E. T. (1987). Self-discrepancy: Theory relating self and affect. *Psychological Review, 94,* 319–340.

Higgins, E. T. (1989). Self-discrepancy theory: What patterns of self-beliefs cause people to suffer? In L. Berkowitz (Ed.), *Advances in experimental social psychology, 22.* New York: Academic Press.

Higgins, E. T. (1990). Self-state representations: Patterns of interconnected beliefs with specific holistic meanings and importance. *Bulletin of the Psychonomic Society, 28,* 248–253.

Higgins, E. T. (1991). Development of self-regulatory and self-evaluative processes: Costs, benefits, and trade-offs. In M. R. Gunnar & L. A. Sroufe (Eds.), *Self processes in development. Twenty-third Minnesota Symposium on Child Psychology.* Hillsdale, NJ: Erlbaum.

Horney, K. (1950). *Neurosis and human growth.* New York: Norton.

James, W. (1890). *Principles of psychology.* Chicago: Encyclopedia Britannica.

James, W. (1892). *Psychology: The briefer course.* New York: Henry Holt & Co.

Jung, C. G. (1928). *Two essays on analytical psychology.* New York: Dodd, Mead.

Kanfer, F. H. (1980). Self-management methods. In F. H. Kanfer & A. P. Goldstein (Eds.), *Helping people change: A textbook of methods* (2nd ed.). New York: Pergamon.

Katz, P. A., & Zigler, E. (1967). Self-image disparity: A developmental approach. *Journal of Personality and Social Psychology, 5,* 186–195.

Katz, P. A., Zigler, E., & Zalk, S. R. (1975). Children's self-image disparity: The effects of age, maladjustment, and action-thought orientation. *Developmental Psychology, 11,* 546–550.

Kelly, G. A. (1955). *The psychology of personal constructs.* New York: Norton.

Kinch, J. W. (1963). A formalized theory of the self-image. *The American Journal of Sociology, 74,* 251–258.

Kohlberg, L. (1976). Moral stages and moralization. In T. Lickona (Ed.), *Moral development and behavior.* New York: Holt, Rinehart & Winston.

Kovacs, M., & Beck, A. T. (1977). An empirical-clinical approach towards a definition of childhood depression. In J. G. Schulterbrandt & A. Raskin (Eds.), *Depression in childhood: Diagnosis, treatment, and conceptual models.* New York: Raven Press.

Kovacs, M., & Beck, A. T. (1978). Maladaptive cognitive structures in depression. *American Journal of Psychiatry, 135,* 525–533.

Kovacs, M., & Beck, A. T. (1986). Maladaptive cognitive structures in depression. In J. C. Coyne (Ed.), *Essential papers on depression.* New York: New York University Press.

Lecky, P. (1945). *Self-consistency: A theory of personality.* New York: Island Press.

Lewis, M., & Brooks-Gunn, J. (1979). *Social cognition and the acquisition of self.* New York: Plenum.

Logan, R. D. (1987). Historical change in prevailing sense of self. In K. Yardley & T. Honess (Eds.), *Self and identity: Psychological perspectives.* Chichester, UK: Wiley.

Maccoby, E. (1980). *Social development.* New York: Wiley.

Markus, H. (1977). Self-schemata and processing information about the self. *Journal of Personality and Social Psychology, 35,* 63–78.

Markus, H. (1980). The self in thought and memory. In D. M. Wegner & R. R. Vallacher (Eds.), *The self in social psychology.* New York: Oxford University Press.

Markus, H., & Herzog, A. R. (1991). The role of the self-concept in aging. In K. W. Schaie (Ed.), *Annual review of gerontology and geriatrics* (Vol. 11). New York: Springer.

Markus, H., & Nurius, P. (1986). Possible selves. *American Psychologist, 41,* 954–969.

Markus, H., & Worf, E. (1987). The dynamic self-concept: A social psychological perspective. In M. R. Rosenweig & L. W. Porter (Eds.), *Annual Review of Psychology, 38,* 299–337.

Marsh, H. W. (1986). Global self-esteem: Its relation to specific facets of self-concept and their importance. *Journal of Personality and Social Psychology, 51,* 1224–1236.

Marsh, H. W. (1987). The hierarchical structure of self-concept and the application of hierarchical confirmatory factor analysis. *Journal of Educational Measurement, 24,* 17–19.

Marsh, H. W. (1990). The structure of academic self-concept: The Marsh/ Shavelson model. *Journal of Educational Psychology, 82,* 623–636.

Marsh, H. W. (1993). Academic self-concept: Theory, measurement, and research. In J. Suls (Ed.), *Psychological perspectives on the self* (Vol. 4). Hillsdale, NJ: Erlbaum.

Maslow, A. H. (1954). *Motivation and personality.* New York: Harper & Row.

Maslow, A. H. (1961). Peak-experience as acute identity-experiences. *American Journal of Psychoanalysis, 21,* 254–260.

Maslow, A. H. (1971). *The farther reaches of human nature.* New York: Viking.

McGuire, W., & McGuire, C. V. (1980). Significant others in self-space: Sex differences and developmental trends in the social self. In J. Suls (Ed.), *Social psychological perspectives on the self.* Hillsdale, NJ: Erlbaum.

Mead, G. H. (1925). The genesis of the self and social control. *International Journal of Ethics, 35,* 251–273.

Mead, G. H. (1934). *Mind, self, and society.* Chicago: University of Chicago Press.

Mischel, W. (1968). *Personality and assessment.* New York: Wiley.

Mischel, W. (1973). Toward a cognitive social learning reconceptualization of personality. *Psychological Review, 80,* 252–283.

Mullener, N., & Laird, J. D. (1971). Some developmental changes in the organization of self-evaluations. *Developmental Psychology, 5,* 233–236.

Nikkari, D., & Harter, S. (1993). *The antecedents of behaviorally-presented self-esteem in young children.* Unpublished manuscript, University of Denver.

Oosterwegel, A., & Oppenheimer, L. (1993). *The self-system: Developmental changes between and within self-concepts.* Hillsdale, NJ: Erlbaum.

Oyserman, D., & Markus, H. (1987). *Possible selves, motivation, and delinquency.* Unpublished manuscript, University of Michigan.

Piaget, J. (1932). *The construction of reality in the child.* New York: Harcourt, Brace & World.

Piaget, J. (1965). *The child's conception of the world.* Paterson, NJ: Littlefield, Adams.

Piers, E. V. (1977). *The Piers-Harris children's self-concept scale* (Research Monograph No. 1). Nashville, TN: Counselor Recordings and Tests.

Reid, M., Landesman, S., Treder, R., & Jaccard, J. (1989). "My family and friends:" Six- to twelve-year-old children's perceptions of social support. *Child Development, 60*(4), 896–910.

Renouf, A. G., & Harter, S. (1990). Low self-worth and anger as components of the depressive experience in young adolescents. *Development and Psychopathology, 2,* 293–310.

Robinson, N. S. (1992). *Evaluating the nature of perceived support and its relation to perceived self-worth in adolescents.* Unpublished manuscript, Peabody College, University of Vanderbilt.

Rogers, C. R. (1950). The significance of the self-regarding attitudes and perceptions. In M. L. Reymert (Ed.), *Feelings and emotions: The Mooseheart symposium* (pp. 78–79). New York: McGraw-Hill.

Rogers, C. R. (1978). The child's perception of other people. In H. McGurk (Ed.), *Issues in childhood social development.* London: Methuen.

Rogers, C. R., & Dymond, R. (1954). *Psychotherapy and personality change.* Chicago: University of Chicago Press.

Rosenberg, M. (1979). *Conceiving the self.* New York: Basic Books.

Russell, A. M., Cahill, M., & Spain, W. H. (1992). *Occupational identity: The self in context.* (Available from the Centre for Educational Research and Development, St. John's, Newfoundland)

Sarbin, T. R. (1962). A preface to a psychological analysis of the self. *Psychological Review, 59,* 11–22.

Selman, R. (1980). *The growth of interpersonal understanding.* New York: Academic Press.

Shavelson, R. J., & Marsh, H. W. (1986). On the structure of self-concept. In R. Schwarzer (Ed.), *Anxiety and cognition.* Hillsdale, NJ: Erlbaum.

Smollar, J., & Youniss, J. (1985). Adolescent self-concept development. In R. L. Leahy (Ed.), *The development of self.* New York: Academic Press.

Stern, D. (1985). *The interpersonal world of the infant.* New York: Basic Books.

Strachen, A., & Jones, D. (1982). Changes in identification during adolescence: A personal construct theory approach. *Journal of Personality Assessment, 46,* 139–148.

Stryker, S. (1987). Identity theory: Developments and extensions. In K. Yardley & T. Honess (Eds.), *Self and identity.* New York: Wiley.

Tesser, A. (1980). Self-esteem maintenance in family dynamics. *Journal of Personality and Social Psychology, 39,* 77–91.

Tesser, A. (1988). Toward a self-evaluation maintenance model of social behavior. In L. Berkowitz (Ed.), *Advances in experimental social psychology* (Vol. 21). New York: Academic Press.

Tesser, A., & Campbell, J. (1980). Self-definition: The impact of the relative performance and similarity of others. *Social Psychology Quarterly, 43,* 341–347.

Trilling, L. (1971). *Sincerity and authenticity.* Cambridge, MA: Harvard University Press.

Vallacher, R. R. (1980). An introduction to self-theory. In D. M. Wegner & R. R. Vallacher (Eds.), *The self in social psychology* (pp. 3–30). New York: Oxford University Press.

Van der Werff, J. J. (1985). *Identity problems: Self-conceptions in psychology.* Muiderberg: Dick Coutinho.

Weiner, B. (1985). An attributional theory of achievement motivation and emotion. *Psychological Review, 92,* 271–282.

Weintraub, K. J. (1978). *The value of the individual: Self and circumstance in autobiography.* Chicago: Chicago University Press.

Wicklund, R. A., & Frey, D. (1980). Self-awareness theory: When the self makes a difference. In D. M. Wegner & R. R. Vallacher (Eds.), *The self in social psychology.* New York: Oxford University Press.

Winnicott, D. W. (1958). *From pediatrics to psychoanalysis.* London: Hogarth Press.

Winnicott, D. W. (1965). *The maturational processes and the facilitating environment.* New York: International Universities Press.

Wylie, R. C. (9161). *The self-concept: A critical survey of pertinent research literature.* Lincoln: University of Nebraska Press.

Wylie, R. C. (1974). *The self-concept. A review of methodological considerations and measuring instruments* (Rev. ed., Vol. 1). Lincoln: University of Nebraska Press.

Wylie, R. C. (1979). *The self concept: Vol. 2. Theory and research on selected topics.* Lincoln: University of Nebraska Press.

Zigler, E., Balla, D., & Watson, N. (1972). Developmental and experiential determinants of self-image disparity in institutionalized and noninstitutionalized retarded and normal children. *Journal of Personality and Social Psychology, 23,* 81–87.

CHAPTER 2

Theoretical Perspectives on the Structure of Self-Concept

HERBERT W. MARSH and JOHN HATTIE

A positive self-concept is a desirable outcome in many disciplines such as educational, developmental, clinical, and social psychology. Self-concept and related variables are frequently posited as mediating or facilitating other desired outcomes such as academic achievement. Researchers with a major focus on other constructs are often interested in how constructs in their research are related to self-concept. Methodologists are also concerned with particular measurement and methodological issues inherent in the study of self-concept. This interest in self-concept has a long and controversial history, and it is one of the oldest areas of research in the social sciences. The longest chapter in William James's 1890 textbook, the first introductory textbook in psychology, was devoted to self-concept and introduced many issues of current relevance.

William James (1890/1963) is generally recognized as the first psychologist to develop a theory of self-concept. Four notions developed by James were particularly important: (a) the I (self-as-knower or active agent) and Me (self-as-known or the content of experience) distinction; (b) the multifaceted, hierarchical nature of self-concept "with the bodily Self at the bottom, the spiritual Self at the top, and the extracorporeal material selves and the various social selves between" (p. 313); (c) the social self based on the recognition individuals receive from their peers or a generalized or potential social self that represents the evaluations of a hypothetical higher authority, a future generation, or God; and (d) the definition of self-esteem as the ratio of success to pretensions and subjective importance so that a person must select carefully "the strongest, truest, deepest self . . . on which to stake his salvation" (p. 310). Hence, James anticipated many subsequent developments in self-concept theories. His social self anticipated the importance of the evaluations by specific and generalized others that was an important focus of symbolic interactionists such as Cooley and Mead. The self-as-knower and self-as-known distinction is acknowledged in nearly all accounts of self-concept and corresponds approximately to the dynamic/process and structural/trait orientations that are currently popular in self-concept research. The development of the self-system described by James is consistent with recently developed cognitive approaches to the study of self. The definition of self-esteem as a function of both accomplishments and aspirations, and also the subjective importance of the activity, proved to be heuristic. The simultaneous self-seeking and self-preserving actions proposed by James may reflect the distinction between self-enhancement and self-consistency that has been the focus of much research. James also anticipated the multifaceted hierarchical model of self-concept that is a major focus of this chapter.

In this chapter, we discuss a wide variety of theoretical models of the structure of self-concept and self-concept instruments that are based (implicitly or explicitly) on such models. In particular, we emphasize the multidimensional, hierarchical model of self-concept proposed by Shavelson, Hubner, and Stanton (1976) and research using the Self Description Questionnaire (SDQ) instruments (Marsh, 1990c; Marsh, Byrne, & Shavelson, 1988; Marsh & Shavelson, 1985) that were developed to test the Shavelson et al. model. This perspective follows from the original Shavelson et al. perspective that theory, measurement, and research are inexorably intertwined such that one cannot be evaluated in isolation from the others. Our major emphasis, however, is on the evaluation of theoretical models of self-concept, and a more systematic evaluation of self-concept instruments is beyond the scope of this chapter (see Wylie, 1989; Chapter 3, this volume).

STRUCTURAL MODELS OF SELF-CONCEPT

Structural models of self-concept have been derived largely through analogy with corresponding models of intelligence. Soares and Soares (1977) proposed models of self-concept in which "theoretical considerations from Spearman, Thurstone, Cattell, Guilford, and Piaget comprise the foundation for the discussion of self-concept theory" (p. 1). Noting the dangers in extrapolating models from one discipline to another, they suggested that there was sufficient overlap in the two areas of research to make the comparison a relevant exercise. Based on their overview, they proposed the unidimensional general factor model, the multidimensional factor model, the hierarchical factor model, and the taxonomic model, which are among those considered here (see Figure 2.1). Although Soares and Soares tested some empirical implications of these models in subsequent empirical studies, they appear not to have developed more fully the theoretical parallels between the two areas of research beyond the brief, heuristic account in their 1977 conference paper. Whereas a review of the structure of intellect is beyond the scope of this chapter, a brief overview (based in part on suggestions by Soares and Soares, but based more on the perspectives of

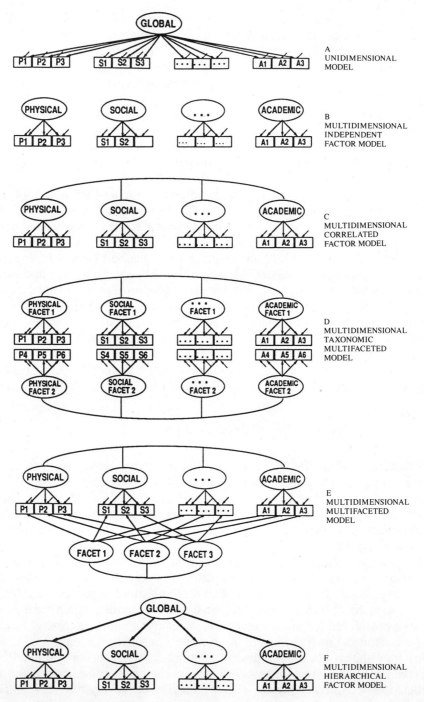

Figure 2.1 Structural models of self-concept derived from related models of ability and intelligence.

other reviewers such as Brody, 1992; Guilford, 1985; Nunnally, 1967; Thorndike, 1990) is instructive. It is also informative that in self-concept research, as in the study of intelligence, support and nonsupport for such models have been substantially influenced by developments in the application of factor analysis and related statistical techniques.

Historical perspectives about the structure of intellect (e.g., Brody, 1992; Guilford, 1985; Nunnally, 1967; Thorndike, 1990) typically begin by noting the methodological and substantive contributions of Darwin, Galton, Pearson, Binet, Burt, and others. Binet developed what is widely credited to be the first practical measure of intelligence, a simple aggregate of performances on 30 diverse tasks. Implicit in Binet's test was the assumption that there was only one factor of intelligence, or at least that different factors were dominated by a single factor. Spearman (1927) pursued this assumption in his two-factor theory of intelligence in which he proposed that performance on a particular task depended on a general ability (his *g* factor) and one or more specific factors that were unique to the particular task. Despite the many subsequent criticisms of Spearman's perspective, the explanatory power of *g* is evident. In any collection of intelligence tasks, there is a substantial common core (e.g., the first principal component) that may be largely responsible for the reliability, stability, and predictions based on the scale.

Other researchers such as E. L. Thorndike and Thurstone argued for multifaceted theories of intelligence. Based in part on further advances in factor analysis, Thurstone (1938) proposed a set of seven primary abilities. He reasoned that most cognitive tasks consisted of various combinations of these relatively independent factors, and so he developed an instrument consisting of relatively pure measures of each factor. However, Thurstone and Thurstone (1941) recognized that the primary mental abilities were correlated, particularly when based on representative samples of subjects. Cattell (1941) noted that the Spearman and Thurstone perspectives could be combined into a hierarchical model, although Cattell subsequently argued for more than one higher-order facet of intelligence. Vernon (1950) also combined Spearman's *g* approach and Thurstone's primary mental abilities approach into a hierarchical model of intelligence that was one basis of the Shavelson et al. model of self-concept emphasized here. At the apex, Vernon posited a single general factor analogous to Spearman's *g*. At the next level, he proposed group factors that were analogous to Thurstone's primary mental abilities. Finally, he proposed specific factors like those acknowledged by Spearman and Thurstone that were unique to narrowly defined tasks. In this sense, the hierarchical model incorporated the general factor and multidimensional perspectives into a single theoretical framework. Guilford (1959, 1969) proposed an alternative structure of intellect as a three-dimensional cube in which each component represented the intersection of 5 operations (what the subject does), 4 contents (the type of information on which operations are performed), and 6 products (type of information resulting from operations applied to contents). Guilford used factor analysis to test for the 120 (5 operations × 4 contents × 6 products) hypothesized components of intelligence. Guilford (1985) subsequently expanded his facet model and proposed a hierarchical representation for his structure of intellect that he suggested was consistent with hierarchical models such as that described by Vernon.

For purposes of this chapter, we distinguish between six models of the structure of self-concept that have been discussed in the literature and are largely based on analogous models in intelligence research (see Figure 2.1).

A Unidimensional, General Factor Model

The unidimensional position, reminiscent of Spearman's two-factor model, suggests that there is only a general factor of self-concept or that a general factor dominates more specific factors (Figure 2.1A). Thus, for example, Coopersmith (1967) and Marx and Winne (1978) argued that the facets of self-concept were so heavily dominated by a general factor that the separate factors could not be adequately differentiated. Further evaluation of these studies, however, reveals that the conclusions may reflect problems in measurement and statistical analysis rather than with the support for unidimensionality of self-concept.

Coopersmith's original 50-item instrument had four subscales: General (26 items), Social (8 items), Home/Parents (8 items), and Academic (8 items). On the basis of preliminary research, however, Coopersmith argued that "preadolescent children make little distinction about their worthiness in different areas of experience or, if such distinctions are made, they are made within the context of the over-all, general appraisal or worthiness that children have already made" (p. 6). Consistent with Coopersmith's conclusions, subsequent factor analyses of this instrument (e.g., Dyer, 1964; Marsh & Smith, 1982) failed to confirm the proposed factor structure or to identify any meaningful alternative structure. Neither of these studies, however, revealed any clear support for a unidimensional perspective. In fact, the Marsh and Smith factor analysis reported 21 eigenvalues greater than 1.0, one widely used criterion for determining the number of factors. The only dominant factor that they found was a "negative item" factor, apparently reflecting the difficulty that children in particular have in responding appropriately to negatively worded items. They concluded, "There appears to be no consistent pattern relating the observed factors to the scales that the Coopersmith instrument was designed to measure" (p. 435; also see Hattie, 1992 for a similar perspective). More importantly for present purposes, the results provided absolutely no support for Coopersmith's widely cited contention that self-concept is dominated by a general factor.

Adopting the simile of flowers, Winne, Marx, and Taylor (1977) argued, "It might be accurate to describe self-concept as a daisy. Much of the construct is shared and relatively undifferentiable, but individual petals or facets may be more or less relevant when self-concept is related to other constructs like achievement." This description resembles the Spearman model of intelligence. Like Spearman's subsequent refinements, however, it leaves open the possibility that there is some "true score" variance associated with specific components of self-concept that may be useful in relating self-concept to other constructs. Soares and Soares (1977) made a similar point in representing a general factor model (based on Spearman's model of intelligence) as a Venn diagram in which there are overlapping ellipses. In their model, the area of overlap among the different domains represents general self-concept, whereas the remaining, nonoverlapping areas reflect aspects of self-concept that are unique to each domain. Interestingly, Bracken (1992) used a similar Venn diagram to represent a multidimensional, hierarchical model of self-concept (see subsequent discussion) rather than a relatively unidimensional model of self-concept.

Marx and Winne (1978) classified the scales from three commonly used self-concept instruments into the academic, social, and physical facets hypothesized by Shavelson et al., and then used multitrait-multimethod (MTMM) analyses to compare responses from different instruments. They found that responses to each of the three facets demonstrated some agreement across instruments (convergence), but responses to the different scales could not be adequately differentiated (divergence). This led them to conclude that "self-concept seems more of a unitary concept than one divided into distinct subparts or facets" (p. 900). Shavelson and Bolus (1982), however, noted important weaknesses in their methodology and reanalyzed the Marx and Winne (1978) data to overcome some of these weaknesses. Although there was evidence for substantial method effects associated with each instrument, Shavelson and Bolus found reasonable support for convergent and divergent validity as well.

In contrast to this early MTMM research, more recent studies based on psychometrically stronger instruments (e.g., Marsh, 1990a; Marsh, Byrne, & Shavelson, 1988; Marsh & Gouvernet, 1989; Marsh & McDonald-Holmes, 1990; Marsh & Richards, 1988b) have shown strong support for the convergent and discriminant validity of self-concept responses from different instruments. In an interesting variation on the MTMM approach, Marsh (1992) examined relations between academic self-concept in specific school subjects and school grades in eight core school subjects. Although not the primary focus of the study, correlations among the achievement scores were substantial (mean $r = .58$), apparently reflecting a g factor, whereas the correlations among the eight components of self-concept (mean $r = .34$) were substantially lower. Consistent with this observation, a variety of structural equation models demonstrated that the set of school grades had a much stronger general component than did the corresponding self-concept scales. Thus, components of academic self-concept were much better differentiated than were the school grades.

In the past 10 to 15 years, researchers have developed self-concept instruments to measure specific facets that are at least loosely based on an explicit theoretical model such as that proposed by Shavelson et al., and then used factor analysis to support these a priori facets (e.g., Boersma & Chapman, 1979; Dusek & Flaherty, 1981; Fleming & Courtney, 1984; Harter, 1982; Marsh, 1990c; Soares & Soares, 1982). Reviews of this research (Byrne, 1984; Marsh & Shavelson, 1985; Shavelson & Marsh, 1986) support the multifaceted structure of self-concept and indicate that self-concept cannot be adequately understood if its multidimensionality is ignored.

In conclusion, there appears to be no support at all for a undimensional perspective of self-concept or, apparently, even a unidimensional perspective of academic self-concept. Critical evaluations of previous research claiming support for the unidimensionality of self-concept suggest that these claims were apparently unwarranted. This conclusion, however, poses a dilemma for many applied researchers who have focused primarily on a general or global component of self-concept like that depicted in the Rosenberg (1965) instrument. The thorny, unresolved issue about the appropriate definition of the global component of self-concept and the relevance of this construct is addressed later.

Multidimensional Independent and Correlated Factor Models

The independent and correlated factor models both represent self-concept as a multidimensional construct but differ in the degree to which the multiple dimensions are correlated. A strong version of the independent factor model requires all the factors to be absolutely uncorrelated (Figure 2.1B) although it may be reasonable to posit a weak version of the model in which the factors are defined to be "relatively" uncorrelated. The independent factor model reflects the antithesis of the undimensional general factor model (Figure 2.1A) in that it hypothesizes that there is no general self-concept—at least not in the sense of Spearman's g. To the best of our knowledge, no self-concept theorists have argued for the strong form of this model, although Soares and Soares (1977, 1982, 1983) and, perhaps, Marsh and Shavelson (1985) may be interpreted as supporting a weak version of the model.

Soares and Soares concluded that "as with research cited supporting a taxonomic model for the meaning of intelligence, the present research results suggest independent factors for explaining self-concept" (1977, p. 4) and that their research fails to support either a general factor model of self-concept or a hierarchical model (1982, 1983). Evidence for these conclusions comes from studies of their Affective Perception Inventory, which measures nine scales: a general self scale, two global academic scales, and six subject-specific scales. Their factor analyses consisted of separate analyses of items *within each scale,* but not factor analyses of items designed to measure different scales. These results apparently showed that none of their scales are undimensional, but are of limited use in determining the relative independence of the scales. Correlations among their nine scales vary from .14 to .66 (median $r = .37$) for U.S. data, from .04 to .61 (median $r = .28$) for Italian data, and from .30 to .76 (median $r = .57$) for Spanish data (Soares & Soares, 1983). In secondary analyses of correlations among their nine scales, Hattie (1992) reported two higher-order factors corresponding to mathematics/science and humanities self-concepts with the general scales loading on both factors. These results seem consistent with Marsh's (1990d) results showing that different components of academic self-concept are quite distinct, but that two second-order factors (Verbal/Academic and Math/Academic) could be identified. Soares and Soares results clearly argue for the multidimensionality of academic self-concept. It is not clear, however, that the results should be interpreted as support for the taxonomic or independent factors models of self-concept, or as failing to support a hierarchical model of self-concept. For example, Hattie (1992, pp. 68–69), based on his review of the research and reanalysis of their published results, concluded that in contrast to claims by Soares and Soares, their data support a hierarchical model of academic self-concept.

Marsh and Shavelson (1985) summarized two studies of SDQIII responses by late-adolescent students. Correlations among the 13 SDQIII scales were small in both studies (median coefficients of .09 and .08). The authors, in apparent support of a multidimensional independent factor model such as that proposed by Soares and Soares, noted this "surprising lack of correlation among facets of self-concept in the late-adolescent data" (p. 122). Although there was strong support for a hierarchical model based on responses by younger children, the authors concluded that "as the self-facets become more distinct as in the late-adolescent data, the utility of the hierarchical ordering becomes questionable" (p. 122). In subsequent research evaluating the hierarchical structure of SDQIII responses, Marsh (1987b) reported three second-order factors and one third-order global factor, but also noted that "the hierarchy was so weak that the first-order facets could not be accurately inferred from the higher-order factors" (p. 17).

In summary, there is clear support for a multidimensional model of self-concept, but apparently little or no support for the strong version of the multidimensional independent factor model. Whereas some studies have reported that correlations among first-order factors are "relatively" uncorrelated, most have found correlations among self-concept factors to be at least modest. Even in studies where correlations among the factors are relatively small, however, there is apparent support for a weak hierarchical ordering of the facets of self-concept that seems inconsistent with the rationale of the independent factor model.

Taxonomic Models

Guilford's structure of intellect model was apparently the inspiration for the taxonomic model of self-concept proposed by Soares and Soares (1977). A unique aspect of Guilford's model is that the components of intellect reflect the intersection of two or more facets, each of which has at least two levels. It is important to distinguish between the meaning of "multifaceted" used here and the typical meaning in self-concept literature. To draw on familiar terminology used in the analysis of variance, this distinction is the difference between a one-way design and a factorial design. In a one-way design that is analogous to most models of self-concept, there is a single facet (the self-concept content domains) with multiple levels (the different self-concept domains such as physical, social, and academic). In the factorial design that is analogous to our interpretation of the taxonomic model (see Figure 2.1D), there are at least two facets, each of which has two or more levels. Thus, for example, Guilford's 120 components of intelligence reflect the multiplicative combination of three different facets: 5 operations $\times$ 4 contents $\times$ 6 products. Although Soares and Soares (1977) proposed a taxonomic model of self-concept and claimed support for it, it appears that they were actually testing the multidimensional independent factor model previously described. Although they derived the term "taxonomic model" from Guilford's model of intelligence, they never described the model in sufficient detail to differentiate it from the independent factors model. Byrne (1984) and Hattie (1992) seemed to take similar perspectives in their reviews of the Soares and Soares "taxonomic" model. Thus, for example, Hattie evaluates the taxonomic model proposed by Soares and Soares in a section entitled "self-concept has no common factor." Furthermore, perhaps, the Soares and Soares interpretation may be inappropriate as Guilford (1985) subsequently noted that factors within his structure were correlated and could be represented as a hierarchical model.

Two forms of the multifaceted self-concept model are presented in Figure 2.1. Figure 2.1D seems most analogous to the description by Soares and Soares based on the Guilford model. As depicted in Figure 2.1D, there are 8 factors representing all multiplicative combinations of 4 levels of the domain facet (the content domain typically considered in self-concept studies) times 2 levels reflecting a second facet. Although the nature of the second facet is not specified, the two levels could reflect identity versus behavior responses as proposed by Fitts (1964), responses to positively and negatively worded items as emphasized by Marsh (1990c), or responses to items reflecting a "personal" perspective indicating how subjects feel about themselves and an "other" perspective indicating how subjects believe they are perceived by others as emphasized by Bracken (1992). Figure 2.1E is an alternative representation of multifaceted data derived from structural equation models of multitrait-multimethod data. As depicted in

Figure 2.1E, there are 7 factors representing 4 levels of the domain facet and 3 levels reflecting a second facet. Thus, instead of positing 12 factors reflecting all combinations of the 4 levels of the first facet and 3 levels of the second facet, only 7 factors are posited. This model proposes that all measures reflecting the same level of each facet can be explained in terms of a single "level" factor (e.g., physical self-concept). As applied in multi-trait-multimethod studies, one facet typically reflects a domain and the other facet reflects multiple methods (e.g., three different self-concept instruments as in Marsh, Byrne & Shavelson, 1988, or, perhaps, ratings by different individuals). Both of these representations could be extended to have more levels in either of the two facets or to have more than two facets.

A number of self-concept instruments implicitly or explicitly posit a taxonomic model although the scores based on the model are not always consistent with the design of the instruments. For example, the structural model underlying the design of the Tennessee Self Concept Instrument (Fitts, 1964) reflects a taxonomic model with three facets. Fitts used a 5 (external frame of reference) × 3 (internal frame of reference) × 2 (positively/negatively worded items) design. The 5 levels of the external facet—Physical, Moral, Personal, Family, and Social—are similar to the self-concept traits proposed in many subsequent instruments. In Fitt's schema, each of these traits could be manifested in relation to three internal frames of reference, the second facet in his test design: Identity (e.g., what I am), Satisfaction (e.g., how I feel about myself), and Behavior (e.g., what I do or how I act). Identity is a private, internal self-concept. Behavior is the self that is observable to others. Satisfaction reflects an actual-ideal discrepancy. The third facet, based on the positive or negative wording of the items, provides a control for various response biases and may or may not be substantively important. Hence the instrument consists of 30 scales (15 if the item wording facet is ignored) and each is represented by 3 of the 90 items in the instrument. In their review of the instrument, Marsh and Richards (1988b) noted that the instrument is often scored in ways that are apparently inconsistent with its design. Thus, for example, the design of the instrument allows three manifestations of social self-concept (identity, satisfaction, behavior), and so it may be inappropriate to summarize social self-concept with a single score that confounds the three manifestations. In their evaluation of support for the underlying structure of the Tennessee instrument, Marsh and Richards concluded that there was little support for the internal facet in TSCS responses and consistent support for only the Physical, Social, and Family traits in the external facet. Whereas there was a clear separation between positively and negatively worded items, it was unclear whether this was substantively important or reflected a substantively unimportant method effect. Although Marsh and Richards (1988b) concluded that "the TSCS was not a psychometrically strong instrument when judged by current test standards," the structural model underlying its development is apparently unique in the self-concept literature. The lack of support for this model apparently reflects limitations in the TSCS instrument and it may be possible that some variation of this model can be more successfully operationalized.

Bracken (1992) also based the design of his new Multidimensional Self Concept Scale (MSCS) on a three-facet taxonomic model. His "context-specific self-concepts" reflect a domain facet having six levels (Social, Competence, Affect, Academic, Family, Physical) based more or less on the Shavelson et al. model (except that Competence and, perhaps, Affect appear to be higher-order domains that overlap with esteem as inferred from instruments like the Rosenberg scale). The "evaluative perspectives" facet has two levels—personal perspective (acquired directly through an individual's evaluations of his or her own behavior) and other perspective (acquired indirectly through inferences about evaluations by others). The "evaluative performance standards" facet has four levels—absolute, ipsative, comparative, and ideal standards. (In addition, the MSCS scale contains both positively and negatively worded items that could reflect a fourth design facet.) Consistent with the taxonomic design, Bracken discusses all eight multiplicative combinations of the two perspectives and four standards (e.g., absolute standard-personal perspective, ideal standard-other perspective). Despite the theoretical importance of the perspectives and standards facets in the acquisition of self-concept in the design of the MSCS, these facets are not employed when scoring the instrument—only six scores reflecting the domain facet are used. Thus, the design of MSCS apparently reflects models 2.1D or 2.1E, whereas the scoring of the MSCS apparently reflects model 2.1C.

Although factor analyses of responses to MSCS items are not presented in the manual, it seems likely that analyses of responses to items within each domain scale would reflect some combination of the perspectives and standards facets, whereas the analyses of all items would reflect various combinations of all three facets as in models 2.1D or 2.1E. Alternatively, model 2.1C that apparently reflects the way the MSCS is scored may be a more appropriate representation of MSCS items, although this may call into question the rationale underlying the design of the instrument. Ultimately, the issue is an empirical one that must be evaluated in relation to systematic tests of the structure underlying the MSCS responses.

In summary, the taxonomic model is apparently consistent with theoretical models underlying some multidimensional self-concept instruments, but it may not be consistent with scores derived from these instruments. More generally, the taxonomic model may permit researchers to combine structural (domain) and process components of self-concept as seems to be the intent of Bracken's environmental-behavioral interactive model. To develop the rich, heuristic potential of the taxonomic model, however, further research is needed on how to determine the most appropriate structure (e.g., Figures 2.1E and 2.1F) and corresponding scores to represent this model, and how scores reflecting various combinations of the facets are differentially related to external criteria.

Compensatory Model

Marx and Winne (1978) proposed a compensatory model with a global self-concept factor and multiple lower-order factors (e.g., social, academic, and physical). This model posits that under some circumstances, the lower-order factors will be negatively correlated. The rationale is that there is an ipsative-like* process such that individuals who, for example, are relatively less successful in the academic area tend to perceive themselves as being more successful in physical and social areas. Support for this unique, provocative model, however, is apparently open to counter-interpretations (Hattie, 1992). It is also ironic that these researchers apparently used the same data to support unidimensional and compensatory models of self-concept.

Marx and Winne (1980) used canonical correlational analysis to examine relations among three self-concept traits measured by each of three instruments. In separate analyses, each instrument was used as the criterion and the other two were used as predictors. After extracting the first pair of canonical variates, they reported that the second and third pairs of canonical variates had some scales loading in opposite directions. However, canonical correlation begins by extracting a pair of canonical variates that are maximally correlated. The second pair of canonical variates are then constructed to be maximally correlated with each other but uncorrelated with the first pair of canonical variates. Because the second pair is explaining residual variance, there is typically a mixture of positive and negative loadings. As noted by Hattie (1992), it may be misleading to claim that these negative loadings reflect a psychological process rather than an interpretational problem associated with canonical correlation. Hattie (1992) reanalyzed the Marx and Winne data based on published correlations among scale scores from the three instruments and concluded, "Overall this evidence does not support Marx and Winne's arguments for a compensatory, bipolar model of self-concept" (p. 74).

It is also instructive to note a parallel finding in the structure of intellect literature and Vernon's (1950) interpretation of apparently bipolar ability factors. In his discussion of interpreting unrotated factors, Vernon noted that there is typically a large first factor that represents a kind of average of the ability tests and additional bipolar factors in which roughly half the

---

*In a truly ipsative set of measures such as a rank ordering, all the scores sum to the same value for each individual; any one score can only be increased if another is decreased. It also follows that across all individuals the average correlation among a set of ipsative scores must be negative, although some individual correlations may be positive. Here, we propose an ipsativelike process in which an increase in any one domain of self-concept must be balanced by a corresponding decrease in some combination of other self-concept domains. Hence, such an ipsativelike process assumes that there is a negative correlation between at least some of the self-concept domains. Because self-concepts in different domains tend to be positively correlated, other processes must exist as well.

factor loadings are negative and half are positive. Vernon argued that although these bipolar factors have no psychological meaning in this form, they reveal that multiple factors are evident. Vernon argued further that rather than interpret these unrotated factors, it is preferable to rotate the factors to approximate simple structure where all the tests have either positive factor loadings or loadings close to zero. Vernon's interpretation of bipolar ability factors and his conclusion that they are not psychologically meaningful is consistent with Hattie's interpretation of Marx and Winne's bipolar self-concept factors.

Winne and Marx (1981) provided additional support for their compensatory model of self-concept. They constructed 12 new scales representing three domains (physical, social, academic) × four response formats (self-ratings compared with other students, feelings about their relative status, rank ordering of the relative importance of high status on the three domains, and rank ordering of low status on the three domains). The design of this instrument resembles in some ways the taxonomic, multifaceted model described earlier. Winne and Marx then related students' responses to their 12 new scales to students' responses to the Sears self-concept instrument and an academic achievement test score. In contrast to previous MTMM studies by these authors, the results strongly supported the convergent and discriminant validity of responses to the three self-concept domains. In support of the compensatory hypothesis, the authors noted academic responses were frequently correlated *negatively* with social and physical responses. However, these negative correlations were apparently an artifact of the ipsative (rank order) format used on the last two of their four response formats. Ipsative scores are necessarily negatively correlated (ranking yourself more highly on one scale necessarily means that rankings on the other scales must be lower) and so negative correlations involving the ipsative scales should not be interpreted as support for the compensatory model. In contrast to the ipsative scales, none of the correlations among any of the remaining scales was significantly negative. In summary, apparent support for compensatory factors claimed by Winne and Marx (1981) seems to reflect an artifact of the use of ipsative rating scales rather than a compensatory process underlying the formation of self-concept in different areas.

Better support for the compensatory model was evident in the pattern of relations between multiple dimensions of self-concept and academic achievement reported by Winne and Marx (1981). Even for the nonipsative ratings, academic self-concept was positively correlated with academic achievement, whereas physical and social self-concepts were negatively related (coefficients ranged from −.12 to −.21). Furthermore, when Marx and Winne (1980) used multiple regression to relate multiple dimensions of self-concept to academic achievement, the beta weights for academic self-concept were positive, whereas the beta weights associated with the nonacademic components were significantly negative.

Bracken (1992) also incorporated a compensatory component—the ipsative standard—into his theoretical model of self-concept. Thus, for example, "As a child gains a sense of what his *overall* ability is, the child evaluates his *specific* areas of functioning by comparing his success in those unique dimensions with his *overall* ability" (Bracken, 1992, p. 7). Bracken, however, did not pursue empirical tests of this theoretical component of his model.

The Internal/External Frame of Reference Model

Stronger empirical support for the compensatory model comes from Marsh's (1986b) research on the internal/external frame of reference (I/E) model that is discussed in more detail in Chapter 7. The model was developed to explain the surprising lack of correlation between math and verbal self-concepts that led to the revision of the original Shavelson et al. (1976) model of self-concept, but seems to be consistent with at least the logic of the compensatory model. Because verbal and mathematics achievements are typically correlated .5 to .8, commonsense as well as the original Shavelson et al. (1976) model suggested that verbal and math self-concepts would also be substantially correlated. Hence it was surprising that these self-concepts were nearly uncorrelated with each other, leading to the revision of the original Shavelson et al. model (Marsh & Shavelson, 1985) and the development of the I/E model. According to the I/E model, individuals form their self-concept judgments in a particular domain by comparing their own competence in that domain with the perceived competences of others in the same domain (an external, social comparison process) and by comparing their own competence in that domain with their own competencies in other domains (an internal, ipsative-like process). Tests of the I/E have been limited thus far to explaining relations between different areas of academic achievement (e.g., verbal and mathematical) and the corresponding areas of academic self-concept. Consistent with common sense, verbal achievement consistently contributes positively to the verbal self-concept and mathematics achievement contributes positively to math self-concept. More surprisingly, however, mathematics achievement contributes negatively to verbal self-concept and verbal achievement contributes negatively to math self-concept. Thus, for example, if I am a weak student in all school subjects but I am relatively better at mathematics (better than my even poorer performances in other school subjects but still below average relative to other students), I may have an average or even above-average math self-concept. Hence the internal comparison process in the I/E model appears to be like the process proposed by Marx and Winne in the compensatory model.

To illustrate the potential breadth of applicability of the I/E model, imagine the following scenario based on a weekend athlete and a professional tennis player. The weekend athlete is reasonably good at both tennis and golf, but is better at golf (with a handicap of 8). The tennis pro is better at tennis than golf but is also a good golfer (with a handicap of 4). When asked to complete yet to be constructed tennis and golf self-concept scales, the weekend athlete had a higher golf self-concept than the tennis pro even though the tennis pro was an objectively better golfer. The apparent discrepancy is due to the operation of the internal comparison process. The weekend athlete has a higher golf self-concept because golf is this person's best sport, whereas golf is not the best sport for the tennis pro.

A Multidimensional, Hierarchical Model

The multidimensional, hierarchical model (see Figure 2.1F) in some respects incorporates each of the other models as a special case. As in the undimensional, global factor model, it hypothesizes a global component at the apex of the hierarchy. Thus, support for the global factor model could also be interpreted as support for a hierarchical model in which the hierarchy is very strong. At the opposite extreme, support for the multidimensional independent factor model could be interpreted as support for a hierarchical model in which the hierarchy is very weak. Only in the extreme cases in which correlations among the self-concept factors approach the reliabilities of the factors or are consistently close to zero would support for the hierarchical model be dubious. Support for the multidimensional correlated factor model automatically implies support for a hierarchical model.

The relations between the taxonomic and hierarchical models are not so clear-cut, but it seems that the two are not incompatible. Indeed, Guilford (1985) posited a hierarchical representation of his taxonomic model of intellect that was apparently the basis of Soares and Soares (1977) taxonomic model of self-concept. Similarly, the compensatory model does not seem to be inconsistent with a hierarchical model, although it may explain why the self-concept hierarchy is apparently weaker than originally anticipated. Indeed, in their original formulation of this model, Marx and Winne (1980) hypothesized a general higher-order factor and second-order, domain-specific factors.

In summary, the multidimensional hierarchical model is apparently consistent—or at least not incompatible—with each of the structural models posited in Figure 2.1. This flexibility, however, is both a strength and a weakness. It is a strength because it provides a broad framework for exploring the structure of self-concept. It is a weakness because the hierarchical model, at least at the level of abstraction considered thus far, may not be falsifiable. Hence, it is critically important that a priori hierarchical models of self-concept are specified in sufficient detail to allow rigorous testing.

Bracken's (1992) Multidimensional, Hierarchical Model

As noted earlier, in what might be considered an alternative representation of a multidimensional, hierarchical model, Bracken (1992) proposed a

Venn diagram (see Figure 12.1, in Chapter 12) like the "daisy" representation proposed by Winne et al. (1977) and that presented by Soares and Soares (1977). Interestingly, these earlier representations—apparently in contrast to Bracken—were used to reflect a relatively undimensional model of self-concept that is analogous to Spearman's model of self-concept. Bracken only provided a cursory description of this model that also serves as a logo for his MCSC instrument. He noted that global self-concept (like Spearman's *g*) is at the center of the Venn diagram—where the specific domains of self-concept overlap with each other and the global component. In the Venn diagram, all the circles reflecting specific domains of self-concept overlap equally with global self-concept, and Bracken specifically proposed that his "model assumes that the various specific self-concept dimensions are of approximately equal importance in their contribution to global self-concept, although it is recognized that some dimensions are likely to be more important for individual children than for others" (p. 5). Elaborating on his model in juxtaposition to an earlier version of this chapter, Bracken (personal communication, December 8, 1993) stated:

> The MSCS Venn diagram depicts both the hierarchical nature of self-concept as well as the correlated nature of the six primary domains. Psychometric *g* is represented where domains overlap with all other domains in the center of the diagram. Where a specific domain overlaps with another domain, the result is variance shared specifically between the two subareas (e.g., where social overlaps with academic as a result of the social interactions that occur within the very specific academic context; where social overlaps with physical, the shared variance represents the influences of physical abilities and appearance on one's social acceptance). Finally, where a domain does not overlap with any other domain, the result is specific variance—or the assessment of a unique and relatively pure construct. Hence, the model reflects *g*, variance shared by pairs of domains, and subscale specificity in a hierarchical fashion.

Bracken's Venn diagram is heuristic but apparently does not provide a sufficiently detailed representation to unambiguously represent his underlying, implicit model. Global self-concept, according to Bracken, reflects the portion of the diagram where all the domains overlap, but in his actual diagram there is no area in which all the domains overlap. The circle representing global self-concept apparently encompasses all areas in which three domains overlap and some—but not all—the areas in which two domains overlap. Bracken specifically refers to the overlap between social and academic self-concepts, but these two domains do not overlap in his diagram. Similarly, there appears to be no overlap between the Affect and Competence domains and between the Physical and Family domains. Hierarchical models of self-concept (see subsequent discussion of Figure 2.2) often depict three or more levels in the hierarchy. Whereas Bracken's Venn

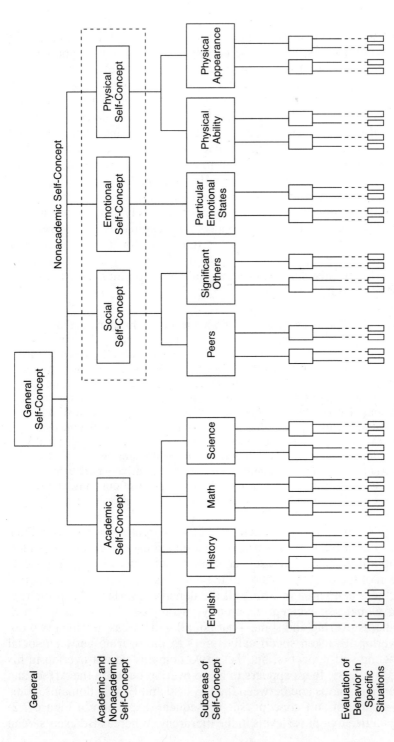

General

Academic and
Nonacademic
Self-Concept

Subareas of
Self-Concept

Evaluation of
Behavior in
Specific
Situations

Figure 2.2 Representation of the hierarchical organization of self-concept as posited in the original Shavelson et al. (1976) model of self concept. From "Validation of Construct Interpretations," by Shavelson, Hubner, and Stanton, 1976, *Review of Educational Research, 46,* 407–441. Copyright 1976 by the American Educational Research Association. Reprinted with permission of the publisher.

diagram could be expanded to include more than two levels and more than one higher-order factor, it would become unwieldy. Although some of the deficits in the particular diagram used by Bracken could be remedied, it seems unlikely that any two-dimensional Venn diagrams would be able to represent Bracken's model.

There are apparently no advantages (except, perhaps, artistic) in representing the multidimensional, hierarchical model as a Venn diagram rather than the more traditional presentation as in Figure 2.1F or in the Shavelson, Hubner, and Stanton (1976) representation (see subsequent discussion of Figure 2.2). Bracken argues that his representation reflects global self-concept, variance shared by pairs of domains, and uniqueness in a hierarchical fashion, but so does the hierarchical model. Whereas Figure 2.1F does not actually depict uniquenesses and correlations among first-order factors that are independent of global self, these are easily added to the figure and are testable with confirmatory factor analysis (CFA) and hierarchical CFA (HCFA) procedures. Also, it is possible to represent correlations among first-order factors as second-order factors (see Figure 2.2) in addition to the global component that appears at the apex. Whereas the degree of overlap among circles can be used to represent relations among different domains in the Bracken's diagram, these can be more easily reflected as predicted or observed parameter estimates in Figure 2.1.

The most important advantage of a representation like that in Figure 2.1F over a Venn diagram representation is that there is a one-to-one correspondence between the diagram and the HCFA procedures used to test the model. Bracken (1992) did not actually pursue rigorous empirical tests of the model depicted in his Venn diagram using statistical techniques such as HCFA. We suspect that if he had, he would have realized the limitations in his Venn diagram representation compared with a more traditional representation of HCFA models such as the one shown in Figure 2.1F.

In summary, despite its heuristic and artistic appeal, Bracken's Venn diagram representation of a multidimensional, hierarchical model of self-concept is unlikely to bear fruit. It seems unable to represent adequately Bracken's underlying, implicit model, to guide HCFA tests of the model, or to represent the results of HCFA analyses. For this reason, we now turn to the hierarchical model proposed by Shavelson et al. (1976) and its subsequent refinements.

THE SHAVELSON, HUBNER, AND STANTON (1976) REVIEW

Despite the rich beginning provided by William James, advances in theory, research, and measurement of self-concept were slow during the heyday of behaviorism. Only in the past 25 years has there been a resurgence in self-concept research. Even during this more recent period, however, interesting peculiarities appear to have undermined the usefulness of this research for understanding self-concept. Unlike many areas of research, self-concept research has not occurred primarily within the structure of a particular discipline. Although many thousands of studies have examined self-concept, until recently only a few researchers had published a significant number of studies or conducted self-concept research over an extended period. In many studies, the major focus is on some other construct (e.g., academic achievement, delinquency), and a measure of self-concept is included because of its assumed relevance to the other construct. It also appears that many self-concept studies lacked sophistication in theory, measurement, or methodology. Prior to the 1980s, reviews of self-concept research (e.g., Burns, 1979; Shavelson, Hubner, & Stanton, 1976; Wells & Marwell, 1976; Wylie, 1974, 1979) typically emphasized the lack of theoretical basis in most studies, the poor quality of measurement instruments used to assess self-concept, methodological shortcomings, and a general lack of consistent findings (except for support for the null hypothesis). This disappointing lack of rigor can, perhaps, be explained by the lack of a disciplinary base for self-concept research. Similar observations led Hattie (1992) to describe this period as one of "dustbowl empiricism" in which the predominant research design in self-concept studies was "throw it in and see what happens." Hattie argued that research during the past 25 years has produced little theoretical understanding of the self-concept construct leading him to lament that only a few self-concept theorists since the 1960s have earned a place in his self-concept hall of fame.

Self-concept, like many other psychological constructs, suffers in that "everybody knows what it is," so that many researchers do not feel compelled to provide any theoretical definition of what they are measuring. Because self-concept is a hypothetical construct, its usefulness must be established by investigations of its construct validity. These investigations can be classified as within-network or between-network studies. Within-network studies explore the internal structure of self-concept. They test, for example, the dimensionality of self-concept and may seek to show that the construct has consistent, distinct multidimensional components (e.g., physical, social, academic self-concept). These studies typically employ empirical techniques such as factor analysis or multi-trait-multimethod (MTMM) analysis. Between-network studies attempt to establish a logical, theoretically consistent pattern of relations between measures of self-concept and other constructs. The resolution of at least some within-construct issues should be a logical prerequisite to conducting between-construct research, but between-network research has predominated self-concept research.

Despite the importance and popularity of the self-concept construct, empirical support for its usefulness based on research conducted prior to the 1980s was weak. Research up to that point had made limited progress toward resolving either the within- or between-construct issues. In fact, most research was directed toward the between-construct issues of relating self-concept to other constructs, whereas insufficient attention had been given to the within-construct issues that should have been the basis of constructing appropriate measurement instruments. In retrospect, this emphasis on between-construct research to the exclusion of within-construct research may have been counterproductive and appears to be one reason findings were not more consistent across different studies. In contrast, studies since the 1980s have made important advances in theory, measurement, and research. An important basis for these advances is the classic review article by Shavelson et al. (1976).

Shavelson et al. (1976) emphasized the increasing importance that researchers, practicioners, and policy makers were placing on the self-concept construct, but noted critical deficiencies in self-concept research. These deficiencies included definitions of the self-concept construct, a dearth of appropriate measurement instruments, and the lack of rigorous tests of counterinterpretations. They concluded "It appears that self-concept research has addressed itself to substantive problems before problems of definition, measurement, and interpretation have been resolved" (p. 470). These concerns with self-concept research were not new. However, what differentiated the Shavelson et al. review from other critiques emphasizing the deficiencies of self-concept research was, in the words of the authors, that "our approach is constructive in that we (a) develop a definition of self-concept from existing definitions, (b) review some steps in validating a construct interpretation of a test score, and (c) apply these steps in examining five popularly used self-concept instruments" (p. 470). Prophetically, they suggested that "perhaps this approach will stimulate further construct validation research" (p. 470). As the contents of this book demonstrate, their research has been hugely heuristic, forming the basis of subsequent research during the next two decades.

Shavelson et al. (1976) began their review by developing a theoretical definition of self-concept. An ideal definition, they emphasized, should consist of the nomological network containing within-network and between-network components. The within-network portion of the network pertains to specific features of the construct—its components, structure, and attributes and theoretical statements relating these features. The between-network portion of the definition locates the construct in a broader conceptual space, indicating how self-concept is related to other constructs. Thus, for example, dividing self-concept into academic, social, and physical components is a within-network proposition, whereas a related between-network proposition is that academic self-concept is more strongly related to academic achievement than are social and physical self-concepts.

In their review of definitions, Shavelson et al. (1976) identified 17 different conceptual components that could be used to classify various definitions. They noted, however:

By integrating various features that are common to the definitions, and by extending the definitions when necessary, it is possible to construct a working definition of self-concept that is consistent with some current research and can be used to begin to integrate empirical evidence on the validity of self-concept interpretations. (p. 411)

Definition of Self-Concept

Self-concept, broadly defined by Shavelson et al. (1976), is a person's self-perceptions formed through experience with and interpretations of his or her environment. They are influenced especially by evaluations by significant others, reinforcements, and attributions for the individual's own behavior. According to Shavelson et al., self-concept is not an entity within the person, but a hypothetical construct that is potentially useful in explaining and predicting how a person acts. These self-perceptions influence the way he or she acts, and these acts in turn influence the person's self-perceptions. Consistent with this perspective, Shavelson et al. noted that self-concept is important as both an outcome and as a mediating variable that helps to explain other outcomes. Shavelson et al. also distinguished between self-concepts based on a person's own self-perceptions and inferred self-concepts that are based on inferences by another person, noting that they would focus on the former. Shavelson et al. identified seven features that were critical to their definition of the self-concept construct:

1. It is organized or structured, in that people categorize the vast amount of information they have about themselves and relate these categories to one another.

2. It is multifaceted, and the particular facets reflect a self-referent category system adopted by a particular individual and/or shared by a group.

3. It is hierarchical, with perceptions of personal behavior in specific situations at the base of the hierarchy, inferences about self in broader domains (e.g., social, physical, and academic) at the middle of the hierarchy, and a global, general self-concept at the apex. Shavelson et al. likened this structure to a hierarchical representation of intellectual abilities with Spearman's g (see Vernon, 1950) at the apex.

4. The hierarchical general self-concept—the apex of the hierarchy—is stable, but as one descends the hierarchy, self-concept becomes increasingly situation-specific and, as a consequence, less stable. Changes in self-perceptions at the base of the hierarchy may be attenuated by conceptualizations at higher levels, and changes in

general self-concept may require changes in many situation-specific instances.

5. Developmentally, self-concept becomes increasingly multifaceted as the individual moves from infancy to adulthood. Infants tend not to differentiate themselves from their environment, young children have self-concepts that are global, undifferentiated, and situation-specific, and it is only with increasing age and the acquisition of verbal labels that self-concept becomes increasingly differentiated and integrated into a multifaceted, hierarchical construct.

6. Self-concept has both a descriptive and an evaluative aspect such that individuals may describe themselves ("I am happy") and evaluate themselves ("I do well in mathematics"). Evaluations can be made against some absolute ideal, a relative standard based on comparisons with peers, or the expectations of significant others. Individuals may differentially weight specific dimensions. Shavelson et al. further noted that the distinction between self-evaluation and self-description has not been clarified conceptually or empirically, so that the term self-concept and self-esteem are used interchangably in the literature.

7. Self-concept can be differentiated from other constructs to which it is theoretically related (the between-network component of the nomological network). Thus for example, academic achievement should be more highly correlated with academic self-concept than with social or physical self-concept, and self-concepts in specific school subjects (e.g., mathematics, English) should be more highly correlated with achievement in matching school subjects than achievements in other subjects.

Shavelson et al. (1976) also presented Figure 2.2 as one possible representation of the hierarchical organization of self-concept. Here, general self-concept at the apex is divided into academic and nonacademic components of self-concept. The academic component is divided into self-concepts specific to general school subjects, and nonacademic self-concept is divided into physical and social components, which are further divided into more specific components. Also, there is a continuum of increasingly more specific components that are not labeled. The evaluations and descriptions of behaviors in specific situations that appear at the base of the hierarchy are consistent with a situation-specific definition of self-concept. Ironically, this heuristic figure has come to be seen as *the* Shavelson et al. model of self-concept although their original intention was that it be just one possible representation of the hierarchical feature of their definition of self-concept. The figure turned out to be so important, in part, because it provided a blueprint for a new generation of multidimensional self-concept instruments that have had significant influence on the field.

Validation of Self-Concept Interpretations

Theory, measurement, and empirical research are inexorably intertwined so that the neglect of one will undermine the others. From this perspective, the Shavelson et al. (1976) definition of the self-concept construct provides a blueprint for constructing self-concept instruments, for designing within-network studies of the proposed structure of self-concept, for testing between-network hypotheses about relations with other constructs and, eventually, rejecting and revising the original construct definition. An important aspect of the Shavelson et al. review was to propose some of the logical, correlational, and experimental procedures for evaluating construct definitions.

Logical analysis examines the logical consistency of the construct definition, measurement instruments (instructions, item format, scoring procedures, etc.), and predictions. The purpose of logical analysis according to Shavelson et al. (1976) is to generate counterhypotheses of the interpretation of test scores that are empirically testable.

Correlational techniques can be used to investigate the (within-network) structure of self-concept and the (between-network) relations between self-concept and other constructs. Shavelson et al. reviewed three correlational techniques that are particularly useful in self-concept research: factor analysis, multitrait-multimethod analysis, and path analysis.

Experimental techniques are also useful in testing the validity of interpretations of self-concept responses. Thus, for example, theory may suggest that a certain intervention should enhance academic self-concept. To the extent that the intervention leads to the enhancement of self-concept, then there is support for the theory and the procedure used to measure self-concept. A potentially useful test of the multidimensionality of self-concept is to test whether the intervention influences those facets of self-concept, but also to ascertain that the intervention does not influence, or has substantially less influence on, those facets of self-concept that it is not intended to influence.

Shavelson et al. (1976) then illustrated these methodological considerations in an evaluation of the construct validity of five popular self-concept instruments.

SUBSEQUENT EXTENSIONS AND REFINEMENTS OF THE SHAVELSON ET AL. MODEL

Between-Network Hypotheses

Shavelson and Bolus (1982) extended the original Shavelson et al. (1976) review in an invited lead article for the *Journal of Educational Psychology*. Here they examined assumptions about the increasing stability of self-concept as one moves toward the apex of the hierarchy and the causal ordering of academic self-concept and achievement. They also demonstrated recent advances in CFA in evaluating measurement, structural, and theoretical issues. Data consisted of measures of self-concept (general, academic, English, mathematics, and science) and school grades (English, mathematics, and science) collected on two occasions 5 months apart. In support of the multidimensionality of self-concept, there was clear separation of the five components of self-concept. In support of a hierarchical model, general self-concept was most highly correlated with general academic self-concept, less correlated with subject-specific components of self-concept, and least correlated with school grades; academic self-concept was most highly correlated with specific subject self-concepts; and subject-specific self-concepts were more highly correlated with marks in the matching area than with marks in other school subjects. In separate analyses of school marks in English, mathematics, and science, there was evidence of the positive contribution of prior academic self-concept to subsequent academic performance beyond the contribution of prior academic achievement. The results did not, however, indicate that self-concept became less stable as one descended the hierarchy as even the subject-specific components of self-concept were very stable. In particular, general academic self-concept appeared to be less stable then subject-specific self-concepts.

Subsequent research (see Marsh, 1990c) further calls into question the validity of the original Shavelson et al. (1976) assumption that global self-concept is the most stable component of the hierarchy. Global self-concepts inferred from measures like the Rosenberg (1965) instrument—compared with more domain-specific, self-concept scales—appear to be less stable over time even though they are as internally consistent at any one occasion.

The Song and Hattie (1984) Model

Song and Hattie (Hattie, 1992; Song & Hattie, 1984) proposed two modifications to the original Shavelson et al. model. First, on the academic side, they proposed a second-order academic factor defined by three first-order factors: achievement self-concept (self-perceptions of actual achievement), ability self-concept (self-perceptions of being capable of achieving), and classroom self-concept (confidence in classroom activities). Second, on the nonacademic side, they proposed two second-order factors: Social self-concept and Self-regard/Presentation self-concept. Social self-concept was defined by the Peer and Family first-order factors. Self-regard/Presentation self-concept was defined in terms of the first-order factors of Physical self-concept that emphasized physical appearance and Confidence, which relates to emotional self-concept in the original Shavelson model, but also overlaps with general esteem as measured by the Rosenberg (1965) instrument.

Hattie (1992) identified seven first-order factors (ability, achievement, classroom, peer, family, confidence, and physical), supporting the design of the instrument and the multidimensionality of self-concept. Hierarchical factor analyses revealed support for three second-order factors, but these differed somewhat from a priori predictions. In particular, the Classroom factor (defined by items such as "I feel left out of things in class" and "Most of my teachers do not understand me") tended to be associated with the second-order social self-concept more than with the second-order academic self-concept. Hattie also noted that the ability and achievement self-concept domains could be extended to include components specific to particular school subjects as in the original Shavelson model and its extensions, whereas the physical domain could be divided into physical appearance and physical skills. With these extensions, the structure described by Hattie is similar to the Shavelson models although the distinction between ability and achievement self-concepts may warrant further consideration.

Hattie (1992) also elaborated and added to features originally proposed by Shavelson et al. (1976). Conceptions of self, according to Hattie, are cognitive self-appraisals that place considerable emphasis on the self as an active appraiser. These self-appraisals are about descriptions, prescriptions, and expectations that individuals attribute to themselves. Although recognizing the multidimensionality of self-concept, Hattie was more concerned with how the specific domains were perceived, organized, weighted, and integrated. He emphasized that self-concept may guide, mediate, or regulate behavior. Hattie also stressed that self-concept is culturally bound and that most of what we know about self-concept comes from Western cultures. In these and other respects, Hattie emphasized a cognitive representation of self in which self-concept has both structural and dynamic process components.

Construct Validity of Academic Self-Concept

Byrne (1984) provided an important review of construct validation research of academic self-concept that was based substantially on the framework provided by Shavelson et al. (1976). She evaluated different (within-network) structural models such as those considered in Figure 2.1, concluding:

> Although no one model to date has been sufficiently supported empirically so as to lay sole claim to the within-structure of the construct, many recent studies, in particular those by Marsh and colleagues (Marsh, Parker, & Smith, 1983; Marsh, Smith, & Barnes, 1983; Marsh, Smith, Barnes, & Butler, 1983) are providing increasingly strong support for the hierarchical model. (p. 50)

On the basis of within-network factor analysis and MTMM studies, Byrne concluded that self-concept is a multidimensional construct with academic self-concept forming one of the facets. She reported a logical pattern of relations among measures of general self-concept, academic self-concept, and subject-specific self-concepts that supported a hierarchical model. She also noted, however, a general lack of support for the Shavelson et al. proposal that self-concept becomes increasingly stable as one ascends the hierarchy. Between-network studies established a strong and logical pattern of relations between academic achievement and academic self-concept (also see Hansford & Hattie, 1982). In particular, relations with achievement became progressively stronger as one descended the hierarchy from general to academic to the corresponding subject-specific component of academic self-concept. Byrne (1984) also reviewed the methodological complications in testing the causal ordering of academic self-concept and achievement, but she concluded that there was too little research to justify clear conclusions.

The Marsh/Shavelson Revised Model

Marsh and Shavelson (1985; Shavelson & Marsh, 1986) brought together more recent research on the Shavelson et al. model and self-concept instrumentation. This article began by reviewing briefly the original Shavelson et al. model and the Shavelson and Bolus (1982) research. Based on the Shavelson and Bolus data, they further commented that the study "suggests that the academic facets of self-concept might be divided further into subareas (math and science vs. English), a possibility not entertained by Shavelson et al. (1976)" (p. 110). The researchers then considered more recent research based on the SDQ instruments. CFA and HCFA analyses were conducted on SDQI responses by preadolescents in Grades 2 through 5. The seven SDQ factors (Physical Ability, Physical Appearance, Peers, Parents, Reading, Math, and General School) based on the Shavelson et al. model were identified in each year group. In tests of alternative hierarchical models, a model with a single higher-order factor fit the data more poorly than a model positing separate second-order academic and nonacademic factors. The best model for each year group, however, posited three second-order factors (nonacademic, Verbal/Academic, and Math/Academic) and a third-order general self-concept. The authors noted that this refinement of the academic portion of the hierarchy was consistent with other SDQ research showing Math and Verbal self-concepts to be almost uncorrelated, apparently precluding their incorporation into a single higher-order academic self-concept factor as originally hypothesized by Shavelson et al. Marsh and Shavelson concluded that their final hierarchical model "is consistent with Shavelson's assumption that self-concept is hierarchically ordered, but the particular form of this higher-order structure is more complicated than previously proposed" (p. 115).

Marsh and Shavelson (1985) then reviewed two studies of late-adolescent responses to the SDQIII. The SDQIII differed from the SDQI in that the peers scale was divided into Same Sex and Opposite Sex scales, and additional scales were constructed to represent Emotional Stability, Problem Solving, Religion/Spirituality, Honesty/Dependability, and a General self-concept scale (based on the Rosenberg, 1965, scale). In the first study, exploratory and confirmatory factor analyses provided support for all 13 scales. The most surprising feature, however, was that even though the pattern of correlations among the different factors was consistent with expectations, the correlations were remarkably small (mean $r = .09$). The authors concluded that "these findings indicate that, although self-concept is multifaceted, the hierarchical structure found in the preadolescent self-concept has nearly vanished. Instead, the SDQIII appears to measure relatively distinct facets of self-concept" (p. 115). As part of this study, the authors also reported that math and English achievement scores were significantly correlated with SDQIII academic scales but were not significantly related to the SDQIII nonacademic scales. Furthermore, mathematics achievement was most highly correlated with Math self-concept and English achievement was most highly correlated with English self-concept.

In the second SDQIII study, Australian university students completed the SDQIII and then asked the person who knew them the best (typically a parent or family member) to complete the SDQIII on their behalf. The small correlations among the 13 SDQIII factors were replicated for self-ratings and were also small for inferred ratings by significant others. In particular, the clear separation between Verbal and Math self-concepts emphasized in the Marsh/Shavelson model was evident in both self-responses ($r = -.03$) and responses by significant others ($r = .00$). The most remarkable finding of the study, however, was the strength and domain specificity of self-other agreement. Applying multitrait-multimethod analysis, there was good support for both convergent and divergent validity; self-other agreement was statistically significant for all 13 SDQIII factors (coefficients of .41 to .79, median = .52), whereas correlations among nonmatching scales were close to zero. These results were subsequently replicated in a large study of Canadian university students (Marsh & Byrne, 1993).

Further Refinements of Theoretical Models of Academic Self-Concept

The Shavelson et al. (1976) model and Marsh/Shavelson revision (Marsh & Shavelson, 1985) were developed within the context of educational psychology, and so it is not surprising that many of the recent developments are specific to academic self-concept. Because this research is reviewed in detail in Chapter 7, it is summarized only briefly in this chapter.

Frame of Reference Effects

Students, to form their academic self-concept, must compare their self-perceived academic accomplishments with some frame of reference. Thus, students with the same academic accomplishments can have very different academic self-concepts if they are using very different frames of reference. A salient source of comparative information is the accomplishments of other students in the same context. Based on this premise and social comparison theory, Marsh (1987a, 1990b, 1991; Marsh & Parker, 1984) developed a model to explain what he called the big-fish-little-pond effect. Consistent with this model, he found that students who attend high schools where the school-average ability level is high (e.g., academically selective schools) have substantially lower academic self-concepts than equally able students who attend high schools where the average ability level is not so high. Furthermore, these poorer academic self-concepts apparently lead to negative effects associated with attending higher-ability high schools on a wide variety of academic outcomes (e.g., coursework selection, educational aspirations, subsequent achievement, and university attendance).

The internal comparison process in the I/E model mentioned earlier posits a different frame of reference in which students compare their performances in any one school subject with their performances in other subjects. Thus, according to this model, a student whose best subject is mathematics will have a higher math self-concept than other students who are equally good at mathematics but even better at other subjects. Although this frame of reference research has focused on academic self-concept in educational contexts, the underlying rationale may apply to other domains of self-concept as well.

Extensions and Refinements of the Marsh/Shavelson Model

Other academic self-concept research has refined and extended the Marsh/Shavelson model. Marsh, Byrne, and Shavelson (1988) found that the revised model performed better than the original Shavelson et al. (1976) model for responses from each of three different self-concept instruments. Marsh (1990d) developed the Academic Self Description Questionnaire (ASDQ) instruments to provide even stronger tests of the revised model. Consistent with the design of the ASDQII, factor analysis identified 15 different first-order factors of academic self-concept corresponding to 15 different school subjects. Although two higher-order factors (Math/Academic and Verbal/Academic) were able to explain relations among eight core school subjects, additional higher-order factors were needed to explain relations among other, noncore subjects (e.g., physical education, art, and music). Furthermore, the hierarchy was weak and much of the variance in first-order factors associated with specific school subjects could not be explained by the higher-order factors.

Marsh (1992) correlated school grades in eight core school subjects to matching ASDQII scales. Although agreement between a single global achievement and a single global academic self-concept scale was substantial ($r = .83$), the CFA model did not fit the data nearly as well as a model positing that self-concept/achievement agreement was specific to each scale. Whereas the eight school grades were substantially intercorrelated, apparently reflecting an academic g factor, the correlations among the eight components of self-concept were substantially lower. Thus, components of academic self-concept are more distinct than the corresponding components of academic achievement. These results have important implications for self-concept theory, measurement, and practice that are discussed in further detail in Chapter 7.

Recent Developments in Physical Self-Concept Research

Physical education and sports science researchers have long been interested in self-concept but until recently have focused primarily on global measures of self-concept. Whereas some instruments such as the Tennessee Self Concept Scales (Fitts, 1964) distinguished between physical and nonphysical components of self-concept, such physical self-concept scales typically confounded self-perceptions in such diverse areas as health, appearance, sexuality, endurance, coordination, and sporting competence (Marsh & Richards, 1988b). SDQ research (Marsh, 1990c, 1993a; Marsh & Jackson, 1986; Marsh & Peart, 1988), however, has shown that objective measures of physical fitness, physical activity, involvement in sports, and interventions designed to enhance physical fitness are substantially related to Physical Ability self-concept, weakly related to Physical Appearance self-concept, and nearly unrelated to nonphysical areas of self-concept.

Recent physical self-concept research (e.g., Fox & Corbin, 1989; Marsh, 1993c; Marsh & Redmayne, 1994; Marsh, Richards, Johnson, Roche, & Tremayne, 1994; Sonstroem, Speliotis, & Fava, 1992), paralleling academic self-concept research described earlier, emphasizes physical self-concept as a multidimensional, hierarchical construct in which there is a global physical component and domain-specific physical components. Based on earlier empirical and theoretical research (Harter, 1982; Marsh, 1987b; Marsh & Shavelson, 1985; Shavelson et al., 1976), Fox and Corbin argued for such a model of physical self-concept. Noting that some self-concept instruments include separate physical scales, they were critical of single-score physical scales that combined and confounded a wide range of apparently differentiable physical components. Consistent with this multidimensional emphasis, their Physical Self Perception Scale instrument measures four physical subdomains (bodily attractiveness, sports competence, physical strength, and physical conditioning/exercise) as well as a global physical self-worth scale. Factor analyses identified the four subdomains, and exploratory factor analysis solutions were reasonably similar for responses by men and by women. Responses to this instrument were able to predict the degree and type of physical activity involvement, and the pattern of relations among the scales supported their hierarchical model of physical self-concept. Fox and Corbin focused primarily on the internal structure of physical self-concept and did not pursue tests of the divergent validity of their physical subdomains.

Marsh and Redmayne (1994) specifically noted the need for divergent validity research showing that specific criteria form a logical pattern of relations with different physical self-concept scales and for multitrait-multimethod tests relating responses to different physical self-concept instruments. They described the development of a preliminary version of the Physical Self Description Questionnaire (PSDQ) and examined relations between six components of physical self-concept and five components of physical fitness. Hierarchical confirmatory factor analyses supported the six components of physical self-concept and a multidimensional, hierarchical model of physical self-concept. The pattern of correlations between specific components of physical self-concept and physical fitness generally supported the construct validity of the self-concept responses, and the correlation between second-order factors representing general physical self-concept and general physical fitness ($r = .76$) was substantial. In contrast to academic self-concept research described earlier, however, correlations among the physical self-concept scales were higher than correlations among the measures of physical fitness. The authors suggested that this may reflect limitations in the particular sample that they used (13- and 14-year-old girls who were generally unfit) and their instrument.

Marsh, Richards, Johnson, Roche, and Tremayne (1994) described a substantially revised version of the PSDQ, which measures 11 scales: Strength, Body Fat, Activity, Endurance/Fitness, Sports Competence, Coordination, Health, Appearance, Flexibility, General Physical Self Concept, and Self-Esteem. The PSDQ scales reflect some scales from the SDQ instruments (Physical Ability, Physical Appearance, and Self-Esteem), scales from the earlier Marsh and Redmayne study, and an attempt to parallel components of physical fitness identified in Marsh's (1993b) CFA of an extensive range of physical fitness indicators from the Australian Health and Fitness Survey. In their study, CFA was used to demonstrate support for these 11 components of physical self-concept and the replicability of the factor structure over gender. Subjects also completed responses to the Physical Self Perception Profile (Fox, 1990) and the Physical Self Concept (Richards, 1988). CFA models of this multitrait-multimethod data provided support for both the convergent and discriminant validity of responses to the three instruments. Comparisons of psychometric, theoretical, and pragmatic considerations of the three instruments led to the recommendation of the PSDQ in a wide variety of research and applied settings. Ongoing research based on a multidimensional, hierarchical model of self-concept and the PSDQ instrument is examining relations between physical self-concept, physical activity, and health-related physical fitness collected on multiple occasions; interventions designed to enhance physical fitness; the influence of perceived importance of different PSDQ scales on their relations with Global Physical Self-concept and Esteem; and the effects of having young elite athletes living and training together (a potential big-fish-little-pond effect in the physical domain).

A Developmental Perspective

Shavelson et al. (1976) did not emphasize developmental aspects of self-concept, but they did hypothesize that self-concept becomes increasingly multifaceted as the individual moves from infancy to adulthood. However, they offered no clear rationale for testing this hypothesis and did not evaluate problems associated with measuring self-concepts for very young children. In apparently related work, Harter (1983, 1985) proposed a development model of self-concept in which self-concept becomes increasingly abstract with age. Her review of previous research suggested that self-conceptions shift from concrete descriptions of behavior in early childhood, to traitlike psychological constructs (e.g., popular, smart, good looking) in middle childhood, to more abstract constructs during adolescence. In subsequent SDQ research, formal tests of this Shavelson et al. hypothesis were evaluated and the ability of very young children to respond to the SDQI was considered.

Increasing Differentiation with Age

One possible test of the hypothesis of increasing differentiation with age is that correlations among multiple dimensions of self-concept become smaller with age. Marsh and Shavelson (1985; also see Marsh, Barnes, Cairns, & Tidman, 1984) reported initial support for this hypothesis in that the average correlation among SDQI scales decreased dramatically with age during early preadolescent ages (Grades 2–5). Marsh (1989) tested the generality of these findings across the preadolescent to early adult period using the normative archive responses to the SDQI, II, and III. For each instrument, he evaluated correlations among all scales, the six scales common to the three instruments, and a set of seven correlations hypothesized a priori to be the smallest. For responses to each SDQ instrument, the mean correlation among all scales was similar to the mean correlation among just the scales common to the three instruments, and the mean correlation among scales selected a priori to be lowest was substantially lower than the mean correlation among all scales or among scales common to the three SDQ instruments. There was a substantial decrease in the size of correlations from Grade 2 to Grade 3, and smaller decreases between Grades 3 and 4, and between Grades 4 and 5. There were no further declines in the average correlation among scales for the rest of the preadolescent (SDQI) data nor for the adolescent (SDQII) and the late-adolescent (SDQIII) data.

An alternative test of the hypothesis of increasing differentiation proposed by Marsh (1989) was that differences among the scale scores for the same person should become larger with age. That is, younger subjects are more likely to have uniformly high or uniformly low self-concepts across all areas, whereas older subjects are more likely to have relatively high self-concepts in some areas and relatively low self-concepts in other areas. He computed the standard deviation of scale scores for each subject (a within-subject standard deviation) for all scales and for the scales common to the three SDQ instruments. Separate within-subject standard deviations were computed for raw scale scores and for factor scores (that were standardized to have a mean of 50 and a standard deviation of 10 across all respondents to each instrument). Within-subject standard deviations increased between Grades 2 and 3, and between Grades 3 and 4, but did not increase further with increases in age for SDQI responses by older subjects or for responses to the SDQII or SDQIII instruments.

Self-Concepts of Very Young Children

Harter (1985), consistent with her proposal that self-concept becomes increasingly integrated with age, proposed that the concept of global self-worth does not evolve before the age of about 8. In support of this claim, Harter and Pike (1984) indicated that children below age 8 either do not understand general self-worth items or do not provide reliable responses, but did not actually present empirical support for this supposition. Subsequent research (Silon & Harter, 1985) suggested that mental age may be more important than chronological age. Factor analyses of Harter's self-concept scale for low-IQ subjects aged 9 to 12 (with mental ages of less than 8) revealed only two self-concept factors instead of the four factors found with normal-IQ children. These low-IQ children did not distinguish between cognitive and physical competence, and the general self-concept items did not cluster together or load on other factors. However, the failure to replicate a factor structure—particularly when using exploratory factor analysis techniques—is a weak basis of support for claims that global self-concept does not exist.

Particularly for responses by young children, the failure to identify the intended factors may reflect difficulties idiosyncratic to a particular instrument or the inability of children to accurately reflect their self-concepts with conventional paper-and-pencil tests. Here, as with research with older children, progress in theory and practice may be stimulated by the development of better measurement procedures. In support of this suggestion, Marsh, Craven, and Debus (1991) described a new, adaptive procedure for assessing multiple dimensions for children aged 5 to 8. In an individual interview format, the SDQI was administered to 501 kindergarten, 1st, and 2nd grade students. Approximately 2 weeks after the

SDQI was individually administered, the SDQI was administered to grade 1 and grade 2 students using the normal group administration procedures.

The critical component of the Marsh, Craven, and Debus (1991) study was the individualized interview format used to collect SDQI responses. Following instructions and sample items, each item was read aloud. The interviewer asked the child if he or she understood the item. If the child did not understand the item, the interviewer explained the sentence further, ascertained that the child understood the item, and read the item again. The child initially responded "Yes" or "No" to each item to indicate whether it was true or false as a description of the child. If the child responded "Yes," the interviewer then asked whether the child meant "yes, always" or "yes, sometimes." Similarly, if the child responded "No," the interviewer asked if the child meant "no always" or "no sometimes." The second probe was always repeated, thus providing a check on the accuracy of the child's first response. Pilot work indicated that some kindergarten students had trouble with a few of the items. These items were initially presented in the original form and then in a paraphrased form. Thus, for example, children were told that mathematics meant work with numbers.

Results of the Marsh, Craven, and Debus (1991) study indicated that internal consistency estimates varied systematically with age. The median reliabilities for the eight SDQI scales were .74, .80, and .82 for kindergarten, Grade 1, and Grade 2 students. Reliability estimates for total academic and total nonacademic self-concepts varied between .85 and .92 for all three ages. At each age level, CFA identified all eight SDQI scales—including the General Self scale. With increasing age, the fit of the eight-factor model improved, the size of correlations among the factors decreased, and self-concept became more differentiated.

There was an initial concern that the 64-item SDQI instrument would be too long for these very young children. Interestingly, items near the end were more effective than earlier items (in contrast to anticipated fatigue effects). Apparently, children learned to respond appropriately so that they were responding more appropriately to items at the end of the instrument than to items at the beginning of the instrument. This observation has important implications for the typically short instruments used with young children.

Correlations between SDQI scales from individual and group administration procedures were statistically significant for all eight SDQI scales (median correlations were .38 and .50 for Grade 1 and Grade 2 students). MTMM analyses of this data indicated support for convergent and discriminant validity, but a substantial method effect was associated with the group administration procedure that was larger for the younger students.

Due in part to this new measurement procedure, Marsh, Craven, and Debus (1991) were able to provide new evidence about issues in the development of self-concept in very young children. In particular, appropriately measured multiple dimensions of self-concept are better differentiated than previously assumed. In current research, this individualized interview procedure for administering the SDQ is being evaluated in Head Start programs in several (U.S.) states.

Other Directions and Relations with Other Constructs

Research reviewed here has focused on the internal structure of self-concept responses and relations with a few external constructs. There also exists, however, a large body of research demonstrating a logical pattern of relations between multiple dimensions of self-concept and other constructs. Employing the logic of construct validation, specific validity criteria should be substantially correlated with the specific areas of self-concept to which they are most logically or theoretically related, and substantially less correlated with other areas of self-concept. The demonstration of this type of pattern for a wide variety of external criteria provides strong support for the construct validity of the self-concept responses and particularly for the multidimensionality of the self-concept construct. Whereas a review of this research is beyond the scope of this chapter each of the following brief summaries illustrates this principle (see Marsh, 1990c, 1993a for more detailed summaries).

Relations with Gender

Gender is weakly related to overall, general, or total self-concept (Marsh, 1989; Hattie, 1992, pp. 176–180). This lack of relation, however, masks well-defined gender differences in specific areas of self-concept—some favoring women and some favoring men—that cancel each other in the formation of total scores. For example, girls and women consistently have higher verbal self-concepts and lower self-concepts in physical ability. Reliance on an overall measure of self-concept does not accurately reflect these content-specific gender differences in multiple dimensions of self-concept (Marsh, 1989).

Relations to Masculinity (M), Femininity (F), and Androgyny

Central postulates in androgyny research (e.g., Marsh & Myers, 1986; Marsh & Byrne, 1991) are that M and F are differentiable constructs and that both M and F contribute to higher levels of self-concept. Whereas appropriately constructed instruments provide clear support for the differentiation of M and F, most research has shown that F is not related to general measures of self-concept after controlling for the effects of M. Marsh and Byrne, however, demonstrated that this apparent lack of support for the importance of F was due in part to an overreliance on general self-concept measures that emphasize stereotypically masculine characteristics such as self-confidence, assertiveness, and a sense of agency (e.g., an internal locus of control). When measures of M and F were related to multidimensional self-concept measures, there was support for a logical, a priori pattern of relations leading to the development of the differentiated additive androgyny model. Consistent with this model, the relative contributions of M and F varied substantially for different areas of self-concept, and F contributed more positively than M for self-concept domains that were more stereotypically feminine. Marsh and Byrne found support for the model was consistent across responses by males and females, across self-responses and responses by significant others, and across five age groups in early-to-middle adolescence.

Although the focus of this research has been on androgyny measure, it provides strong support for the need to consider multiple dimensions of self-concept. Relations with M and F cannot be adequately understood if the multidimensionality of self-concept is ignored. Marsh and Myers further argued that M and F should also be considered as multidimensional, hierarchically ordered constructs and proposed a theoretical model of M and F that was based substantially on the original Shavelson et al. model.

Relations to Self-Concept Inferred by Significant Others

Ratings by others have been used widely to validate self-concept responses, but empirical support for self-other agreement has typically been weak (coefficients of about .2). The problem, however, is apparently related to an overreliance on general measures of self-concept and psychometrically weak instruments that attempt to infer specific self-concept domains from single-item scales. When both subjects and significant others complete a psychometrically strong instrument in which multiple dimensions are each inferred from multi-item scales, self-other agreement is substantially stronger than typically found and is very content specific. Marsh and Byrne (1993), for example, reported that the average self-other correlation for the 13 SDQIII scales was .56 in two different studies. MTMM analyses provided strong support for the convergent and divergent validity of responses in these studies. In both studies, self-other agreement on general self-concept tended to be weaker than for the other self-concept scales.

Relations to Interventions Designed to Enhance
Specific Areas of Self-Concept

A more general review and meta-analysis of programs designed to enhance self-concept is provided by Hattie (1992, pp. 221–240). Different interventions designed to enhance specific areas of self-concept have been shown to have more impact on those areas of self-concept than on other areas of self-concept (e.g., Craven, Marsh, & Debus, 1991; Marsh & Peart, 1988; Marsh & Richards, 1988a; Marsh, Richards, & Barnes, 1986a, 1986b). This pattern of relations also provides a control for placebolike effects that are posited to influence all areas of self-concept. Thus, for example, academic interventions have substantial effects on academic components of self-concept but little effect on nonacademic components, whereas physical interventions have substantial effects on physical self-concept but little effect on academic components of self. Considerable information would have been lost if these interventions had been evaluated in terms of just an overall, general, or total self-concept score.

RELATIONS BETWEEN SPECIFIC AND GLOBAL COMPONENTS OF SELF-CONCEPT

In this chapter, we have focused on the structure of self-concept and domain-specific measure of self. Less attention has been given to the role of global self-concept and specific self-concept processes. This focus on domain-specific components of self-concept has been necessary, perhaps, to correct what seems to have been a counterproductive, historical overemphasis on global measures of self-concept. Particularly during the period between 1960 and the early 1980s—the heyday of dustbowl empiricism in self-concept research (Hattie, 1992)—many researchers related general self-concept to a bewildering array of other constructs apparently without any clear theoretical basis for predicting how and why the measures should be related. Research summarized in this chapter and other chapters in this volume demonstrates the inappropriateness of this research strategy. As researchers focus increasingly on domain-specific measures of self-concept, however, we are left with an important dilemma. What is the role of global self-concept, and how is it related to domain-specific measures of self-concept? Theoretical approaches to such relations also require researchers to examine specific processes that individuals use to integrate specific self-concept information. These vexing questions have plagued self-concept researchers since the time of William James, who provided the inspiration for many approaches currently used in the self-concept literature.

James (1890/1963) proposed that the best representation of a person's overall self-evaluation is an appropriately weighted average of self-evaluations in specific domains. Because a person cannot be all things, each individual must select carefully "the strongest, truest, deepest self . . . on which to stake his salvation" (p. 310) so that "I, who for the time have staked my all on being a psychologist, am mortified if others know much more psychology than I. But I am contented to wallow in the grossest ignorance of Greek" (p. 310). Objective accomplishments are evaluated in relation to internal frames of reference so that "we have the paradox of a man shamed to death because he is only the second pugilist or the second oarsman in the world . . . Yonder puny fellow, however, whom everyone can beat, suffers no chagrin about it, for he has long ago abandoned the attempt to 'carry that line'" (p. 310). Putting these two ideas together, James concludes that our self-feeling "depends entirely on what we back ourselves to be and do" (p. 310).

Theoretical Approaches to Defining Global Self Concept

Following James (1890/1963), researchers have proposed that the relations between global and domain-specific self-concepts should be a function of the importance that an individual places on each domain, of individual standards of excellence or ideals for each domain and, perhaps, of the certainty of an individual's views about each domain. In the general paradigm used to test such hypotheses, individuals respond to a global self-concept scale or self-esteem scale, respond to content-specific domains, and indicate their importance, certainty, or ideals for each domain. Domain-specific ratings may consist of single-item responses or, preferably, scale scores or factor scores derived from multi-item scales with good psychometric properties. Esteem is defined by responses to generalized characteristics such as self-confidence and self-competence that are superordinate to, but not specific to, particular domains. This approach is illustrated by the widely used Rosenberg (1965) scale and the general-self or self-esteem scales on many multidimensional instruments such as those developed by Marsh (1990c), Harter (1982), and others. (Examples of items from the SDQIII are "Overall, I have a lot of self-confidence" and "Overall, nothing I do is very important.") Items from such scales are reasonably homogeneous and typically define a separate factor in factor analyses.

A critical test of these weighted-average approaches is whether domain-specific ratings in combination with other information about individual importance, individual certainty, or individual actual/ideal discrepancies are better able to predict esteem than the domain-specific ratings. Despite their intuitive appeal, such approaches have received limited empirical support, although methodological problems and ambiguities about the appropriate question to address preclude any clear conclusions (e.g., Marsh, 1986a, 1993d; Pelham & Swann, 1989; Wells & Marwell, 1976; Wylie, 1974, 1979).

In an evaluation of such approaches, it is important to distinguish between three ways in which domain-specific ratings can be averaged to form a total score. *Simple unweighted averages* require the weights to be constant across domains and individuals. For example, this approach requires weighting physical attractiveness and mathematics competence equally when computing a total score for all individuals. *Constant weighted averages* allow weights to differ according to the domain but not according to individuals. Thus, for example, physical attractiveness can be weighted more than mathematics competence, but the same (larger) weight must be assigned to all individuals for physical attractiveness and the same (smaller) weight must be assigned to all individuals for mathematical competence. The different weights for each domain may be assigned a priori on the basis of theory or design, derived from group-level variables (e.g., the group average importance rating of each domain), obtained by empirical procedures that employ only information from the domains ratings using techniques such as factor analysis or by empirical procedures such as multiple regression that determine an empirically optimal set of weights in relation to a specific criterion (e.g., global self-esteem). *Individually weighted averages* allow the weights to differ according to the domain and allow the weights assigned to each domain to vary from individual to individual. Thus, for example, physical attractiveness may be weighted more than mathematical competence for some individuals, whereas mathematical competence may be weighted more than physical attractiveness for other individuals.

The simple unweighted approach is the most parsimonious and provides a basis of comparison for evaluating more complicated approaches. Similarly, the constant weighted approaches are more parsimonious than individually weighted approaches. Support for an individually weighted approach requires that it is able to explain significantly more variance than either the unweighted or constant weighted approaches. In the self-concept literature, the term weighted average approach typically refers to an individually weighted average approach. Self-concept researchers, at least implicitly, have used a variety of weighted-average definitions of global self-concept (Harter, 1985, 1986, 1989; Harter & Marold, 1991; Hattie, 1992; Marsh, 1986a, 1990c, 1993a; Marsh & Shavelson, 1985; Pelham & Swann, 1989; Rosenberg, 1965; Wells & Marwell, 1976; Wigfield & Karpathian, 1991; Wylie, 1974), and here we discuss some that appear to be most widely used or most theoretically interesting.

Agglomerate Global Self-Concept

The total score in this approach represents a broad, typically ill-defined collection of self-report items. This is the implicit basis of total scores for many idiosyncratic instruments that have been so pervasive in self-concept research and for many older instruments (e.g., the Coopersmith, 1967) that were not designed to measure specific components of self-concept. On some such instruments, there is an attempt to measure a diverse set of facets, but the different facets have not been empirically verified, nor have their contributions been balanced. Instead, responses are simply summed to form a total score that is taken to be a measure of global self-concept. Such a construct cannot be adequately characterized, and is idiosyncratic to particular instruments.

Hierarchical Approach

This approach is represented by the general self-concept that appears at the apex of the Shavelson et al. model (see Figure 2.2) and the highest-order factor in the HCFAs by Marsh (1987b). Whereas this approach to global self-concept has important theoretical implications, the distinction between it and the other uses of general self needs clarification. This general self is an unobserved construct that is itself defined by unobserved constructs (it is a higher-order factor). Like the weighted and unweighted total scores, it represents some average of specific facets of self-concept, and its breadth is limited by the scope of specific scales that are included in the analysis. Thus, in a study that only examined different areas of *academic* self-concept, such a general self would necessarily be a general academic self-concept. Like the general-self scale, the hierarchical general self is superordinate to the specific self facets. The hierarchical factor analysis of SDQIII responses by Marsh (1987b) is particularly relevant to this discussion because it includes both a separate general self scale and a hierarchical self. The General-self scale was hypothesized to contribute directly to the hierarchical general self-concept that was at the apex of the hierarchy. This hypothesis was supported and correlations between the two forms of general self-concept were consistently close to .9 suggesting that the two are very similar when inferred on the basis of responses to the SDQIII. It is also interesting to note that the hierarchical approach is a special case of the constant weighted approach in that the weight assigned to any particular domain (based on the factor analysis) is the same for each individual but varies for different domains.

Importance-Weighted Averages

This approach is based on the assumption that the contribution of a specific component of self-concept to overall self-concept should be based on the saliency or importance of the specific component to a particular individual. Whereas it would be reasonable to consider an importance-weighted average in which the group averages of importance are used (a constant weighted approach instead of an individually weighted approach), this approach is not typically considered except, perhaps, as a basis of comparison for individually weighted average approaches. Critical assumptions implicit in the use of this weighted average approach are that the weighted average correlates with global self-concept more than an unweighted average and that the contribution of a particular domain varies systematically with the importance placed on that domain. Thus, for example, academic competence will contribute more strongly (more positively if academic self-concept is high, more negatively if it is low) to the prediction of global self-concept for individuals who judge academic competence to be more important. In the terminology of ANOVA, the effect of a particular domain interacts with its perceived importance.

Actual/Ideal Discrepancies

In this approach, general self is defined as a function of differences between actual and ideal self-concepts. High self-perceptions in each domain contribute positively to global self-concept, but high ideals or standards contribute negatively to global self-concept. This approach fell out of favor after considerable application (see review by Wylie, 1974, 1979), but a resurgence of cognitive models has led to renewed interest in discrepancy measures. For example, Markus and Nurius (1986; Markus & Wurf, 1987) introduced the related notion of possible selves (what you might become, what you hope to become, or what you are afraid of becoming) and Higgins (1987) considered discrepancies between actual, ideal, and ought selves from the perspective of self and of significant others. In related research on multiple discrepancy theory, Michalos (1991) related seven discrepancy scores—actual with best past, expected by now, expected in future, deserves, needs, wants, and had by others—to happiness and life satisfaction.

Marsh (1993d) distinguished between calculated discrepancies and perceived discrepancies. Calculated discrepancy scores are simply the difference between separate ratings of actual self-concept and ideal self-concept. There is not, however, much support for these calculated discrepancies; ideal ratings typically do not contribute beyond what can be explained by actual ratings alone, and the mean discrepancy scores have no more and, perhaps, less explanatory power than the mean of actual ratings (see reviews by Wells & Marwell, 1976; Wylie, 1974, 1979; also see Michalos, 1991). Perceived discrepancy scores are based on subjects' judgments of their perceived differences between actual and ideal self-concept on a response scale that may vary from "very short of my ideal self" to "very much like my ideal self." Whereas this approach apparently circumvents difficulties associated with collecting and combining separate ratings of actual and ideal self-ratings, it also introduces new complications in testing the underlying model. For example, perceived discrepancy ratings confound the presumably positive effects of high actual ratings and the presumably negative effects of high ideal self-ratings. Because researchers typically do not collect perceived discrepancy, actual, and ideal ratings, assumptions underlying this approach are often untested.

Actual/Ideal Discrepancies Weighted by Importance

In this approach, the perceived or calculated (actual/ideal) discrepancy for each domain is weighted by the importance of the domain. This approach is a logical hybrid of the importance weighting and discrepancy approaches proposed by Marsh (1993d) that is implicit in William James's observation that the second best pugilist in the world is shamed to death because he is not the best. Apparently, the boxer's pugilistic competence contributes negatively to his esteem because he has a very high, unachieved ideal to be the best and because he judges this domain to be very important. Unachieved ideals do not affect esteem in domains judged to be of no importance.

Actual/Importance Discrepancy Approach

In Harter's (1985, 1986, 1989) formulation of this approach, global self-concept is defined by discrepancies between (actual) domain ratings and domain importance ratings. Harter (1986) noted that her approach combined aspects of the importance-weighted and the actual/ideal discrepancy approaches. When discussing the pragmatic basis for her approach, Harter noted that there are different forms of ideal self (e.g., committed ideal, fantasy ideal) and that, particularly for children, there are methodological and conceptual complexities when making ideal-self ratings. For these reasons, she focused on importance rather than ideal self. Harter (1986) also pointed out:

> It should be noted that James' formula constitutes a ratio in which successes (competence) were divided by pretensions (importance). We opted to subtract these two scores from one another, rather than divide, because the former operation appeared to be a better analogue of the actual psychological processes involved. (pp. 154–155)

Harter (1986, 1989) claimed support for the construct validity of her actual/importance discrepancy approach based on a pattern of relations between her discrepancy scores, esteem, and a variety of other constructs, but she did not report whether self-concept/importance discrepancies had more explanatory power than just the (actual) self-concept ratings. Without such empirical evidence, interpretations of Harter's discrepancy scores and claims for their construct validity should be viewed cautiously. Other research (e.g., Marsh, 1986a, 1993d) indicates that scores based on this approach are substantially less correlated with esteem than the simple unweighted average.

Weighted Certainty Approach

In this approach, each specific domain is weighted by the certainty each respondent has about his or her rating. It was proposed by Pelham and Swann (1989), and also follows from the James's (1890/1963) contention that individuals emphasize areas of self that are "the strongest, truest, and deepest" (p. 310).

Profile Similarity Indexes

A profile similarity index (Pelham & Swann, 1989) is merely the relation between two sets of scores (e.g., self-concept and importance ratings) computed separately for each subject. Like any other correlation coefficient, scores can vary between +1.0 and −1.0 with positive scores reflecting a similarity in the pattern of self-concept and importance ratings, negative scores reflecting a dissimilarity, and a 0 score reflecting no relation. These profile similarity indexes bear a close relation to individually weighted-average approaches (Marsh, 1993d). For example, in the actual/importance profile similarity index, similar profiles of actual and importance ratings (e.g., feeling most positive about domains judged to be most important) are posited to reflect higher esteem, whereas dissimilar profiles reflect lower esteem. Logically, profile similarity indexes can be defined for any two sets of scores (e.g., actual and ideal, actual and certainty, or perceived discrepancy and importance). This approach is related to earlier work by Rogers (1951; Rogers & Dymond, 1954) in which individuals performed independent Q-sorts in terms of actual self and ideal self, and the two sets of scores were correlated to create a profile similarity index. Despite its intuitive appeal, major disadvantages with the Rogers approach included the confounding of the contributions of actual and ideal self-ratings, typically untested psychometric properties of the congruency measures, the added time and complications in collecting Q-sort data, and a failure to demonstrate the increased explanatory power of these measures over actual self-concept ratings (see Wylie, 1974, 1979). Pelham and Swann modified Rogers' approach by using simple ratings instead of the more cumbersome Q-sorts. Also, whereas earlier studies compared the predictive power of similarity indexes and unweighted averages, Pelham and Swann only required that the similarity indexes and unweighted averages together are able to predict esteem better than the unweighted average alone.

Empirical Tests of Different Approaches

Marsh (1986a) evaluated methodological issues in the importance-weighted-average approach and proposed a general multiple regression model to test it. He focused initially on Hoge and McCarthy's (1984) paradoxical finding that esteem was more highly correlated with the unweighted mean domain-specific, self-concept rating than with the mean rating weighted by individual importance ratings. After replicating this result with SDQIII responses, Marsh noted several potential problems that might explain this paradoxical finding. Whereas researchers typically use raw, untransformed ratings of importance and self-concept, Marsh recommended the use of a z-score transformation of the self-concept ratings and "ipsatized" importance ratings (in which the importance ratings by each respondent are divided by the mean importance rating for that respondent so that the sum of the ipsatized importance ratings is 1.0 for each respondent). He also identified other methodological problems in previous research, including the use of single-item ratings to infer specific areas of self-concept and ambiguities in how the weighted average model should be tested. Even after implementing proposed solutions to many of these problems, however, Marsh (1986a) found little support for the individually weighted importance approach.

Previous research has focused on relations between importance-weighted ratings of specific domains of self-concept and general esteem. Analogously, however, global academic self-concept can be inferred from responses from a global academic scale like the general school scale on the SDQ and ASDQ instruments or from an appropriately weighted average of self-concepts in specific school subjects like those on the ASDQ instruments. Pursuing this approach with ASDQ responses, Marsh (1993d) examined relations among multi-item self-concept scales for 15 school subjects, importance ratings for the 15 school subjects, and global school self-concept. This application of the importance-weighted model to global academic self-concept may be stronger than previous tests based on global self-esteem, because the universe of specific (school subject) domains was more completely sampled by the ASDQII than is typically possible in studies of global esteem. Another interesting feature of this study was a clear a priori basis of importance, in that within the context of the school where the study was conducted the different subjects were designated as core and noncore subjects.

The unweighted mean of the 15 subject-specific self-concept scales correlated substantially with global school self-concept (.73). The first principal component of the 15 self-concept ratings did marginally better (.76), whereas using multiple regression to differentially weight the 15 self-concept scores did best (.85). As hypothesized, global school self-concept was substantially more correlated with the mean of the 9 self-concepts in core school subjects ($r = .79$) than the mean of the 6 noncore self-concepts ($r = .42$). Hence, assigning the noncore self-concepts an a priori importance weighting of zero improved the explanatory power of the mean self-concept score. These results provided preliminary support for the a priori distinction between core and noncore subjects and the usefulness of a constant weighted average approach with a priori weights.

Consistent with earlier results, Marsh (1993d) found that the typical operationalization of the weighted importance model (the mean crossproduct of 15 untransformed self-concept ratings and untransformed importance ratings) did substantially *poorer* than just the mean self-concept rating (.623 vs. .730). Weighted averages based on standardized self-concept responses and ipsatized importance ratings performed better, but none of the importance-weighted averages did better than the unweighted averages of the 9 core self-concepts or the multiple regression weighted average of all 15 self-concepts.

The most appropriate test of the individually weighted importance approach is a test of self-concept × importance interactions in a multiple regression model (Marsh, 1986a). When Marsh (1993d) applied this multiple regression, the 45 predictor variables—15 academic self-concept scales, 15 importance ratings, and 15 self-concept × importance interaction terms—explained 75.5% of the variance in global school self-concept. The variance uniquely explained by the 15 interaction terms (0.6%), however, was not statistically significant.

Marsh (1993d) further demonstrated how this multiple regression approach could be generalized to test each of the different weighted average models considered earlier as well as the profile similarity indexes like those proposed by Pelham and Swann (1989). However, application of this multiple regression approach to Pelham and Swann's original data and ASDQII responses provided little support for their profile similarity index based on importance ratings. In further analyses of data from Pelham and

Swann, Marsh (1993d) found little or no support for importance-weighted averages, certainty-weighted averages, perceived discrepancy averages, actual/importance discrepancy scores, or the profile similarity indexes.

Fox (1990; Fox & Corbin, 1989) incorporated importance ratings into his multidimensional, hierarchical model of physical self-concept. Marsh (1994) evaluated this extension in a study of relations between PSDQ scales, perceived importance ratings of the PSDQ scales, global measures of physical self-concept, and global self-esteem. As with earlier research that focused on academic and general self-concepts, he found little or no support for importance-weighted averages, perceived discrepancy scores, or profile similarity indexes in the physical domain.

Discussion and Summary of Relations between Specific and Global Components of Self-Concept

Here we have examined the relations between global and specific domains of self-concept, operationalizing a variety of theoretical approaches to combining the specific domains. Marsh (1993d) found support for differentially weighting the specific domains of academic self-concept in that global academic self-concept was much more strongly related to self-concepts in core subjects than in noncore subjects. This result apparently provides stronger evidence for differentially weighting specific domains than has typically been reported in previous research. Marsh's support of differential weighting, however, should be interpreted cautiously. The results supported a constant weighted model using the core/noncore distinction to assign weights of zero or one to the different domains. The results, however, provided no support for an individually weighted approach in which the weight assigned to each domain varied from individual to individual. Total scores based on weighting each domain by individual ratings of importance by each student were substantially less correlated with global school self-concept than the simple mean of the nine core school subjects. In this sense, there is little support for differentially weighting specific domains for each respondent according to individual ratings of importance in any of the research considered in this chapter. The effect of any specific domain on global measures does not vary much for respondents who rated the domain as more or less important.

It is useful to place these results into the broader context of Wainer's (1976) classic research on differential weighting. He began by reviewing research showing that simple unweighted averages of predictors consistently performed better than expert human judgment. He then demonstrated mathematically that by using a simple unweighted average, "the resulting prediction is apt to be very close to the optimal one, were the optimal weights known, and often better than one which does not use optimal weights" (p. 217), "these equal weights have greater robustness than least squares coefficients" (p. 213), and that "this sort of scheme works well even when an operational criterion is not available" (p. 217). Based on his research, he recommended that the best approach to weighting predictions is to "(a) orient all predictors in the proper direction, discarding equivocal ones; (b) scale them into standardized form; and (c) add them up" because in relation to choosing optimal weights "it don't make no nevermind" (p. 213). Whereas researchers are sometimes loath to accept such simple truths and there have been numerous challenges to his claims, the practical implications of Wainer's recommendations have not been seriously threatened by subsequent research—including the results based on weighted-average models of self-concept such as those reviewed here.

IMPLICATIONS

Research summarized in this chapter reflects a natural extension of empirical and theoretical trends toward considering more specific components of self-concept. Historically, researchers typically did not distinguish academic from nonacademic or general components of self-concept. The original Shavelson et al. (1976) model of self-concept emphasized this distinction theoretically but offered little empirical support for it. Byrne (1984), in her classic review of within- and between-network studies, provided empirical support for the Shavelson et al. model and the usefulness of an academic specific component of self-concept. The original Shavelson et al. model of self-concept hypothesized that self-concepts in specific school subjects could be explained in terms of a single higher-order dimension of academic self-concept. Subsequent research demonstrated, however, that at least two higher-order academic factors—Math/Academic and Verbal/Academic—were required and led to the Marsh/Shavelson model. Marsh (1990d) continued this trend in a (within-network) factor analysis of ASDQ responses showing that students have distinct self-concepts in a wide variety of specific school subjects, and that this domain specificity is reflected in a (between-network) study of relations with corresponding academic achievement scores. This research clearly demonstrates that self-concept and its relation to other variables cannot be adequately understood if its multidimensional, domain-specific nature is ignored. More recently, Marsh (1993c; Marsh & Redmayne, 1994; Marsh, Richards, Johnson, Roche, & Tremayne, 1994), proposed a multidimensional, hierarchically ordered structure of physical self-concept. Research with the PSDQ provided support for this hierarchical structure and the domain specificity of relations between specific components of physical self-concept and matching components of physical fitness. B. M. Byrne (personal communication, October 18, 1993) also noted that she is currently working on a multidimensional, hierarchical model of self-concepts in the social domain. In each case, there appears to be increasing emphasis on developing multidimensional, hierarchical models of self-concept that are specific to particular domains.

In a similar vein, Vispoel (1993) argued that self-concepts in the performing arts has been largely ignored and he designed the high school version of the Arts Self-Perception Inventory (ASPI) to parallel the SDQII. Students completed the ASPI, SDQII, and a background survey of interest, grades, and noteworthy accomplishments in performing arts. Factor analysis identified the four factors that the ASPI is designed to measure (dance, drama, music, and visual arts). Each ASPI scale was relatively uncorrelated with other ASPI scales (median $r = .26$) and with the SDQII scales (median $r = .17$) and was most highly correlated with criteria in the same area of performing arts. Vispoel (1995; Vispoel, Wang, Bleiler, & Tzou, 1993) subsequently developed an adult version of the ASPI to parallel the SDQIII instrument and conducted a similar study with university students. He replicated the hierarchical structure of SDQIII responses and demonstrated that ASPI responses could be explained in terms of four first-order factors consistent with the design of the instrument and a second-order performing arts factor. Although the second-order performing arts factor was modestly related to global self-concept in his HCFA, it was reasonably independent of the other self-concept factors. Vispoel (1995) proposed an extension of the Marsh/Shavelson hierarchical model in which performing arts defined a distinct higher-order component of self-concept.

The central focus of this chapter has been on theoretical models of self-concept rather than instruments used to infer self-concept. Nevertheless, empirical tests of theoretical models and instrument construction should be evaluated simultaneously. Hence, tests of theoretical models must also be concerned with the quality of measures used to evaluate the models. From this perspective, it is useful to summarize important measurement criteria that facilitate the evaluation of theoretical models. Self-concept instruments and the scales they purport to measure should be based on an explicit theoretical model such as those considered here. Within-network research should provide support for the a priori scales and their psychometric properties. In particular, factor analyses should provide evidence for the relative unidimensionality of responses representing each scale, for the a priori factor structure that was the basis for the design of the instrument, and for the replicability and generalizability of the factor structure. Support for the instrument should also address the breadth of each scale. Thus, for example, should academic self-concept be considered a single domain, divided into verbal, math, and general components as on the SDQ, or divided into even more specific components associated with particular school subjects as on the ASDQ? Should physical self-concept be considered a single domain, divided into physical appearance and ability as on the SDQ, or divided into more specific physical components as on the PSDQ? Whatever the answer to such questions, the appropriate compromise should be supported on the basis of theory, intended purpose, instrument construction, and empirical results. Between-network studies should provide support for the convergent and divergent validity of the multiple self-concept scales. Each scale should be more highly correlated to external criteria (e.g., other constructs, known group differences, experimental interventions) to which it is most logically or theoretically related, and less correlated to criteria to which it is less logically or theoretically related. Particularly when a more global domain (e.g., academic or physical) is divided into specific subdomains that are supported by factor analysis, there should also be support for their separation from between-network studies. Consistent with the construct validation approach that is appropriate for self-concept research, this pattern of results provides support for both the interpretation of responses to a particular self-concept instrument and the theoretical model on which the instrument was based. This construct validation approach was a central feature in the original Shavelson et al. (1976) article and subsequent research based on it. This approach also provides an important basis for evaluating the usefulness of advances in self-concept theory, new self-concept instruments and the domains they purport to measure, and empirical findings and generalizations summarized in subsequent chapters in this book.

REFERENCES

Boersma, F. J., & Chapman, J. W. (1979). *Student's Perception of Ability Scale manual.* Edmonton, Canada: University of Alberta.

Bracken, B. A. (1992). *Multidimensional Self Concept Scale.* Austin, TX: Pro-Ed.

Brody, N. (1992). *Intelligence* (2nd ed.). San Diego, CA: Academic Press.

Byrne, B. M. (1984). The general/academic self-concept nomological network: A review of construct validation research. *Review of Educational Research, 54,* 427–456.

Cattell, R. B. (1941). Some theoretical issues in adult intelligence testing. *Psychological Bulletin, 38,* 592.

Coopersmith, S. A. (1967). *The antecedents of self-esteem.* San Francisco: Freeman.

Craven, R. G., Marsh, H. W., & Debus, R. (1991). Effects of internally focused feedback and attributional feedback on the enhancement of academic self-concept. *Journal of Educational Psychology, 83,* 17–26.

Dusek, J. B., & Flaherty, J. F. (1981). The development of self-concept during adolescent years. *Monographs of the Society for Research in Child Development, 46*(4. Serial No. 191).

Dyer, C. O. (1964). Construct validity of self-concept by a multitrait-multimethod analysis (Doctoral dissertation, University of Michigan, 1963). *Dissertation Abstracts International, 25,* 8154. (University Microfilms No. 64–8154)

Fitts, W. H. (1964). *Tennessee Self Concept Scale: Test Booklet.* Nashville, TN: Counselor Recordings and Tests.

Fleming, J. S., & Courtney, B. E. (1984). The dimensionality of self-esteem: II: Hierarchical facet model for revised measurement scales. *Journal of Personality and Social Psychology, 46,* 404–421.

Fox, K. R. (1990). *The physical self-perception profile manual.* DeKalb: Northern Illinois University, Office for Health Promotion.

Fox, K. R., & Corbin, C. B. (1989). The Physical Self-Perception Profile: Development and preliminary validation. *Journal of Sport & Exercise Psychology, 11,* 408–430.

Guilford, J. P. (1959). Three facets of intellect model. *American Psychologist, 14,* 469–479.

Guilford, J. P. (1969). *The nature of human intelligence.* New York: McGraw-Hill.

Guilford, J. P. (1985). The structure-of-intellect model. In B. B. Wolman (Ed.), *Handbook on intelligence: Theory, measurements and applications.* New York: Wiley.

Hansford, B. C. & Hattie, J. A. (1982). The relationship between self and achievement/performance measures. *Review of Educational Research, 52,* 123–142.

Harter, S. (1982). The Perceived Competence Scale for Children. *Child Development, 53,* 87–97.

Harter, S. (1983). Developmental perspectives on the self-system. In P. H. Mussen (Ed.), *Handbook of child psychology* (4th ed., Vol. 4, pp. 275–285). New York: Wiley.

Harter, S. (1985). Competence as dimensions of self-evaluation: Toward a comprehensive model of self-worth. In R. L. Leahy (Ed.), *The development of self* (pp. 55–122). New York: Academic Press.

Harter, S. (1986). Processes underlying the construction, maintenance and enhancement of self-concept in children. In J. Suls & A. Greenwald (Eds.), *Psychological perspective on the self* (Vol. 3, pp. 136–182). Hillsdale, NJ: Erlbaum.

Harter, S. (1989). Causes, correlated, and the functional role of global self-worth: A life-span perspective. In J. Kolligian & R. Sternberg (Eds.), *Perceptions of competence and incompetence across the life-span* (pp. 67–97). New Haven, CT: Yale University Press.

Harter, S., & Marold, D. B. (1991). A model of the determinants and mediational role of self-worth: Implications for adolescent depression and suicidal ideation. In J. Strauss & G. R. Goethals (Eds.), *The self: Interdisciplinary approaches* (pp. 66–92). New York: Springer-Verlag.

Harter, S., & Pike, R. (1984). The Pictorial Perceived Competence Scale and Social Acceptance Scale for young children. *Child Development, 55,* 1969–1982.

Hattie, J. (1992). *Self-concept.* Hillsdale, NJ: Erlbaum.

Higgins, E. T. (1987). Self-discrepancy: A theory relating self and affect. *Psychological Review, 84,* 319–340.

Hoge, D. R., & McCarthy, J. D. (1984). Influence of individual and group identity salience in the global self-esteem of youth. *Journal of Personality and Social Psychology, 47,* 403–414.

James, W. (1963). *The principles of psychology.* New York: Holt, Rinehart & Winston. (Original work published 1890)

Markus, H., & Nurius, P. (1986). Possible selves. *American Psychologist, 41,* 954–969.

Markus, H., & Wurf, E. (1987). The dynamic self-concept: A social psychological perspective. *Annual review of psychology, 38,* 299–337.

Marsh, H. W. (1986a). Global self esteem: Its relation to specific facets of self-concept and their importance. *Journal of Personality and Social Psychology, 51,* 1224–1236.

Marsh, H. W. (1986b). Verbal and math self-concepts: An internal/external frame of reference model. *American Educational Research Journal, 23,* 129–149.

Marsh, H. W. (1987a). The big-fish-little-pond effect on academic self-concept. *Journal of Educational Psychology, 79,* 280–295.

Marsh, H. W. (1987b). The hierarchical structure of self-concept and the application of hierarchical confirmatory factor analysis. *Journal of Educational Measurement, 24,* 17–19.

Marsh, H. W. (1989). Age and sex effects in multiple dimensions of self-concept: Preadolescence to adulthood. *Journal of Educational Psychology, 81,* 417–430.

Marsh, H. W. (1990a). Confirmatory factor analysis of multitrait-multimethod data: The construct validation of multidimensional self-concept responses. *Journal of Personality, 58,* 661–692.

Marsh, H. W. (1990b). The influence of internal and external frames of reference on the formation of math and English self-concepts. *Journal of Educational Psychology, 82,* 107–116.

Marsh, H. W. (1990c). A multidimensional, hierarchical self-concept: Theoretical and empirical justification. *Educational Psychology Review, 2,* 77–172.

Marsh, H. W. (1990d). The structure of academic self-concept: The Marsh/Shavelson model. *Journal of Educational Psychology, 82,* 623–636.

Marsh, H. W. (1991). The failure of high ability high schools to deliver academic benefits: The importance of academic self-concept and educational aspirations. *American Educational Research Journal, 28,* 445–480.

Marsh, H. W. (1992). The content specificity of relations between academic achievement and academic self-concept. *Journal of Educational Psychology, 84,* 35–42.

Marsh, H. W. (1993a). Academic self-concept: Theory measurement and research. In J. Suls (Ed.), *Psychological perspectives on the self* (Vol. 4). Hillsdale, NJ: Erlbaum.

Marsh, H. W. (1993b). The multidimentional structure of physical fitness: Invariance over gender and age. *Research Quarterly for Exercise and Sport, 64,* 256–273.

Marsh, H. W. (1993c). Physical fitness self-concept: Relations to field and technical indicators of physical fitness for boys and girls aged 9–15. *Journal of Sports and Exercise Psychology, 15,* 184–206.

Marsh, H. W. (1993d). Relations between global and specific domains of self: The importance of individual importance, certainty, and ideals. *Journal of Personality and Social Psychology, 65,* 975–992.

Marsh, H. W. (1994). *The importance of being important: Theoretical models of relations between specific and global components of physical self-concept.*

Journal of Sport and Exercise Psychology, 16, 306–325. Manuscript submitted for publication.

Marsh, H. W., Barnes, J., Cairns, L., & Tidman, M. (1984). The Self Description Questionnaire (SDQ): Age and sex effects in the structure and level of self-concept for preadolescent children. *Journal of Educational Psychology, 76,* 940–956.

Marsh, H. W., & Byrne, B. M. (1991). The differentiated additive androgyny model: Relations between masculinity, femininity, and multiple dimensions of self-concept. *Journal of Personality and Social Psychology, 61,* 811–828.

Marsh, H. W., & Byrne, B. M. (1993). Do we see ourselves as others infer: A comparison of self-other agreement on multiple dimensions of self-concept from two continents. *Australian Journal of Psychology, 45,* 49–58.

Marsh, H. W., Byrne, B. M., & Shavelson, R. (1988). A multifaceted academic self-concept: Its hierarchical structure and its relation to academic achievement. *Journal of Educational Psychology, 80,* 366–380.

Marsh, H. W., Craven, R. G., & Debus, R. (1991). Self-concepts of young children 5 to 8 years of age: Measurement and multidimensional structure. *Journal of Educational Psychology, 83,* 377–392.

Marsh, H. W., & Gouvernet, P. (1989). Multidimensional self-concepts and perceptions of control. Construct validation of responses by children. *Journal of Educational Psychology, 81,* 57–69.

Marsh, H. W., & Jackson, S. A. (1986). Multidimensional self-concepts, masculinity and femininity as a function of women's involvement in athletics. *Sex Roles, 15,* 391–416.

Marsh, H. W., & McDonald-Holmes, I. W. (1990). Multidimensional self-concepts: Construct validation of responses by children. *American Education Research Journal, 27,* 89–117.

Marsh, H. W., & Myers, M. R. (1986). Masculinity, femininity, and androgyny: A methodological and theoretical critique. *Sex Roles, 14,* 397–430.

Marsh, H. W., & Parker, J. W. (1984). Determinants of self-concept: Is it better to be a relatively large fish in a small pond even if you don't learn to swim as well? *Journal of Personality and Social Psychology, 47,* 213–231.

Marsh, H. W., Parker, J. W., & Smith, I. D. (1983). Preadolescent self-concept: Its relation to self-concept inferred by teachers and to academic ability. *British Journal of Educational Psychology, 53,* 60–78.

Marsh, H. W., & Peart, N. (1988). Competitive and cooperative physical fitness training programs for girls: Effects on physical fitness and on multidimensional self-concepts. *Journal of Sport and Exercise Psychology, 10,* 390–407.

Marsh, H. W., & Redmayne, R. S. (1994). A multidimensional physical self-concept and its relations to multiple components of physical fitness. *Journal of Sports and Exercise Psychology, 16,* 43–55.

Marsh, H. W., & Richards, G. (1988a). The Outward Bound Bridging Course for low achieving high-school males: Effect on academic achievement and multidimensional self-concepts. *Australian Journal of Psychology, 40,* 281–298.

Marsh, H. W., & Richards, G. E. (1988b). The Tennessee Self Concept Scales: Reliability, internal structure, and construct validity. *Journal of Personality and Social Psychology, 55,* 612–624.

Marsh, H. W., Richards, G., & Barnes, J. (1986a). Multidimensional self-concepts: The effect of participation in an Outward Bound program. *Journal of Personality and Social Psychology, 45,* 173–187.

Marsh, H. W., Richards, G., & Barnes, J. (1986b). Multidimensional self-concepts: A long-term follow-up of the effect of participation in an Outward Bound program. *Personality and Social Psychology Bulletin, 12,* 475–492.

Marsh, H. W., Richards, G., Johnson, S., Roche, L., & Tremayne, P. (1994). Physical Self Description Questionnaire: Psychometric properties and a multitrait-multimethod analysis of relations to existing instruments. *Journal of Sport & Exercise Psychology, 16,* 270–305. Manuscript submitted for publication.

Marsh, H. W., & Shavelson, R. J. (1985). Self-concept: Its multifaceted, hierarchical structure. *Educational Psychologist, 20,* 107–125.

Marsh, H. W., & Smith, I. D. (1982). Multitrait-multimethod analyses of two self-concept instruments. *Journal of Educational Psychology, 74,* 430–440.

Marsh, H. W., Smith, I. D., & Barnes, J. (1983). Multitrait-multimethod analyses of the Self Description Questionnaire: Student-teacher agreement on multi-dimensional ratings of student self-concept. *American Educational Research Journal, 20,* 333–357.

Marsh, H. W., Smith, I. D., Barnes, J., & Butler, S. (1983). Self-concept: Reliability, stability, dimensionality, validity and the measurement of change. *Journal of Educational Psychology, 75,* 772–790.

Marx, R. W., & Winne, P. H. (1978). Construct interpretations of three self-concept inventories. *American Educational Research Journal, 15,* 99–108.

Marx, R. W., & Winne, P. H. (1980). Self-concept validation research: Some current complexities. *Measurement and Evaluation in Guidance, 13,* 72–82.

Michalos, A. C. (1991). Global report on student well-being. Volume I: Life satisfaction and happiness. New York: Springer-Verlag.

Nunnally, J. C. (1967). Psychometric theory. New York: McGraw-Hill

Pelham, B. W., & Swann, W. B. (1989). From self-conceptions to self-worth: On the sources and structure of global self-esteem. *Journal of Personality and Social Psychology, 57,* 672–680.

Richards, G. E. (1988). *Physical Self Concept Scale.* Sydney: Australian Outward Bound Foundation.

Rogers, C. R. (1951). *Client-centered therapy.* Boston: Houghton Mifflin.

Rogers, C. R., & Dymond, R. F. (1954). *Psychotherapy and personality change.* Chicago: University of Chicago Press.

Rosenberg, M. (1965). *Society and the adolescent child.* Princeton: Princeton University Press.

Shavelson, R. J., & Bolus, R. (1982). Self-concept: The interplay of theory and methods. *Journal of Educational Psychology, 74,* 3–17.

Shavelson, R. J., Hubner, J. J., & Stanton, G. C. (1976). Validation of construct interpretations. *Review of Educational Research, 46,* 407–441.

Shavelson, R. J., & Marsh, H. W. (1986). On the structure of self-concept. In R. Schwarzer (Ed.), *Anxiety and cognitions.* Hillsdale, NJ: Erlbaum.

Sillon, E. L., & Harter, S. (1985). Assessment of perceived competence, motivational orientation, and anxiety in segregated and mainstreamed educable mentally retarded children. *Journal of Educational Psychology, 77,* 217–230.

Soares, L. M. & Soares, A. T. (1977, April). *The self-concept: Mini, maxi, multi.* Paper presented at the annual meeting of the American Educational Research Association, New York.

Soares, L. M. & Soares, A. T. (1982, July). *Convergence and discrimination in academic self-concepts.* Paper presented at the 20th Congress of the International Association of Applied Psychology, Edinburgh, Scotland.

Soares, L. M., & Soares, A. T. (1983, April). *Components of students' self-related cognitions.* Paper presented at the annual meeting of the American Educational Research Association, Montreal, Quebec, Canada.

Song, I. S., & Hattie, J. A. (1984). Home environment, self-concept, and academic achievement: A causal modeling approach. *Journal of Educational Psychology, 76,* 1269–1281.

Sonstroem, R. J., Speliotis, E. D., & Fava, J. L. (1992). Perceived physical competence in adults: An examination of the Physical Self-Perception Scale. *Journal of Sport and Exercise Psychology, 10,* 207–221.

Spearman, C. (1927). *The abilities of man.* London: Macmillan.

Thorndike, R. M. (1990). Origins of intelligence and its measurement. *Journal of Psychological Assessment, 8,* 223–230.

Thurstone, L. L. (1938). *Primary mental abilities.* Chicago: University of Chicago Press.

Thurstone, L. L., & Thurstone, T. G. (1941). *Factorial studies of intelligence.* Chicago: University of Chicago Press.

Vernon, P. E. (1950). *The structure of human abilities.* London: Methuen.

Vispoel, W. P. (1993). The development and validation of the Arts Self-Perception Inventory for Adolescents. *Educational and Psychological Measurement, 53,* 1023–1033.

Vispoel, W. P. (1995). Self-concept in the arts: An extension of the Shavelson model. *Journal of Educational Psychology, 87,* 134–145.

Vispoel, W. P., Wang, T., Bleiler, T., & Tzou, H. (April, 1993). *Validation studies for early adolescent and adult versions of the Arts Self-Perception Inventory.* Paper presented at the annual meeting of the American Educational Research Association, Atlanta, GA.

Wainer, H. (1976). Estimation coefficients in linear models: It don't make no nevermind. *Psychological Bulletin, 83,* 213–217.

Wells, L. E., & Marwell, G. (1976). *Self-esteem: Its conceptualization and measurement.* Beverly Hills, CA: Sage.

Wigfield, A., & Karpathian, M. (1991). Who am I and what can I do? Children's self-concepts and motivation in achievement situations. *Educational Psychologist, 26,* 233–261.

Winne, P. H., & Marx, R. W. (1981, April). *Convergent and discriminant validity in self-concept measurement.* Paper presented at the annual meeting of the American Educational Research Association, Los Angeles, CA.

Winne, P. H., Marx, R. W., & Taylor, T. D. (1977). A multitrait-multimethod study of three self-concept instruments. *Child Development, 48,* 893–901.

Wylie, R. C. (1974). *The self-concept* (Rev. ed., Vol. 1). Lincoln: University of Nebraska Press.

Wylie, R. C. (1979). *The self-concept* (Vol. 2). Lincoln: University of Nebraska Press.

Wylie, R. C. (1989). *Measures of self-concept.* Lincoln: University of Nebraska Press.

CHAPTER 3

Self-Concept Instrumentation:
A Historical and Evaluative Review

LORI K. KEITH and BRUCE A. BRACKEN

In the century since William James (1890/1983) began the discussion of
the conscious self by defining it as a ratio of an individual's successes to
his or her pretensions, theories and definitions of self-concept have prolif-
erated. Cooley (1902), for instance, described the "looking-glass self" as
an internalization of others' reactions to oneself. Although James provided
an enormous impetus for the study of the self, it was not until the 1940s
and 1950s when the early definitions were expanded and self-concept was
conceptualized as a cognitive (Rogers, 1951; Sarbin, 1952) as well as an
affective construct (Mead, 1934; Sullivan, 1953) that instruments for measuring self-concept began to proliferate (Rosenberg, 1989).

Consistent with the evolving theoretical orientations, authors of early
self-concept instrumentation created scales that purported to measure a
cognitive or affective construct and that were characterized by unidimensionality and an emphasis on global self-concept (e.g., the Rosenberg Self
Esteem Scale; Rosenberg, 1965). As the basis for his instrument, Rosenberg described self-esteem as the individual's self-regard or feelings of
self-worth. Similarly, the Coopersmith Self-Esteem Inventory (Coopersmith, 1967, 1981) was based on a unitary notion of self-concept that the
author defined as "a set of attitudes and beliefs that a person brings with
him- or herself when facing the world" (p. 1). The most recently developed
cognitively based instruments depict self-concept as part of a larger "self-
system" (Harter, 1985, 1988, 1990; Messer & Harter, 1986; Neeman &
Harter, 1986; Renick & Harter, 1988).

In contrast to the cognitivist perspective, some investigators have conceptualized self-concept as a behavioral construct and have developed instruments that integrate behavioral principles (e.g., Boersma & Chapman,
1992; Bracken, 1992). Regardless of the theorists' basic orientations, most
theorists accept the multidimensionality of self-concept (e.g., Byrne &
Shavelson, 1986; Harter, 1982, 1990; Marsh, 1987; Marsh, Barnes, & Hocevar, 1985; Marsh & Hocevar, 1985; Shavelson, Hubner, & Stanton,

1976). As a result of the theoretical movement away from a unitary construct toward a multidimensional construct, most instruments developed since the mid-1970s assess several facets of self-concept in addition to a global component. The exact structure of these dimensions, the particular facets, and their relationship to overall self-concept vary widely across instruments.

Just as the underlying theories and definitions of self-concept have varied widely across instruments and researchers, so has the assessment methodology taken many forms. Specific forms of self-concept assessment include semantic differentials, adjective checklists, drawing tasks, Q-sorts, projective tests, actual-ideal measures, third-party report, and questionnaires. Although a plethora of self-concept instruments have been developed, the majority have been used only in research and appear in the professional literature only once. Relatively few instruments are thoroughly developed, commercially published, or used widely in research or clinical practice. Therefore, very little information is available about the majority of instruments cited in the literature. The unfortunate result of researchers having used such a collection of questionable instrumentation is that equivocal findings pervade the self-concept literature.

A brief review of common methodology used to assess self-concept illustrates this predicament. For example, the semantic differential technique consists of a presentation of bipolar continua (e.g., "happy-sad"; "strong-weak") with which respondents rate themselves. Although commonly used in research, authors seldom identify the specific semantic pairs employed, making it impossible to discern the extent to which the stimuli are related to self-concept. Hattie (1992) concluded, "The semantic differential seems to have been poorly used for measuring self-concept" (p. 160). Moreover, in a review of semantic differential based research, Wylie (1974) concluded that only about 40% of the 81 articles surveyed used Osgood's semantic differential *and* reported the particular stimulus pairs used. According to Wylie, these limitations lead to uninterpretable results across investigations.

The adjective checklist, a frequently used technique in self-concept research during the 1950s and 1960s, requires an examinee to indicate adjectives that are self-describing (Hattie, 1992). Similar to the semantic differential, many forms of the adjective checklist have been used in research, with investigators most often failing to identify the specific adjectives included on their respective research protocols. Wylie (1974) contended that adjective checklists are insufficiently reliable or valid to use in either research or clinical practice.

Also popular in the 1950s and 1960s, the Q-sort technique has been widely used for research and clinical purposes. The individual, by sorting cards imprinted with descriptive statements into several stacks according to the extent to which the statement applies to him- or herself, creates a continuum that purportedly reflects a range between the "true self" and the "ideal self." Wylie (1961) questioned the underlying premise for the

Q-sort, asking whether discrepancies between the true and ideal self are attributable to unrealistic expectations represented by the ideal self or an overly negative view of the true self.

Similar to the basic premise of the Q-sort, "actual-ideal" techniques have been used in research and clinical practice. Typically, subjects complete a questionnaire that asks about their "true selves" and then they answer the same questions with regard to an "ideal self." The discrepancy between the two "selves" is computed as a measure of self-concept. As with the Q-sort, it is unclear whether the discrepancy is best interpreted as a measure of self-concept (for certainly it is an indirect one at best), a measure of how close the person is to a negative self-image or simply a measure of maturity because discrepancies increase as a function of age. Additionally, Hattie (1992) cites numerous psychometric inadequacies of the actual/ideal procedure including regression to the mean, low test reliability due to high correlations between true and ideal scores, and variability of stimulus salience among respondents.

Projective tests such as the Rorshach, the Thematic Apperception Test, and the Behavioral Interpretation Inventory have been used in the assessment of the self; however, these procedures are generally considered peripheral measures of self-concept. Because these techniques were intended primarily to detect and categorize pathology and describe the nonphenomenal self, and because the procedures rely on subjective attributions made by the examiner, the validity of such techniques as measures of self-concept is highly suspect. Wylie (1974) emphatically rejects such techniques for measuring self-concept by stating, ". . . conceptual and methodological problems of establishing construct validity of indices purporting to reveal the unconscious self-concept have not been clearly recognized or coped with, and consequently, no measure in use has been demonstrated to be adequate for this purpose" (p. 287).

Subjective human figure drawings also have been used to infer self-concept, particularly among young children. Such tasks instruct the child to draw a picture of a person, which according to the "Body Image" hypothesis (Machover, 1949) is purportedly a reflection of him- or herself. It is from this proposed "self-drawing" that the child's self-concept is inferred. Other tests present pictures or drawings of children and require the respondent to identify the person who is most like him- or herself. Projective drawing techniques possess the same inadequacies as other "peripheral" measures. Furthermore, the assumption that self-concept can be validly inferred from a person's self-drawing remains scientifically indefensible (Wylie, 1974). The proliferation of questionable procedures such as the semantic differential, Q-sort, and other projective and construction tasks have contributed to the vast array of equivocal findings in the self-concept literature.

The most widely used technique for assessing self-concept is the self-report questionnaire. Most commercially produced and currently used self-concept instruments employ this self-report technique. As a more direct measure of an individual's self-concept than many of the techniques previously discussed, the self-report questionnaire is appropriate for young children, adolescents, and adults, depending on their reading abilities and the readability of the respective questionnaires. In general, the technical adequacy of self-report measures is stronger and more directly assessed than that of the previously discussed methods.

Following her most recent review of the research and available methods for measuring self-concept, Wylie (1989) indicated that she was encouraged by recent developments in self-concept instrumentation; however, she cautioned users, "None of the published information warrants using any of these instruments as tools for diagnosing individuals" (p. 121).

Shavelson, Hubner, and Stanton (1976), along with Wylie, decried the state of self-concept research and called for uniformity among self-concept definitions. They suggested seven characteristics critical to defining the construct of self-concept: (a) organization, (b) multifaceted nature, (c) hierarchical structure, (d) stability, (e) developmental progression, (f) an evaluative component, and (g) differentiable characteristics.

Several researchers followed the recommendations of Shavelson et al. (1976) and developed instruments that reflect these essential characteristics (Boersma & Chapman, 1992; Bracken, 1992; Marsh, 1988, 1990). Additionally, previously published scales have been revised to align the scales more closely with emerging theory and methodology (e.g., Coopersmith, 1987; Piers, 1984). Better integration of theory and methodology has improved the psychometric quality of self-concept instruments. However, many self-concept measures continue to lack a clear operational definition, a sound theoretical basis, or evidence for strong technical adequacy.

Despite the improvements in current instrumentation, researchers continue to use project-developed instruments of questionable substance. Hattie (1992) contended, "The time has long passed when substantive studies based on unevaluated instruments should be considered publishable" (p. 140). Equally disturbing is the persistent use of poorly normed, outdated, and inappropriate measures for diagnosis and evaluation in clinical settings.

Self-concept research must continue to refine the construct and validate the current instrumentation. Recent studies employing factor analysis and multitrait-multimethod techniques are helpful and important in this regard (e.g., Bracken, Bunch, Keith, & Keith, 1992; Keith & Bracken, 1994; Marsh & Hocevar, 1985). Future self-concept research should continue to investigate the relative importance of domain-specific self-concepts as compared with global self-concept.

The remainder of this chapter provides comprehensive reviews and evaluations for self-concept instruments that are historically significant, widely used in research, or recently developed. We begin with early instruments and proceed on the basis of publication date and the unique contribution the instrument makes to the evolution of self-concept instrumentation and theory.

EVALUATIVE STANDARDS

Each instrument was evaluated in terms of its development and construction, standardization and norming, administration and interpretation, and its foundational psychometric characteristics and qualities. Furthermore, qualitative as well as quantitative characteristics were examined, including the incorporation of a theoretical orientation, the presence of a definition of the construct measured, the representativeness of the standardization sample, the number and types of subdomains included in the instrument, administration time, appropriate age or grade level of the scale, reading level required for completion, level of internal consistency, level of test-retest reliability, evidence of validity, types of scores produced and interpretive guidelines, and suggestions for remediation and intervention.

Because of the subjective nature of several of these characteristics, including theoretical orientation and definition, interpretive guidelines, and recommendations for remediation and intervention, an evaluative description of each is presented. Additionally, in the consideration of support for an instrument's validity, both the type (e.g., construct, content, criterion-related) and strength of support was evaluated (Carmines & Zeller, 1979). Finally, validity coefficients were rated as high (.80 or greater), moderately high (.60 to .79), moderate (.30 to .59) and low (below .30).

The adequacy of standardization samples was evaluated based on the recommendation of the American Educational Research Association, American Psychological Association, National Council on Measurement in Education (1985) for 200 subjects for each age interval for a "good" rating, and 100 subjects per age level for an "adequate" rating. In addition, an objective assessment of the internal consistency of each instrument was made based on the following criteria suggested by Bracken (1987) and Salvia and Ysseldyke (1988): (a) median internal consistency of .80 or greater for subtest interpretation; (b) internal consistency of .90 or greater for scale interpretation; (c) median stability coefficients of .80 or greater for subtest interpretation; and (d) test-retest reliability of .90 or greater for scale interpretation.

SELF-CONCEPT SCALES EVALUATED

Rosenberg Self-Esteem Scale

First published in 1965, the Rosenberg Self-Esteem Scale (RSES; Rosenberg, 1979) is one of the earliest measures of overall self-concept and is the forerunner of modern self-concept instrumentation. The RSES is a 10-item unidimensional measure of global self-esteem based on Rosenberg's theory of self-concept as "an organization of parts, pieces, and components, . . . hierarchically organized and interrelated in complex ways" (Rosenberg, 1979, p. 73). Rosenberg described these "parts" as separate entities that should be studied and measured independently. Rosenberg does not explicitly state goals or intended purposes for the RSES, but he defines self-concept as "the totality of the individual's thoughts and feelings having reference to himself as an object" (p. 7).

Development and Standardization

No rationale, either logical or empirical, is presented for the selection of items on the RSES; however, Rosenberg indicated that the 10 items have face validity and assess positive and negative global self-attitudes. Although no age range is suggested for the scale, item vocabulary appears appropriate for examinees as young as approximately 12 years; item content and format are presented in a relatively straightforward fashion. The RSES uses a Guttman method of scaling, with a 7-point scale summed across the 10 items in various combinations. This scoring method is cumbersome to use and is without any obvious advantages over simpler scoring schemes (e.g., Likert). According to Rosenberg, the scale is often scored according to the simpler Likert format, which appears to produce similar scores.

The RSES was originally administered to a sample of 5,024 juniors and seniors attending 10 "randomly" chosen high schools in New York State. The sample was stratified by community size; however, no other demographic information is reported. Because the sample is from only one state, and because important demographic variables such as race, gender, and SES were not included as stratification variables, and all comparisons to population percentages were omitted from the examiner's manual, generalizability of the sample to the U.S. population is not possible. Even more serious is the outdated nature of the sample; the norms were collected in 1965, thus greatly diminishing the utility and generalizability of the original sample to contemporary respondents.

Administration and Interpretation

The RSES is appropriate for group or individual administration; however, very little information is provided regarding administration or interpretation procedures. No standardized administration instructions are presented in the examiner's manual. Furthermore, neither the estimated reading level nor the scale's administration time are discussed. Based on the Guttman scaling method, a raw score ranging from zero to six is produced for each item, which in turn is classified as reflecting High, Medium, or Low self-esteem. Although specific guidelines for scale or item interpretation are not discussed, implications and outcomes related to these categories are presented in the broader context of studies that employed the RSES (Rosenberg, 1979).

Psychometric Characteristics

With a reported alpha coefficient of .77 for the total scale score, the RSES does not meet the minimum suggested criterion of .90 for internal consistency. A substantial amount of error is associated with the total scale score (e.g., 23% of the score is due to measurement error); therefore, considerable caution is warranted when interpreting students' scores. No estimates of scale stability are reported for the original sample; however two independent studies reported stability coefficients of .85 and .88 for small college samples over 2-week intervals (Silber & Tippett, 1965; McCullough, cited in Rosenberg, 1979).

Numerous validity studies have been conducted on the RSES and reported in the professional literature; however, many of these studies were not addressed in the revised Rosenberg manual and the author provides no rationale why some studies were reported and others were not. In addition to the studies selected for presentation, however, some validity evidence was presented based on the original norming sample. For example, Rosenberg studied the relationship between students' self-concept and depressed affect; 4% of the high self-esteem adolescents compared with 80% of adolescents identified as possessing low self-esteem, were described as depressed.

Two supplemental studies by Silber and Tippett (1965) and Tippett and Silber (1965) summarized by Rosenberg (1979) provided convergent and discriminant validity of the RSES. Finally, factor-analytic studies reported by Rosenberg (1979) identified two factors for the 10 RSES items; Carmines and Zeller (1974) labeled these factors as positive and negative self-esteem items. Kohn (1969) and Kohn and Schooler (1969) described the two factors as self-confidence and self-deprecation. Although support for the unidimensionality of the RSES might be considered questionable based on the factor analyses, the two identified factors appear to be related more to method variance associated with positive and negative item types rather than any theoretically defensible or clinically relevant explanation.

Summary

As one of the earliest measures of self-concept, the RSES is a historical landmark in the field of self-concept instrumentation. Despite its serious limitations (e.g., outdated norms, low internal consistency), the RSES continues to be used in the interest of brevity and ease of administration. Although its contributions to the development of self-concept cannot be denied, the incongruence of the RSES with current theory, its relatively poor psychometric quality, and its outdated normative sample suggest that the RSES is of questionable utility as a tool for either research or clinical applications.

Coopersmith Self-Esteem Inventories

First published in 1967, the Coopersmith (CSEI; Coopersmith, 1981) was designed as a unitary measure of self-esteem. The CSEI was a definite improvement on the RSES, with more extensive content sampling and a more cogently presented theory and rationale. Coopersmith defined self-esteem as "the evaluation a person makes, and customarily maintains, of him- or herself; that is, overall self-esteem is an expression of approval or disapproval, indicating the extent to which a person believes him- or herself competent, successful, significant, and worthy" (pp. 1–2). Revised in 1981 to incorporate theoretical advances in the structure of self-concept, the CSEI purports to measure "self" attitudes in the areas of social, academic, family, and personal experience. Recommended uses for the CSEI include individual assessment, classroom screening, instructional planning for building self-esteem, program evaluation, and research.

Development and Standardization

Two basic forms of the CSEI were developed, one for children and one for adults, the School and Adult Forms, respectively. The School Form is appropriate for children aged 8 to 15 years and comprises 50 items, which constitute four subscales—General Self, Social Self-Peers, Home-Parents, and School-Academic. Eight additional items create a Lie Scale that is intended to measure response defensiveness. An abbreviated version is also available by administering only the first 25 items. According to the manual, item content for the School Form was based largely on the work of Rogers and Dymond (1954). Items also were reviewed by five psychologists for content and were field tested on a group of 30 children. The Adult Form is recommended for use with persons 16 years old and older and consists of 25 items modified from the School Form.

The original normative sample for the CSEI included 44 boys and 43 girls in Grades 5 and 6. Several subsequent studies on larger samples are cited in the examiner's manual; however, the current norms for the School Form are based on research by Kimball (1973). The Kimball sample comprised 7,593 children in Grades 4 through 8, and included all socioeconomic levels along with "Black and Spanish-surnamed students" (Coopersmith, 1981, p. 17). Additionally, the Kimball sample includes approximately equal numbers of boys and girls and approximately equal numbers of subjects in each grade. Although this sample appears more than adequate in size, the sample is limited in other respects (e.g., all subjects reside in the same state).

The norms for the Adult Form are based on a sample of 226 college students with a mean age of 21.5 years from a community college and a state university in northern California. The sample is divided into two age groups (16–19 years and 20–34 years) based on data indicating slightly lower scores for adolescents. Because the number of subjects for each age level is unspecified, determination of sample size adequacy is not possible. Furthermore, this sample does not meet the criterion for a nationally representative sample due to the inclusion of only one geographic region, overrepresentation of highly educated adults, and the lack of information about race, ethnicity, and gender characteristics of the sample.

Administration and Interpretation

Guidelines for administration and scoring are provided explicitly in the examiner's manual. With an estimated administration time of approximately 10 minutes, the CSEI may be administered individually or in a group format. Although the manual states that the School Form is appropriate for ages 8 to 15 years, the scale's readability is not provided. Both forms include items with short statements to which the respondent must reply "Like me" or "Unlike me." With the exception of two items on the School Form that include noncontemporary vocabulary (e.g., scolded), the item content of the CSEI is straightforward.

Scoring keys for the School and Adult Forms are recommended to reduce scoring time as well as scoring errors. Specific scoring instructions are provided in the event that scoring keys are unavailable. Additionally, a computer scoring service is available through the Center for Self-Esteem Development, but its use is not described in detail. With 26 independent items, the General-Self scale is weighted more heavily than the remaining content scales, each of which comprises 8 items. Therefore, the CSEI Total Score is influenced considerably by general self-concept content.

In lieu of standard scores and classifications, percentile ranks corresponding to total scores are provided. The author recommends two procedures for interpreting examinees' performances: the development of local norms and the supplemental use of behavior observations. Although these techniques may be useful when conducting a comprehensive evaluation, they do not compensate for the lack of suitable norms. As stated in the manual, these techniques must be used with caution; however, no guidelines for cautious interpretation are provided. Because the CSEI norms are over 25 years old and are very restricted geographically, additional caution is warranted when using and interpreting the instrument.

Psychometric Characteristics

Total scale internal consistency based on Kimball's (1973) data indicates acceptable reliability for Grades 4 and 8 with coefficients of .90 and .92, respectively. However, internal consistencies for Grades 5, 6, and 7 fall below the recommended criterion of .90 for total scores with coefficients of .87, .88 and .89, respectively. Short Form internal consistencies were predictably lower (.74 and .71) when computed for a sample of 103 college students (Bedian, Geagud, & Zmud, 1977).

Short-term stability of the total scale falls slightly below accepted levels with a test-retest correlation of .88 over a 5-week interval. Not surprisingly, coefficients are even lower for longer intervals (.64 for 1 year; .42 to .70 for 3 years).

Although the manual suggests that subscales may be scored separately, the author provides neither the means (norms tables) nor the support (e.g., information regarding technical adequacy of the subscales) to make such a practice possible. No information is provided in the examiner's manual to allow users to judge the technical adequacy of the Adult Form.

Although numerous validity studies are reported in the manual, only sparse data are actually presented to support the authors' claims of validity. For instance, although the author claims that "Her (Kokenes, 1974, 1978) study confirmed the construct validity of the subscales proposed by Coopersmith as measuring sources of self-esteem" (p. 13), no data are provided to support the interpretation. Similarly, several factor analyses are discussed in support of construct validity; however, the number of factors produced ranged from four to nine, which indicates that Coopersmith's original unidimensional design is not supported. Additional supplemental data including concurrent, predictive, convergent, and discriminant validity are cited in the manual, but one cannot judge the validity of the CSEI due to the omission of actual supporting data.

Summary

The CSEI is a brief, easily scored measure of self-esteem. Although the author suggests that the CSEI can be used for individual and group screening, instructional planning, program evaluation, and clinical or research uses, it would not be the measure of choice for any of these purposes. The 1981 CSEI revision uses normative data gathered nearly 10 years earlier (Kimball, 1973). A primary limitation of the scale is that the scale does not produce standard scores; only percentile ranks in fifth percentile units are available. Additionally, the Coopersmith exhibits only moderate reliability and meager support of validity.

Tennessee Self-Concept Scale

Originally published in 1965 as a unidimensional measure, the Tennessee Self-Concept Scale (TSCS; Roid & Fitts, 1988) was revised in 1988 to provide an examinee-friendly, multidimensional measure of self-concept. With 100 items and response choices including "completely false," "mostly false," "partly false and partly true," "mostly true," "completely true," the authors intended to capture the respondent's "self-picture." Beyond attempting to capture an examinee's self-picture, no further definition or theory of self-concept is offered. Without theoretical linkages, the TSCS subscales include Identity, Satisfaction, Behavior, Physical, Moral-Ethical, Personal, Family, and Social. Stated uses of the TSCS include counseling, clinical assessment, diagnosis, personnel selection, and research.

Development and Standardization

Through a logical approach to item construction, a large pool of self-descriptive statements was initially produced. The statements were classified as positive or negative and were evaluated with regard to scale appropriateness by clinicians. Although this is a step in scale construction, such a process is subjective and does not reflect an explicit definition or theoretical rationale. In the revision of the TSCS, six scales were developed empirically by analyzing responses of selected groups: normative, psychotic, neurotic, personality disordered, defensive positive, and personality integration. Items that distinguished each of these groups from the others were retained to create a scale for the identification of that group. With these empirically derived scales, the authors expanded the usefulness of the TSCS and, as an early multidimensional measure, contributed to the progression of self-concept instrumentation.

The TSCS standardization sample included 626 subjects from various parts of the United States who ranged in age from 12 to 68 years. Additionally, the sample included ". . . an approximate balance of males and females, blacks and whites, representatives of all social, economic, and intellectual levels, and of educational levels. . . ." (p. 56); however, college students, white participants, and subjects from 12 to 30 years of age are overrepresented according to the manual. Because no further demographic information or clarification is provided, the representativeness of the TSCS standardization sample is impossible to determine. Specifically, one cannot determine which or how many geographic locations were sampled, even though "various parts of the United States" (p. 56) are represented according to the manual. Although the TSCS serves an expansive age range, an average of only 11 participants per age level was included in the normative sample. No new standardization sample is reported for the Adult Form; however, several samples were collected for research purposes (age range = 19–64 years). The average score across these samples differed from the original TSCS normative sample by only 1.81 raw score units indicating, according to the authors, "the robustness and general representativeness of the TSCS normative sample for United States adults . . ." (p. 58).

Mean differences of greater magnitude were found between independent adolescent groups and the original sample, which prompted the authors to calculate new adolescent norms based on independent studies. Generally, small samples of highly restricted segments of the population were gathered for the supplementary scales. For example, the standardization sample for the Stanwyck-Garrison Faking Good Scale included 69 graduate nursing students, 40 dental hygienist students, and 29 college freshmen. No further demographic information is provided regarding gender, age, ethnicity, or location of that sample. The most serious concern regarding the norms for the TSCS is that although the examiner's manual was revised in

1988, there is no evidence that any norms were updated. The "new" adolescent norms, which were developed in a very questionable fashion by averaging scores across individual TSCS studies and matching them to a sample from one particular study, used data published between 1969 and 1983. The method used to "norm" the TSCS is a practice that is not commonly used by commercial test publishers. The TSCS is in dire need of a thorough revision and competent restandardization.

Administration and Interpretation

With a fourth-grade reading level and an estimated administration time of 10 to 20 minutes, the TSCS is brief and appropriate for both group and individual administrations. The simple administration format should be self-explanatory to respondents of all ages for which the test was designed (12–68 years). The items are easily understood, with only a few items that should use more contemporary vocabulary. Examples of dated language include "I try to understand the other fellow's point of view" and "Sometimes, when I am not feeling well, I am cross."

Items from the various TSCS subscales form a grid of rows and columns which facilitate scoring and interpretation. Interpretation of the Total Scale score as a general measure of self-esteem is based on equal contributions from the column subscales of Physical, Moral-Ethical, Personal, Family, Social, and the row subscales of Identity, Self-Satisfaction, and Behavior. However, items are not independent and contribute to more than one scale, which results in content contamination across supposedly independent scales. Supplementary scales do not contribute to the Total Scale score.

For interpretive purposes, two forms of the TSCS are available; however, no differences in item content or administration formats exist for the two forms. The only differences between the two forms are the profiles and available scores that are produced. The Counseling Form (Form C) includes 14 basic scales, whereas the Clinical and Research Form (Form C&R) provides 29 scores. Forms C and C&R both include the basic subscales (Identity, Satisfaction, Behavior, Physical, Moral-Ethical, Personal, Family, Social, Self-Criticism) and supplementary scales. Form C&R adds to these basic and supplementary scales a number of additional clinical "indicators" and "indices." Form C&R provides more quantitative information than Form C, which may be useful, if not overwhelming, when making clinical diagnoses. Form C is a simpler version to score and use, but it still provides information about several basic areas of self-concept. According to the manual, Form C was designed for users "who emphasize the Total Score and Basic Row and Column scores, rather than the more clinically oriented empirical scales of Form C&R" (p. 8).

Clear but complex instructions for the calculation and interpretation of scale scores are provided in the examiner's manual. Additionally, case studies using both forms are provided as interpretive examples. Because hand-scoring of the TSCS can be arduous, both forms may be scored by computer through a mail-in service or with the scoring program. A separate chapter of the manual provides detailed instructions regarding preparation for and interpretation of computerized scoring.

Normalized T scores and percentile ranks for the total scale and subscales are provided on profile sheets that provide a graphic representation of the scores. In addition to the norm-referenced interpretation, ipsative subscale analysis (intra-examinee variability) is permitted using subscale raw scores.

Although a large amount of diverse information about the examinee is generated by the TSCS, the authors offer only a few brief suggestions as to how this information can be used to guide remediation or intervention efforts. The TSCS manual, its record and scoring forms, and the profile analysis procedures have very little examiner appeal. The manual is poorly organized and unnecessarily difficult to wade through. Furthermore, it provides an abundance of superfluous information about the instrument's supplementary scales, but very little meaningful information about the instrument's major subscales. Hand-scoring and profile analysis is exceedingly cumbersome, making computer scoring mandatory or at least highly desirable.

Psychometric Characteristics

Internal consistency estimates are not provided for the original standardization sample, but were computed for a sample collected during the revision of the TSCS. Cronbach's alpha was computed for 472 adolescents and adults, which produced a Total Score coefficient of .94 and subscale reliabilities between .81 and .87 (median = .83). As such, the TSCS meets the criteria for acceptable internal consistency at both the total scale and subscale levels for this sample. Internal consistencies for the supplementary scales are also provided in this study and range from .40 on the Stanwyck-Garrison Faking Good Scale to .84 on the General Maladjustment Scale (median = .76). For this sample, only three of the eight supplementary scores for which internal consistencies are provided meet the criterion of .80. Internal consistency coefficients are reported for smaller samples from additional studies and range from .66 to .94, inclusive of total and subscale scores.

Fitts (1965) reported a .92 Total Score stability coefficient over a 2-week interval for 60 college students. In addition to acceptable Total Score stability, the eight major subscales also meet the recommended criterion (range = .80 to .91; median = .88). Stability coefficients are also provided for the supplementary scales and range from .60 to .92 (median = .85); 12 of the 21 supplemental scales met the .80 criterion.

The TSCS examiner's manual addresses construct, content and criterion-related validity primarily from studies selected from extant literature, with no rationale for which studies were included or excluded. As evidence for construct validity, the authors cite total scale correlations of .80 and .73 with the Piers-Harris Children's Self-Concept Scale. Additionally, the authors suggest support exists for the TSCS hierarchical model; however, the manual does not present supporting data and no particular theoretical model is specified or presented. Further, the authors conclude that the TSCS "has some empirically based connections with each of the recognized models of self-concept." (p. 70). In general, it appears that the construct assessed by the TSCS was defined on a post hoc basis and matched to existing models only after analyses of existing data. The method used by Roid and Fitts is antithetical to traditional construct validation practices that require specification of an a priori theoretical or empirical relationship between measures and the consequent interpretation of empirical evidence with respect to the proposed relationship (Carmines & Zeller, 1979).

As a further support for TSCS construct validity, moderate correlations with the Minnesota Multiphasic Personality Inventory scales are reported in directions expected by the authors. Also, low correlations between the TSCS and the Edwards Personal Preference Schedule provide some evidence for discriminant validity of the TSCS.

Several factor analyses of the TSCS are discussed that provide equivocal support for the dimensionality of the TSCS. In support of the TSCS structure, one confirmatory factor analysis resulted in 79% of the row items and 80% of the column items loading on their expected factors (McGuire & Tinsley, 1981). On the other hand, a subsequent confirmatory factor analysis cited in the manual found that fewer than 25% of the items fit with their hypothesized factors. These conflicting results may be due to disparate methodologies, samples, or to the structure of the TSCS itself.

For content validity, the authors cite item categorization by clinicians, with consensus on the 90 items included in the final form. Second, the authors reference the facet-design work by Levin et al. (1978) as support for the three-by-five facet model of the TSCS. The authors do not, however, provide a theoretical match between the assessed content and the overall construct of self-concept.

Criterion-related validity is addressed by the authors in summaries of studies comparing the TSCS to various outcome variables. The original norm group is among the myriad samples studied for this purpose. Mean score differences were observed between psychiatric patient groups and normals at one extreme, as well as between normals and a group who rated high on personality integration at the other extreme. Additional evidence of discrimination among clinical groups is provided in summary form from the literature and through a discussion of profile cluster analysis studies, although some diagnostic groups (e.g., schizophrenic, manic, paranoid) are not readily discriminated in the profile analyses.

Summary

By incorporating areas such as Satisfaction and Moral-Ethical self-concept, the TSCS contributes a broader perspective to self-concept instrumentation than available previously and purports to be a measure of overall affectivity. Given its broader content sampling, it is ironic that the TSCS includes no items that assess academic self-concept. The TSCS is a reliable and temporally stable measure and TSCS validity has been extensively investigated. Weaknesses of the TSCS include a poorly organized examiner's manual and extremely difficult scoring and interpretation procedures, particularly for the supplementary scales. A major limitation of the TSCS, even though it is a fairly recently revised instrument, is the inappropriate fashion in which the normative sample was based on data extracted from independent studies published between 1969 and 1983.

The Piers-Harris Children's Self-Concept Scale

Originally published in 1969, the Piers-Harris Children's Self-Concept Scale (PHSCS; Piers, 1984) is a unidimensional measure of self-concept with items reflecting content from the behavior, intellectual/school, physical appearance/attributes, anxiety, popularity, and happiness/satisfaction domains. The PHSCS represents a significant contribution to the field of self-concept instrumentation in that items were developed to reflect these specific areas even before the current focus on multidimensionality. The definition of self-concept according to Piers is a "relatively stable set of self-attitudes reflecting both a description and an evaluation of one's own behavior and attitudes" (p. 1). A framework of theoretical assumptions is described in the examiner's manual. These include a phenomenological view of self-concept that is best suited to measurement through self-report. Additionally, self-concept is assumed to be expressed differentially throughout various stages of development and it is assumed to be a relatively stable construct. Self-concept is also described as both a global and domain-specific construct.

The stated purpose of the PHSCS is to assess conscious self-perceptions in children rather than to make inferences based on third-party report or behavioral observation. Recommended uses of the scale include screening in clinical settings for children in need of further psychological assessment, incorporation into comprehensive clinical evaluations, and a variety of research applications.

Development and Standardization

The PHSCS consists of 80 items designed to reflect general self-concept. Four pilot tests were conducted with large item pools to eliminate items that did not contribute to the reliability or validity of the scale. Retained items included approximately equal numbers of positively and negatively connoted phrases. To obtain the total scale score, items endorsed in the positive direction are summed.

Based on the results of several factor analyses, items were assigned to one or more cluster scales to reflect the following six factors: Behavior, Intellectual and School Status, Physical Appearance and Attributes, Anxiety,

Popularity, and Happiness and Satisfaction. These scales were identified after the original scale was developed; thus they are not an integral part of the total scale. Additionally, the items that constitute the cluster scales are not mutually exclusive, nor are they equal in number. As a result, this aspect of the scale development appears to have been haphazard and nonsystematic. Because many items are found on more than one scale and also contribute unequally to cluster scales, interpretation of scales as discrete facets of self-concept is not possible.

A unique feature of the PHSCS is the inclusion of two supplementary validity scales, the Inconsistency Index and the Response Bias Index. Although both these indexes aid the examiner in judging the validity of the respondent's self-report, the samples used for standardization are separate from and much smaller than the total scale standardization sample. Also, the payoff for the time and effort needed to compute the Response Bias Index is relatively small because examinees who respond in an extremely positive or negative manner are likely to be apparent to the examiner without computing additional veracity scores. Because inconsistency in responding generally requires closer examiner scrutiny, the Inconsistency Index may be a useful index.

The 1966 standardization sample for the PHSCS comprised 1,183 public school children in Grades 4 through 12, ages 8 through 18 from a small town in Pennsylvania. No other characteristics of the sample are provided in the PHSCS manual. With 107 children per age level, the sample is adequate in size; however, the sample is not nationally representative and does not easily generalize beyond the small unnamed town in Pennsylvania. Additionally, norms for the cluster scales are based on a sample of 485 children (248 girls and 237 boys) in public schools. The PHSCS manual reports that 279 of these children were elementary school age, 55 were in junior high, and 151 were in high school. Further specification of age or grade levels, geographic location, and ethnicity are not indicated and therefore, the generalizability of these indexes is extremely limited.

Administration and Interpretation

With a third-grade readability level and an approximate administration time of 20 minutes, the PHSCS is appropriate even for the youngest recommended age level of 8 years. Administration may be conducted individually or in group format, and a combination of computer administration and scoring options are also available through the publisher. In general, items are simply stated and easily interpreted with the occasional exception of items with frequency qualifiers such as "often" and "usually." Such items are subject to a variety of interpretations; however, only 7 of 80 items incorporate such a term. Conversely, many items include behavioral statements with the word "I," which personalizes the item affect, cognition, or behavior.

Total scale and cluster scale raw scores may be converted into stanines, percentile ranks and normalized T scores. Caution should be exercised when comparing cluster scale scores to total scale scores due to the separate standardization samples. As with the total scale, cluster scales were standardized on a very small, regional sample, which also restricts the representativeness and generalizability of the norms.

The PHSCS examiner's manual suggests a strategy for interpreting the scale and encourages integration of PHSCS scores with information gained from additional sources. The possible range for the total score is 0 to 80 (-5 SD to $+3$ SD). A low total score may suggest low overall self-concept or it may indicate a very negative domain-specific self-concept. This is a difficult distinction to make, however, because of the unequal numbers of items from specific subscales that contribute to the total scale score. Each of the six self-concept dimensions contribute between 10 and 17 items to the total scale.

In addition to norm-referenced interpretation strategies, instructions for ipsative, or intrachild, interpretations are provided. Critical values for difference scores are provided for each of the six cluster scales along with guidelines for computing domain-specific strengths and weaknesses. Item level interpretation is facilitated by information in the manual that identifies items that have been shown to differentiate between clinical and nonclinical groups and between male and female respondents.

An entire chapter of the Examiner's Manual is devoted to the discussion of research findings regarding self-concept as well as studies that have employed the PHSCS. The studies often present conflicting results, however, and do not lead to meaningful recommendations for intervention or remediation.

Psychometric Characteristics

With reliability estimates of .90 and .93 for the total scale, the PHSCS possesses good internal consistency for boys at Grades 6 and 10, respectively. However, internal consistency of .88 for girls at these same grade levels falls slightly below the suggested criterion. Internal consistency estimates for other age and grade levels were determined through independent research studies and are similar in magnitude to the estimates based on the standardization sample (.89 to .92), suggesting that the total scale is adequately reliable at most age levels. However, due to the grade- and gender-specific samples included in these supplemental data, caution should be exercised in generalizing the results.

With a range of internal consistency at the subscale level of .73 to .81 (median = .765), five of the six cluster scales fail to meet the minimum level of internal consistency of .80. This limitation suggests that examiners should use cluster scale scores cautiously when making clinical or educational decisions based on these subscales.

Based on several supplemental studies, PHSCS total scale stability coefficients ranged from .42 to .96. As one would expect, studies that used longer intervals (8–12 months) reported lower reliabilities (.42 and .51, respectively) than those that employed 3- to 4-week intervals (.96 and .86, respectively). For 20 studies with a median interval of 4 months, the median test-retest reliability is .725. Though self-concept is known to be a stable construct, the stability of the PHSCS does not generally meet the criterion of .90 for total scale scores. Only one study, with 10 students in third and fourth grades reported adequate stability with a coefficient of .96.

The authors discuss several types of validity in the examiner's manual, including content, concurrent, contrasted groups, and construct. The majority of the supportive evidence, however, is supplemental data that has been summarized but not presented in sufficient detail to evaluate critically.

Content validity for the PHSCS is argued on the basis of the construction of items reflecting a framework of domains recommended by Jersild (1952), and subsequent elimination of items with low discriminatory power based on statistical analyses. Concurrent validity studies indicate moderate correlations between the PHSCS and other measures of self-concept (range = .32 to .85). Additionally, the PHSCS correlated moderately with indicators of adjustment: −.64 to −.48 with emotional and behavioral problems; −.54 to −.69 with anxiety; −.27 with psychoticism; −.34 to −.47 with neuroticism; .25 to .45 with the Children's Social Desirability Scale; .41 to .49 with extroversion as defined by the Junior Eysenck Personality Questionnaire; .19 to .27 with the Intellectual Achievement Responsibility Questionnaire Total Scale; and .25 to .57 with the Intellectual Achievement Responsibility Questionnaire Success Scale. These studies provide a moderate amount of evidence that the PHSCS relates to measures of other constructs as expected.

Modest support for construct validity is also provided by several factor analyses; however, with individual items loading on different factors in the separate analyses, only coarse approximations of the original set of factors that formed the basis for the cluster scales are evident in subsequent studies. Therefore, caution is advised when interpreting cluster scales of the PHSCS. Several independent investigations are also summarized in the examiner's manual as support for PHSCS validity.

Summary

Since its publication in 1963, the PHSCS has been widely used in research and clinical endeavors. With better technical qualities than preceding instruments and item development based on specific areas of functioning, the PHSCS has contributed significantly to the field. Strengths of the PHSCS include items appropriate for examinees of all intended ages and adequate levels of internal consistency at the total scale level. Weaknesses of the PHSCS, however, far outweigh these strengths. Inadequate test-retest reliability at most age levels and a lack of validity data gathered during the standardization are limiting factors. Furthermore, although it is commendable that the scale was converted to a multifaceted measure through addition of cluster scales, the total scale PHSCS continues to assess a unitary construct and is therefore incongruent with the current consensus on the multidimensional nature of self-concept. The principal limitation of the PHSCS is its outdated and geographically restricted normative sample.

Offer Self-Image Questionnaire–Revised

The Offer Self-Image Questionnaire–Revised (OSIQ-R; Offer, Ostrov, Howard, & Dolan, 1992) consists of 129 objective self-report items. Along with the Rosenberg Self-Esteem Scale (1965), the original OSIQ was one of the earliest instruments to address adolescent self-image. The OSIQ-R is a multidimensional instrument that assesses 12 self-concept domains: Emotional Tone, Impulse Control, Mental Health, Social Functioning, Family Functioning, Vocational Attitudes, Self-Confidence, Self-Reliance, Body Image, Sexuality, Ethical Values, and Idealism. Although the OSIQ-R assesses these multiple dimensions, no explicit definition of self-image is given.

In the beginning, the OSIQ was used chiefly to study the development of normal adolescents. Other stated uses included employment in research regarding adolescents' self-views, as a clinical tool for practitioners working with both troubled and normal adolescents, and as a research tool to explore the nature of the self.

The OSIQ-R is based on two basic theoretical assumptions: (a) Because "an individual can master one aspect of experience while failing to adjust to another . . ." evaluation of multiple areas of self-image is necessary (Offer, Ostrov, Howard, & Dolan, 1992; p. 16); and (b) adolescents are sufficiently insightful to describe their own feelings and thoughts.

Development and Standardization

The OSIQ-R was based on the results of Q-sort analyses of item content stemming from several studies cited in the examiner's manual. Following a pilot study, the scale was reduced to 130 items and 11 categories that "on the basis of theory, clinical experience, and a review of empirical findings—were believed to be important to the psychological life of the adolescent" (Offer, Ostrov, Howard, & Dolan, 1992; p. 16). Subsequent revisions resulted in the current version of 129 items that assess the previously mentioned 12 areas. Although the OSIQ-R appears to be empirically based, only limited discussion of its theoretical foundation is presented in the examiner's manual.

The total standardization sample is adequate in size with 964 adolescents between the ages of 13 and 18; however, undersampling of the extreme ages (49 subjects at age 13 and 83 at 18) resulted in less than adequate normative groups at these levels. With the inclusion of subjects from eight states and the District of Columbia, the normative sample is fairly regional; however, it overrepresents the Northeastern region and underrepresents the South, Central and Western United States. The sample is closely matched to 1985 U.S. Census data with regard to ethnicity. Subjects in the sample appear to have been exposed to a much higher level of parental education than the general population; only 3% of parents did not graduate high school compared with 20% in the population. Also, 40% of the parents were college graduates in contrast to 21% in the general population. Relatively equal numbers of males and females were included in the sample.

Administration and Interpretation

The OSIQ-R was designed for use with adolescents between 13 and 18 years of age. As a self-report inventory, its 29 items are rated on a six-point Likert style format that ranges from "Describes me very well" to "Does not describe me at all." Readability is reported at the mid-fifth-grade level and should therefore be appropriate for most teenagers. Several of the statements, however, are awkwardly worded and unclear. Examples include "I do not have many fears which I cannot understand" and "Very often parents don't understand a person because they had an unhappy childhood." Additionally, several items are "double-barreled" in nature. For instance, "At times, I feel like a leader and feel that other kids can learn something from me" and "Sometimes I feel so ashamed of myself that I just want to hide in a corner and cry." Because these and several other items are unclear, it is likely that avoidable measurement error will be introduced due to differential interpretations of the item across respondents.

The OSIQ-R may be administered in group or individual format. Instructions for administration are provided on the front of the Administration Booklet given to the respondent and may also be read by the examiner.

Scoring options for the OSIQ-R are limited to sending record form facsimiles or mailing in record forms for computer scoring by the publisher (cost is included in cost of answer sheets) or through a microcomputer scoring system supplied by the publisher. Hand scoring is not an option. Although computer scoring conserves scoring time for the examiner, the usefulness of the OSIQ-R for the examiner who needs immediate results or who has limited access to a computer, is diminished. Computer scoring does provide extensive interpretive information including profiled T scores and confidence intervals, interpretive text that discusses several checks on the validity of examinees' responses, normative and ipsative interpretation of the results, analysis of critical items that are rarely extremely endorsed, and profile analyses compared with several diagnostic groups. Also included are the client's responses as displayed in the response booklet, allowing examination of individual items by the examiner, and a color, graphic summary of the results.

OSIQ-R interpretation guidelines suggest that T scores below 40 indicate "troublesome" adjustment, and scores below 30 indicate "very unmanageable" areas of adjustment. Scores above 60 indicate good adjustment, while scores above 70 define an area as one in which the teenager is "unusually well-adjusted."

This interpretive scheme applies to all subscales with the exception of the Sexuality scale for which both extremely low or extremely high scores deviate from conventional norms and suggest problematic thoughts, behavior, or feelings. Because the well-adjusted adolescent tends to score close to the mean on this scale and the scale does not have a linear relationship with the other 11 scales, the Sexuality scale is not included in the Total Self-Image score. Although the authors apparently believe that this scale contains important information, further explanation of its relationship to the composite score is not provided.

The scales that do contribute to the Total Self-Image score have differing numbers of items and thereby contribute unequally to the composite score. Thus, a respondent's Total Self-Image is influenced much more by the Family Functioning scale, which contains 19 items, than by the Body Image scale which has only 9 items. Additionally, due to differences in content and a low correlation with the total scale, the Idealism scale does not contribute to the Total score. Although these decisions regarding scale inclusion in the composite score are empirically based, there is no theoretical rationale for these decisions. A practical discussion of the importance and interpretation of critical items, as well as a brief interpretation of four sample profiles is included; however, specific guidelines for intervention are not presented.

Psychometric Characteristics

Internal consistency estimates were computed by age levels (younger = 13–15; older = 16–18) and gender. For both age levels and genders, total scale internal consistency is at or above the .90 criterion. The subscales, however, generally fall well below the .80 criterion for acceptable internal consistency (range = .45 to .90; median = .69). Only the Family Functioning scale meets the criterion for both age levels and genders (.83 to .90). The Emotional Tone scale demonstrates adequate internal consistency at both age levels for females only with coefficients of .81. The OSIQ-R subscale internal consistencies are too low to support clinical interpretation; furthermore, no information is provided to determine whether the subscale possesses enough unique variance to warrant independent interpretation.

With a Total Scale stability coefficient of .63 and a median subscale coefficient of .58, both over a time interval of 2 years, the OSIQ-R evidences moderate test-retest reliability. On short-term stability, estimates likely would be higher.

The OSIQ-R subscales and the total score are moderately intercorrelated (median r = .48). Additionally, factor analysis resulted in only two factors. Included on the first factor with significant loadings are the Emotional Tone, Impulse Control, Mental Health, Social Functioning, Family Functioning, Vocational Attitudes, Self-Confidence, Self-Reliance, and Body-Image scales. The second factor included Sexuality, Ethical Values, and Idealism scales, in addition to the Impulse Control, Family Functioning, Vocational Attitudes, and Self-Reliance scales. The results of the factor analysis do not support the hypothesized structure of the OSIQ-R, but the author contended that the first factor is a "general, intra-individual self-image factor, while the second factor encompass[es] (sic) areas of self-image that are more effected (sic) by societal image, morality, and social change" (p. 22). It appears, however, that due to the low internal consistency for most scales and a factor structure that does not provide strong support for the scales, the OSIQ-R items assess constructs other than those intended.

Most of the validity studies reported in the examiner's manual were conducted with the original OSIQ, rather than the revised instrument. Because that information addresses the original scale, not the one in current use, it will not be detailed here. Although the original version of the OSIQ has been widely used in research, the validity of the OSIQ-R is not well established in the current revised manual, and is only referred to as "other research." Because several scales were added to the OSIQ-R and because the OSIQ was first published in 1969, presentation of information on the latest version is imperative.

Summary

As one of the early measures of self-image for adolescents, the OSIQ has contributed to the study of normal adolescent self-concepts. Because support exists for its use as a measure of general affectivity, the OSIQ has broadened the perspective and the clinical usefulness of self-concept measurement. Strengths of the OSIQ-R include a large standardization sample and good total scale internal consistency. A major weakness of the OSIQ-R, however, is that validity studies reported in the examiner's manual were conducted with the OSIQ, not the revised version of the scale. Additionally, factor analyses do not support the structure of the OSIQ-R.

The Self-Perception Inventory

The Self-Perception Inventory (SPI; Soares & Soares, 1985) is based on a forced-choice semantic differential format in which items are presented as two opposite adjectives or sentences. Four forms of the inventory are available including the Student, Adult, Teacher, and Nursing forms. Furthermore, translations are available in Spanish, Italian and French. Self-concept is defined in the SPI manual as "the system of perceptions formulated of the self in awareness of its distinctive existence" (p. 10). The underlying theoretical model of the SPI describes self-concept as a relatively stable construct which develops over time through interaction with the environment. A multidimensional "clustering model" with self-concept at the core of many "self-pictures" is described (p. 14). The model is multifaceted, and although fairly stable, reflects changing roles of and demands on the individual. Self-report scales comprising the Student Form include Self Concept, Reflected Self/Classmates, Reflected Self/Teachers, Reflected

Self/Parents, Ideal Concept, and Student Self. Additionally, two Perceptions of Others scales are completed by people associated with the student. Similarly, the Adult Form comprises the following scales: Self Concept, Reflected Self/Friends, Reflected Self/Teachers, Reflected Self/Parents, Reflected Self/Partners, Ideal Concept, and Student Self. Again, two Perceptions of Others scales are completed by relevant others. The primary purpose of the SPI, according to the authors, is to serve as a research tool. Additional uses cited include description of children and adults in affective terms, comparison of self- and other-ratings, contribution to a larger assessment battery, and identification of clinical disorders. Because the SPI is available in several translations, includes forms for specific populations, and employs a widely researched semantic differential format, the SPI contributes uniquely to existing self-concept instrumentation.

Development and Standardization

Development of the SPI as stated in the examiner's manual is unclear. According to the authors, the SPI Student Form was developed by first comparing "ratings" and "analyses" from students, teachers, university educators, psychologists and researchers regarding single adjectives. Again, the method of assembly and the purpose and criteria for the ratings are unclear; however, those adjectives with the "greatest degree of rater-agreement were changed to phrases and tested further" (p. 16). As a result of a pilot project conducted with third and fourth graders in the spring of 1967, an instrument with 20 pairs of traits was created. Because the authors found that children needed a larger context for the adjectives, these traits were presented as complete sentences.

The SPI Adult Form was similarly developed; however, the final form comprises 36 items, each with two opposing adjectives (e.g., happy-sad). The traits for the Adult Form were validated against other personality measures including the Minnesota Multiphasic Personality Inventory (MMPI).

Although large standardization samples are reported for both the Student and Adult Forms, information regarding the normative sample of the SPI is limited. The total sample for the Student Form includes 10,712 subjects; however, this data set is a compilation of 14 independent studies with 5 studies having been conducted outside the United States. The remaining 9 samples were gathered from undisclosed regions identified only as urban or suburban locations. For each sample, the number of males and females is identified, and for some, the number of "disadvantaged" versus "advantaged" students is identified; however, these terms are not defined. Grades 2 through 12 are represented in the norms, but no percentages are provided to indicate the number of students representing each grade level. Further, none of the information matches sample characteristics to population characteristics. The authors do not indicate a time frame for the collection of the normative sample, and because of the long history of research with this instrument, it is important that users know, for example, whether the samples were collected in 1967 or 1990. Given such scant information regarding the standardization sample, the examiner cannot make an informed determination of the representativeness of any of the subsamples or generalizability of the norms.

Similarly, the standardization sample for the Adult Form comprised 2,650 subjects compiled from 10 different studies. Again, means and standard deviations are presented for each SPI scale and are divided by male and female subjects with the sample size of each provided. Subjects across the 10 studies ranged from ninth graders to "working adult" subjects with an unspecified age range; however, various levels of college students and workers from a variety of settings are included. As with the Student Form, representativeness of these samples is indeterminable given the limited amount of information reported in the manual.

Administration and Interpretation

Instructions for both group and individual administration of the SPI are provided and clearly written. Each item is presented as a four-point continuum between two terms that are opposite in meaning (e.g., the available responses between the terms happy and unhappy are "very happy," "more happy than unhappy," "more unhappy than happy," and "very unhappy"). The respondent is instructed to choose the option that best describes him or her, thereby providing information regarding the direction and intensity of the response.

Completion time for the scale is estimated between 5 and 20 minutes "depending upon age group and reading ability" (p. 5); however, the readability of the SPI is not indicated. Item content on the Student Form includes several global descriptors that are likely difficult for elementary students to evaluate (e.g., "sure of my self—not sure of myself" and "satisfied—feel sorry for myself"). Additionally, several items include figurative language that is likely to be interpreted literally by elementary school children. These include "stand on my own two feet—go along with the gang"; "can wait for things—want things right away" (p. 17). Items for the Adult Form contain adjectives that are fairly sophisticated and require global descriptions of oneself on abstract characteristics; these may be difficult for some adults to comprehend. Most adults of average cognitive ability should, however, be comfortable with the task.

For both the Student and Adult Forms, positive and negative responses are assigned dichotomous value (two points for extreme responses; one point for less extreme responses). An index raw score is obtained for each subscale by summing the item scores. Raw scores may also be converted to stanines for normative comparisons. Additionally, some guidance is provided for determining significant discrepancies between traits represented by the different subscales, between trait-pairs across different subscales, and between subscale total scores. Limited information regarding interpretation of the SPI is provided. For example, some consideration is given to the interpretation of discrepancies, but no evidence is provided to support the interpretability of individual subscales (e.g., subscale specificity, factor support). Furthermore, no examples or illustrative case studies are provided in the SPI manual. Because recommended uses include clinical identification, more interpretive guidance and intervention suggestions are warranted.

Psychometric Characteristics

It appears that internal consistency estimates are provided only for the self-report Self Concept and Student Self subscales of the Student Form. With internal consistency of .94, the Self Concept subscale evidences good reliability; however, the Student Self subscale falls slightly below acceptable levels ($r = .79$). Although difficult to infer from the manual, it appears that internal consistency estimates are also provided for the scales rated by others; however, no internal consistency estimates are reported for the Adult Form.

Test-retest reliability is addressed for each of the four subscales and for peer-rated, teacher-rated and self-rated versions of the Reflected Self Concept. Ranging from .74 to .89 (median = .855) over an interval of 7 to 8 weeks, adequate stability is evident for four of the six scales reported. Test-retest reliability is also indicated for the seven subscales of the Adult Form and ranges from .68 to .86 (median = .79) over an interval of 8 weeks. Four of the seven subscales fell below the criterion for adequate test-retest reliability, suggesting that interpretation of the Reflected Self subscales, which purport to measure how the respondent believes others perceive him or her, is not very stable.

As evidence of content validity, the authors report correlations between the SPI Student Form and the Coopersmith Self-Esteem Inventory (Coopersmith, 1981). Low to moderately high correlations are reported (range = .29 to .68; median = .49) between five SPI scales and the Coopersmith Full Scale score. Separately, a coefficient of .63 is indicated between the SPI Self Concept scale and the Coopersmith Full Scale. Additionally, a moderate correlation of .44 is indicated between the SPI (scale unspecified) and the Tennessee Self-Concept Scale (Roid & Fitts, 1988).

Construct validity is addressed for the Student Self scale only, and the evidence is stated as "$r = .50$ [for] elementary school students, [and] $r = .74$ [for] secondary school students" (p. 25). No explanation regarding the nature of these apparent correlations is provided. Without additional information, this "evidence" for construct validity is inadequate and uninterpretable.

In support of the concurrent validity of the SPI Student Form, self-ratings and other-ratings were compared. Significant differences are reported between "Teachers' perceptions" and the Self Concept and Reflected Self-Teacher scales, both of which are completed by the child, with absolute mean differences of 8.74 ($p = .001$) and 7.56 ($p = .05$), respectively. "Teachers' Perceptions," however, are not defined and no SPI scale had been previously labeled as such. Therefore, examiners cannot judge the concurrent validity of the SPI based on this information. Additionally, the authors state that ratings by parents and children are consistent, but no evidence is presented to support the claim. Finally, the authors conclude that "peer ratings have generally fallen somewhere between those of the other two groups" (p. 25); however, no information regarding peer ratings is explicitly presented in the accompanying table. In sum, the vague and casual presentation in the examiner's manual is confusing and does not provide strong support for the validity of the instrument.

The authors report intercorrelations of the SPI Adult Form and the MMPI as evidence for content validity. Correlations between the identified scales range from $-.01$ to $-.38$, with only three correlations in the moderate range. Furthermore, no predictions are set forth regarding the expectations for the relationship between the SPI and the MMPI (convergent or discriminant validity) and no attempt is made to explain the data presented.

Summary

Caution should be exercised when interpreting the SPI scales and various versions because inadequate information is provided about the instrument's reliability, stability, validity, and the representativeness and size of the standardization sample. Furthermore, the examiner's manual is very poorly organized. It is primarily written in outline form and foregoes text to describe anything that is presented in table form. Further, information presented in tables is not readily interpreted due to unexplained abbreviations. Although several features of the SPI are unique including multiple translations and forms for specific populations, the manual is so disorganized and information presented so scant that any contribution made to the development of self-concept instrumentation is negated by these limitations.

Inferred Self-Concept Scale

The Inferred Self-Concept Scale (ISCS; McDaniel, 1986) is a unidimensional, 30-item Likert-type questionnaire designed to measure the self-concepts of children within a school setting. The ISCS is a third-party report scale that is completed, not by the child, but by the child's teacher. In this regard, the ISCS contributes uniquely to the measurement of self-concept, which is typically based on self-report. Furthermore, the ISCS format allows for measurement of self-concept in children too young to respond to a questionnaire.

Several assumptions stated in the literature are endorsed by the authors as the underlying theoretical structure of the ISCS. These include the belief that self-concept is a construct that can be "inferred from behavior";

". . . is acquired and, therefore, can be changed"; and ". . . is complex, made up of many facets," and " 'that the individual can predict success or failure in connection with behavior that pertains to a given facet . . .' (Sears & Sherman, 1964, p. 10)" (p. 2). Self-concept is further defined by the author as "a psychological construct which enables teachers, counselors, parents, and others to achieve deeper understanding of the behavior and development of children . . ." (p. 1). Stated purposes for the ICSC include research and individual evaluation.

Development and Standardization

ISCS items were determined by examination of relevant literature and the final item set was extracted from 100 items reviewed by professionals in the field. Reviewers unanimously agreed on 37 items as indicators of a student's self-concept. After deletion of seven redundant items, 30 items comprised the final scale.

The normative sample for the ISCS is comprised of 180 students, 90 boys and 90 girls, in Grades 1 through 6 at 16 public elementary schools in Austin, Texas. In each grade level, 30 children were observed by their teachers and school counselors. The schools selected for participation had a high percentage of low-income families as reported by the 1960 Census. Group means from two administrations of the ISCS in the same school year are presented for several variables including gender, ethnic group, family size, birth order, and grade level. No indication of the match between these variables and population percentages is provided. Overall, the sample is inadequate in size and representativeness because with only 30 subjects for each grade level, the criterion of at least 100 subjects is not met. Furthermore, with only one city represented, the sample cannot confidently be generalized to other geographic areas. The final and perhaps most serious threat to generalizability to a contemporary respondent is that the normative data appear to have been collected in 1967, nearly 30 years ago.

Administration and Interpretation

Administration of the ISCS is simple and explicit with instructions on each Record Sheet for the respondent's convenience. No particular requirement is stated for the length of observation of the child and direct observation while completing the Record Sheet is not implied. Column totals for each of the five points on the Likert-type scale are computed and summed to yield a total self-concept score. The author suggests that this total raw score be conceptualized as a point on a continuum of possible scores from 30 to 150, with the higher scores representing positive self-concept and the low extreme indicating negative self-concept. No standard scores or additional interpretive guides are provided in the examiner's manual. Because self-concept tends to be negatively skewed, a score slightly greater than the mid-point (90) might well be below average, but beyond the middle of this "continuum." Furthermore, comparison of an examinee's performance to the standardization group is limited; means but no standard deviations are reported. Finally, the author makes no recommendations for intervention or remediation based on the instrument.

Psychometric Characteristics

The ISCS possesses good internal consistency at the total scale level with a split-half reliability coefficient of .90 for a combined sample of teachers and counselors as raters. With estimates of .86 each for two separate samples of teachers and counselors, internal consistency is slightly below the recommended criterion.

Test-retest reliability was examined with the standardization sample for an interval of 6 months and reported by ethnic group, gender, family size, birth order, and grade level. Overall, only moderate stability for the total sample is indicated ($r = .66$). At each of the six grade levels, test-retest reliability fell below the .90 criterion (range $= .49$ at the sixth-grade level to .84 at the first-grade level; median stability $= .70$).

In support of the validity of the ISCS, the examiner's manual discusses content and construct validity. As evidence for content validity, McDaniel cites the item selection procedure whereby professionals chose the items from a larger pool. In the discussion of construct validity, the author takes the position that no other instrument existed at the time of validation of the ISCS that could be used as a criterion measure due to the unique format of the ISCS and the variability among self-concept instruments. This rationale is indefensible since some useful comparison is possible even if the criterion instrument is not universally accepted as a measure of the construct or of the same format. It would be expected that if separate instruments measured the same construct, scale format would be less important. Instead, the author chose to compare the ISCS with measures of intelligence, academic achievement, and other variables including grade level, age in months, and family size. These variables might be predicted to evidence discriminant validity, but do not provide convincing evidence for construct validity. The author states that because the ISCS correlated significantly with these variables, "construct validity is upheld" (p. 7). These modest correlations ($r = .25$ to .32) only demonstrate that "language IQ," "non language IQ," and Total IQ (measured by the California Tests of Mental Maturity) possess less than 10% shared variance with the ISCS. Similarly, academic achievement as measured by the Metropolitan Achievement Tests demonstrated discriminant validity with correlations from .09 to .20 (median $= .185$) with the ISCS but does not lend support for the claim that the ISCS measures self-concept. Rather, support is demonstrated for the expectation that the ISCS does not measure academic achievement.

Although the manual states the author's objections to the self-report format, many of these problems are not eliminated by use of other-report, which perhaps creates a new set of difficulties. For instance, teachers and counselors can have "differences in word-meaning and in the test-taking experience" just as those completing self-reports. Further, "differences in response set, . . . intelligence, . . . [and] socioeconomic status" (p. 2) may all affect responses of teachers and counselors. Observations of professionals are problematic in that the raters are associated closely with students and may have strong personal feelings that may impair objectivity. Additionally, the teacher/counselor is called on to recall the student's past behaviors and interpret those behaviors. Further, a comparison between teacher/counselor ratings and child self-reported ratings would seem to further construct validation of the ISCS more than comparisons with intelligence, academic achievement, and known lesser-related variables.

Finally, McDaniel reports the results of a factor analysis that indicated the emergence of two factors. Based on content, these factors were labeled "self-conformance" and "self-attitude." The results are only briefly discussed, but do not support the unidimensional model proposed by the author.

Summary

Because it relies on the reports of significant others in the child's life, the ISCS is a unique measure of self-concept. For this same reason, it may be less desirable when a more direct assessment through self-report is feasible. Furthermore, because it is based on a unidimensional model, the ISCS lags behind the current multidimensional view of self-concept. Although the ISCS possesses acceptable internal consistency, low stability, lack of a large, representative standardization sample, and little evidence for construct validity are its weaknesses.

Self-Perception Profile for Children

First published in 1979, the Self-Perception Profile for Children (SPPC; Harter, 1985) was revised in 1982 to include additional subscales and to refine the original scales. The revised SPPC includes six domains: Scholastic Competence, Social Acceptance, Athletic Competence, Physical Appearance, Behavioral Conduct, and Global Self-Worth, and was designed as a measure of "children's perceptions of themselves . . . across the various domains of his/her life" (p. 5).

Development and Standardization

Based on the work of James (1890/1983) and Cooley (1902), Harter (1985) contends that "perceived competence or adequacy in domains rated as important is strongly predictive of self-worth" (p. 7). Another predictor is the degree of positive regard from others. Further, Harter purports that these two sources are independent of one another; thus global self-worth and domain-specific competence are viewed as distinct constructs. The two-step response format whereby children must first choose the direction and then the intensity of their response is a unique contribution to self-concept instrumentation.

Harter focuses considerable attention on research surrounding the study of children's self-regard, somewhat to the expense of other pertinent information. In particular, very little information regarding scale development or the rationale for the selection of particular domains is provided.

The SPPC was administered to four samples of children, which collectively consisted of 1,543 lower-middle-class to upper-middle-class children from Colorado. Children in Grades 3 through 8 were sampled, with approximately equal numbers of girls and boys. At each grade level, the sample met the minimum criterion for size with the smallest group composed of 107 fifth-grade students. Although the normative sample is sufficiently large, it falls short in other important areas. With only one state and a narrow range of socioeconomic classes sampled, the normative sample cannot be construed as representative of the population. The author states that the sample was approximately 90% Caucasian, but more specific information is not presented regarding race and ethnicity of the remaining 10%. Furthermore, no comparison is made between the match of sample percentages and population percentages on other relevant variables. Because of the sparse information provided about the four samples, determination of generalizability to children from other locations is limited.

Administration and Interpretation

Comprising 36 self-report items, 6 items for each of the six scales, the SPPC is appropriate for either group or individual administration and for children in third through sixth grades. The manual does not estimate administration time or readability, both important considerations in the evaluation of young children. Furthermore, the SPPC response format may be somewhat cumbersome for children of this age since students must evaluate each item twice. The second of these evaluations results in a mark being placed on their answer sheet, but the first choice must be determined mentally. Harter states that this response format, which includes a positively and a negatively worded phrase, was designed to eliminate the "pull" for socially desirable responses. For instance, "Some kids have a lot of friends BUT Other kids don't have very many friends" is typical of the 36 items on the scale. A sample item is provided to ensure that respondents understand the nature of the response format. Additionally, detailed instructions are provided to aid in administration of the sample item, as well as the entire questionnaire. No evidence is provided to support the claim that such an item type reduces socially desirable responses.

SPPC items are assigned a value of 1 to 4 according to which item option is selected, with a score of 1 representing the least positive self-perception and 4 being the most positive. Scores are transferred to data coding sheets on which items are grouped according to subscale. The examiner can then easily compute the mean for each subscale. Because only raw scores are computed, no norm-referenced comparisons are possible. Additionally, the clinical utility of the SPPC is limited because the scale raw scores cannot be compared easily with other normative evaluations of a child's abilities or social-emotional adjustment.

Evaluation of the discrepancy between a child's judgment of his or her own competence and the relative importance of that domain as perceived by the child is possible; however, a separate administration of a 10-item measure is necessary. For each of 10 items, the respondent is asked "How important are these things to how you feel about yourself as a person?" with available responses of "really true of me" and "sort of true of me" in either a positive or negative direction. The item format parallels that of the SPPC, and a scoring key is provided. Instructions for computing the discrepancy scores are provided in detail, along with some interpretive guidance for this particular index. For example, Harter indicates that the "critical consideration involves how adequate the child feels in just those areas judged as important" (p. 24). By subtracting Importance Ratings from their respective Competence scores in each domain, the examiner can determine the magnitude and direction of the Discrepancy score. When summed, a large negative Total Discrepancy score indicates low self-worth due to low perceived competence in areas of importance. A small negative, zero, or positive Total Discrepancy score should be interpreted as the result of high perceived competence in areas of importance, and thus high self-worth. Norms for the relationship between the mean Discrepancy score and Global Self-Worth are provided in graphic form. Interpretive aids for the entire scale, such as examples of score interpretations are not indicated.

Psychometric Characteristics

At the subscale level, three of the six scales possess adequate internal consistency with median alpha coefficients of .83, .81, and .81; however, three scales fall slightly below the minimum criterion with estimates of .79, .78, and .74. Even with moderate scale reliability, one must question whether content domains were adequately sampled given only six items per scale. Estimates of test-retest reliability are not reported for the SPPC; therefore, examiners cannot be confident of SPPC stability.

Construct validity of the SPPC is addressed through factor analysis based on the responses of three separate samples. Because sample size is not reported and because adequate sample size is crucial to valid factor analytic findings, confident conclusions cannot be reached. Factor loadings for five of the six domains appear to support the Scholastic Competence, Social Acceptance, Athletic Competence, Physical Appearance, and Behavioral Conduct dimensions. Item loadings on nontarget factors are reportedly below .18 and nonsignificant. However, the sixth domain, Global Self-Worth, which Harter contends is independent of other domains, was not included in the factor analysis. Harter stated that because domains of importance which contribute more heavily to Global Self-Worth are unique to the individual, it is "unlikely that self-worth will systematically emerge as a distinctive factor" (p. 18). Her rationale for failing to include the sixth domain in the factor analysis appears inconsistent with the theoretical position that global self-worth is independent, a position which should have been tested empirically. Given the sparse evidence for the construct validity of the SPPC, the true nature of the construct measured by the SPPC is uncertain.

Summary

A major strength of the SPPC is its foundation on a strong theoretical model. Because many historical instruments were largely atheoretical in nature, Harter's contribution in this regard is a significant improvement to the field. With adequate internal consistency for three scales and slightly less than adequate estimates for the remaining three, the SPPC possesses borderline internal consistency for clinical usage. Importantly, with only six items per scale, content sampling in each domain is very restricted.

Extensions of the SPPC

Harter and her colleagues developed several extensions of the Self-Perception Profile designed for specific populations. These include the Self-Perception Profile for College Students (Neeman & Harter, 1986); the Self-Perception Profile for Adults (Messer & Harter, 1986); the Self-Perception Profile for Adolescents (Harter, 1988); and the Self-Perception Profile for Learning Disabled Students (Renick & Harter, 1988). These scales have many elements in common with one another and with the Self-Perception Profile for Children (Harter, 1985) previously reviewed. Therefore, the following is a brief delineation of features common to all the scales, followed by a discussion of characteristics specific to each version.

Harter's theoretical orientation is consistent throughout the five scales; each scale is appropriate for group or individual administration; and each scale employs Harter's unique response format which she contends reduces responses due to social desirability. Throughout the scales, items beginning with negative and positive stems are alternated to avoid an examinee response set. For each item, the respondent must make two decisions after reading sometimes double-barreled items. For example, the child may respond to either or both of two ideas in one question for the item, "Some kids wish something about their face or hair looked different BUT Other kids like their face and hair the way they are." Explicit administration and scoring guidelines, as well as suggestions for posttest questions provide a clear understanding of the subject's responses and thus, provide a basis for interpretation. Additionally, because only raw scores and local standardization samples are available, interpretation of examinees' responses and generalizability of results is severely limited. Limited discussion of the purposes or applications, as well as sparse information regarding scale development is also common across the scales. Finally, a profile of subscales is easily constructed for each instrument; however, administration of separate questionnaires to assess the perceived importance of each subscale is necessary.

With regard to psychometric characteristics, the five instruments each present borderline levels of internal consistency (range = .65 to .92). Because internal consistency represents the homogeneity of items within a subscale, it is not surprising that reliabilities approach the acceptable criterion given that each subscale consists of a small number of very similar items, with limited content sampling. Finally, for each of the instruments, test-retest reliability is not reported and evidence for validity is sparse. In summary, all five Harter instruments share a common theoretical foundation, a unique but unrefined response format, and lack of support for acceptable stability and validity. Consequently, the five versions of the Self-Perception Profile share common limitations that reduce the instruments' usefulness.

Self-Perception Profile for Adolescents

The Self-Perception Profile for Adolescents (SPPA) (Harter, 1988) is an upward extension of the SPPC and shares six domains with the original instrument. Additionally, three scales were designed specifically for measurement of adolescent self-regard in the areas of Job Competence, Close Friendship, and Romantic Appeal. With five additional items for each subscale, the SPPA comprises a total of 45 items. Harter recommends that the SPPA be used with 9th through 12th graders.

Four samples of adolescents in Grades 8 through 11 were administered the SPPA. All subjects were selected from lower-middle-class to upper-middle-class neighborhoods in Colorado. The sample is divided by grade and age with 165 eighth-grade, 161 ninth-grade, 110 tenth-grade, and 215 eleventh-grade students. Additionally, boys and girls are approximately balanced across each grade level. The manual states that the samples were 90% Caucasian, but no further details regarding race and ethnicity are provided. Further, no comparison is made between the standardization sample and population percentages for relevant demographic variables. Therefore, generalizability to adolescents outside Colorado or of lower socioeconomic status (SES) levels is limited.

Of the four samples of adolescents to whom the SPPA was administered, only the fourth sample, which comprised 123 ninth-grade students, responded to the final revision of the instrument with all nine subscales. Therefore, only the internal consistency estimates for this group are discussed here. With internal consistency ranging from .74 to .92, and a median of .81, six of the nine subscales possess good internal consistency.

Three subscales, however, including Social Acceptance, Behavioral Conduct, and Job Competence, fall slightly below the minimum recommended criterion. Furthermore, because each subscale is composed of five very homogeneous items, content sampling appears to be woefully inadequate. For example, Athletic Competence, the subscale with the highest internal consistency (.92), assesses the respondent's feelings of adequacy in "sports," "athletic activities," and "outdoor games," or whether the respondent feels "athletic." Consequently, the larger domain of overall physical competence, which includes many possibilities for experiencing adequacy or inadequacy, is poorly represented.

Some support for the construct validity of the SPPA is provided by an exploratory factor analysis, which was conducted on only the fourth sample. Although three additional samples were factor analyzed, the entire scale was not administered and therefore, is not reported here. Thirty-eight of 40 items loaded significantly on target factors; items on the Acceptance and Job Competence subscales indicated somewhat weaker factor patterns,

Self-Perception Profile for College Students

The authors believe that college students' self-perceptions are similar in many ways, but different in other ways from those of children, adolescents, and adults. In the Self-Perception Profile for College Students (SPPCS) Neeman and Harter (1986) integrated the Scholastic Competence, Athletic Competence, and Social Acceptance scales from the SPPC; Job Competence, Romantic Relations, and Close Friendships from the SPPA; Intellectual Ability and Morality from the adult version; and Appearance and General Self-Worth which are common to all five instruments. Additionally, Neeman and Harter added three scales designed specifically for the college population: Creativity, Parent Relations, and Finding Humor in One's Life.

Two pilot studies with college students were conducted to create the final scale. Three hundred subjects were included in the standardization sample, 182 from Colorado State University and 118 from the University of Denver. Women were greatly oversampled (230 women to 70 men), as were freshmen (142) and sophomores (94) compared with juniors (41) and seniors (23). According to the manual, 93% of the respondents were Caucasian and 94% were never married. Although more information about the sample is reported relative to the two previously discussed versions of the Self-Perception Profile, its usefulness would have been greatly enhanced had it been compared with population percentages. The standardization sample was also administered the 24-item Importance Ratings Scale.

With 54 items, administration time for the SPPCS is estimated at 30 minutes. As with Harter's other instruments, additional administration of the Importance Ratings Scale is necessary to determine discrepancies between perceived competence and importance of the domain. Additionally, the examiner's manual includes a brief discussion of the 20-item Social Support Scale, which is based on Cooley's (1902) "looking-glass self."

This scale is designed to measure "the degree to which children feel that significant others acknowledge their worth as a person" (p. 36). Administration and scoring for both the Importance Ratings and Social Support Scale is conducted in the same manner as the SPPCS. The target population for all these scales is traditional undergraduate students attending college on a full-time basis.

For the three scales presented in the SPPCS manual, more interpretive guides, including an illustration of profile construction and an example of respondents who discount the importance of domains, is provided. Research and therapeutic applications for the SPPCS are discussed in greater detail than for the SPPC and SPPA.

Information regarding psychometric quality is presented for all three scales included in the manual. For the SPPCS, good internal consistency is evidenced for 11 of 12 subscales (range = .76 to .92; median = .84); however, internal consistency is not reported for the General Self-Worth subscale. Additionally, the one subscale that does not demonstrate adequate internal consistency, Job Competence, is cited in the manual as more reliable in the summer (.84) "perhaps because the items were more salient" (p. 11). Given this discrepancy and questionable rationale of temporal saliency, it seems all the more important that information regarding stability be reported; however, the authors do not report any investigation of test-retest reliability. Furthermore, with four very similar items per subscale, high estimates of internal consistency but very poor content sampling would be expected. Internal consistency for the Importance Ratings Scale is generally less than adequate (range = .53 to .84), for each of the 10 subscales with a median reliability of .76. Considerably higher internal consistency is reported for the 5 Social Support subscales, ranging from .76 for Campus Organizations to .90 for Close Friend (median = .88). Similar to the other subscales, however, each scale consists of four closely related items employing similar terms. Additionally, no test-retest reliability is reported for the Importance Ratings Scale or the Social Support Scale.

To investigate construct validity, factor analyses were conducted for the SPPCS and the Social Support Scale. For the SPPCS, results indicated 12 factors that corresponded to the 12 subscales with significant loadings for each item of each factor. Additionally, no cross-loadings above .35 were indicated. The General Self-Worth subscale was not included in the analysis. Similarly, results for the Social Support Scale indicated five strong factors with no nontarget loadings above .25. Therefore, support for the construct validity of the SPPCS is indicated.

In summary, the psychometric qualities of the SPPCS and its two related scales are described in more detail than those of the SPPC and SPPA; still, many critical elements are omitted. In particular, discussion of how the three scales are integrated for interpretation is not clear. Furthermore, the rationale for three scales rather than only one is questionable. Of most concern is the limited content sampling and the nongeneralizable Colorado standardization sample, which overrepresents women and college freshmen.

The Adult Self-Perception Scale

Based on the theoretical orientation and structural format of the SPPC, the Adult Self-Perception Scale (ASPS; Messer & Harter, 1986) was designed for research purposes, including enhancement of knowledge regarding multidimensional self-concept, and clinical purposes, including diagnosis and measurement of change during treatment. Because the authors contend that an adult's self-concept is more differentiated than that of a child, the ASPS includes subscales analogous to the SPPC, along with other relevant adult subscales. The 12 subscales of the ASPS are Sociability, Job Competence, Nurturance, Athletic Abilities, Physical Appearance, Adequate Provider, Morality, Household Management, Intimate Relationships, Intelligence, Sense of Humor, and Global Self-Worth. With a total of 50 items, the Global Self-Worth subscale is composed of six items, while the remaining subscales are each represented by four items. Limited content sampling common among all the previous Harter scales is again evident in this adult extension of the SPPC.

Administration to two standardization samples is reported in the examiner's manual. Sample A comprised 151 parents ranging in age from 30 to 50 years. With 97 women and 44 men, women were greatly overrepresented in the normative sample. Furthermore, information regarding sample demographics such as race, family status, and level of education are vague. For example, Sample A was composed of a "majority [of subjects who] were part of intact, upper middle class families. . . . had completed high school with the majority having completed college." Even so, it is apparent from the sample description that an extremely homogeneous group was included.

Sample B consisted of only 250 mothers of children under age 3 years. Sample B demographic characteristics include an average age of 26 for middle-class mothers and 22 for lower-class mothers. The number of subjects in each SES group, however, is not reported. Additionally, 90% of the mothers had completed high school and "over 50% . . . attended college," yielding an average educational level of 14.67 years (p. 15). The authors report that 98% of the sample was Caucasian. Similar to the norms of the other versions, no comparison is made between the sample and population percentages; therefore, the generalizability of this sample to other adults across the country is impossible to determine. Given that in total the two samples include 401 women and 44 men, generalizability to adult males is very limited.

Internal consistencies are reported for the total samples as well as for the subgroups that constitute Sample A. For both samples A and B, six subscales possess good internal consistency (range = .65 to .91; median = .81); however, the Nurturance, Adequate Provider, Morality, Sociability, Sense of Humor, and Job Competence subscales fail to meet the minimum criterion for one or both samples.

A factor analysis conducted with responses of Sample B on all subscales except General Self-Worth, indicated a 10-factor solution. Only the Job Competence subscale was not represented by a corresponding factor. The authors theorize that in a sample of fewer homemakers, this factor might be stronger. Moderate to moderately high loadings are indicated for each factor (range = .65 to .89; median = .775). Additionally, cross-loadings of items on other scales are not significant, providing support for the construct validity of the ASPS.

As with previously discussed versions, the procedure for calculating discrepancies among subscales is presented and includes separate administration of an Importance Ratings Scale. No information is reported, however, on the psychometric soundness or the validity of this scale.

In a separate section of the manual devoted to applications of the ASPS, the authors have expanded the explanations and interpretive guides beyond those presented in the previously discussed Harter instruments. Particularly, use in the therapeutic setting is discussed and four clinical examples are provided in some detail.

Overall, the ASPS, with less than adequate reliability for several of the subscales, no norm-referenced scores, and little evidence of validity, should be used only in research settings, as insufficient support is available for clinical use. Also, with such limited content sampling and overrepresentation of women in the two Colorado-based standardization samples, the ASPS should be used with caution.

Self-Perception Profile for Learning Disabled Students

As an adaptation of the SPPC, the Self-Perception Profile for Learning Disabled Students (SPPLD; Renick & Harter, 1988) was designed to assess "both learning disabled and normally-achieving children's domain-specific judgments of their competence or adequacy and their perceived worth or esteem as a person" (p. 1). The structure of the SPPLD is based on the authors' findings that children classified as learning disabled responded differently to the Perceived Competence Scale for Children (an earlier version of the Self-Perception Profile for Children) by differentiating between subsets of items from the Scholastic Competence subscale. Therefore, the SPPLD comprises five subscales from the PCSC: Social Acceptance, Athletic Competence, Behavioral Conduct, Physical Appearance, and Global Self-Worth. Additionally, five new scales were developed: General Intellectual Ability, Reading Competence, Spelling Competence, Writing Competence, and Math Competence. Because the authors state that the SPPLD is appropriate for learning-disabled children as well as normally achieving children for whom a more differentiated measure of self-concept is desired, a uniform theoretical structure of self-concept is not represented.

The SPPLD consists of 45 items, with 5 items for each of the more generally labeled subscales and 4 items for those assessing specific academic areas. As with other versions of the Self-Perception Profile, even the broadly defined subscales only sample a narrow range of content. Instructions for administration are similar to the other versions, with an added recommendation that items be read aloud because many children with learning disabilities have difficulty reading. Also, the authors suggest using an index card to cover items not being considered to facilitate attention and concentration. With regard to interpretation of the SPPLD, the manual presents consideration of bases for social comparison, information regarding differences between LD and normally achieving children, and guidelines for interpretation, including cut scores and instructions for overall profile, subscale, and item analyses. As with previously discussed Harter instruments, the Importance Ratings Scale must be completed to determine discrepancies between perceived competence and importance of specific domains.

Two standardization samples are discussed in the SPPLD manual. One sample included 201 children in Grades 4 through 8 identified as having a learning disability according to the Colorado state criteria. The second group included 367 normally achieving fourth through eighth graders attending the same schools in suburban Denver as the children in the LD group. For the learning-disabled sample, 97% were Caucasian, 1% were Chicano, and 2% were described as "Other." All students were categorized as middle to upper-middle socioeconomic status. Although boys ($n = 140$) were oversampled relative to girls ($n = 50$), the proportion of boys to girls with learning disabilities is closer to a six-to-one ratio. Furthermore, with less than 100 subjects for each grade level, the sample size is inadequate.

For the sample of normally achieving children, boys and girls were approximately equally sampled; however, the sample size fails to meet the minimum criterion of 100 subjects for each grade level. Information on variables such as race, ethnicity, and socioeconomic status for the normally achieving sample is not reported.

Good internal consistency is indicated for both samples, with only one subscale falling slightly below the .80 criterion. Internal consistency for the Writing Competence subscale is .78, for the LD sample, and .84 for the normally achieving sample. The range of internal consistency estimates for both samples is .78 to .90, with a median of .84. Because test-retest reliability is not reported for either sample, the scale's usefulness for the evaluation of interventions is limited.

Exploratory factor analyses also were conducted with both samples. The pattern of significant target loading for all items provides support for the theoretical structure of the SPPLD, and only six nontarget loadings significant above .20 are reported. Subscale intercorrelations reported for both samples provide some support for SPPLD discriminant validity. Moderate correlations between most of the subscales indicate that different facets of self-concept are measured by the various subscales.

Overall, the SPPLD seems to be a reliable and valid tool for the assessment of domain-specific self-concepts for students with learning disabilities as well as normally achieving children. More analyses and explanation in support of construct and discriminant validity of the scale, as well as information for interpretation, is presented in the SPPLD manual than for other Harter instruments. The principal limitations of the SPPLD are its very restricted Colorado sample and content sampling.

The Pictorial Scale of Perceived Competence and Acceptance for Young Children

Designed as a downward extension of the PCSC, the Pictorial Scale of Perceived Competence and Acceptance for Young Children (PSPC; Harter & Pike, 1981) is intended for children in "pre-school to second grade"; however, no ages are indicated and the minimum age requirement is unclear. No rationale is presented for the downward extension, but the major difference between the version for older children and the preschool version is that pictures are used in the administration of the PSPC rather than the standard self-report questionnaire. Factor analysis of the PSPC yielded two factors, Competence and Acceptance. Each of these factor is further divided into two subscales, though not supported factor analytically. The Competence scale includes Cognitive and Physical Competence, and the Acceptance scale includes Peer and Maternal Acceptance. Each subscale includes six items with accompanying pictures. Separate forms with some overlapping items were designed for two age groups, first- and second-grade students, and preschool and kindergarten children; however, no rationale for the distinction is provided.

The PSPC is appropriate only for individual administration, and is accomplished by presenting two pictures to the child that are representative of the item read aloud by the examiner. The child must first choose the picture that shows a child most like him or her, and then indicate, by pointing to a large or small circle, whether that child is "a lot like him or her" or "just a little like him or her" (p. 4). The items are counterbalanced such that 12 item stems describe a more competent child and 12 begin with a description of a less competent child. A sample item is presented to teach the test format to the child. The child's responses are scored by the examiner on a scale of 1 to 4. The scores for each item are summed and a raw score is computed for each subscale. An individual profile sheet is provided to facilitate visual inspection of an individual child's responses. Thus, clear instructions for administration and scoring are provided; however, no standard scores or instructions are presented to guide interpretation of the information obtained.

Information regarding scale development is extremely sparse and is limited to a brief discussion of the adaptation of the PCSC and a factor analysis that resulted in the two-factor structure of the scale. No information regarding a standardization sample is reported.

Furthermore, no information regarding the theoretical basis for the scale, definition of construct measured, or the psychometric characteristics of the scale is presented in the manual. The examiner is referred to a published article for this information (Harter & Pike, 1984). Because examiners in both research and clinical settings need much more information than is provided in the examiner's manual for the PSPC, information from the article should be incorporated into the manual.

The administration approach of the PSPC is novel and appears most appropriate for young children, thus contributing to the development of self-concept instrumentation in the very difficult area of preschool assessment. Little evidence, however, is presented in the examiner's manual to support the use of this scale. Neither purposes and applications of the scale, nor information regarding technical adequacy (reliability and validity) are stated. Some support for the scale's construct validity is provided by the factor analysis indicating two factors; however, the discussion of the results is limited to two sentences with regard to scale development. Although clear instructions for administration and scoring are provided, much more information is required before a determination of the soundness or usefulness of the scale can be made.

In summary, the extensions of the Self-Perception Profiles share a common theoretical orientation. The various scales, however, are largely "project-developed" instruments developed and normed solely in Colorado, and mostly in the greater Denver area. The instruments, therefore, lack generalizability to the national population and often lack generalizability to various ethnic groups or gender groups even within Colorado. The scales are typically brief, which reduces administration time; however, with so few items per subscale, the instruments typically fall short on reliability and content sampling. As project-developed instruments with multiple different authors across the various versions, there is a lack of uniformity in content among the various examiner's manuals and an overall shortage of support for the instruments' validity.

Joseph Pre-School and Primary Self-Concept Screening Test

Designed primarily to fill the gap in assessment of self-concept down to the preschool years, the Joseph Pre-School and Primary Self-Concept Screening Test (JPPSST; Joseph, 1979) is appropriate for children between the ages of 3 years 6 months and 9 years 11 months. Ample information regarding the theoretical orientation of the scale is reported in the examiner's manual, along with a good overview of the research related to the measurement of self-concept. Based on the work of Erikson (1963), Smart and Smart (1973), Perkins (1975), and Wylie (1961), Joseph concludes that self-concept develops early in a child's life. Additionally, he considers self-concept to be the center of a child's social-emotional development, and the best predictor of general success. Joseph defines self-concept as "the way an individual perceives himself, his behaviors, how others view him, and the feelings of personal worth and satisfaction that are attached to these perceptions" (p. 8).

Five domains are assessed by the JPPSST—Significance, Competence, Power, General Evaluative Contentment, and Virtue. The author states, however, that the first two dimensions are primary as they measure the extent to which children feel valued by others and their own perceptions of competence, respectively. The Power and General Evaluative Contentment subscales are described as secondary, and purportedly measure the child's perceived ability to control others and feelings of life satisfaction, respectively. Finally, the Virtue subscale is described as the least important to characteristically egocentric children because it measures perceived compliance with moral standards.

Several purposes and potential uses of the JPPSST are presented. The chief purpose was to respond to the need for an instrument for screening and identification of high-risk children in preschool and primary grades. The author points out that with the passage of Public Law 94-142, and consequently, the requirement to reliably assess the emotional status of young children, the JPPSST can be useful in school settings. Potential use as a tool for monitoring early childhood programs and for measuring self-concept in special populations including minority groups and nonverbal children is stated. Finally, the JPPSST manual suggests that the scale may be useful as a research tool.

Development and Standardization

The JPPSST was developed through logical and empirical efforts and analyses. Original test items were developed based on the five subscales along with those situations thought to be common among most children. The pictorial format attempted to circumvent the test-taking limitations (limited reading abilities) of young children. Two pilot investigations assessed the usefulness of stimulus illustrations and item stems. The final draft of the scale is composed of 15 items and an Identity Reference Drawing that is administered to establish rapport and remind the child that he or she is describing him- or herself.

The standardization sample for the JPPSST includes 1,245 children from rural, suburban, and urban areas within Illinois, and includes children receiving special education services. A range of socioeconomic status is reported for the normative sample, although no quantitative description is provided. Additionally, 91% of the normative sample was Caucasian, with 9% of the children belonging to minority racial groups. The sample was divided into three age groups. For each of these, an ample number of children was included to meet the minimum criterion of 100 subjects; 285 children aged 3 years 6 months to 4 years 6 months were tested; 328 children 4 years 7 months to 5 years 11 months participated; and for the broadest age range of 6 years to 9 years 11 months, 632 were included. The division of the normative sample into three age groups was based on "developmental scoring patterns related to behavioral observations and socially desirable responding tendencies" (p. 12). It is unclear whether adequate numbers of children of various ages were sampled across the latter age range. The overall sample included children from several school programs; however, the author notes that no significant differences were found in children's self-concepts based on location or gender. Therefore, these variables were collapsed within the three age groups. Although the standardization sample is fairly heterogeneous, examiners cannot assume that the norms apply to children from other regions of the United States. Additionally, no comparison is made between sample and population percentages on variables deemed important by the author. Specifically, Caucasian children were oversampled.

Administration and Interpretation

Clear instructions for administration and scoring are provided in the examiner's manual. The JPPSST is appropriate only for individual administration and is estimated to take approximately 5 to 7 minutes. Twenty-seven laminated stimulus cards, a set for boys and one for girls, are included in the test kit along with boy and girl Identity Reference Drawings. To administer the scale, the examiner presents two simple drawings illustrating opposite extremes of a concept such as "clean" and "dirty." The examiner then asks the child which picture corresponds to each descriptor. After discriminating between the two drawings, the examinee is directed to indicate which picture is most like him or her.

Scoring is accomplished by crediting responses indicative of positive self-concept with two points on the record form, while giving no credit to negative responses. Ambivalent responses for which the child indicates that both pictures are representative of him- or herself are credited with one point. Points for the 15 items are summed to yield a global score that, when compared with the appropriate age norms, is classified as High Positive, Moderate Positive, Watch List, Poor, or High Risk Negative. Although Joseph explicitly states that the scale's separate dimensions are not equally important, a systematic theoretical contribution to the total score is not apparent. Equal, or at least systematically distributed weight would be desirable to yield a total score that is representative of the child's global self-concept. Responses of examinees for whom Global Self Concept is classified as Poor or High Negative Risk can be further evaluated using the Diagnostic Dimensional Evaluation on the Record Form. By summing the number of items for each dimension that did not receive a score of two, areas most in need of remediation are easily identified.

To facilitate interpretation, Joseph discusses each item with regard to the particular dimension measured, typical response patterns and whether the item is more or less predictive of the total score relative to other items. Additionally, analysis of the Identity Reference Drawing is facilitated by Joseph's discussion of emotional indicators in children's drawings (Koppitz, 1968). Qualitative information from the child's drawing of him- or herself may be integrated with the Global Self Concept score and the

Diagnostic Dimensional Evaluation when making decisions regarding the need for further evaluation. A number of case examples at various ages are presented to illustrate scoring and interpretation procedures. Additionally, a resource guide to self-concept enhancement strategies is included.

Psychometric Characteristics

Internal consistencies for the JPPSST range from .59 to .81. With a median reliability of .73, the JPPSST falls short of the .90 criterion for total scale reliability. Furthermore, with a correlation of .87 over a 4-week interval, test-retest reliability falls slightly below the criterion of .90 for total test stability for a small sample of 18 children with a median age of 4 years 10 months.

The author reports investigations that support the concurrent and criterion-related validity of the JPPSST. A moderate correlation of .51 with the Inferred Self Concept Judgment Scale and a moderately high correlation of .65 between the Behavior Rating Form (Coopersmith, 1967) and the JPPSST Global Self Concept score provide concurrent validity support for the scale.

The author presents comparisons of Global Self Concept scores with measures of cognitive functioning and academic achievement as evidence for criterion-related validity. Correlations of .66 with the Slosson Intelligence Test, .63 with the Preschool Language Scale IQs, and .69 with the Developmental Test of Visual Motor Integration, suggest a positive relationship between Global Self Concept on the JPPSST and cognitive functioning as measured by these instruments. In contrast, nonsignificant correlations were found between a more reliable measure of intelligence, the Wechsler Preschool and Primary Scales of Intelligence.

Concurrent validity was explored through investigation of the JPPSST's relationship to academic success. On the basis of readiness skills, the top and bottom 15% of preschoolers and kindergarten classes were administered the JPPSST. Mean score differences were highly significant with the highest achievers demonstrating higher overall self-concept, particularly at the preschool level. Finally, support for the validity of the JPPSST as a screening tool was provided with a study of 20 children referred for special education services due primarily to emotional difficulties. On the basis of Global Self Concept, 85% of these children were identified accurately as being at "high risk."

Summary

Based on a multidimensional theoretical model, and a developmentally appropriate response format, the JPPSST contributes significantly to the assessment of self-concept in young children. Furthermore, the examiner's manual is informative and well organized, incorporating several case examples and interpretive guidelines. Because estimates of internal consistency and stability fall slightly below minimum levels for technical adequacy and because the standardization sample is fairly homogeneous and regional, caution is warranted when interpreting results from the JPPSST. Finally, based on validity studies, the JPPSST appears most appropriate as an early childhood self-concept screening device.

Culture-Free Self-Esteem Inventories, Second Edition

First published in 1981, the Culture-Free Self-Esteem Inventories, Second Edition (CFSEI-2; Battle, 1992) is founded on Battle's definition of self-esteem:

> Self-esteem refers to the perception the individual possesses of his or her own worth. . . . It is, thus, a composite of an individual's feelings, hopes, fears, thoughts, and views of who he is, what she is, what he has been, and what she might become. Perception of self-worth, once established, tends to be fairly stable and resistant to change. (p. 3)

Although no explicit theoretical rationale is provided, the author's definition purportedly follows from premises forwarded by James (1890/1983). Battle further claims that the CFSEI-2 assesses several components of self-concept that, for children, include general, social, academic, and parent-related domains. For adults, the CFSEI-2 measures the areas of general, social, and personal self-concept. The author identifies several purposes for the CFSEI-2 including use as both a clinical and a research tool. Screening and identification of children and adults in need of further psychological assistance and intervention planning are explicitly stated as clinical uses for the CFSEI.

Development and Standardization

As a basis for the creation of subscales, the author reported that experts in the field of self-esteem are in agreement regarding the multifaceted nature of the construct. However, the author provides no rationale for the particular areas included. Additionally, several generally recognized foundational dimensions, including physical and affective self-concept are not included in Battle's scale. Omission of the latter is particularly questionable given that the definition provided by Battle indicates that self-concept includes a person's "feelings." Similarly, although a chapter entitled "Development" is included, the majority of the research contained in this chapter was conducted following the development of the CFSEI. No rationale is provided for the initial selection of items; however, inclusion of final items was based on their contribution to alpha coefficients. Although this is a reasonable method for refining scales, no clear theoretical underpinnings provide a rationale for the initial scales.

Form A, which consists of 60 forced-choice items, was designed for elementary school and junior high students. Form B is comprised of a subset of 30 items taken from Form A, and was designed exclusively for elementary school students. Form AD was developed for high school students and adults. Information regarding standardization of the three CFSEI-2 forms is scant. From the normative tables, it appears that the sample for Form A is sufficiently large with 1,679 children in elementary school and 873 junior high students. Furthermore, the number of boys and girls is approximately equal. The standardization sample for Form B, however, is seriously lacking with only 116 elementary-age subjects; an average of 19 students per grade level. This sample is also approximately equal in number of boys and girls. Furthermore, it is unclear why the authors also included a supplemental standardization sample of 274 junior high students for Form B, since the form was intended for use with only elementary school students. This supplemental sample, too, contains less than 200 students per grade level. For Form AD, 585 adults ages 16 to 65, comprise the standardization sample; these included significantly more women (337) than men (248).

For all three forms, information regarding geographic representation of the standardization sample is vague or missing. The only indication of location is that Forms A and B were standardized in the United States and Canada. Furthermore, information regarding race and ethnicity of the sample, along with comparisons to population percentages, is missing altogether.

Administration and Interpretation

Administration of each of the CFSEI-2 forms is relatively simple when done in either group or individual formats. Respondents check "yes" or "no" after reading or hearing an audiotaped declarative statement. Scale readability level is not reported, although the examiner's manual states that children below Grade 2 should be administered the CFSEI-2 in oral format, whereas children in second grade or higher can respond independently. A cassette tape is available for oral administration but is not required. Most of the items appear appropriate for elementary school students; however, respondents may experience difficulty with the "yes, no" response format for items stated in the negative. For example, the item, "I never worry about anything" results in a double-negative when answered "no." This can be confusing for adults and uninterpretable for young children. Administration time is estimated at 10 to 15 minutes for each of the forms, whether presented orally or read independently.

Scoring of the CFSEI-2 is accomplished by comparing examinee responses to the key in the manual which displays the response for each item that is indicative of high self-esteem. This comparison process is tedious; however, templates are available to facilitate scoring. Because items are intermingled across scales, the task of scoring each subscale is even more tedious. Once raw scores are calculated, conversion to percentile ranks and T scores for both the total and subscales is possible. No scheme for ipsative analysis is explicitly provided; however, because each subscale is converted to *T* scores, normative comparisons on this basis can be done.

Further interpretive guides include seven brief case reports that demonstrate suggested uses of the CFSEI-2. Overviews of outcome research on several programs designed to enhance self-esteem are also discussed. Although the author states in the beginning of the manual that self-concept is multidimensional and that the CFSEI-2 is designed to measure this multifaceted construct, no discussion of the appropriate uses of this information is provided (e.g., comparison of subscales; usefulness of independent subscales).

Psychometric Characteristics

The CFSEI-2 reports internal consistency estimates for Form A computed on a sample of 117 seventh-, eighth-, and ninth-grade students with alpha coefficients as follows: General, .71; Social, .66; Academic, .67; parents, .76; and Lie, .70. Without explanation, no estimate of internal consistency is reported for the Total scale. Additionally, no internal consistency estimates are reported for Form B. Form AD evidences slightly lower internal consistencies than Form A: General, .78; Social, .57; Personal, .72; and Lie, .54. Because all of these coefficients fall well below the recommended subscale criterion of .80, considerable error is associated with the CFSEI-2 subscales and examiners must use considerable caution when interpreting scores at this level.

Based on a study of 198 elementary children in Grades 3 through 6, Form A demonstrated less than adequate stability over an unreported time interval. At all grade levels, the total score stability coefficient fell below the .90 criterion, ranging from .81 to .89. Furthermore, subscale stability coefficients fell below the criterion of .80 at all grade levels, with a range of .26 to .76 (median = .65). Higher stability coefficients were reported for Form A for Grades 7 through 9; however, the total score fell slightly below the .90 criterion at two of the three grade levels with coefficients of .88 and .89 for Grades 8 and 9, respectively. The seventh-grade stability coefficient of .96 indicates good total test reliability.

Based on a study of 110 elementary students reported in the examiner's manual, test-retest reliability for Form B is adequate at Grades 4 and 5 ($r = .91$ and .92, respectively). Form B total scale stability is lower than the criterion with a coefficient of .79 for Grades 3 and 6. Additionally, subscale stability estimates are below acceptable levels with a range of .49 to .80 and a median of .67. Only the Social scale at the fourth-grade level meets the criterion for adequate stability, indicating that for most respondents, scores may fluctuate markedly over time as a function of error and not as a result of true changes in self-concept.

For a sample of 127 college students over an unreported time interval, Form AD evidences below-criterion test-retest reliability at the total scale level with a stability coefficient of .82. Adequate stability is reported for the General (.82) subscale, but a slightly less than adequate coefficient is reported for the Personal (.78) subscale; and, grossly inadequate stability is indicated for the Social scale ($r = .56$).

As evidence that the CFSEI-2 measures the construct of self-esteem, the author addresses issues of content and concurrent validity. The author's development of a definition of self-esteem and item construction according to this definition are cited as evidence of content validity. Without a rationale for the inclusion of particular subscales, however, support for content validity is incomplete. As evidence of concurrent validity, the manual presents correlations between the CFSEI-2 and the Coopersmith Self-Esteem Index (Coopersmith, 1967). The coefficients are moderately high and range from .71 to .82 for Grades 3 through 6.

Negative correlations between CFSEI-2 Form AD of Beck's Depression Inventory ($-.53$ to $-.56$) and the Depression scale of the Mini-Mult (Minnesota Multiphasic Personality Inventory short form; Kincannon, 1968) ($-.34$ to $-.78$) were found in a study of 26 referred high school students, indicating that a negative relationship exists between self-esteem and depression. Several additional studies reported in the examiner's manual found significant negative correlations between the CFSEI-2 and measures of depression. Further support for CFSEI-2 construct validity is based on significant negative correlations between the CFSEI-2 and measures of anxiety for children, junior high students, and adults (range = $-.68$ to $-.77$).

Several researchers have contributed supplemental validity data to the manual, providing support for the discriminant validity of the CFSEI-2 for groups of learning-disabled students (Stevenson & Romney, 1984) and children with attention deficit/hyperactivity disorder (Battle & Shea, 1989). Other studies cited in the examiner's manual provide support for the construct validity and multidimensionality of the CFSEI-2 by reporting significant correlations between academic achievement and the Academic scale. For each of these studies, the author presents data in a cogent format that can be readily examined by test users.

Summary

The CFSEI-2 provides a well-organized examiner's manual that clearly delineates research results and available psychometric and interpretive information. Furthermore, by reporting several investigations of the relationship between the CFSEI-2 and measures of depression and anxiety disorders, the author has provided support of the broader clinical use of self-concept. Serious weaknesses of the CFSEI-2 include lack of information regarding the standardization sample, internal consistency estimates that are either below recommended levels or unreported, and lack of a clearly articulated theoretical basis.

Self-Esteem Index

The Self-Esteem Index (SEI; Brown & Alexander, 1991) is a multidimensional self-report measure of self-concept that includes four 20-item scales (Familial Acceptance, Academic Competence, Peer Popularity, Personal Security). Additionally, the Self-Esteem Quotient is an aggregate score of all items. Each statement is rated by the respondent on a four-point Likert-type scale with options of "Always true," "Usually true," "Usually false," "Always false." Brown and Alexander define self-concept as ". . . the way that individuals perceive and value themselves. . . . a learned characteristic that is acquired inferentially" (p. 3). No specific theoretical rationale is cited as the basis for the SEI; however, the authors believe sufficient support exists for designing an instrument to assess multiple domains of self-concept. Stated purposes for the SEI include both clinical and research uses, with several specific clinical goals outlined including identifying children with behavioral or emotional difficulties and guiding interventions.

Development and Standardization

The SEI was developed through both logical and empirical means. The authors began by building an item pool based on the relevant literature, similar instruments, and opinions of professionals in the field. Professionals in various roles were then asked to select the items they believed would best identify children with low self-esteem. A pilot test of the 120 items selected most frequently and subsequent analyses of item discrimination and item difficulty resulted in the final 80 items. No theoretical rationale is provided to support the choice of the four particular dimensions assessed by the SEI.

The SEI was standardized in 19 states from various regions of the United States. The sample comprised 2,455 subjects ranging in age from 8 years to 18 years 11 months. Students from selected schools were chosen at random and included in the study with the exception of those previously identified as Seriously Emotionally Disturbed. In comparison with the U.S. population based on the Statistical Abstract of the United States (1985), the SEI standardization sample matches population percentages on variables of gender, domicile, race, geographic location, ethnicity, and educational attainment of parents. On the variable of principal language spoken in the home, English-speaking children were oversampled by 8.9% while Spanish-speaking children were undersampled by 3.7% and "other" languages were undersampled by 5.2%. Sampling deviations on all other variables are even smaller, indicating that the SEI normative sample is very representative of the national population.

Additionally, at each of 11 one-year age intervals, the number of subjects in the sample exceeds the criterion of 100. The median number of subjects per age interval is 212 with a range of 132 to 340. Therefore, the

SEI possesses an excellent standardization sample that is not only nationally representative but is also adequate in size at each age level.

Administration and Interpretation

As a self-report questionnaire, the SEI is easily administered in about 30 minutes in either group or individual formats. Because items for each of the four scales are intermingled, single scales cannot be administered individually. Specific guidelines for administration are provided in the examiner's manual, and the instructions to be read to respondents are also provided on the front of the SEI Student Response Booklet.

Straightforward scoring procedures are outlined in the examiner's manual and are facilitated by the use of the SEI Profile and Record Form. Scoring of reversed item weights for negatively connoted items is cued by circles, and squares connote positive items. Three types of normative scores are provided including scaled scores, deviation quotients, and percentile ranks. Scaled scores, with a mean of 10 and a standard deviation of 3, are provided for subscales. The SEI total score, the Self-Esteem Quotient, has a mean of 100 and a standard deviation of 15. Qualitative descriptors corresponding to standard scores and deviation quotients also are provided for interpretive purposes, and percentile ranks are available for the scale scores and total test score.

The authors point out that the Self-Esteem Quotient should be interpreted as "the best predictor of global or general self-esteem" (p. 20). Further diagnostic information can be gleaned from analysis of the subtests. Information about subscale specific variance is not reported, even though the authors encourage independent interpretation of subscale scores. Although no specific case study examples are given, detailed guidelines for communicating information gained from the SEI are discussed.

Psychometric Characteristics

The SEI evidences high internal consistencies for both the subscale and total scale scores. The SEI mean subscale internal consistency estimates are .80 for Personal Security, .82 for Peer Popularity, .85 for Academic Competence, and .90 for Familial Acceptance. Additionally, the SEI total scale internal consistency is reported as .93. Although the SEI meets the recommended internal consistency criteria at both the subscale and total scale levels, it does not provide estimates of test-retest reliability.

The authors cite support for content, construct, concurrent, and contrasted groups validity. In support of the content validity, Brown and Alexander indicate the use of both logical and empirical scale development. Additionally, construct validity is supported through significant item-to-total correlations, which demonstrate item homogeneity. These correlations are presented in the form of medians for each scale at each of the 11 age ranges. All the medians, with the exception of the Self-Esteem Quotient at age 8 (.27), are .30 or above, suggesting that each item contributes meaningfully to its respective scale. Similarly, subscale intercorrelations of the SEI ranged from .31 to .53, indicating support for the construct validity of the SEI in that each scale appears to measure a unique aspect of self-concept while correlating moderately to strongly with the total score (.67 to .83).

Additionally, the authors found support for the factor structure of the SEI with a principal components factor analysis with varimax rotation. They reported a general factor corresponding to the total score, and four factors that coincide with each of the four scales. Because most of the SEI items load significantly and moderately on the respective target factors, and because the nontarget loadings are generally low, there appears to be strong within-network support for the SEI construct validity.

When concurrently compared with the Piers-Harris Children's Self-Concept Scale, Revised (Piers, 1984), the SEI total scores correlated moderately highly at .77. Additionally, when compared with the Coopersmith Self-Esteem Inventories, School Form (Coopersmith, 1981), the resulting total score correlation of .83, was sufficiently high to support the concurrent validity of the SEI.

Finally, the authors investigated the ability of the SEI to identify groups expected to score in the deviant extremes of the SEI. A group of students previously identified as emotionally disturbed scored one standard deviation below normals on both the SEI Academic Competence Scale and the Self-Esteem Quotient. Similarly, a group of students previously identified as learning disabled scored significantly below the mean of the normative group on the Personal Security scale, but was near normal on other scales including the total score. A group of behavior-disordered students scored one standard deviation below the normative group on the Academic Competence Scale, but also scored near normal levels on all other scales. Contrary to expectations, gifted students' mean SEI scores were not significantly different from the normative group means. The contrasted-groups study provided partial support for the SEI; however, the most reliable score, the Self-Esteem Quotient, differed significantly for only one group.

Summary

As one of the first multidimensional self-concept measures to combine high internal consistency, content, construct, concurrent and contrasted groups validity, and a large, nationally representative standardization sample, the SEI offers improved psychometric quality to existing self-concept instrumentation. Furthermore, the SEI manual is written in an organized, cogent manner, and the scale provides several types of scores for interpretation. Weaknesses of the SEI include its lack of a stated theoretical base, and its inadequate sampling of generally recognized foundational domains of self-concept including physical self-concept. Additionally, although the SEI is progressive in its demonstration of psychometric quality, its lack of reported test-retest reliability is a weakness.

Perception of Ability Scale for Students

The Perception of Ability Scale for Students (PASS; Boersma & Chapman, 1992) is a 70-item forced choice questionnaire designed to measure academic self-concept in students from elementary to low middle school grades. The authors define academic self-concept as:

> a relatively stable set of attitudes and feelings reflecting self-evaluation of one's ability to successfully perform basic school-related tasks such as reading, writing, spelling, and math. . . . academic self-concept is seen as a factor related to, yet distinct from, general self-concept or self-esteem. (p. 1)

Because the PASS focuses narrowly on one aspect of self-concept, it contributes a very facet-specific model to self-concept instrumentation.

The theoretical underpinnings of the PASS include the multifaceted model proposed by Shavelson, Hubner, and Stanton (1976); the work of Bloom (1976) who pointed out the importance of "specific school-related self-perceptions, and argued that they are a crucial influence in motivation and perseverance in school tasks" (p. 33); and Brookover and Gotlieb's (1964) argument that self-concept is a "functionally limiting factor" in school achievement in that it defines a student's perceived upper and lower limits of ability (p. 33). The PASS authors addressed only one domain in the Shavelson et al. (1976) model in an attempt to produce a measure of both general and specific academic self-concept. The six subscales are Perception of General Ability, Perception of Math Ability, Perception of Reading/Spelling Ability, Perception of Penmanship and Neatness Skills, School Satisfaction, and Confidence in Academic Ability. The stated purposes of the PASS include screening children in need of further psychological evaluations, as well as monitoring special and regular educational programming. Additionally, the PASS may be used as part of an overall psychological assessment in educational or counseling settings. Research purposes include use as a quantitative measure of academic self-concept, including the relationship between academic self-concept and achievement, and the relationship between academic self-concept and other psychoeducational constructs.

Development and Standardization

The six scales of the PASS were determined based on the authors' extension of the Shavelson et al. (1976) model, which identifies specific academic content areas. The authors created an initial pool of about 200 items that addressed the areas of "general self-perceptions of ability; perceptions of subject-specific competence; and feelings, attitudes, and self-confidence about school in general" (p. 34). Pilot tests were conducted with 143 items assessing self-perceptions in each of five elementary grade content areas, as well as general academic statements. A Principal Components factor analysis resulted in six factors; the first 12 items that had the strongest loadings on each of the specific factors were chosen to represent the scale. The 10 items with the strongest factor loadings on the general component were chosen for the Confidence in Academic Ability Scale. Difficulty indexes were also examined as a basis for item retention. A second pilot test and analyses were conducted with the resulting 70 items. Sixty-three of 70 items loaded significantly on their respective factors, thus supporting a six-factor model. With a median interscale correlation range of .27 to .39, the six scales are fairly independent; however, moderately high correlations between each scale and the Full Scale indicate measurement of a common construct, presumably academic self-concept.

The standardization sample comprised 831 children in Grades 3 through 6 drawn from nine schools within a single geographic region of the United States. Sample sizes are generally adequate at each grade level, although oversampling of sixth graders and undersampling of fifth graders is evident. The authors claim that the sample included both rural and urban students, as well as children from all socioeconomic backgrounds, but no percentages for these variables are presented. Percentages are presented for ethnicity, but no comparison is made to the national or regional population percentages. Generalizability of the normative sample is unknown for the variables of gender, ethnicity, socioeconomic status and rural/urban status. Moreover, the sample is clearly regional and not representative of children from across the United States.

Administration and Interpretation

With 70 brief self-descriptive statements that require a yes or no response, the PASS can be easily administered in group or individual formats. Administration time is estimated at 15 to 20 minutes, and items may be read aloud by the examiner or silently by the respondent. With a mid-second-grade readability level, the PASS is appropriate for most children in Grades 3 through 6.

Clear guidelines for scoring and interpreting the PASS are presented in the examiner's manual with abbreviated scoring instructions on the response booklet and scoring profile. Additionally, guidelines for three validity checks including response bias, inconsistency, and misrepresentation are provided. These checks only require a count of yes or no responses and comparison to the criterion for indication of an invalid assessment. The scoring system relies on a carbon copy test booklet that allows the examiner to compute raw scores for each scale easily even though the items are integrated across subscales. Raw scores are transferred to a scoring profile that yields *T* scores and percentile ranks for subscales and the Full Scale. Stanines and confidence intervals are also available in the examiner's manual. A mail-in computer scoring service is available as an alternative to hand scoring and is suggested for large volumes of questionnaires.

The PASS manual provides ample information regarding the interpretation of test results including general guidelines, integrative information, and several examples of case studies. A step-by-step interpretation approach is presented in which the first step is consideration of validity issues, followed by interpretation of Full Scale and subscale scores, determination of relative strengths and weaknesses, and finally, individual item interpretations.

Psychometric Characteristics

Moderate subscale intercorrelations (range = .29 to .60; median = .42) suggest that each scale is somewhat independent from the others. Moderately strong correlations between the Full Scale score and subscales (range = .65 to .79; median = .74) reflect a common core that is measured. Furthermore, the PASS demonstrates very good internal consistencies at the Full Scale level ($r = .93$), and for four of six subscales. Only the School Satisfaction and Confidence scales fail to meet the .80 suggested criterion, with estimates of .75 and .69, respectively.

In a separate study, Chapman, Boersma, and Maguire's (1977) sample demonstrated Full Scale internal consistency of .91, and again four of six subscales met the .80 criterion. However, unlike the normative sample, the School Satisfaction scale evidenced .83 internal consistency, but the Penmanship and Neatness scale and the Confidence scale fell below the .80 criterion.

Scale stability was investigated in two independent studies; neither employed the standardization sample. With 603 children in Grades 3 through 6, stability estimates ranged from .71 to .83 (median = .76) for a 4- to 6-week interval and from .55 to .75 (median = .64) over one year. At the briefest interval, the Full Scale correlated .83, which fails to meet the minimum recommended level of stability of .90. Additionally, only the Reading/Spelling scale ($r = .82$) demonstrated an acceptable level of stability. Given these results, the PASS appears to have acceptable internal consistency; however, it is somewhat lacking in stability.

A number of investigations into the content, concurrent, convergent, and discriminant validity of the PASS are reported. Content validity is claimed by the authors in that items were created to reflect self-concept in several common academic content areas.

Concurrent validity was investigated by comparing the PASS to similar instruments including the Piers-Harris Children's Self-Concept Scale (PHSCS), the Brookover Self-Concept of Ability Scales, the Canadian Self-Esteem Inventory for Children-Form A, and the Tennessee Self-Concept Scale (range = .25 to .74). In a study with the standardization sample, the PASS and the Intellectual and School Status subscales of the PHSCS demonstrated moderately strong support for concurrent validity with a correlation of .74. Additionally, PASS subscale correlations with the PHSCS Intellectual and School Status subscale were in the moderate range (.45 to .60).

Support for PASS discriminant validity was demonstrated by low correlations between theoretically dissimilar scales of the PASS and the PHSCS. For example, the PASS Math Ability scale correlated .38 with the PHSCS Physical Appearance and Attributes scale and .35 with the Popularity scale. Low to moderate correlations between the PASS and grades (range = .03 to .52) are reported, although higher correlations were indicated for subscales and grades in the same subject area. The highest correlation was for the Reading/Spelling scale and grades in spelling (.52) and reading (.47). Similarly, the Math Ability scale and the Penmanship scale both correlated .40 with grades in the respective content areas.

Moderate correlations were also indicated between the PASS and the Canadian Test of Basic Skills, a standardized measure of achievement. The PASS Full Scale and the CTBS Composite score correlated .37, whereas PASS Math and Reading/Spelling scales correlated .37 and .41 with their respective skill areas. Low correlations were generally found between the PASS and measures of intelligence, including the WISC-R (.03) and the Stanford-Binet Intelligence Scales, Fourth Edition (.16). A moderate correlation of .40 was found between the PASS and the Pupil Rating Scale, indicating a moderate relationship between teacher ratings of students and students' academic self-concept. Likewise, when parents were asked to complete the PASS as they believed their child would, a correlation of .36 resulted between parent and child perceptions. Overall, then, the PASS evidences moderate correlations with many logically related academic variables.

Summary

As a measure of one specific self-concept domain, the PASS contributes to the available self-concept instrumentation. The benefits of assessing academic self-concept are easy to imagine. The PASS manual is thorough and well-organized, relating the strengths of the instrument in a cogent manner. In particular, many independent investigations that provide support for the content, concurrent, convergent, and discriminant validity of the PASS are reported. Additionally, good internal consistency and a large, although geographically restricted, standardization sample are noted. Weaknesses of the PASS include less than desirable test-retest reliability and its regional standardization sample.

Self-Description Questionnaire, I

Based on the multifaceted, hierarchical model proposed by Shavelson, Hubner, and Stanton (1976), the Self-Description Questionnaire, I (SDQI;

Marsh, 1988) was designed as a multidimensional measure of self-concept. It consists of 76 Likert-type items designed to assess four nonacademic domains of self-concept: Physical Abilities, Physical Appearance, Peer Relations, and Parent Relations—along with three academic domains: Reading, Mathematics, and General School. Although the original SDQI did not include a measure of general self-concept, a separate scale was later added for this purpose. According to Marsh (1990), self-concept is a "person's perceptions regarding himself or herself; these perceptions are formed through experience with and interpretations of one's environment. They are especially influenced by evaluations by significant others, reinforcements, and attributions for one's own behavior" (p. 27). The SDQI is appropriate for group or individual assessment; however, the examiner's manual describes no explicit purposes for the instrument.

Development and Standardization

Items for the seven domains measured by the SDQI were based on the Shavelson model of self-concept, which is clearly delineated in the examiner's manual. Preliminary analyses including item- and factor-analyses and item difficulty levels, led to revisions of the items. The original SDQI was revised to include a General Self scale after the development of the SDQII and SDQIII. The author provides results of exploratory and confirmatory factor analyses as evidence in support of the SDQI scales. Although target loadings in most cases at the 4th- and 5th-grade level are significant, with few significant cross-loadings, these analyses are less convincing at the second- and third-grade levels. The academic scales are less well-defined at Grades 2 and 3.

The seven scales of the SDQI were standardized on a sample of 3,564 elementary school students in New South Wales, Australia. With 388 boys and 408 girls in Grades 2 through 4, and 1,583 boys and 1,185 girls in Grades 5 through 6, older students as well as boys are overrepresented. The author does not offer a comparison of sample demographic data on current Australian census information; therefore, determination of generalizability to the Australian population is difficult. Furthermore, generalization to the U.S. population cannot be assumed without empirical demonstration. The General-Self Scale was normed separately on 739 subjects, most of whom were fifth-grade students. No norms for Grades 2 through 4 are provided for this scale, and the author warns that students in Grades 5 and 6 should be compared with this norm group cautiously. Even more difficult to support is generalizability to other countries. Although Marsh devotes a chapter to this topic in the examiner's manual, he fails to provide evidence that the SDQI is suitable for cross-cultural populations. Some support for use with children in urban areas of northwest England is provided; however, as the author himself points out, this sample may not generalize to the whole country. Similarly, the SDQI norms that were developed only in New South Wales, Australia, are likely not representative of all Australian children. The author details the significant limitations of the SDQI for cross-cultural assessment including variations in the connotations of words used in items, differences in openness to self-description, and possible differences in the relationship of dimensions of self-concept.

Administration and Interpretation

The SDQI is easily administered with clear guidelines that instruct the examiner to read aloud the items to either groups of children or individual children. The SDQI was designed for students between the ages of 8 and 12, corresponding to Grades 4 through 6, but has norms for Grades 2 through 6. A readability level is not reported, but should be determined prior to use to ensure that the items are not too difficult to comprehend by children in this age range. The estimated administration time for the SDQI is 20 minutes.

Several items are awkwardly worded and not likely to be easily understood by U.S. children in the intended age range. For instance, the item "I get good marks in Mathematics," should be changed to read "I get good grades in Mathematics"; parallel items on the Reading and General School scales are similarly inappropriate.

In addition to the nine scales that produce scores, three total scores can be computed. The Total Nonacademic raw score is an average of the five nonacademic scales, and the Total Academic raw score is an average of the four academic scales. The average of these two scores results in the Total Self raw score. However, the author indicates that low correlations between the Total Academic and Total Nonacademic scores show that these scales are more distinct than expected; therefore, the rationale for combining them into one Total Self score is not supported empirically. Further caution regarding interpretation of these scores is issued and users are encouraged to analyze specific areas of self-concept rather than total scores. For each scale score as well as the three total scores, mid-interval percentile ranks and nonnormalized T scores are provided with the previously noted exception of the General-Self scale for Grades 2 through 4. A veracity scale is incorporated in the SDQI, with raw scores that can be converted to percentile ranks and T scores.

The author recommends SDQI interpretation based on several types of scores; however, no systematic scheme of interpretation is applicable to all scales. For instance, comparison of scale raw scores is suggested for the academic scales because the items are written in parallel form. The author further recommends the use of percentile ranks, but cautions that only scores at the low end of the distribution are "readily interpretable and diagnostically meaningful" (p. 21). The manual also prescribes comparison of nonnormalized T scores of the three total scale scores, but not of individual scales with the total scales due to dissimilar distributions. Although rationale is provided for each of these recommended interpretation schemes, this "system" is cumbersome and hinders both normative and ipsative interpretation of the scale. The author summarizes the interpretation section of the SDQI manual by stating, "Because there are as yet unresolved difficulties with the appropriate scaling of the SDQI scale scores, users should be cautious about making interpretations of overall profiles based on responses by an individual child" (p. 26). Overall, scant information for interpretation of the SDQI is provided with no further general interpretive guidelines or examples. Additionally, the author does not make suggestions for remediation or intervention based on the SDQI beyond a broad discussion of the research in this area.

Psychometric Characteristics

With internal consistency estimates ranging from .80 to .92 and a median alpha coefficient of .88 for the eight scale scores, the SDQI possesses good internal consistency. For the three total scores, internal consistency also meets the recommended criterion; .91 for the Total Nonacademic score, .92 for the Total Academic score, and .94 for the Total Self score.

In contrast, a mean stability correlation of .65 is reported for the total scale scores and .61 for the individual scales (range = .27 to .74) over a 6-month interval. None of the SDQI scales meet the minimal criterion for stability, suggesting that score changes over time are due to scale instability rather than true changes in self-concept. The author attempts to dismiss the limited stability by stating that because the construct itself is subject to change, higher stability is not expected; however, the author makes the case elsewhere in the manual that "self-concept is . . . relatively stable over time" (p. 105). Certainly 6 months is not such a long interval that stability estimates this low would be expected as a result of change in the self-concepts of individuals.

Marsh addresses three areas of SDQI validity: content, construct, and concurrent. Evidence for content validity is provided in the description of item development and refinement, which was based on the Shavelson et al. (1976) model. Items were modified from previous research or developed to represent the components of the Shavelson et al. model.

Additionally, Marsh provides evidence of construct validity through both within-network and between-network studies. Results of an exploratory factor analysis, a within-network technique, based on the entire standardization sample yielded a median item target loading of .73 (range = .46 to .85), and a median nontarget loading of .03 (range = −.02 to .19). It should be noted that only the positively worded items from each scale were used in the factor analysis; that is, all negatively connoted items were excluded.

Results of a series of exploratory factor analyses conducted separately for each grade level yielded target loadings ranging from .27 to .70, for Grade 2 (n = 170); .08 to .74 for Grade 3 (n = 103); .36 to .85 for Grade 3 (n = 134); and .38 to .83 for Grade 3 (n = 251). (Note: Although the last three groups are labeled "Grade 3" in the examiner's manual, it seems that the latter two groups represent Grades 4 and 5 respectively, as indicated in

the text.) Overall, the Reading, Math, and School factors are less well defined for Grades 2 and 3 than for fourth- and fifth-grade students. Confirmatory factor analyses were also conducted and results are discussed in the
manual as supportive of the construct validity of the SDQI; however, no
data are presented and the reader is referred to outside sources.

Exploratory and confirmatory factor analyses with the revised SDQI included the General-Self scale and provide support for eight factors. Because correlations between the General-Self and other factors are low (.16
to .43), with a median of .23, support for the General-Self as a separate
factor is evidenced.

Moderately high correlations are reported between the SDQI and the
Perceived Competence Scale (PCS; Harter, 1982, 1983) on theoretically
similar scales including General Self scales (.57), Physical scales (.67),
SDQI Academic and PCS Cognitive scales (.60), and SDQI Peers and PCS
Social scales (.74). Additionally, with a mean correlation of .30 for the remaining row/column comparisons, support for the discriminant validity of
the SDQI is indicated.

Summary

As the first instrument based on the Shavelson et al. (1976) model, the
SDQI contributes significantly to the development of self-concept instrumentation by demonstrating adherence to a strong theoretical base and
definition. Furthermore, thorough investigation of the fit between the
Shavelson et al. model and the SDQI through exploratory and confirmatory factor analyses as well as by multitrait-multimethod studies is an important step in the refinement and sophistication of the measurement of
self-concept. The SDQI examiner's manual, however, presents scant information regarding the scale itself and is concerned more broadly with the
construct of self-concept. An abundance of space is devoted to recapping
previous research efforts with other instruments to the neglect of information regarding the clinical utility of the SDQI. Good internal consistency and evidence for the validity of the SDQI, along with examiner and
examinee friendliness are indicated; however, lack of evidence for scale
integration and interpretation and limited stability are problematic. Especially problematic for North American use is the SDQI normative sample
which was collected solely in Australia.

Self-Description Questionnaire, II

Published in 1990, the Self-Description Questionnaire, II (SDQII; Marsh,
1990) like the SDQI, is based on the multidimensional and hierarchical
theoretical model of self-concept posited by Shavelson, Hubner, and Stanton (1976). For students in Grades 7 through 10, the SDQII was designed
to assess self-concept in the same domains from the same theoretical foundation as previously mentioned for the SDQI.

Development and Standardization

Marsh retained the seven SDQI scales in the SDQII, but he divided the Peer scale into Same and Opposite Sex Relations scales. Additionally, the SDQII includes two new scales: Emotional Stability and Honesty/Truthfulness. The SDQII also includes a General-Self scale that is based on the Rosenberg Self-Esteem Scale (Rosenberg, 1965, 1979) and Rosenberg's belief in a supraordinate general self-concept. Each scale contains either 8 or 10 items; that were selected after two revisions and item tryouts.

SDQII norms were based on 5,494 students from various regions of Sydney, Australia. The sample was approximately equally divided by gender with 2,658 boys and 2,836 girls. Though the sample was described as including working-, middle-, and upper-class communities, coed and single-sex Catholic and public schools, no further demographics are provided, making examination of representativeness on these and other variables impossible. Generalizability to other countries, and possibly other areas within Australia, from a single metropolitan community in Australia is untenable.

Administration and Interpretation

The self-report format of the SDQII is easily administered to either individuals or groups, and average completion time is estimated at 20 minutes. No readability level is indicated for the scale; however, the items generally appear easily interpretable by adolescent students with only a few exceptions. Several items include words not commonly used by adolescents in the United States. For example, "I get good marks in Mathematics" and "I'm hopeless in English classes" would be misunderstood items by most American teenagers. The structure of the response options are very confusing with choices of "six shades of truth" ("false," "mostly false," "more false than true," "more true than false," "mostly true," and "true") for each of the 102 items.

Scoring guidelines are clearly set out in the manual and are provided in summary form on the individual scoring and profile booklet. Interpretation is based on mid-interval percentile ranks and nonnormalized T scores for each of the 11 scales as well as the Total Self-Concept score. An explanation of the use of these scores is provided. When transformed to T scores, both normative and ipsative analyses are possible.

Independently, the Total Self-Concept score is the sum of the 11 individual scales, including General Self-Concept and is intended to be interpreted as a "global evaluation of self" (p. 23). Because the General scale is included in the Total score, and because these two scores are highly correlated, independent interpretation of these scales is not supported and the need for a separate set of general items is unclear. Further, because four scales comprise 8 items each and seven scales consist of 10 items each, all scales do not contribute equally to Total Self-Concept. Therefore, aside from logical problems of interpretation, this aggregate measure is less in-fluenced by physical appearance, physical abilities, parent relations, and opposite sex relations than by the other scales, with no rationale for such disproportionate assignment of values. The SDQII provides no interpretive guides, such as case study examples, and no guidelines or suggestions are provided for scale intervention and remediation strategies.

Psychometric Characteristics

The SDQII meets the accepted criteria for internal consistency at both the total scale (.94) and subscale levels, with a median subscale alpha co-efficient of .86 (range = .83 to .91). Test-retest reliability was deter-mined for a sample of 137 high school girls in a study of the effects of a physical fitness intervention. For a 7-week interval, the median stability estimate of .79 fell just below the .80 criterion. With a range from .72 to .88, 6 of 11 scales demonstrated inadequate stability; no estimate of Total Self-Concept stability is reported.

Through the description of a theoretical basis and item development, content validity is supported. A factor analysis provides support for the SDQII with a median target loading of .68 (range = .48 to .80) and a me-dian nontarget loading of .03 (range = −.12 to .27). Further evidence of construct validity is presented through comparisons of the SDQII with in-struments designed to measure related constructs. Additionally, math abil-ity correlated more highly with the academic scales (Math = .48; Verbal = .39; and General School = .55) than with nonacademic scales (range = −.08 to .23).

Summary

As a companion to the SDQI, the SDQII contributes to the advancement of self-concept instrumentation in that it is a multidimensional and hierarchi-cal measure based on a strong theoretical model. The manual discusses a brief history of self-concept methodology as well as recent investigations into the relationship between self-concept and such variables as age and gender. Furthermore, the SDQII possesses excellent internal consistency and strong evidence for construct and content validity. It is not compared, however, with other purported measures of self-concept. Finally, the SDQII evidences the same weaknesses as the SDQI; that is, a lack of inte-grated interpretation guidelines and an inappropriate standardization sam-ple for use anywhere except Sydney, Australia.

Multidimensional Self Concept Scale

The Multidimensional Self Concept Scale (MSCS; Bracken, 1992) is a 150-item self-report inventory with a Likert-type format designed to mea-sure self-concept in children aged 9 to 19. Bracken defines self-concept as "a multidimensional and context-dependent learned behavioral pattern that reflects an individual's evaluation of past behaviors and experiences, influences an individual's current behaviors, and predicts an individual's future behaviors" (p. 10). Along with this definition, the MSCS is based on the Shavelson et al. (1976) hierarchical, multidimensional model of self-concept. The MSCS is composed of six subdomains contributing equally to global self-concept. The six domains are represented by six 25-item subscales including social, competence, affect, family, physical and academic.

In addition to the multidimensional, context-dependent aspects of the MSCS theoretical model, Bracken proposes a theoretical model for the acquisition of self-concept. This model proposes that children acquire evaluative information about themselves through two perspectives (i.e., Personal and Other Perspectives). That is, they gain information about themselves directly through their interactions with the environment and from feedback from other people in their environments (after Cooley's Looking-glass self). Additionally, information that is gained through these dual perspectives is evaluated against four standards (absolute, comparative, ipsative, ideal). In combination, the two perspectives and four evaluative standards represent the means by which children gain information about themselves, evaluate themselves, and adopt a unified self-image within each of the six primary self-concept domains.

The MSCS was designed chiefly as a comprehensive clinical assessment tool for use in various settings including schools, hospitals, correctional facilities, and mental health centers. Additionally, the MSCS may serve as a measure of global and/or domain-specific self-concept in a variety of research applications. As one of the most recently developed self-concept scales, the MSCS contributes significantly to the measurement of self-concept in that it provides a comprehensive assessment tool based on a strong multidimensional theoretical model.

Development and Standardization

A clear rationale is presented for inclusion of the six domains, including support from literature, existing instrumentation, and children's primary areas of engagement. Similarly, the manual presents a step-by-step discussion of item construction that incorporates the underlying theoretical model. The scale underwent two tryouts and a large field testing to establish the final set of items.

The standardization sample for the MSCS includes 2,501 children, ages 9 to 19, residing in 17 diverse sites from the four major regions of the United States. The sample is nationally representative, closely matching the 1990 U.S. Census with regard to gender, race, ethnicity, and geographic region. The MSCS standardization sample exceeds the minimum standards for size and national representativeness.

Administration and Interpretation

Because the readability level of the MSCS is reported as third-grade level, and administration time is approximately 20 to 30 minutes, the MSCS appears appropriate for most children in the age range of 9 to 19 years.

Depending on the cognitive abilities of the examinee, some items contain phrases or words that may be slightly difficult; however, items are generally short and easily interpreted. Additionally, examiners are instructed to define difficult words or phrases when necessary. The respondent's evaluations of him- or herself are facilitated by objective, behavioral item content. Due to ease of administration, either group or individual administration is appropriate.

Standard scores are provided for both the total scale and each of the subscales. Additionally, percentile ranks, standard scores (both deviation quotients and *T* scores), self-concept classifications, confidence intervals, and scale deviations are provided, which allow for both comprehensive normative and ipsative interpretations. Because the MSCS subscales are shown to possess ample specific variance, each can be interpreted as a unique aspect of self-concept, and can be used and interpreted in conjunction with other scales or independently. Furthermore, because the items from the six subscales are included only on their single respective scales, any of the subscales may be administered individually or in combination.

A framework for the interpretation of the MSCS, either individually or in combination with other psychoeducational instruments, is provided based on the context-dependent, multidimensional model of self-concept. The author presents and discusses several case examples to further guide interpretation. Additionally, an appendix that includes over 70 commonly used psychological and educational instruments is provided to facilitate the synthesis of children's MSCS domain-specific performance with their performance on the same domains assessed by tests included in comprehensive psychoeducational batteries.

The author dedicates a significant portion of the MSCS manual to MSCS-based intervention strategies. Bracken recommends direct instruction and skill building, modeling, selective reinforcement, cognitive-behavioral reframing, and modifications to the environment as a sample of methods for self-concept improvement. Additionally, the author demonstrates how the MSCS self-concept acquisition model, which includes the dual perspectives and four evaluative standards, can be used to improve children's and adolescents' self-concepts.

Psychometric Characteristics

MSCS Total Scale internal consistency exceeds the recommended criterion of .90, as well as the ideal standard of .95 proposed by Nunnally (1978), at all grade levels with a range of reliability coefficients from .97 to .99 (Total sample internal consistency = .98). Likewise, at the subscale level, the MSCS evidences excellent internal consistency with a range of coefficients between .87 to .97. Given these strong estimates of internal consistency and comprehensive content sampling (25 items per scale), examiners should have considerable confidence in the MSCS Total Scale and its subscales for the instrument's intended purposes, including clinical and research applications.

With a Total Scale stability coefficient of .90 over a 4-week interval, the MSCS also meets the proposed stability criterion. Furthermore, the median test-retest coefficient for the subscales is .79 (range = .73 to .81), indicating sufficient stability of the MSCS subscales.

Bracken (1992) presents support for the content, concurrent, contrasted groups, and discriminant validity of the MSCS. Moderately strong total scale correlations between the MSCS and theoretically similar instruments including the Coopersmith Self-Esteem Inventory (Coopersmith, 1981), (.73); the Piers-Harris Children's Self-Concept Scale (Piers, 1984), (.85); the Self-Description Questionnaire, I (Marsh, 1988), (.69); and the Self-Description Questionnaire, II (Marsh, 1990), (.80) provide evidence for the concurrent validity of the MSCS.

In studies of contrasted groups, support for the MSCS as a discriminator of students' problematic social-emotional functioning is indicated. Bardos (1992) found that children previously identified as exhibiting low self-esteem scored lower on all MSCS scales than a randomly selected group. Further, Bardos found that children in need of further assessment scored lower than a nonidentified group on the MSCS.

Support for the discriminant validity of the MSCS is indicated with a moderate Total Scale Score correlation (.55) with the Assessment of Interpersonal Relations (AIR; Bracken, 1993), a scale designed to assess relationship quality in three of the primary contexts assessed by the MSCS (social, family, academic). Additionally, a five-instrument factor analysis that included the MSCS and four other theoretically similar scales was conducted (Bracken, Bunch, Keith, & Keith, 1992). The emergence of six factors corresponding to the six MSCS subscales provides support for the content and construct validity of the MSCS and its underlying theoretical model.

Summary

The MSCS is the most recently developed scale for the assessment of multidimensional self-concept. Through excellent psychometric characteristics, a diverse nationally representative standardization sample, a wide age range, third-grade readability, ease of administration and scoring, and an empirically supported theoretical framework, the MSCS has addressed many areas of weakness in earlier instruments. Furthermore, the MSCS and its underlying theory provide a cogent definition of self-concept, a reliable and valid instrument for assessing self-concept, and a comprehensive framework for scale interpretation and intervention planning.

CONCLUSION

Systematic evaluations of 20 self-concept measures revealed that many instruments continue to demonstrate serious qualitative weaknesses; however, more recently developed instruments serve as reliable and valid measures for use in clinical and research settings. Examiner's manuals for each instrument were reviewed for the following objective components: standardization sample size and geographic origination; inclusion of explicit purpose(s); number and types of domains assessed; age/grade appropriateness; administration time; readability of the scale; presence of a stated theoretical foundation; inclusion of a definition of self-concept; internal consistency; test-retest reliability; evidence of validity reported in the manual; and types of scores produced by the instrument.

Table 3.1 summarizes information regarding the instruments' standardization samples. Based on information provided in the examiner's manuals, only 4 of the 20 manuals indicate a national standardization sample: These are the MSCS, OSIQ-R, SEI, and TSCS. With 2,501 respondents between the ages of 9 to 19 years residing in four regions of the United States, the MSCS sample is representative of the U.S. population. Additionally, the OSIQ-R sample is based on 964 adolescents, aged 13 to 18, from eight states and the District of Columbia, representing diverse regions of the United States. The SEI sample comprised 2,455 children and adolescents between the ages of 8 and 8 years 11 months from 19 states. Likewise, the TSCS reports a sample of 626 respondents from "various parts of the U.S." (Roid & Fitts, 1988; p. 56). The remaining 16 instruments' have standardization samples that represent restricted geographic regions and were generally normed in a single city, state, or region (e.g., Coopersmith, Central Connecticut; ISCS, Austin, Texas; JPPSST, suburban and urban Illinois; PASS, Idaho, Oregon, and Washington; PHSCS, one town in Pennsylvania; SPPC, Colorado). Other instruments include a non-U.S. standardization sample (e.g., SDQI and SDQII, Australia). Size and publication date of the standardization sample are also determinants of representativeness. Based on the criterion of at least 100 subjects for each age or grade level, most examiner's manuals report adequate samples. Only the Coopersmith with 87 subjects, the ISCS with 180 children in Grades 1 through 6, the PSPC with no information provided, and the TSCS with 626 subjects over a broad age range, are apparently inadequate. Also, the norms for most instruments are quite dated with only 6 of the 20 scales normed or renormed since 1990.

Table 3.1 also indicates the purpose(s) indicated by test authors. Purposes including individual and group evaluation, screening for children in need of further assessment, program evaluation, intervention design, and research are cited in 10 examiner's manuals; however, the remaining 10 manuals fail to propose what uses are appropriate for the instrument. Finally, Table 3.1 lists the domains purportedly assessed by each self-concept instrument. Because the development of self-concept theory has produced fairly high agreement on a multidimensional model, most instruments include several domains.

Information regarding age/grade appropriateness, administration time, readability, and the inclusion of a stated theoretical basis and definition is

**TABLE 3.1   Standardization Samples, Purposes, and Domains
Assessed by Twenty Self-Concept Instruments Based on Information in
Test Manuals and Supplemental Data**

Instrument	Standardization Sample Assessed	Purposes	Domains
Adult Self-Perception Scale (ASPS)	151 parents ages 30–50, and 250 mothers of children under age 3 years	Research Clinical diagnosis Measurement of trmt. change	Sociability Job Competence Nurturance Athletic Abilities Intimate Relationships Physical Appearance Morality Adequate Provider Sense of Humor Intelligence Household mgmt. Global Self-Worth
Coopersmith Self-Esteem Inventories (CSEI)	*School Form:* 87 children in Grades 5 and 6 in one state; 7,593 children in Grades 4–8; *Adult Form:* 226 college students in Northern Calif.	Assessment Screening Program evaluation Research	General Self Social Self-Peers Home-Parents School/Academic Total Self Lie Scale
Culture-Free Self-Esteem Inventories, Second Edition (CFSEI-2)	*Form A:* 1,679 children in elem. grades in Canada; 873 in junior high grades in Canada *Form B:* 116 children in elem. grades in Canada *Form AD:* 585 adults ages 16–65 from Canada	Screening and identification Research Intervention planning	*Forms A & B:* Total General Social Academic Parental *Form AD:* Total General Social Personal
Inferred Self-Concept Scale (ISCS)	180 children in Grades 1–6 from Austin, Texas	Research Individual evaluation	Unidimensional
Joseph Pre-School and Primary Self-Concept Screening Test (JPPSST)	1,245 children ages 3-6–9-11 from Illinois	Screening to identify "high risk" young children Research	Significance Competence Power General Evaluative Competence Virtue
Multidimensional Self Concept Scale (MSCS)	2,501 children ages 9–19 in Grades 5–12 from the four major U. S. regions	Clinical assessment in various settings Research	Global Self Concept Social Academic Affect Competence Family Physical

(Continued)

TABLE 3.1   *(Continued)*

Instrument	Standardization Sample Assessed	Purposes	Domains
Offer Self-Image Questionnaire, Revised (OSIQ-R)	964 adolescents ages 13–18 from eight states and the District of Columbia	Research regarding normal adolescent development Clinical tool Research	Emotional Tone Impulse Control Mental Health Social Family Vocational Self-Confidence Self-Reliance Body Image Sexuality Ethical Values Idealism
Perception of Ability Scale for Students (PASS)	831 children in Grades 3–6 from one U.S. region	Screening Program evaluation Research	General Ability Math Reading/Spelling School Satisfaction Penmanship/Neatness Confidence in Academic Ability
Pictorial Scale of Perceived Competence and Acceptance for Young Children (PSPC)	No information reported	Not reported	Cognitive Competence Physical Maternal Acceptance Peer Acceptance
Piers-Harris Children's Self-Concept Scale (PHSCS)	1,183 children ages 8–18 in Grades 4–12 from one Pennsylvania town	Clinical screening, assessment Research	Total Self Behavior Intellectual/School Physical Appearance/ Attributes Anxiety Popularity Happiness/ Satisfaction
Rosenberg Self-Esteem Scale (RSES)	5,024 adolescents from 10 high schools in New York	Not reported	Unidimensional
Self-Description Questionnaire, I (SDQ-I)	3,562 children from primary schools in New South Wales, Australia; General Self: 739 fifth-grade students	Not reported	Physical Abilities Physical Appearance Peer Relations Parent Relations Reading Mathematics General School

TABLE 3.1   *(Continued)*

Instrument	Standardization Sample Assessed	Purposes	Domains
Self-Description Questionnaire, II (SDQ-2)	5,494 students from Sydney, Australia	Not reported	Physical Abilities Opposite Sex Relations Same Sex Relations Honesty/Truthfulness Math Emotional Stability Verbal General School General Self
Self-Esteem Index (SEI)	2,455 children ages 8–18-11 from 19 states	Clinical evaluation Intervention planning Research	Academic Competence Familial Acceptance Peer Popularity Personal Security Total Self
Self-Perception Inventory (SPI)	*Student Form:* 10,712 children in Grades 2–12 *Adult Form:* 2,650 subjects from Grade 9 to "working adults"	Research	*Student Form:* Self Concept Reflected self/classmates Reflected self/teachers Reflected self/parents Ideal Concept Student Self *Adult Form:* Self Concept Reflected self/friends Reflected self/teachers Reflected self/parents Reflected self/partners Ideal Concept Student Self
Self-Perception Profile for Adolescents (SPPA)	651 adolescents in Grades 8–11 from Colorado	Not reported	Scholastic Competence Behavioral Conduct Athletic Competence Close Friendship Global Self-Worth Physical Appearance Romantic Appeal Social Acceptance Job Competence
Self-Perception Profile for Children (SPPC)	1,543 children in Grades 3–8 from Colorado	Not reported	Scholastic Competence Social Acceptance Physical Appearance Behavioral Conduct Global Self-Worth

(Continued)

TABLE 3.1 *(Continued)*

Instrument	Standardization Sample Assessed	Purposes	Domains
Self-Perception Profile for College Students (SPPCS)	318 college students from Colorado	Not reported	Scholastic Competence Athletic Competence Social Acceptance Job Competence Romantic Relations Close Friendships Intellectual Ability Morality Parent Relations Creativity Finding Humor in One's Life Appearance General Self-Worth
Self-Perception Profile for Learning Disabled Students (SPPLD)	201 children in Grades 4–8 identified as having a learning disability, and 367 normally achieving children in Grade 4, all from suburban Denver	Assessment of learning-disabled and normally achieving children	Social Acceptance Athletic Competence Behavioral Conduct Physical Global Self-Worth
Tennessee Self-Concept Scale (TSCS)	626 subjects ages 12–68 from "various parts of the U.S."	Counseling tool Clinical assessment and diagnosis Personnel selection Research	Identity Behavior Satisfaction Physical Moral-Ethical Personal Family Social

summarized in Table 3.2. Self-concept scales intended for use with a broad age or grade range (MSCS, PHSCS, SEI, TSCS) are most useful for clinicians and researchers; however, some scales were designed to address assessment needs for specific populations (JPPSST and PSPC for very young children; OSIQ-R for adolescents; ASPS for adults). The instruments (CFSEI, ISCS, RSES, SPPLD, SPI) that fail to report intended age ranges are most problematic on this dimension.

As indicated in Table 3.2, 11 instruments report estimates of administration time ranging from 5 to 30 minutes. Furthermore, all estimated times appear appropriate for both clinical and research settings. For the remaining 9 scales that do not provide time estimates, Bracken and Mills (1994) estimate that students generally respond to items at a rate of approximately 50 items per 10 minutes. Therefore, relative administration

TABLE 3.2 Administration and Interpretation Guides for Twenty Self-Concept Instruments

Instrument	Administration Time (in minutes)	Readability	Theoretical Foundation	Definition	Intended Age/Grade of Examinee
Adult Self-Perception (ASPS)	Not reported	Not reported	Yes	Yes	Adults
Coopersmith Self-Esteem Inventories (CSEI)	30	Not reported	Yes	Yes	School Form: Ages 8–15 Adult Form: Ages 16 and older
Culture-Free Self-Esteem Inventories, Second Edition (CFSEI-2)	Not reported	Not reported	No	Yes	Form A: Elem. and Junior High Form B: Elem. Form AD: Adults
Inferred Self-Concept Scale (ISCS)	Not reported	Not reported	Yes	Yes	School-age children
Joseph Pre-School and Primary Self-Concept Screening Test (JPPST)	5–7	Not applicable	Yes	Yes	Children in primary and preschool grades
Multidimensional Self Concept Scale (MSCS)	20–30	Third grade	Yes	Yes	Ages 9–19 Grades 5–12
Offer Self-Image Questionnaire, Revised (OSIQ-R)	Not reported	Mid-fifth grade	Yes	No	Ages 13–18
Perception of Ability Scale for Students (PASS)	15–20	Mid-second grade	Yes	Yes	Grades 3–6
Pictorial Scale of Perceived Competence and Acceptance for Young Children (PSPC)	Not reported	Not applicable	No	No	Preschool–Grade 2

(Continued)

TABLE 3.2 (*Continued*)

Instrument	Administration Time (in minutes)	Readability	Theoretical Foundation	Definition	Intended Age/Grade of Examinee
Piers-Harris Children's Self-Concept Scale (PHSCS)	20	Third grade	Yes	Yes	Ages 8–18 Grades 4–12
Rosenberg Self-Esteem Scale (RSES)	Not reported	Not reported	Yes	Yes	Not reported
Self-Description Questionnaire, I (SDQ-I)	20	Not reported	Yes	Yes	Ages 8–12 Grades 2–6
Self-Description Questionnaire, II (SDQ-2)	20	Not reported	Yes	Yes	Grades 7–10
Self-Esteem Index (SEI)	30	Not reported	No	Yes	Ages 8–18-11
Self-Perception Inventory (SPI)	20	Not reported	Yes	Yes	Student Form: Elem. and secondary students Adult Form: High school students and adults
Self-Perception Profile for Adolescents (SPPA)	Not reported	Not reported	Yes	Yes	Grades 9–12
Self-Perception Profile for Children (SPPC)	Not reported	Not reported	Yes	Yes	Grades 3–6
Self-Perception Profile for College Students (SPPCS)	30	Not reported	Yes	Yes	Ages 17–23
Self-Perception Profile for Learning Disabled Students (SPPLD)	Not reported	Not reported	Yes	Yes	Not reported
Tennessee Self-Concept Scale (TSCS)	10–20	Fourth grade	No	No	Ages 12–68

time can be estimated by considering the number of items in each scale. With only 10 items, the RSES would likely require the least amount of time (5 minutes or less).

From viewing Table 3.2, it is evident that most examiner's manuals do not report scale readability. Because many children referred to psychologists in school and clinical settings demonstrate low self-concept as well as educational deficiencies, the examiner must have information regarding the necessary reading level for successful completion of the scale. Because items are presented pictorially for the JPPSST and the PSPC, this variable is not applicable; however, with a range of mid-second to mid-fifth grade, the MSCS, OSIQ-R, PASS, PHSCS, and the TSCS are the only instruments that provide an estimate of reading level. Without this information, it is difficult for the test user to determine the appropriateness of the scale for clients or research participants, particularly in cases of young or low-functioning respondents.

Finally, Table 3.2 indicates whether each examiner's manual explicitly states a theoretical foundation for the instrument and a definition of the construct assessed. Although most instruments provide both a definition and a theory, the CFSEI-2, PSCS, SEI, and TSCS manuals do not present a specific theoretical basis. Furthermore, the OSIQ-R, PSCS, and TSCS manuals do not define the construct. Overall, the theoretical bases vary from behavioral (e.g., MSCS, PASS) to cognitive in orientation (e.g., PSCS, SPPC); however, self-concept definitions are quite similar across instruments, indicating that the terms self-esteem, self-concept, and self-image are referents to the same general construct.

Psychometric characteristics of the 20 instruments are summarized in Table 3.3. As suggested by Bracken (1987) and Salvia and Ysseldyke (1988), $\geq .90$ and $\geq .80$ are considered adequate levels of internal consistency for total scales and subscales, respectively. Total scale internal consistencies are reported for all scales except the CFSEI-2, PSPC, SPI, and the Self-Perception Profiles (SPPA, SPPC, SPPCS, SPPLD, ASPP). The MSCS, OSIQ-R, PASS, SDQI, SDQII, SEI, and TSCS consistently meet the .90 criterion for adequate internal consistency at the total scale level. Subscale internal consistencies are reported by all multidimensional instruments except the Coopersmith and the PSPC. Acceptable levels of median subscale internal consistencies are reported in Table 3.3 for the MSCS, PASS, SDQI, SDQII, SEI, SPPA, SPPC, SPPCS, SPPLD, ASPS, and the TSCS; however, particular subscales for several of these instruments fall below the .80 criterion. Furthermore, the SPI reported internal consistencies for only two subscales, Self Concept (.94), which exceeded the .80 criterion, and Student Self (.79), which fell slightly below the criterion.

Because researchers and test authors generally agree that self-concept is a stable construct, short-term test-retest reliability estimates of $\geq .90$ for total scales and $\geq .80$ for subscales is considered minimally adequate

TABLE 3.3 Psychometric Characteristics of Twenty Self-Concept Instruments Based on Examiner's Manuals and Supplemental Data

Instrument	Internal Consistency	Test-Retest Reliability	Validity Reported in Manual	Scores Produced
Adult Self-Perception Scale (ASPS)	Subscale: .81	Not reported	Construct	Raw Scores
Coopersmith Self-Esteem Inventories (CSEI)	*School Form:* Total Scale: .80–.92 Subscales: Not reported *Adult Form:* Not reported	*School Form:* Total Scale: .88 (5 weeks) .42 to .70 (3 yrs) .64 (12 months) *Adult Form:* Not reported	*Concurrent* *Construct* *Criterion-Related* *Predictive* *Discriminant*	*Percentile Ranks* *Total Scale in 5th per-centile units*
Culture-Free Self-Esteem Inventories, Second Edition (CFSEI-2)	*Form A:* (Grades 7–9) Total Scale: Not reported Subscale: .70* *Form B:* Not reported *Form AD:* Total scale: Not reported Subscale: .65*	*Form A:* (grades 3–6) Total Scale: .81 to .89 Subscale: .68* (no interval reported) *Form A:* (grades 7–9) Total Scale: .88 to .96 Subscale: .83* (no interval reported) *Form B:* (grades 3–6) Total Scale: .79 to .92 Subscale: .96* (no interval reported)	Content Concurrent *Discriminant* Construct	Percentile Ranks *T* scores

Instrument			Validity	Scores
Inferred Self-Concept Scale (ISCS)	Total Scale: .86 to .90	*Form AD:* Total Scale: .82 Subscale: .78* (no interval reported) Total Scale: .49 to .84 (6 months)	Construct Content	Raw Scores
Joseph Pre-School and Primary Self-Concept Screening Test (JPPSST)	Total Scale: .59 to .81	Total Scale: .87 (4 weeks)	Construct Criterion-related	Raw Scores Classifications
Multidimensional Self Concept Scale (MSCS)	Total Scale: .98 Subscale: .92*	Total Scale: .90 (4 weeks) Subscale: .79 (4 weeks)*	Content Construct Concurrent Discriminant *Contrasted Groups*	Normalized IQ Metric Normalized *T* Scores Percentile Ranks Classifications
Offer Self-Image Questionnaire, Revised (OSIQ-R)	Total Scale: .90 Subscale: .70*	Total Scale: .63 (2 years) Subscale: .58 (2 years)*	Construct Predictive *Discriminant Concurrent Contrasted Groups*	*T* Scores Classifications
Perception of Ability Scale for Students (PASS)	Total Scale: .93 Subscale: .80*	Total Scale: .83 (4–6 weeks) Subscale: .76 (4–6 weeks)*	*Content Concurrent Convergent Discriminant*	*T* Scores Percentile Ranks Stanines

(Continued)

TABLE 3.3 (*Continued*)

Instrument	Internal Consistency	Test-Retest Reliability	Validity Reported in Manual	Scores Produced
Pictorial Scale of Perceived Competence and Acceptance for Young Children (PSPC)	Not reported	Not reported	Not reported	Raw Scores
Piers-Harris Children's Self-Concept Scale (PHSCS)	Total Scale: .88 to .93 Subscale: .77*	Total Scale: .96 (3–4 weeks) Subscale: Not reported	Content Concurrent Contrasted Groups *Construct Convergent Discriminant*	Normalized *T* Scores Stanines Percentile Ranks
Rosenberg Self-Esteem Scale (RSES)	Total Scale: .77	Total Scale: .85 to .88 (2 weeks)	Convergent Discriminant Construct	Classifications
Self-Description Questionnaire-I (SDQ-I)	Total Self: .94 Subscale: .88*	Total Self: Not reported Subscale: .61*	Content Construct Concurrent	Midinterval Percentile Ranks Nonnormalized *T* Scores
Self-Description Questionnaire-II (SDQ-II)	Total Scale: .94 Subscale: .86*	Total Scale: Not reported Subscale: .79*	Content Construct	Midinterval Percentile Ranks Nonnormalized *T* Scores
Self-Esteem Index (SEI)	Total Scale: .93 Subscale: .83*	Total Scale: Not reported	Content Construct Concurrent Contrasted Groups	Percentile Ranks Scaled Scores Deviation Quotients

164

	Internal Consistency	Test-Retest	Validity	Scores
Self-Perception Inventory (SP1)	*Student Form:* Total Scale: Not reported Subscales: Self-concept .94* Student/Self .79* (remaining scales not reported)	*Student Form:* Total Scale: Not reported Subscale: .86* *Adult Form:* Total Scale: Not reported Subscale: .79*	Construct	Stanines
Self-Perception Profile for Adolescents (SPPA)	Subscale: .81*	Not reported	Construct	Raw Scores
Self-Perception Profile for Children (SPPC)	Subscale: .80*	Not reported	Construct	Raw Scores
Self-Perception Profile for College Students (SPPCS)	Subscale: .84*	Not reported	Construct Discriminant	Raw Scores
Self-Perception Profile for Learning Disabled Children (SPPLD)	Subscale: .84*	Not reported	Construct	Raw Scores
Tennessee Self-Concept Scale (TSCS)	Total Scale: .94 Subscale: .83*	Total Scale: .92 (2 weeks) Subscale: .88 (2 weeks)*	Content Construct *Criterion-related Discriminant*	Percentile Ranks Normalized *T* Scores

* Median subscale coefficient.

(Bracken, 1987; Salvia & Ysseldyke, 1988). Total scale stability coefficients are reported in 11 of 20 manuals; however, only three instruments, the MSCS, the PHSCS, and the TSCS consistently meet the .90 criterion (see Table 3.3). At the subscale level, stability coefficients are reported for eight instruments. Only the CFSEI (Form A), SPI (Student Form), the TSCS (with supplemental data) meet the .80 criterion for all subscales. Other instruments including the MSCS and the SDQII with median coefficients of .79, and the PASS with a median coefficient of .76, fell only slightly below the criterion.

Each instrument's presentation of evidence for validity was closely examined and summarized in the review of the particular scale; however, when comparing across instruments, only indications of validity presented by the test author were considered (Table 3.3). Because validity is not an objective variable, the presence of any evidence of valid information was credited. Only the Pictorial Scale of Perceived Competence and Acceptance for Young Children failed to include evidence of validity. Many instruments presented support for validity by summarizing the research literature but did not conduct studies as part of the original scale development. Furthermore, many of the summarized studies present little or no actual data and provide equivocal support, making decisions about the validity of the instrument difficult to determine.

Finally, as illustrated in Table 3.3, the 20 instruments employ a wide range of types of scores including T scores, Deviation Quotients, percentile ranks, classifications, and raw scores. For clinical practice, however, standard scores are the most useful when making comparisons between a client's performance and the norm group and when comparing the client's performance across instruments within a battery. Eleven of the 20 scales provide at least one type of standard score; however, several scales provide very restricted score reporting options. For example, the Coopersmith only provides Total Score percentile ranks for every fifth percentile interval. Additionally, the RSES and the JPPSST only provide qualitative classifications based on raw scores. The utility of these instruments and those providing only raw scores (e.g., ISCS, PSPC) is very limited.

In summary, the 20 instruments evaluated herein demonstrate the evolution of a more coherent construct of self-concept than that described by Wylie (1974). With inclusion of a theoretical foundation, a definition of the construct assessed, and several domains represented by multidimensional scales, most instruments have shown great evolutionary strides in the measurement of self-concept. Additionally, improvement in psychometric soundness of instruments is evidenced by more total scale internal consistencies that meet recommended criteria and more evidence of scale validity presented in most manuals. Limitations, however, remain as indicated by less than adequate levels of total scale and subscale stability, lack of nationally representative standardization samples, and restricted scoring options. In general, more recently developed instruments (e.g., MSCS,

OSIQ-R, PASS, SEI) should be considered the instruments of choice when measuring self-concept in most clinical and research situations. Because these scales most consistently meet high standards of technical adequacy, their use may reduce the number of equivocal findings in research and improve clinical assessment practice.

REFERENCES

American Educational Research Association, American Psychological Association, National Council on Measurement in Education. (1985). *Standards for educational and psychological testing.* Washington, DC: American Educational Research Association.

Bardos, A. N. (1992). Relationship between the Multidimensional Self Concept Scale, Draw a Person: Screening Procedure for Emotional Disturbance, and the Emotional and Behavioral Problem Scale for a sample of emotionally/behaviorally disturbed children. In B. A. Bracken (1992), *Multidimensional Self Concept Scale.* Austin, TX: Pro-Ed.

Battle, J. (1992). *Culture-Free Self-Esteem Inventories* (2nd ed.). Austin, TX: Pro-Ed.

Battle, J., & Shea, R. (1989). *The relationship between attention-deficit-hyperactivity disorder and self-esteem.* Edmonton, Canada: Edmonton Public Schools.

Bedian, A. G., Geagud, R. J., & Zmud, R. W. (1977). Test-retest reliability and internal consistency of the short form of Coopersmith's Self-Esteem Inventory. *Psychological Reports, 41,* 1041–1042.

Bloom, B. S. (1976). *Human characteristics and school learning.* New York: McGraw-Hill.

Boersma, F. J., & Chapman, J. W. (1992). *Perception of ability scale for students.* Los Angeles, CA: Western Psychological services.

Bracken, B. A. (1987). Limitations of preschool assessment and standards for minimal levels of technical adequacy. *Journal of Psychoeducational Assessment, 5,* 313–326.

Bracken, B. A. (1992). *Multidimensional Self Concept Scale.* Austin, TX: Pro-Ed.

Bracken, B. A. (1993). *Assessment of Interpersonal Relations.* Austin, TX: Pro-Ed.

Bracken, B. A., Bunch, S., Keith, T. Z., & Keith, P. B. (1992, August). *Multidimensional self concept: A five instrument factor analysis.* Paper presented at the annual conference of the American Psychological Association, Washington, DC.

Bracken, B. A., & Mills, B. C. (1994). School counselors' assessment of self-concept: A comprehensive review of ten instruments. *The School Counselor, 42,* 14–31.

Brookover, W. B., & Gotlieb, D. (1964). *Sociology of education.* New York: American Book Company.

Brown, L., & Alexander, J. (1991). *Self-Esteem Index.* Austin, TX: Pro-Ed.

Byrne, B., & Shavelson, R. J. (1986). On the structure of adolescent self-concept. *Educational psychologist, 78,* 474–481.

Carmines, E. G., & Zeller, R. A. (1974). On establishing the empirical dimensionality of theoretical terms: An analytical example. *Political Methodology, 1,* 75–96.

Carmines, E. G., & Zeller, R. A. (1979). *Reliability and validity assessment.* Newbury Park, CA: Sage.

Chapman, J. W., Boersma, F. J., & Maguire, T. O. (1977). *Some preliminary findings with the student's perception of ability scale; Implications for research with learning disabled children.* Paper presented at the annual meeting of the Canadian Psychological Association, Vancouver.

Cooley, C. H. (1902). *Human nature and the social order.* New York: Scribners.

Coopersmith, S. (1967). *The Antecedents of Self-Esteem.* Palo Alto, CA: Consulting Psychologists Press, Inc.

Coopersmith, S. (1981). *Coopersmith Self-Esteem Inventory.* Palo Alto, CA: Consulting Psychologists Press, Inc.

Erikson, E. (1963). *Childhood and society* (2nd ed.). New York: Norton.

Fitts, W. H. (1965). *Tennessee Self-Concept Scale.* Nashville, TN: Counselor Recordings and Tests.

Harter, S. (1982). The Perceived Competence Scale for Children. *Child Development, 53,* 87–97.

Harter, S. (1985). *Self-Perception Profile for Children.* Denver, CO: University of Denver Press.

Harter, S. (1988). *Self-Perception Profile for Adolescents.* Denver, CO: University of Denver Press.

Harter, S. (1990). Self and identity development. In S. S. Feldman & G. Elliot (Eds.), *At the threshold: The developing adolescent.* Cambridge, MA: Harvard University Press.

Harter, S., & Pike, R. G. (1981). *The Pictorial Scale of Perceived Competence and Acceptance for Young Children.* Denver, CO: University of Denver Press.

Harter, S., & Pike, R. (1984). The pictorial scale of perceived competence and social acceptance for young children. *Child Development, 55,* 1969–1982.

Hattie, J. B. (1992). *Self-concept.* Hillsdale, NJ: Erlbaum.

James, W. (1983). *Principles of psychology* (Vol. 1). Cambridge, MA: Harvard University Press. (Original work published in 1890)

Jersild, A. T. (1952). *In search of self.* New York: Teachers College Bureau of Publications.

Joseph, J. (1979). *Joseph Pre-School & Primary Self-Concept Screening Test.* Wood Dale, IL: Stoelting Company.

Keith, L. K., & Bracken, B. A. (1994, March). *Self concept or self concepts: Factor analytic study of a multidimensional model.* Paper presented at the National Association of School Psychologists Annual Conference, Seattle, WA.

Kimball, O. M. (1973). Development of norms for the Coopersmith self-esteem inventory: Grades four through eight. (Doctoral dissertation, Northern Illinois University, 1972). *Dissertation Abstracts International, 34,* 1131–1132.

Kincannon, J. C. (1968). Prediction of the standard MMPI scale scores from 71 items: The mini-mult. *Journal of Consulting and Clinical Psychology, 32,* 319–325.

Kohn, M. L. (1969). *Class and conformity: A study in values.* Homewood, IL: Dorsey Press.

Kohn, M. L., & Schooler, C. (1969). Class, occupation, and orientation. *American Sociological Review, 34,* 659–678.

Kokenes, B. (1974). Grade level differences in factors of self-esteem. *Developmental Psychology, 10,* 954–958.

Kokenes, B. (1978). A factor analytic study of the Coopersmith self-esteem inventory. *Adolescence, 13,* 149–155.

Koppitz, E. (1968). *Psychological evaluation of children's human figure drawings.* Needham Heights, MA: Allyn and Bacon.

Levin, J., Karnie, E., & Frankel, Y. (1978). Analysis of the Tennessee Self-Concept Scale as a faceted instrument. *Psychological Reports, 43,* 619–623.

Machover, K. (1949). *Personality projection in the drawing of the human figure.* Springfield, IL: Thomas.

Marsh, H. W. (1987). The hierarchical structure of self-concept: An application of hierarchical confirmatory factor analysis. *Journal of Educational Measurement, 24,* 17–39.

Marsh, H. W. (1988). *Self-Description Questionnaire, I.* San Antonio, TX: The Psychological Corporation.

Marsh, H. W. (1990). *Self-Description Questionnaire, II.* San Antonio, TX: The Psychological Corporation.

Marsh, H. W., Barnes, J., & Hocevar, D. (1985). Self-other agreement on multi-dimensional self-concept ratings: Factor analysis and multitrait-multi-method analysis. *Journal of Personality and Social Psychology, 49,* 1360–1377.

Marsh, H. W., & Hocevar, D. (1985). The application of confirmatory factor analysis to the study of self-concept: First and higher order factor structures and their invariance across age groups. *Psychological Bulletin, 97,* 562–582.

McDaniel, E. L. (1986). *Inferred Self-Concept Scale.* Los Angeles, CA: Western Psychological Services.

McGuire, B., & Tinsley, H. E. A. (1981). A contribution to the construct validity of the Tennessee Self-Concept Scale: A confirmatory factor analysis. *Applied Psychological Measure, 5,* 449–457.

Mead, G. H. (1934). *Mind, self, and society.* Chicago: University of Chicago Press.

Messer, B., & Harter, S. (1986). *Adult Self-Perception Profile.* Denver, CO: University of Denver Press.

Neeman, J., & Harter, S. (1986). *Self-Perception Profile for College Students.* Denver, CO: University of Denver Press.

Nunnally, J. C. (1978). *Psychometric theory* (2nd ed.). New York: McGraw-Hill.

Offer, D., Ostrov, E., Howard, K. I., & Dolan, S. (1992). *Offer Self-Image Questionnaire, Revised.* Los Angeles, CA: Western Psychological Services.

Perkins, H. V. (1975). *Human development.* Belmont, CA: Wadsworth.

Piers, E. V. (1984). *Piers-Harris Children's Self-Concept Scale: Revised manual.* Los Angeles, CA: Western Psychological Services.

Renick, M. J., & Harter, S. (1988). *Self-Perception Profile for Learning Disabled Students.* Denver, CO: University of Denver Press.

Rogers, C. R. (1951). *Client-centered therapy.* New York: Houghton Mifflin.

Rogers, C. R., & Dymond, R. F. (Eds.). (1954). *Psychotherapy and personality change: Coordinated studies in the client-centered approach.* Chicago: University of Chicago Press.

Roid, G. H., & Fitts, W. H. (1988). *Tennessee Self-Concept Scale, Revised manual.* Los Angeles, CA: Western Psychological Services.

Rosenberg, M. (1965). *Society and the adolescent self-image.* Princeton, NJ: Princeton University Press.

Rosenberg, M. (1979). *Conceiving the self.* New York: Basic Books.

Rosenberg, M. (1989). Self-concept research: A historical overview. *Social Forces, 68*(1), 34–44.

Salvia, J., & Ysseldyke, J. E. (1988). *Assessment in special and remedial education* (3rd ed.). Boston, MA: Houghton Mifflin.

Sarbin, T. R. (1952). A preface to a psychological analysis of the self. *Psychological Review, 59,* 11–22.

Sears, P. S., & Sherman, V. S. (1964). *In pursuit of self-esteem.* Belmont, CA: Wadsworth.

Shavelson, R. J., Hubner, J. J., & Stanton, G. C. (1976). Self-concept: Validation of construct interpretations. *Review of Educational Research, 46,* 407–441.

Silber, E., & Tippett, J. S. (1965). Self-esteem: Clinical assessment and measurement validation. *Psychological Reports, 16,* 1017–1071.

Smart, M. S., & Smart, R. C. (1973). *Preschool children, development and relationships.* New York: Macmillan.

Soares, A. T., & Soares, L. M. (1985). *The Self-Perception Inventory, Revised edition.* Bridgeport, CT: Author.

Statistical Abstract of the United States. (1985). Washington, DC: U.S. Department of Commerce, Bureau of the Census.

Stevenson, D. T., & Romney, D. M. (1984). Depression in learning-disabled children. *Journal of Learning Disabilities, 10,* 579–582.

Sullivan, H. S. (1953). *The interpersonal theory of psychiatry.* New York: Norton.

Tippett, J. S., & Silber, E. (1965). Self-image stability: The problem of validation. *Psychological Reports, 17,* 323–329.

Wylie, R. C. (1961). *The self-concept: A critical survey of pertinent research literature.* Lincoln: University of Nebraska Press.

Wylie, R. C. (1974). *The self-concept: A review of methodological considerations and measuring instruments* (2nd ed., Vol. 1). Lincoln: University of Nebraska Press.

Wylie, R. C. (1989). *Measures of self-concept.* Lincoln: University of Nebraska Press.

CHAPTER 4

Social Self-Concept

THOMAS J. BERNDT and LEAH BURGY

The idea of a social self-concept originated more than a century ago, when William James wrote:

> A *man's social self* is the recognition which he gets from his mates. We are not only gregarious animals, liking to be in sight of our fellows, but we have an innate propensity to get ourselves noticed, and noticed favorably, by our kind. (1890, p. 293, italics original)

The link between the social self and social recognition was reinforced early in the 20th century by Charles Cooley (1922). He wrote perhaps the most poetic hypothesis in social science, saying that "Each to each a looking glass/Reflects the other that doth pass." Cooley explained:

> As we see our face, figure, and dress in the glass, and are interested in them because they are ours, . . . so in imagination we perceive in another's mind some thought of our appearance, manners, aims, deeds, character, friends, and so on, and are variously affected by it. (p. 184)

To both James and Cooley, then, the social self-concept referred to people's perceptions of how much other people liked and admired them. In other words, these theorists defined the social self-concept by self-perceptions of social acceptance.

Other scholars have defined the social self-concept by people's perceptions of their social competence or social skill. Fitts (1965) said that the Social subscale on his Tennessee Self-Concept Scale was designed to measure "a person's sense of adequacy and worth in social interactions with other people" (p. 3). Another self-concept scale, the Texas Social Behavior Inventory (Helmreich, Stapp, & Ervin, 1974), has been viewed as measuring people's evaluations of their social skill (Blascovich & Tomaka, 1991). For example, people are assumed to have a positive social self-concept when they feel at ease with other people, feel comfortable talking to strangers, and are confident about their social competence.

In practice, the two definitions of the social self-concept probably over-lap. People who perceive themselves as more accepted by other people are likely to perceive themselves as more socially skilled. However, the defini-tion suggested by James and Cooley is inherently more specific than the al-ternative. When the social self-concept is defined in terms of social acceptance, it is natural to raise the question, acceptance by *whom?* James answered this question by saying, "A man has as many social selves as there are individuals who recognize him." James continued, "We may practically say that he has as many different social selves as there are dis-tinct groups of people about whose opinion he cares" (p. 294). For James, the social self-concept refers to people's evaluations of their acceptance by specific groups of other people. By contrast, self-evaluations of social skill do not imply, or have a necessary reference to, any specific group of other people.

We emphasize the distinction between the two definitions of the social self-concept throughout this chapter. In the first section, current measures of the social self-concept are discussed. As noted in that section, the most widely used measures are part of multidimensional self-concept scales. Many researchers have used measures that focus on people's perceptions of their social acceptance. Measures that focus on people's appraisal of their social skill have been used in fewer studies.

The second section of the chapter focuses on the relations of social self-concepts to other self-report measures. The relation of people's social self-concepts to their general self-esteem is considered first. Then the relations of social self-concepts to other facets of the multidimensional self-concept are considered. Next, measures of the social self-concept are compared with measures of other constructs that are also assessed through self-reports. The correlations of social self-concepts with some self-report measures are so strong that the discriminant validity of the measures is doubtful. In particular, self-perceptions of social acceptance seem equiva-lent to measures of loneliness. They overlap greatly with measures of per-ceived social support.

The third section of the chapter focuses on the relations of people's so-cial self-concepts to their actual social acceptance and to indicators of social competence not derived from self-reports. From one perspective, these relations show the degree to which social self-concepts are based in reality. Using Cooley's (1922) metaphor, the relations indicate whether people see themselves through a looking glass that is sharp and clear, or one that is blurred and perhaps distorted. Recent evidence confirms that the relation between perceived and actual social acceptance is far from perfect. Few researchers, however, have carefully explored the sources of the discrepancies between the two.

The third section also includes information on the relations between the social self-concepts of school-age children and their academic achievement. Several writers have suggested that students' academic achievement should relate to the academic facets of the self-concept rather than its social facets. Some research, however, has shown that students higher in achievement tend to be more accepted by peers. These findings imply that academic achievement might affect both academic and social self-concepts. A review of self-concept research indicates that students' achievement is largely unrelated to their perceptions of their peer acceptance and social skill.

The final section of the chapter focuses on some general problems in current theories and research on the social self-concept. One problem is that few writers have carefully evaluated the theoretical and practical significance of the social self-concept. All writers assume that positive social self-concepts are desirable, and a few researchers have evaluated programs to enhance the social self-concepts of children and adolescents. These programs lack a firm foundation in theories of the antecedents and consequences of variations in social self-concepts. Providing this foundation would be a worthwhile goal for future work.

MEASURING THE SOCIAL SELF-CONCEPT

The most widely used measures of the social self-concept are part of multidimensional self-concept scales. Unidimensional self-concept measures like those created by Coopersmith (1967) and Rosenberg (1965) do not provide information about people's social self-perceptions, so they are not discussed in this chapter. The social subscales on most multidimensional scales were designed for use with children and adolescents. These subscales usually assess children's and adolescents' perceptions of their social acceptance by peers. The alternative definition of the social self-concept, in terms of people's appraisal of their social skills, is also represented by several measures. Some measures of this type are part of multidimensional scales; others were designed for use on their own. These measures are discussed after those that assess perceptions of peer acceptance.

A few multidimensional scales include subscales for children's perceptions of their acceptance by parents (e.g., Harter & Pike, 1984). Those subscales are not discussed in this chapter because they are more closely linked to the family self-concept, which is discussed in Chapter 8 in this volume. In addition, the psychometric characteristics of social self-concept measures are discussed only briefly in this section. Another chapter of this *Handbook* provides a comprehensive analysis of psychometric issues relevant to all self-concept measures (Chapter 3, this volume).

Harter's Measures of the Social Self-Concept

Susan Harter has devised several multidimensional self-concept scales for use with preschool children, school-age children, adolescents, and adults (see Table 4.1). Harter (1983) argues that the content of the self-concept

TABLE 4.1   Harter's Measures of Social Acceptance

Source	Measure	Items	Sample Items	Alpha	Age Range
Harter & Pike (1984)	Pictorial Scale of Perceived Competence and Social Acceptance for Young Children (two versions)	6	1. This girl has lots of friends, BUT This girl doesn't have lots of friends 2. This boy has friends to play games with, BUT This boy doesn't have friends to play games with 3a. This girl stays overnight at friends', BUT This girl doesn't stay overnight at friends' (Preschool and Kindergarten) 3b. Others share their toys with this boy, BUT Others don't share their toys with this boy (1st and 2nd grade)	.74 to .83	Preschool to Grade 2
Harter (1982)	Social Competence subscale of the Perceived Competence Scale	7	1. Some kids find it hard to make friends, BUT For other kids it's pretty easy 2. Some kids have a lot of friends, BUT Other kids don't have very many friends 3. Some kids don't think they are a very important member of their class, BUT Other kids think they are pretty important to their classmates	.78	Grades 3–9
Harter (1985)	Social Acceptance subscale of The Self-Perception Profile for Children	6	1. Some kids find it hard to make friends, BUT Other kids find it's pretty easy to make friends 2. Some kids have a lot of friends, BUT Other kids don't have very many friends 3. Some kids would like to have a lot more friends, BUT Other kids have as many friends as they want	.75 to .80	Grades 3–8

changes as children develop. She assumes, first, that self-concepts become more differentiated with age because older children distinguish more precisely between their performance or success in different domains of life. Therefore, self-concept measures should assess more specific domains, or include more subscales, when intended for older children. For example, Harter and Pike (1984) concluded that preschool children differentiate little between their level of acceptance by peers and by mothers. Therefore, these researchers suggested that items assessing the two types of acceptance should be combined into a single scale. By contrast, Harter's (1985) scale for school-age children has a separate subscale for peer acceptance.

Second, Harter assumes that the other people whose evaluations are most significant for the social self-concept change with age. Although maternal acceptance is assessed on the scale for preschool children (Harter & Pike, 1984), it is not assessed on the scale for school-age children (Harter, 1985). Similarly, the scale for school-age children does not distinguish between friendships and acceptance by a group of peers. On the scale designed for adolescents (Harter, 1988), there are separate subscales for these two facets of peer relationships.

Third, Harter (1983) has argued that self-concept measures must be adapted to fit children's level of cognitive development. At the simplest level, items must be worded in language that children of the intended age range for a scale can easily understand. In addition, measures for children who have not yet learned to read must be administered orally. Harter also suggested that children who are not yet reading benefit when items presented orally are supplemented by pictures. Her scale for preschool and early elementary-school children (Harter & Pike, 1984) includes pictures that illustrate the contrasts between children who are high and low in self-esteem. These pictures are designed to help children select a statement (corresponding to a level of self-esteem) that best describes how they see themselves.

Finally, the examples in Table 4.1 show that Harter's measures have a somewhat unusual response format. Each item describes two types of children. For example, the first item on the Social Competence subscale (Harter, 1982) reads, "Some kids find it hard to make friends, BUT for other kids it's pretty easy." Children are instructed first to decide which type of kid is more like them. Once they have chosen one type (e.g., the kids who find it hard to make friends), they are asked to decide whether the statement about that type of kid is "sort of true" or "really true" for them. Children are credited with the most positive self-concept if they choose the positive statement and say it is really true for them; they are credited with the least positive self-concept if they choose the negative statement and say it is really true for them.

Harter (1979) suggested that the unusual response format would increase children's willingness to report their self-perceptions accurately, rather than giving what they view as socially desirable responses. Children are told explicitly that there are kids who have problems (e.g., find it hard to make friends), so they may be more willing to indicate that they have similar difficulties. However, some researchers have reported problems with the response format of Harter's measures (e.g., Marsh & Holmes, 1990). Some children misunderstand the instructions and assume they should say how much *each* of the two statements linked to a single item are true for them. They say, for example, how true it is that they find it hard to make friends, and how true it is that it's pretty easy for them.

Nevertheless, most researchers have used Harter's scales without such problems. Whether the unusual response format has important advantages is uncertain. As noted later, scores on social self-concept measures with more traditional response formats correlate strongly with comparable measures on Harter's scales, so the need for an unusual format to reduce social-desirability biases might be doubted.

The first versions of Harter's measures were devised in the late 1970s. In this review, the measures are described in order of their creation, because that order shows some subtle but significant changes in Harter's definition of the social self-concept.

The Social Competence Subscale of the Perceived Competence Scale

Harter's Perceived Competence Scale (PCS) was intended for use with students in the third through the ninth grades. Information about the reliability and validity of this scale was presented in a manual (Harter, 1979) and a later journal article (Harter, 1982). The scale includes subscales for global self-worth and for perceived competence in the cognitive, physical, and social domains.

Harter (1979) described the Social Competence subscale by saying, "The emphasis is on popularity with one's peers" (p. 1). The subscale includes one item that refers to popularity specifically ("Some kids are popular with others their own age, but other kids are not very popular"). Yet as already noted, the first item on the social subscale refers to friendship (or making friends) rather than popularity per se. The third item on the subscale, shown in Table 4.1, refers neither to friendship nor popularity explicitly. It asks whether children believe they are an important member of their class. This item seems ambiguous because children might consider themselves important for their academic performance, their athletic ability, or other skills unrelated to social acceptance. However, students apparently interpret these various items as referring to the same domain, because the internal consistency of the subscale is fairly high (see Table 4.1).

Harter (1979, 1982) reported that mean scores on the social competence subscale do not change significantly between second and ninth grade. In her samples, scores were similar for boys and girls. Other researchers have obtained similar results (e.g., Nottelman, 1987).

The Peer Acceptance Subscale of the Pictorial Scale of Perceived Competence and Social Acceptance

Harter and Pike (1984) described two versions of a pictorial self-esteem scale for use with young children. One version is for preschool children; the other is for first and second graders. Both versions are administered in individual interviews rather than in the paper-and-pencil format of the PCS. As noted earlier, the oral presentation of the items is supplemented by pictures.

Harter and Pike (1984) included separate items for children's perceptions of their acceptance by peers and by their mothers. When they did a factor analysis of young children's responses to the items, however, they found that young children did not clearly distinguish between them. Therefore, they recommended that the two types of items be combined into one subscale for social acceptance.

The peer acceptance items on the pictorial scale are more heterogeneous than those on the PCS. For example, Table 4.1 shows that one item refers neither to friendships nor to popularity but to the frequency with which peers show prosocial behavior (e.g., sharing toys) when playing with the child. Another item refers to the frequency of interaction with friends (e.g., how often a child stays overnight at a friend's house). These items seem to go beyond the boundaries of either social acceptance or social skill and, in fact, seem to be indicators of the quality and intensity of children's peer relationships. Therefore, they overlap with items used in other research to assess children's perceptions of the support they receive from peers (e.g., Dubow & Ullman, 1989). This issue is discussed explicitly later in this chapter.

Little published research on Harter and Pike's scale is available. In their original report, Harter and Pike (1984) reported that mean scores on the peer acceptance subscale changed little between 4 and 8 years of age. Harter and Pike did not mention whether boys' and girls' scores differed significantly, but Das and Berndt (1992) found no sex difference in preschoolers' scores on the peer-acceptance subscale.

The Social Acceptance Subscale of the Self-Perception Profile for Children

During the early 1980s, Harter (1985) revised the PCS and changed its title to the Self-Perception Profile for Children (SPPC). The greatest change was the addition of subscales for students' perceptions of their behavioral conduct and their physical appearance. To accommodate these additions without greatly increasing the length of the scale, she reduced each subscale from seven items to six.

The changes in the social subscale were less dramatic but still important. The name of the scale was changed from *Social Competence* to *Social Acceptance*. Harter (1985) explained that, "A closer examination of the item content, as well as interview data with children, has suggested that this subscale basically taps the degree to which the child is accepted by peers or is popular. The items do not tap competence directly in the sense that they do not refer to social skills. Rather, they tap the degree to which one has friends, feels one is popular, and feels that most kids like them" (p. 6, italics omitted). In other words, Harter recognized the distinction between the James-Cooley definition of social self-concept in terms of social acceptance and the alternative definition in terms of social skill. She further recognized that her subscale reflected the former much more than the latter.

Most items on the Social Acceptance subscale are the same or similar to those on the older Social Competence subscale of the PCS. However, the item about being "an important member of the class" was dropped. Another item about being "easy to like" was also dropped, perhaps because it did not say specifically who liked the subject (e.g., peers or adults). The remaining items refer sometimes to friendships and sometimes to popularity, as on the older scale.

Age differences in mean scores on the Social Acceptance subscale are minimal. In one study of several hundred gifted students from the 5th to the 11th grade (Cornell et al., 1990), no significant differences between the Social Acceptance scores of students in different grades were found. Another study of gifted students in the 5th through the 8th grade also showed no significant age differences (Hoge & McScheffrey, 1991).

The sex differences in mean scores on the subscale also are minimal. In two studies of gifted students (Cornell et al., 1990; Hoge & McScheffrey, 1991), sex differences were nonsignificant. Nonsignificant sex differences were also found in studies of children in low-income, single-parent families (Alessandri, 1992) and Chinese children (Meredith, Abbott, & Ming, 1992).

Self-Perceptions in Adolescence and Adulthood

Harter's scales for adolescents and for college students have been used less often by researchers. As noted already, the Self-Perception Profile for Adolescents (SPPA, Harter, 1988) includes subscales for peer acceptance and for close friendships. The scale also includes subscales for perceptions of opposite-sex romantic relationships and for perceived job competence. The addition of these subscales is consistent with Harter's hypothesis about developmental changes in the differentiation of self-concepts. The subscales also reflect Harter's beliefs about the domains of competence that are most important to general self-esteem at different stages of life.

Only a few reports of research using the SPPA have been published. In one study, adolescents with a history of grade retention scored lower than a comparison group of nonretained students on the Academic Competence subscale of the SPPA (Hagborg, Masella, Palladino, & Shepardson, 1991). However, the two groups of students did not differ in their scores on the

Social Acceptance and Close Friendship subscales. In a second study with a small sample (Lavoritano & Segal, 1992), girls had higher scores than boys on the Close Friendship subscale of the SPPA, but sex differences on the Social Acceptance subscale were nonsignificant.

Even less information is available on the Self-Perception Profile for College Students (Neeman & Harter, 1986). This scale includes subscales for domains not assessed with younger subjects (e.g., creativity). The scanty data currently available suggest that women may have higher self-concepts in the domain of close friendships, just as on the SPPA, but the available data are inconsistent (Masciuch, McRae, & Young, 1990).

In summary, Harter and her coworkers have devised many scales for assessing the self-concepts of children and adults. The scales that have been used most often are the older PCS and the newer SPPC. The Social Competence subscale on the PCS is similar to the Social Acceptance subscale on the SPPC. The name *Social Acceptance* describes the items on these subscales better than the name *Social Competence*.

Marsh's Measures of the Peer Self-Concept

Herbert Marsh has created three multidimensional self-concept measures (see Table 4.2). The measures are based on the hierarchical model of the self-concept proposed by Shavelson, Hubner, and Stanton (1976). The primary distinction in the model is between facets of the academic self-concept (e.g., reading and math) and facets of the nonacademic self-concept (e.g., physical ability and emotional states). Of the nonacademic facets, the most indicative of the social self-concept is the one that reflects relationships with peers.

Like Harter, Marsh assumes that the differentiation of the self-concept increases with age. Therefore, his measures for adolescents and adults have more subscales than those for elementary school students. In particular, the measure for young children includes a single subscale for peer relationships. The measures for adolescents and adults include separate subscales for relationships with same-sex peers and with opposite-sex peers.

Like Harter, Marsh also assumes that self-concept items for younger children must be worded more simply than those for adolescents and adults. Thus he created different measures for use with subjects in different age ranges. All measures are based on the same theoretical model, so the original measure is described more fully in the following sections than are the measures devised for adolescents and adults.

The Peer Relationships Subscale of the
Self-Description Questionnaire I (SDQI)

Marsh, Parker, and Smith (1983) created the SDQI for use with second-through ninth-grade students. In describing the measure, these researchers said little about their definition of the peer self-concept. However, an

TABLE 4.2   Marsh's Measures of Peer Acceptance

Source	Measure	Items	Sample Items	Alpha	Age Range
Marsh, Parker, & Smith (1983)	Peer Relationships subscale of the Self Description Questionnaire I (SDQI)	8	1. I have lots of friends 2. I make friends easily 3. Most kids have more friends than I do	.86	Grades 2–9
Marsh, Parker, & Barnes (1985)	Peer Relationships subscales of the Self Description Questionnaire II (SDQII)	10	1. I enjoy spending time with friends of the same sex 2. I do not get along well with girls 3. Boys often make fun of me	.86	Grades 7–11
Marsh & O'Niell (1984)	Peer Relationships subscale of the Self Description Questionnaire III (SDQIII)	10	1. I have few friends of the same sex that I can really count on 2. I don't get along very well with members of the same sex 3. I am comfortable talking to members of the same sex	.87	15 years and older

examination of the items (see Table 4.2) suggests that they intended the subscale to measure children's acceptance by peers rather than their social skill.

The peer-relationships items on the SDQI are very similar to those on the Social Acceptance subscale of Harter's (1985) SPPC. Some items refer to friendship explicitly; others that are not shown in Table 4.2 refer to popularity or liking by classmates. Marsh's items are more simply worded than Harter's, because he does not ask children to choose between statements about two types of children. In responding to Marsh's measures, children simply rate on a 5-point scale the degree to which each statement is true or false for them.

Marsh, Craven, and Debus (1991) suggested that the SDQI is appropriate for use with children as young as 5 years of age. When examining children between 5 and 8 years of age, Marsh and his colleagues did not adopt Harter and Pike's (1984) procedure of using pictures to supplement verbal items. The primary adaptation for these children was to administer items orally, during an individual interview.

Marsh et al. (1991) reported a confirmatory factor analysis of the responses by young children. Unlike the exploratory factor analysis of Harter and Pike (1984), this factor analysis suggested that even 5-year-olds differentiate between the various facets of self-concept assessed by the SDQI.

Marsh et al. (1991) argued that their results showed the advantages of confirmatory factor analysis. They also argued that the total length of the SDQI, 64 items, might be an advantage rather than a disadvantage when assessing young children's self-concepts. In their sample, the correlations among items intended to represent the same facet of the self-concept were stronger for the second half of the testing session than the first half, which suggests a practice effect in responding to the instrument. They concluded that this effect and other details of their procedure made their measure superior to Harter and Pike's (1984) scale for assessing preschoolers' self-concepts.

In Marsh et al. (1991), 8-year-olds had lower scores on the Peer Relationships subscale than 5-year-olds. Marsh (1989) reported that scores on this subscale decrease further between second and ninth grade. According to Marsh, the age change reflects a shift from unrealistically high self-concepts to more realistic views of self. This explanation is plausible, because young children's scores on most self-concept measures are near ceiling, or the maximum point on response scales. Marsh suggests that as children grow older, they begin to appraise their relative status and performance more accurately. Thus many children begin to assume, correctly, that they are not the most popular, most intelligent, and best-looking children in their class.

Marsh's hypothesis has a firm foundation in theory. In Cooley's (1922) terms, when older children evaluate themselves, they seem to use a less distorted mirror (or looking glass) than that used by younger children. Perceptions of one's reputation, social status, and performance seem to become more accurate as children grow, and the links between these perceptions and self-evaluations become stronger (Ruble, 1983).

As noted earlier, however, scores for perceived social acceptance do not decrease with age on Harter's SPPC (e.g., Cornell et al., 1990; Harter, 1982). The contrasting results are unlikely to reflect differences in item content, because scores on Harter's Social Acceptance subscale correlate strongly with those on Marsh's Peer Acceptance scale. In one sample, the correlation between the two was .68 (Marsh, 1990); in another sample the correlation was .74 (Marsh & Gouvernet, 1989). These correlations are close to the reliability of the measures (see Table 4.1), which suggests that the two measures are virtually identical.

Recall, however, that the two measures differ in their response format. The traditional format of Marsh's measure may be partly responsible for the age changes he has observed. There are consistent individual differences in people's tendencies to choose, or avoid, the extreme points on a response scale (Nunnally, 1978). The tendency to avoid the extremes is stronger in older and better educated subjects. A developmental change in this response bias might account for the modest age changes in self-concepts reported by Marsh (1989). By contrast, the nontraditional format of Harter's measures might make them less susceptible to the response bias. This speculation would be worth more careful study, because it raises questions about the theoretical and clinical significance of age changes in scores on self-concept measures.

The Same- and Opposite-Sex Peer Subscales of the Self-Description Questionnaires, II and III (SDQII and SDQIII)

Marsh's SDQII was designed for use with adolescents in the 7th through 11th grades (Marsh, Parker, & Barnes, 1985). His SDQIII was designed for use with adolescents and adults more than 15 years old (Marsh & O'Niell, 1984). Both scales, as noted earlier, include separate subscales for same-sex and for opposite-sex peer relationships.

Table 4.2 lists example items from both scales. These items are surprisingly different from those on the SDQI. The first item from the SDQII, "I enjoy spending time with friends of the same sex," refers not to adolescents' social acceptance but to their sociability. The second item, "I do not get along well with girls," is scored on the same-sex peer subscale when answered by girls and on the opposite-sex peer subscale when answered by boys. This item seems to assess self-perceptions of social skill as much as or more than social acceptance. The third item, "Boys often make fun of me," is scored on the same-sex scale when answered by boys and the opposite-sex scale when answered by girls. This item refers explicitly to aggression received from peers rather than to social acceptance.

The SDQIII items are explicitly worded in terms of same- and opposite-sex peer relationships, so their scoring does not depend on the sex of the subject responding to them. However, some items again refer to social skill while others refer to social acceptance. Of the examples in Table 4.2, those concerning how well a person gets along with peers and how comfortable a person is when talking to peers seem to assess self-perceptions of social skill. The other item in the table, concerning the number of dependable friends that a person has, seems to assess perceptions of social acceptance.

Table 4.2 also shows that the internal consistency of the peer subscales on the SDQII and SDQIII is high. The high degree of internal consistency might suggest that the distinction between self-concept measures focusing on social acceptance and on social skill is unimportant. However, this issue is so important theoretically that researchers should examine it more directly by comparing unidimensional measures of both types of self-concept measures. Researchers should not only examine the correlation between them, but also see how they correlate with other measures.

On the SDQII and SDQIII, subjects' reports of their same- and opposite-sex relationships are only modestly correlated. Marsh et al. (1985) reported that scores on the Same-Sex and Opposite-Sex Peer subscales of the SDQII correlated .21. On the SDQIII, the correlation among the comparable subscales was .34 in a sample of high school girls and .21 in a sample of college students (Marsh & O'Niell, 1984). These low correlations strengthen the argument that the two facets of peer relationships should be assessed separately, at least during adolescence and young adulthood.

Age and sex differences in responses to the subscales have been inconsistent. Marsh (1989) reported irregular changes between 7th and 11th grade in scores on the Same-Sex Peer scale of the SDQII. Scores on the Same-Sex Peer scale of the SDQIII decreased linearly after 15 years of age, but the decrease accounted for less than 1% of the variance in subjects' scores. Marsh (1989) also reported higher scores for girls than boys on the Same-Sex Peer scale of the SDQII, higher scores for boys than girls on the (single) Peer subscale of the SDQI, and no sex difference in scores on the SDQIII. The inconsistencies suggest that boys and girls respond similarly to the social items on the Self-Description Questionnaires.

Bracken's Social Subscale on the Multidimensional Self Concept Scale

Recently, Bracken (1992) published a detailed manual for a new self-concept scale. His Multidimensional Self Concept Scale (MSCS) differs in several ways from those devised by Harter and Marsh. First, he assumes that the same facets of the self-concept are important throughout middle childhood and adolescence. Therefore, instead of creating different measures for different age ranges, he created a single measure, written at a third-grade reading level, for students from 9 to 19 years of age. Second, his scale includes more items for each facet of the self-concept than Harter's and Marsh's scales. The scale has subscales for six facets of the self-concept—academic, affect, competence, family, physical, and social—and each subscale has 25 items. Because of their lengths, these subscales generally have greater internal consistency than do the corresponding subscales on Harter's and Marsh's measures.

Third, and most important for this chapter, Bracken's Social subscale does not focus on social acceptance by peers. Table 4.3 shows the first three items on the subscale. Many of the items, such as the second example in the table, assess self-evaluations of social relationships with people in general rather than peers specifically. In the manual for the scale, Bracken (1992) explained the reason for this decision explicitly. He stated that the social scale could be divided into subscales on social relationships with male peers, female peers, parents, and other categories of people, "but such minute discriminations would likely allow little environmental generalization, tend to be assessed less reliably, and significantly increase the length of the scale" (p. 13).

The items in Table 4.3 also suggest that the social self-concept is operationally defined on the MSCS by a combination of perceived social acceptance and perceived social skill. The item, "People do not seem interested in talking with me," reflects social acceptance. The items "I am usually a

TABLE 4.3   Other Measures of the Social Self-Concept

Source	Measure	Items	Sample Items	Alpha	Age Range
Bracken (1992)	Social subscale of the Multidimensional Self Concept Scale (MSCS)	25	1. I am usually a lot of fun to be with 2. People do not seem interested in talking with me 3. I am too shy	.88 to .92	9–19 years
Fitts (1965)	Social subscale of the Tennessee Self-Concept Scale (TSCS)	18	1. I am a friendly person 2. I am popular with men 3. I am not interested in what other people do	.89 to .94	12 years and older
Helmreich, Stapp, & Ervin (1974)	Texas Social Behavior Inventory (TSBI)	16	1. I would describe myself as self-confident 2. I am not likely to speak to people until they speak to me 3. I feel confident of my appearance	.92	18 years and older

lot of fun to be with" and "I am too shy" reflect social skill. Other items assess perceived popularity or social acceptance directly (e.g., "Most people like me") or assess the characteristics of a person's friendship (e.g., "I get a lot of phone calls from friends"). A few items refer specifically to relationships with the opposite sex (e.g., "I feel desired by members of the opposite sex"). A few refer to how a child is treated by other people (e.g., "People pick on me"). Taken together, these items ask people to report both on their social standing and on their competence in social interactions.

In a sample of fifth and sixth graders (Delugach, Bracken, Bracken, & Schicke, 1992), scores on the Social subscale of the MSCS correlated above .80 with those on the Peer Relationships subscale of the SDQI. In a second sample, somewhat lower correlations were found between the MSCS Social subscale and the subscales for Same- and Opposite-Sex Peer Relationships on the SDQII. In both samples, scores on the MSCS Social subscale varied little with age or sex. Age and sex differences in scores on the Social subscale also were minimal in the standardization sample for the scale (Bracken, 1992).

Measures of the Social Self-Concept of Adults

The oldest measure of the social self-concept in widespread use is the Social subscale on the Tennessee Self-Concept Scale (TSCS). The scale was originally published by Fitts in 1965. A revised version of the manual was published by Roid and Fitts in 1988. The Social subscale is intended to measure people's perceptions of their social skill. Several items are similar to those on standard personality inventories. Examples from Table 4.3 include "I am a friendly person," and "I am not interested in what other people do." Other items refer explicitly to people's evaluations of their social competence. Examples include "I am satisfied with the way I treat other people," and "I should be more polite to others."

Although the TSCS was designed for use with individuals as young as 12 years old, its primary use has been with adults. In one sample of adults, scores on the original Social subscale correlated .61 and .59 with the Same- and Opposite-Sex Peer subscales of the SDQIII (Marsh & Richards, 1988). However, other researchers have rarely focused on the Social subscale. They have instead used the mean scores across all subscales of the TSCS as a general measure of self-esteem (Blascovich & Tomaka, 1991).

One final measure of the social self-concept, the Texas Social Behavior Inventory (TSBI), was devised by Helmreich, Stapp, and Ervin (1974). The scale is at the opposite extreme from those by Harter and Marsh, because the items refer hardly at all to a person's social acceptance. As Table 4.3 shows, the items assess self-perceptions of social competence and ease in social interactions. This emphasis is so pronounced that Blascovich and Tomaka (1991) questioned whether the scale measures self-esteem or social skill. Stated differently, examination of this scale raises questions about the distinction between self-concept measures and other kinds of self-report measures. In particular, what makes a measure of the social self-concept different from a self-report measure of social skill, or self-reports on one's social relationships? This question is one focus of the next section.

RELATIONS OF SOCIAL SELF-CONCEPTS TO OTHER KINDS OF SELF-REPORTS

Many questions about the social self-concept can be addressed by correlating measures of this construct with other self-report measures. As just mentioned, the relations of self-concept measures to other kinds of self-reports can be useful in defining the social self-concept and showing how it differs from other types of self-perceptions. Before examining other kinds of self-reports, however, it is useful to examine the relations of social self-concepts to other facets of the self-concept and to general self-esteem.

The Social Self-Concept and Other Facets of the Self-Concept

The multidimensional scales of Harter, Marsh, and Bracken are all based on the assumption that different facets of the self-concept are somewhat independent. Marsh's Self-Description Questionnaires are based on the added assumption, from the model of Shavelson et al. (1976), that self-concept facets are arranged in a hierarchy. In this model, academic facets of the self-concept are distinguished from nonacademic facets. For example, students' evaluations of their performance in reading and in math, two academic subjects, should be more strongly related to each other than they are to self-evaluations in nonacademic areas, such as the social domain.

Evidence on the intercorrelations of self-concept subscales not only can test the degree to which self-concept facets are hierarchically arranged but can also shed light on the origins of the social self-concept. For example, if measures of the social self-concept are strongly related to measures of perceived athletic competence, then success in sports might be assumed to enhance a person's social success.

Harter (1982) reported intercorrelations among the subscales of the PCS that are consistent with both these assumptions. Students' scores on the Social subscale were strongly correlated with those on the Physical subscale, which measures perceptions of ability and performance in athletics. Scores on the Social subscale were less strongly correlated with those for perceived cognitive competence. However, the correlations of the Social and Cognitive subscales were moderate, around .30. These data indicate that students who perceive themselves as more accepted by peers also tend to perceive themselves as intelligent and good at schoolwork.

Later research has largely confirmed Harter's (1982) findings. Researchers have found strong correlations between measures of perceived social acceptance and measures of perceived physical or athletic competence (e.g., Harter, 1985; Marsh & Gouvernet, 1989; Marsh & Holmes, 1990). In one study (Boivin & Begin, 1989), the correlation between the two subscales on the PCS was so strong that the researchers concluded the subscales lacked discriminant validity. The correlation between the Social and Cognitive subscales is usually lower, although in some samples these correlations are above .40 (Harter, 1985; Marsh & Holmes, 1990).

With Harter's SPPC, perceived social acceptance can be correlated with perceived athletic competence and with perceived physical appearance. In some of Harter's (1985) samples, children's perceptions of their social acceptance were more strongly correlated with their perceived athletic competence than with their perceived physical appearance, but there were exceptions and the differences were slight. In another study (Boivin, Vitaro, & Gagnon, 1992), both correlations were strong, but the correlation of social acceptance with athletic competence was stronger than that with physical appearance.

Marsh's SDQI has comparable subscales for peer relationships, physical abilities, physical appearance, and academic self-concepts, so the same questions about the intercorrelations among subscales can be examined. Marsh and his colleagues have presented these intercorrelations in many publications (e.g., Marsh, Barnes, Cairns, & Tidman, 1984; Marsh et al., 1991; Marsh & Gouvernet, 1989; Marsh, Smith, Barnes, & Butler, 1983), so general patterns are easy to identify.

As on Harter's measures, scores for the social self-concept (perceived peer relationships) are strongly correlated with those for perceived physical or athletic abilities and perceived physical appearance. The correlation between the Social and Physical Abilities subscales is stronger in some samples than that between the Social and Physical Appearance subscales, but the opposite is true in other samples. Taken together, the data suggest that students who view themselves as more accepted by peers also view themselves as more athletically competent and more physically attractive. Moreover, these judgments usually have a basis in reality. Popular children and adolescents typically have greater athletic ability and are more physically attractive than unpopular children and adolescents (Hartup, 1983; Savin-Williams, 1987).

On Marsh's measures, the correlations between the social and the academic facets of the self-concept are consistently lower than those among academic facets (e.g., perceptions of reading and math achievement). The correlations between social and academic self-concepts are not zero, although they seem to be lower than the corresponding correlations on Harter's PCS and SPPC (see, e.g., Marsh & Gouvernet, 1989). These moderate relations between social and academic self-concepts probably have a basis in reality, too. More popular children and adolescents are typically higher in academic achievement than their less popular classmates (Coie & Krehbiel, 1984; Wentzel & Erdley, 1993).

The pattern of intercorrelations for Harter's and Marsh's scales may not hold for other self-concept measures. Bracken (1992) reported that scores on the Social subscale of his MSCS are most strongly correlated with scores on his Competence and Affect subscales ($rs > .60$). The correlation between the Social and Physical Appearance subscales is high (.53), but not as high as for the former subscales.

Recall that the Social subscale on the MSCS differs from those on Harter's and Marsh's measures because it focuses on a combination of social skills and peer acceptance rather than peer acceptance per se. Bracken's Social scale overlaps to a greater extent with traditional items on personality inventories. The items on the Competence subscale (e.g., "I am honest") and the Affect subscale (e.g., "I feel insecure") also overlap with self-reports of personality traits. This overlap probably accounts for the pattern of intercorrelations among subscales.

The Social Self-Concept and General Self-Esteem

Hierarchical models of the self-concept (Harter, 1983; Shavelson et al., 1976) imply that self-evaluations in specific domains are aggregated in some way to form a general self-concept. Evidence regarding this aggregation process can be obtained by correlating specific self-concept subscales with measures of general self-esteem. In particular, correlations between measures of the social self-concept and of general self-esteem can suggest how much self-evaluations of social success affect people's overall sense of self-worth.

Harter (1993) stated that general self-esteem is most strongly related to self-perceptions of physical appearance. In her view, children and adolescents who feel they are good-looking, or who are most happy about their physical appearance, are also likely to have high general self-esteem. Children and adolescents who are not happy with the way they look are likely to have low general self-esteem. Thus, according to Harter, perceptions of physical appearance matter more for general self-esteem than do perceptions of social acceptance.

Evidence regarding the relations of self-concepts in specific domains to general self-esteem is not consistent. In the manual for the SPPC, Harter (1985) reported that scores for students' global self-worth correlated above .60 with scores for their perceived physical appearance, but only between .45 and .60 with scores for their perceived social acceptance. Li (1988) and Boivin et al. (1992) reported the same pattern. However, Boivin and his colleagues suggested a different explanation for the pattern than Harter did. They noted that the SPPC items for physical appearance and for global self-worth are worded similarly. For example, one item on the Physical Appearance subscale asks how happy kids are with the way they look. One item on the Global Self-Worth subscale asks how happy kids are with themselves as a person. Children who are not reading the items carefully may respond to them similarly not because their physical appearance strongly affects their general self-esteem, but merely because the items seem the same to them.

In other research with Harter's measures, children's general self-esteem was more strongly related to their perceived social acceptance than to their perceived physical appearance. This pattern was reported by Hoge and McScheffrey (1991) for a large sample of gifted children in the fifth to eighth grades, and by Marsh and Holmes (1990) with a more representative sample of students in the fifth grade.

Research with Marsh's questionnaires has also yielded data on the correlations between general and specific facets of the self-concept. As with Harter's measures, patterns have varied across studies. In one study with the SDQI (Marsh & Gouvernet, 1989), the General subscale was more strongly related to that for Peer Relationships than for Physical Appearance. The opposite pattern was found in a second study (Marsh & Holmes, 1990). In other studies (Marsh, Smith, & Barnes, 1983; Marsh et al., 1991), the correlations for the two subscales were about equal.

Limited data are also available on the correlations among subscales of the SDQII and SDQIII. In one sample that was given the SDQII (Marsh et al., 1985), general self-concepts were more strongly related to perceived physical appearance than to perceptions of same- and opposite-sex peer relationships. In studies with the SDQIII, the correlations of general self-concepts with perceived physical appearance and with same- and opposite-sex peer relationships were similar (Marsh, 1986; Marsh & O'Niell, 1984).

Before drawing conclusions about the relations of social self-concepts to general self-esteem, an alternative approach to the issue should be mentioned. The alternative approach derives from a hypothesis of William James (1890), who argued that the relation of success in any domain to a person's sense of overall worth depends on the importance that the person attaches to success in specific domains.

James illustrated his hypothesis with a much-quoted example. He said:

> So we have the paradox of a man shamed to death because he is only the second pugilist or the second oarsman in the world. That he is able to beat the whole population of the globe minus one is nothing; he has "pitted" himself to beat that one; and as long as he doesn't do that nothing else counts . . . Yonder puny fellow, however, whom every one can beat, suffers no chagrin about it, for he has long ago abandoned the attempt to "carry that line," as the merchants say, of self at all. (p. 310)

In terms of this chapter, James's (1890) hypothesis is that the correlation of people's social self-concept to their general self-esteem should depend on the importance that they attach to success in social life. The correlation should be strong only for people who greatly value their social standing or social acceptance.

This hypothesis seems sensible, but empirical research has provided little support for it. In two large-scale studies, Marsh (1986, 1993) examined how well people's general self-esteem could be predicted from their self-evaluations in specific domains such as social life and academics. He systematically tested whether the prediction of self-esteem could be improved by taking into account the importance that individuals said they attached to specific domains. These tests showed little or no improvement in the prediction of self-esteem when individuals' importance ratings were taken into account. Marsh (1993) also discussed previous research that had yielded findings interpreted as supporting James's hypothesis. Marsh concluded that the previous research was flawed either in its design or in the analyses of the data.

Finally, Marsh (1993) suggested why James's hypothesis has not been confirmed by empirical research. As the earlier quotation implies, James was thinking of domains of human achievement whose importance varies greatly across individuals. Some people set a goal of being great pugilists, but most do not. Some set a goal of being great oarsmen, but most do not. By contrast, the domains assessed in modern self-concept measures are much broader and, therefore, are important to virtually all people. Almost all of us care whether we have friends and are liked by other people; almost all of us care whether we are good at academic tasks and are viewed by other people as physically attractive. In this sense, modern self-concept measures are not the most appropriate for testing James's hypothesis. The measures are appropriate for showing the limits of the hypothesis and, conversely, the types of self-perceptions that affect nearly all people's general self-evaluations.

Taken together, previous research suggests that physical appearance is strongly related to general self-esteem, but so is acceptance by peers. Correlation of perceived physical appearance with general self-esteem may partly reflect an artifact of similarities in item wording. Without these similarities, perceptions of social acceptance might be the strongest correlate of general self-esteem. Stated more boldly, one possible interpretation of previous research is that individuals' appraisals of their social self affect their general self-esteem more than any other facet of the self-concept.

The Social Self-Concept and Related Self-Reports

Many writers have discussed the possible effects of people's social self-concepts on their social interactions and social relationships (e.g., Harter, 1993; Hymel & Franke, 1985). These discussions are rarely based on, or linked to, an explicit theory of self-concepts and their effects. However, the guiding assumption in most discussions seems to be a version of the well-known hypothesis of the self-fulfilling prophecy (e.g., Fiske & Taylor, 1984).

People have low social self-concepts, by one definition, when they believe that they are not accepted by other people. These people are likely to assume that other people will behave negatively toward them. This prophecy becomes self-fulfilling when it leads to negative behavior, caused by anxiety or anger, toward other people. Their negative behavior reduces other people's willingness to interact with them, and so reduces their opportunities for practicing their social skills. The net result of these processes is that people with low social self-concepts are persistently lonely and avoid or behave inappropriately in social situations.

This unhappy portrait of individuals with low social self-concepts may be accurate, but it is difficult to examine rigorously. One major problem in studying the effects of social self-concepts was addressed indirectly by Nicholls, Licht, and Pearl (1982). They wrote a provocative article with the title, "Some Dangers of Using Personality Questionnaires to Study Personality." The central message of the article was that the standard measures of supposedly different constructs, such as masculinity and self-esteem, often include the same or very similar items. Therefore, when researchers say that masculine individuals have high self-esteem, they may simply be saying that people who describe themselves as self-confident when completing a masculinity scale also describe themselves as self-confident when completing a self-esteem scale. In short, the correlations between measures of personality constructs with different *labels* are misleading, or meaningless, when those measures have very similar *items*.

The same problem exists in research on the possible effects of social self-concepts. Many researchers have correlated measures of the social self-concept with measures of other constructs that are also assessed by self-reports and that have similar items. Several measures whose items overlap with those on measures of the social self-concept are listed in Table 4.4.

Perhaps the greatest overlap exists between social self-concept and loneliness measures. The Loneliness scale of Asher, Hymel, and Renshaw (1984) was designed to assess children's feelings about their peer relations, or their happiness with their social situation. Table 4.4 lists the first three items on the scale. The first item, "It's hard for me to make friends," is virtually identical, except for response format, to the first item on the social competence subscale of the PCS (see Table 4.1). The other two items in Table 4.4 do not match items on the PCS (or the SPPC) as closely. However, an exact match for all items would be impossible because the loneliness measure has 16 items and Harter's measure has only 7. Our inspection of the two scales suggested that 6 of the 7 items on Harter's scale have close equivalents on the scale created by Asher et al. (1984).

This similarity between the two scales suggests that they should be strongly correlated. In two studies with third through fifth grade students (Dubow & Ullman, 1989; Hymel, Rubin, Rowden, & LeMare, 1990), the correlations between the scales were above .70. These correlations are very close to the reliability of the shorter measure, the Social subscale of the PCS (see Table 4.1). The correlations suggest that the two measures lack discriminant validity. In simpler terms, both are measuring the same construct.

Asher et al. (1984) described their scale as measuring not loneliness by itself, but loneliness and social dissatisfaction. This label suggests why the overlap with social self-concepts is so great. The most common definition of the social self-concept emphasizes people's perceptions of their social acceptance. People who view themselves as low in social acceptance are also likely to report dissatisfaction with their social relationships.

Great overlap also exists between social self-concepts and measures of perceived social support. During the past 20 years, researchers have done hundreds of studies of the effects of supportive social relationships on people's physical and mental health (see Belle, 1989; Sarason, Sarason, & Pierce, 1990). The central measure in most studies is derived from people's reports about whether they have other people on whom they can rely for help and advice. In other words, self-reports are used to assess people's access to, or involvement in, supportive social relationships.

Many measures of social support have items similar to those used to assess social self-concepts. Table 4.4 lists the first three items on Dubow and Ullman's (1989) measure of perceived support from friends. Other items on the measure are even more similar to those on self-concept measures that assess perceived social acceptance. It is not surprising, then, that the

TABLE 4.4   Other Measures of Social Perception

Source	Measure	Items	Sample Items	Alpha	Age Group
Asher, Hymel, & Renshaw (1984)	Questionnaire for Perceived Loneliness and Social Dissatisfaction	16	1. It's hard for me to make friends 2. I have nobody to talk to 3. I'm good at working with other children	.90	Grades 3–6
Connolly (1989)	Adolescent Social Self-Efficacy Scale	25	1. How easy is it for you to start a conversation with a boy or girl you don't know very well? 2. How easy is it for you to express your opinion to a group of kids discussing a topic which is of interest to you? 3. How easy is it for you to join a group of kids in the school cafeteria for lunch?	.90 to .95	Grades 6–12
Dubow & Ullman (1989)	Peer Support Subscale of the Social Support Appraisals Scale	15	1. Do you feel left out by your friends? 2. Are you well-liked by your friends? 3. Do you get picked on or teased by your friends?	.91	Grades 3–5
Wheeler & Ladd (1982)	Children's Self-Efficacy for Peer Interaction Scale	22	1. Some kids want to play a game. Asking them if you can play is *easy/hard* for you 2. Some kids are arguing about how to play a game. Telling them the rules is *easy/hard* for you 3. Some kids are teasing your friend. Telling them to stop is *easy/hard* for you	.85	Grades 3–5

correlation of perceived friends' support with the Social subscale on Harter's PCS is greater than .50 (Dubow & Ullman, 1989).

Similar findings have been reported in studies of adults. Cuffel and Akamatsu (1989) analyzed responses on several measures including the UCLA Loneliness Scale, the TSBI, and measures of social relationships. They concluded, "Loneliness and, to a certain extent, social self-esteem may be best characterized by subjective levels of satisfaction with casual and close friendships" (p. 470). One implication that might be drawn from this statement is that all three types of measures assess the same construct.

Harter (1993) drew a similar conclusion about the connections between low self-esteem, depression, and feelings of hopelessness. She said the correlations between measures of these constructs are so strong that they cannot be distinguished from one another. Consequently, it makes no sense to ask whether low self-esteem causes depression and hopelessness or vice versa. The three measures are inextricably intertwined, so which is cause and which is effect cannot be determined.

Our analysis suggests that the same conclusion should be drawn about the connections between low social self-concepts, loneliness, and perceptions of a general lack of support from peers. Hypotheses about the causal links among these three cannot be tested and should not even be advanced. Although different labels are attached to the three types of measures, the labels merely reflect the origins of the measures in different theoretical and research traditions. Viewed from the most important perspective, that of individual items, the measures do not differ in important ways.

Strictly speaking, our conclusion holds only for measures of the social self-concept that assess perceptions of social acceptance. However, comparable issues arise with social self-concept measures that assess people's perceptions of their social skill. These measures overlap with ones designed explicitly to assess social skill or social competence through self-reports.

Wheeler and Ladd (1982) created the self-report measure of Children's Self-Efficacy for Peer Interaction. The first item on this measure, shown in Table 4.4, refers to a child's ability to approach a group of peers and ask to join their game. This item differs from those on social self-concept measures that focus on social acceptance, but it is similar to items on other self-concept measures. Table 4.3 shows that Bracken's (1992) MSCS includes the item, "I am too shy." Table 4.3 also shows that the TSBI includes the item, "I am not likely to speak to people until they speak to me." Because of these similarities, strong correlations might be expected between these measures of the social self-concept and self-report measures of social skill.

In one study (Ladd & Price, 1986), the correlation between the Social subscale on Harter's PCS and the Self-Efficacy scale of Wheeler and Ladd (1982) was only .29. By contrast, when Connolly (1989) adapted Wheeler and Ladd's scale for use with adolescents, she found its correlation with the Social subscale on the PCS was greater than .60 in one sample.

In another study (Buhrmester, Furman, Wittenberg, & Reis, 1988), college students' scores on the TSBI were correlated with their scores on a new self-report measure of interpersonal competence. The new measure was designed to assess five domains of interpersonal competence, from initiating relationships to managing interpersonal conflicts. Students'

TSBI scores were significantly correlated with their scores on the five domains of competence. The multiple correlation between TSBI and interpersonal-competence scores was .71. In discussing this high correlation, the researchers concluded, "Taken together, the [interpersonal competence] scales capture most of what is assessed by the TSBI" (p. 1003).

Of course, this overlap between measures need not be seen as a problem. The overlap may simply clarify the interpretation of data on the social self-concept. Still, a critic might argue that measures of the social self-concept are less useful, because less well-defined, than measures of perceived social support or perceived social skill.

RELATIONS OF SOCIAL SELF-CONCEPTS TO SOCIAL ACCEPTANCE AND COMPETENCE

The early theories of James (1890) and Cooley (1922) suggest that people's social self-concepts should be strongly related to their actual social position or social acceptance. For James, the actual recognition that a person receives from other people should determine how favorably the person sees himself or herself. For Cooley, other people are the looking glass in which a person sees his or her reflection.

The degree to which empirical data support the hypotheses of James and Cooley has been debated. After reviewing previous research, Shrauger and Schoeneman (1979) concluded, "There is no consistent agreement between people's self-perceptions and how they are actually viewed by others" (p. 549). However, research reported since their review suggests that this conclusion is overly negative. Significant relations exist not only between social self-concepts and actual social acceptance, but also between social self-concept and some aspects of peer reputation and social competence.

Perceived Social Acceptance and Actual Acceptance by Peers

Table 4.5 summarizes recent studies of the relation between social self-concept and actual social acceptance. The studies are ordered by the age or grade in school of the subjects in a study. No studies involved adults, probably for two reasons. First, the social self-concept measures that researchers have used most often in recent years—those from Harter's PCS or SPPC—are only suitable for school-age children and adolescents. Second, and more important, research on children's social acceptance has flourished recently, as researchers have tried to identify the possible negative effects of a lack of peer acceptance during childhood (Asher & Coie, 1990; Parker & Asher, 1987). Social acceptance is also easier to study in childhood or adolescence than in adulthood, because the social groups in which adults participate are more diverse and less easy to contact for research purposes than are the classmates of school-age children.

TABLE 4.5   Correlations between Social Self-Concept and
Actual Social Acceptance

Study	Grade Level of Subjects	N	Self-Concept Measure	Actual Competence Measure	Correlation
Das & Berndt (1992)	Preschool	59	Pictorial Scale of Perceived Competence and Social Acceptance	Ratings of Liking	.23 (boys) .04 (girls)
Harter & Pike (1984)	Preschool–2	255	Pictorial Scale of Perceived Competence and Social Acceptance	Teacher Ratings on Same Items	.06
Boivin, Vitaro, & Gagnon (1992)	2 3 4	466 350 274	Harter's SPPC	Social Preference Scores	.27 .32 .38
Hymel, Rubin, Rowden, & LeMare (1990)	2 5	87 87	Harter's PCS	Ratings of Liking	.27 .31
Kurdek & Krile (1982)	3–5 4–5 6–7 6–8	115 54 49 102	Harter's PCS	Social Preference Scores	.09 .54 .26 .18
Ladd & Price (1986)	3 4 5	36 37 41	Harter's PCS	Positive Nominations & Ratings of Liking	.14 & .04; .25 & .24; .56 & .48
Harter (1982)	4–6	85	Harter's PCS	Ratings of Liking	.59
Cornell et al. (1990)	5–6 7–11	281 184	Harter's SPPC	Social Preference Scores	.42 (boys), .26 (girls); .39 (boys), .29 (girls)
Bohrnstedt & Felson (1993)	6–8	415	Two Questions Provided by Experimenters	Positive Nominations	.26 (girls); .42 (boys)
Cauce (1987)	7	89	Harter's SPPC	Positive Nominations	.44
Chambliss, Muller, Hulnick, & Wood (1978)	7–9	93	Self Descriptive Questionnaire	Ratings of Liking	.29

For all studies listed in Table 4.5, the social self-concept was defined in terms of peer acceptance, not a self-appraisal of social skill. Actual peer acceptance was assessed most often with sociometric techniques. Sociometry, or measurement of social relationships, originated in the 1930s with the work of Moreno (1934). Currently, the standard procedure for assessing peer acceptance is to ask groups of students to name three classmates whom they especially like and three classmates whom they especially dislike. Then the number of positive nominations and negative nominations received by each student in the group is calculated. Next, a social-preference score is computed by subtracting the number of negative nominations received by each child from the positive nominations that the child received. This difference score, standardized to take account of differences between the number of students in different classrooms, is defined as a measure of children's social preference (Bukowski & Hoza, 1989).

In some studies, researchers obtained only positive nominations (asking whom children liked or with whom they were friends), not negative nominations. In some studies, researchers asked children to use a multipoint scale to rate how much they liked or disliked each of their classmates. These variations in the assessment of social acceptance are indicated in Table 4.5, although they seem not to have an important effect on the relations between social self-concepts and social preference.

The relations between perceived and actual acceptance by peers are lowest for preschool children. Harter and Pike (1984) reported a nonsignificant correlation between preschoolers' ratings of their acceptance by peers and teachers' ratings of the preschoolers' peer acceptance, even though teachers made their ratings on the same items that the preschoolers answered. Das and Berndt (1992) found nonsignificant correlations between preschoolers' scores on the Harter and Pike peer subscale and actual ratings of liking by peers. These findings might be taken as evidence that preschoolers are poor at judging how much they are accepted by peers. Another possibility is that Harter and Pike's (1984) peer subscale is low in validity, so it underestimates the relations between perceived and actual acceptance.

The hypothesis that the findings reflect preschoolers' immaturity, not defects in measurement, is supported by other evidence that young children have difficulty accurately comparing themselves with peers (Ruble, 1983). Improvements in children's ability to make social comparisons would be expected to increase the relation between their perceived social acceptance and their actual acceptance by peers. As Table 4.5 shows, both Ladd and Price (1986) and Boivin et al. (1992) reported data consistent with this hypothesis. In these studies, however, the age differences in the correlations were small, and probably not statistically significant.

The correlation between perceived and actual peer acceptance seems to vary as much across samples and measures as it varies with age. These variations are most obvious, in Table 4.5, for the samples assessed by Kurdek and Krile (1982). Moreover, among seventh graders and older adolescents, perceived and actual acceptance by peers are no more strongly related than among elementary school students. Age differences in the correlation between perceived and actual acceptance were small even when students of different ages were assessed with the same procedures (e.g., Cornell et al., 1990). In sum, current evidence does not suggest that the correspondence between self-perceptions and actual peer acceptance increases or decreases regularly with age.

Table 4.5 also includes data from a few studies in which the correlation between perceived and actual acceptance was computed separately for boys and for girls. In each sample, the correlation was stronger for boys than girls. Because of small sample sizes, however, the sex differences in the correlations are not significant. Further research on this issue might confirm that boys' self-reports of their acceptance by peers match their actual acceptance somewhat more closely than is true for girls. Yet until more evidence is available, conclusions on this issue would be premature.

Not reported in Table 4.5 are a few studies in which researchers compared children's social self-concepts with their sociometric status. For these studies, children were classified into categories of sociometric status based on their social preference score and on the total number of positive and negative nominations they received from peers (Coie, Dodge, & Coppotelli, 1982). Children were classified as (a) popular if they were high in social preference and received many nominations, (b) rejected if they were low in social preference and received many negative nominations, (c) neglected if their social preference score was near zero because they received few positive or negative nominations, (d) controversial if their social-preference score was near zero but they received many positive and negative nominations, or (e) average, if they did not fit into any of the previous groups.

In one study with a small sample (Rubin, Hymel, LeMare, & Rowden, 1989), mean scores on the Social subscale of the PCS did not differ significantly for popular, average, neglected, and rejected children. In another study with a larger sample (Boivin & Begin, 1989), popular children had higher scores on the Social subscale of the PCS than average children. As in the first study, neglected children's social self-concepts did not differ significantly from those of average children. Most important, one subgroup of rejected children had lower scores for their social self-concepts than average children, but another subgroup had scores similar to those of average children.

In a third study with an even larger sample (Patterson, Kupersmidt, & Griesler, 1990), only neglected children had scores on the Social Acceptance subscale of the SPPC that differed from those of average children. However, the researchers then standardized children's scores on the Social

Acceptance subscale. They also standardized ratings of liking that children received from peers. Comparisons of the two standardized scores showed significant differences for most sociometric-status groups. For rejected children, the scores for perceived acceptance were significantly higher than those for actual liking by peers. For popular and average children, the scores for perceived acceptance were significantly lower than those for liking.

Patterson et al. (1990) concluded that rejected children overestimate their peer acceptance while popular and average children underestimate it. This conclusion may be correct, but other interpretations of the findings are possible. Boivin and Begin (1989) suggested that some rejected children may have positive social self-concepts because they have good relationships with peers outside their classroom. These children may not be well accepted by their classmates, but they may have good friends in their neighborhood, on athletic teams, or in other groups. Therefore, they are not overestimating their peer acceptance when they report positive social self-concepts. Instead, they are thinking about their acceptance by different peers than those who complete the supposedly objective measure of their peer acceptance.

To avoid this problem, Bohrnstedt and Felson (1983) used more specific measures of perceived and actual acceptance than is customary. These researchers asked students in the sixth to eighth grades to name the other students in their fourth-period class whom they liked best. Then they asked the students to report how much they were liked by the other students in the same fourth-period class. An analogous procedure was used by Chambliss, Muller, Hulnick, and Wood (1978). With this procedure, students' perceptions of their acceptance are assessed for the same reference group as for the measure of actual acceptance.

Table 4.5 shows that in these two studies the correlation between perceived and actual peer acceptance was significant but modest, just as in other studies with more traditional measures. Unfortunately, children were not classified into social-status groups in the two studies. Therefore, whether the modest correlation was due partly to rejected children's overestimating their peer acceptance, or popular children underestimating it, cannot be determined.

Previous research has shown that discrepancies between perceived and actual acceptance by peers may have many sources (John & Robins, 1994; Shrauger & Schoeneman, 1979). To some extent, discrepancies are inevitable because of random error or unreliability of measurement. In addition, self-perceptions may be systematically biased. A self-enhancement bias, or a desire to see oneself positively, can make self-perceptions more positive than objective indicators. For example, rejected children may be unwilling to admit that they are disliked by many of their classmates. Conversely, a bias toward modesty can make self-perceptions less positive than objective indicators. Popular children, for example, may choose to view themselves as less outstanding in their peer group than they actually are (Patterson et al., 1990).

Tendencies toward self-enhancement or modesty may be affected not only by children's social status, but also by their personality traits. John and Robins (1994) discovered that self-enhancement biases are greatest for people high in narcissism. People low in narcissism are likely to show modesty or self-diminishment biases. In addition, Bohrnstedt and Felson (1983) discovered that adolescents perceive their social acceptance more positively when they are higher in general self-esteem. Adolescents' perceptions of their social acceptance are also more positive when they are higher in athletic ability. These findings imply that people's perceptions of their social acceptance are not determined solely by their actual acceptance. People who feel generally more positive about themselves, or more positive about specific areas of competence, may attach some of that rosy glow to their perceptions of social acceptance.

Finally, the discussion thus far has been based on an implicit assumption that people receive unambiguous information about their social acceptance, and then incorporate either an accurate or a distorted version of that information into their self-concepts. However, the information that most people receive is limited and often distorted. Stated in terms of Cooley's (1922) metaphor, most people see themselves in a looking glass that provides a dim, blurred, and selective reflection.

People low in social acceptance are especially likely to see themselves in a flawed mirror (Shrauger & Schoeneman, 1979). Norms of politeness dictate that people don't directly tell other people that they dislike them. Disliked individuals may also misinterpret the feedback they receive, assuming that other people dislike some of their actions but do not dislike them personally. Moreover, individuals who are disliked often change their pattern of social interaction to minimize the time they spend with people who criticize them.

Given these biases in social feedback, the question about the relations between perceived and actual social acceptance might be turned on its head. Instead of asking why perceptions of social acceptance are inaccurate, researchers might ask why any relation exists between social self-concepts and actual social acceptance!

One longitudinal study has shown not only that children's perceptions of their social acceptance are related to their actual acceptance, but that actual acceptance affects self-perceptions. In the study (Cole, 1991), fourth graders responded to Harter's SPPC and reported on their liking for classmates in both the fall and the spring of a school year. Regression analyses showed that the students' acceptance by peers in the fall was a predictor of their scores on the Social Acceptance subscale of the SPPC in the spring, even after fall scores on the same subscale were taken into account. These analyses imply that the students' acceptance by peers influenced the changes during the year in their perceptions of their social acceptance.

Additional research of this kind is needed. New studies should be designed not simply to show that peer acceptance affects self-concepts, but to examine the influences on social self-concepts directly. One foundation for these studies should be theoretical writings on the formation of self-perceptions and the sources of inaccuracies in self-perceptions (see John & Robins, 1994; Shrauger & Schoeneman, 1979).

Social Self-Concepts, Peer Reputation, and Academic Achievement

Children's acceptance by peers is heavily influenced by their social behavior (Asher & Coie, 1990; Hartup, 1983). Children who are aggressive and disruptive, who often disagree with others, and who behave inappropriately in social situations are often rejected. Children who are shy and withdrawn are often neglected. Popular children are usually sociable, cooperative, and skilled at organizing enjoyable activities.

Because children's social self-concepts are related to their peer acceptance, at least after the preschool years, relations also would be expected between children's social self-concepts and their social behavior toward peers. The data on this issue are limited but consistent with expectations. Children who perceive their social acceptance more positively are rated by peers as less aggressive and as less isolated and withdrawn (Hymel, Rubin, Rowden, & LeMare, 1990). They are also rated by peers as more socially competent (Cauce, 1987). Parents describe children with low social self-concepts as high in externalizing problems such as aggression and high in internalizing problems such as anxiety (Durrant, Cunningham, & Voelker, 1990).

A more controversial question is how the social self-concepts of school-age children are related to their academic achievement. On one hand, hierarchical models of the self-concept (e.g., Shavelson et al., 1976) rest on the assumption that different facets of the self-concept are linked to different kinds of performance. In particular, social self-concepts should be linked mainly to social success and not to academic success. On the other hand, research cited earlier has shown that peer acceptance is related to academic achievement. More popular children have higher grades and achievement test scores at school (Wentzel & Erdley, 1993). Because of the relation between perceived and actual acceptance by peers, children with better social self-concepts might also be expected to display better achievement in school.

The evidence on this question is greater and more consistent than on most other topics discussed in the chapter. Students' scores on measures of the social self-concept are rarely correlated with measures of their academic achievement. In one study of fifth and sixth graders (Marsh et al., 1983), scores on the peer subscale of Marsh's SDQI showed few significant correlations with multiple measures of academic achievement. In another study of seventh to ninth graders (Marsh & Gouvernet, 1989), scores on the same scale and on Harter's social scale from the PCS were not correlated with students' test scores in reading and math. Research with other samples and with the social scales on the SDQII and SDQIII yielded similar results (Marsh, 1990; Marsh et al., 1985; Marsh & O'Niell, 1984).

For practical reasons, educators have been especially concerned about the social self-concepts of children unusually high or low in academic achievement. Educators have wondered whether intellectually gifted children pay a price, in terms of social acceptance, for their superior academic performance. Educators have wondered whether low-achieving students likewise pay a price, or are less accepted by their classmates, because of their poor academic performance.

These concerns seem unwarranted, at least for the majority of gifted and low-achieving students. No significant difference between the social self-concepts of gifted students and students average in academic achievement was found in a recent meta-analysis (Hoge & Renzulli, 1993). One exception to the rule was a study of gifted adolescent girls (Callahan, Cornell, & Loyd, 1990). Among this group of high achievers, those with higher IQs had lower scores on the social subscale of the SPPC. This finding might be attributed to chance, but it is consistent with biographical data that suggest children with extremely high IQs sometimes have difficulties in groups with more average peers (Schneider, 1987). Gifted students in general, however, view their social acceptance and social skills neither more positively nor more negatively than average students.

Researchers have also examined the social self-concepts of students with reading or learning disabilities. In several studies, learning-disabled students perceived their social acceptance about as positively as did other students with average levels of achievement (Casey, Levy, Brown, & Brooks-Gunn, 1992; Clever, Bear, & Juvonen, 1992; Durrant et al., 1990). The weight of the evidence suggests that low achievement in school has little effect on students' social self-concepts. Although a link exists between students' achievement and their social status (Wentzel & Erdley, 1993), the link apparently is not strong enough to connect students' achievement to their perceptions of their peer acceptance.

One partly inconsistent finding should be noted. In a study with a small sample of fourth through sixth graders (la Greca & Stone, 1990), learning-disabled students had lower scores on the social subscale of the SPPC than did average to high achievers. However, the difference was not directly related to their poor achievement, because low-achieving students who were not identified as learning-disabled perceived their social acceptance more positively than the learning-disabled students. These results suggest that under certain conditions classification as a learning-disabled student, and the special educational programming associated with that classification, may affect social self-concepts. To explore these issues further, research should examine not only the social self-concepts of learning-disabled students, but also the frequency and quality of their peer interactions.

CONCLUSION

One message of this chapter, perhaps the most obvious one, is that the creation of multidimensional self-concept measures has sparked a great increase in research on the social self-concept. Before these measures were published, research on this facet of the self-concept was scarce. Since their publication, many researchers have reported data on the relations of social self-concepts to other constructs.

The publication of multidimensional measures has been a mixed blessing, however. In the creation of these measures, the nature and significance of the social self-concept was not a central issue. Indeed, it is only a slight exaggeration to say that the social self-concept was almost tangential to the creation of the measures. In the description of some measures, even an explicit definition of the social self-concept is absent.

One consequence of this history is that measurement issues have received more attention in recent literature than theoretical issues. With a few notable exceptions that are discussed later, researchers have reported data on the social self-concept mainly because they used a multidimensional scale that included a social subscale. Recent data have shown the reliability and validity of the new scales, so attention should now turn toward generating and testing hypotheses about the social self-concept per se.

The most fundamental theoretical issue concerns the definition of the social self-concept. The contrast between definitions that refer to social acceptance and those that refer to social skills was introduced at the beginning of the chapter. This contrast was important in understanding the correlations of social self-concepts with other measures. The contrast is also linked to major theoretical issues.

The first of these issues might be called the "reference-group problem." When the social self-concept is defined by people's perceptions of their social acceptance, the reference group for these perceptions must be specified. The items in current self-concept measures most often refer to peers, or the friends and classmates of school-age children. However, peer groups are heterogeneous. Children and adolescents, the subjects in most recent research on the social self-concept, have different relationships with same-sex peers and with opposite-sex peers. In addition, they have different relationships with peers at school, in their neighborhood, on their athletic teams, and in other organized groups.

Researchers need to be more thoughtful in handling these variations. Harter and Marsh included separate subscales for same- and opposite-sex relationships in the adolescent and adult versions of their scales. Yet for some elementary-school children, opposite-sex peers may be an important reference group. For some adolescents and adults, opposite-sex peers may not be an important reference group. A "one-size-fits-all" self-concept measure may obscure rather than clarify these variations.

Self-concept measures for general use may also fail to match the requirements for specific research projects. Their failure may take two forms that relate to a second and a third issue for future research. The second issue might be called the "overlapping-items problem." As shown earlier, items on social self-concept subscales are often similar or even identical to items on measures of other constructs such as loneliness and social support. The similarities cast doubt on the discriminant validity of social self-concept scales and have important implications for the interpretation of research findings.

One implication is that any statement about the relation between such overlapping measures should be treated not as an intriguing hypothesis but as a tautology, a statement that must logically be true. To avoid tautological thinking, researchers must look beyond the label for a measure and examine the content of the items when deciding whether a correlation between two measures is meaningful.

The third issue might be called the "criterion problem" (John & Robins, 1994). Several researchers have examined the correlation between people's social self-concepts, defined by their perceptions of their peer acceptance, and their actual acceptance by peers. The hypothesis guiding this research is not often stated explicitly, but it usually seems to be a variant of the James-Cooley hypothesis that people's self-perceptions of their peer acceptance should be highly correlated with their actual acceptance.

The problem with recent tests of this hypothesis is that researchers have rarely established that the criterion, actual social acceptance, refers to the peers in subjects' minds when they report their perceptions of peer acceptance. This problem seems impossible to solve with standard measures of the social self-concept. To solve the problem, researchers need to tailor the measure of the social self-concept to the group for which measures of actual peer acceptance are available. Researchers who take the effort to adapt existing measures may also be more likely to consider the purposes and requirements for a specific project carefully before collecting data. Their data should then be more interpretable and more valuable.

A fourth theoretical issue might be called the "origins problem." The origins of people's social self-concepts have been examined from a very limited perspective in previous studies. As noted earlier, researchers have commonly assumed that individuals who are more accepted by their peers will perceive their social relationships more positively. That is, however, only part of the story. People's perceptions of their social success may depend partly on their general attitude toward themselves and the world, or the degree to which they view themselves and other people positively or negatively (Bohrnstedt & Felson, 1983; Watson & Clark, 1984). Little attention has been given to this issue, or to the processes by which the realities of people's social lives affect their self-perceptions and self-evaluations.

A final issue might be called the "significance problem." Surprisingly few writers have discussed the significance of the social self-concept critically. Certainly, people are better off when they have a positive view of their social self than when they have a negative one. However, the implications of this truism for research and practice are not immediately obvious.

Interpreted simplistically, the truism implies that researchers and practitioners should try to boost the social self-concepts of children who perceive their social acceptance or social skill as lacking. Some interventions of this type have been empirically evaluated, and not all findings have been encouraging. For example, adolescents in one counseling program rated their social acceptance and close friendships less positively on Harter's scale for adolescents after the program than before (Lavoritano & Segal, 1992).

Other programs have had more positive effects. The central element of successful programs is apparently the formation of cohesive groups of peers who learn about each other and begin to care for one another (Amerikaner & Summerlin, 1982; Culp, Little, Letts, & Lawrence, 1991; Omizo & Omizo, 1987). In other words, participants in the programs begin to feel more positively about their peer acceptance because they become part of a peer group in which they are accepted and valued. The participants show improved social self-concepts because they become friends with each other.

If this explanation of the programs' effectiveness is correct, social self-concepts are not significant in themselves. They are merely one indicator, and an indirect one, of the quality of the social relationships among the participants. If the quality of these relationships was assessed more directly, measures of participants' social self-concepts would not be necessary.

Are measures of social self-concepts necessary? If not necessary, are they valuable? There is no general answer to these questions. For some researchers and practitioners, the answers will be no. More direct measures of children's social acceptance or social skill will be preferable. For other researchers and practitioners, the answers will be yes. Understanding people's perceptions of their social position and social skills can be valuable for explaining their behavior and improving their psychological adjustment. The most important goal for future research is to present explicit hypotheses about when an assessment of people's social perceptions is valuable, and then to test those hypotheses directly. Such tests would resolve the significance problem in research on the social self-concept.

REFERENCES

Alessandri, S. M. (1992). Effects of maternal work status in single-parent families on children's perception of self and family and school achievement. *Journal of Experimental Child Psychology, 54,* 471–433.

Amerikaner, M., & Summerlin, M. L. (1982). Group counseling with learning disabled children: Effects of social skills and relaxation training on self-concept and classroom behavior. *Journal of Learning Disabilities, 15,* 340–343.

Asher, S. R., & Coie, J. D. (Eds.). (1990). *Peer rejection in childhood.* New York: Cambridge University Press.

Asher, S. R., Hymel, S., & Renshaw, P. D. (1984). Loneliness in children. *Child Development, 55,* 1456–1464.

Belle, D. (Ed.). (1989). *Children's social networks and social supports.* New York: Wiley.

Blascovich, J., & Tomaka, J. (1991). Measures of self-esteem. In J. P. Robinson, P. R. Shaver, & L. S. Wrightsman (Eds.), *Measures of personality and social psychological attitudes* (pp. 115–160). San Diego, CA: Academic Press.

Bohrnstedt, G. W., & Felson, R. B. (1983). Explaining the relationship among children's actual and perceived performances and self esteem: A comparison of several causal models. *Journal of Personality and Social Psychology, 45,* 43–56.

Boivin, M., & Begin, G. (1989). Peer status and self-perception among early elementary school children: The case of rejected children. *Child Development, 60,* 591–596.

Boivin, M., Vitaro, F., & Gagnon, C. (1992). A reassessment of the self-perception profile for children: Factor structure, reliability, and convergent validity of a French version among second through sixth grade children. *International Journal of Behavioral Development, 15,* 275–290.

Bracken, B. (1992). *The Multidimensional Self Concept Scale.* Austin, TX: Pro-Ed.

Buhrmester, D., Furman, W., Wittenberg, M. T., & Reis, H. T. (1988). Five domains of interpersonal competence in peer relationships. *Journal of Personality and Social Psychology, 55,* 991–1008.

Bukowski, W. M., & Hoza, B. (1989). Popularity and friendship: Issues in theory, measurement, and outcome. In T. J. Berndt & G. W. Ladd (Eds.), *Peer relationships in child development* (pp. 14–45). New York: Wiley.

Callahan, C. M., Cornell, D. G., & Loyd, B. (1990). Perceived competence and parent-adolescent communication in high ability adolescent females. *Journal for the Education of the Gifted, 13,* 256–269.

Casey, R., Levy, S. E., Brown, K., & Brooks-Gunn, J. (1992). Impaired emotional health in children with mild reading disability. *Journal of Developmental and Behavioral Pediatrics, 13,* 256–260.

Cauce, A. (1987). School and peer competence in early adolescence: A test of domain-specific self-perceived competence. *Developmental Psychology, 23,* 287–291.

Chambliss, J., Muller, D., Hulnick, R., & Wood, M. (1978). Relationships between self-concept, self-esteem, popularity, and social judgments of junior high school students. *Journal of Psychology, 98,* 91–98.

Clever, A., Bear, G. G., & Juvonen, J. (1992). Discrepancies between competence and importance in self-perceptions of children in integrated classes. *Journal of Special Education, 26,* 125–138.

Coie, J., Dodge, K., & Coppotelli, H. (1982). Dimensions and types of social status: A cross-age perspective. *Developmental Psychology, 18,* 557–570.

Coie, J. D., & Krehbiel, G. (1984). Effects of academic tutoring on the social status of low-achieving, socially rejected children. *Child Development, 55,* 1465–1478.

Cole, D. A. (1991). Change in self-perceived competence as a function of peer and teacher evaluation. *Developmental Psychology, 27,* 682–688.

Connolly, J. (1989). Social self-efficacy in adolescence: Relations with self-concept, social adjustment, and mental health. *Canadian Journal of Behavioural Science, 21,* 258–269.

Cooley, C. (1922). *Human nature and social order* (rev. ed.). New York: Scribner's.

Coopersmith, S. (1967). *The antecedents of self esteem.* San Francisco: Freeman.

Cornell, D. G., Pelton, G. M., Bassin, L. E., Landrum, M., Ramsay, S G., Cooley, M. R., Lynch, K. A., & Hamrick, E. (1990). Self-concept and peer status among gifted program youth. *Journal of Educational Psychology, 82,* 456–463.

Cuffel, B. J., & Akamatsu, T. J. (1989). The structure of loneliness: A factor-analytic investigation. *Cognitive Therapy and Research, 13,* 459–474.

Culp, R., Little, V., Letts, D., & Lawrence, H. (1991). Maltreated children's self-concept: Effects of a comprehensive treatment program. *American Journal of Orthopsychiatry, 61,* 114–121.

Das, R., & Berndt, T. J. (1992). Relations of preschoolers' social acceptance to peer ratings and self-perceptions. *Early Education and Development, 3,* 221–231.

Delugach, R. R., Bracken, B. A., Bracken, M. J., & Schicke, M. C. (1992). Self concept: Multidimensional construct exploration. *Psychology in the Schools, 10,* 213–223.

Dubow, E. F., & Ullman, D. G. (1989). Assessing social support in elementary school children: The survey of children's social support. *Journal of Clinical Child Psychology, 18,* 52–64.

Durrant, J. E., Cunningham, C. E., & Voelker, S. (1990). Academic, social and general self-concepts of behavioral subgroups of learning disabled children. *Journal of Educational Psychology, 82,* 657–663.

Fiske, S. T., & Taylor, S. E. (1984). *Social cognition.* New York: Random House.

Fitts, W. H. (1965). *Tennessee Self-Concept Scale Manual.* Nashville, TN: Counselor Recording and Tests.

Hagborg, W. J., Masella, G., Palladino, P., & Shepardson, J. (1991). A follow-up study of high school students with a history of grade retention. *Psychology in the Schools, 28,* 310–317.

Harter, S. (1979). *Perceived Competence Scale for Children.* Unpublished manual, University of Denver.

Harter, S. (1982). The perceived competence scale for children. *Child Development, 53,* 87–97.

Harter, S. (1983). Developmental perspectives on the self system. In P. H. Mussen (Series Ed.) and E. M. Hetherington (Vol. Ed.), *Handbook of child psychology: Vol. 4. Socialization, personality, and social development* (pp. 275–385). New York: Wiley.

Harter, S. (1985). *Manual for the Self-Perception Profile for Children.* Unpublished manuscript, University of Denver.

Harter, S. (1988). *The Self-Perception Profile for Adolescents.* Unpublished manual, University of Denver.

Harter, S. (1993). Causes and consequences of low self-esteem in children and adolescents. In R. F. Baumeister (Ed.), *Self-esteem: The puzzle of low self-regard* (pp. 87–116). New York: Plenum.

Harter, S., & Pike, R. (1984). The pictorial scale of perceived competence and social acceptance for young children. *Child Development, 55,* 1969–1982.

Hartup, W. W. (1983). Peer relations. In P. H. Mussen (Series Ed.), E. M. Hetherington (Vol. Ed.), *Handbook of child psychology: Vol. 4. Socialization, personality, and social development* (pp. 103–196). New York: Wiley.

Helmreich, R., Stapp, J., & Ervin, C. (1974). The Texas Social Behavior Inventory (TSBI): An objective measure of self-esteem or social competence. *Journal Supplement Abstract Service Catalogue of Selected Documents in Psychology, 4,* 79. (Ms. No. 681)

Hoge, R. D., & McScheffrey, R. (1991). An investigation of self-concept in gifted children. *Exceptional Children, 57,* 238–245.

Hoge, R. D., & Renzulli, J. S. (1993). Exploring the link between giftedness and self-concept. *Review of Educational Research, 63,* 449–465.

Hymel, S., & Franke, S. (1985). Children's peer relations: Assessing self-perceptions. In B. H. Schneider, K. H. Rubin, & J. E. Ledingham (Eds.), *Children's peer relations: Issues in assessment and intervention* (pp. 75–91). New York: Springer-Verlag.

Hymel, S., Rubin, K. H., Rowden, L., & LeMare, L. (1990). Children's peer relationships: Longitudinal prediction of internalizing and externalizing problems from middle to late childhood. *Child Development, 61,* 2004–2021.

James, W. (1890). *The principles of psychology.* New York: Henry Holt & Co.

John, O. P., & Robins, R. W. (1994). Accuracy and bias in self-perception: Individual differences in self-enhancement and the role of narcissism. *Journal of Personality and Social Psychology, 66,* 206–219.

Kurdek, L. A., & Krile, D. A. (1982). A developmental analysis of the relation between peer acceptance and both interpersonal understanding and perceived social self competence. *Child Development, 53,* 1485–1491.

Ladd, G. W., & Price, J. M. (1986). Promoting children's cognitive and social competence: The relation between parents' perceptions of task difficulty and children's perceived and actual competence. *Child Development, 57,* 446–460.

la Greca, A. M., & Stone, W. L. (1990). LD status and achievement: Confounding variables in the study of children's social status, self-esteem, and behavioral functioning. *Journal of Learning Disabilities, 23,* 483–490.

Lavoritano, J. E., & Segal, P. B. (1992). Evaluating the efficacy of short-term counseling on adolescents in a school setting. *Adolescence, 27,* 535–543.

Li, A. K. (1988). Self-perception and motivational orientation in gifted children. *Roeper Review, 10,* 175–180.

Marsh, H. W. (1986). Global self-esteem: Its relation to specific facets of self-concept and their importance. *Journal of Personality and Social Psychology, 51,* 1224–1236.

Marsh, H. W. (1989). Age and sex effects in multiple dimensions of self concept: Preadolescence to early adulthood. *Journal of Educational Psychology, 81,* 417–430.

Marsh, H. W. (1990). Confirmatory factor analysis of multitrait-multimethod data: The construct validation of multidimensional self-concept responses. *Journal of Personality, 58,* 661–692.

Marsh, H. W. (1993). Relations between global and specific domains of self: The importance of individual importance, certainty, and ideals. *Journal of Personality and Social Psychology, 65,* 975–992.

Marsh, H. W., Barnes, J., Cairns, L., & Tidman, M. (1984). The Self Description Questionnaire (SDQ): Age effects in the structure and level of self-concept for preadolescent children. *Journal of Educational Psychology, 76,* 940–956.

Marsh, H. W., Craven, R., & Debus, R. (1991). Self concepts of children 5 to 8 years of age: Measurement and multidimensional structure. *Journal of Educational Psychology, 83,* 377–392.

Marsh, H. W., & Gouvernet, P. J. (1989). Multidimensional self-concepts and perceptions of control: Construct validation of responses by children. *Journal of Educational Psychology, 81,* 57–69.

Marsh, H. W., & Holmes, I. (1990). Multidimensional self concepts: Construct validation of responses by children. *American Educational Research Journal, 27,* 89–118.

Marsh, H. W., & O'Niell, R. (1984). Self-Description Questionnaire, III (SDQIII): The construct validity of multidimensional self-concept ratings by late-adolescents. *Journal of Educational Measurement, 21,* 153–174.

Marsh, H. W., Parker, J., & Barnes, J. (1985). Multidimensional adolescent self-concepts: Their relationship to age, sex, and academic measures. *American Educational Research Journal, 22,* 422–444.

Marsh, H. W., Parker, J. W., & Smith, I. D. (1983). Preadolescent self-concept: Its relation to self-concept as inferred by teachers and to academic ability. *British Journal of Educational Psychology, 53,* 60–78.

Marsh, H. W., & Richards, G. E. (1988). Tennessee Self-Concept Scale: Reliability, internal structure, and construct validity. *Journal of Personality and Social Psychology, 55,* 612–624.

Marsh, H. W., Smith, I., Barnes, J., & Butler, S. (1983). Self concept: Reliability, stability, dimensionality, and measurement of change. *Journal of Educational Psychology, 75,* 772–790.

Mascuich, S. W., McRae, L. S., & Young, J. D. (1990). The Harter Self-Perception Profile: Some normative and psychometric data. *Psychological Reports, 67,* 1299–1303.

Meredith, W. H., Abbott, D. A., & Ming, Z. F. (1992). Self-concept and sociometric outcomes: A comparison of only children and sibling children from urban and rural areas in the People's Republic of China. *Journal of Psychology, 126,* 411–419.

Moreno, J. L. (1934). *Who shall survive? Foundations of sociometry, group psychotherapy, and sociodrama* (3rd ed.). Beacon, NY: Beacon House.

Neeman, J., & Harter, S. (1986). *The Self-Perception Profile for College Students*. Unpublished manual, University of Denver.

Nicholls, J. G., Licht, B. G., & Pearl, R. A. (1982). Some dangers of using personality questionnaires to study personality. *Psychological Bulletin, 92,* 572–580.

Nunnally, J. C. (1978). *Psychometric theory* (2nd ed.). New York: McGraw-Hill.

Omizo, M. M., & Omizo, S. A. (1987). The effects of group counselling on classroom behaviour and self-concept among elementary school learning disabled children. *Exceptional Child, 34,* 57–64.

Parker, J., & Asher, S. (1987). Peer relations and later personality adjustment: Are low accepted children "at risk"? *Psychological Bulletin, 102,* 357–389.

Patterson, C., Kupersmidt, J., & Griesler, P. (1990). Children's perceptions of self and of relationships with others as a function of sociometric status. *Child Development, 61,* 1335–1349.

Roid, G. H., & Fitts, W. H. (1988). *Tennessee Self-Concept Scale* (revised manual). Los Angeles: Western Psychological Services.

Rosenberg, M. (1965). *Society and the adolescent self-image.* Princeton, NJ: Princeton University Press.

Rubin, K., Hymel, S., LeMare, L., & Rowden, L. (1989). Children experiencing social difficulties: Sociometric neglect reconsidered. *Canadian Journal of Behavioral Science, 21,* 94–111.

Ruble, D. N. (1983). The development of social-comparison processes and their role in achievement-related self-socialization. In E. T. Higgins, D. N. Ruble, & W. W. Hartup (Eds.), *Social cognition and social development: A sociocultural perspective* (pp. 134–157). Cambridge, England: Cambridge University Press.

Sarason, B. R., Sarason, I. G., & Pierce, G. R. (Eds.). (1990). *Social support: An interactional view.* New York: Wiley.

Savin-Williams, R. C. (1987). *Adolescence: An ethological perspective.* New York: Springer-Verlag.

Schneider, B. H. (1987). *The gifted child in peer group perspective.* New York: Springer-Verlag.

Shavelson, R., Hubner, J., & Stanton, G. (1976). Self concept: Validation and construct interpretations. *Review of Educational Research, 46,* 407–441.

Shrauger, J. S., & Schoeneman, T. J. (1979). Symbolic interactionist view of self-concept: Through the looking glass darkly. *Psychological Bulletin, 86,* 549–573.

Watson, D., & Clark, L. A. (1984). Negative affectivity: The disposition to experience aversive emotional states. *Psychological Bulletin, 96,* 465–490.

Wentzel, K. R., & Erdley, C. A. (1993). Strategies for making friends: Relations to social behavior and peer acceptance in early adolescence. *Developmental Psychology, 29,* 819–826.

Wheeler, V. A., & Ladd, G. W. (1982). Assessment of children's self-efficacy for social interactions with peers. *Developmental Psychology, 18,* 795–805.

CHAPTER 5

Competence Self-Concept

NATALIE NOVICK, ANA MARI CAUCE, and KWAI GROVE

Researchers have long postulated a tendency in children to master the environment because this activity was satisfying in itself (Berlyne, 1950; Montgomery, 1954; Piaget, 1954). The perception of one's own ability to master or deal effectively with the environment, a construct we refer to as "competence self-concept," has figured prominently in research from a number of theoretical perspectives (e.g., Abramson, Seligman, & Teasdale, 1978; Adler, 1927; Bandura, 1977; Bem, 1972; Coopersmith, 1967; deCharms, 1968; Deci, 1975, 1980; Gurin & Brim, 1984; Harter, 1978; Hendrick, 1943; Kelley, 1971; Kelly, 1955; Lepper & Greene, 1978; Skinner & Chapman, 1984; Weiner, 1972; Weisz & Stipek, 1982; White, 1959, 1963; Woodworth, 1958). Virtually all self-theorists would agree that at the core of this construct is Bandura's (1982) postulate that the "basic phenomenon being addressed centers on people's sense of personal efficacy to produce and regulate events in their lives" (p. 122). Nonetheless, there is no clear conceptualization of competence self-concept. Consequently, it is difficult to operationalize and measure the construct and determine its role relative to other domains of the concept.

Competence self-concept is not the same thing as competent behavior. The behavioral aspect of competence involves active, adaptive, and effective engagement with the environment in pursuit of personal goals (Palenzuela, 1987; Short & Hess, 1983) and is characterized by a number of factors, including an active coping orientation, realistic goal-setting, initiative, planning, persistence, and effort in the service of goal-directed behavior, and an ability to enjoy success and cope with failures while benefiting from both (Tyler & Gatz, 1977). Cognitive self-perceptions of competence, on the other hand, may be totally unrelated to competent behavior. For example, we might demonstrate behavioral competence by publishing far more empirical studies than our colleagues, yet nevertheless have a low opinion of our research capabilities. Conversely, strong competence beliefs that are not justified by performance are also possible. In fact, people's competence self-judgments tend to be influenced much more by how they interpret their performance than by the actual performance itself (Bandura, 1977; Nicholls, 1982).

Although differences between cognitive and behavioral aspects of competence may be clear, a distinction between competence self-concept and other constructs involving self-relevant evaluative processes is more difficult to discern. This distinction becomes especially blurred in the case of Bandura's (1977, 1984) perceived self-efficacy construct, which appears to resemble White's (1963) classic formulation of sense of competence as "the subjective side of one's actual competence" (p. 39). According to Bandura (1984), perceived self-efficacy involves "people's judgments of their capabilities to deal with different realities" (p. 231), and White's description of perceived competence implies a judgment of one's ability to deal with the environment. These conceptualizations appear to be equivalent or very closely related (Palenzuela, 1987a; Weisz & Stipek, 1982), although White focuses on the motivational aspects of competence, and Bandura emphasizes its cognitive aspects. However, neither researcher addresses competence within the context of its interrelated behavioral, cognitive, motivational, and affective components to arrive at a complete understanding of the dynamic quality of the construct.

There is some empirical validation for competence self-concept as a distinct component of the multidimensional self-concept (Bracken, Bunch, Keith, & Keith, 1992). However, while one might assume that competence self-concept exerts a pervasive influence on behavior in comparison with other, more clearly limited, self-concept domains, little empirical research has directly addressed this assumption. Nevertheless, to the extent that perceived self-efficacy and competence self-concept are related, the latter construct is likely a very important determinant of behavior. Extensive research has been conducted on perceived self-efficacy, yielding compelling evidence that it is highly predictive of behavior in certain contexts. For example, in complex decision-making situations, those who possess strong convictions about their problem-solving capabilities tend to display highly efficient analytic thinking in comparison with those who are plagued by self-doubt (Bandura & Wood, 1989; Wood & Bandura, 1989). Furthermore, individuals with a strong sense of self-efficacy are more apt to anticipate success and visualize scenarios that help guide performance (Bandura, 1986, 1989; Corbin, 1972; Kazdin, 1978). In contrast, those who see themselves as incompetent tend to dwell on their personal deficiencies and exaggerate the severity of potential problems (Beck, 1976; Lazarus & Launier, 1978; Sarason, 1975), often undermining their actual performance (Bandura, 1989).

Thus, it may be inferred from evidence on perceived self-efficacy that competence self-concept exerts a similar and pervasive influence on performance-related behavior and cognition. Yet, without precise definitions of these constructs it is difficult to determine whether research that specifically addresses perceived self-efficacy is actually examining the same thing as competence self-concept or something different. The few empirical studies that have purported to look at competence self-concept per se tend to focus on career decision-making, finding that perceptions of competence substantially influence both career planning and preparation for careers (Betz & Hackett, 1986; Lent & Hackett, 1987). For example, in comparison with those who doubt their competence in the work world, people who judge themselves as competent tend to consider a wider range of career options and prepare themselves educationally for these occupations. In addition, those who limit their career choices do so more out of perceived incompetence than from actual inability (Hackett & Betz, 1981). However, despite the emphasis on "competence self-concept," precise definition of the construct is generally assumed.

Because of the ambiguity in conceptualizing and measuring competence self-concept, the purpose of this chapter is to clarify both its meaning and its relevance to similar terms that have often been used interchangeably with the construct, such as perceived self-efficacy. To accomplish this purpose, our discussion is organized into four sections. In the first, we review and integrate selected theoretical perspectives of competence self-concept—focusing particularly on motivational, social, and behavioral formulations—outlining a general framework for conceptualizing the construct based on affect. In fact, we argue, without emotional engagement, performance achievements have no impact on competence self-judgments. Next, we examine competence self-concept from a developmental perspective, summarizing research on changes in perceived competence over the life span. Based on the literature, it appears that children do not formulate a sense of competence until middle childhood; then, what is initially a general, diffuse conception of competence begins to differentiate into discrete behavioral domains as a child matures to adulthood. In the third section, we look at a number of personal and environmental components that are viewed as basic resources for the development of competence self-concept. To a great extent, family of origin determines access to many of the resources that are vital in the formation of a strong sense of personal efficacy. Finally, the last section of this chapter looks at the relation between competence self-concept and self-esteem. Judgments of personal ability to interact effectively with the environment not only play a large role in determining our behavior, these beliefs also exert profound influence on the way we feel about ourselves.

IN SEARCH OF AN ELUSIVE CONSTRUCT

Early conceptualizations of competence neglected self-relevant cognitive aspects of the construct and focused instead on its motivational and behavioral manifestations. Until the middle part of this century, all human behavior—including competence—was thought to be explained by biologically based energies. It was only the nature of these energies or instincts that was in dispute. According to Freud (1949), behavior originated in libidinal and aggressive urges. In other words, we are motivated to behave in a particular way because of instinct. Recognizing unique aspects of mastery behavior (e.g., exploration, manipulation, play, creativity) that differentiated it from libidinal and aggressive behaviors, other researchers interested in the competence construct began to explore theoretical alternatives to Freud's original drive theory. For example, Hendrick (1942) proposed that a third instinct might account for mastery behavior, in particular, a drive "to do and to learn how to do" (p. 33). According to Hendrick's theory, we experience pleasure when efficient mastery of the environment enables us to control and alter our world.

Motivational theories of the origins of competence have ranged from strictly intrapersonal rationales to explanations that heavily emphasize environmental feedback. Focusing on processes that occur within the individual, Fenichel (1945) was one of the first to entertain a notion that physiological arousal may be instrumental in competence motivation. In particular, he suggested that successful performance stemmed from a need to reduce physical sensations of anxiety associated with ineffective functioning. In a similar vein, Mittelmann (1954) proposed that motility itself was a drive, originating in an individual's innate need to distinguish the self from objects in the environment. Shifting to a more environmental perspective, Hartmann (1950) suggested that skills and abilities were the ultimate result of constant interplay between a child's actions and environmental feedback regarding those actions.

When Piaget (1952) began to observe and study his own children's behavior as infants, he took for granted the motivational aspect of mastery behavior and avoided the issue altogether. He described an infant as actively engaged in a process of building schemata, or cognitive-behavioral structures, incorporating environmental information consistent with these schemata while adjusting to inconsistent information at the same time. As the infant constantly practices and improves on an increasing number of mastery behaviors, these schemata gradually permit increasing control over the environment. Thus, while never giving explicit recognition to motivation in competence development, the relevance of Piaget's observations to the motivational origins of efficacious behavior were evident and stimulated subsequent researchers to explore a connection between competence motivation and competence behavior.

By the middle part of the 20th century, research on competence had begun to diverge into three distinct, but sometimes overlapping, perspectives: (a) motivational theories, which looked at competence behavior in terms of intrinsic urges or drives; (b) social theories, which viewed competence in terms of symbolic interaction or "system responsiveness"; and (c) cognitive theories, which conceptualized competence in terms of expectancies and perceptions of control. Contemporary theories of competence are now beginning to integrate these theoretical perspectives, recognizing the dynamic, interactive effect of thoughts, feelings, behavior, and motivation on all aspects of self-conception.

Motivational Theories

A number of researchers have viewed competence from a motivational perspective, conceptualizing the construct as either a biological drive to effectively deal with the environment or as an impetus for accomplishing goals. In his seminal theory on effectance motivation, White (1959) addresses the origin of exploratory and manipulative behaviors originally described by Piaget (1952). According to White (1959), we are born with an urge to engage effectively with the environment. This intrinsic drive for transactions with our surroundings, or "effectance motive," is presumed to derive from novel stimulation in the environment. Exploratory, creative, and playful activity causes changes in the environment, and the perception of agency in producing these changes (perceived self-efficacy) generates pleasurable sensations that are intrinsically satisfying. To recreate these hedonic effects, an infant is motivated to produce more efficacious behavior. By continuing to explore and manipulate the environment, the child establishes a cybernetic process linking behavior, environmental consequence, intrinsic reward, and motivation. Gradually, this feedback loop leads to cumulative acquisition of knowledge and skills for dealing effectively with the environment. Thus, by means of a continuous process of effective interaction with the environment and feedback about the results of this interaction, the child develops a desire for mastery based on intrinsic motivation.

Hunt (1961) also sees in Piaget's descriptions of infant behavior evidence for intrinsic motivation, which he characterizes as motivation involved in information processing and behavior. As originally suggested by McClelland, Atkinson, Clark, and Lowell (1953), Hunt (1961) postulates that the affective value of pleasant (reinforcing) or unpleasant (aversive) information is based on its relation to an individual's current state of arousal. Small discrepancies between arousal generated by a stimulus and baseline arousal produce positive affect; large discrepancies produce negative affect. Thus, motivation might be viewed as a desire for the positive hedonic effects that are associated with slight increases in physiological arousal. However, as an infant matures, familiar objects begin to lose some of their appeal (their ability to cause small changes in an individual's baseline arousal), and novel stimuli are sought. Consequently, the child begins to be attracted to challenges that have an intermediate, rather than large, probability of success. Over time, by increasing level of goal difficulty after each successful performance, the child begins to feel a sense of efficacy.

A second way of looking at competence from a motivational perspective is represented in research on goal-setting. The study of goals in relation to performance began with the work of Lewin, Dembo, Festinger, and Sears (1944), who studied effects of performance outcomes on level of aspiration and expectancies for future performance. Expanding on this approach, later theorists (e.g., Latham & Yukl, 1975; Locke, 1968; Rotter, 1954; Steers & Porter, 1974) suggested that certain properties of goals, such as value, specificity, and level, served to clarify standards of adequacy for the individual. More recently, Nicholls (1982) theorized that goals may be distinguished by their relation to task *performance* or to task *mastery*. Individuals who are performance/outcome oriented seek to demonstrate their abilities to themselves or to others in order to maintain or acquire positive perceptions of personal competence. In contrast, individuals who are mastery/learning oriented seek to increase their abilities or master new tasks and prefer personal effort over other causal factors when accounting for performance (Dweck, 1986; Dweck & Elliott, 1983). For example, a child who is primarily mastery motivated might view learning to ride a bicycle in terms of the personal satisfaction to be gained from accomplishing this task, whereas a child who is primarily performance oriented might focus on impressing his or her friends.

Performance goals tend to have a social context, whereas mastery goals tend to be personal. When performance goals are salient, outcome relative to peers is viewed as a major determinant of success and satisfaction (Ames & Ames, 1981; Ames & Felker, 1979; Butler, 1987). However, when mastery goals are salient, competence assessments also involve factors such as previous performance, interest, and effort, whereas achievement and social comparison are relatively less important. In addition, mastery-oriented people tend to use more personal and flexible standards than performance-oriented people (Dweck & Elliott, 1983) because their tendency to interpret negative outcomes in a more constructive way produces an affective result that tends to reinforce intrinsic motivation. Consequently, mastery-oriented people are generally able to experience considerable satisfaction about what they have learned, even when they have failed to accomplish their goals. In contrast, performance goals appear to make people particularly vulnerable to a helpless response in the face of failure (Elliott & Dweck, 1988). When performance goals motivate behaviors, attributions to low ability, negative affect, and deterioration in performance characterize attempts to cope with failure. This style of coping is characterized by attributions to low ability, negative affect, and deterioration in performance. However, behavior can also be motivated by mastery and performance goals simultaneously. That is, internal and external sources of effectance motivation can occur in response to a single task and fuse (Smith, 1969). For example, an individual may be motivated to work both by the possibility of earning a financial bonus and by the intrinsically rewarding nature of the work. Furthermore, one form of motivation can also come to supplant the other, as when extrinsic rewards such as grades replace the intrinsic satisfaction of performing well in school.

Regardless of whether primary reinforcements for efficacious behavior come from internal or external factors, effectance motivation is instrumental in development of actual behavioral competencies and perception of those competencies. However, sometimes motivation to achieve can be too strong. For early researchers who examined motivation to succeed, need for achievement meant striving to attain standards of excellence, which was considered a positive personality trait (McClelland et al., 1953). However, later research suggested that there might be a negative aspect to need for achievement. For example, compared with mothers of boys who scored low in need for achievement, Rosen and D'Andrade (1959) found that mothers of boys who scored high in this area tended to be more intrusive, setting high standards for their sons' behavior and insisting on superior performance. Furthermore, these mothers appeared to restrict the amount of autonomy their sons could exercise in decision making. Thus, a key element in the acquisition of a debilitating level of achievement motivation may be related to parents' conditional approval.

When people apply a too-stringent standard of achievement, objective successes tend to be regarded as failures (Atkinson, 1964; Atkinson & Feather, 1966). Furthermore, individuals who evaluate their behavior in terms of high performance standards and interpret actual accomplishments as failures because they fall short of these standards tend to be particularly susceptible to depression (Kanfer & Hagerman, 1980; Rehm, 1977). Depressive rumination about subjective judgments of failure not only impairs ability to initiate and sustain efficacious behavior, it also exacerbates self-perceptions of incompetence (Kavanagh & Bower, 1985; Nolen-Hoeksema, 1987). Ultimately, clinical depression can result when a perception of failure affects evaluative feelings about the self, or self-esteem.

Thus, from its early instinct-based origins, a motivational approach to competence gradually expanded to incorporate social, as well as personal, factors. However, although the development of competence may be motivated by either internal or external factors, the frame of reference in motivational theories has tended to be internal, and emphasis has been on either the need to experience, or actual experience of, causal agency in the service of personal goals. In contrast to this dispositional approach, social theories of competence have emphasized the environment rather than the individual. From a social perspective, competence is presumed to develop as a result of responsiveness from either significant individuals in one's life or from the "system" in general, rather than as a result of characterological response to significant factors in a person's life.

Social Theories

Self theory in sociology is based largely on symbolic interaction theory, which emphasizes an active, creative view of the self. Mead's (1934) concept of "I" in the reflective self is seen as an actor in the environment, shaping and affecting his or her world while simultaneously being shaped by it. This active, efficacious self is a source of agentive qualities such as creativity and spontaneity (Gecas, 1989). Expanding on Mead's formulation and adding elements of neo-Freudian psychology, Foote and Cottrell (1955) place mastery behavior in an interpersonal context and emphasize the importance of role performance and successful socialization in development of a sense of competence. These researchers define competence as the ability to control "the outcomes of episodes of interaction" (p. 36) and postulate that it is a multidimensional construct composed of health, intelligence, empathy, autonomy, judgment, and creativity. Drawing from Foote and Cottrell's (1955) formulation, Gladwin (1967) proposes that competence develops from three interrelated sets of abilities: effective use of appropriate goal-directed behaviors, effective use of social systems to achieve personal goals, and effective use of reality testing to determine the success of one's efforts. Diverging somewhat, Franks and Marolla (1976) distinguish between "inner self-esteem," involving personal competence, and "outer self-esteem," involving reflected appraisals from others. In addition, Rosenberg (1979) postulates that self-confidence, or confidence in one's ability to behave effectively, is a dimension of self-concept.

Adding a structural context to the analysis of competence, other researchers have viewed competence judgments in terms of the social structure (e.g., Gecas & Schwalbe, 1983; Giddens, 1979; Inkeles, 1966). For example, Inkeles (1966) focuses on the adequacy of performance in light of role requirements inherent in an individual's social network and defines competence as an ability to attain and perform in three kinds of roles: (a) roles assigned to an individual by society; (b) roles in the social system that the individual may reasonably aspire to; and (c) roles that the individual might develop for him- or herself. Finally, Giddens (1979) uses the term "power" instead of "competence" and views the construct as a capacity of social actors to achieve intended outcomes.

The variety of conceptualizations in the sociological literature suggests that psychologists have not been the only researchers to struggle with a precise definition of competence self-concept. However, regardless of discipline, there appears to be general agreement that the distinction between personal and environmental or social components of competence self-attitudes is very important. From an external perspective, sociological researchers conceptualize competence as effective role performance for both the individual and the society in which the individual functions. From a dispositional perspective, motivational researchers view competence in terms of response to either mastery (personal) or performance (social) goals. Finally, from a social learning perspective, cognitive researchers also distinguish between personal and social aspects of competence, emphasizing an individual's unique interpretation of a task or situation.

Cognitive Theories

Nowhere is the distinction between social and personal elements of competence more evident than in cognitive theories. Similar to social theories, where performance appraisal is informational rather than evaluative (Harackiewicz, Sansone, & Manderlink, 1985), cognitive conceptualizations of competence are derived largely from attribution and social learning theories and emphasize beliefs about personal agency or control. Bridging the gap between personal and interpersonal origins of behavioral competence, Bandura (1977, 1978) has argued that sense of competence, although based on environmental feedback, is primarily a product of the individual's perception of that feedback. Competence, or self-efficacy as he terms it, develops gradually as a result of direct and mediated transactions with the environment. Each transaction, in turn, produces an affective reaction and expectancies for future similar transactions that together impact motivation to engage in a particular behavior. In other words, rather than being born with an effectance motive, we learn to be competent by setting goals (discrepancy production) and then interpreting the effects of our actions on the environment (Bandura, 1989). These interpretations, in turn, produce an affective reaction (e.g., positive feelings in the case of discrepancy reduction) and expectancies for future similar transactions that together impact competence self-judgments. Thus, competence self-concept has a temporal dimension involving attributions for past performance attainments and expectancies for future performance outcomes. An individual develops motivation to behave competently by developing expectancies of future efficacy based in part on attributions made for past behaviors.

During the attribution process, information from a number of personal and environmental sources is evaluated and transformed, which affect competence self-judgments. Consequently, attaining a goal is not inherently enlightening. However, if an individual attributes important goal achievements to personal agentic control, attributions are likely to support self-attitudes of competence. In particular, research has found that perceptions of personal competence increase when people ascribe achievements to their own capabilities rather than to situational factors (Bem, 1972; Weiner, 1972). In fact, Wortman (1975) has found that merely causing a chance outcome, but having foreknowledge about the consequences of one's behavior, induces perceptions of control. Generally, the more agentic control an individual *believes* he or she has over an intended outcome, the more likely the person is to attribute performance achievement to personal competence.

Like perceived self-efficacy, personal agency beliefs (personal, as opposed to situational, causation) and perceived control (personal capacity to cause an intended outcome) serve an important behavior regulation function (Ford, 1984, 1985). They provide information useful when making attributions for performance outcomes, when developing expectancies for future performance attempts, and when deciding whether to activate or inhibit goal-directed behavior. Furthermore, theory and research support the belief that both personal agency and control beliefs are critical in the development of competence judgments (Ford & Thompson, 1985), although there is some confusion about their roles relative to competence self-concept and to each other. For example, Weisz and Stipek (1982) conceptualize personal agency and perceived control as analogous constructs, consisting of two more specific components, "perceived competence of self" and "perceived contingency of outcomes." For these researchers, then, competence self-concept is a subcomponent of a more general personal agency domain. Making a similar distinction, Bandura (1982) uses the labels "self-efficacy" and "behavior-outcome" expectancies to characterize two different perspectives on personal agency, suggesting that he, too, sees competence self-concept as a subcomponent of personal agency. Many other researchers (e.g., Ford & Thompson, 1985; Palenzuela, 1987a, 1987b; Weisz, 1980; Weisz & Stipek, 1982) tend to agree, postulating that personal agency is a function of two interrelated but conceptually distinct motivational components, perceived control (beliefs about how responsive the environment is to one's efforts to attain desired outcomes) and perceived competence (beliefs about one's own ability actually to achieve those outcomes).

Some theorists, however, argue that perceived control is the master construct. For instance, deCharms (1979) distinguishes between "personal causation," or an *experience of agency* in controlling and being controlled, and "locus of control," or *perception of control.* Thus, it is not yet clear how agency, control, and perceived competence interrelate. What does seem apparent, however, is that agency and control have an external orientation and refer to a person's capacity to influence performance outcomes, whereas perceived competence is based on an internal orientation and refers to judgments of personal ability to perform effectively, regardless of environmental responsiveness.

Perceptions of agentic control (personal agency and perceived control) mediate the effect of performance attributions on competence self-concept by influencing the way an individual psychologically positions him- or herself in relation to the environment. According to Vallacher and Wegner (1989), high-level agents tend to perceive their behavior as personally controlled, whereas low-level agents see their behavior as being under situational control. Furthermore, high-level agents, or "why" people, view their behavior in the context of future consequences and implications. This farsighted perspective promotes behavioral consistency and stability, enabling the high-level person to maintain a course of action that facilitates effective performance and self-attitudes of competence. In contrast, low-level agents, or "how" people, tend to be sensitive to contextual cues for purposes of behavior regulation. That is, low-level agents focus on the immediate situation and may be less self-motivated and less consistent in their behavior over time, and more external in their locus of control than their high level counterparts (Vallacher & Wegner, 1989). In short, low-level agents' conscious concern with action details makes them more dependent on the environment and less self-reliant than high-level agents, resulting in self-attitudes of incompetence and decreased effectiveness in dealing with challenge.

Differential impact of high- and low-level agency orientations on attributions for performance outcomes and on competence self-attitudes is noteworthy. Because low-level agents tend to see achievements as situationally caused, these outcomes are therefore irrelevant to competence self-concept (Vallacher & Wegner, 1989). Conversely, high-level agents are more inclined to view achievements as personally caused and therefore relevant to competence self-concept. Moreover, perceptions of control by high-level agents can impact performance attributions even when these judgments are inaccurate. Assigning a probability of success to a performance effort that is inappropriately higher than objective probability would warrant is termed "illusion of control" (Langer, 1975). It is this illusion of controllability, rather than the experience of controllability itself, that affects competence processes (Brown & Inouye, 1978). Furthermore, people can even develop perceptions of control in direct opposition to veridical evidence, implying that contextual factors may be more psychologically significant than outcome valence (Harter, 1978, 1981; Langer & Benvenuto, 1978). For instance, Langer and Benvenuto (1978) find that, despite successful performance, being assigned an "inferior" label relative to others results in beliefs of incompetence and self-induced dependence. Thus, regardless of an individual's actual ability to control an outcome, perceptions of personal control over the outcome appear to determine the effect of performance attributions on competence self-judgments.

Even when an individual has implemented an action strategy, achieved an important goal, and attributed success to personal capability based on perceptions of personal agency and perceived control, the impact of the achievement on competence self-concept is moderated by two other considerations in the attribution process. First, accomplishments with minimal physical effort are ascribed primarily to ability and therefore tend to reinforce feelings of competence, whereas successes achieved with great effort connote less ability and are likely to have a weaker effect on perceived self-efficacy (Bandura, 1982). Furthermore, high levels of arousal associated with increased effort not only influence attributions and competence judgments, they can hinder actual performance as well. For example, a student who normally obtains very high grades suddenly begins to experience test anxiety because he is applying to graduate school and questions whether he has a competitive grade average. As a result, he studies more but begins to perform poorly on exams because of his assumption that he is not as capable as his peers. Consequently, not only do his negative attributions decrease his sense of academic competence, his actual performance also suffers in response to increased levels of arousal.

In addition to ascribing behavior to either ability or effort, a second factor that moderates effect of performance achievements on competence self-concept is contextual in nature and involves judgments of task difficulty. For example, if a task is viewed as easy, success has little impact on perceived self-efficacy. However, if a task is seen as challenging, mastery provides salient evidence in support of competence self-judgments (Bandura, 1982). Thus, if the student in the previous example overcomes his test anxiety and begins to perform better on exams he believes are difficult, his competence self-concept is likely to improve.

Identification of the importance of agentic control in the attribution literature adds a cognitive dimension to factors identified in motivational and sociological research as being critical to competence self-concept. As a result, three elements now appear important to the formation of self-efficacy judgments: (a) foreknowledge of the outcome desired (a specific performance goal based on personal and social considerations); (b) the performance goal must be considered important enough to trigger an affective response; and (c) the person must believe he or she has agentic control over an adequate action strategy. In other words, if the individual initiates behavior in pursuit of an important, identified goal and believes behavioral outcome is contingent on his or her performance, evaluation of the outcome takes on personal relevance and affects competence self-concept. Regardless of actual level of performance, then, it is how the individual evaluates performance that determines competence self-judgments. Moreover, if a performance goal is viewed as challenging rather than easy, yet is performed without great effort, the impact of attributions of "success" on competence self-concept is even stronger.

Not only do attributions for past performance efforts affect competence self-concept, expectancies for future performance also mediate one's sense of personal efficacy. The expectancy construct figures prominently in cognitive theories of competence or self-efficacy. Rotter (1954) defines expectancy as "the probability held by an individual that a particular reinforcement will occur as a function of a specific behavior on his part in a specific situation or situations" (p. 107). Not surprisingly, these probabilities manifest in two ways: *self-efficacy* expectancies and *response-outcome* expectancies (Bandura, 1977). The former is a belief about one's competence, while the latter is a belief about environmental response (Gecas, 1989). Another way of looking at this distinction is that perceived competence is a factor in self-efficacy expectancies, whereas performance outcomes have to do with agentic control. Compared with outcome expectancies, research strongly suggests that self-efficacy expectancies are a more powerful predictor of behavior, including coping behavior, performance achievement, and positive affect (Bandura, 1977; Bandura, Adams, & Beyer, 1977; Bandura, Reese, & Adams, 1982; Bandura & Schunk,

1981; Betz & Hackett, 1981; Hackett & Betz, 1981; Schunk, 1981). However, Bandura (1982) himself has suggested that "in any given instance behavior would be best predicted by considering both self-efficacy and outcome beliefs" (p. 140).

Credited as being one of the first to examine expectancies from a perspective of personal versus environmental control, Rotter (1966) determined that behavior varies as a function of generalized expectations that outcomes are either self-determined or determined by forces outside one's control. Since then, a number of other studies have compared "internals" with "externals" on diverse measures of competence (e.g., Lefcourt, 1966, 1972, 1976, 1981; Levenson, 1981; Phares, 1976; Rothbaum, Wolfer, & Visintainer, 1979; Strickland, 1977; Thornhill, Thornhill, & Youngman, 1975; Throop & MacDonald, 1971), finding that internals tend to make greater efforts to master and cope with their environment than externals, who tend to perceive events as uncontrollable. This research, however, has generally been limited by its failure to consider perceptions of personal competence in relation to control orientation.

Expectations about the instrumentality of behavior in the context of the environment are considered to be a product of one's history of reinforcement (Rotter, 1966). Thus, perceptions of personal control for past performance efforts contribute directly to expectations of control for future efforts. For those whose experiences result in beliefs that desirable consequences are under their own internal control (e.g., skill or effort), rather than under the external control of environmental influences (e.g., chance or fate), successes tend to support or increase beliefs of personal competence (Bandura, 1977). Furthermore, individuals with an internal locus of control may have strong perceptions of personal control that tend to override environmental messages that threaten performance effectiveness. For example, a competitive skier who ignores foggy weather conditions because she believes in her ability to "feel" her way down a mountain is allowing strong convictions of personal control to outweigh negative messages from the environment. In fact, strong internal locus of control that makes an individual less vulnerable to environmental contingencies may provide a protective resiliency that safeguards both performance outcomes and efficacy expectancies. However, taken to its extreme, a strong sense of personal control can also result in taking excessive risks.

An environment in which competence goes unrewarded or is punished may have negative effects on expectancies. Thus, although we may have high expectations of personal competence for a given task, if we don't have similar confidence in the responsiveness of the environment to our efforts, we may have low outcome expectancies. Relation between outcome and efficacy expectancies is important because it influences initiation of goal-directed behavior (Bandura, 1977, 1982). Furthermore, the strength of our competence convictions in light of certain environmental contingencies not only affects motivation to engage in a given activity but even choices we make about behavioral settings (Bandura, 1989). In addition, both efficacy and outcome expectancies also determine how much effort people will expend in an activity and how long they will continue their efforts in the face of obstacles and aversive experiences (Bandura, 1977, 1982). Individuals who doubt their performance capabilities tend to decrease their efforts or give up entirely when goal achievement is difficult, whereas those with a strong expectation of efficacy expend additional effort to overcome the obstacle (Bandura & Schunk, 1981; Brown & Inouye, 1978; Schunk, 1981). In general, the stronger the expectation of personal competence and belief that the outcome is contingent on personal performance, the more active the task mastery efforts (Bandura, 1989).

Although an internal locus of control often contributes to positive efficacy expectancies, this is not always the case, nor does an internal locus of control always result in positive outcome expectancies. An individual may be high on internal control, yet, depending on assessment of task-related environmental contingencies, may be high, moderate, or low on expectancy of task success (Rotter, 1966). Thus, if one regards an outcome as personally determined (internal control) but believes he or she lacks the specific skills required to attain that outcome (low self-efficacy expectancies), the individual may feel less competent and view the task with an attitude of futility (low outcome expectancies). Therefore, for people with an internal locus of control, expectancies are likely to make a positive contribution to competence self-concept only when both self-efficacy expectancies and outcome expectancies are positive, or when positive competence expectancies outweigh negative outcome expectancies (as in the case of the skier).

Self-efficacy expectancies vary on several dimensions that have important implications for perceptions of competence, such as level of difficulty, specificity, and strength (Bandura, 1977, 1982). For example, if a task is perceived as being relatively easy, and an individual believes strongly that he or she has the specific skills it takes to succeed, self-efficacy expectancies will generally be positive. Furthermore, people who experience success in a number of competence domains may be expected to have positive self-efficacy expectancies in a greater number of situations than those who have more limited success (Bandura, 1977). Over time, domain-specific expectancies of competence form a general set of expectations that an individual carries into new situations. These expectations may contribute to generalized orientations of competence or incompetence that are relatively stable across situations and relationships (Smith, 1969).

In addition to the contribution that attributions make to self-efficacy expectancies, there are also two important external sources of expectancy input: (a) vicarious experiences; and (b) social influence from significant sources (Bandura, 1982). For example, seeing similar others perform a task successfully can raise efficacy expectations if we judge ourselves capable of mastering the same kind of activity (Bandura, 1971). In light of successful performance by others, we tend to make inferences about our own ability to succeed, which raises our expectancy of success accordingly. Once we form a conception of how to behave through modeling, we apply what we have learned to the task at hand. Our initial performance efforts are then refined over time through self-corrective adjustments. By observing the differential effects of our own actions, we determine appropriate responses for the task and thereby increase our actual level of competency (Dulany, 1968).

Verbal influence is another way in which efficacy expectancies are affected by interpersonal factors (Bandura, 1982). If someone whose opinion we respect gives us reason to believe we can master a difficult task, even if we initially doubt our ability, our expectancy of success tends to increase. On the other hand, strong expectancies of competence can also be shaken if the message from an influential source is negative. Although social persuasion alone may be limited in its power to change competence self-concept, it can influence performance level and thereby make an indirect contribution. For example, after receiving praise from a teacher on a math assignment, a child with average mathematics skills may expend more effort and consequently perform better than usual on a math test. In fact, research has shown that efficacy information from others is most effective for people who have some reason to believe that they can produce positive results through their own actions (Chambliss & Murray, 1979a, 1979b).

When people have strong expectations of personal competence but negative outcome expectancies, they may try to change the environment to improve its responsiveness. Research has found that when individuals with high levels of self-efficacy are confronted with environmental unresponsiveness, they tend to respond with resentment, protest, and collective efforts to change existing conditions (Bandura, 1973; Short & Wolfgang, 1972). However, if both outcome and personal efficacy expectancies are weak in a particular situation, instead of trying to change environmental factors, an individual may not even want to attempt the task. In the original theory of learned helplessness (Seligman, 1975), people become inactive and depressed if they believe their actions do not affect what happens to them. In other words, personal competence expectancies may be high, but outcome expectancies are low. In the reformulated theory (Abramson, Seligman, & Teasdale, 1978), causal locus of helplessness is shifted to a belief that one cannot produce the requisite performance. That is, competence expectancies, rather than outcome expectancies, are implicated. Specifically, the theory postulates three aspects of failure judgments: (a) internality (personal versus environmental causes), (b) stability (enduring versus transient cause), and (c) generality (causes with pervasive effects versus causes that only apply in a few situations). Attributing "failures" to personal deficiencies of a generalized and enduring nature has a major impact on efficacy expectancies, and together the two factors contribute to low levels of self-perceived competence and effectance motivation. Ultimately, if this negative pattern of attributions and expectancies persists, despondency and depression can result (Seligman, Abramson, Semmel, & von Baeyer, 1979).

The relative effect of personal and social influences on performance expectancies differs depending on theoretical perspective. From an internal frame of reference, White (1959, 1963) has emphasized intrinsic factors that create an expectation of self-efficacy. In this view, social influence plays a minor role in performance expectancy. On the other hand, symbolic interactionists have argued that self-concept is not self-generated but is rather a looking-glass reflection of others' perceptions of us (Cooley, 1902). That is, interpersonal processes are the dominant source of efficacy information. However, in a review of studies that correlated judgments by others with self-evaluations, Shrauger and Schoeneman (1979) could not find consistent agreement between people's self-perceptions and how they were regarded by others. This may be due to the decreasing significance of social information and increasing importance of personal information as an individual matures and becomes better able to accurately incorporate self-relevant information from a variety of sources (Harter, 1986).

Reconciling internal and external conceptualizations of expectancy, expectancy formulations in research on work and task accomplishment have long recognized the importance of looking at environmental influences as well as trait components of expectancies. According to Motowidlo, Loehr, and Dunnette (1978), expectancy of successful performance is a function of two elements: (a) an individual's perception of task characteristics (environmental factors), and (b) his or her self-perceptions of competence (interpersonal factors). Thus, "generalized expectancy of task success" refers to a person's overall competence self-concept plus the expectancy of meeting a successful performance standard in a particular task situation (Motowidlo et al., 1978; Moulton, 1974). The individual reaches a general expectation of task mastery by determining from situational cues the objective probability of achieving a particular performance standard and by determining personal competence from appraisal of relevant skills and previous experience.

As is the case with attributions for past performance efforts, expectancies for future performance efforts do not have to be accurate to affect competence self-concept. Illusory expectancies are based in part on erroneous attributions and tend to occur when the individual incorrectly attributes an achievement to personal skill, rather than to fortuitous environmental circumstances. Chapman and Chapman (1967) postulate that "illusory correlations" develop whenever two events are inaccurately presumed to be associated with each other. Once an erroneous correlation has been established, occasional observations of cases where the two events coincide tend to reconfirm the belief, and inconsistent cases are either ignored or forgotten. For example, if a visitor to Las Vegas plays "21" for the first time and begins to win, he may develop an expectation of success. Unfortunately, if he starts placing large bets because he attributes his winning streak to personal competence, the odds are that he will eventually be out of money and disappointed. Ultimately, inflated expectancies of self-efficacy for future performance efforts may generalize to competence self-attitudes, thereby inflating an individual's sense of competence in a particular domain.

In summary, expectancies make an important contribution to competence self-concept. Influenced indirectly by attributions, which accommodate both motivational (performance goals and vested interest) and cognitive (perceptions of agentic control) factors, and by social factors (vicarious information and social persuasion), it is not surprising that expectancies have been shown to be a reliable predictor of behavior. Furthermore, when expectancies arouse affect by implicating the self (self-efficacy expectancies) rather than the environment (outcome expectancies), their influence on competence self-concept is likely to be similarly profound.

Contemporary Theories

Recent conceptualizations of competence tend to provide a more thorough explanation of how we come to view ourselves as competent individuals, including emphasis on affect, as well as motivation, behavior, and cognition. In particular, several researchers (Harackiewicz, Sansone, & Manderlink, 1985; Harter, 1978, 1986; Kanfer, 1980; Wicklund, 1978) postulate that self-evaluative responses to performance outcomes provoke affective reactions that ultimately affect an individual's motivation to engage in given behaviors. For example, Harter (1978) proposes a model in which an infant's initial effectance urges produce two immediate outcomes: a self-perception of success or failure and a response from socializing agents in the environment. As a consequence, both perception of personal control over outcomes and feedback from significant others trigger an affective response in the child that may contribute directly to motivation. Her model further postulates that for each incidence of mastery behavior, a combination of factors in this chain of influence will have a direct impact on the child's perceived sense of competence and will carry with it its own affective and motivational consequences. Thus, in a circular fashion the motivational orientation stemming from perceived competence will, in turn, modify initial mastery urges and provoke new behaviors and consequences.

Although James (1890) was one of the first to acknowledge importance of affect in self-conceptions, emotions have only recently emerged as an important focus of research in self theory. In this research, emotions have taken on important significance and involve not only feelings, but also processes of initiating, maintaining, and terminating relations between the individual and the environment (Barrett & Campos, 1987; Frijda, 1986). Moreover, emotion is now regarded as the way in which a person, an event, and the person's evaluation of the significance of that event are interrelated (Campos, Campos, & Barrett, 1989). Thus, feelings of satisfaction and pleasure following successful performance outcomes might be considered an affective catalyst that promotes competence self-evaluation. In other words, when we perform an important task successfully, we view our behavior as efficacious and regard ourselves as competent. Associated positive feelings contribute, in turn, to motivation. Therefore, we are compelled to repeat our "successful" behavior to attain the same affective result.

It is postulated that for goal-directed behavior to impact competence self-concept, a task must be relevant to our goals and important enough to generate interest (physiological arousal). With interest and self-relevance, cognitive processes take on affective significance. That is, instead of being merely informational, appraisals are now evaluative as well. In particular, a growing body of evidence shows that the nature of attributions we make for performance outcomes strongly influences the kind of affect we experience (Weiner & Graham, 1983). If these appraisals are positive, we experience positive, self-relevant emotion; if these appraisals are negative, we experience negative, self-relevant emotion. In addition, social reinforcement from others can also influence both the nature and strength of the hedonic response during the appraisal process. Ultimately, cognitive aspects of performance appraisal transfer to attitudes about the self (competence self-concept), whereas evaluative aspects transfer to feelings about the self (self-esteem) (see Figure 5.1).

Investigators (Campos, Campos, & Barrett, 1989) have found that three elements make an action affectively significant: (a) relevance of the action to an individual's goals; (b) hedonic nature of the action (whether the action produces intrinsically positive or negative feelings); and (c) emotional reinforcement from others, such as facial expressions and verbalizations. Thus, efficacy-related emotions have both intrapersonal and

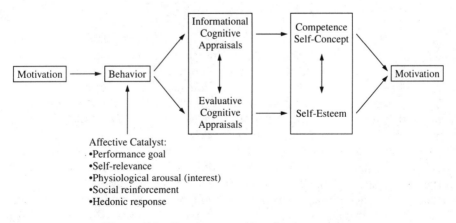

Figure 5.1   Competence self-evaluation process.

interpersonal regulatory consequences for behavior. For example, if a child performs a goal-directed task, receives encouragement for that performance from significant others, and feels good about his or her behavior, the behavior is likely to be repeated. By repeating the action, the child not only maintains positive affect but simultaneously signals to others that they should continue their support of his or her behavior (Emde, 1988). Therefore, efficacy-related affect is not only an impetus for goal-directed behavior, it is also a means of generating expressive signals that have environmental consequences (Frijda, 1986).

Conceptualizing affective response to efficacious behavior as a relational experience, rather than a strictly personal phenomenon, has important implications. First, emotional signals from others not only guide an individual's action, they may also generate similar emotions in a perceiver (Campos, Campos, & Barrett, 1989), a process known as social referencing (Campos & Stenberg, 1981). For instance, if a child's parents respond positively to her report card, even though it is average, she might feel delighted by her performance. On the other hand, if her parents express disappointment, the child might feel sadness and embarrassment. Second, ecological factors also impact feelings of efficacy (Campos, Campos, & Barrett, 1989). Two obvious examples are the amount of encouragement a parent gives to a young child's exploratory behavior and a family's emotional climate, or proportion of time a child encounters emotional feedback that supports mastery efforts. Thus, just as motivation and cognition have both personal and social aspects, affective consequences of task-related behavior are likewise bidimensional. Cumulatively, these internal and external components play a critical role in motivation, behavior, interpretations of that behavior, and, ultimately, formation of competence self-concept.

DEVELOPMENT OF THE COMPETENT SELF

Not only do researchers from a number of disciplines vary widely in the way they view competence self-concept, there is also some disagreement with regard to *when* we acquire a conception of ourselves as competent individuals. Some theorists (e.g., deCharms, 1968; Malinowski, 1955; White, 1959) presume that we are born with an incipient sense of competence that develops more fully after practice and reinforcement from the environment. For example, defining "executive competence" as an ability to initiate and sustain exploratory and manipulative behavior, Wenar (1964) postulates that a child is aware of his or her competence as early as the age of one. On the other hand, Mead (1934) ties the origin of competence self-concept to the advent of symbolization and language. Still others argue that self-conceptions of competence only emerge after the child has accomplished other achievements underlying selfhood (e.g., Smith, 1969).

Although there is compelling empirical evidence to suggest that perceptions of personal agency develop in the first year of life (see Lamb, 1981; Suomi, 1981, for reviews), other empirical data link emergence of a generalized sense of competence with early childhood (Harter, 1985, 1986; Marton, Golombek, Stein, & Korenblum, 1988; Nicholls, 1978; Stipek, 1981). Overall, cross-sectional evidence from infancy through late childhood suggests that levels of perceived competence grow increasingly more modest, and competence self-concept grows increasingly more accurate, with development (Weisz, 1986). Furthermore, the literature suggests that acquisition of competent styles of behaving and self-conceptions of competence is a lifelong task (Ford & Thompson, 1985).

Early perceptions of personal agency make significant contributions to competence development in the first year of life by regulating goal-directed behavior through affective arousal. Operant conditioning studies suggest that infants are capable of perceiving contingencies between their behavior and events in the environment (Rovee-Collier & Lipsitt, 1981) and experiencing related arousal as early as the first few weeks of life. This contingency awareness appears to be based on development of memorial ability and capacity to understand means-end relationships (Piaget, 1952), as well as perceptual sensitivity to environmental stimuli such as distance perception and discrimination of facial features (Suomi, 1981; Watson, 1979). Although by the 2nd month, infants are able to demonstrate stable learning that is retained over several days or weeks, the 4th month seems to mark the beginning of a nascent sense of personal agency when an infant's perceptions of personal control begin to transfer to new situations (Ford & Thompson, 1985). For example, Finkelstein and Ramey (1977) found that infants between 4 and 9 months who were previously exposed to a series of contingent experiences later learned new operant responses more rapidly than did nonexposed infants. However, this finding did not hold for 3-month-olds in a follow-up study (Ramey & Finkelstein, 1978). By the second half of the first year, with a growing sense of means-ends relationships (McCall, 1979; Piaget, 1952), increasing ability to behave intentionally (Weisz, 1983), and the memorial and associative skills required to perceive contingencies over time (Weisz, 1983), infants' conceptions of personal agency became more complex and sophisticated.

Experiences of contingency or control by infants elicit interest and other positive emotions that affect goal-directed behavior. Crucial to this emotional responding is contingent responding by a primary caregiver, usually the mother. It is thought that contingent responding fosters well-modulated fluctuations in arousal that are keyed to an infant's tolerance to stimulation (Thompson & Lamb, 1983). A process of following infant actions such as smiling and gazing with appropriate and predictable maternal responses likely reinforces the functional efficacy of behaviors that the infant has learned regulate interpersonal interaction (Ford & Thompson, 1985). Tronick and colleagues (1982) conclude, "When infants are able to accomplish their interactive goals, when their displays are responded to appropriately, a feeling of effectance cumulates; when interactive goals are thwarted, a sense of helplessness develops" (p. 97). For example, when mothers are asked to remain nonresponsive to their infants' behavior, the infants typically react with intense social behavior, followed by quieting, sobering, withdrawal, and occasional distress (e.g., Tronick, Als, Adamson, Wise, & Brazelton, 1978; Trevarthen, 1977). Ultimately, repeated experiences of this kind may generate anxious feelings of ineffectance in a baby (Tronick et al., 1978).

A primary goal of early mastery attempts in infancy is to modulate arousal by developing familiarity with the environment. This is an interactive process in which an infant discovers how self-initiated actions affect the environment and how the environment, in turn, responds to the behavior. Eventually, as the child develops a sense of autonomy and becomes able to initiate and maintain effective transactions with the environment, a diffuse sense of competence emerges that encompasses the child's beliefs about his or her capabilities (Harter, 1989). Thus, out of the interaction between child and environment, the environment's *responsiveness* to the child's behavior is critical in development of competence self-concept. Furthermore, the quality of this individual-environmental interaction, particularly the opportunities it provides for efficacious behavior (e.g., stimulation, challenge, lack of constraints), continues to be a major condition for competence self-concept development throughout the child's life (Gecas, 1989).

Although the process of interacting with the environment begins in infancy (or even before), and the experience of personal agency develops as early as the 4th month, it appears to take several years before young children can make judgments about their competence or adequacy. For example, researchers have found that children as young as 4 can make competence-related judgments of their classmates if questions address concrete, observable behaviors (Stipek, 1984). Similarly, Harter (1989) has found that children between the ages of 4 and 7 can express attitudes about their cognitive competence, physical competence, and general behavioral conduct. However, these domains of competence behavior are not clearly differentiated from each other in terms of value. In contrast to older children, who attach evaluative significance to success in specific domains, young children seem unable to make discriminating judgments about the relative importance of different domains of competence.

Not only do young children seem to have difficulty rating the importance of different kinds of competence, their diffuse self-judgments of competence are not necessarily accurate. In fact, several researchers (e.g., Harter, 1989; Nicholls, 1978; Nicholls & Miller, 1983) have determined that perceptions of competence in early childhood are likely to be inaccurately high. The reason for this inaccuracy may be inability to use social comparison information for the purpose of self-evaluation (see review by

Ruble, 1983), a process that requires three subskills: (a) ability to perform seriation; (b) ability to observe personal performance and position from a detached perspective; and (c) ability to relate temporally separate outcomes to one another (Nicholls, 1978). As a result of their inability to perform these skills, young children's judgments of their own competence tend to reflect the inflated image they see in their parents' eyes.

Using a different approach to explain differences in competence judgments between children and adults, Kun (1977) postulates that a "halo scheme" may interfere with children's ability to make accurate self-judgments of competence. In particular, children tend to equate competence with effort, such that successful performance attained with considerable effort is seen as more competent than similar achievement with relatively little effort. Thus, to understand developmental change in competence judgments, it may also be important to understand how children themselves conceptualize competence (Weisz, 1986). Nicholls and Miller (1984) suggest that development of a *concept* of competence goes through a three-stage process. In the first stage, children below the age of 5 cannot distinguish between task difficulty and personal ability but can differentiate tasks on a basis of subjective expectancy of success. In the next stage, children between the ages of 5 and 8 are able to see that difficult tasks require more ability than easier tasks but do not distinguish unique contributions of task difficulty and ability to outcomes. Finally, by the age of 7 or 8, children are able to differentiate ability and task difficulty and use social comparison information to make ability judgments.

Once a child reaches middle childhood, several other changes begin to take place that improve ability to make accurate and relevant self-judgments. First, there is an increasing tendency to attach affective significance to behavior (Harter, 1989). Whether self-generated or influenced by significant others in a child's life, some domains of behavior become more important than others and, presumably, exert more potent influence on self-relevant attitudes. For example, if a child has a poor perception of his or her athletic ability but cares little about excelling in sports, judgments of athletic competence are likely to have negligible affective impact and, consequently, little effect on competence self-judgments. However, if athletic skill is important to the child, negative affective consequences stemming from appraisals of incompetence are likely to result. These feelings of disappointment or unhappiness make competence appraisals particularly salient, thereby increasing the possibility that they might generalize to the child's overall sense of self-worth.

A second change that takes place during middle childhood is an increasing ability to incorporate environmental information and social comparison into accurate self-perceptions. There is considerable evidence that children spontaneously compare peers' performance to their own by about the age of 7 or 8 (Ruble, Feldman, & Boggiano, 1976). Although initially unable to discriminate between objective performance and subjective feedback from others related to that performance, children in middle childhood gradually become able to determine when feedback is inconsistent with personal perceptions of behavior. In addition, a tendency to equate ability with amount of effort expended in task performance is replaced with normative judgments of competence. Not nearly as dependent on direct sources of performance feedback as they were in early childhood, older children become more adept at forming perceptions of competence based on an awareness of their place in a social hierarchy of competence (Nicholls & Miller, 1983).

Finally, a third change that takes place in middle childhood is the separation of general self-conceptions into discrete behavioral domains, a phenomenon White (1963) predicted in his early examination of effectance motivation and competence. Thus, what was initially a diffuse sense of competence in early childhood becomes more differentiated, diverging into specific categories of behavior that incorporate relevant arenas of activity in a child's life. Current researchers place this point of differentiation in competence self-attitudes at about the age of 8 (Harter, 1989; Marton et al., 1988). From this point on, competence self-concept becomes more and more compartmentalized until adulthood, when an individual's array of competence self-conceptions is likely to comprise a large number of domain-specific judgments (Harter, 1989).

The transition from a diffuse sense of competence in infancy and early childhood to self-judgments in specific domains of ability has been a primary focus in Harter's (e.g., 1986, 1989) research on the development of self-attitudes in children and adolescents. According to her findings, in middle childhood an increasing number of competence domains can be articulated, as well as differentiated, and the structure of the self-concept changes to reflect this increasingly more complex view of self-efficacy. In particular, she has found that children between the ages of 8 and 12 can clearly distinguish among 5 domains of competence or adequacy: scholastic competence, athletic competence, behavioral conduct, peer social acceptance, and physical appearance. Once a child reaches adolescence, 3 new domains have been added: close friendships, romantic appeal, and job competence. Further articulation and differentiation among college students results in 12 domains of competence: scholastic competence, intellectual ability, creativity, job competence, athletic competence, physical appearance, romantic relationships, peer social acceptance, close friendship, parent relationships, sense of humor, and morality. Finally, adults are able to articulate and differentiate among 11 domains: intelligence, sense of humor, job competence, morality, athletic ability, physical appearance, sociability, intimate relationships, nurturance, adequacy as a provider, and household management.

Although Harter (1992) and others (e.g., Cauce, 1987; Glick & Zigler, 1985; Higgins, 1987, 1991; Markus & Nurius, 1986; Rosenberg, 1979; Tesser, 1988; Tesser & Campbell, 1983) have concluded that self-judgments in a number of domains contribute in varying degree to self-esteem, it is not clear from the research how this process occurs. Nor is it clear how competence self-concept in specific domains relate to a general sense of competence. We suspect that a general sense of competence cuts across, or comprises, all the more specific competence domains that are self-relevant. If these self-relevant domains also carry affective significance, they likely affect self-esteem. For instance, if perceived job competence carries affective weight with a person, job competence self-concept would be positively related to both overall competence self-concept and self-esteem. If the individual is not affectively invested in job competence, as might be the case for someone working solely for the monetary reward, job competence self-concept would be unrelated to general competence self-concept and feelings of self-worth. This proposition receives partial support in the work of Cauce (1987), who found that both perceived peer competence and perceived school competence were positively and moderately ($r = .35$) with perceived general competence among early adolescents. Furthermore, both of these aspects of competence are rated as being highly desirable by the youths, a finding that may have implications for self-esteem (see final section of this chapter for a more complete analysis of the link between competence self-concept and self-esteem).

Developmental research on competence self-concept or perceived self-efficacy in adults in less extensive than comparable research in children and adolescents. However, studies that have been conducted on adult populations suggest relative stability in self-judgments of competence over much of the life course, with the possibility of a slight decrease in the last decades of life (Gurin & Brim, 1984; Mortimer, Lorence, & Kumka, 1986). Based largely on cross-sectional analyses of specific age groups, adult studies have generally found a slight curvilinear pattern: level of competence self-concept increases through adolescence and early adulthood, peaks at middle age, and begins to decline around the age of 60 (Brim, 1974; Dowd, 1975; Gurin & Brim, 1984). Noteworthy is one study on a large sample of adults ($n = 1,212$) that found a decrease in sense of competence during early middle age, stability through the 40s and 50s, and a slight increase in the early 60s (Lachman, 1986). However, based on a review of the literature on aging and self-concept, Bengston, Reedy, and Gordon (1985) conclude it is more likely that cohort membership, gender, sociocultural trends, and life-stage experiences have greater influence on self-conceptions (including self-efficacy) than maturation level itself.

Researchers have found that changes in adult self-concept appear to be most closely associated with particular events in development, such as graduation from school, marriage, parenthood, and retirement. Furthermore, it is often not the event itself that is significant, but rather the timing of the event. According to Gurin and Brim (1984), unexpected or atypical events convey information that there is something unique or special about the individual, making this information self-relevant and therefore pertinent to competence appraisals. Because it is not necessarily the event itself that affects competence self-judgments as much as it is its timing in relation to social custom, *atypical* and *off-time* events trigger negative social comparison with agemates who typically experience these events at a different time in their lives (Gurin & Brim, 1984). In addition, studies have shown that economic or social disruption (McLanahan, 1983), role strain, and decreased control and responsibility (Langer & Rodin, 1976; Schulz, 1980) can also reduce competence self-concept, particularly if an individual's sense of self-efficacy is initially low (Clausan, 1986; Gecas & Mortimer, 1987; Mortimer, Finch, & Kumka, 1982). Interventions that have been found to counteract some of the negative impacts of these events focus on improving social-role performance, adaptive capacity, and perceptions of control (Kuypers & Bengston, 1973).

Thus, reciprocity between self and environment, so important during formation of self-perceptions of competence in early childhood, appears to remain a critical factor throughout an individual's life. Moreover, self-judgments of competence developed early in childhood may generate a lifelong pattern of behavior by creating self-fulfilling prophecies (Gecas & Mortimer, 1987). For instance, children with positive competence self-judgments may tend to take more risks when they approach challenging tasks, and subsequent success in these efforts may foster an increasing sense of competence over time. Conversely, children who view their competence in less positive terms may retreat from challenge and risk, behavior that is likely to have a cumulative and negative effect on competence self-concept.

In summary, evidence from the developmental literature suggests that our sense of competence develops from two kinds of input: internal sources of information, or appraisals of the effects of our actions on the immediate world of physical objects, and external sources of information, or reflected appraisals from individuals in our environment. Although intrinsic motivation may guide initial exploration and mastery efforts, a developing sense of competence is directly linked to responsiveness of the environment and only develops after other basic achievements in selfhood have already occurred. Furthermore, once an initial sense of competence emerges in early childhood, this self-perception may determine a characteristic coping style that influences the way challenges are approached throughout life. In middle childhood, as we become adept at integrating personal and environmental sources of information to form more accurate competence judgments and begin to attach emotional significance to performance outcomes, competence self-concept becomes differentiated. Moreover, once we attach value judgments to behavior in specific domains of competence, these evaluations likely generalize to our sense of self-worth. By adulthood, sense of competence is multifaceted, integrating into the self-structure a vast amount of information from internal and external sources, and weighted according to importance assigned to relevant

TABLE 5.1   Critical Factors in the Development of Competence Self-Concept

Developmental Stage	Achievement
Newborns (0–4 months)	Perceptual sensitivity to environmental stimuli Memorial ability Understanding of means/ends relationships Contingency awareness
Infancy (4 months–2 years)	Intentional behavior Contingency awareness over time Sense of personal agency
Early childhood (2–7 years)	Specific competence judgments of peers Undifferentiated, inaccurate competence self-judgments
Middle childhood (7–12 years)	Performance behavior attains affective significance Self-perceptions become more accurate Competence self-judgments become domain-specific
Adolescence/ young adulthood (12–21 years)	Continuing differentiation of competence self-judgments Level of competence self-concept increases slightly
Adulthood (21–39 years)	Domain-specific competence self-concept Level of competence self-concept increases slightly
Middle age (39–59 years)	Level of competence self-concept peaks
Old age (60+ years)	Level of competence self-concept decreases slightly

domains of competence. Unless we experience untimely or atypical events, we are unlikely to see any major changes in competence self-concept throughout the remainder of our lives. The developmental pattern of this progression is summarized in Table 5.1.

RESOURCES FOR A COMPETENT SELF

In general, the "competent self" can be conceptualized as a combination of elements from both internal and environmental sources of input that inform the self about capabilities and skills. Because there are many behavioral domains where competence behavior is displayed, a wide variety of personal and environmental characteristics may serve as resources for emerging self-attitudes of competence (Amato & Ochiltree, 1986). For example, some resources for competence self-concept, such as disposition, gender, health, size, and physical strength, are biological in nature. Although subject to modification by the environment, these resources are largely determined at birth. Other resources are interpersonal in nature and involve relationships with significant others in the environment.

Finally, a third set of resources involves social-cultural systems. The way society distributes wealth, education, status, and power to different families, social groups, and classes gives some individuals an advantage over those with less access to these opportunities. On an even larger scale, by virtue of their shared knowledge, worldview, and way of life, individual cultures support and encourage the development of some forms of competence at the expense of others (Amato & Ochiltree, 1986).

Biological Resources

Biological resources for competence consist of inherited physiological capacities and dispositions that affect a child's skill at dealing effectively with the environment. For example, a temperament in infancy characterized by attentiveness, curiosity, and exploration is evidence of intrinsic motivation and predictive of competent behavior as the infant matures (Hunt, 1961; White, 1959). When exploration and manipulation evoke positive feelings (e.g., satisfaction and pleasure), the child is motivated to produce similar behaviors. Conversely, if such activity evokes negative feelings (e.g., frustration, disappointment, or anger), the child ceases active exploration of the environment. Very quickly after birth, environmental responsiveness to a child's initial mastery efforts begins to affect the primacy of dispositional control over behavior, gradually becoming a more and more important competence-related resource as the child matures.

Health, size, and physical strength are other biological factors that affect competence development. For example, if a child is genetically susceptible to a particular illness or disease and succumbs to the condition, there may be negative effects on many other aspects of the individual's life, including competence self-concept. Likewise, if a person is atypical with regard to size, strength, or appearance, sense of competence may be affected. For example, an adolescent who is short relative to his peers may not feel competent enough to try out for the football team, even though he is athletic and would likely make the team. As is true with atypical life events, it is the unusual or unexpected factor that provides salient self-relevant information and, consequently, has a capacity to influence competence self-judgments.

Another obvious biological resource for competence self-attitudes is gender. A great deal of evidence suggests that men have a greater sense of self-efficacy, personal control, and mastery than do women (Block, 1976, 1983; Maccoby & Jacklin, 1974). This difference in competence self-concept is even more evident when it relates to a task that is considered masculine in sex type (Lenney, 1981; McMahon, 1982). For example, because leadership positions have traditionally been regarded as appropriate for men, and women are stereotypically viewed as having fewer of the qualities necessary to be an effective leader (e.g., Bem, 1974; Broverman, Vogel, Broverman, Clarkson, & Rosenkrantz, 1972), women in these roles tend to have lower expectancies of success and less confidence in their competence than men (Heilman, Lucas, & Kaplow, 1990). Gecas (1989) attributes these differences to cultural factors (e.g., sex-role stereotypes) and structural factors (e.g., different social environments). For example, gender differences may reflect cultural conceptions of "masculinity" (emphasizing agency, potency, and assertiveness) and "femininity" (emphasizing passivity, dependence, and conformity). With regard to a structural perspective, gender differences in perceived competence may relate to power differences between men and women in society, restricted opportunities for women, and the nature of housework and jobs that women typically hold (Mirowsky & Ross, 1986). As cultural and structural factors change over time, the extent to which decreasing gender bias will be reflected in self-attitudes of competence depends largely on how patterns of interaction within the family and workplace support these changes (Gecas, 1989).

Interpersonal Resources

Although biologically determined resources make an important contribution to an individual's sense of competence, interpersonal factors also play a major role according to the developmental literature. The importance of social contexts in the development of self-conceptions has a long history in social psychology (see theories of Cooley, 1902, and Mead, 1934, for early examples), and it is generally acknowledged that the way significant others view attempts at mastery can affect competence self-concept both in terms of a child's initiation of mastery behavior and evaluation of performance. In particular, family context is usually the most important environmental influence on a child's developing sense of competence, particularly in infancy (White, 1979). Generally, if parents are supportive of an infant's active attempts to master the physical and interpersonal environment, the result tends to be a mutually satisfying relationship that engenders a sense of efficacy in the child (Edgar, 1980; Schaffer, Rudolph, & Crook, 1978).

Research on parenting styles has determined that a combination of parental support and encouragement, plus use of inductive control (a style that relies more on reasoning than on coercive control), is conducive to development of both competent behavior and self-judgments of competence among children (Baumrind, 1978; Gecas, 1971). In their review of studies that examined family influence on competence development, Amato and Ochiltree (1986) find that high-competence family environments are those in which parents communicate frequently with their children and encourage them to explore and manipulate the environment (White, 1979); the relationship between parents and child is close and supportive (Frodi, Bridges, & Grolnick, 1985; Rollins & Thomas, 1979); parents have high educational expectations for their child and help with schoolwork (Henderson, 1981); parents use induction techniques and point out consequences of behavior to their child (Rollins & Thomas, 1979); parents use authoritative, rather than authoritarian or permissive, styles of parenting (Baumrind, 1978); and there is an absence of overt conflict between family members (Emery, 1982; Rutter, 1971). There is also some evidence that vicarious experience, or seeing parents performing efficacious behavior, also contributes to a developing sense of competence (Bandura, 1977; Whitbeck, 1987). However, as Gecas and Schwalbe (1986) note, it is a child's ongoing interpretation of the parent-child relationship that has an impact on competence self-concept, rather than the parents' actual behavior.

In addition to family relationships, family structure also contributes to a child's developing sense of competence (Gecas, 1989). For example, Rodin (1976) finds that the impact of family size on density of living conditions has an effect on children's self-perceptions of control: the denser the living conditions, the less control children feel they have. Although this finding may reflect the effects of diminished privacy on self-determined behavior and an associated increase in environmental unpredictability, factors related to parenting style likely also played a role. In particular, as family density increases, parental control may become more rigid and authoritarian (Elder & Browerman, 1963), thereby restricting a child's opportunities for efficacious behavior (Gecas, 1989).

Smith (1969) describes positive parent-child relationships that support mastery efforts as "benign circles of socialization." In this formulation, a child behaves, and this behavior generally receives a supportive response from the family, thereby motivating similar future behaviors. However, rather than viewing this process as circular, Harter (1989) conceptualizes the reciprocal interaction between parents and child as a spiraling process, changing in both content and level of interaction as the child develops. The results of this dynamic relationship are varying levels of competence relevant to particular behavioral domains (e.g., different self-conceptions of academic competence, physical competence, and social competence). Thus, in benign situations where a family supports mastery efforts, successful performance encourages a child to attempt new challenges and attain even higher levels of achievement, thereby supporting development of a variety of competence self-conceptions that relate to normal domains of activity for the child.

Not only are parent-child relationships important in development of self-attitudes of competence, interpersonal influences can also provoke a sense of incompetence in a young child. Described by Smith (1969) as "vicious circles of socialization," nonsupportive relationships create an environment that does not respond to the child's efforts at mastery and control. These interpersonal influences can instill a sense of incompetence that is unwarranted by the child's actual performance. That is, the child may develop an attitude of illusory incompetence that impairs the exercise of abilities that actually exist. A likely outcome for a child caught in this situation is fewer mastery efforts over time and lower competence self-concept relative to his or her peers (Langer, 1979).

A number of factors have been shown to limit a family's ability to provide a supportive environment, such as parental depression and stressful situations within the family (Downey & Coyne, 1990). A critical aspect of support appears to be conditionality, or extent to which a child believes that support is contingent on meeting high parental performance standards (Harter, 1991). Similar in concept to an atmosphere of unconditional positive regard (see Rogers & Dymond, 1954), in which a child is loved and supported as an individual rather than because his or her behavior meets the expectations of others, conditionality may undermine attitudes of competence by impacting feelings of satisfaction and pleasure associated with personal performance. In particular, Harter's (1991) research has revealed a close link between conditional support and self-esteem: the more conditional the support from parents, the lower a child's self-esteem. Thus, regardless of level of parental support, if this support is provided only when a child meets parental expectations, lower perceptions of competence may result.

Parent-child relationships are not the only interpersonal source of competence-related information. Mead (1934) suggests that development of self-conceptions depends on an expanding and increasingly complex set of role relationships that comprise all contexts in which the individual is a participant. These relationships begin with a child and his or her primary caregiver, extend to more complicated role relationships in the immediate family, and, with the advent of daycare or school, broaden to include peer group, extrafamilial adult authorities, and, ultimately, the entire structure of society. With role relationships expanding in number and complexity, reflected appraisals gradually become more generalized, and self-conceptions become progressively more objective and less dependent on contingencies of particular role relationships.

Sociocultural Resources

In addition to the influence of biological and interpersonal resources on competence self-concept, social and cultural factors also contribute to development of self-relevant competence judgments. Because families differ in access to social resources by virtue of their position in the social structure, children may have more or less exposure to opportunities for mastery experiences. Resources such as wealth, political power, social influence, and access to information can have a substantial impact not only on how much effort a child expends on mastery attempts, but also on whether the child even initiates mastery behavior. In particular, children born into high-resource families are likely to have more opportunity for mastery efforts than children with limited exposure to these resources (Gladwin, 1967). As a result of differential access to social resources, relative inaccessibility reduces an individual's ability to acquire knowledge and skills necessary to develop a competence in dealing with the environment (Smith, 1969).

Much of the research on social antecedents of competence self-concept has focused on social stratification, which affects opportunities to engage in efficacious behavior, especially in the workplace, and ideological belief systems, which produce differential evaluation of people's actions (Gecas & Schwalbe, 1983). Although correlations are not strong, socioeconomic status (as determined by occupational prestige and education level) has been found to be positively related to self-efficacy and mastery and negatively related to powerlessness (Gecas & Seff, 1987; Gurin, Gurin, & Morrison, 1978). More specifically, research has shown that some of the factors that appear to be positively linked to competence self-concept in the workplace include employee self-direction, challenge, and work complexity (Gecas & Seff, 1987; Kohn & Schooler, 1983; Mortimer & Lorence, 1979; Mortimer, Lorence, & Kumka, 1986; Schwalbe, 1986; Staples, Schwalbe, & Gecas, 1984). In addition, other important class-related factors that contribute to increased competence self-concept are education (Kohn & Schooler, 1983; Mirowsky & Ross, 1983) and income (Downey & Moen, 1987; Duncan & Liker, 1983). Not surprisingly, disruptions in employment status (e.g., termination, demotion, losing one's job because of injury or illness) tend to decrease sense of competence and increase powerlessness and psychological distress (Gecas & Seff, 1987).

Race and ethnicity have also been found to play a role in the development of competence self-concept (Gurin, Gurin, & Morrison, 1978). Much of the work in this area has focused on differences between African Americans and whites (Franks & Marolla, 1976; Hughes & Demo, 1989; Tashakkori & Thompson, 1991). Compared with whites, African Americans have been found to have lower perceived self-efficacy (Gurin, Gurin, & Morrison, 1978), a finding several researchers (e.g., Franks & Marolla, 1976; Gecas, 1989; Hughes & Demo, 1989) attribute to consequences of racial discrimination on power, control, and access to resources that support efficacious action. In particular, Hughes and Demo (1989) argue that African Americans are often deprived of opportunities in relation to whites, which hinders development of a strong sense of competence. Similarly, Tashakkori and Thompson (1991) suggest that, compared with whites, African Americans feel less personal control over environmental responsiveness. However, despite difference in competence self-concept, research has not demonstrated similar differences in self-esteem (see Gecas, 1982, for review). One possible explanation for this lack of correlation may be that self-esteem is primarily influenced by interpersonal relationships, whereas self-efficacy may be more influenced by sociocultural factors (Gecas & Schwalbe, 1983).

Finally, even the culture we live in has a strong impact on shaping competence self-concept because it affords certain individuals more access to opportunities than others (Franks & Marolla, 1976). For example, Western culture emphasizes values such as mastery, individualism, freedom, self-reliance, and achievement. Consequently, forms of competence involving language and numeric ability (Inkeles, 1966), leadership (Inkeles, 1966), autonomy (Erikson, 1959; Smith, 1969), and initiative and industry (Erikson, 1959; Smith, 1969) have been highly valued. Conversely, cultural and ideological values that emphasize fatalistic beliefs have been found to be associated with lower perceptions of self-efficacy and greater beliefs in external control (Gecas, 1989). Thus, in Western society, individuals who possess valued skills are more likely to "succeed" and thereby reap personal and social benefits associated with this success (Amato & Ochiltree, 1986), one of these benefits being a strong sense of competence.

COMPETENCE AND SELF-ESTEEM

Self-esteem is thought to be closely linked to competence self-concept. Although a few see self-esteem as synonymous with a sense of competence in dealing with the environment (e.g., Bracken, 1992; Lawler, 1973), most "self" researchers assign a more global definition to the construct that involves general regard for the self as a person (e.g., Epstein, 1973, 1991; Harter, 1986; Harter & Marold, 1992; Rosenberg, 1979, 1986). Thus, self-esteem might be viewed as the affective, or evaluative, counterpart to cognitive representations of the self. However, despite some ambiguity in the way the two constructs relate to each other, self-esteem is widely acknowledged as having a strong influence on psychological orientation to the world, including motivation to engage in efficacious behavior. Likewise, the way a person views his or her competence is generally accepted as an important determinant of feelings of self-esteem.

At the turn of the century, James (1890) was one of the first to suggest that competence self-concept was a critical element in evaluative feelings about self-worth. Recognizing the multidimensional nature of self-attitudes, he postulated that abilities in only those areas deemed important were relevant to self-esteem. In other words, self-esteem resulted from how an individual weighted his or her competencies. According to this conceptualization, if we see ourselves as competent in domains where we aspire to success, we have high self-esteem. On the other hand, if we see ourselves as unsuccessful in these areas, we have low self-esteem. Thus, the importance we ascribe to mastery efforts actually determines the kind of self-related affect we will experience (Weiner & Graham, 1983).

Contemporary research has confirmed James's presumption of a systematic relation between perceptions of competence in domains deemed important and an individual's self-esteem. Not only do correlational studies demonstrate an association between attitudes of competence in important domains and feelings about the self (see Glick & Zigler, 1985; Higgins, 1987, 1991; Markus & Nurius, 1986; Rosenberg, 1979; Tesser, 1988; Tesser & Campbell, 1983), causal modeling techniques also suggest that discrepancy between "ideal" and "real" self is an important determinant of self-worth (Harter, 1990). Furthermore, the close association between competence self-concept and self-esteem appears to hold for all but the youngest age categories. From a developmental perspective, researchers have determined that a discrepancy model does not apply to young children and that competence does not appear to be critical to self-esteem of children under the age of 8 (Harter, 1985, 1986, 1990), primarily because a young person does not appear to have a concept of his or her worth as a person until middle childhood. For example, when Harter (1989) asked teachers in one study to identify behaviors that did not discriminate between high and low self-esteem in young children, among those behaviors selected were competence (performs tasks competently, performs tasks without difficulty, uses materials in imaginative ways) and motivation to complete tasks (stays on task until finished, tries to do very best, does not complete things). Thus, competence self-concept and self-esteem appear to be unrelated in young children who have not yet developed an ability to make domain-specific evaluations of their competence and formulate a more global concept of their worth as a person (Harter, 1985, 1986, 1989).

However, by the age of 8, a link between judgments of personal competence and evaluative feelings about the self becomes evident. For example, Harter (1990) finds clear evidence in children between the ages of 8 and 15 that self-worth is based in part on real/ideal competence discrepancy scores for domains of importance to the individual. In fact, she also obtains the same pattern of results for older adolescents and college students, for gifted and learning-disabled children, and for adults. Furthermore, the larger the discrepancy between importance judgments and perceived competence, the more negative impact this difference appears to have on self-esteem. She finds it particularly noteworthy that low self-esteem was related to perceptions of incompetence in domains where individuals had aspirations of success. Furthermore, Higgins (1987, 1989) concludes that such importance/competence discrepancies not only predict self-esteem, but depression and anxiety as well.

Other researchers have confirmed Harter's findings. In one study (Marton et al., 1988), self-esteem of young male and female adolescents was found to be related to two specific domains of competence: objective measures of adaptive skills (e.g., verbal and nonverbal skills, fine-motor coordination) and competence in personality function as measured by psychiatrists (maintenance of identity, reality testing regarding self and others, relatedness, verbal communication, self-evaluation, identity crystallization, and role assumption). The authors concluded that competence in adaptive skills and competence in personality functions were not only equally related to self-esteem, but that the behaviors involved in these domains of competence were similar to behaviors that distinguished securely from insecurely attached infants in attachment theory (e.g., Ainsworth, 1979; Sroufe, 1978, 1979a, 1979b).

Without aspirations and affective involvement in performance efforts, we tend to be bored, unmotivated, uncertain of our competence, and dependent on momentary external stimulation for satisfaction (Bandura, 1991). However, personal aspirations create interest in our own behavior in the form of physiological arousal and heightened self- and environmental awareness. When our actions cause noticeable increases in arousal, we conduct a personal and environmental inventory to determine the valence of this arousal. Regardless of objective level of performance, if our appraisals tell us we have been successful at performing a task that is important to us, we perceive this arousal as "positive" and experience feelings of pleasure and satisfaction. In addition, because these feelings stem from our own behavior, they also provoke an affective evaluation of the self. Although some investigators (e.g., Weiner, Russell, & Lerman, 1978) have suggested that successful performance results in a number of different affects (e.g., affects related to outcome, sense of control, and feedback from others), Harter (1978, 1986) postulates that affect produced by perceptions of competence relates directly to self-evaluation. In other words, positive affect stemming from perceived successes enhances self-esteem.

Thus, association between competence self-concept and self-esteem may not be as direct as is assumed by much of the literature. Rather, nature and intensity of affect generated in task performance efforts may mediate the process by which personal competence appraisals influence self-esteem. Moreover, compared with those who have an external locus of control, people who internalize performance standards and believe outcomes are under their personal control are likely to experience stronger affective response to performance efforts. That is, the more performance outcomes implicate the self, the greater the intensity of self-relevant affect. Therefore, not only does affect serve as a catalyst for making task performance appraisals relevant to competence self-concept, it also may be instrumental in making competence judgments relevant to self-esteem.

Given the empirical evidence for a relation between competence self-concept and self-esteem, investigators might presume that we could improve self-esteem by raising our level of competence. In fact, James (1890) asserted that there were two ways to improve self-esteem: We can either raise our actual level of competence or lower our aspirations. Both alternatives serve to reduce discrepancy between competence and importance and, thereby, increase level of self-esteem. However, improving level of competent behavior as a strategy for improving self-esteem is problematic because there are natural limits on the extent to which an individual can increase actual capability (Harter, 1991). In addition, Epstein (1991) postulates two other reasons why perceptions of competence in important domains may be resistant to change. First, assuming that the individual's self-theory is hierarchically organized with more general attitudes and feelings (e.g., overall sense of competence and self-esteem) overlying discrete, situation-specific self-conceptions, and that general self-conceptions have more of an impact on self-esteem than specific self-thoughts, the postulates that higher-order schemata may be far more resistant to modification than lower-order, situation-specific constructs. Higher-order beliefs are typically acquired without conscious awareness in early childhood from emotionally charged experience that make these beliefs difficult to alter. Second, he notes that "people have a vested interest in maintaining the stability of their personal theories of reality, for they are the only systems they have for making sense of their world and guiding their behavior" (p. 97). Because any threat to the stability of one's personal theory likely evokes stress and anxiety, changes in important self-related beliefs and judgments are therefore to be avoided (Harter, 1991).

Furthermore, not only might it be difficult to increase actual level of competence, there are also psychological roadblocks to discounting the relevance of domains that are considered important (Harter, 1991). In particular, we are living in a society where certain competencies such as scholastic and athletic ability are highly valued. Therefore, aspirations and standards in these areas are typically quite high, making it difficult for those who feel inadequate to discount their importance. In addition, these domains are often considered important by others, particularly parents and peers. Research shows that competence in domains important to others is just as highly correlated with self-esteem as is competence in domains important to the self (Harter & Marold, 1992), a correlation that likely grows stronger over the course of development (Ruble, 1983; Suls & Sanders, 1982). Therefore, even if a person feels inadequate in particular domains, social factors make it difficult to reduce subjective importance of these domains to improve evaluative feelings about the self.

CONCLUSION

Competence self-concept is not simply a matter of knowing that we can behave efficaciously. Rather, conceptualizing one's competence involves transforming personal and social information into self-efficacy judgments in the presence of an affective stimulus. That is, emotion mediates the transfer of self-related appraisals to self-relevant conceptions. For emotion to generate physiological arousal of sufficient strength to impact the self-conception process, three elements appear to be necessary: (a) a goal that is considered "important" to both the self and to others; (b) behavior that is in direct service of that goal; and (c) agentic control over performance. Without these elements, affective arousal is minimal. Without affective arousal, cognitive appraisals of personal and environmental information do not implicate the self and consequently have little effect on self-judgments of personal competence.

Once the competence evaluation process is engaged in early infancy, it is maintained by a dynamic feedback system in which motivation, behavior, cognition, and feelings continuously interact and evolve to accommodate changing input from the environment. However, rather than objective behavior itself, it is *appraisal* of our behavior that appears to matter most to self-conceptions. Furthermore, environmental responsiveness to early mastery attempts from primary caregivers appears to be the critical external factor that determines nature and strength of performance-related affect and subsequent motivation to repeat efficacious behavior. Presumably, the better we become at monitoring and adjusting our behavior in response to environmental contingencies, the more often we experience positive affect during the behavior evaluation process, and the stronger our competence self-concept becomes.

In addition, not only does emotional arousal influence the extent to which cognitive appraisals of behavior impact self-conceptions of competence, competence self-concept has a reciprocal effect on feelings. For example, regarding self-behavior as efficacious generates emotions such as satisfaction and pleasure, whereas perceiving self-behavior as incompetent may lead to feelings of frustration, disappointment, and unhappiness. Moreover, the way we view personal performance efforts in important tasks over which we have control gives rise to positive or negative feelings regarding these competence judgments that, in turn, affect the way we evaluate our worth as a person. The positive feelings that accompany behavior perceived as "competent" generalize to feelings about the self. Thus, competence self-concept is an important source of self-esteem. Beginning in infancy, the results of these reciprocal processes are cumulative, appear to be domain-specific, and gradually become more resistant to change as patterns of behavior in each competence domain and evaluation of that behavior become habitual. Although there may be some decrease in competence self-concept and self-esteem in adolescence, generally, the patterns established in childhood tend to remain in place for a lifetime.

REFERENCES

Abramson, L. Y., Seligman, M. E. P., & Teasdale, J. D. (1978). Learned helplessness in humans: Critique and reformulation. *Abnormal Psychology, 87,* 49–74.

Adler, A. (1927). *The theory and practice of individual psychology.* New York: Harcourt.

Ainsworth, M. D. S. (1979). Infant-mother attachment. *American Psychologist, 34,* 932–937.

Amato, P. R., & Ochiltree, G. (1986). Family resources and the development of child competence. *Journal of Marriage and the Family, 48,* 47–56.

Ames, C., & Ames, R. (1981). Competitive versus individualistic goal structures: The salience of past performance information for causal attributions and effect. *Journal of Educational Psychology, 73,* 411–418.

Ames, C., & Felker, D. (1979). An examination of children's attributions and achievement-related evaluations in competitive, cooperative, and individualistic reward structures. *Journal of Educational Psychology, 71,* 413–420.

Atkinson, J. W. (1964). *An introduction to motivation.* Princeton, NJ: Van Nostrand.

Atkinson, J. W., & Feather, N. T. (1966). *A theory of achievement motivation.* New York: Wiley.

Bandura, A. (1971). Psychological modeling. *Conflicting theories.* Chicago: Aldine-Atherton.

Bandura, A. (1973). *Aggression: A social learning analysis.* Englewood Cliffs, NJ: Prentice-Hall.

Bandura, A. (1977). Self-efficacy: Toward a unifying theory of behavioral change. *Psychological Review, 84,* 191–215.

Bandura, A. (1978). The self system in reciprocal determinism. *American Psychologist, 33,* 122–147.

Bandura, A. (1982). Self-efficacy mechanism in human agency. *American Psychologist, 37,* 122–147.

Bandura, A. (1984). Recycling misconceptions of perceived self-efficacy. *Therapy Research, 8,* 231–255.

Bandura, A. (1986). *Social foundations of thought and action: A social cognitive theory.* Englewood Cliffs, NJ: Prentice-Hall.

Bandura, A. (1989). Human agency in social cognitive theory. *American Psychologist, 44,* 1175–1184.

Bandura, A. (1991). Social cognitive theory of self-regulation. *Organizational Behavior and Human Decision Processes, 50,* 248–287.

Bandura, A., Adams, N. E., & Beyer, J. (1977). Cognitive processes mediating behavioral change. *Journal of Personality and Social Psychology, 35,* 125–139.

Bandura, A., Reese, L., & Adams, N. E. (1982). Microanalysis of action and fear arousal as a function of differential levels of perceived self-efficacy. *Journal of Personality and Social Psychology, 43,* 5–21.

Bandura, A., & Schunk, D. H. (1981). Cultivating competence, self-efficacy, and intrinsic interest through proximal self-motivation. *Journal of Personality and Social Psychology, 41,* 586–598.

Bandura, A., & Wood, R. E. (1989). Effect of perceived controllability and performance standards on self-regulation of complex decision-making. *Journal of Personality and Social Psychology, 56,* 805–814.

Barrett, K., & Campos, J. (1987). Perspectives on emotional development: II. A functionalist approach to emotions. In J. Osofsky (Ed.), *Handbook of infant development* (2nd ed., pp. 555–578). New York: Wiley.

Baumrind, D. (1978). Parental disciplinary patterns and social competence in children. *Youth and Society, 9,* 239–276.

Beck, A. T. (1976). *Cognitive theory and the emotional disorders.* New York: International Universities Press.

Bem, D. J. (1972). Self-perception theory. In L. Berkowitz (Ed.), *Advances in experimental social psychology* (Vol. 6, pp. 2–62). New York: Academic Press.

Ben, S. L. (1974). The measurement of psychological androgyny. *Journal of Consulting and Clinical Psychology, 42,* 155–162.

Bengston, V. L., Reedy, M. N., & Gordon, C. (1985). Aging and self-conceptions: Personality processes and social contexts. In J. E. Birren & K. W. Schaie (Eds.), *Handbook of the psychology of aging* (pp. 544–593). New York: Van Nostrand-Reinhold.

Berlyne, D. E. (1950). Novelty and curiosity as determinants of exploratory behavior. *British Journal of Psychology, 41,* 68–80.

Betz, N. E., & Hackett, G. (1981). The relationship of career-related self-efficacy expectations to perceived career options in college women and men. *Journal of Counseling Psychology, 28,* 399–410.

Betz, N. E., & Hackett, G. (1986). Applications of self-efficacy theory to understanding career choice behavior. *Journal of Social and Clinical Psychology, 4,* 279–289.

Block, J. H. (1976). Issues, problems, and pitfalls in assessing sex differences: A critical review of *The Psychology of Sex Differences. Merrill-Palmer Quarterly, 22,* 283–308.

Block, J. H. (1983). Differential premises arising from differential socialization of the sexes: Some conjectures. *Child Development, 54,* 1335–1354.

Bracken, B. A. (1992). *Multidimensional self concept scale.* Austin, TX: Pro-Ed.

Bracken, B. A., Bunch, S., Keith, T. Z., & Keith, P. B. (1992, August 12). *Multidimensional self concept: A five instrument factor analysis.* Paper presented at the American Psychological Association Meeting, Washington, DC.

Brim, O. G., Jr. (1974, August 15). *The sense of personal control over one's life.* Paper presented at the American Psychological Association Meeting, New Orleans, LA.

Broverman, I. K., Vogel, S. K., Broverman, D. M., Clarkson, F. E., & Rosenkrantz, P. S. (1972). Sex-role stereotypes: A current reappraisal. *Journal of Social Issues, 28,* 59–78.

Brown, I., & Inouye, D. K. (1978). Learned helplessness through modeling: The role of perceived similarity in competence. *Journal of Personality and Social Psychology, 36,* 900–908.

Butler, R. (1987). Task-involving and ego-involving properties of evaluation: Effects of different feedback conditions on motivational perceptions, interest and performance. *Journal of Educational Psychology, 79,* 474–482.

Campos, J. J., Campos, R. G., & Barrett, K. C. (1989). Emergent themes in the study of emotional development and emotional regulation. *Developmental Psychology, 25,* 394–402.

Campos, J. J., & Stenberg, C. (1981). Perception, appraisal, and emotion: The onset of social referencing. In M. E. Lamb & L. R. Sherrod (Eds.), *Infant social cognition: Empirical and theoretical considerations* (pp. 217–314). Hillsdale, NJ: Erlbaum.

Cauce, A. M. (1987). School and peer competence in early adolescence: A test of domain-specific self-perceived competence. *Developmental Psychology, 23,* 287–291.

Chambliss, C. A., & Murray, E. J. (1979a). Cognitive procedures for smoking re-duction: Symptom attribution versus efficacy attribution. *Cognitive Therapy and Research, 3,* 91–96.

Chambliss, C. A., & Murray, E. J. (1979b). Efficacy attributions, locus of con-trol, and weight loss. *Cognitive Therapy and Research, 3,* 349–354.

Chapman, L. J., & Chapman, J. P. (1967). Genesis of popular but erroneous psy-chodiagnostic categories. *Journal of Abnormal Psychology, 72,* 193–204.

Clausan, J. A. (1986, June 8). *Early adult choices and the life course.* Paper pre-sented at the American Sociological Association Annual Meeting, New York.

Cooley, C. H. (1902). *Human nature and the social order.* New York: Scribner's.

Coopersmith, S. (1967). *The antecedents of self-esteem.* San Francisco: Freeman.

Corbin, C. (1972). Mental practice. In W. Morgan (Ed.), *Ergogenic aids and mus-cular performance* (pp. 93–118). New York: Academic Press.

deCharms, R. (1968). *Personal causation.* New York: Academic Press.

deCharms, R. (1979). Personal causation and perceived control. In L. C. Perl-muter & R. A. Monty (Eds.), *Choice and perceived control.* Hillsdale, NJ: Erlbaum.

Deci, E. L. (1975). *Intrinsic motivation.* New York: Plenum.

Deci, E. L. (1980). *The psychology of self-determination.* Lexington, MA: Lex-ington Books.

Dowd, J. (1975). Aging as exchange: Preface to theory. *Journal of Gerontology, 30,* 584–594.

Downey, G., & Coyne, J. C. (1990). Children of depressed parents: An integra-tive review. *Psychological Bulletin, 108,* 50–76.

Downey, G., & Moen, P. (1987). Personal efficacy, income, and family transi-tions: A longitudinal study of women heading households. *Journal of Health and Social Behavior, 28,* 320–333.

Dulany, D. E. (1968). Awareness, rules, and propositional control. In T. R. Dixon & D. L. Horton (Eds.), *Verbal behavior and general behavior theory.* Engle-wood Cliffs, NJ: Prentice-Hall.

Duncan, G. J., & Liker, J. (1983). Disentangling the efficacy-earnings relation-ship among white men. In G. J. Duncan & J. N. Morgan (Eds.), *Five thousand American families: Patterns of economic progress* (pp. 218–248). Ann Arbor, MI: Institute for Social Research.

Dweck, C. (1986). Motivational processes affecting learning. *American Psychol-ogist, 41,* 1040–1048.

Dweck, C., & Elliott, E. S. (1983). Achievement motivation. In E. M. Hethering-ton (Ed.), *Handbook of child psychology: Socialization, personality, and social development* (Vol. 4). New York: Wiley.

Edgar, D. (1980). *Introduction to Australian society.* Sydney: Prentice-Hall.

Elder, G. J., Jr., & Browerman, C. (1963). Family structure and childrearing pat-terns: The effects of family size and sex composition. *American Sociological Review, 28,* 891–905.

Elliott, E. S., & Dweck, C. S. (1988). Goals: An approach to motivation and achievement. *Journal of Personality and Social Psychology, 54,* 5–12.

Emde, R. (1988). Development terminable and interminable: I. Innate and motivational factors from infancy. *International Journal of Psychoanalysis, 69,* 23–42.

Emery, R. (1982). Intraparental conflict and the children of discord and divorce. *Psychological Bulletin, 92,* 310–330.

Epstein, S. (1973). The self-concept revisited or a theory of a theory. *American Psychologist, 28,* 405–416.

Epstein, S. (1991). Cognitive-experiential self theory. Implications for developmental psychology. In M. R. Gunnar & L. A. Sroufe (Eds.), *Self processes and development: The Minnesota Symposium on Child Development* (Vol. 23). Hillsdale, NJ: Erlbaum.

Erikson, E. (1959). Identity and the life cycle. *Psychological issues, v. 1, Monograph 1.* New York: International Universities Press.

Fenichel, O. (1945). *The psychoanalytic theory of neurosis.* New York: Norton.

Finkelstein, N. W., & Ramey, C. T. (1977). Learning to control the environment in infancy. *Child Development, 48,* 806–819.

Foote, N. N., & Cottrell, L. S. (1955). *Identity and interpersonal competence: A new direction in family research.* Chicago: University of Chicago Press.

Ford, M. E. (1984). Linking social-cognitive processes with effective social behavior: A living systems approach. In P. C. Kendall (Ed.), *Advances in cognitive-behavioral research and therapy* (Vol. 3). New York: Academic Press.

Ford, M. E. (1985). A living systems conceptualization of social intelligence: Outcomes, processes, and developmental change. In R. Sternberg (Ed.), *Advances in the psychology of human intelligence* (Vol. 3). Hillsdale, NJ: Erlbaum.

Ford, M. E., & Thompson, R. A. (1985). Perceptions of personal agency and infant attachment: Toward a life-span perspective on competence development. *International Journal of Behavioral Development, 8,* 377–406.

Franks, D. D., & Marolla, J. (1976). Efficacious action and social approval as interacting dimensions of self-esteem: A tentative formulation through construct validation. *Sociometry, 39,* 324–341.

Freud, S. (1949). *An outline of psycho-analysis* (J. Strachey, Trans.). New York: Norton.

Frijda, N. (1986). *The emotions: Part III, Synthesis.* New York: Cambridge University Press.

Frodi, A., Bridges, L., & Grolnick, W. (1985). Correlates of mastery-related behavior: A short-term longitudinal study of infants in their second year. *Child Development, 56,* 1291–1298.

Gecas, V. (1971). Parental behavior and dimensions of adolescent self-evaluation. *Sociometry, 34,* 466–482.

Gecas, V. (1982). The self-concept. *Annual Review of Sociology, 8,* 1–33.

Gecas, V. (1989). The social psychology of self-efficacy. *Annual Review of Sociology, 15,* 291–316.

Gecas, V., & Mortimer, J. T. (1987). Stability and change in the self-concept from adolescence to adulthood. In T. Honess & K. Yarkley (Eds.), *Self and identity: Perspectives across the lifespan* (pp. 265–286). London: Routledge & Kegan Paul.

Gecas, V., & Schwalbe, M. L. (1983). Beyond the looking-glass self: Social structure and efficacy-based self-esteem. *Social Psychology Quarterly, 46,* 77–88.

Gecas, V., & Schwalbe, M. L. (1986). Parental behavior and adolescent self-esteem. *Journal of Marriage and the Family, 48,* 37–46.

Gecas, V., & Seff, M. A. (1987, June 11). *Social class, occupational conditions, and self-esteem.* Paper presented at the American Sociological Association Annual Meeting.

Giddens, A. (1979). *Central problems in social theory.* Berkeley, CA: University of California Press.

Gladwin, T. (1967). Social competence and clinical practice. *Psychiatry, 30,* 30–43.

Glick, M., & Zigler, E. (1985). Self-image: A cognitive-developmental approach. In R. Leahy (Ed.), *The development of the self.* New York: Academic Press.

Gurin, P., & Brim, O. G., Jr. (1984). Change in self in adulthood: The example of sense of control. In P. B. Baltes & D. G. Brim, Jr. (Eds.), *Life-span development and behavior.* New York: Academic Press.

Gurin, P., Gurin, G., & Morrison, B. M. (1978). Personal and ideological aspects of internal and external control. *Social Psychology, 41,* 275–296.

Hackett, G., & Betz, N. E. (1981). A self-efficacy approach to the career development of women. *Journal of Vocational Behavior, 18,* 326–339.

Harackiewicz, J. M., Sansone, C., & Manderlink, G. (1985). Competence, achievement-orientation, and intrinsic motivation: A process analysis. *Journal of Personality and Social Psychology, 48,* 493–508.

Harter, S. (1978). Effectance motivation reconsidered: Toward a developmental model. *Human Development, 21,* 34–64.

Harter, S. (1981). A model of intrinsic mastery motivation in children: Individual differences and developmental change. *Minnesota Symposium on Child Psychology* (Vol. 14). Hillsdale, NJ: Erlbaum.

Harter, S. (1985). Competence as a dimension of self-evaluation: Toward a comprehensive model of self-worth. In R. Leahy (Ed.), *The development of the self.* New York: Academic Press.

Harter, S. (1986). The relationship between perceived competence, affect, and motivational orientation within the classroom: Process and patterns of change. In A. K. Boggiano & T. Pittman (Eds.), *Achievement and motivation: A social-developmental perspective.* Cambridge, MA: Cambridge University Press.

Harter, S. (1989). Causes, correlates, and the functional role of global self-worth: A life-span perspective. In J. Kolligian & R. Sternberg (Eds.), *Perceptions of competence and incompetence across the life-span.* New Haven, CT: Yale University Press.

Harter, S. (1990). Adolescent self and identity development. In S. S. Feldman & G. R. Elliott (Eds.), *At the threshold: The developing adolescent* (pp. 352–387). Cambridge, MA: Harvard University Press.

Harter, S. (1991). Causes and consequences of low self-esteem in children and adolescents. In R. F. Baumeister (Ed.), *Self-esteem: The puzzle of low self-regard.* New York: Plenum.

Harter, S. (1992). Visions of self: Beyond the me in the mirror. Manuscript submitted for publication.

Harter, S., & Marold, D. B. (1992). The directionality of the link between self-esteem and affect: Beyond causal modeling. In D. Cicchetti & S. L. Toth (Eds.), *The self and its disorders: Rochester Symposium on Developmental Psychopathology.* Rochester, NY: University of Rochester Press.

Hartmann, H. (1950). Comments on the psychoanalytic theory of the ego. *Psychoanalytic Studies of the Child, 5,* 74–95.

Heilman, M. E., Lucas, J. A., & Kaplow, S. R. (1990). Self-derogating consequences of sex-based preferential selection: The moderating role of initial self-confidence. *Organizational Behavior and Human Decision Processes, 46,* 202–216.

Henderson, R. W. (1981). Home environment and intellectual performance. In R. W. Henderson (Ed.), *Parent-child interaction: Theory, research, and prospects* (pp. 3–29). New York: Academic Press.

Hendrick, I. (1942). Instinct and the ego during infancy. *Psychoanalytic Quarterly, 11,* 33–58.

Hendrick, I. (1943). The discussion of the "instinct to master." *Psychoanalytic Quarterly, 12,* 561–565.

Higgins, E. T. (1987). Self-discrepancy: Theory relating self and affect. *Psychological Review, 94,* 319–340.

Higgins, E. T. (1989). Self-discrepancy theory: What patterns of self-beliefs cause people to suffer? In L. Berkowitz (Ed.), *Advances in experimental social psychology* (Vol. 22). New York: Academic Press.

Higgins, E. T. (1991). Development of self-regulatory and self-evaluative processes: Costs, benefits, and trade-offs. In M. R. Gunnar & L. A. Sroufe (Eds.), *Self processes in development: Minnesota Symposium on Child Psychology* (Vol. 23). Hillsdale, NJ: Erlbaum.

Hughes, M., & Demo, D. H. (1989). Self-perceptions of Black Americans: Self-esteem and personal efficacy. *American Journal of Sociology, 95,* 132–159.

Hunt, J. M. (1961). *Intelligence and experience.* New York: Ronald.

Inkeles, A. (1966). Social structure and the socialization of competence. *Harvard Educational Review, 36,* 265–283.

James, W. (1890). *The principles of psychology* (Vol. 1). New York: Henry Holt & Co.

Kanfer, F. H. (1980). Self-management methods. In F. H. Kanfer & A. P. Goldstein (Eds.), *Helping people change: A textbook of methods* (2nd ed.). New York: Pergamon.

Kanfer, F. H., & Hagerman, S. (1980). The role of self-regulation. In L. P. Rehm (Ed.), *Behavior therapy and depression: Present status and future directions.* New York: Academic Press.

Kavanagh, D. J., & Bower, G. H. (1985). Mood and self-efficacy: Impact of joy and sadness on perceived capabilities. *Cognitive Therapy and Research, 9,* 507–525.

Kazdin, A. E. (1978). Covert modeling: Therapeutic application of imagined rehearsal. In J. L. Singer & K. S. Pope (Eds.), *The power of human imagination: New methods in psychotherapy. Emotions, personality, and psychotherapy* (pp. 255–278). New York: Plenum.

Kelley, H. H. (1971). *Attributions in social interaction.* Morristown, NJ: General Learning.

Kelly, G. A. (1955). *The psychology of personal constructs.* New York: Norton.

Kohn, M. L., & Schooler, C. (1983). *Work and personality: An inquiry into the impact of social stratification.* Norwood, NJ: Ablex.

Kun, A. (1977). Development of the magnitude-covariation and compensation schemata in ability and effort attributions of performance. *Child Development, 48,* 862–873.

Kuypers, J. A., & Bengston, V. L. (1973). Social breakdown and competence. *Human Development, 16,* 181–201.

Lachman, M. E. (1986). Personal control in later life: Stability, change, and cognitive correlates. In M. M. Baltes & P. B. Baltes (Eds.), *Psychology of control and aging.* Hillsdale, NJ: Erlbaum.

Lamb, M. E. (1981). Developing trust and perceived effectance in infancy. In L. P. Lipsitt (Ed.), *Advances in infancy research* (Vol. 1). Norwood, NJ: Ablex.

Langer, E. J. (1975). The illusion of control. *Journal of Personality and Social Psychology, 32,* 311–328.

Langer, E. J. (1979). The illusion of incompetence. In L. C. Perlmuter & R. A. Monty (Eds.), *Choice and perceived control.* Hillsdale, NJ: Erlbaum.

Langer, E. J., & Benvenuto, A. (1978). Self-induced dependence. *Journal of Personality and Social Psychology, 36,* 886–893.

Langer, E. J., & Rodin, J. (1976). The effects of choice and enhanced responsibility for the aged: A field experiment in an institutional setting. *Journal of Personality and Social Psychology, 34,* 191–198.

Latham, G. P., & Yukl, G. A. (1975). A review of research on the application of goal setting in organizations. *Academy of Management Journal, 18,* 824–845.

Lawler, E. E. (1973). *Motivation in work organizations.* Monterey, CA: Brooks/Cole.

Lazarus, R. S., & Launier, R. (1978). Stress-related transactions between person and environment. In L. A. Pervin & M. Lewis (Eds.), *Perspectives in interactional psychology.* New York: Plenum.

Lefcourt, H. M. (1966). Internal versus external control of reinforcement: A review. *Psychological Bulletin, 65,* 206–220.

Lefcourt, H. M. (1972). Recent developments in the study of locus of control. In B. A. Maher (Ed.), *Progress in experimental personality research* (Vol. 6). New York: Academic Press.

Lefcourt, H. M. (1976). *Locus of control: Current trends in therapy and research.* Hillsdale, NJ: Erlbaum.

Lefcourt, H. M. (1981). *Research with the locus of control construct: Vol. I. Assessment methods.* New York: Academic Press.

Lenney, E. (1981). What's fine for the gander isn't always good for the goose: Sex differences in self-confidence as a function of ability area and comparison with others. *Sex Roles, 7,* 905–923.

Lent, R. W., & Hackett, G. (1987). Career self-efficacy: Empirical status and future directions. *Journal of Vocational Behavior, 30,* 347–382.

Lepper, M. R., & Greene, D. (1978). Overjustification research and beyond: Toward a means-ends analysis. In M. R. Lepper & D. Greene (Eds.), *The hidden cost of reward.* Hillsdale, NJ: Erlbaum.

Levenson, H. (1981). Differentiating among internality, powerful others, and chance. In H. Lefcourt (Ed.), *Research with the locus of control construct: Vol. I. Assessment methods* (pp. 15–63). New York: Academic Press.

Lewin, K., Dembo, T., Festinger, L., & Sears, P. S. (1944). Level of aspiration. In J. M. Hunt (Ed.), *Personality and the behavior disorders* (Vol. 1, pp. 333–378). New York: Ronald.

Locke, E. A. (1968). Toward a theory of task motivation and incentives. *Organizational Behavior and Human Performance, 3,* 157–189.

Maccoby, E. E., & Jacklin, C. N. (1974). *The psychology of sex differences.* Stanford, CA: Stanford University Press.

Malinowski, B. (1955). *Magic, science, and religion.* New York: Anchor Books.

Markus, H., & Nurius, P. (1986). Possible selves. *American Psychologist, 41,* 954–969.

Marton, P., Golombek, H., Stein, B., & Korenblum, M. (1988). The relation of personality functions and adaptive skills to self-esteem in early adolescence. *Journal of Youth and Adolescence, 17,* 393–401.

McCall, R. B. (1979). Qualitative transitions in behavioral development in the first two years of life. In M. H. Bornstein & W. Kessen (Eds.), *Psychological development from infancy: Image to intention.* Hillsdale, NJ: Erlbaum.

McCleland, D. C., Atkinson, J. W., Clark, R. A., & Lowell, E. J. (1953). *The achievement motive.* New York: Appleton-Century.

McLanahan, S. S. (1983). Family structure and stress: A longitudinal comparison of two-parent and female-headed families. *Journal of Marriage and the Family, 45,* 47–55.

McMahon, I. D. (1982). Expectancy of success on sex-linked tasks. *Sex Roles, 8,* 949–958.

Mead, G. H. (1934). *Mind, self, and society.* Chicago: University of Chicago Press.

Mirowsky, J., & Ross, C. E. (1983). Paranoia and the structure of powerlessness. *American Sociological Review, 48,* 228–239.

Mirowsky, J., & Ross, C. E. (1986). Social patterns of distress. *Annual Review of Sociology, 12,* 23–45.

Mittelmann, B. (1954). Motility in infants, children, and adults. *Psychoanalytic Studies of the Child, 9,* 142–177.

Montgomery, K. C. (1954). The role of the exploratory drive in learning. *Journal of Comparative Physiology and Psychology, 47,* 60–64.

Mortimer, J. T., Finch, M. D., & Kumka, D. (1982). Persistence and change in human development: The multidimensional self-concept. In P. B. Baltes & O. G. Brim, Jr. (Eds.), *Life-span development and behavior* (Vol. 4, pp. 263–312). New York: Academic Press.

Mortimer, J. T., & Lorence, J. (1979). Occupational experience and the self-concept: A longitudinal study. *Social Psychology Quarterly, 42,* 307–323.

Mortimer, J. T., Lorence, J., & Kumka, D. S. (1986). *Work, family, and personality: Transition to adulthood.* Norwood, NJ: Ablex.

Motowidlo, S. J., Loehr, J., & Dunnette, M. D. (1978). A laboratory study of the effects of goal specificity on the relationship between probability of success and performance. *Journal of Applied Psychology, 63,* 172–179.

Moulton, R. W. (1974). Motivational implications of individual differences in competence. In J. W. Atkinson & J. O. Raynor (Eds.), *Motivation and achievement.* Washington, DC: Winston.

Nicholls, J. G. (1978). The development of the concepts of effort and ability, perception of own attainment and the understanding that difficult tasks require more ability. *Child Development, 49,* 800–814.

Nicholls, J. G. (1982). Conceptions of ability and achievement motivation. In R. Ames & C. Ames (Eds.), *Research on motivation in education: Student motivation* (pp. 37–73). New York: Academic Press.

Nicholls, J. G., & Miller, A. T. (1983). The differentiation of the concepts of difficulty and ability. *Child Development, 54,* 951–959.

Nicholls, J. G., & Miller, A. T. (1984). Development and its discontents: The differentiation of the concept of ability. In J. G. Nicholls (Ed.), *The development of achievement motivation.* Greenwich, CT: JAI Press.

Nolen-Hoeksema, S. (1987). Sex differences in unipolar depression: Evidence and theory. *Psychological Bulletin, 101,* 259–282.

Palenzuela, D. L. (1987a). The expectancy construct within the social-learning theories of Rotter and Bandura: A reply to Kirsch's approach. *Journal of Social Behavior and Personality, 2,* 437–452.

Palenzuela, D. L. (1987b). Sphere-specific measures of perceived control: Perceived contingency, perceived competence, or what? A critical evaluation of Paulhus and Christie's approach. *Journal of Research in Personality, 21,* 264–286.

Phares, E. J. (1976). *Locus of control in personality.* Morristown, NJ: General Learning Press.

Piaget, J. (1952). *The origins of intelligence in children.* New York: International Universities Press.

Piaget, J. (1954). *The construction of reality in the child.* New York: Basic Books.

Ramey, C. T., & Finkelstein, N. W. (1978). Contingent stimulation and infant competence. *Journal of Pediatric Psychology, 3,* 89–96.

Rehm, L. P. (1977). A self-concept model of depression. *Behavior Therapy, 8,* 787–804.

Rodin, J. (1976). Density, perceived choice, and response to controllable and uncontrollable outcomes. *Journal of Experimental Social Psychology, 12,* 564–578.

Rogers, C., & Dymond, R. (1954). *Psychotherapy and personality change.* Chicago: University of Chicago Press.

Rollins, B. C., & Thomas, D. L. (1979). Parental support, power, and control techniques in the socialization of children. In W. R. Burr, R. Hill, F. I. Nye, & I. L. Reiss (Eds.), *Contemporary theories about the family* (Vol. 1, pp. 317–364). New York: Free Press.

Rosen, B. C., & D'Andrade, R. (1959). The psycho-social origins of achievement motivation. *Sociometry, 22,* 185–218.

Rosenberg, M. (1979). *Conceiving the self.* New York: Basic Books.

Rosenberg, M. (1986). Self-concept from middle childhood through adolescence. In J. Suls & A. G. Greenwald (Eds.), *Psychological perspectives on the self* (Vol. 3, pp. 107–136). Hillsdale, NJ: Erlbaum.

Rothbaum, F., Wolfer, J., & Visintainer, M. (1979). Coping behavior and control in children. *Journal of Personality, 47,* 118–135.

Rotter, J. B. (1954). *Social learning and clinical psychology.* Englewood Cliffs, NJ: Prentice-Hall.

Rotter, J. B. (1966). Generalized expectancies for internal versus external control of reinforcement. *Psychological Monographs, 80*(1, Whole No. 609).

Rovee-Collier, C. K., & Lipsitt, L. P. (1981). Learning, adaptation, and memory. In P. M. Stratton (Ed.), *Psychobiology of the human newborn.* New York: Wiley.

Ruble, D. N. (1983). The development of social comparison processes and their role in achievement-related self-socialization. In E. T. Higgins, D. N. Ruble, & W. W. Hartup (Eds.), *Social cognition and social development: A sociocultural perspective* (pp. 134–157). Cambridge, England: Cambridge University Press.

Ruble, D. N., Feldman, N. S., & Boggiano, A. K. (1976). Social comparison between young children in achievement situations. *Developmental Psychology, 12,* 192–197.

Rutter, M. (1971). Parent-child separation: Psychological effects on the children. *Child Development, 50,* 283–305.

Sarason, I. G. (1975). Anxiety and self-preoccupation. In I. G. Sarason & D. C. Spielberger (Eds.), *Stress and anxiety* (Vol. 2). Washington, DC: Hemisphere.

Schaffer, H., Rudolph, M., & Crook, C. K. (1978). The role of the mother in early social development. In H. McGurk (Eds.), *Issues in childhood social development* (pp. 51–77). London: Methuen.

Schulz, R. (1980). Aging and control. In J. Garber & M. E. P. Seligman (Eds.), *Human helplessness: Theory and applications* (pp. 261–277). New York: Academic Press.

Schunk, D. H. (1981). Modeling and attributional effects on children's achievement: A self-efficacy analysis. *Journal of Educational Psychology, 73,* 93–105.

Schwalbe, M. L. (1986). *The psychosocial consequences of natural and alienated labor.* Albany, NY: State University of New York Press.

Seligman, M. E. P. (1975). *Helplessness: On depression, development, and death.* San Francisco: Freeman.

Seligman, M. E. P., Abramson, L. Y., Semmel, A., & von Baeyer, C. (1979). Depressive attributional style. *Journal of Abnormal Psychology, 88,* 242– 247.

Short, R. H., & Hess, G. C. (1983). Adaptive processes of coping, defending, and mastery. *International Journal for the Advancement of Counseling, 6,* 201–217.

Short, J. F., Jr., & Wolfgang, M. E. (1972). *Collective violence.* Chicago: Aldine-Atherton.

Shrauger, J. S., & Schoeneman, T. J. (1979). Symbolic interactionist view of self-concept: Through the looking glass darkly. *Psychological Bulletin, 86,* 549–573.

Skinner, E., & Chapman, M. (1984). Control beliefs in an action perspective. *Human Development, 72,* 129–133.

Smith, M. B. (1969). *Social psychology and human values.* Chicago: Aldine.

Sroufe, L. A. (1978). Attachment and the roots of competence. *Human Development, 1,* 50–57.

Sroufe, L. A. (1979a). The coherence of individual development: Early care, attachment, and subsequent developmental issues. *American Psychologist, 34,* 834–841.

Sroufe, L. A. (1979b). Socioemotional development. In J. Osofsky (Ed.), *Handbook of infant development* (pp. 462–516). New York: Wiley.

Staples, C., Schwalbe, M. L., & Gecas, V. (1984). Social class, occupational conditions, and efficacy-based self-esteem. *Social Perspectives, 27,* 85–109.

Steers, R. M., & Porter, L. W. (1974). The role of task-goal attributes in employee performance. *Psychological Bulletin, 81,* 434–452.

Stipek, D. (1981). Children's perceptions of their own and their classmates' ability. *Journal of Educational Psychology, 73,* 404–410.

Stipek, D. J. (1984). Young children's performance expectations: Logical analysis or wishful thinking? In J. Nicholls (Ed.), *The development of achievement motivation* (pp. 33–56). Greenwich, CT: JAI Press.

Strickland, B. R. (1977). Internal-external control of reinforcement. In T. Bliss (Ed.), *Personality variables in social behavior* (pp. 219–279). Hillsdale, NJ: Erlbaum.

Suls, J., & Sanders, G. (1982). Self-evaluation via social comparison: A developmental analysis. In I. Wheeler (Ed.), *Review of personality and social psychology* (Vol. 3). Beverly Hills, CA: Sage.

Suomi, S. J. (1981). The perception of contingency and social development. In M. E. Lamb & L. R. Sherrod (Eds.), *Infant social cognition.* Hillsdale, NJ: Erlbaum.

Tashakkori, A., & Thompson, V. D. (1991). Race differences in self-perception and locus of control during adolescence and early adulthood: Methodological implications. *Genetic, Social, and General Psychology Monographs, 117,* 133–152.

Tesser, A. (1988). Toward a self-evaluation maintenance model of social behavior. In L. Berkowitz (Ed.), *Advances in experimental social psychology* (Vol. 21). New York: Academic Press.

Tesser, A., & Campbell, J. (1983). Self-definition and self-evaluation maintenance. In J. Suls & A. G. Greenwald (Eds.), *Psychological perspectives on the
self* (Vol. 2, pp. 1–32). Hillsdale, NJ: Erlbaum.

Thompson, R. A., & Lamb, M. E. (1983). Security of attachment and stranger sociability in infancy. *Developmental Psychology, 19,* 184–191.

Thornhill, M. A., Thornhill, M. A., & Youngman, M. B. (1975). A computerized
and categorized bibliography on locus of control. *Psychological Reports, 36,*
505–506.

Throop, W. F., & MacDonald, A. P. (1971). Internal-external locus of control: A
bibliography. *Psychological Reports, 28,* 175–190.

Trevarthen, C. (1977). Descriptive analyses of infant communicative behavior. In
H. R. Schaffer (Ed.), *Studies in mother-infant interaction.* London: Academic
Press.

Tronick, E. Z., Als, H., Adamson, L., Wise, S., & Brazelton, T. B. (1978). The infant's response to entrapment between contradictory messages in face-to-face
interaction. *Journal of the American Academy of Child Psychiatry, 17,* 1–13.

Tyler, F. B., & Gatz, M. (1977). Development of individual psychosocial competence in a high school setting. *Journal of Consulting and Clinical Psychology,
45,* 441–449.

Vallacher, R. R., & Wegner, D. M. (1989). Levels of personal agency: Individual
variation in action identification. *Journal of Personality and Social Psychology, 89,* 660–671.

Watson, J. S. (1979). Perception of contingency as a determinant of social responsiveness. In E. B. Thoman (Ed.), *Origins of the infant's social responsiveness.* Hillsdale, NJ: Erlbaum.

Weiner, B. (1972). *Theories of motivation.* Chicago: Markham.

Weiner, B., & Graham, S. (1983). An attributional approach to emotional development. In C. Izard, J. Kagan, & R. Zajonc (Eds.), *Emotion, cognition and behavior.* Hillsdale, NJ: Erlbaum.

Weiner, B., Russell, D., & Lerman, D. (1978). Affective consequences of causal
ascriptions. In J. H. Harvey, W. J. Ickes, & R. F. Kidd (Eds.), *New directions in
attribution research* (Vol. 2). Hillsdale, NJ: Erlbaum.

Weisz, J. R. (1980). Developmental change in perceived control: Recognizing
noncontingency in the laboratory and perceiving it in the world. *Developmental Psychology, 16,* 385–390.

Weisz, J. R. (1983). Can I control it? The pursuit of veridical answers across the
life span. In P. B. Baltes & O. G. Brim, Jr. (Eds.), *Life span development and
behavior* (pp. 233–300). New York: Academic Press.

Weisz, J. R. (1986). Understanding the developing understanding of control. In
M. Perlmutter (Ed.), *Cognitive perspectives on children's social and behavioral
development: The Minnesota Symposium on Child Psychology* (Vol. 18,
pp. 219–278). Hillsdale, NJ: Erlbaum.

Weisz, J. R., & Stipek, D. J. (1982). Competence, contingency and the development of perceived control. *Human Development, 25,* 250–281.

Wenar, C. (1964). Competence at one. *Merrill-Parlmer Quarterly, 10,* 329–342.

Whitbeck, L. B. (1987). Modeling efficacy: The effect of perceived parental efficacy on the self-efficacy of early adolescents. *Journal of Early Adolescence, 7,* 215–225.

White, B. L. (1979). The family: The major influence on the development of competence. In N. Stinnett, B. Chesser, & J. DeFrain (Eds.), *Building family strengths: Blueprints for action* (pp. 175–193). Lincoln: University of Nebraska Press.

White, R. W. (1959). Motivation reconsidered: The concept of competence. *Psychological Review, 66,* 297–333.

White, R. W. (1963). Ego and reality in psychoanalytic theory. A proposal for independent ego energies. *Psychological Issues, 3,* 3.

Wicklund, R. A. (1978). Year years later. In L. Berkowitz (Ed.), *Cognitive theories in social psychology.* New York: Academic Press.

Wood, R. E., & Bandura, A. (1989). Impact of conceptions of ability on self-regulatory mechanisms and complex decision-making. *Journal of Personality and Social Psychology, 56,* 407–415.

Woodworth, R. S. (1958). *Dynamics of behavior.* New York: Holt.

Wortman, C. B. (1975). Some determinants of perceived control. *Journal of Personality and Social Psychology, 31,* 282–294.

CHAPTER 6

Global Self-Concept and Its Relationship to Stressful Life Conditions

H. THOMPSON PROUT and SUSAN M. PROUT

As evidenced by this volume, self-concept is a complex psychological construct that has a long history and pervades a wide variety of psychological theory and practice. In clinical practice, self-concept issues are often the base of psychological and educational referrals, a focus of clinical assessment, and a target for treatment and intervention. Many wide-ranging psychotherapeutic approaches (from psychodynamic to cognitive-behavioral) point to self-concept and its associated variables as significant in their theoretical formulations. There have been numerous clinical and theoretical articles about improving the self-concept of individuals presenting a wide range of problems, and numerous books and structured programs detail educational and therapeutic interventions for enhancing self-esteem in either group or individual formats. Also, instruments that assess self-concept or self-esteem are often used as outcome measures in counseling and psychotherapy outcome studies.

As professionals, we have sat in numerous staffings and team meetings in both educational and clinical settings where issues related to self-concept and self-esteem have been extensively discussed. In fact, self-concept and self-esteem are so frequently mentioned in case discussions, one wonders about the uniformity of clinical definition among professionals. When the generic "self-concept" problem is mentioned in clinical discussion, it is often unclear whether all parties are referring to the same issues and constructs. Additionally, on a subjective level, there may be a tendency to be overly inclusive in the assumption that individuals who present with adjustment problems or disabilities also have self-concept problems. It is also easy for professionals to fall back on diminished self-concept to explain some identified emotional or behavioral phenomena. As will be seen from the following discussion, some writers assume that impaired self-concept or lowered self-esteem is almost always associated with many educational and psychological problems. Yet, the empirical literature does not support this absolute association.

Despite the abundance and ascribed importance of self-concept in the clinical literature and in clinical practice, the construct most often plays a secondary role to other disorders. In most accepted diagnostic and classification schemas, there is no "Self-Concept Disorder." Moreover, lowered self-esteem or self-concept problems are generally viewed as diagnostic criteria for other disorders. The overall purpose of this chapter is to examine the role of general or global self-concept in relation to other clinical disorders.

ISSUES IN CLINICAL CONSIDERATION OF SELF-CONCEPT PROBLEMS

Two relevant issues in the relationship between self-concept and other educational or psychological disorders, conditions, or disabilities are the causative/reactive dimension of self-concept problems and the generality or specificity of self-views. Both issues need to be considered when analyzing the clinical importance and pervasiveness of self-concept problems.

Although some models have been proposed (e.g., Harter, 1989) that suggest directionality between global self-worth and other psychological variables, this issue remains largely unresolved. When self-concept problems are apparent and coexist (comorbid conditions) with another disorder, disability, or problem, it may be difficult to determine whether diminished self-concept is a result of the disorder or caused by the disorder. For example, a 14-year-old boy presents with clinical depression and apparent low self-esteem. Is the low self-esteem a result of depression or its base cause? Typically, clinicians assume that self-concept problems are reactive in individuals with disabilities. When students with learning disabilities also present with self-concept problems, it is often assumed that the lowered self-esteem is related to self-perceptions of academic failure and/or negative feedback from the environment related to the academic difficulties. However, because self-concept problems can occur in individuals without disabilities, the self-concept problems may have another causal base. The relevance of this causative/reactive dimension is related to the importance assigned to self-concept in the clinical analysis of individual cases. Issues related to the development of self-concept are discussed in other chapters in this volume, and it is beyond the scope of this chapter to detail these. However, in relation to the clinical relevance of self-concept, the following categorization appears helpful:

- *Primary* self-concept problems are those in which diminished self-concept preceded the development of a disorder and appears to play a central role in the disorder/problem. In effect, self-concept is the primary cause or a primary cause in the development and maintenance of the disorder. Example: A child with well-documented low self-esteem presents with problems that evolve into clinical depression.

- *Secondary* self-concept problems are those in which diminished self-concept appears reactive to a disorder, disability, or condition. Theoretically, if the condition did not exist, there would not be a self-concept problem. Example: An individual with mild mental retardation develops self-esteem problems.

- *Secondary/Primary* self-concept problems are those in which diminished self-concept was initially reactive or secondary, but the self-concept problem assumes a central and pervasive role in the individual's functioning and is related to development of additional problems or disorders. Example: An individual with a learning disability develops low self-esteem, which evolves into clinical depression.

It would appear that those persons with primary or secondary/primary types of self-concept problems should have some element of their treatment focus on self-esteem enhancement. Although the actual sequencing of the development of self-concept problems may not always be possible, this categorization can be useful in determining the centrality of self-concept problems in the overall analysis of a case.

The second issue addresses the generality versus specificity of self-concept problems. Although, self-concept is multidimensional and many scales assess self-concept across several primary dimensions, this chapter, for the most part, will focus on global aspects of self-concept. In some cases, diminished self-concept may be a realistic reflection of some personal situation or condition. For example, Prout, Marcal, and Marcal (1992), in a meta-analysis of self-reported personality characteristics of individuals with learning disabilities found that trends on academically focused self-concept measures showed more deviance from the norm than trends on global measures. This finding is not surprising since some degree of academic failure is inherent in learning disabilities. Similarly, Dunham and Dunham (1978) discussed the role of body image and physical limitations among persons with physical disabilities. Thus, it would not be surprising for individuals with physical disabilities to show indexes of self-concept problems in physical or body image areas. These more specific self-concept "problems" need to be viewed in the context of the other conditions and disorders, and their overall contribution to more global self-concept needs to be assessed.

SELF-CONCEPT AND PSYCHOPATHOLOGY

The role of self-concept in psychopathology is not totally clear, although lowered self-esteem is generally considered an indication to more fully examine an individual's overall social-emotional functioning. This type of diminished self-concept may be primarily related to problems with the affective aspects of self-esteem. In more psychodynamic formulations, the issues of identity formation and self-conceiving are important adolescent developmental phases, often viewed within a developmental crisis framework. The ability to know oneself and behave accordingly in a consistent manner is deemed necessary for adjustment. Failure to resolve this crisis not only affects behavior at the time but also influences further development. More extreme problems in this area can underlie psychopathology and maladjustment (Van der Werff, 1990).

Rosenberg (1989) addressed the issue of the relationship of anxiety and self-esteem, in particular the etiologic or directional aspect of the relationship: Does anxiety cause low self-esteem or does low self-esteem cause anxiety? It would appear that this directional issue could apply to other social-emotional variables as well. In particular, Rosenberg has found indications of self-esteem relationships with a variety of anxiety-related symptoms including psychosomatic symptoms, loneliness, and oversensitivity. Harter (1989) has hypothesized that global self-worth and self-esteem serve as mediators of social-emotional functioning, particularly affective and motivational states. Mediation of this sort may be particularly related to depression and suicidal ideation.

As mentioned previously, diagnostic and classification schemata do not have identity disorders that are specifically designated as "Self-Concept Disorders." However, a review of the fourth edition of the *Diagnostic and Statistical Manual of Mental Disorders* (DSM-IV; American Psychiatric Association [APA], 1994) shows that self-concept and self-esteem issues play a significant role in a variety of disorders. A review of diagnostic criteria and related clinical information across these disorders shows that self-perception is a key component in both the etiologic and descriptive aspects of many disorders. Self-perception can play a causative role as well as be a reaction to the disorder, similar to the primary/secondary distinction described previously. In the Child and Adolescent Disorders, "low self-esteem" is noted as an associated feature with Learning Disorders, Conduct Disorders, and Oppositional Defiant Disorder. In discussion of the Elimination Disorders of Enuresis and Encopresis, it is also noted that there are often resulting effects on self-esteem and that the degree of limitation and impairment of the elimination disorder can be related to the extent of the impact on self-esteem. Children whose self-esteem is considerably influenced by an elimination problem also have concomitant effects on their social functioning. Mood Disorders cite self-perception diagnostic criteria as part of the diagnostic criteria. The diagnostic category of Major Depressive Disorder includes "feelings of worthlessness" (p. 327) as a symptom and symptoms for Dysthymic Disorder include "low self-esteem" (p. 349). Conversely, a symptom for Hypomanic Episode is "inflated self-esteem" (p. 338). In the Anxiety Disorder classification, individuals with Panic Disorder may attribute their problems to "lack of strength of character" (p. 398). Individuals with Social Phobia may be hypersensitive to criticism, rejection, and negative evaluation, and may display low self-esteem; a symptom that includes fear of social or performance situations. The Body

Dysmorphic Disorder, one of several Somatoform Disorders, cites several behaviors associated with checking for personal defects as associated features and lists as a primary diagnostic feature "preoccupation with an imagined defect in appearance" (p. 468). In the Sexual and Gender Identity Disorders classification, individuals with Hypoactive Sexual Desire Disorder may display problems with body image, while persons with Gender Identity Disorder often experience "isolation and ostracism" (p. 533) that contribute to low self-esteem. In the Eating Disorders classification, a feature of Anorexia Nervosa is a "disturbance in the way in which one's body weight or shape is experienced" (p. 545) and "undue influence of body weight on self-evaluation" (p. 545). Similarly, under Bulimia Nervosa "self-evaluation is unduly influenced by body shape and weight" (p. 547) is an associated feature. Under general diagnostic criteria for Personality Disorder, a pattern of impairment in cognition includes problems in "ways of perceiving and interpreting self" (p. 630). Self-concept problems also are associated with Antisocial, Histrionic, Narcissistic, Avoidant, and Dependent Personality Disorders, whereas Borderline Personality Disorder notes a general feature of instability in self-image, and a more specific diagnostic feature of "identity disturbance: markedly and persistently unstable self-image or sense of self" (p. 654). Lastly, although this may be beyond what is typically considered within the realm of self-concept problems, one could regard multiple personality disorder (now called Dissociative Identity Disorder in the Dissociative Disorders classification) as an extreme case of self-concept disorder: A primary feature is the presence of at least two identities that episodically control the person's behavior.

SELF-CONCEPT AND DISABILITIES

It has long been theorized that a significant limitation or disability will invariably affect a person's overall evaluation of self. The specific nature of the disability can be related to the area of self-perception affected. For example, it has been reported that children with learning disabilities will inevitably have a negative self-concept (Gordon, 1970; Russell, 1974) due to the effects of academic failure on self-perception. McWhirter (1988), in addressing more general psychosocial adjustment states, "virtually every learning disabled child has some emotional difficulties" (p. 14), due to the lack of success in school and other areas of functioning. Despite this contention, previous reviews and analyses (Chapman, 1988; Prout, Marcal, & Marcal, 1992) have not found absolute trends in self-reported self-concept and other social-emotional variables. Chapman (1988) in a review of earlier studies of self-concepts of learning-disabled children, found that most children with learning disabilities score generally in the normal ranges on measures of global self-worth. Prout, Marcal, and Marcal

(1992) found only a mild trend toward lower general self-concept, but a stronger trend on more specific academically related or school-related self-ratings. Chapman (1988) maintains that the only way to answer the question of whether children with learning disabilities have lower self-concepts than "normally achieving" students is to make the distinction between academic self-concept and global self-concept. Chapman notes that some children with learning disabilities may enhance their self-views with nonacademic pursuits, thus diminishing or compensating for the effect of lack of success in school.

It is well established that mental retardation is related to higher incidence and prevalence of psychological disturbance (Jacobson & Ackerman, 1989; Sevin & Matson, 1994). Matson (1985) presented a biosocial theory of psychopathology in persons with mental retardation and noted that various social factors contribute to psychopathology. Inability to perform basic tasks and social skills impairs relationships and can have profound effects on an individual's self-concept. Balla and Zigler (1979) note that individuals with mental retardation are generally expected to display more adverse self-concepts than individuals with higher levels of cognitive ability. This is thought to be due to individuals' recognition of their intellectual and related limitations as well as the presumed stigmatization that accompanies such limited abilities. However, in their review of earlier studies of self-concept and mental retardation, Bella and Zigler found that the support for this view (mental retardation associated with lowered self-concept) was "mixed," with several studies showing no differences in self-concept between persons with mental retardation and those without mental retardation.

There has been considerable debate in educational circles regarding the nature of special education services for children and adolescents with disabilities. One issue revolves around the degree of integration or inclusion of children with disabilities into regular education classrooms. Further, there is the question of whether there should be any self-contained or segregated services for these disabled children. Two contrasting views on the effect of class placement on self-esteem have been offered. Sinclair and Forness (1983) concluded that the relationship between special class placement and self-concept was largely unresolved; yet they noted the potential negative effects of labeling and categorical designations of the more segregated types of placements (e.g., fully self-contained classes, separate schools for children with disabilities). Gurney (1988), on the other hand, using a social comparison theory base, proposed that full integration might have negative influences on students with special educational needs. Some students with special needs may become more aware of their limitations due to self-comparisons with students without disabilities, and develop lower self-esteems as a result. Gurney, also noting the inconclusiveness of the research literature on this issue, suggested that practitioners consider self-esteem when planning educational programs for individual students with special needs.

Dunham and Dunham (1978) addressed the multitude of factors that can affect individuals with physical handicaps, in particular, body image and a physical sense of self. Because of readily apparent or noticeable limitations, persons with visible physical disabilities may attract more attention than other less visible disability groups. Further, there may be a tendency for others to assume additional deficits (e.g., cognitive) in persons with physical limitations. Limited physical abilities also attenuate the individual's involvement with the full array of life experiences, and social interactions consequently can be seriously affected. Dunham and Dunham cite the example of a person confined to a wheelchair who is forced to engage in social interactions at a physically lower level when in a group of others who are standing. Physical and social self-concepts can be negatively influenced as a result of physical disabilities and the responses of others to those disabilities. As a result, activities to enhance self-esteem are seen as central to the rehabilitation process.

SELF-CONCEPT AND SITUATIONAL PROBLEMS

Factors external to the individual are known to affect the development of self-esteem. Levant (1984) noted that the general link between family functioning and psychosocial adjustment is well established, both from an empirical and theoretical standpoint. Elevated levels of family dysfunction are related to higher incidence of individual psychopathology. Family process theories often address the sense of self-worth or identity with its base in family interaction and individual psychosocial adjustment. Further, stress affects overall psychological functioning (Milgram, 1989). Although high self-esteem can help a person cope with stressors, stress can also reduce coping capacity and alter cognitive appraisal, including self-appraisal. The individual's affect-oriented self-concept is influenced by the ability to cope effectively with life's stressors.

Wolfe and St. Pierre (1989), in their review of the literature on psychological sequelae of child abuse noted that lowered self-esteem has been reported in empirical studies as well as noted in the clinical literature. Abused children often attribute the reason for the abuse to themselves, and engage in self-blame as a result. Thompson and Rudolph (1992) note that therapists who counsel victims of child abuse should include strategies to help overcome feelings of worthlessness and to enhance self-esteem. Similarly, children of divorce may also engage in self-blaming (Thompson & Rudolph, 1992). Wallerstein and Blakeslee (1989) describe a wide range of psychological reactions to parental divorce that interact with the developmental level of the child. Diminished self-esteem can result from parental divorce, but such problems are more likely to be seen in children who were above the age of 6 when the divorce occurred; in particular, children between 6 and 8 years are more likely to blame themselves for the divorce and develop less healthy self-images as a result.

REVIEW OF STUDIES

The review that follows is based on research covering a span from the early 1980s and the 1990s. This research focused on variables that affect global or general self-concept, self-esteem, or self-image. We did not consider related variables or measures such as "perceived competence" or "self-attribution" unless the description clearly reflected the measured construct as general self-esteem or self-concept. For the most part, this literature base included studies that used the better known instruments for assessing self-concept. These instruments were commercially published scales or those that had an adequate independent research base. Generally, we chose studies that compared some "special" group with either a control group, some other published sample, or the scale normative sample. In addition to comparison studies, we also reviewed correlational studies that considered variables related to global self-concept. We did not include treatment studies in our review unless the pretreatment self-concept was a source of comparison or correlational analysis. Our goal was to determine the extent to which each study reached a data-based conclusion about the relationship of self-concept to the identified disorders, problems, conditions, disabilities, or context-related situations. In many of the studies reviewed, self-concept was one of several constructs considered.

DISABILITIES AND HEALTH PROBLEMS

As previously discussed, there is considerable opinion and theory about the relationship of self-concept and disability status. This section reviews studies that have addressed the relationship between self-concept and learning disabilities, mental retardation, and physical handicaps. Additionally, the relationship between self-concept and health problems was examined.

Learning Disabilities

Most studies that have examined self-concept among individuals with learning disabilities have focused on differences between children with learning disabilities and their nondisabled peers. Further, virtually all the studies in this area have focused on child and/or adolescent populations. Hettinger (1982), however, examined the relationship between global self-concept and reading achievement among adolescents (eighth-grade students) with reading problems. Overall, there was little relationship between reading problems and global self-concept; a modest inverse relationship between achievement and self-concept was found among girls, but not boys. These inconclusive findings raised some questions about the hypothesized link between self-concept and school achievement among children with educational problems.

Among younger students with learning disabilities, the findings have been equivocal. Winne, Woodlands, and Wong (1982) found no differences in general self-concept among fourth- to seventh-grade students with learning disabilities when compared with normal (nondisabled) and gifted nondisabled students. However, Carroll, Friedrich, and Hund (1984) compared students with learning disabilities and students with educable mental impairments (IQs between 50 and 69), with normal or nondisabled elementary students ages 7 to 11 years. Both groups of students with handicaps exhibited lower self-concepts than the nondisabled students. The students with learning disabilities reported somewhat higher self-concepts than the children with mental retardation. Similarly, Karper and Martinek (1983) examined self-concept in a mixed sample of students enrolled in kindergarten through third-grade integrated physical education classes. Mildly handicapped students identified as learning disabled and/or hyperactive did not differ on general self-concept assessments conducted at either the beginning of the school year or the end of the academic year. Further, there was no relationship between global self-concept and measures of motor performance on either assessment.

Stone (1984) examined self-concept, socioeconomic status, and parental expectations among 7- to 13-year-old students with learning disabilities. No significant trends were found when learning disability status alone was considered; further analysis suggested that parental expectations and family attitudes may have more impact on self-concept than the children's actual learning problems. In similar studies with elementary and middle school students, DeFrancesco and Taylor (1985) and Hall and Richmond (1985) both found that students with learning disabilities showed lower self-concepts than their nondisabled peers. Nielsen and Mortorff (1989) examined the issue of self-concept among gifted third- through fifth-grade students diagnosed as learning disabled. The students' self-concept scores were compared with scale norms and the means of other published samples. The gifted students evidenced higher self-concepts than both the general population and nongifted students with learning disabilities. The gifted students with learning disabilities displayed only slightly (nonsignificant) lower scores than gifted students without learning disabilities.

Among adolescents and secondary students, Beck, Roblee, and Hanson (1982) studied differences in self-concept among 4th- through 12th-grade students, including students in learning-disability classes. No significant differences were found between the three groups of special education students (learning disability, emotional disturbance, and educable mental retardation), and none of the groups differed from a comparison group of students without exceptional educational needs. Similarly, Silverman and Zigmond (1983) found that a group of 6th- to 12th-grade adolescents exhibited no differences in self-concept between students with learning disabilities, a normal control group, and children in the scale's normative samples. And, Pickar and Ton (1986) found that the global self-concept of

10th- and 11th-grade adolescents with learning disabilities was the same as from a comparable sample of adolescents without learning disabilities.

The popular notion that children and adolescents with learning disabilities present lower global or general self-esteems does not appear to be supported by studies that compared these individuals with individuals without learning disabilities. Of the 12 analyses reviewed here, 9 reported no significant differences while 3 report that students with learning disabilities evidenced lower self-esteem. As this review focused on general self-esteem, the possibility of more domain-specific self-concept problems is not precluded (e.g., diminished academic self-concept).

Mental Retardation

The examination of self-concept among persons with mental retardation is confounded somewhat by issues related to measurement and assessment problems more so than with other populations. Zetlin, Heriot, and Turner (1985) examined response styles of adults with mental retardation on self-concept measures. Although the investigators used an oral administration, they reported a number of problematic response patterns that confounded the assessments. Although not totally negating research in this area, it was concluded that there was a need to revise methods of assessing self-concept within this population. Further, some caution should be exercised when evaluating both clinical assessment of self-concept with individuals with mental retardation and interpretation of the relevant research. The findings in this area are offered with this caution.

Wolf (1981) investigated the self-concepts of a group of black adolescents (ages 11 to 16) with mental retardation who also presented some degree of emotional disturbance. These individuals scored lower in global self-concept when compared with other samples of individuals without mental retardation or disturbance. It was also found that self-concept was negatively related to measures of deviant behavior. Thus, the coexistence of behavior disorder in persons with mental retardation may moderate the assessment of their global self-concepts. The Beck et al. (1982) study, mentioned previously, found that students with mental retardation did not differ in self-concept from other students in special education or regular education students. And, Carroll and colleagues (1984; cited previously) found that elementary students with mental retardation scored lower in self-concept than students in regular education and students with learning disabilities.

Strohmer, Prout, and Gorsky (1994) compared a sample of college students with the normative sample of a personality inventory designed specifically for adolescents and adults with mild mental retardation and borderline intelligence (Prout & Strohmer, 1991). The college students were unaware of the nature of the instrument and assumed that they were completing a general inventory. On the instrument's general self-concept scale, the sample with mild mental retardation and borderline intelligence scored lower than the nondisabled college students.

Although there are relatively few recent studies in this area, there appears to be a modest relationship between mental retardation and global self-concept. Three of the four studies reviewed reported that individuals with mental retardation exhibited lower self-concepts than nondisabled persons. These findings are noted within the context of the cautions and limitations detailed by Zetlin et al. (1985). These findings show a somewhat stronger trend than the earlier review by Balla and Zigler (1979); however, this current review represents a fairly small number of studies. Nonetheless, it is possible that due to the nature of mental retardation and the pervasive limitations across areas of functioning, that global self-concept (as opposed to domain-specific self-esteem) is more likely to be affected in persons with mental retardation than in persons with other disabilities. This increased certainty is in contrast to the equivocal findings among children with learning disabilities, which may be more domain-specific disabilities that are sensitive to domain-specific, self-concept measures.

Physical Handicaps

It has been hypothesized that physical limitations, especially the more visible nature of the disability and the associated influences on social functioning may affect global self-concept among persons with physical disabilities. However, as mentioned previously, there may be domain-specific (physical self-concept) self-perception deficits with this group. A variety of physical disabilities have been studied, and it is somewhat questionable whether these diverse disabilities represent a sufficiently homogeneous group to synthesize results across disabilities.

Sethi and Sen (1981) compared the self-esteem of orthopedically handicapped 8- to 12-year-olds with control children matched for age and IQ. The children with physical handicaps reported higher, but not significantly higher, self-concept scores than the sample of children without physical handicaps. This moderately surprising, nonsignificant finding may be partially related to the matched IQ aspect of the study because the disabled children did not differ from the nonhandicapped children on other areas of functioning. Harvey and Greenway (1984) compared two groups of 9- to 11-year-old children with physical handicaps. One group was enrolled in a special school and the other group attended school in a regular education setting. Both groups, regardless of type of school placement, evidenced lower self-concepts than a matched group of children without physical handicaps.

MacBriar (1983) studied 8- to 17-year-old children with meningomyelocele and compared their self-concepts with those of their siblings without the disorder. No significant differences were found between the self-concepts of children with handicaps and the self-concepts of their siblings. However, Kazak and Clark (1986) studied younger children with meningomyelocele and compared their responses with a group of age-matched control children without meningomyelocele. This younger group of children with meningomyelocele reported lower self-concepts than the control group. Magill and Hurlbut (1986) investigated self-concept patterns of boys and girls aged 13 to 18 with cerebral palsy. In separate analyses, differences were found for girls in the more negative direction, but not for boys, when compared with adolescents without cerebral palsy or other disabilities.

Loeb and Sarigiani (1986) compared visually-impaired and hearing-impaired children (ages 8–15) with children having neither of these impairments. The children with hearing impairments reported lower self-concepts when compared with the non-hearing-impaired comparison sample. No pattern of differences was observed for the children with visual impairments.

Children with broadly defined physical handicaps also do not show a clear pattern of diminished self-concepts. Half (four) of the analyses considered here showed patterns that suggest a tendency toward lower self-concept, while half (four) showed no such tendency. Again, although global self-concept may not be as sensitive to physical handicaps, physical self-esteem may be related more to the specific aspects of physical disabilities.

Health-Related Problems

Psychological status has been investigated among individuals who have a fairly wide variety of diseases and conditions. Issues related to the interface of medical disease and psychological adjustment are complex and beyond the scope of this chapter; however, the interrelationships of general health and self-concept have been examined and will be discussed. Parkerson, Broadhead, and Tse (1990) investigated the relationship of health status and self-concept. They found that an increase in health-related problems and concerns was associated with lower self-concept among adult primary care patients. Similarly, Larson, Boyle, and Boaz (1984) found that self-concept was negatively correlated with the number of medical problems reported by a broad sample of medical and psychiatric inpatients at a Veteran's Administration medical center. Further, for some of the health-related problems considered, it is not totally clear whether the disorders have physical or psychological bases (e.g., enuresis).

Among those problems that appear to have a predominately physical base, Hazzard and Engert (1986) found that asthmatic children between the ages of 7 and 15 years scored higher on self-concept measures than the instrument's normative means. The authors hypothesized that this unexpected finding may be related to a compensatory or denial defense mechanism that helps individuals maintain more positive self-views. Kashani,

Konig, Shepperd, and Wilfley (1988) also compared asthmatic children (ages 7–15) with matched controls and found no differences between the two groups on global self-concept. Brown (1985) assessed self-concept in 8- to 10-year-old children with diabetes and found that these children did not differ from the normative average. Moreover, Ferrari, Matthews, and Barabas (1983) compared 6- to 12-year-old children with diabetes and children with epilepsy, with matched controls without chronic disease. Whereas, the children with epilepsy reported lower self-concepts, the children with diabetes did not differ from the controls. Simmons (1985) studied early adolescents with cystic fibrosis (ages 12–15) and found that these individuals' self-reported self-concept did not differ from the norm means. Similarly, Fritz and Williams (1988) studied adolescents who had survived childhood cancer. These adolescents, with a mean age of 17 years, displayed global self-concept that exceeded the normative means.

Of the six analyses considered here of individuals with a predominately medically based chronic disease, only one showed results that would indicate children with chronic disease have more negative self-concept than children without disease. Although other literature and additional aspects of the studies reviewed here suggest some nature of psychological impact of chronic illness, the influence of disease on global self-concept does not appear to be significant. It might be hypothesized, however, that children's domain-specific self-concepts might be more adversely affected, given relationships between physical illness and physical self-concept.

As mentioned previously, self-concept has also been studied in children with diseases that arguably have more of a psychological basis. Adams and Weaver (1986), for example, examined the relationship between functional pain (nonorganic) and self-concept among 10- to 16-year-old pediatric outpatients. Those children with functional pain of a presumed psychological base, scored lower on a global self-concept measure than a group of children with physically based chronic disease. Because children with physically based diseases tend to score within normal ranges, the lower self-concepts of children with functional pain is consistent with the presumed psychological base.

Strauss, Smith, Frame, and Forehand (1985) compared the self-concepts of obese 2nd- through 5th-grade children with nonobese children. The obese children reported lower global self-concepts. However, Kimm, Sweeney, and Janosky (1991) found that 8- to 17-year-old children being treated in an outpatient children's obesity clinic scored within the normative ranges on a measure of global self-concept. In an investigation of older individuals, Dykens and Gerrard (1986) studied female college students with eating disorders and weight concerns. One group consisted of individuals who met diagnostic criteria for bulimia and one group included individuals who reported being dissatisfied with their weight and had engaged in repeat dieting. These groups were compared with students who had reported satisfaction with their current weight and had not dieted within the past year. Both the bulimic and repeat dieting groups reported lower self-concepts than the nondieting, weight-satisfied group.

Wagner and Geffken (1986) assessed the self-concepts of 5- to 14-year-old children prior to their entering a treatment program for primary nocturnal enuresis (night elimination problems only). At the initiation of treatment, these children did not display diminished self-concepts. Also, Wagner, Smith, and Norris (1988) studied children (ages 5–16) with two types of enuresis, nocturnal and nocturnal/diurnal (elimination problems at night and during the day). Although the nocturnal children were within normal limits, those children with nocturnal/diurnal elimination problems reported below-average self-esteem and lower self-concepts than the children with nocturnal enuresis. These results, considered with the findings of the other enuresis study, indicate that the diurnal component appears to be more crucial to self-esteem problems. The diurnal pattern would be more noticeable and visible, whereas knowledge of the nocturnal, bed-wetting pattern would be more likely restricted to the family unit. Finally, Owens-Stively (1987) compared 7- to 11-year-old children with encopresis to a matched group of children without encopresis. The encopretic children reported lower self-concepts than the matched controls. Again, it appears that the more noticeable the elimination problem, the lower the child's self-concept.

Within this group of studies that focused on health-related problems with more of a psychological component, there appears to be a stronger relationship with self-concept. Six of the 10 analyses showed some negative impact or relationship between self-concept and psychologically related health problems. This is in contrast to the meager findings in those studies where there was a clear organic or medical base for the medical condition. Overall, including the correlational studies with adult medical patients, half of the analyses (9 of 18) showed some negative relationship between self-concept and disease or health problems. The relationship appears stronger with more psychologically related conditions.

Summary

Across this heterogeneous list of disabilities and medical conditions, there is a modest overall relationship between global self-concept and disabilities/conditions. Of 42 analyses, 19 (45%) showed trends of diminished self-concept among individuals with disabilities or medical conditions. Admittedly, the groupings of these widely varied conditions is somewhat arbitrary and caution is offered against overgeneralizing the findings. However, some tentative conclusions can be made. First, it appears that the more defined or specific a condition is, the less impact it has on global self-concept (e.g., learning disabilities, medical conditions with a clear organic base). Global disabilities such as mental retardation that affect global functioning are more likely to adversely affect global self-concept.

Also, medical conditions that appear to have some degree of psychological etiology or component appear to have a more deleterious relationship with self-concept.

SELF-CONCEPT AND PSYCHOLOGICAL PROBLEMS

This section of the chapter will review research findings between self-concept, depression, juvenile delinquency, and more generalized emotional disturbance in children, adolescents, and adults. The studies reviewed were generally comparisons of individuals with an identified psychological disorder or maladaptive behavior pattern with those in a nonclinical group. Some studies compared different subgroups within a broader clinical group.

Depression/Anxiety

Studies involving depressed or anxious children, adolescents, and adults have consistently reported a moderate relationship between depression or anxiety and self-concept. This is not unexpected given the importance of self-concept in theoretical and clinical discussions of these disorders. Teri (1982) in a study of adolescents between 9th and 12th grades found a negative relationship between self-reported depression and self-concept. In fact, according to the study results, one of the best predictors of depression was found to be the subject's self-image. In a similar study with younger subjects, Strauss, Forehand, Frame, and Smith (1984) reported that an inverse relationship was found between depression and self-concept measures for 2nd- through 5th-grade students. With adults, Beck, Steer, Epstein and Brown (1990) also found a significant correlation between self-reported depressive symptoms and self-esteem among outpatient adults identified with mood or anxiety disorders. Also using self-report measures, Patton (1991) found that a significant relationship existed between depression and self-concept in adolescents aged 14 to 16.

These studies, using primarily correlational analyses, have consistently showed a significant negative relationship between self-concept and depression. All four studies yielded similar negative relationships. Further, this relationship was observed in child, adolescent, and adult populations.

Juvenile Delinquency

The studies reviewed in this section involved primarily adolescents who had been adjudicated as juvenile delinquents and compared their self-concept ratings with nonadjudicated peers. A small number of studies also compared adolescents based on ethnic background, residential setting, or sex.

Haddock and Sporakowski (1982) compared adolescent status offenders, criminal offenders, and nondelinquents on a measure of global self-concept and found no difference on self-concept scores between the latter two groups. However, the status offenders, who were primarily female (vs. primarily male criminal offenders), reported lower self-concepts than the nondelinquents or the criminal offender group. Although the gender variable is a possible confound, it appears that the nature of the adolescent's involvement with the legal system may influence self-perception at the time of assessment. Himes-Chapman and Hansen (1983) found in a study that compared adolescents in each of three living situations (youth homes, mental health facility, and a control group), that while the control group had higher self-concept scores than the other two groups, there were no significant differences between the adolescents in the two residential treatment groups. In a study that also examined ethnic background, Calhoun, Connley, and Bolton (1984) compared African American, Mexican American, and Caucasian incarcerated delinquents with similarly matched nondelinquents. They found no differences between African Americans and Caucasians on measures of self-esteem and self-concept. However, nondelinquent Mexican-American adolescents had significantly higher self-perception scores than delinquents of the same background. The authors attributed these low self-perception scores among the Mexican American youths to the negative effects of incarceration and loss of independence. Mexican American family cultural values may attach more negative affect to this loss of independence. Jurich and Andrews (1984) compared two groups of adolescents, adjudicated and nonadjudicated adolescents between the ages of 12 and 15, who were matched on the basis of sex, age, and demographics. They reported significant differences in global self-concept between the delinquent and nondelinquent adolescents. A study by Hains (1984) also compared nondelinquent and delinquent adolescents on three measures, one of which was a self-concept scale. Hains's results indicated that the delinquents' mean self-concept scores were not significantly different from the nondelinquent adolescents' scores. Further, Evans, Levy, Sullenberger, and Vyas (1991) found significantly lower self-concept scores among male and female delinquents when compared with nondelinquent peers, especially among those who were younger and female. Self-concept scores also appeared to be related to the length of a child's incarceration; the longer the confinement, the lower the child's self-concept.

These studies compared primarily delinquent and nondelinquent adolescents. There was a modest trend toward lower self-concepts among the delinquent samples, as compared with their nondelinquent cohorts. Six of the 10 analyses showed a difference in the direction of lower global self-concept for delinquent youth.

Emotional Disturbance

The studies reviewed in this section involve children, adolescents, and adults in residential treatment, special education, day treatment, and outpatient programs. The majority of the studies compared individuals with emotional/behavioral problems against a control group with no diagnosed disorder. This review includes a wide variety of disorders; several studies described subjects generically as "emotionally disturbed." Some of the studies also compared subjects with different diagnoses.

In a study of elementary children identified as having attention deficit disorder with hyperactivity (ADD-H) and those with attention deficit disorder without hyperactivity (ADD-WO), Lahey, Schaughency, Strauss, and Frame (1984) found that both ADD groups demonstrated poor global self-concepts. Koenig, Howard, Offer, and Cremerius (1984) studied 12- to 19-year-old adolescents in psychiatric facilities, and attempted to differentiate between levels of self-image and psychiatric disorder. They found that within the diagnostic groups of depression, conduct disorder, eating disorders, and psychosis, all four groups had global self-image difficulties. In a study of hospitalized adults, Larson, Boyle, and Boaz (1984) found that negative self-concept was related to factors such as alcoholism, psychiatric diagnosis, functional disability, and number of medical problems. Richman, Brown and Clark (1984) found that the self-concepts of 11th- and 12th-grade public high school students were inversely related to variables associated with maladaptive behavior. Lund (1987), in a study of primary and secondary school children with emotional/behavioral problems who attended a special day school, found that the global self-esteem of the children in the program was significantly lower than those of children in regular schools. In a later study, Lund (1989) found that the self-esteem of children in a day treatment school for children with emotional/behavioral problems was also low but that the children showed nonsignificant gains in self-esteem over a 24-month period. In a study of children beginning a psychiatric treatment program, Zimet and Farley (1987) found that the self-concepts of the children in treatment, when compared with a similar group of children and a control group, were primarily positive, with no significant self-concept deficits evident.

Hundert, Cassie, and Johnston (1988) compared children between the ages of 6 and 12, who were attending a variety of treatment programs for emotionally disturbed children. The programs ranged from minimally intrusive (e.g., resource, part-time programs) to more intrusive programs (e.g., special class placement and day treatment programs). No differences were found in children's self-concepts across groups, and the authors reported that the children's self-concepts did not differ significantly from the normal ranges as described in the test manuals. Kelly (1988), in a study of adolescent and elementary conduct disordered and emotionally disturbed children, found that the two groups did not differ significantly from each other on subtests or total scores on two self-concept scales. In a similar study that compared self-concept scores between children with identified emotional/behavioral problems and normal control groups, Schneider and Leitenburg (1989) found that children identified as aggressive had higher self-esteem than withdrawn or aggressive-withdrawn children.

However, control group children yielded the highest self-esteem scores of all the groups. Politino and Smith (1989) compared the self-concepts of normal and emotionally disturbed children between the ages of 8 and 13 years. The results indicated that the emotionally disturbed group had significantly lower self-concepts than the normal subjects.

The studies of self-concept among children, adolescents, and adults with various types of emotional disturbance show a moderate trend indicating somewhat lower self-concepts than nondisturbed or behavior-disordered children. In this varied grouping of emotional disorders, 11 of 15 analyses found a significant difference or relationship.

Summary

Overall, across these groups of individuals with "psychological disorders," there is a moderate relationship between self-concept and broadly defined indexes of emotional disturbance. Of 29 analyses, 21 (72%) revealed findings that global self-concept tends to be lower in groups with some type of identified disturbance. As discussed earlier, the etiologic and/or directionality of global self-concept problems and psychopathology is not completely clear. However, these studies appear generally to support the importance of global self-concept as a concern in mental health issues.

SELF-CONCEPT AND SITUATIONAL FACTORS

This section will examine the effect of psychosocial stressors on self-concept. Psychosocial stressors are broadly considered, with the stressor generally regarded as external to the individual. We will include studies that have examined a variety of family situations, including children who have been victims of child abuse and adolescents who were pregnant or were teenage mothers.

Family Situations

Family functioning and structure long have been thought to have an effect on individuals within the family unit. Studies examined here include children of divorce or homelessness, and children affected by death or illness within the family.

A number of studies have focused on children of divorce. Parrish (1987) compared third- through eighth-grade students who lived in intact, divorced, and nonremarried families, or divorced and remarried families (reconstituted families). Those children from intact families demonstrated higher self-concepts than either of the groups in which there had been a divorce. In two similar studies, Beer (1989b) compared fifth- and sixth-grade children from divorced homes with a group of controls from nondivorced homes. The children from the divorced homes reported lower self-concepts than the control children on two self-concept measures. In the second study, Beer (1989a) found that a sample of fifth-grade children from divorced homes also reported lower self-concepts than children from nondivorced homes. Garber (1991) examined the long-term impact of divorce on young adults. The effects of divorce alone on self-concept were not evident in this college student population. However, there was a significant negative influence of perceived parental conflict; a modest trend toward lower self-concepts related to perception of more parental conflict. In another study with college students, Parrish and Parrish (1991) found that lower self-concept was associated with having experienced a parental divorce at any time in the student's life. There appears to be a generally consistent finding that divorce negatively affects children's self-concepts, with some indications that the impact is moderately long term.

The issue of self-concept among homeless children also has been addressed. Miner (1991) compared Australian adolescents who had been homeless for at least 6 months with a group of adolescents living at home. A generalized pattern of lowered self-concept was found among the homeless adolescents. Although the topic of homelessness has received considerable attention in the media, this topic has received little attention in the research literature.

Three studies have focused on illness and death of a family member. Harvey and Greenway (1984), in addition to studying children with physical handicaps, examined the self-concepts of the children's siblings. The siblings of the children with physical handicaps evidenced lower self-concepts than the siblings of children without physical handicaps. Ferrari (1984) also studied siblings of male children with pervasive developmental disability or diabetes. The siblings were compared with a group of children who did not have siblings with known chronic illnesses. No differences in self-concept were found between the two sibling groups. Balk (1990) examined the effects of sibling death on a group of 14- to 19-year-old adolescent survivors. No global self-concept problems were evident.

In these studies, there was an overall pattern of family factors that influence self-esteem, with seven of nine analyses showing some negative impact on self-esteem. However, almost all the studies showing negative effects dealt with family situations where some degree of familial conflict or dysfunction was evident. Family self-concept might be anticipated to be more greatly affected than global self-concept in these circumstances.

Child Abuse

As noted previously, it has been generally accepted that child abuse is very likely to diminish a child's psychological functioning. Victims of both physical and sexual abuse have been studied and are reviewed. Allen and

Tarnowski (1989) compared physically abused children, aged 7 to 13 years, with a nonabused control group. The physically abused children demonstrated lower self-concepts than the control children. In a similar study, Johnson and Eastburg (1992) compared the self-concepts of physically abused elementary school students (ages 5–13) with those of a matched group of nonabused children. The abused children in this study also reported lower self-concepts than the nonabused children. Orr and Downes (1985) evaluated the self-concept of 9- to 15-year-old girls referred to a sexual abuse clinic. Overall, the global self-concepts of these girls was in the normal range when compared with the scales' normative samples. In addressing the issue of the source of sexual abuse, Wagner (1991) compared victims of intrafamilial abuse and extrafamilial abuse with nonabused children. Across groups, the average age was 11. Victims of intrafamilial abuse showed lower self-concepts than either the extrafamilial abused or nonabused children. These latter groups did not significantly differ from each other. It would appear that the intrafamilial abuse may have had a stronger effect on self-concept, apparently due to the closer relationships within the family unit. It is also possible that the victim may accept some degree of responsibility for the abuse. In a somewhat surprising study, Mannarino, Cohen, Smith, and Moore-Motily (1991) found that sexually abused girls, ages 7 to 13, reported significantly *higher* self-concepts than either a clinical control group or a group of normal controls. The clinical control group consisted of girls presenting other types of behavioral or mental health problems and who therefore were not true controls. The higher self-concepts of the abused girls may represent some form of coping.

Across these studies of children who have been abused, half (3 of 6) of the analyses showed some negative impact on self-concept. Taken together, there also appears to be some influence from the degree of the dysfunctional nature of abusive families. That is, the more directly the abuse is related to or based in the family functioning, the greater the influence on self-concept. This hypothesis would be generally consistent with the findings in other family-related areas such as divorce; greater family dysfunction or perceived conflict is associated with lower self-concept.

Adolescent Pregnancy and Teenage Motherhood

Adolescent pregnancy and teenage motherhood can be viewed as a significant psychosocial stressor. In most cases, pregnancy interrupts typical adolescent development and activity and often occurs without the beneficial support of the father. Several studies have addressed the self-concepts of girls faced with this stressor. Horn and Rudolph (1987), for example, studied the self-concepts of 13- to 19-year-old adolescent mothers. These young, unwed mothers showed lower self-concepts when compared with published norms. However, Matsuhashi and Felice (1991) compared first-time pregnant girls, aged 14 to 17, with a sample of girls who had never been pregnant. The girls with the first-time pregnancies did not differ from the girls who had never been pregnant and generally displayed relatively high levels of self-esteem. Drummond and Hansford (1991) examined the self-esteem of unwed, pregnant 10th- through 12th-grade girls attending an alternative high school program for teen mothers. The findings were mixed in this study, with the girls showing lower than norm self-concepts on one instrument but not on another measure. Paik (1992) also studied pregnant teenagers, ages 12 to 19, in a school for pregnant girls. These girls reported lower than norm self-concepts.

The studies that have investigated self-concept and teenage pregnancy and/or motherhood have reported mixed results. Three of the five analyses in these studies show some degree of negative impact, while two showed no differences.

Summary

Across these various special situations, there is some modest support for the influence of psychosocial stressors on self-esteem. Again, the studies in this area are a heterogeneous grouping, and it is somewhat arbitrary to treat these studies as representing a common theme in the research. Nonetheless, they all represent stressors external to the individual and all the stressors could be termed significant life events. Of 20 analyses in this review, 13 (65%) revealed some negative relationship between life stressors and self-concept. Perhaps the strongest trend showed that events associated with family dysfunction appear to have the potential for having the most impact on individuals. It is likely that family dysfunction would influence family self-concept even more than global self-concept.

CONCLUSIONS

Across all the studies included in this review, slightly over half (58%) of the analyses showed some type of negative relationship with global self-concept. This finding may be attenuated due to other sources of variation in these studies. It is possible that the relationship is stronger when other design variables and factors (e.g., accuracy of diagnosis, severity of disorder, severity of stressors) in the studies are considered. In fact, on a subjective level, it would appear that the more pervasive and severe the stressor in a person's life, the more deleterious effect it has on self-concept. Nonetheless, this general finding supports the notion that self-concept plays an influential role in a variety of other conditions. The weakest relationship appeared to be with disabilities and medical conditions that have a more specific type of impairment and those that do not necessarily have a direct or clear psychological component. The clinical relevance of self-concept in these types of cases is more likely to be related to domain-specific, or perhaps even disorder-specific issues. More specific self-concept instruments appear necessary in such cases. Being affected by a condition or disability does not necessarily appear to yield negative impact on global self-concept; that is, possessing a certain specific characteristic may not negatively affect the individual's self-perception. The stronger predictors of self-concept appear to be disorders that have a more pronounced or clearer psychological component. Thus, self-concept in clinical cases may be more of a "mental health" variable than a "personal characteristic" variable. These conclusions would appear most relevant for children and adolescents because the vast majority of the research has been done with these younger populations. In fact, research with adults is very limited; adult self-concept would appear to be a viable direction for future research.

Although this chapter focused on global self-concept, self-concept should be considered as a multidimensional variable in clinical practice (see Chapter 12, this volume). The specifics of the range of conditions considered here suggests that global self-concept should be viewed in the context of the specific problem or condition. In fact, understanding self-concept in areas other than those most directly affected by a disability or condition may reveal more about social-emotional functioning. Finding domain-specific diminished self-concepts (e.g., academic self-concept in children with learning disabilities) may be expected in some conditions; finding diminished self-concepts in less directly related areas (e.g., affect self-concept in children with learning disabilities) may be more useful in understanding problems in psychosocial adjustment.

This review provides relatively strong support for the importance of self-concept as a mental health variable. Although sound clinical practice dictates that cases be dealt with on an individual basis, self-concept as a focus in clinical personality assessment and therapeutic interventions appears to be warranted. Further, the continued use of self-concept as an outcome variable in counseling and psychotherapy studies also appears to be a worthwhile endeavor.

REFERENCES

Adams, J. A., & Weaver, S. J. (1986). Self-esteem and perceived stress in young adolescents with chronic disease: Unexpected findings. *Journal of Adolescent Health Care, 7,* 173–177.

Allen, D. M., & Tarnowski, K. J. (1989). Depressive characteristics of physically abused children. *Journal of Abnormal Psychology, 17,* 1–11.

American Psychiatric Association. (1994). *Diagnostic and statistical manual of mental disorders* (4th ed.). Washington, DC: Author.

Balk, D. E. (1990). The self-concepts of bereaved adolescents: Sibling death and its aftermath. *Journal of Adolescent Research, 5,* 112–132.

Balla, D., & Zigler, E. (1979). Personality development in retarded persons. In N. R. Ellis (Ed.), *Handbook of mental deficiency, psychological theory and research* (2nd ed., pp. 143–168). Hillsdale, NJ: Erlbaum.

Beck, A., Steer, R. A., Epstein, N., & Brown, G. (1990). Beck Self Concept Test. *Psychological Assessment, 2,* 191–197.

Beck, M. A., Roblee, K., & Hanson, J. (1982). Special education/regular education: A comparison of self-concept. *Education, 102,* 277–279.

Beer, J. (1989a.). The relation of divorce to self-concepts and grade point average of fifth grade school children. *Psychological Reports, 65,* 104–106.

Beer, J. (1989b). The relationship of divorce to self-concept, self-esteem, and grade point average of fifth and sixth grade children. *Psychological Reports, 65,* 1379–1383.

Brown, A. J. (1985). School-age children with diabetes: Knowledge and management of the disease and adequacy of self-concept. *Maternal Child Nursing Journal, 14,* 47–61.

Calhoun, G., Connley, S., & Bolton, J. (1984). Comparison of delinquents and nondelinquents in ethnicity, ordinal position and self-perception. *Journal of Clinical Psychology, 40,* 323–328.

Carroll, J. J., Friedrich, D., & Hund, J. (1984). Academic self-concept and teachers' perceptions of normal, mentally retarded, and learning disabled elementary students. *Psychology in the Schools, 21,* 343–348.

Chapman, J. W. (1988). Learning disabled children's self-concepts. *Review of Educational Research, 58,* 347–371.

DeFrancesco, J. J., & Taylor, J. (1985). Dimensions of self-concept in primary and middle school learning disabled and nondisabled students. *Child Study Journal, 15,* 99–105.

Drummond, R. J., & Hansford, S. G. (1991). Dimensions of self-concept of pregnant unwed teens. *Journal of Psychology, 125,* 65–69.

Dunham, J. R., & Dunham, C. S. (1978). Psychosocial aspects of disability. In R. M. Goldenson, J. R. Dunham, & C. S. Dunham (Eds.), *Disability and rehabilitation handbook* (pp. 12–20). New York: McGraw-Hill.

Dykens, E. M., & Gerrard, M. (1986). Psychological profiles of purging bulimics, repeat dieters, and controls. *Journal of Consulting and Clinical Psychology, 54,* 283–288.

Evans, R., Levy, L., Sullenberger, T., & Vyas, A. (1991). Self concept and delinquency: The on-going debate. *Journal of Offender Rehabilitation, 16,* 59–74.

Ferrari, M. (1984). Psychosocial effects on children: I. Chronically ill boys. *Journal of Child Psychology and Psychiatry and Allied Disciplines, 25,* 459–476.

Ferrari, M., Matthews, W. S., & Barabas, G. (1983). The family and the child with epilepsy. *Family Process, 22,* 53–59.

Fritz, G. K., & Williams, J. R. (1988). Issues of adolescent development for survivors of childhood cancer. *Journal of the American Academy of Child and Adolescent Psychiatry, 27,* 712–715.

Garber, R. J. (1991). Long-term effects of divorce on the self-esteem of young adults. *Journal of Divorce and Remarriage, 17,* 131–137.

Gordon, S. (1970). Reversing a negative self-image. In L. Anderson (Ed.), *Helping the adolescent with the hidden handicap* (pp. 71–86). Belomont, CA: Fearon.

Gurney, P. W. (1988). *Self-esteem in children with special educational needs*. London: Rutledge.

Haddock, B. L., & Sporakowski, M. J. (1982). Self-concept and family communication: A comparison of status and criminal offenders and non-offenders. *Journal of Offender Counseling, Services and Rehabilitation, 7,* 61–74.

Hains, A. A. (1984). Variables in social cognitive development: Moral judgment, role-taking, cognitive processes, and self-concept in delinquents and non-delinquents. *Journal of Early Adolescence, 4,* 66–74.

Hall, C. W., & Richmond, B. O. (1985). Non-verbal communication, self-esteem, and interpersonal relations of learning disabled and non-learning disabled students. *The Exceptional Child, 32,* 87–91.

Harter, S. (1989). Causes, correlates, and the functional role of global self-worth: A life-span perspective. In J. Kolligan & R. Sternberg, (Eds.), *Perceptions of competence and incompetence across the life-span* (pp. 67–99). New Haven, CT: Yale University Press.

Harvey, D. H., & Greenway, A. P. (1984). The self-concept of physically handicapped children and their non-handicapped siblings: An empirical investigation. *Journal of Child Psychology and Psychiatry and Allied Disciplines, 25,* 273–284.

Hazzard, A., & Engert, L. (1986). Knowledge, attitudes, and behavior in children with asthma. *Journal of Asthma, 23,* 61–67.

Hettinger, C. C. (1982). The impact of reading deficiency on the global self-concept of the adolescent. *Journal of Early Adolescence, 2,* 293–300.

Himes-Chapman, B. S., & Hansen, J. C. (1983). Family environments and self-concepts of delinquent and mentally ill adolescents. *Family Therapy, 10,* 289–298.

Horn, M. F., & Rudolph, L. B. (1987). An investigation of verbal interaction, knowledge of sexual behavior and self-concept in adolescent mothers. *Adolescence, 22,* 591–598.

Hundert, J., Cassie, J. B., & Johnston, N. (1988). Characteristics of emotionally disturbed children referred to day treatment, special class, outpatient and assessment services. *Journal of Clinical Child Psychology, 17,* 121–130.

Jacobson, J. W., & Ackerman, J. J. (1989). Psychological services for persons with mental retardation and psychiatric impairments. *Mental Retardation, 27,* 33–36.

Johnson, W. B., & Eastburg, M. C. (1992). God, parent and self-concepts in abused and nonabused children. *Journal of Psychology and Christianity, 11,* 235–243.

Jurich, A. P., & Andrews, D. (1984). Self-concepts of rural early adolescent juvenile delinquents. *Journal of Early Adolescence, 4,* 41–46.

Karper, W. B., & Martinek, T. J. (1983). Motor performance and self-concept of handicapped and non-handicapped children in integrated physical education classes. *American Corrective Therapy Journal, 37,* 91–95.

Kashani, J. H., Konig, R., & Shepperd, J. A., & Wilfley, D. E. (1988). Psychopathology and self-concept in asthmatic children. *Journal of Pediatric Psychology, 13,* 509–520.

Kazak, A. E., & Clark, M. N. (1986). Stress in families of children with meningmyeolocele. *Developmental Medicine and Child Neurology, 28,* 220–228.

Kelly, E. J. (1988). Use of self-concept tests in differentiating between conduct disordered and emotionally disturbed students. *Psychological Reports, 62,* 363–367.

Kimm, S. Y., Sweeney, C. G., & Janosky, J. E. (1991). Self-concept measures and childhood obesity: A descriptive analysis. *Journal of Developmental and Behavioral Pediatrics, 12,* 19–24.

Koenig, L., Howard, K. I., Offer, D., & Cremerius, M. (1984). Psychopathology and adolescent self-image. *New Directions for Mental Health Services, 22,* 57–71.

Lahey, B. B., Schaughency, E. A., Strauss, C. C., & Frame, C. (1984). Are attention deficit disorders with and without hyperactivity similar or disimilar disorders? *Journal of the American Academy of child Psychiatry, 23,* 302–309.

Larson, P. C., Boyle, E. S., & Boaz, M. E. (1984). The relationship of self-concept to age, disability, and institutional residency. *Gerontologist, 24,* 401–407.

Levant, R. F. (1984). *Family therapy: A comprehensive overview.* Englewood Cliffs, NJ: Prentice-Hall.

Loeb, R. C., & Sarigiani, P. (1986). The impact of hearing impairment on self-perceptions of children. *Volta Review, 88,* 89–100.

Lund, R. (1987). The self-esteem of children with emotional and behavioural difficulties. *Maladjustment and Therapeutic Education, 5,* 26–33.

Lund, R. (1989). Self-esteem and long term placement in day schools for children with emotional and behavioural difficulties. *Maladjustment and Therapeutic Education, 7,* 55–57.

MacBriar, B. R. (1983). Self-concept of preadolescent and adolescent children with meningmyelocele. *Issues in Comprehensive Nursing, 6,* 1–11.

Magill, J., & Hurlbut, N. (1986). The self-esteem of adolescents with cerebral palsy. *American Journal of Occupational Therapy, 40,* 402–407.

Mannarino, A. P., Cohen, J. A., Smith, J. A., & Moore-Motily, S. (1991). Six and twelve month follow-up of sexually abused girls. *Journal of Interpersonal Violence, 6,* 494–511.

Matson, J. L. (1985). Biosocial theory of psychopathology: A three by three factor model. *Applied Research in Mental Retardation, 6,* 199–227.

Matsuhashi, Y., & Felice, M. E. (1991). Adolescent body image during pregnancy. *Journal of Adolescent Health, 12,* 313–315.

McWhirter, J. J. (1988). *The learning disabled child: School and family.* Lanham, MD: University Press of America.

Milgram, N. A. (1989). Children under stress. In T. H. Ollendick & M. Herson (Eds.), *Handbook of child psychopathology* (2nd ed., pp. 399–418). New York: Plenum.

Miner, M. H. (1991). The self-concept of homeless adolescents. *Journal of Youth and Adolescence, 20,* 545–560.

Nielsen, M. E., & Mortorff, A. S. (1989). Self-concept in learning disabled gifted students. *Roeper Review, 12,* 29–36.

Orr, D. P., & Downes, M. C. (1985). Self-concept of adolescent sexual abuse victims. *Journal of Youth and Adolescence, 14,* 401–410.

Owens-Stively, J. A. (1987). Self-esteem in encopretic children. *Child Psychiatry and Human Development, 18,* 13–21.

Paik, S. J. (1992). Self-concept of pregnant teenagers. *Journal of Health and Social Policy, 3,* 93–111.

Parkerson, G. R., Broadhead, W. E., & Tse, C. J. (1990). The Duke Health Profile: A 17 item measure of health and dysfunction. *Medical Care, 28,* 1056–1072.

Parrish, T. S. (1987). Children's self-concepts: Are they affected by parental divorce and remarriage? *Journal of Social Behavior and Personality, 2,* 559–562.

Parrish, T. S., & Parrish, J. G. (1991). The effects of family configuration and support system failures during childhood and adolescence on college students' self-concepts and social skills. *Adolescence, 26,* 441–447.

Patton, W. (1991). Relationship between self-image and depression in adolescents. *Psychological Reports, 68,* 867–870.

Pickar, D. B., & Ton, C. D. (1986). The learning disabled adolescent: Eriksonian psychosocial development, self-concept, and delinquent behavior. *Journal of Youth and Adolescence, 15,* 429–440.

Politino, V., & Smith, S. L. (1989). Attitude toward physical activity and self-concept of emotionally disturbed and normal children. *Adapted Physical Activity Quarterly, 6,* 371–378.

Prout, H. T., Marcal, S. D., & Marcal, D. C. (1992). A meta-analysis of self-reported personality characteristics of children and adolescents with learning disabilities. *Journal of Psychoeducational Assessment, 10,* 59–64.

Prout, H. T., & Strohmer, D. C. (1991). *Emotional Problems Scales: The Self-Report Inventory.* Odessa, FL: Psychological Assessment Resources.

Richman, C. L., Brown, K. P., & Clark, M. L. (1984). The relationship between self-esteem and maladaptive behaviors in high school students. *Social, Behavior and Personality, 12,* 177–185.

Rosenberg, M. (1989). *Society and the adolescent self-image.* Middletown, CT: Wesleyan University Press.

Russell, R. W. (1974). The dilemma of the handicapped adolescent. In R. E. Weber (Ed.), *Handbook of learning disabilities* (pp. 111–132). Englewood Cliffs, NJ: Prentice-Hall.

Schneider, M. J., & Leitenburg, H. (1989). A comparison of aggressive and withdrawn children's self-esteem, optimism and pessimism and causal attributions for success and failure. *Journal of Abnormal Child Psychology, 17,* 133–144.

Sethi, M., & Sen, A. (1981). A comparative study of orthopedically handicapped children with their normal peers on some psychological variables. *Personality Study and Group Behavior, 1,* 83–95.

Sevin, J. A., & Matson, J. L. (1994). An overview of psychopathology. In D. C. Strohmer & H. T. Prout (Eds.), *Counseling and psychotherapy with persons with mental retardation and borderline intelligence* (pp. 21–78). Brandon, VT: Clinical Psychology Publishing.

Silverman, R., & Zigmond, N. (1983). Self-concept in learning disabled adolescents. *Journal of Learning Disabilities, 16,* 478–482.

Simmons, R. J. (1985). Emotional adjustment of early adolescents with cystic fibrosis. *Psychosomatic Medicine, 47,* 111–122.

Sinclair, E., & Forness, S. (1983). Classification and educational issues. In J. L. Matson & J. A. Mulick (Eds.), *Handbook of mental retardation* (pp. 171–184). New York: Plenum.

Stone, B. (1984). Ecological view of self-concept. *RASE: Remedial and Special Education, 5,* 43–44.

Strauss, C. C., Forehand, R. L., Frame, C., & Smith, K. (1984). Characteristics of children with extreme scores on the Children's Depression Inventory. *Journal of Clinical Child Psychology, 13,* 227–231.

Strauss, C. C., Smith, K., Frame, C., & Forehand, R. (1985). Personal and interpersonal characteristics associated with childhood obesity. *Journal of Pediatric Psychology, 10,* 337–343.

Strohmer, D. C., Prout, H. T., & Gorsky, J. (1994). The development of a personality inventory for adolescents and adults with mild mental retardation and borderline intelligence. *Assessment in Rehabilitation and Exceptionality, 1,* 78–89.

Teri, L. (1982). Depression in adolescence: Its relationship to assertion and various aspects of self-image. *Journal of Clinical Child Psychology, 11,* 101–106.

Thompson, C. L., & Rudolph, L. B. (1992). *Counseling children* (3rd ed.). Pacific Grove, CA: Brooks/Cole.

Van der Werff, J. (1990). The problem of self-conceiving. In H. Bosma & S. Jackson (Eds.), *Coping and self-concept in adolescence* (pp. 13–33). New York: Springer-Verlag.

Wagner, W. G. (1991). Brief-term psychological adjustment of sexually abused children. *Child Study Journal, 21,* 263–276.

Wagner, W. G., & Geffken, G. (1986). Enuretic children: How they view their wetting behavior. *Child Study Journal, 16,* 13–18.

Wagner, W. G., Smith, D., & Norris, W. R. (1988). The psychological adjustment of enuretic children: A comparison of two types. *Journal of Pediatric Psychology, 13,* 33–38.

Wallerstein, J., & Blakeslee, S. (1989). *Second chances.* New York, NY: Ticknor & Fields.

Winne, P. H., Woodlands, M. J., & Wong, B. Y. (1982). Comparability of self-concept among learning disabled, normal, and gifted students. *Journal of Learning Disabilities, 15,* 470–475.

Wolf, T. M. (1981). Measures of deviant behavior, activity level, and self-concept for educable mentally retarded/emotionally disturbed students. *Psychological Reports, 48,* 903–910.

Wolfe, D. A., & St. Pierre, J. (1989). Child abuse and neglect. In T. H. Ollendick & M. Herson (Eds.), *Handbook of child psychopathology* (2nd ed., pp. 377–398). New York: Plenum.

Zetlin, A. G., Heriot, M. J., & Turner, J. L. (1985). Self-concept measurement in mentally retarded adults: A micro-analysis of response styles. *Applied Research in Mental Retardation, 6,* 113–125.

Zimet, S. G., & Farley, G. K. (1987). How do emotionally disturbed children report their competencies and self-worth? *Journal of the American Academy of Child and Adolescent Psychiatry, 26,* 33–38.

CHAPTER 7

Academic Self-Concept: Its Structure, Measurement, and Relation to Academic Achievement

BARBARA M. BYRNE

In a state-of-the-art review of self-concept research, Shavelson, Hubner, and Stanton (1976) reported that most research had been of a substantive nature with scant attention paid to methodological issues related to the construct. As a consequence, most of these early studies considered the structure of self-concept to be unidimensional and used assessment instruments that were designed to measure general (global) self-concept. Because the lion's share of this research (prior to 1976) addressed substantive issues related to students' perceptions of self within an academic context, it is not surprising that findings were inconsistent, confounded, and ambiguous (for reviews, see Byrne, 1984; Hansford & Hattie, 1982; Shavelson et al., 1976; West, Fish, & Stevens, 1980; Wylie, 1974).

In response to Shavelson et al.'s (1976) call for critically needed construct validation research in the area of self-concept, a growing number of studies have since addressed issues related to the structure and measurement of the construct. This work has yielded a literature that is rich in methodological as well as substantive information related to self-concept. Accordingly, it now seems evident not only that self-concept is a multifaceted construct but that at least one of its domain-specific facets, *academic self-concept*, is itself multidimensionally structured; convergence of findings from myriad studies conducted over the past 15 years provide strong endorsement for this statement. That the inculcation of this important finding has precipitated other changes in the direction of self-concept research is reflected in the literature in at least two ways: (a) Most, if not all, newly developed self-concept instruments are designed to measure multiple facets of the construct, (see Byrne, in press), and (b) increasingly more substantive self-concept research is being designed to take these multiple facets into account.

One area of self-concept research that has undergone extensive examination is the construct validation of academic self-concept. In particular, great strides have been made with respect to knowledge of (a) its theoretical structure, (b) its linkage to other important variables in its nomological net such as academic achievement, and (c) the development of instruments designed to measure domain-specific aspects of academic self-concept. For a comprehensive review of each of these factors, readers are referred to Byrne (in press).

THE STRUCTURE OF ACADEMIC SELF-CONCEPT

To fully comprehend the structure of academic self-concept, it is necessary first to orient the construct within the framework of a theoretical model. Although self-concept theory has been modeled from four known perspectives (see Byrne, 1984; Strein, 1993), the one that has provided the basis for most of the validation work associated with academic self-concept is the Shavelson model (Shavelson et al., 1976). In their seminal review, Shavelson and associates postulated that self-concept, in general terms, represents perceptions of self as derived from self-attributions, interaction with significant others, and other experiential aspects of the social environment. They proposed a model of self-concept that portrayed a multidimensional and hierarchically ordered structure, with global perceptions of self as a person (general self-concept) at the apex, and actual behavior at the base. Moving from the top to the bottom of the hierarchy, the structure became increasingly differentiated. More specifically, global self-concept was shown to split into two facets—academic and nonacademic (physical, social, emotional) self-concepts; these facets, in turn, divided into separate and more specific components (e.g., mathematics self-concept). For purposes of this chapter, however, only the academic half of the original model is relevant, and is so portrayed in Figure 7.1.

Shavelson et al. (1976) argued that perceptions of self are formulated relative to some particular behavior and thus, direction of causal flow progresses from actual performance at the base, to overall perceptions of self at the apex. For example, the model as schematically presented in Figure 7.1, hypothesizes that self-perceptions of mathematic competence "cause" self-perceptions of overall academic competence, which in turn, impacts perceptions of self in general.

In addition to their schematic representation of academic self-concept structure, Shavelson et al. (1976) suggested that the construct becomes increasingly multifaceted with age, and is discriminable from related behavioral constructs such as, for example, mathematics achievement. Moreover, based on their failure to find adequate conceptual or empirical justification for distinguishing between self-description and self-evaluation, Shavelson and associates argued for the evaluative character of academic

General

Academic
Self-Concept

Subareas of
Self-Concept

Evaluation of
Behavior in
Specific
Situations

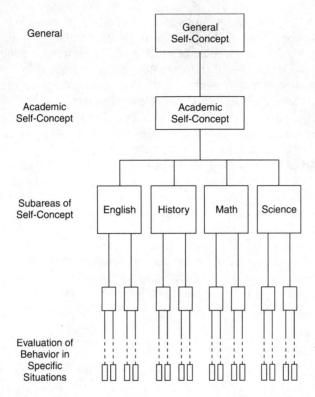

Figure 7.1 Structure of Academic Self-Concept as postulated by Shavelson, Hubner, and Stanton (1976). From "Self-Concept: Validation of Construct Interpretations" by R. J. Shavelson, J. J. Hubner, and G. C. Stanton, 1976, *Review of Educational Research, 46,* p. 413. Copyright 1976 by the American Educational Research Association. Adapted by permission of the publisher.

self-concept. These evaluations are based on either absolute standards, or on relative ones such as comparison with one's peers; evaluative importance can vary for each component in the model.

One consequence of the murky differentiation between self-description and self-evaluation is that the terms "self-concept" and "self-esteem" have tended to be used interchangeably in the literature (Hughes, 1984; Marsh, 1993a); this ambiguity prevails, regardless of the particular facet of self-concept under study. Despite some consensus that the term "self-concept" connotes a broad definition of the construct that includes cognitive, affective, and behavioral aspects whereas the term "self-esteem" is thought to be a more limited evaluative component of the broader self-concept term, and despite substantial empirical work that addressed this discriminability issue (Marsh, 1993a), clarification of their separate construct status has not yet been definitively established. Because the contents of this chapter reflect a review of this literature, the terms "self-concept" and "self-esteem" are used here in the same synonymous manner. (But, for a counter cross-cultural perspective, see Cheng, 1992; Watkins & Dhawan, 1989.)

Although there is no precise definition of academic self-concept, Strein (1993) has noted that use of the term can be characterized by two elements common to most research, both of which are consistent with the Shavelson model. First, academic self-concept reflects descriptive (e.g., "I like math") as well as evaluative (e.g., "I am good at math") aspects of self-perception. Second, self-perceptions associated with academic self-concept tend to focus on scholastic competence, rather than attitude.

When the Shavelson model was proposed in 1976, it had not been formally tested. Rather, the intent was to provide a heuristic and plausible model of self-concept that might well serve as a springboard for further construct validation work in the area. Today, almost two decades later, a review of the literature yields ample evidence that it is currently the most empirically tested model of self-concept available. We turn now to a summary of studies that were instrumental in both validating and restructuring the academic portion of the originally proposed Shavelson model; this review is limited to tests of its multidimensionality and its hierarchical ordering.

Validation of a Multidimensional Structure

Early attempts to validate the multidimensionality of the Shavelson model utilized zero-order correlational analyses. Based on consistent findings that revealed academic self-concept to be related to, albeit clearly discriminable from both general and subject-matter self-concepts, two independent studies of seventh- and eighth-grade students argued strongly for a multidimensional structure (Shavelson & Bolus, 1982; Shavelson, Bolus, & Keesling, 1980). Similar findings were subsequently reported for Canadian (Byrne, 1986) and Filipino (Watkins & Gutierrez, 1989) high school students.

Later validity research bearing on the multidimensional structure of self-concept has used a confirmatory factor-analytic approach that allowed for an examination of relations among the latent constructs themselves, rather than among the observed measures presumed to represent them. Indeed, results from a multitude of studies that tested for multidimensionality across age (for reviews, see Byrne, 1984, 1990a; Marsh, 1990c, 1993a; Marsh & Shavelson, 1985), gender (e.g., Byrne & Shavelson, 1987; Marsh, 1993b), and cultures (e.g., Song & Hattie, 1984; Watkins, Fleming, & Alfon, 1989) are overwhelmingly consistent in supporting this aspect of the Shavelson et al. model. Unquestionably, the most extensive testing of the multidimensionality of academic self-concept structure has come from the work of Marsh and colleagues. Based on more than two dozen factor analyses of 12,266 sets of responses to items comprising the Self-Description Questionnaires (SDQI, Marsh, 1992b;

SDQII, 1992c; SDQIII, 1992d), Marsh (1990b) has demonstrated impressive support for the multidimensionality of self-concept and the Shavelson model from which these instruments were developed. In particular, recent research based on responses to the Academic Self-Description Questionnaires (ASDQ-I, and ASDQ-II; Marsh, 1990c) has revealed the remarkably strong multidimensionality of academic self-concept.

One interesting complication associated with the multidimensional academic self-concept structure modeled by Shavelson et al. (1976), however, is the replicated finding of negligible correlation between Math and English self-concepts. Yet, as portrayed in Figure 7.1, both facets are presumed to be explained by the higher-order factor of academic self-concept which, by definition, assumes their substantial correlation. Paradoxically, although the correlation between Math and English self-concepts is close to zero, the correlation between Math and English achievement is relatively high; such findings have been consistent across all three SDQ instruments (Marsh, 1990b) as well as across other self-concept measures (Byrne & Shavelson, 1986; Marsh, Byrne, & Shavelson, 1988). In search of answers to this conundrum, Marsh subsequently proposed (a) a revised version of the Shavelson model, labeled the Marsh/Shavelson model (Marsh & Shavelson, 1985), and (b) the Internal/External Frame of Reference model (Marsh, 1986), both of which are described later.

Validation of a Hierarchical Structure

Because hypotheses bearing on the hierarchical structure of self-concept are most appropriately tested within a confirmatory factor-analytic framework, only research designed in this manner is reviewed here. In an initial validation of the hierarchical ordering of self-concept facets, Shavelson and Bolus (1982) examined a series of alternative models ranging from one that postulated a unidimensional structure (general self-concept only) to a multidimensional structure comprising five facets (general, academic, English, math, and science self-concepts); findings revealed the five-factor model to best describe the data for students in seventh and eighth grades. Consistent with the Shavelson model, relations among the facets produced a pattern whereby the correlation between subject-matter self-concepts and academic self-concept was the strongest; between academic and general self-concepts the next strongest, and between subject-matter self-concepts and general self-concept, the weakest. Later studies by Byrne (1986; Byrne & Shavelson, 1986), and Fleming and Courtney (1984) replicated these findings for high school and college samples, respectively.

Nonetheless, in a series of studies across a range of grades, Marsh (Marsh, Parker, & Smith, 1983; Marsh, Relich, & Smith, 1983; Marsh, Smith, Barnes, & Butler, 1983) reported the hierarchical structure to weaken with increasing age. Whereas for preadolescents, less distinct subject-matter self-concepts yielded a clear hierarchical structure, such an ordering was barely evident for late adolescents, due to the more highly independent nature of self-concept relations. Marsh and colleagues argued that the negligible correlation between English and math self-concepts necessarily produced a slightly different hierarchical structure than the one proposed by Shavelson et al. (1976).

In a reanalysis of Marsh's SDQI data for students in Grades 1 through 5, Marsh and Shavelson (1985) used second-order factor analyses and found that English and math self-concepts each combined separately with academic self-concept to form two academic self-concept facets—academic/English self-concept and academic/math self-concept. In light of the inability of these two academic facets to form a single academic dimension, the authors argued for a modification of the original Shavelson model that reflected these findings; this revised model is known as the Marsh/Shavelson model.

Validation of the Marsh/Shavelson Model

Based on SDQIII responses by late adolescents, Marsh (1987b) tested and found strong support for the revised model of academic self-concept, and in particular, the need for two separate higher-order academic factors. In a more extensive testing of the academic portion of both the Marsh/Shavelson model and the original Shavelson model (with a single academic self-concept higher-order factor) based on self-concept responses from three different measuring instruments, Marsh et al. (1988) concluded the former to be superior in representing the hierarchical structure of self-concept facets. Despite this support for two higher-order academic facets, however, Marsh et al. noted that the adequacy of this support was relatively weak. Arguing that the revised model had not fully reflected the specificity of academic self-concepts, they proposed a more explicit Marsh/Shavelson model that included additional first-order, academic-specific self-concepts related to other core subject areas representative of a typical academic curriculum. This proposed model is presented in Figure 7.2.

Subsequent validation of this more academically specific model for both preadolescents and adolescents (Grades 5 through 10), based on the more appropriately constructed ASDQ-I and ASDQ-II scales, yielded support for the two higher-order academic factors, albeit the hierarchical linkage was still relatively weak (Marsh, 1990d). Nonetheless, this factor-analytic study was important because it pointed out the extent to which multiple components of academic self-concept could be clearly distinguished from one another. These findings underscore the domain specificity of academic self-concept and, thus, the need to use instrumentation designed to measure specific rather than global dimensions of academic self-concept for research that bears on perceptions of self relative to particular academic subject areas.

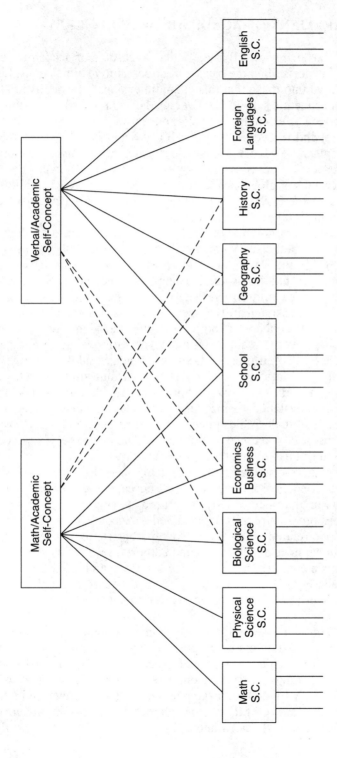

Figure 7.2 Structure of Academic Self-Concept as postulated by Marsh, Byrne, and Shavelson (1988). From "A Multifaceted Academic Self-Concept: Its Hierarchical Structure and Its Relation to Academic Achievement" by H. W. Marsh, B. M. Byrne, and R. J. Shavelson, 1988, *Journal of Educational Psychology, 80,* pp. 366–380. Adapted by permission.

THE MEASUREMENT OF ACADEMIC SELF-CONCEPT

As noted in an earlier review (Byrne, 1990a), measures of academic self-concept can be categorized on the basis of four descriptive dimensions. First they can be divided into those that take a unidimensional perspective to the measurement of academic self-concept versus those that take a multidimensional perspective. For example, the Self-Concept of Ability Scale (SCAS; Brookover, 1962) and the Perception of Ability Scale for Children (PASS; Boersma & Chapman, 1992) are both single instruments devoted to the measurement of academic self-concept. However, whereas all items on the SCAS tap perceptions of global academic self-concept (it takes a unidimensional perspective), the PASS is designed to measure several aspects of academic self-concept (it takes a multidimensional perspective).

A second categorization of academic self-concept measures can be made according to whether they constitute single instruments, as was the case with the SCAS and PASS, or whether they represent subscales of a larger instrument. A unidimensional example of the latter is the Self-Perception Profile for Children (SPPC; Harter, 1985). Although this instrument is multidimensional in the sense that it is designed to measure multiple facets of self-concept, it comprises a single academic self-concept subscale. For purposes of establishing a categorization of academic self-concept scales here, then, it represents the unidimensional perspective. In contrast, the SDQI (Marsh, 1992b) constitutes a multidimensional perspective because, in addition to several nonacademic subscales, it has three different subscales designed to measure particular aspects of academic self-concept; one subscale is designed to measure global perceptions of academic (or school) competence, the other two, the more specific perceptions of math and English competence, respectively.

As an aid to readers who may have a particular need to select a measure of academic self-concept from one of these four categories, Table 7.1 provides a summary of unidimensionally structured instruments, and Table 7.2 lists multidimensionally structured instruments. Accompanying each measure is information related to the grade level appropriate to its use, the item scale format, the number of subscales, and author(s) responsible for its development. Instruments are included if (a) after a search of the PsychLit and ERIC databases, it was found that they had been cited at least five times since 1980, or (b) they were recently developed, albeit commercially published instruments.

Although a thorough assessment of psychometric soundness associated with each of these instruments is not possible here, I considered it worthwhile to include a brief description and psychometric summary for two well-validated multidimensional academic self-concept scales; they have been normed for use with different age populations and are reviewed in the following sections. However, for valuable comparative information bearing on other multidimensional instruments that include academic subscales,

TABLE 7.1 Measures of Academic Self-Concept: The Unidimensional Perspective

Instruments	Grade Level	Scale Format	Authors(s)
Single Instruments			
Self-Concept of Ability Scale	7–12	5-pt Guttman	Brookover (1962)
Instrument Subscales			
Culture-Free Self-Esteem Inventory for Children	3–9	Yes/no Checklist	Battle (1992)[a]
Multidimensional Self-Concept Scale	5–12	4-pt Likert	Bracken (1992)
Piers-Harris Children's Self-Concept Scale	4–12	Yes/no Checklist	Piers & Harris (1984)
Self-Esteem Index	4–12	4-pt Likert	Brown & Alexander (1991)
Self-Esteem Inventory	3–10	2-pt Checklist	Coopersmith (1984)
Self-Perception Profile for Children	3–8	4-pt Checklist	Harter (1985)[b]
Student Self-Concept Scale	3–12	3-pt Likert	Gresham, Elliott, & Evans-Fernandez (1993)

[a] Originally published by Special Child Publications, Seattle.
[b] Formerly called the Perceived Social Competence Scale for Children (Harter, 1982).

TABLE 7.2 **Measures of Academic Self-Concept: The Multidimensional Perspective**

Instruments	Grade Level	Scale Format	Academic Subscales	Authors(s)
Single Instruments				
Academic Self-Concept Scale	College	4-pt Likert	7	Reynolds (in press)[a]
Academic Self-Description Questionnaire (SDQ-I)	3–6	6-pt Likert	12	Marsh (1990d)
Academic SDQ-II	7–11	6-pt Likert	15	Marsh (1990d)
Dimensions of Self-Concept (DOSC) (Forms E, S)	4–12	3-pt Likert	5	Michael, Smith, & Michael (1984)
DOSC (Form H)	College	3-pt Likert	5	Michael, Denny, Knapp-Lee, & Michael (1984)
Perception of Ability Scale for Students	1–8	Yes/no Checklist	6	Boersma & Chapman (1992)[b]
Instrument Subscales				
Affective Perception Inventory (API) (Primary)	1–3	4-pt SD[c]	8	Soares & Soares (1985)
API (Intermediate)	4–8	4-pt SD	8	Soares & Soares (1985)
API (Advanced)	9–12	4-pt SD	8	Soares & Soares (1985)
Self-Concept and Motivation Inventory	pre/K	3-choice face	1	Milchus, Farrah, & Reitz (1968)
Self Description Questionnaire (SDQ-I)	2–6	5-pt Likert	3	Marsh (1992b)[d]
SDQ-II	7–11	6-pt Likert	3	Marsh (1992c)[d]
SDQ-III	11–college	8-pt Likert	3	Marsh (1992d)[d]

[a] Formerly Reynolds, Ramirez, Magrina, & Allen, 1980.
[b] Formerly called Student's Perception of Ability Scale (Boersma & Chapman, 1977).
[c] Semantic Differential.
[d] Formerly published by The Psychological Corporation.

readers are referred to Bracken and Mills (1994), Byrne (in press), Hughes (1984), Keith and Bracken (Chapter 3, this volume) and Marsh & Holmes (1990).

Measuring Academic Self-Concepts for Elementary School Students

Perception of Ability Scale for Children (PASS)

The PASS (Boersma & Chapman, 1992) is a 70-item self-report scale[1] designed to measure how students feel about themselves with respect to their lives at school. The instrument was originally developed in the late 1970s for use with children in Grades 1 through 6, and was formerly known as the Student's Perception of Ability Scale (SPAS; Boersma & Chapman, 1977). Multidimensional academic self-concepts are measured on the basis of six subscales: Perception of General Ability, Perception of Mathematics Ability, Perception of Reading and Spelling ability, Perception of Penmanship and Neatness, General School Satisfaction (each of which contains 12 items), and Confidence in Academic Ability (10 items). Item format elicits a forced-choice yes/no response, and all items are scored in the positive direction. Although reading level of the items is mid-second grade, the authors recommend that individual items be read aloud for children below Grade 3. The PASS can be administered either in groups or individually and requires approximately 15 minutes.

Research spanning the past 15 years has yielded an abundance of psychometric data for the instrument. Internal consistency reliability for the entire scale was consistent across normative samples of American ($n = 831$; $\alpha = .93$) and Canadian ($n = 310$; $\alpha = .91$) children; subscale reliabilities ranged from .64 to .93 (mean $\alpha = .80$). Test-retest reliability has been reported at .83, with values for subscales ranging from .71 to .82 (mean $r = .77$). The PASS has demonstrated moderate to strong concurrent validity with other related scales, the highest coefficient being with the Intellectual and School Status subscale of the Pier-Harris Children's Self-Concept Scale ($r = .74$) (see the PASS Manual for a more comprehensive breakdown). Finally, this research has shown the PASS to significantly predict grade point average, to usefully discriminate between learning-disabled, mentally-retarded, gifted, and normal-achieving students, to be sensitive to change following remedial intervention programs, and to be substantially related to academic locus of control and achievement expectations (Boersma & Chapman, 1992). In addition, the PASS has been used successfully to measure the academic self-concepts of other ethnic groups such as New Zealand Maoris, Canadian Native Indians, and Spanish-speaking Mexican-Americans (Arellano & Chapman, 1992).

---

[1] A 35-item short-form version is also available.

Another unique characteristic of the PASS is its valid and reliable use with learning-disabled children. Indeed, a large body of literature now provides strong support for its use with this population (Chapman & Boersma, 1991, 1992). The PASS has been shown to be very consistent in its identification of low achievers and, in particular, learning-disabled students.

Measuring Academic Self-Concepts for High School Students

Academic Self Description Questionnaire (ASDQ-II)

As noted earlier, development of the ASDQ-II evolved from construct validity research bearing on the Shavelson model and its subsequent revision, the Marsh/Shavelson model. To adequately test the validity of the revised model, an instrument was needed that was capable of measuring self-concept facets reflective of multiple aspects of academic performance; the ASDQ-II was therefore designed to address this need. In consultation with school administrators, Marsh (1990d, 1993a) determined a set of school subjects taken by all students, and a separate self-concept scale was constructed to match each content area.

The ASDQ-II (Marsh, 1990a) is a 96-item scale designed for use with adolescents (late elementary through high school). It comprises 15 subject-matter subscales and one General School subscale, each of which is composed of six items. The subject-matter subscales measure self-perceived competence related to nine core subjects (English language, English literature, foreign language, mathematics, science, history, geography, commerce, computer studies) and six noncore subjects (physical education, health, music, art, industrial arts, and religion). The phrasing of the six item stems in each subscale is identical, with only the subject area being changed. For example, "Compared with others my age, I am good at . . ."; "I get good marks in . . . classes" (Marsh, 1990d). For the General School subscale, the term "most school subjects" replaced the specific academic area. Items are constructed on a six-point Likert scale—false, mostly false, more false than true, more true than false, mostly true, true.

Marsh (1992a) has reported internal consistency reliability coefficients ranging from .89 to .95 (Md $\alpha = .92$) for the 15 subject-matter subscales. Both exploratory and confirmatory factor analyses have yielded well-defined solutions related to each of these academic areas (Marsh, 1990d).

Although the ASDQ-II is a relatively new instrument, its design was patterned after the SDQII (Marsh, 1992a).[2] Given the abundance of sound psychometric data available on all three SDQ scales, it can generally be expected that the ASDQ-II will accrue the same high quality and thorough psychometric information as its parent instrument.

---

[2] Although the reference is dated as 1992 as consequence of a recent change in its location of distribution, the instrument has been established since the early 1980s.

ACADEMIC SELF-CONCEPT/ACHIEVEMENT RELATIONS

That the link between self-concept and academic performance has provided a constant source of intrigue for researchers is evidenced by the
plethora of studies devoted to the topic over the past 30 years or so (see
Hattie, 1992). Questions raised by this research have been:

1. What is the relation between academic self-concept and academic
   achievement?
2. Is there evidence of causal predominance between self-concept and
   academic achievement?
3. What are the social referents that underlie the formation of self-
   concept as it relates to academic achievement?

We now review findings related to each of these issues.

The Link between Self-Concept and Academic Achievement

It has been generally assumed, and particularly so by educators (Wylie,
1979), that academic achievement and perceptions of self within an academic context are strongly related, and a review of findings from this research is generally consistent in reporting a positive relation between the
two constructs. However, the strength of the relation between the two constructs has been widely discrepant. For example, in their review of the literature, West et al. (1980) reported correlation coefficients that ranged
from 0.18 to 0.50 between general self-concept and academic achievement,
and from 0.27 to 0.70 between academic self-concept and academic
achievement. Likewise, Hansford and Hattie (1982) found general self-
concept and academic achievement correlations to average around 0.20,
and academic self-concept and academic achievement correlations around
0.40. In a recent meta-analytic study of 128 studies, Hattie (1992) reported 944 of the 1,136 correlations to be positive, 22 to be zero, and 170
to be negative; the average correlation between self-concept and academic
performance was 0.21.

When drawing conclusions from these reviews, at least one important
consideration should be the time frame in which the studies were conducted. Indeed, all the studies reviewed in the West et al. (1980) and Hansford and Hattie (1982) investigations and, likely, most of those reviewed by
Hattie (1992)[3] would have been conducted prior to 1980. In light of limited
knowledge of self-concept structure, and generally inferior self-concept
instrumentation at that time (Byrne, 1984; Shavelson et al., 1976; Wylie,

---

[3] A footnote associated with Chapter 9, from which my information here is drawn, states
that it was based on the earlier Hansford and Hattie (1982) article.

1974, 1979), it is not surprising that the findings are somewhat confusing, ambiguous, and lower than might be expected, thereby leading Wylie (1979) to conclude, "The correlations of achievement indices and overall self-regard indices tend to be small in absolute terms, offering no support to the commonly accepted lore that achievement and self-regard are strongly associated" (p. 406).

Specifically, the range of self-concept and achievement correlations reported is a function of several factors. *First,* the operationalization of self-concept and academic achievement has varied widely across studies. In the case of self-concept, for example, some studies used general self-concept measurements as indicators of self-concept, whereas others used academic self-concept measurements (Byrne, 1984). Further complicating the issue has been the use of diverse "self" terms (e.g., self-concept, self-esteem, self-regard, self-attitude), with no guarantee that the construct, as termed, was actually operationalized as such (Hattie, 1992). In a similar manner, academic achievement has been operationalized variously as subject grades, standardized achievement scores, self-reported grades, grade-point averages, teacher ratings of perceived academic competence, self-reports of grades, and the like.

Second, the instruments themselves have varied in terms of scaling format (e.g., Likert, semantic differential), number of scale points, number of items, and specificity of item content. It certainly seems unlikely that scores based on such a diversity of instruments are comparable across studies. Because academic achievement scores too have been represented by a variety of indicators (e.g., grades, achievement test scores), it is easy to see why reported correlations between the two constructs are so diverse.

Third, construct validity associated with the measuring instruments of both self-concept and academic achievement have also varied extensively. For example, whereas some instruments have undergone substantial construct validation, others have been project developed solely for specific studies, with little or no previous examination of their psychometric properties (Byrne, 1984; Hattie, 1992; Wylie, 1974, 1979).

Fourth, samples have also been widely discrepant with respect to their size, as well as demographic factors related to gender, age, grade level, academic ability, ethnicity, and socioeconomic status (Hattie, 1992). Taking all these various factors into account, it seems quite amazing that there is any consistency whatsoever in findings related to the link between self-concept and academic achievement! (For an excellent summary of statistics related to all the preceding factors, see Hattie, 1992.)

In light of problems associated with these early studies investigating the relation between self-concept and academic achievement, and to gain a more precise conceptualization of the constructs, it seems reasonable to base conclusions on later studies that have been consistent in both the definition and measurement of these two constructs. In particular, it is important to know that the self-concept facets being measured are grounded in a well-tested body of theory. In this regard, the research of Marsh and associates is exemplary. Thus, based on their work with the SDQ and ASDQ instruments, which were developed from the Shavelson and Marsh/Shavelson models, respectively, one can feel confident in reporting well-replicated correlations between particular aspects of academic self-concept and academic achievement. We turn now to a review of their reported findings.

In research based on the SDQs (I, II, and III), Marsh has been emphatic in operationalizing the distinctiveness of academic and nonacademic self-concepts, in addition to the more specific academic self-concepts related to English (verbal) and math self-concepts. From 11 studies relating SDQI responses by preadolescents to English, mathematics, and general academic achievement as measured by objective tests and teacher ratings, Marsh (1993a) reported that correlations between academic achievement and the nonacademic self-concepts were mostly nonsignificant and negative, that English achievement was substantially correlated with English self-concept (Md $r = 0.39$), and less correlated with general academic self-concept (Md $r = 0.21$), that correlation between English self-concept and math self-concept, consistent with previous research, was negligible (Md $r = 0.04$), and that mathematics achievement was substantially correlated with math self-concept (Md $r = 0.33$), but less correlated with general academic self-concept (Md $r = 0.26$) and English self-concept (Md $r = 0.10$). Results have demonstrated even stronger domain specificity based on adolescent data. Findings from these studies yielded correlations of 0.58, 0.27 and 0.11 between math achievement and math, general academic, and English self-concepts, respectively; correlations were 0.42, 0.24, and 0.19 between English achievement and English, general academic, and math self-concepts, respectively. Nonacademic self-concepts were found not to be related significantly to any of the achievement scores.

Research based on the ASDQ-II follow from these earlier investigations into the relation between self-concept and academic achievement, and yield more precise correlations between specific facets of academic self-concept and their matched subject-matter achievement scores. Marsh (1992a) reported that all correlations between matching areas of achievement and self-concept were substantial, with values ranging from 0.45 to 0.70 (mean $r = 0.57$). In the same study, Marsh found correlations among the achievement scores (0.42 to 0.72; mean $r = 0.58$) to be substantially larger than correlations related to matching self-concept scores (0.21 to 0.53; mean $r = 0.34$). Accordingly, these findings argue for the greater distinctiveness of academic self-concept facets than their matching academic subject areas.

Of import here, then, is that research involving the ASDQ-II has yielded correlations between self-concepts and academic achievement that are substantially higher than those typically reported (e.g., Byrne, 1984; Hattie, 1992; Hansford & Hattie, 1982; West et al., 1980). Indeed, earlier research has shown the relation between self-concept and academic achievement to be stronger when self-concept measurements reflect academic, rather than nonacademic domains. Thus, it is not surprising that when these relations represent an even more domain-specific match between an academic self-concept facet and its related subject matter achievement score, the correlations will be yet higher.

Causal Predominance between Self-Concept and Academic Achievement

Of all the issues addressed concerning self-concept and academic achievement relations, the one that has been the most perplexing and illusory has been the question of whether academic self-concept causes academic achievement, or whether instead, academic achievement causes academic self-concept. In reviewing such claims of causal predominance, I (Byrne, 1984) found that for every study that argued for the impact of academic self-concept on academic achievement, there was a comparable one that claimed the reverse to be true. Of these 23 studies, 11 argued for causal flow from self-concept to academic achievement, 11 for an academic achievement to self-concept flow, and one was unable to determine direction. Additionally, I noted three review papers that were also split in their conclusions regarding this causal issue. Following a review of published studies and 18 doctoral dissertations concerned with the impact of intervention programs on the self-concept and academic achievement of schoolchildren, Scheirer and Kraut (1979) reported no evidence of causal connection between the two constructs; these same conclusions were drawn earlier by Rubin, Dorle, and Sandidge (1977). In sharp contrast, however, the West et al. (1980) review concluded, "Findings are now sufficient to indicate that school achievement is 'causally predominant' over self-concept of academic ability" (p. 194). Two later studies have similarly produced mixed findings. Whereas Pottebaum, Keith, and Ehly (1986) found neither self-concept, nor academic achievement to be causally predominant, Skaalvik and Hagtvet (1990) reported findings of causal flow from academic achievement to self-concept based on one sample, and from self-concept to academic achievement based on the other. Taken together, this melange of claims provides clear evidence that causal predominance remains yet an unresolved issue.

One major limitation of the preceding studies, however, is that with the exception of four, all were cross-sectional studies and therefore failed to meet the necessary criterion of temporal precedence in the determination of cause (Cook & Campbell, 1979; Kenny, 1979). This criterion demands that to assess, for example, whether self-concept influences academic achievement, self-concept must precede academic achievement in time. To meet this criterion, then, a longitudinal research design is required. One type of longitudinal design that has been used to untangle the self-concept or academic achievement predominance issue is the cross-lagged panel correlation (CLPC) design (see Cook & Campbell, 1979); a literature review reveals four such studies, two of which were noted in my earlier review (Byrne, 1984). Of these four studies, two reported the causal predominance of academic self-concept over academic achievement for elementary (Chapman, Cullen, Boersma, & Maguire, 1981) and secondary students (Moyer, 1980), respectively; one reported the causal predominance of academic achievement over self-concept for secondary students (Calsyn & Kenny, 1977), and one (Watkins & Astilla, 1987) was unable to establish any causal direction for secondary students. Here again, we find no consistency in reported findings. However, in explaining this discrepancy, we could note the known limitations of the CLPC design (see, e.g., Rogosa, 1980).

A statistically more sophisticated approach to the analysis of longitudinal data is the use of structural equation modeling (SEM) procedures. This technique addresses a number of limitations associated with the CLPC design. *First,* unlike CLPC, which cannot define a causal effect, SEM provides for the specification of causal effects in the hypothesized model.

Second, whereas CLPC analyses are based on observed variables that are presumed to represent exactly (no measurement error) their underlying latent constructs, SEM analyses are based on latent unobserved variables as measured by multiple indicators; SEM can estimate measurement error.

Third, comparison of cross-lagged correlations in CLPC assumes that each variable's structure and variance remains stable across time; inasmuch as it does not, CLPC will favor the less stable variable in assigning causal predominance; SEM, in contrast, takes this variability into account.

Fourth, although both CLPC and SEM presume the ,hypothesized model to be correct, SEM is able to correct for subsequently determined misspecification, whereas CLPC is incapable of doing so.

Fifth, although Kenny (1979) provided a means for testing the comparison of cross-lagged correlations statistically and noted the low power associated with this test, most research has disregarded this admonition. Such omission is likely due to the time and effort involved in manually computing the results; in contrast, testing for statistical significance in SEM is straightforward and easily performed with a related statistical computer package. (For a didactic application using the EQS program, see Byrne, 1994. For a more extensive discussion of deficiencies associated with CLPC, see Rogosa, 1980.) Given the statistical rigor of the SEM methodology, then, we turn now to a review of studies that tested for causal direction between self-concept and academic achievement over two or more time points.

Based on two-wave data, Shavelson and Bolus (1982) reported causal direction flowing from academic self-concept to academic achievement based on data for seventh- and eighth-grade students. Although this academic self-concept to academic achievement flow replicated for each of three subject-matter self-concepts (English self-concept, math self-concept, science self-concept), the authors cautioned that the size ($N = 99$) and nature of their sample (time lag of 4 months; sample from one school) warranted only tentative generalization to the population. Despite a much larger sample of high school students ($N = 929$), data from two schools, and a longer time span (7 months), however, Byrne (1986) was not able to demonstrate evidence of causal predominance. In a third study that spanned three time points, (Newman, 1984) tested for causal predominance between mathematics academic achievement and math self-concept in 2nd, 5th, and 10th grades. His results showed that although academic achievement in 2nd grade led to changes in math self-concept in Grade 5, this causal effect diminished between Grades 5 and 10. Following a critique and reanalysis of these data, however, Marsh (1988) argued for the flow from math self-concept to math academic achievement. In a review of these three SEM studies, Marsh (1990a) brought to light an interesting factor related to the academic achievement indicators that may have led to the causal results reported. He noted that Shavelson and Bolus (1982) inferred academic achievement from grades and concluded causal direction to flow from academic self-concept to academic achievement. Newman (1984) inferred academic achievement from standardized test scores and argued for causal flow from academic achievement to academic self-concept. Finally, Byrne (1986) inferred academic achievement from two measures (grades, standardized test scores) and was unable to establish causal predominance. On the basis of this pattern of results, Marsh (1990a) argues for its support of his previous contention (1987a) that prior academic self-concept is more likely to affect subsequent achievement if achievement is inferred from school grades rather than from standardized test scores.

The most recent investigation of causal relations between academic self-concept and academic achievement is a four-wave panel study of the Youth in Transition data ($N = 1,456$; Bachman & O'Malley, 1975) conducted by Marsh (1990a). Analyses focused on data at Times 1 (early Grade 10, 2 (late Grade 11), 3 (late Grade 12), and 4 (one year after normal high school graduation). Three latent constructs were of interest as follows: (a) academic ability (T1 only), as measured by four standardized test scores, (b) academic self-concept (T1, T2, T4) as measured by responses to multiple self-rating items, and (c) school grades (T1, T2, T3). Results showed that whereas grade averages in Grades 11 and 12 were significantly affected by academic self-concept measured in the previous year, prior reported grades had no effect on subsequent measurements of academic self-concept. On the basis that this study represents the most rigorous design to date for testing these causal relations, Marsh contends that results show, convincingly, that academic self-concept is causally predominant over academic achievement. Nonetheless, as with scientific inquiry in general, and construct validity research in particular, further testing is needed to establish a pattern of replication that can provide a basis for confirmation or disconfirmation of Marsh's conclusions.

Frame-of-Reference Effects on Self-Concept/Achievement Relations

Despite the import of concrete information such as school grades in providing students with benchmarks by which to judge their own academic ability, formation of their academic self-concepts seems to require the additional comparison of their ability with some standard or frame of reference. Because students have different frames of reference, the same objective indicators of achievement would likely lead to diverse perceptions of academic competence (Marsh, 1993a). Study of these frames of reference, as they bear on the relation between self-concept and academic achievement, has yielded two important perspectives on the topic. One perspective is grounded in social comparison theory and embodies the notion that academic self-concept is derived from one's comparison of his or her own ability with the ability of members of a significant other reference group. A second perspective, proposed by Marsh (1986), contends that in addition to comparisons with a reference group, students internally compare their ability in one subject with that in another. He termed this perspective the "internal/external frame of reference model." The following sections review each of these theoretical perspectives.

The Reference-Group Comparison

There seems to be little doubt that social comparison processes play a vital role in self-concept development (see Suls & Miller, 1977). In particular, in achievement-related environments such as schools, social comparison processes bear importantly on the formation of self-perceived academic competence. Social comparison theory (Festinger, 1954) argues that people use significant others in their environment as frames of reference in forming self-assessments. Because students spend most of their time within the school environment, teachers and fellow students serve as important significant others in the formation of their self-conceptions.

Historically, investigations of this comparative practice have focused, for the most part, on the academic self-concepts of low-ability students within one of two school contexts: (a) the academically tracked high school in which high- and low-track students share the same school milieu (see Kulik & Kulik, 1982), or (b) the mainstreamed school in which learning- and/or mentally-disabled children share the same school milieu with normally-achieving children (see Chapman, 1988). Marsh (1987b; Marsh & Parker, 1984), however, developed an area of research that has investigated the effects of social comparison processes on the formation of academic self-concepts within the school environment. Marsh's approach considered the student body as a whole, rather than particular student subgroups. Marsh referred to this process as the "big-frog-little-pond effect (BFLPE)."

Academically Tracked Schools.   Schools that practice ability grouping (the placement of low- and high-ability students in separate classrooms) provide a fertile environment for the operation of social comparison

processes. This is particularly so at the high school level, where such practices have been shown to segregate students into distinct within-school societies. Each school-based society has its own social structure and norms
(Rosenbaum, 1976), and the unique characteristics of each group are readily recognized by students and teachers alike (Finley, 1984; Rosenbaum,
1976). The salience of these ability groups, then, makes them effective social referents for adolescents in their development of perceptions of self
(see Richer, 1976).

Over the years, ability grouping in high school, commonly known as
"academic tracking," has sparked considerable debate regarding its relative advantages and disadvantages. Attention has swung from the 1950s
focus on positive aspects of ability grouping for high-track students, to its
negative effect on low-track students—especially with respect to their
academic self-concepts (Kulik & Kulik, 1982). Although these concerns
have precipitated numerous investigations of track differences in academic self-concepts, findings have largely been inconsistent and indeter-
minate. In reviews of this literature (Byrne, 1988; see also Kulik & Kulik,
1982), it is notable that most research (a) had focused on only the general
and academic facets of self-concept and had not considered the more specific subject-matter self-concepts; (b) had not been linked to a specific
theoretical model; (c) used analyses based on observed, rather than on latent variable relations; and (d) had relied on traditional statistical procedures that were incapable of assessing the underlying latent constructs and
taking measurement error into account.

Based on analyses of covariance and mean structures, Byrne (1988)
subsequently tested for latent mean differences between high- ($n = 582$)
and low- ($n = 248$) track adolescents with respect to their general, academic, English, and math self-concepts. Results yielded significant track
differences in all three academic self-concepts, with low-track student
scores lower than their high-track peers; however, differences in general
self-concept were not significant between the groups (see also Byrne,
1990b). For low-track students, in particular, findings suggest that, despite
their negative academic experiences and concomitantly low academic self-
concepts, their overall perception of self remains on a par with high-track
students. Consistent with Rosenberg's (1968) views on self-concept development, it is possible that low-track students, albeit cognizant of their
inferior academic abilities, do not place a high value on academic attainment. Relatedly, it may be that low-ability students place more importance
on their social and/or physical, rather than academic competencies (see,
e.g., Renick & Harter, 1989; Winne, Woodlands, & Wong, 1982). As such,
their self-concepts in these areas may be better than, or at least equal to
their high-track peers. If this is true, school counselors, psychologists, and
others concerned with the well-being of low-ability students may well consider placing more emphasis on assessments of their nonacademic, rather
than on their academic self-concepts.

Mainstreamed Schools. Research in the area of mainstreamed schools has focused largely on the impact of social comparison processes on the general and academic self-concepts of children with learning and mental disabilities. Typically, studies of children with learning disabilities (LD) have examined self-concept differences between students placed in special remedial programs within the schools and those who are "mainstreamed" (share the same classroom as nondisabled children). Studies of children who are mentally retarded have typically compared students who attend special segregated schools with those who have been integrated into a regular school and share the same classroom with normally-achieving children.

In a meta-analytic review of 21 studies of general self-concept, and 20 of academic self-concepts, Chapman (1988) reported that while students with LD, overall, tend to have lower self-concepts than their normal achieving peers, this decrement is more consistent and dramatic for academic self-concept than for general self-concept. For example, it is not that general self-concept scores for LD students are typically low, but rather, that when compared with non-LD children, general self-concept scores for children with LD tend to be lower than those for non-LD children. In contrast, results related to academic self-concept were unequivocal; students with LD consistently reported substantially lower academic self-concept scores than their non-LD peers.

Findings related to children with mental retardation, however, tend to be more variable. Regardless of whether placed in special classes or integrated into regular classes, children with LD tend to compare themselves with normally-achieving students, whereas mentally-retarded children most often compare themselves with other retarded children (Silon & Harter, 1985; Renick & Harter, 1989). On the other hand, Renick and Harter reported that when children with LD were requested to compare themselves with their LD peers, they perceived themselves as being much more academically competent.

As a consequence of measuring multiple facets of self-concepts, Renick and Harter (1989) found that perceptions of academic competence for children with LD placed in regular classrooms were more highly correlated with feelings of general self-worth than they were with perceptions of either social acceptance or athletic competence. These results suggest that, for children with LD at least, perceptions of how well they perform academically may have an overriding effect on the extent to which they like themselves as persons in general.

Developmental differences related to children with LD were somewhat inconsistent across the Chapman (1988) and Renick and Harter (1989) studies. Whereas Renick and Harter found that academic self-concepts decreased with increasing age for children with LD in regular classrooms, Chapman's (1988) review did not conclude that this was the case. Nonetheless, he did report a strong and consistent relation between children's academic self-concepts and teachers' feedback and level of academic achievement. Chapman further determined that decrements in academic self-concept, consistent with other work in this area, were found to be established by Grade 3.

Two interesting and consistent findings that evolved from both the Chapman (1988) review and the work of Renick and Harter (1989) are important for future research on children with learning disabilities. First, both studies revealed the importance of measuring multiple domains of self-concept for children with LD. Chapman reported more consistent results when a multidimensional instrument was used to measure multiple facets of academic self-concept (e.g., PASS; Boersma & Chapman, 1992); Renick & Harter found that whereas children with LD felt inadequate in terms of their academic competence, they exhibited relatively higher perceptions of their social acceptance, athletic competence, and global self-worth. Second, both studies reported the Piers-Harris Children's Self-Concept Scale (Piers, 1984) to be an inadequate measure of academic self-concept.

The BFLPE.   According to Marsh (1984a, 1984b, 1987a; Marsh & Parker, 1984), the BFLPE occurs when equally able students exhibit lower academic self-concepts following comparison of themselves with more able students, and higher academic self-concepts following a comparison with less able students. This model contends that academic self-concept and individual academic achievement are correlated positively, whereas academic self-concept and school-average achievement[4] are correlated negatively. In contrast to studies of social comparison processes related to subgroups within a school, as discussed earlier regarding academically tracked and mainstreamed schools, Marsh's research focuses on how students evaluate their abilities relative to the mean achievement level of the school as a whole. As such, the comparative framework in Marsh's work is provided at the school level in terms of the average ability of its student body (whether the school is deemed to be representative of high- vs. low-ability students), and the extent to which student abilities within a particular school are homogeneous.

Based on data from two large national studies (Youth in Transition; High School and Beyond) for which academic ability was held constant, Marsh (1993a) reported that students who attended higher-ability schools were more apt to select less demanding coursework, and to have lower academic self-concepts, lower grade-point averages, lower educational aspirations, and lower occupational aspirations in both their second and last years of high school than their counterparts in lower-ability schools. The BFLPE was found to be related to academic performance as

---

[4] Marsh has operationalized this term as "average IQ or standardized achievement score in a school (based on the whole school or a random sample)" (H. W. Marsh, personal communication, January 18, 1994).

measured by grades ($r = \approx .15$), but not as measured by standardized achievement tests.

As noted by Strein (1993), frame-of-reference effects have several implications for school psychologists in their advising of parents and educators regarding the placement of children in remedial and accelerated programs, as well as transfers to or from other schools. Consistent with the BFLPE findings, Strein suggested that psychologists should strengthen the academic self-concepts of children with low academic achievement by recommending placement in classrooms comprising students who are similarly achieving. On the other hand, placement of students with low academic achievement in heterogeneously grouped classrooms would likely lead to decrements in the students' academic self-perceptions. Nonetheless, Slavin (1987, 1990) provides a counterargument based on achievement outcomes as derived from a meta-analytic investigation of elementary and secondary schools.

The Internal/External Comparison

Marsh contends that, in addition to a natural inclination to compare their academic abilities with the abilities of other students in their immediate school environment, students also compare their ability in one academic subject with their ability in other subjects. He refers to this comparative process as the "internal/external (I/E) frame-of-reference model" (Marsh, 1986). This concept is derived from construct validation of the Shavelson model of self-concept, wherein Marsh (1986; Marsh et al., 1988) uncovered intriguing relations between English and math self-concepts, and between English and math academic achievement. Specifically, English and math achievement correlated at approximately 0.5 to 0.8, whereas the correlations between respective self-concepts were near zero. The I/E model was designed specifically to explain why English and math self-concepts are so distinct.

According to the I/E/ frame-of-reference perspective, the formation of students' perceptions of their own academic competence is based on two sets of comparisons—an *external comparison,* by which students compare their abilities in particular subjects with the abilities of other students in their classroom or school, and an *internal ipsativelike comparison,* by which students compare their own abilities in one subject relative to their ability in another subject. (Development of the I/E model, however, grew out of research related only to the areas of math and English.)

For example (see Marsh, 1993a), suppose a student accurately perceives him- or herself as performing below average in both math and English but is better at math than English. Although his or her math skills are below average relative to other students (external comparison), but higher than average relative to English (internal comparison), the student may exhibit an average or above-average math self-concept depending on how these two factors are weighted. Because math and English achievement test scores are substantially correlated, the external comparison should yield a positive correlation between their matching self-concepts. In contrast, because math and English achievements are compared with each other, and it is the differential between these two scores that results in a higher self-concept in one area or another, the internal comparison should lead to a negative correlation. Depending on the relative strength of each, then, the joint operation of both sets of comparisons will lead to a near-zero correlation between English and math self-concepts.[5]

A second aspect of the I/E model argues that the impact of math achievement on English self-concept should be negative, and vice versa. That is to say, a high math self-concept is expected when a student's math skills are good compared with those of other students (external) and high compared with one's own English skills (internal). Holding math achievement constant, then, it is the *difference* between math and English achievement that is predictive of math self-concept; high English achievement serves only to weaken a high math self-concept (Marsh, 1993a).

Marsh and colleagues have empirically tested the basic tenets of the I/E model with data from Australian (Marsh, 1986), American (Marsh, 1990b), and Canadian (Marsh et al., 1988) students at various levels of the educative system; near-zero correlations between math and English self-concepts were reported in all studies, thereby providing ample evidence in support of the I/E model. Although the consistently small correlation between math and English self-concepts is inconsistent with the original Shavelson model, it is nonetheless consonant with the revised Marsh/Shavelson model (Marsh, 1993a).

CONCLUSION

This chapter has summarized important construct validity research bearing on the structure and measurement of academic self-concept, and on the relation between academic self-concept and academic achievement. Findings from this work provide evidence that academic self-concept is both multidimensionally and hierarchically structured, albeit the latter is more complex than originally conceptualized by Shavelson et al. (1976). Despite substantial correlation with academic achievement, this association is logically stronger when a specific facet of academic self-concept, rather than a global academic self-concept is considered.

Not addressed in this chapter are the methodological and substantive consequences of gender, age, ability, socioeconomic status, ethnicity, and other demographic variables on academic self-concept. Methodologically,

---

[5] The I/E model does not require that the math/English self-concept correlation be zero; however, it must be substantially less than the math/English achievement correlation (Marsh, 1993a).

these variables raise the question of whether the structure and measurement of academic self-concept, and its nomological link with academic achievement remain unchanged across populations; of substantive interest is the extent to which specific academic self-concept scores differ across groups. Although most academic self-concept research is of a substantive nature, there is an urgent need for methodological work in this area since any testing for group differences implicitly assumes invariant academic self-concept measurement and structure.

REFERENCES

Arellano, O. R., & Chapman, J. W. (1992). Academic self-concepts among English- and Spanish-speaking Mexican-American students. *School Psychology International, 13,* 271–281.

Bachman, J. G., & O'Malley, P. M. (1975). *Youth in transition, data file documentation* (Vol 2). Ann Arbor, MI: Institute for Social Research.

Battle, J. (1992). *Culture-Free Self-Esteem Inventories.* Austin TX: Pro-Ed.

Boersma, F. J., & Chapman, J. W. (1977). *The Student's Perception of Ability Scale.* Edmonton Alberta, Canada: University of Alberta.

Boersma, F. J., & Chapman, J. W. (1992). *Perception of Ability Scale for Students.* Los Angeles: Western Psychological Services.

Bracken, B. A. (1992). *Multidimensional Self Concept Scale.* Austin, TX: Pro-Ed.

Bracken, B. A., & Mills, B. C. (1994). School counselor's assessment of self-concept: A comprehensive review of ten instruments. *School Counselor.*

Brookover, W. B. (1962). *Self-Concept of Ability Scale.* East Lansing, MI: Educational Publications Services.

Brown, L., & Alexander, J. (1991). *Self-Esteem Index.* Austin, TX: Pro-Ed.

Byrne, B. M. (1984). The general/academic self-concept nomological network: A review of construct validation research. *Review of Educational Research, 54,* 427–456.

Byrne, B. M. (1986). Self-concept/academic achievement relations: An investigation of dimensionality, stability, and causality. *Canadian Journal of Behavioural Science, 18,* 173–186.

Byrne, B. M. (1988). Adolescent self-concept, ability grouping, and social comparison: Reexamining academic track differences in high school. *Youth and Society, 20,* 46–67.

Byrne, B. M. (1990a). Methodological approaches to the validation of academic self-concept: The construct and its measures. *Applied Measurement in Education, 3,* 185–207.

Byrne, B. M. (1990b). Self-concept and academic achievement: Investigating their importance as discriminators of academic track membership in high school. *Canadian Journal of Education, 15,* 173–182.

Byrne, B. M. (1994). *Structural equation modeling with EQS and EQS/Windows: Basic concepts, applications, and programming.* Newbury Park, CA: Sage.

Byrne, B. M. (in press). *Measuring self-concept across the lifespan: Issues and instrumentation.* Washington, DC: American Psychological Association.

Byrne, B. M., & Shavelson, R. J. (1986). On the structure of adolescent self-concept. *Journal of Educational Psychology, 78,* 474–481.

Byrne, B. M., & Shavelson, R. J. (1987). Adolescent self-concept: Testing the assumption of equivalent structure across gender. *American Educational Research Journal, 24,* 365–385.

Calsyn, R. J., & Kenny, D. A. (1977). Self-concept of ability and perceived evaluation of others: Cause or effect of academic achievement? *Journal of Educational Psychology, 69,* 136–145.

Chapman, J. W. (1988). Learning disabled children's self-concepts. *Review of Educational Research, 58,* 347–371.

Chapman, J. W., & Boersma, F. J. (1991). Assessment of learning disabled students' academic self-concepts with the PASS: Findings from 15 years of research. *Developmental Disabilities Bulletin, 19,* 81–104.

Chapman, J. W., & Boersma, F. J. (1992). Performance of students with learning disabilities on validity indexes of the Perception of Ability Scale for Students. *Perceptual and Motor Skills, 75,* 27–34.

Chapman, J. W., Cullen, J. L., Boersma, F. J., & Maguire, T. D. (1981). Affective variables and school achievement: A study of possible causal influences. *Canadian Journal of Behavioural Science, 13,* 181–192.

Cheng, C. H. K. (1992). *Towards a culturally relevant model of self-concept for Hong Kong Chinese.* Paper presented at the Fourth Asian Regional Congress of the International Association for Cross-Cultural Psychology, Kathmandu, Nepal.

Cook, T. D., & Campbell, D. T. (1979). *Quasi-experimentation: Design and analysis issues for field settings.* Chicago: Rand McNally.

Coopersmith, S. (1984). *Coopersmith Self-Esteem Inventory.* Palo Alto, CA: Consulting Psychologist Press.

Festinger, L. (1954). A theory of social comparison processes. *Human Relations, 7,* 117–140.

Finley, M. K. (1984). Teachers and tracking in a comprehensive high school. *Sociology of Education, 57,* 233–243.

Fleming, J. S., & Courtney, B. E. (1984). The dimensionality of self-esteem: II. Hierarchical facet model for revised measurement scales. *Journal of Personality and Social Psychology, 46,* 404–421.

Gresham, F. M., Elliott, S. N., & Evans-Fernandez, S. E. (1993). *Student's Self-Concept Scale.* Circle Pines, MN: American Guidance Service.

Hansford, B. D., & Hattie, J. A. (1982). The relationship between self and achievement/performance measures. *Review of Educational Research, 52,* 123–142.

Harter, S. (1982). The Perceived Competence Scale for Children. *Child Development, 53,* 87–97.

Harter, S. (1985). *Manual for the Self-perception Profile for Children.* Denver, CO: University of Denver.

Hattie, J. (1992). *Self-concept.* Hillsdale, NJ: Erlbaum.

Hughes, H. M. (1984). Measures of self-concept and self-esteem for children ages 3–12 years: A review and recommendations. *Clinical Psychology Review, 4*, 657–692.

Kenny, D. A. (1979). *Correlation and causality.* New York: Wiley.

Kulik, C. C., & Kulik, J. A. (1982). Effects of ability grouping on secondary school students: A meta-analysis of evaluation findings. *American Educational Research Journal, 19*, 415–428.

Marsh, H. W. (1984a). Self-concept: The application of a frame of reference model to explain paradoxical results. *Australian Journal of Education, 28*, 165–181.

Marsh, H. W. (1984b). Self-concept, social comparison, and ability grouping: A reply to Kulik and Kulik. *American Educational Research Journal, 21*, 799–806.

Marsh, H. W. (1986). Verbal and math self-concepts: An internal/external frame of reference model. *American Educational Research Journal, 23*, 129–149.

Marsh, H. W. (1987a). The big-fish-little-pond effect on academic self-concept. *Journal of Educational Psychology, 79*, 280–295.

Marsh, H. W. (1987b). The hierarchical structure of self-concept and the application of hierarchical confirmatory factor analysis. *Journal of Educational Measurement, 24*, 17–39.

Marsh, H. W. (1988). Causal effects of academic self-concept on academic achievement: A reanalysis of Newman (1984). *Journal of Experimental Education, 56*, 100–104.

Marsh, H. W. (1990a). Causal ordering of academic self-concept and academic achievement: A multiwave, longitudinal panel analysis. *Journal of Educational Psychology, 82*, 646–656.

Marsh, H. W. (1990b). The influence of internal and external frames of reference on the formation of math and English self-concepts. *Journal of Educational Psychology, 82*, 646–656.

Marsh, H. W. (1990c). A multidimensional, hierarchical model of self-concept: Theoretical and empirical justification. *Educational Psychology Review, 2*, 77–172.

Marsh, H. W. (1990d). The structure of academic self-concept: The Marsh/Shavelson model. *Journal of Educational Psychology, 82*, 623–636.

Marsh, H. W. (1992a). Content specificity of relations between academic achievement and academic self-concept. *Journal of Educational Psychology, 84*, 35–42.

Marsh, H. W. (1992b). *Self Description Questionnaire (SDQ) I: A theoretical and empirical basis for the measurement of multiple dimensions of preadolescent self-concept: A test manual and research monograph.* Macarthur, NSW Australia: Faculty of Education, University of Western Sydney.

Marsh, H. W. (1992c). *Self Description Questionnaire (SDQ) II: A theoretical and empirical basis for the measurement of multiple dimensions of adolescent self-concept: An interim test manual and research monograph.* Macarthur, NSW Australia: Faculty of Education, University of Western Sydney.

Marsh, H. W. (1992d). *Self Description Questionnaire (SDQ) III: A theoretical and empirical basis for the measurement of multiple dimensions of late adolescent self-concept: An interim test manual and research monograph.* Macarthur, NSW Australia: Faculty of Education, University of Western Sydney.

Marsh, H. W. (1993a). Academic self-concept: Theory, measurement, and research. In J. Suls (Ed.), *Psychological perspectives on the self* (Vol. 4). Hillsdale, NJ: Erlbaum.

Marsh, H. W. (1993b). The multidimensional structure of academic self-concept: Invariance over gender and age. *American Educational Research Journal, 30,* 841–860.

Marsh, H. W., Byrne, B. M., & Shavelson, R. J. (1988). A multifaceted academic self-concept: Its hierarchical structure and its relation to academic achievement. *Journal of Educational Psychology, 80,* 366–380.

Marsh, H. W., & Holmes, I. W. M. (1990). Multidimensional self-concepts: Construct validation of responses by children. *American Educational Research Journal, 27,* 89–117.

Marsh, H. W., & Parker, J. W. (1984). Determinants of self-concept: Is it better to be a relatively large fish in a little pond even if you don't learn to swim as well. *Journal of Personality and Social Psychology, 47,* 213–231.

Marsh, H. W., Parker, J. W., & Smith, I. D. (1983). Preadolescent self-concept: Its relation to self-concept as inferred by teachers and to academic ability. *British Journal of Educational Psychology, 53,* 60–78.

Marsh, H. W., Relich, J. D., & Smith, I. D. (1983). Self-concept: The construct validity of interpretations based upon the SDQ. *Journal of Personality and Social Psychology, 45,* 173–187.

Marsh, H. W., & Shavelson, R. J. (1985). Self-concept: Its multifaceted, hierarchical structure. *Educational Psychologist, 20,* 107–125.

Marsh, H. W., Smith, I. D., Barnes, J., & Butler, S. (1983). Self-concept: Reliability, stability, dimensionality, validity, and the measurement of change. *Journal of Educational Psychology, 75,* 772–790.

Michael, W. B., Denny, B., Knapp-Lee, L., & Michael, J. J. (1984). The development and validation of a preliminary research form of an academic self-concept measure for college students. *Educational and Psychological Measurement, 44,* 373–381.

Michael, W. B., Smith, R. A., & Michael, J. J. (1984). *Dimensions of Self-Concept (DOSC): A self-report inventory of five school-related factors of self-concept, Forms E and S.* San Diego, CA: EDITS.

Milchus, N., Farrah, G., & Reitz, W. (1968). *The Self-Concept and Motivation Inventory: What face would you wear? Preschool/Kindergarten Form.* Dearborne Heights, MI: Person-o-Metrics.

Moyer, D. C. (1980). Academic achievement, self-concept and locus of control: A causal analysis of the National Longitudinal Study. *Dissertation Abstracts International, 40,* 4496A. (University Microfilms No. 8003756)

Newman, R. S. (1984). Children's achievement and self-evaluations in mathematics: A longitudinal study. *Journal of Educational Psychology, 76,* 857–873.

Piers, E. V. (1984). *Revised manual for the Pier-Harris Children's Self-Concept Scale.* Los Angeles: Western Psychological Services.

Pottebaum, K. A., Keith, T. Z., & Ehly, S. W. (1986). Is there a causal relation between self-concept and academic achievement? *Journal of Educational Research, 79,* 140–144.

Renick, M. J., & Harter, S. (1989). Impact of social comparisons on the developing self-perceptions of learning disabled students. *Journal of Educational Psychology, 81,* 631–638.

Reynolds, W. M. (in press). *Academic Self-Concept Scale.* Odessa, FL: Psychological Assessment Resources.

Reynolds, W. M., Ramirez, M. P., Magrina, A., & Allen, J. E. (1980). Initial development and validation of the academic self-concept scale. *Educational and Psychological Measurement, 40,* 1013–1016.

Richer, S. (1976). Reference-group theory and ability grouping: A convergence of sociological theory and educational research. *Sociology of Education, 49,* 65–71.

Rogosa, D. (1980). A critique of cross-lagged correlation. *Psychological Bulletin, 88,* 245–258.

Rosenbaum, J. E. (1976). *Making inequality: The hidden curriculum of high school tracking.* New York: Wiley.

Rosenberg, M. (1968). Psychological selectivity in self-esteem formation. In C. Gordon & K. Gergen (Eds.), *The self in social interaction.* New York: Wiley.

Rubin, R. A., Dorle, J., & Sandidge, S. (1977). Self-esteem and school performance. *Psychology in the Schools, 14,* 503–507.

Scheirer, M. A., & Kraut, R. E. (1979). Increasing educational achievement via self-concept change. *Review of Educational Research, 49,* 131–150.

Shavelson, R. J., & Bolus, R. (1982). Self-concept: The interplay of theory and methods. *Journal of Educational Psychology, 74,* 3–17.

Shavelson, R. J., Bolus, R., & Keesling, J. W. (1980). Self-concept: Recent developments in theory and methods. *New Directions for Testing and Measurement, 7,* 25–43.

Shavelson, R. J., Hubner, J. J., & Stanton, G. C. (1976). Self-concept: Validation of construct interpretations. *Review of Educational Research, 46,* 407–441.

Silon, E. L., & Harter, S. (1985). Assessment of perceived competence, motivational orientation, and anxiety in segregated and mainstreamed educable mentally retarded children. *Journal of Educational Psychology, 77,* 217–230.

Skaalvik, E. M., & Hagtvet, K. A. (1990). Academic achievement and self-concept: An analysis of causal predominance in a developmental perspective. *Journal of Personality and Social Psychology, 58,* 292–307.

Slavin, R. E. (1987). Ability grouping and student achievement in elementary schools: A best-evidence synthesis. *Review of Educational Research, 57,* 293–336.

Slavin, R. E. (1990). Achievement effects of ability grouping in secondary schools: A best-ever synthesis. *Review of Educational Research, 60,* 471–499.

Soares, L. M., & Soares, A. T. (1985). *The Affective Perception Inventory (API)/composite test manual.* Trumbell, CT: SOARES Associates.

Song, I. S., & Hattie, J. (1984). Home environment, self-concept, and academic achievement: A causal modeling approach. *Journal of Educational Psychology, 76,* 1269–1281.

Strein, W. (1993). Advances in research on academic self-concept: Implications for school psychology. *School Psychology Review, 22,* 273–284.

Suls, J. M., & Miller, R. L. (1977). *Social comparison processes: Theoretical and empirical perspectives.* Washington, DC: Hemisphere.

Watkins, D., & Astilla, E. (1987). Causal dominance among self-concept, locus of control, and academic achievement. *The Journal of Psychology, 120,* 627–633.

Watkins, D., & Dhawan, N. (1989). Do we need to distinguish the constructs of self-concept and self-esteem? *Journal of Social Behavior and Personality, 4,* 555–562.

Watkins, D., Fleming, J. S., & Alfon, M. C. A. (1989). A test of Shavelson's hierarchical, multifaceted self-concept model in a Filipino college sample. *International Journal of Psychology, 24,* 367–379.

Watkins, D., & Gutierrez, M. (1989). The structure of self-concept: Some Filipino evidence. *Australian Psychologist, 24,* 401–410.

Wells, L. E., & Marwell, G. (1976). *Self-esteem: Its conceptualization and measurement.* Beverly Hills, CA: Sage.

West, C. K., Fish, J. A., & Stevens, R. J. (1980). General self-concept, self-concept of academic ability and school achievement: Implications for "causes" of self-concept. *The Australian Journal of Education, 24,* 194–213.

Winne, P. H., Woodlands, M. J., & Wong, B. Y. L. (1982). Comparability of self-concept among learning disabled, normal, and gifted students. *Journal of Learning Disabilities, 15,* 470–475.

Wylie, R. C. (1974). *The self-concept: A review of methodological considerations and measuring instruments.* Lincoln: University of Nebraska Press.

Wylie, R. C. (1979). *The self-concept (Vol 2): Theory and research on selected topics.* Lincoln: University of Nebraska Press.

CHAPTER 8

Family Self-Concept:
Ideas on Its Meaning

CANDICE FEIRING and LYNN S. TASKA

In the novel *Martha Quest,* Doris Lessing describes Martha's adolescent search for self-identity. Part of Martha's struggle to define herself centers on her relationships with family members—who she is and how she is with her mother, father, and younger brother:

> She knew, too, that she was bad-tempered and boorish. She made resolutions day after day that from now on she would be quite different. And yet a fatal demon always took possession of her, so that at the slightest remark from her mother she was impelled to take it up, examine it, and hand it back, like a challenge . . . . (p. 5)
>
> Martha had never thought of herself as a pacifist, but it seemed she was one; she played this part against her father's need . . . . (p. 25)
>
> Jonathan Quest, the younger brother, came home for the holidays from his expensive school, like a visitor from a more prosperous world. For the first time, Martha found herself consciously resenting him. Why, she asked herself, was it that he, with half her brains, should be sent to a "good school." Why was it he should inevitably be given the advantages? (p. 26)

Martha's self-descriptions differ as does her relationship with each family member. In this chapter, we explore the meaning of the family self-concept and how this term may be useful in understanding the development of the social self. The term "family self-concept" does not immediately evoke a clear meaning. This is not surprising because the terms "self-concept" and "family" are each open to a broad spectrum of interpretation. For this discussion, we will use family self-concept as a general term to indicate several possible components. In particular, we focus on the self in relation to mother, father, and siblings, as well as the self in relation to the entire family.

We would like to thank Richard Ashmore, Bruce Bracken, Wyndol Furman, and Saul Rosenthal for their thoughtful feedback.

Our analysis of family self-concept includes four specific features. First, we focus on the social self; that is, the aspects of the self that are derived through the individual's relationships with other people and in particular family members. Second, the family is viewed as a social system, and it is within the family system that the family self-concept evolves. Third, the family system is embedded in a larger social network of kin and nonkin children and adults. The family self-concept and the intrafamilial relationships from which it derives are affected by extrafamilial relationships. Fourth, family self-concept changes with development. The form, content, and centrality of self-concepts change with development as do relationships with family members.

This chapter considers how concepts of the self with family members and the self in family relationships relates to global self-concepts. We begin by presenting some of our basic assumptions about self-concepts, in general, and family self-concepts, in particular. Next, we examine the meaning of the family self-concept by using a social systems approach. After a brief consideration of systems characteristics, we explore how features of relationships are relevant for conceptualization of family self-concepts. Theory and research concerning the mother-child, father-child, parent-child, sibling-child, and family-child relationships are reviewed in regard to their significance for our definition of the family self-concept. We conclude the chapter by presenting a heuristic model for describing the factors that we believe are important for understanding the significance of the family self-concept within, as well as across, particular developmental periods.

THE CONCEPT OF SELF IN THE FAMILY

The Existential and Categorical Self

We begin our discussion of the concept of self in the family with the classic distinction first described by James (1890) between the self as subject and the self as object—the "I" compared with the "Me." The self as subject possesses the sense of personal agency and control, whereas the self as object contains the person's information and evaluation of the self (Dickstein, 1977). The duality of the self as subject and object can be thought of in terms of two general structural components—the existential self and the categorical self (Lewis & Brooks-Gunn, 1979). The existential self is the recognition of the self as being distinct from other people and objects. Such recognition occurs early in development, in the second half of the first year of life. It is reflected in the infant's demonstration of self-permanence in the ability to maintain an identity independent of interactions with others or setting.

The categorical self, which develops after self-permanence becomes stable between 8 to 9 months, is the self as object defined in relation to other people and objects. The categorical self is that part of the self comprising the ways the individual thinks about the self. Some common and early categories include sex, age, valence (good/bad), and family membership. For example, the young female child will learn that she belongs to the category of girl not boy, child not grown-up, and my family of mother, father, and younger brother, not strangers. The earliest understanding of family membership and identity may be in terms of those people who are familiar; that is, those people with whom the infant most frequently interacts compared with those who are not known or frequently interacted with (Lewis & Feiring, 1978). It is of interest to note that the term "familiar" which has come to mean that which is a common or everyday occurrence originally indicated that which pertained to the family. The sense of self as part of one's family and as distinct from each family member is probably the earliest to emerge and the most enduring across the life span (Lewis & Brooks-Gunn, 1979; Mahler, Pine, & Bergman, 1975; Troll, 1987).

The existential self as subject in the family is the actor who interacts and forms relationships with family members. Later on in this chapter, we will examine how the individual's interactions with specific family members reflect their sense of agency within and outside the family. The self as object in the family concerns the individual's knowledge and evaluation of what I am like—how I behave, how I feel, how the other behaves, how the other feels with each family member separately and with the family as a whole. It is to this self as object within the family that we devote the greater part of our discussion.

The Social Self-Concept

A central aspect of the self-concept is its relational quality (Cooley, 1902; Deaux, 1991; Mead, 1934; Ogilvie & Ashmore, 1991; Sroufe & Fleeson, 1986; Tomkins, 1987). The self is a social construction that represents in large part the internalization of the attitudes significant others hold about one's self (Harter, 1986). The extent to which the content of the self-concept is social, rather than individual, has received considerable debate. In line with the looking-glass-self theorists and the symbolic interactionists, we hold a strong social perspective whereby the sense of identity is always formulated in the context of some specific social world (Berger, 1966; Cooley, 1902; Felson, 1985; Mead, 1934; Schafer & Keith, 1985).

Social identity is the part of an individual's self-concept that derives from knowledge of group memberships (Tajfel, 1981). The infant is born into a social network, the most immediate and important of which is the family. Thus, the first group to which most children belong is the family. Initially, through parents and siblings and, later, on the child's own initiative as well, his or her network will expand to include significant others beyond the family such as friends, teachers, and, eventually, mates. The infant learns to adapt to a changing array of people, behavior, goals, and institutions, and the development of the self and relationships takes place within this array (Cochran & Brassard, 1979; Lewis & Feiring, 1978).

Investigations of the phenomenological sense of self indicate that when children and adolescents are asked to "tell me about yourself," the thoughts elicited are highly social (McGuire & McGuire, 1982; McGuire, McGuire, & Cheever, 1986). The generally recognized social origins of the self, dictate that a large portion of the self-space should be occupied by other people. In one study, using free self-descriptions, 23% of all the noun concepts used were references to significant others (McGuire & McGuire, 1988). It is also not surprising that the people particularly relevant for children's and adolescents' self-descriptions are kin, with nuclear family members predominating; of the self-descriptions involving others, 47% are of kin, including parents (14%), siblings (20%), the nuclear family in general (7%), and extended family members (5%).

The Self-Concept as a Multiplicity of Self-Representations

Before our discussion proceeds further, it is necessary to clarify our use of the term "self-concept." We do not regard self-concept as a static, generalized, or average view of the self. Rather, self-concept is used as a term to denote a system of self-generalizations or schemas (Markus & Sentis, 1982). These schemas are generated from past social experiences and, simultaneously, include both the existential self and the categorical self; that is, self-schemas have the capacity to represent the self as subject and object (Markus & Wurf, 1987). It is also important to consider the concept of other in the same terms as the self-concept. The concept of other is not an average or generalized view of the other person, but rather a system of other schemas formed from past social experiences. Other schemas characterize others as objects, both in terms of personal qualities and expectations for interaction. As objects, the concepts of self and other are mutually defining as they are derived from shared interactions. Lewis and Brooks-Gunn (1979) emphasize how the knowledge of the self and other are interdependent. "What can be demonstrated to be known about the self can be said to be known about the other and what is known about the other can be said to be known about the self" (p. 231). Consequently, the family self-concept is a term we use to summarize the idea that an individual has multiple schemas of the self and other with each family member. We will now consider how best to characterize these multiple schemas or representations of self and other within the family.

Self with Other Representations

Much of the formation and reformation of the self-concept takes place within the real or imagined interaction with others and in particular significant others. Similar to the concept of self, the concept of other is also constructed and reconstructed through consideration of interactions. A particularly important construct for our conceptualization is the *self-with-other unit* delineated by Ogilvie and Ashmore (1991). Individuals form representations of what they are like, how they behave, and what they feel when they are with specific people. What gets internalized is the self, the specific other, and the relationship of self and specific other.

The self-with-other unit is a hypothetical construct. It is defined as a mental representation of the personal qualities that individuals believe describe themselves when with particular other people. At the very least, the self-with-other unit includes one self-quality, one affect, and one object of that affect. The critical elements of important self-with-other experiences are mentally encoded. The mentally encoded, affectively valenced, events are used by the existential self to identify current social interactions as similar to or different from previous patterns of self-with-other interactions. In general, the self-with-other unit is a composite created from an average of repeated self-with-specific-other experiences. Of course, some experiences may have greater significance for the formation of the self-with-other unit, such as highly affective interactions of a positive or negative nature. Constellations of experientially similar self-with-other units are psychologically grouped together.

Not all the self-with-other representations that compose the self-concept are identical. Some key ways they differ are in centrality (degree of importance), valence (positive or negative quality) and time reference point (past, present, and future). Perhaps the most distinct difference in self-with-other representations is their centrality. Some self-representations are salient identities or core conceptions (Gergen, 1968; Stryker, 1987), whereas others are more peripheral. Central self-conceptions are usually the most well elaborated and are hypothesized to have the strongest influence on information processing and behavior. For many individuals, self-with-family-member representations, particularly self-with-parent representations, are the most central during childhood.

Although the idea of a self-with-other representation unit is based primarily in work with adults, it has been suggested that relationships with family members are important for the development of later self-with units (Ogilvie & Ashmore, 1991). The attachment theorists have most clearly articulated the processes involved in the development of the self in parent-child relationships. In particular, Bowlby (1969, 1973, 1980) suggests that the interaction patterns with parents, and primarily the mother, are the sources from which infants come to construct internal working models of the self and others in attachment relationships. The purpose of these models is to understand and anticipate others' behavior as well as to guide or plan one's own behavior in the relationship. In a similar vein, Stern (1985) describes a relational model in which internal representations of interactions with the primary caregiver, usually the mother, become generalized.

These internal representations of generalized interactions exist in the infant's mind based on repeated interactions with the other who provides regulation of the self. Through the development of these internal representations, the infant gains information about the social world, the self, and how to behave and feel with particular others.

We propose that in infancy the most central self-with-other representations are with immediate family members or consistently available others involved in the infant's life, such as grandparent or day-care provider. Two important distinctions to be made are (a) the degree to which others are consistently available for interaction, and (b) the affective quality of the interaction. In addition to being regularly available for interaction, studies of network membership and support provisions find that immediate family members are key sources of emotional support, instrumental help, and cognitive guidance (Furman & Buhrmester, 1985; Nair & Jason, 1985; Zelkowitz, 1989). In general, family members are an ongoing part of the infant's social world and available for interactions involving multiple functions, such as caregiving, play, nurturance, and learning/exploration. It is important to note that not only caregiving experiences give rise to self-with-other representations. Although the newborn's experiences with others primarily involve the functions of caregiving and nurturance, play and exploration are also occurring and rapidly increase in salience for the infant's daily social interactions.

Multiplexity, or the performance of more than one support function by network members, has been related to greater satisfaction of children with their networks (Nair & Jason, 1985; Sandler, Wolchik, & Braver, 1985). Multiplexity can be considered an index or salience and centrality of a particular network member in a given individual's network. Relationships with immediate family members are characterized by multiplexity and a high frequency of interaction (Zelkowitz, 1989). The combination of multiplexity and frequent interaction should facilitate the development of self-with-other representations with family members. In addition, this combination helps define the extent to which the self-with-other family member representations are central, compared with each other as well as to extended kin and nonkin significant friends and adults.

Some would argue that the most important self-with-other experiences in infancy are those with the primary caregiver, in most instances, the mother (Bowlby, 1969; Ogilvie & Ashmore, 1991; Sroufe & Fleeson, 1986; Stern, 1985). This epigenetic view of the development of self and relationships assumes that the infant first adapts to the mother and, from this primary relationship, all representations of self and others follow. Whereas there may be multiple internal representations of self with mother, such as self-with-mom when she is singing me to sleep and self-with-mom when she is telling me "no," it is these self-with-mother experiences that determine in a linear fashion self-with-other experiences with other immediate family members, extended kin, and nonkin adults and peers. Alternatively, we would argue along with others that multiple relationships and consequently multiple internal representations of self-with-others are formed within the first year of life (Ainsworth, Blehar, Waters, & Wall, 1978; Lewis, 1982; Lewis & Feiring, 1979). The immediate family members are clearly within young children's most important set of social network members in regard to the range of social functions they engage in with the child, frequency of contact, and the importance society places on family membership.

Internalized self-with-other-family-member representations created and organized in infancy and early childhood may form the nonconscious foundations for later self-with-other experiences and representations. These representations inform the individual about how to interpret events, what to feel during and about certain interactions, and how to behave in different interaction sequences with current and future partners. Depending on the theme of particular interaction sequences, different self-with-other-family-member representations may emerge as more informative. For example, new interactions involving attachment experiences may be based on self-with-mother or self-with-father representations, and interactions involving affiliation experiences may be based on self-with-father or sibling representations. It is possible that children form constellations of self-with-mother, self-with-father and self-with-siblings that vary in centrality and evaluative tone. These self-with-family-member constellations can be viewed as family self-concepts.

Although we consider self-with-other-family-member representations to be quite important, we do not mean to ignore the salience of significant extended family and nonkin adults and peers. Through both child interview and maternal report, it is evident that grandparents, friends, and other caregivers are important members of children's social worlds. Furthermore, we do not intend to overemphasize the influence early self-with-other-family-member experiences have on later interpersonal development in childhood, adolescence, and adulthood. Internalized self-with-other-family-member representations are not static structures into which new interpersonal experiences are merely assimilated into unchanging fixed earlier representations. Rather, the family self-concept is characterized by the change processes of modifying, updating, regrouping, and transforming representations to accommodate current experiences. In other words, we view the family self-concept as an open system with the tendency to respond and act selectively to the great range and variety of input from interaction with family members and others.

Having described a broad framework for our basic assumptions about the family self-concept, we now turn to a more specific consideration of the self with the particular family members of mother, father, and sibling. We will undertake this task within a social systems approach and will also, whenever possible, examine how the family self-concept changes with developmental period.

THE FAMILY SELF-CONCEPT AND A SYSTEMS APPROACH

From a systems perspective, the family is an open system with organized patterns of interaction that form a complex integrated whole (Minuchin, 1988). From this perspective, each family member's behavior both contributes to and is constrained by an ongoing family pattern. Characteristics of the family system include shared values, such as general comfort with confrontation and conflict or the value placed on the achievement of social, academic, and economic goals. Other characteristics include patterns that define each family member's unique role in maintaining the family system (e.g., the peacemaker, the angry one).

As we explore the meaning of the self in the family system, we will examine individual family members, as the basic elements of the system, and relationships, as the fundamental subsystems, that the family members construct as they interact with each other. The family system consists of elements that are combined into multiple, interdependent subsystems that can function separately, such as mother-father, wife-husband, mother-father-child, mother-child-sibling but which, when taken together, are greater than the sum of elements and subsystems. Social systems and family systems, in particular, can be characterized by several attributes. Our discussion of the family self-concept will focus on the following systems attributes:

1. Systems have elements and these elements can be combined to form subsystems.
2. Elements are interdependent.
3. Elements are nonadditive.
4. Systems operate according to a steady state principle so that family relationships and interactions presuppose variation and constraint in a family system in which flexibility and stability exist.

A system comprises a set of interrelated elements (Monane, 1967; Von Bertalanffy, 1967). Complex systems, such as the family, have many elements or subsystems that can combine or interact with each other in a potentially large number of ways. Although elements have an enormous number of degrees of freedom for behavior, they self-organize to generate patterned behavior.

Frequently, the family system contains the individual elements of mother, father, child, and sibling. Of particular interest here are the subsystems made up of two elements or more: for example the dyads, triads, and the total system of four members. In this family of four persons, there are, in addition to the 4 individual elements, 6 dyads, 4 triads, and the entire system, yielding a total of 15 units to consider. Each subsystem has its own boundaries and unique qualities of interaction. At the same time, all subsystems are interrelated to each other as part of the larger family system and interactions and effects across subsystems are governed by implicit rules and patterns. Thus, it is important to recognize that the self in one subsystem of the family is influenced by the self in other subsystems and the entire system as a whole.

It is important to specify that in talking about the self in various subsystems we will assume the child's point of view. This means consideration of (a) the child as daughter or son—the child in the parent-child subsystems; (b) the child as sister or brother—the child in the sibling-child subsystem; and (c) the child as daughter or son *and* sister or brother—the child in the parent-sibling-child subsystem. Over time, the child becomes an adolescent, then an adult, and during either of these periods, the individual may take on the role of parent. We will, however, not be focusing on the family self-concept from this particular perspective in this chapter. We will limit our focus to an examination of the self in regard to family of origin, rather than family of procreation.

As a point of reference, we use the average although not typical U.S. family of two parents and two children. We recognize the increasing prevalence of a wide variety of family constellations including single-parent, divorced, and reconstituted families. Although an examination of the issues relevant to these family types is beyond the scope of the present chapter, two related points offer some general guidance. First, the importance of family constellation for self-development may be best understood when the focus is on studying the processes that characterize particular family structures. Thus, examination of the relationships that compose the family system and their relation to particular self-with-family-member representations may reveal important information on how the functioning of such families influence children's self-development. This chapter provides a framework for considering what family processes may be of interest when considering the family self-concept of so called "nontraditional" families. Second, attention must be paid to the ways in which developmental processes vary as a function of the context in which they occur (Bronfenbrenner, 1986; Bronfenbrenner & Crouter, 1983). Consequently, the salience or importance of specific family processes for self-with-family-member representations may be moderated by family structure.

Subsystems, Interactions, and Relationships

Before we elaborate the family self-concept within various subsystems, it is necessary to articulate issues concerning the meaning of interactions and relationships for the development and description of self-with-other-family-member units. Previously, we have indicated that subsystems are in essence the relationships that family members construct with each other. At the same time, self-with-other units are said to be derived from past social experiences and interactions. The question thus arises of how to go conceptually from interactions to relationships and from relationships to self-with-other representations.

Many studies imply that social interactions and relationships are the same, perhaps in part because interactions are easier to define and measure. Social interactions are specific behaviors or patterns of behavior between two or more individuals. Relationships may be inferred from interactions, but there is not a one-to-one correspondence between interactions and relationships. At the behavioral level, a relationship comprises a series of past interactions between the same individuals that influence current and future interactions (Hinde, 1988). Relationships persist in the absence of interactions and are characterized by the subjective components of memories of past interactions and expectations for future ones. Specific relationships have unique qualities, develop over time, and are affected by individual and extraindividual factors (Bracken & Cain, 1994). Self-with-other-family-member representations are based on specific relationships that define particular subsystems. The relationship that defines the subsystem is manifested in social interactions.

Specification of particular relationship qualities (Hinde, 1976, 1979) should be useful as they will help us describe individual subsystems and their self-with-other units. As we have indicated previously, what is known about the self is known about the other. In this sense, characteristics that have been used to describe relationships (e.g., Hinde, 1979; Lewis, 1987), should also provide important aspects of the self-with-other representations. The following qualities do not constitute an exhaustive list, but rather are an indication of those we believe are particularly relevant for the family self-concept.

Relationships Vary in Their Content or Function.   Consider a range of functions as delineated by Sullivan (1953) and elaborated by Weiss (1974) and Furman (1987): enhancement of self-worth, companionship, affection, intimacy, nurturance, caregiving, and instrumental aid. At any given point in time, as well as across developmental periods, subsystems may be characterized by some of these functions or provisions more than others. Depending on the particular combination of functions, different aspects of the self-with-other unit may be more or less likely to develop. Thus, for example, a relationship characterized by play and competition is perhaps more typical of certain same-sex, child-sibling relationships. The self-with-same-sex-sibling representation may be described by references to the self as a competent soccer player and one who is better or worse than the same-sex sibling. In contrast, the self-with-mother relationship may be characterized by the functions of caregiving, nurturance, and instrumental aid. The self-with-mother representation may be described in terms of lovability and interpersonal connectedness.

Duration and Frequency Are Two Time-Oriented Qualities of Relationships.   The duration of self-with-other family representations may be among the longest as they begin to evolve soon after birth. This may contribute to their impact on the development of other self-conceptions and relationships outside the family. The frequency of interaction within a particular family subsystem and, therefore, in part, the frequency with which a particular self-with-other representation is utilized may, of course, vary between subsystems and across time. Although extended duration in combination with high frequency of interaction may be related to the salience of a particular self-with-other representation, this is not always the case. Consider the child whose father dies when the child is 9 years old. No interactions except those in the mind of the child take place, but few would doubt that the relationship persists. Not only through imagination and memories can the child evoke the self with father, but other family members can evoke this self as well through discussion of the father with the child.

Multiplexity as Compared with Uniplexity Is an Important Aspect of Relationships.   As we have indicated, the extent to which a relationship comprises multiple functions is in many cases an index of centrality. This should be true not only of a relationship but of the self-with-other representation that is evoked in that relationship.

Relationships Can Be Characterized by Their Reciprocity versus Complementarity.   This status or power aspect of relationships has particular significance for self-with-other representations in the child-parent subsystems. Parent-child relationships have been thought of as primarily unilateral early in development, with an important transformation taking place in adolescence, whereby adolescents and their parents move away from the structure of unilateral authority and begin to interact more cooperatively (Youniss & Smollar, 1985). The process which involves both the formation of a unique identity that is differentiated from parents and the maintenance of connectedness with them is referred to as individuation (Grotevant & Cooper, 1985; Olson, Sprenkle, & Russell, 1979; Sroufe, 1983). Individuation is fundamentally related to the issue of power in a relationship and how such power is related to the development of the self. Individuality is defined by a sense of the distinctiveness of self from others and the expression of the person's own point of view. Connectedness is defined by mutuality as seen in the person's sensitivity, openness, and respect for the views of others. Individuation is a relationship property (Huston & Robins, 1982). It is not a characteristic of individuals or entire families because a person can have individuated relationships with some people and not with others. Within the family system, it is quite possible for the child or adolescent to have different levels of individuation for one subsystem or relationship compared with another. Although, as already indicated, individuation has usually been thought of in terms of parent-child relationships, this process can also be seen as relevant for the child-sibling relationship.

From our point of view, we see the process of individuation as particularly important for the nature of self-with-other representations in the family. The balance of connectedness and individuality and the unilateral compared with the reciprocal quality of relationships influences the structure and content of self-with-other representations. The self-with-other, as close and intimate, and the self-with-other, as independent or autonomous, are critical features of the various self-with-other-family-member representations. As we examine particular family subsystems and their self-with-other representations, the significance of individuation will be highlighted.

The Child-Mother Subsystem

Perhaps due to the mother's unique biological relationship, she has held a special role in theory and research on the development of the self and relationships. Early psychoanalytic theory has described the central role and significance of the mother in the child's life (Freud, 1915/1959). Although mother is generally used to designate the child's principal caretaker, whether or not this is the biological mother, the primary role of the mother has continued to hold a central place in current theories of social and self-development. Freud's model was epigenetic in form; it proposed a deterministic fixed sequence of development from mother to other social objects (Lewis, 1982). In general, this model and others based on it hold that the mother is the first and primary person in the child's social world and that all subsequent relationships and selves in relationships are affected by this early and unique interaction. If the relationship with mother is the first to be constructed, then the self-with-mother is the earliest self-with-other representation to emerge. From this, it follows that if the mother-child relationship is a good one, as defined by responsivity and sensitivity, then the child will develop a positive competent sense of self and "good" social relationships. Conversely, if the child-mother relationship is a poor one, then the child will develop a negative sense of self and "poor" social relationships.

Working Models of the Self and Mother

Any current discussion of the self-with-mother must begin with the work of Bowlby. Most of what we know about the family self-concept of self-with-mother grows out of Bowlby's theoretical work and the literature it has inspired regarding the attachment system. According to Bowlby (1969, 1973, 1980), the attachment behavioral system is a psychological organization hypothesized to exist within the person. The attachment system's set goal is to regulate behaviors that maintain or provide proximity to and contact with the attachment figure(s). Attachment behaviors are most evident when the individual is stressed, for example, frightened, sick, or tired. They are alleviated when the attachment figure responds with protection, help, and comfort. The attachment system is directed to maintain a balance between attachment and exploratory behaviors across a broad range of situations and contexts. In familiar non-threatening contexts, the balance favors exploration with periodic referencing of the attachment figure's location. In threatening situations, the balance tips in favor of physical contact. Threatening situations may involve risk of injury or predation from the environment, such as those to which humans have become adapted. They can also entail situations that have been associated with negative consequences in the individual child's experience. The awareness that an attachment figure is available and responsive engenders a pervasive sense of felt security. Felt security facilitates the child's ability to play an active role in his or her own social and cognitive development.

The relative safety or threatening aspect of particular situations and the attachment figure's availability and responsiveness are not newly evaluated each time they are encountered. Through repeated interactions with people and objects, the child forms increasingly complex representations of people, objects, and the self. Representations of attachment figures are constructed early in childhood. These representations are called "representational models" or "working models" and are described as the conceptions the child forms about the characteristics, nature, and behavior of the social world and the people in it, including the self. Note that the term "working model" is used rather than "representation" to indicate dynamic rather than static structure about the self and others. These models, which vary in their flexibility and adaptability, are derived from the child's repeated interactions with attachment figures. They are seen as typically based on daily interactions that are primarily with parents. However, it is in fact the mother that is seen as the most important attachment figure. In the research to be reviewed here, the mother is clearly the focus, particularly in the work on infants and children. Although neither parent plays an exclusive role in terms of the functions of attachment, play, or teaching, the relative predominance of which parent is involved in what function varies. In Western cultures, the mother tends to become the preferred attachment figure, whereas the father tends to become the preferred playmate (Lamb, 1976, 1977; Lytton, 1980; Main, Kaplan, & Cassidy, 1985). This is not surprising because mothers remain the primary caregivers even when they are employed outside the home and fathers play an increased role in caregiving (Pleck, 1985).

Both the quality and substance of the working models are related to the balance of appropriate nurturance and caregiving with exploration. The extent to which the parent is sensitively perceptive of the child's signals, contingently responsive to these signals, giving of comfort when necessary, and accepting, is the foundation for the secure base from which the child feels capable to explore the environment. Such a secure base encourages the formation of agency in the existential self and the capacity for self-reflection as well (Fonagy, Steele, Steele, Moran, & Higgitt, 1991).

In Bowlby's work, the representational model of the child's attachment figure is highly interdependent with the representational model of the self. Given that the child's primary source of learning about the self is the mother, interactions with the mother are the most salient for the child's self-construction. Working models of self and mother are complementary as they develop from dyadic transactional patterns (Bretherton, 1990). If the young child experiences a supportive parent-child relationship, then the complementary working model of the self as deserving of support and love should emerge. On the other hand, if the child experiences a rejecting parent-child relationship then a consequent working model of the parent as rejecting is complemented by a working model of the self as unlovable.

Working models of the self and mother, once organized, are seen as operating outside conscious awareness. Because new experiences and information are assimilated into existing models that are not conscious, the models tend to be stable and resistant to change (Bowlby, 1980). Working models of the self and mother are, however, revised as the child's cognitive and affective skills become more sophisticated. In this way, behaviors—both actions and thoughts—that regulate the attachment system are transformed considerably with development, although the basic interrelationships among the component subsystems of self and attachment figure remain unchanged. Attachment behaviors become more subtle as children's coping skills and ability to anticipate and assess the motivations and actions of the attachment figure improve. This suggests that the self-with-mother representations become more elaborated as well. In general, Bowlby's work offers a more complete theoretical picture of the particular family self-concept of self-with-mother. The major source of self-with-mother representation is the attachment function, although other functions may be a part of it as well. Fundamental self-conceptions of agency, self-reflection, and self-worth are rooted in the self-with-mother representation.

Relationship Properties and Self-with-Mother Representations

In accord with Bowlby's conceptualization, Sroufe and Fleeson (1986) have suggested that learning about the self in early childhood takes place primarily within the context of relationships. The components of the attachment figure become incorporated into the self through the process of the child learning the other and self roles within the relationship. Several propositions about relationships and how they function are stipulated and it is of interest to consider how some of these bear on the representation of self-with-mother as well as other family members.

Relationships Are Wholes.   This proposition indicates that relationships are not the simple combination of two partners' individual characteristics. Thus, consistent with the systems principle of nonadditivity, the child's characteristics are not a constant added to relationship with mother or father or sibling. This proposition applied to the self suggests that the self-with-mother is different from the self-with-each-other-family-member. In some sense, this is another way of articulating the concept of multiplicity of selves. We would also add, however, that there is an inter-dependency between the different selves that make up the family self-concept. This is in part because there may be overlap in the ways family members relate to and construe each other and the social world outside the boundaries of family (Reiss, 1981; Reiss & Oliveri, 1983a).

Close Relationships Have Coherence and Continuity over Time. This proposition indicates that whereas specific behaviors change, the na-ture of the attachment relationship remains the same over development. For example, infants who were secure in their early attachment at 1 year of age, as evidenced by seeking and receiving comfort from the mother when stressed, show cooperative give-and-take with their mothers in a tool-solving problem at 2 years (Matas, Arend, & Sroufe, 1978). This proposi-tion applied to the self suggests that the self-with-mother representation has coherence and continuity over time. Such a notion is compatible with self theorists ideas concerning the properties of coherence in the self across situations (Epstein, 1991). Based on this, we would suggest that self-with-mother representations in regard to the attachment function would tend toward coherence and continuity. As we shall discuss shortly, however, there is an important issue of whether it is the internalized self-with-mother representation from infancy that influences consistency or whether it is the mother-child relationship that remains consistent.

Early Close Relationships Are Carried Forward to Later Close Re-lationships. The personality of the self is viewed as an organization of attitudes, expectations, and behaviors of the individual that operates across situations (Block & Block, 1980; Sroufe, 1979). The initial organization of the infant or the anlage of personality is a feature of the mother-infant dyad, not the infant. With development, a new organization emerges around the self rather than the mother. Thus, self-regulation grows out of dyadic regulation between the infant and the mother. The mothers' capac-ity to effectively regulate the dyadic relationship is of critical importance because it profoundly shapes the organization of the self-with-mother, and this representation is the framework from which the child explores new relationships.

In contrast to Sroufe and Fleeson, we would argue that the self-with-mother representation is the most central in infancy but is not the frame-work from which the child explores new relationships. Self-with-father and sibling representations are central, if not most central, to the child's under-standing of the self and social relationships.

The Strange Situation and Inferred Self-Representations

Ainsworth and colleagues have developed a method to assess the quality of the mother-infant relationship (Ainsworth, Blehar, Waters, & Wall, 1978) that enables us to infer critical properties of the infant's self-with-mother representations. This laboratory technique, known as the "Strange Situation," remains the most widely used systematic method for observing individual differences in the security of attachment to the caregiver. In this procedure, the infant experiences an accumulation of anxiety-provoking circumstances due to repeated separations from the mother which are meant to evoke behaviors that would be expected to cause the child to seek comfort from the mother. From the infant's behavior, in particular his or her ability to find comfort in the mother's presence and to return to exploration without becoming withdrawn, angry, or petulant, individual differences in the quality of attachment are inferred. These differences are assessed and described in terms of the infant's confidence in the caregiver's availability/responsiveness in contrast to anxious concern and inability to be comforted.

In general, three different patterns of behavior are observed. Approximately 50% of the infants greet their mother and seek proximity and/or comfort from her before returning to exploratory play. These children are seen as having a secure relationship with the mother. From this we can infer that the self-with-mother representation is one of self as secure when with mother. Note that in infants we must infer the nature of the self from the nature of the relationship which, in turn, is inferred from the specific behavioral interactions. Thus, for example, an infant should be distressed when separated from the mother in an unfamiliar situation. On reunion with her, the infant should seek contact with the mother perhaps by clinging to her leg. If the mother responds by hugging her infant, the infant should calm and return to limited exploration of the new environment. A secure sense of self-with-mother comprises behaviors that are summarized by the two statements: "I can be comforted by my mother when stressed," and "I can explore the social and object world when I feel safe." These two general self-with-mother representations essentially describe the process of individuation in young children, whereby the self can be connected to others or autonomous, depending on the degree of threat in a situation.

Our statements about young children's self-thoughts are not meant to be taken literally as the children thinking, "I am counting on my mother's comfort since she has been available in the past." In accordance with Sroufe (1990), our interpretation of the young child's self-with-mother representation is as a metaphor. The emerging self-with-mother representation is viewed as an unconscious organization of the relation among arousal (due to externally or internally perceived threat), social behavior, and expectations about the mother's availability and sensitivity to the child's signals and needs. Maternal responsivity to the child's signals of distress has positive consequences for the child's regulation of emotions, and it is from these patterns of infant-mother regulation that internal self-with-mother organization and regulation develops. When the mother-infant relationship is not characterized by regulation of affect and maintenance of behavioral organization when confronted with threat, this can be a factor that contributes to less optimal self-organization in regard to dealing with stress and close relationships.

There are two major insecure patterns in the quality of the mother-infant relationship. Approximately 25% of infants appear to avoid proximity with the mother following reunion. They do not appear to be stressed by the separations in terms of outward behavior such as crying or attempts to find the mother, although there is evidence that they do show a physiological stress response (Dozier & Kobak, 1992). These children are seen as having an insecure avoidant relationship with the mother. From this, we can infer that the self-with-mother representation can be summarized by the statement, "I do not expect to be comforted by my mother when stressed, and I will focus on objects rather than people."

A third group of infants, approximately 12%, seek proximity to mother during reunion, but also display anger (fighting) toward her or passivity. These children are seen as having an insecure ambivalent relationship with the mother. From this, we can infer that the self-with-mother representation can be summarized by the statement, "I am uncertain about whether I will be comforted by my mother when stressed, and I will focus my behavior on getting her to respond to me or watching her rather than other people or objects."

Two major lines of research and theory have followed the contributions of Bowlby and Ainsworth. The first has been concerned with individual differences in the quality of attachment as a result of the quality of early care, specifically the psychological availability and responsiveness of the mother. The second has been concerned with whether and how the quality of the attachment relationship lays the foundation for the sense of self and the way a person behaves in intimate relationships. It is this second line of work that is most closely related to our examination of the family self-concept and the self-with-mother representation.

Attachment Research and Self-Functioning

We now consider a brief review of studies interested in the link between the child's early attachment with mother and subsequent self-functioning. As we describe these studies, it will become clear that most work concerns the existential self as perceived by others in contexts other than the family. A fundamental premise of this work is that the secure or insecure organization of the self rooted in the self-with-mother working model is reflected in the child's functioning with other adults and peers. Thus, the majority of such studies infer the nature of the working model of self with mother, not from observations of the child with the mother, but from the association between the quality of the early mother-child attachment and subsequent qualities of the self with persons outside of the family.

We begin our review with an early exception to this generalization. Two-year-olds with secure compared with insecure infant-mother attachment histories have been observed to show a more complex organized pattern of autonomous functioning (Matas et al., 1978). Assessment of problem solving in a frustrating situation indicated that secure children were more effective in using maternal assistance and showed more enthusiasm, positive affect, and persistence. Such a pattern of behavior is viewed as demonstrating the influence of an early positive self-with-mother representation, that is reflected in the child's current ability to use the mother to regulate him- or herself in an emotionally stressful situation.

In an older sample of 3.5-year-olds, Waters, Wippman, and Sroufe (1979) reported that security of attachment in infancy was associated with individual differences in ego strength/effectance and peer competence. As measured by a Q-sort procedure completed by preschool teachers blind to attachment quality, secure children scored higher than insecure children on both peer competence and ego strength with the former association being the strongest. Similarly, Arend, Gove, and Sroufe (1979) found that 4- to 5-year-old children with secure attachment histories were higher on teacher Q-sort ratings of ego resiliency (flexibility and resourcefulness) than children with insecure histories.

These significant associations, for middle-class samples, between a secure infant-mother relationship and, by inference, a secure self-with-mother representation, and ego resiliency have also been observed in a high-risk (e.g., unplanned pregnancy, less than high school education), low socioeconomic sample (LaFreniere & Sroufe, 1985; Sroufe, 1983). Based on extensive observations by teachers and independent observers over several months at a laboratory preschool, 4- to 5-year-old children who had been securely attached as infants received higher scores than those with insecure histories on measures of ego resiliency, self-esteem, social competence, and agency. The children with secure histories were also rated as less dependent and as displaying negative affect less frequently. A follow-up study of a subsample of these high-risk children when they were 11 years old, observed during a summer camp experience, also suggested a link between current self-functioning and past self-with-mother attachment history (Elicker, Englund, & Sroufe, 1992). Specifically, camp counselors rated children with secure infant-mother attachment histories as higher in self-esteem and self-confidence. Unfortunately, this study did not attempt to examine the children's current working model of the self-with-mother and whether it was related to past attachment history and current self-functioning as rated by the child or others.

In general, attachment researchers have of necessity used measurement at the behavioral level because until recently their work has focused on the early childhood period. In a study of 6-year-olds conducted by Cassidy (1988), we find a more direct examination of the relation between the mother-child relationship in regard to the attachment function, self-with-mother working models, and global self-esteem. The quality of the mother-child attachment relationship was measured by observing and rating the child's reunion behavior following a one-hour separation (Main & Cassidy, 1985). Reunion behaviors were classified into four patterns. Secure relationships were those in which the quality of interaction was warm, intimate, and personal. Upon reunion with their mother, securely attached children showed pleasure and either initiated interaction or were positively responsive to her initiations. Avoidant/insecure relationships were those in which the quality of the interaction was limited and neutral. Avoidant children avoided the mother upon reunion in a nonconfrontational way. Ambivalent/insecure children were clearly ambivalent about seeking proximity to their mother upon reunion and evidenced sadness, avoidance, fear, and hostility. These first three patterns correspond to the classifications derived from the Strange Situation methodology. The fourth pattern, controlling/insecure, was felt to represent a disorganized style (Main & Cassidy, 1988) and took one of two forms: (a) confronting and punitively rejecting her; or (b) giving the mother helpful directions in an attempt to comfort her.

Assessment of the working model of the self with mother was done by asking the child to complete stories using a doll family. These stories were intended to reflect the mental representation of the self in regard to the attachment relationship with mother (Main et al., 1985). The stories dealt with conflict and vulnerability within the family as well as threats from outside the family. Responses to the stories were classified according to the three types of self-with-mother representations. Secure/confident representations were those in which the protagonist was described as valuable and worthy, and the relationship with the mother was warm, special, and valued. There was open negotiation in the stories of conflict with mother and reliance on her for protection and help in stories about external threats. Insecure/avoidant representations featured protagonists that were isolated and/or rejected and the mother-child relationship was not described as special or valued. When problems were solved, this was accomplished without maternal input. Insecure/hostile representations were those in which the protagonist was described as hostile, violent, and negative, and the relationship with the mother was disorganized. The description of this doll-play methodology is of interest in and of itself for it highlights and supports the idea of the complementary nature of the self and mother representations.

More global measures of the self-concept were obtained by using both the Pictorial Scale of Perceived Competence and Social Acceptance for Young Children (Harter & Pike, 1984) and an open-ended interview. This latter assessment involved asking children to tell about themselves using specific open-ended questions. Responses to this interview were classified into four types: open/flexible, avoidant/perfect, negative, and body-preoccupied.

The results of this study indicated that the self-with-mother representation was significantly related to the pattern of attachment quality with mother. Secure attachment quality with mother was related to a confident self-with-mother representation, and insecure/avoidant attachment quality with mother was related to an avoidant rejected self-with-mother representation. Self-with-mother representations of the insecure/ambivalent and insecure/controlling attachment quality groups did not show any recognizable pattern. The failure to differentiate patterns of insecurity in regard to outcomes has been a recurrent problem for attachment researchers (Lamb, Thompson, Gardner, & Charnov, 1985). In some instances, this is due to small sample sizes in the insecure groups necessitating analyses which combine the samples of avoidant and ambivalent children. In Cassidy's study, these groups were analyzed separately even though the avoidant and ambivalent groups had 8 and 6 children respectively. Certainly for the study of self-with-mother representations, it is important to separate and show differential patterns for these groups, because the theory indicates clear differences in how the self-with-mother would be represented.

Self-with-mother representations were related to the open-ended measure of self-concept, but not to the Harter measures of social acceptance (peer and maternal acceptance) and competence (cognitive and physical). In the former case, in regard to the open-ended measure of the self, the more the self-with-mother representation was confident, the more open/flexible were the general self-descriptions. It is of interest that the current security of the mother-child relationship was related to the measures of social acceptance and competence. Taken together, these findings suggest that the self-with-mother representation may not be the central link between general self functioning and past attachment history, but that the current mother-child relationship is a major determinant. This study does not have early measures of attachment history from infancy so it is not possible to examine the extent to which the quality of the past attachment relationship is related to current self-with-mother representations or the current child-mother relationship.

According to Cassidy, the results of her study support the idea that there is a connection between the self and the child-mother relationship in young children. However, the relation observed regards the self-with-mother representation only in the context of the attachment function. The self-with-mother representation, while related to open-ended description about the self, does not appear to be related to the more global rating of competence and peer acceptance. In contrast, the measure of current attachment relationship quality with mother is related to all others. In reviewing Cassidy's findings, we first must note that we have taken the space to describe her work in detail because it may constitute one of the only studies that considers the child-with-mother relationship at a representational level. We believe that the methodology used in this study offers a good framework for examining self-with-other-family-member representations. It certainly would be of interest to observe the child's reunion behavior with the father and relate this to representations of the self-with-father using the doll-story technique. It would also be important to explore self-with-parent representations for other functions in addition to attachment, such as learning and companionship. This would mean writing doll stories that reflected themes concerning these functions and observing family interactions that reflected the nature of relationships relevant to them. Self-with-sibling representations could also be studied using this type of methodology.

Cassidy's findings raise the problem of the extent to which it is the self-with-mother in the past or present compared with the current relationship that influences adaptation and self-competence in or outside the family. There are actually several issues to be considered and disentangled. First, we can consider the extent to which past self-with-mother representations are related to current ones. As far as we know, there are no data on this relation, although attachment theory would predict at least a moderate relationship. Exactly how early patterns of these self-with-mother representations would change with development has not been specified. Investigation of this issue would require a longitudinal assessment of interactions with mother, relationship quality in regard to a specific function (attachment, of course, being a particularly important one), and the self-with-mother representation. A second issue is how or whether the quality of past attachment relationships influences current self-with-mother representations. Thus far, this issue has been studied to some degree in retrospective examinations of adult's descriptions of their memories of early attachment relationships with parents (e.g., Kobak & Sceery, 1988; Main et al., 1985). The third issue concerns the extent to which or whether current global self-competence and functioning is related to a combination of past and current experience or only current circumstances.

All major theories of adaptation assign a central role to the contemporaneous environment as an influence on competence and functioning. However, they differ considerably in regard to the role played by prior experience and, in particular, attachment experiences with the mother. For attachment theorists, the family self-concept and specifically self-with-mother attachment representations can explain continuity from past to current self-functioning. Other theories assert that continuity in competence over time is the result of stability in the environment and is not a function of self-organization grounded in early attachment history (Lamb et al., 1985; Lewis, 1982; Lewis & Feiring, 1991; Lewis & Feiring, in press; Waters, Kondo-Ikemura, Posada, & Richters, 1990). Two recent studies offer some insight into the importance of early attachment relationships with mother compared with the current family environment for later functioning. Although these studies do not directly measure self-with-mother representations but require an inference about such representations based on observations of attachment quality, they provide an initial gauge of the centrality of past self-with-mother representations.

Sroufe, Egeland, and Kreutzer (1990) examined the differential resiliency of two groups of children that showed poor adaptation in the preschool period. One group had a secure mother-infant history ($N = 11$) as assessed from behavior in the Strange Situation procedure, whereas the other had an insecure history ($N = 16$). Also examined in a larger sample ($N = 190$) was the extent to which early attachment history (12–18 months) contributed additional predictive power to variation in outcome (in early elementary school—1–3 grade) once intervening (30 months) and contemporary (6 years) measures of the family environment had been considered. The analyses collapsed the two anxious attachment patterns making it impossible to infer differences in the adaptation or inferred self-representations of avoidant compared with ambivalent youngsters. The primary outcome measures were composite teacher ratings of the sample's emotional health and peer competence in early elementary school. The measure of the intervening and contemporaneous family environment was the HOME Scale (Caldwell & Bradley, 1984), which was completed by trained observers. A composite measure of the HOME subscales, indexing mother's verbal and emotional responsivity, her acceptance and involvement with the child, and provision of an organized and stimulating environment, was used.

The results of the analysis of the two small groups with different attachment histories and similar poor preschool functioning indicated that the secure group showed a better adaptation in early elementary school. This is argued as evidence for a rebound effect due to the effects of early attachment history. However, no data are presented to refute the claim that the observed secure-in-infancy, poor preschool adjustment, positive elementary school adaptation pattern is not due to a mother-child relationship that follows this same pattern. Furthermore, there is no demonstration that an internal representation of the self-with-mother is an enduring organizing principle that guides adaptation rather than the current mother-child relationship. Additional regression analyses on the larger sample in which the mother-child relationship/home environment is used as a predictor along with attachment history do not lend support to the idea that early attachment history plays a significant role. It is the mother-child relationship/home environment that is repeatedly the most powerful predictor. Even considering the simple correlation between attachment history and subsequent adaptation, the relation is quite small ($r = .19$).

A study by Lewis and Feiring (1991) examined attachment history and the contemporary family environment as predictors of behavior problems in 6-year-olds. Attachment history was measured using a modified version of the Strange Situation procedure when the child was 1 year old. The family environment was indexed by the mother's ratings of cohesion and conflict in the family at 6 years on the Family Environment Scale (FES; Moos & Moos, 1976). Adaptation was measured using the mother's ratings on the Child Behavior Checklist at the same time point (Achenbach, 1979). Both attachment history and contemporary family environment significantly predicted behavior problems, but only for boys, not for girls. The environmental measure was somewhat more powerful than the attachment history in explaining outcome.

Overall, these studies do not provide confirmation of the idea that the relationship quality with mother as represented in the self-with-mother working model is predictive of subsequent adaptation in addition to or as a determinant of the current mother-child relationship. None of the research cited has provided a direct examination of the association between the mother-child relationship over time and the self-with-mother representation as they may influence each other and current or subsequent self-competence or functioning.

The Child-Father Subsystem

Discussion of the father-child subsystem requires consideration of the mother because much of our knowledge about fathers centers on how they are different from mothers. In their classic analysis of the qualitative differences in father and mother roles in child development, Parsons and Bales (1955) claimed that fathers' and mothers' roles or social functions are divided according to instrumental and expressive functions. The father's function is delineated as primarily instrumental and is characterized by a concern with mastery and competence. The mother's function is viewed primarily as an expressive one and is characterized by a concern with interpersonal relationships, emotional support, nurturance, and caregiving. Empirical work that focuses on the form and content of parenting behavior supports the idea that child-father and child-mother relationships are distinct from each other.

Both naturalistic in-home observations and laboratory-based studies indicate that fathers differ from mothers in the quantity of time spent with the child and in the quality or function of the activities in which the child is engaged. Although some research suggests that fathers have increased their involvement with their children, mothers continue to spend more time with their young children. Differences in the quantity of time fathers and mothers spend with their children, however, do not necessarily imply that fathers are of less significance than mothers in the development of the family self-concept or global self-concepts. If we restricted our focus to the attachment system and the functions of caregiving and nurturance, we might conclude that fathers were less important and that given the frequency of interaction with mother, self-with-mother representations should be the most central. But this is not the case because families engage in other functions and these functions are important for self-development. Fathers make significant contributions to their children's socialization although they do not appear to take major responsibility for their daily care or needs.

The affiliative system and the function of play are most closely tied to the father. Fathers spend proportionally more of their interaction time in play compared with mothers (e.g., Bronstein, 1984; Clarke-Stewart, 1978, 1980; Kotelchuck, 1976; Lamb, 1977; Russell & Russell, 1987). Their play is more physical (although as children become older it becomes increasingly verbal), idiosyncratic, and emotionally arousing compared with that of mothers. In contrast, mothers tend to be responsible for most of the caregiving compared with fathers and are more directive (e.g., Belsky, Gilstrap, & Rovine, 1984; Pedersen & Robson, 1969; Pleck, 1985; Radin & Russell, 1983; Russell & Russell, 1987). When they do play, mothers tend to do so in ways that are less arousing, more verbal, and more often entail conventional games and toys (Clarke-Stewart, 1978; Lamb, 1977; MacDonald & Parke, 1984).

The behavior of young children toward their parents in stressful and nonstressful contexts is consistent with the findings of distinct roles for fathers and mothers. When not distressed, young children tend to direct more playful distal behaviors toward their fathers compared with their mothers (Clarke-Stewart, 1978; Lamb, 1982). When distressed, they tend to direct more attachment-related behaviors, such as contact seeking, to the mother. Such behaviors are consistent with the suggestion that the roles of attachment figure and playmate are conceptually distinct (Bowlby, 1969). Some theorists have indicated that a primary role of the father is as an affiliative as opposed to attachment agent and that playful interactions with the father may be of particular importance in the development of social skills and social competence (Bailey, 1982; Lamb, 1982; Parke, MacDonald, Beitel, & Bhavnagri, 1988). It has been hypothesized that physical play with father is important in the development of affective skills, such as communicating and interpreting emotional states (Parke et al., 1988). In one study, paternal physical play with preschool boys was found to be related to their positive social attributes as rated by teachers (MacDonald & Parke, 1984). Paternal characteristics and relationships have also been associated with the emotional quality of social interactions in infancy (Bridges, Connell, & Belsky, 1988; Kotelchuck, 1976) and with the development of adolescent's friendship networks (Oliveri & Reiss, 1987).

As children become older, the father's role in the family is likely to increase, in part due to the declining need for caregiving activities and the increasing need for play, exploration, and self-initiated action (Lewis & Weinraub, 1976). Across many cultures, it has been shown that fathers' interactions with children in public places, such as zoos, public streets, and malls, are quite different from those seen in the home (Mackey, 1985). Although not adequately studied, an important aspect of fathers' involvement with their children may be in public settings compared with mothers' involvement, which may be more evidenced in private familiar settings (Feiring & Coates, 1987; Lewis, 1987). For example, for both females and males, the relationships with kin are determined primarily by their mother's kin network (Oliveri & Reiss, 1987; Troll, 1987). In contrast, it may be that fathers are most influential in providing contacts with people other than kin (Feiring & Coates, 1987). This difference in role performance by context, with mothers dominating in the home, may explain to some degree our rather limited information and theory about the father's role in the development of self and relationships in childhood.

Taken together, these results suggest that self-with-father representations may be organized more elaborately with regard to the behavioral system of affiliation compared with attachment. They also indicate that self-with-father representations may be particularly relevant for behavior toward and representations of self-with-strangers, acquaintances, and friends. Of course, we are not arguing that children do not form attachments to their fathers or that self-with-father representations do not influence the development of close relationships with friends or lovers. Evidence exists to show that children are attached to their fathers (Lamb, 1981; Russell & Russell, 1987) and that relationships with fathers can influence the development of self-attributes and competence (Allen, Hauser, Bell, & O'Connor, 1994; Buhrmester et al., 1992; Phares & Compas, 1992; Youniss & Smollar, 1985). Our argument is thus one of relative degrees of influence, rather than one of absolutes.

The Child-Parent Subsystem

Although self-with-father representations may be relatively more organized around the affiliation function and those with the mother around attachment, we believe that both representations are equally central for the developing child. This argument is based on the premise that behavioral involvement and commitment to parents first evidenced in early attachment and affiliative relationships makes the child receptive to parents as socialization agents and makes self-with-parent representations core identities. Note that we have included affiliation as well as the attachment function as a foundation for the child's commitment to the family system because we believe that in addition to protection and comfort from threat, engagement in enjoyable social interaction is another critical ingredient for development of the social self, relationships, and competence.

Identification with both parents makes self-with-mother-and-father representations the most central and important for self-definition in childhood. Following Richters and Waters (1991), we use the term "identification" to indicate the child's investment in the family system of behavior patterns, rules, and perceptions as predominantly defined by the parents. It comprises the child's readiness to accept the parents' demands for behavior, the parents' view of the child, and the child's role in the relationship with his or her parents. As long as the child's social world is primarily focused on the family, identification with the parents is a process that can help explain the centrality of the self-with-parent representations. Perceived parental attitudes toward the self are by far the most important for self-esteem in childhood, whereas in adolescence classmate support gains in significance (Harter, 1990; Rosenberg, 1979). Thus, the degree of parental influence on the self appears to evidence a developmental shift. In adolescence, there is a greater emphasis on the formation of identities outside the family. Consequently, we move from the concept of identification, a term primarily used to describe socialization in childhood, to that of individuation, a term frequently used to describe socialization in adolescence. In examining the individuation process, we consider a literature that is substantially grounded in the contribution of both parents to development of self-concept.

The Parent-Adolescent Subsystem and Individuation

The concept of individuation describes how adolescents transform as opposed to abandon the centrality of their relationship with parents. Individuation may be viewed as two complementary processes (Grotevant & Cooper, 1985; Youniss & Smollar, 1985). One process involves moving away from the development of the self that was valid during childhood to construct a self that fits with the adolescent's own experiences rather than parental demands or desires. The other process involves remaining connected to parents so that validation can be received from parents for the self-concepts the adolescent has constructed.

Individuation entails the child's ability to use parents as resources (e.g., emotional, informational, material) *and* the ability to be autonomous; that is, to govern him- or herself and make important life decisions. Being autonomous does not require lack of dependence on parents (Memmi, 1984). Individuation is thus something that happens with parents rather than from them (Ryan & Lynch, 1989). It is a process that begins in adolescence and continues into adulthood. As described by the following quote from the *New York Times Metropolitan Diary* (October 1993), autonomy as a label for freedom from parental attachment is misleading and ignores the normative closeness that characterizes the parent-child relationship in the second and later decades of life (Hill & Holmbeck, 1986).

> Dr. F.L., who has a 22-year-old son and a 26-year-old daughter, writes that he has formulated the following answering-machine message to respond to calls from "grown" off-spring: "If you require financial assistance, PRESS ONE. If you are in an emotional turmoil over an impending breakup with a romantic partner and require a few hours of sympathetic discussion, PRESS TWO. If you are being treated unfairly at work or school and wish to displace your anger to a nuclear-family member, PRESS THREE. If your car or household appliances need immediate repair or replacement, PRESS FOUR. If you are telephoning to inquire about our well-being or to pass a few moments of pleasant topical conversation, please check the number you intended to dial."

The consolidation of self-identity draws selectively from previous identifications and relationships and integrates them into an autonomous self

(Damon, 1983). Prior and current relationships with parents are seen as very important for this identity process. We believe that current self-with-parent representations and the parent-adolescent relationships that underlie such representations form one basis for emerging self-definitions.

Many of the cognitive capabilities for revising concepts of self and relationships emerge during adolescence. Self-reflection, or the ability to see the self as an object of thought, transforms the way that concepts of self and parents are updated and revised (Kobak & Cole, 1994). Selman (1980) suggests that the acquisition of perspective-taking is essential for the development of self-reflection, since one must first be aware that others are observing and evaluating the self. Whereas preadolescents generally operate at Level 2 (self-reflective thinking characterized by recognizing the self as the possible target of others' perspectives), adolescents become capable of Level 3 thinking, characterized by a mutual or third-person perspective. In interpersonal situations, this type of thinking allows the individual to step outside a two-person interaction to identify mutual interests or goals. In thinking about the self, Level 3 reasoning allows the individual to step outside or establish an autonomous perspective. This then creates the possibility of evaluating and integrating conflicting aspects of self and family members.

Three related literatures lend support to the notion that autonomy and self-development are linked to parental relationships in adolescence and young adulthood: attachment, ego identity, and identity-formation studies. Although these bodies of work do not examine self-with-parent representations directly, we use them to expand our ideas about the ways in which such representations may be important for the developing self-concept.

Researchers working within an attachment framework have focused on how the quality of attachment relationships as currently constructed is related to general self-qualities. These studies are based on self-report of family relationships and self-attributes. Some of this work has relied on the use of a structured interview originally designed to tap adults' working models (Kobak & Cole, 1994; Kobak & Sceery, 1988). This interview (George, Kaplan, & Main, 1985) asks the adolescent to describe early relationships with parents, generate adjectives describing each parent, and provide memories supporting these adjectives. Adolescents are asked to recall incidents of distress as a child, including being upset, separated from parents, rejected by parents, and threatened by parental separation. They are then asked to consider the effects of their upbringing on their personality, why their parents behaved as they did, changes in, as well as the current status of, their relationships with their parents, and to think about the most important thing learned from attachment experiences.

The interview is seen as providing a context for assessing how individuals think and feel about themselves and their relationship with their parents. It asks the adolescent (or adult) to focus on his or her working model of parents and the self, and to link generalizations about attachment relationships to specific memories of the self with parents. Individuals vary in their ability to access information about the models and in their ability to discuss them in an organized and coherent fashion. The extent to which an individual can sustain attention to the model, tolerate uncertainty, and experience emotional appraisal of model-relevant memories indicates the degree to which models are open to change and revision.

In analyzing an individual's responses to the interview, emphasis is placed on the organization to a greater extent than the content of discourse. This approach allows for the identification of three different "states of mind" that describe the structure and nature of the person's working model (Main & Goldwyn, 1985). These states of mind correspond to the infant classifications of secure, avoidant, and anxious/resistant; they are free-to-evaluate, dismissing, and preoccupied. Work with adults (Main et al., 1985; Main & Goldwyn, 1985) indicates that the free-to-evaluate group values attachment, is at ease recalling attachment-related events, and regards attachment experiences as influential while being relatively objective in evaluating a particular experience or relationship. The dismissing group tends to devalue the importance of attachment relationships, discounts the importance of attachment relationships for current functioning, and has trouble recalling specific events or recalls events that involve rejection and lack of affection. The preoccupied group has trouble integrating positive and negative experiences with parents; although attachment is valued, confusion or conflict is evident in evaluating attachment-related experiences.

Research using this interview suggests that the preceding three patterns first identified for adults (who were parents of young children) are applicable to adolescents (Kobak & Sceery, 1988). Free-to-evaluate adolescents are the most coherent in describing their parental relationships, are more likely to see themselves as being loved, and are less likely to idealize their parents compared with the other insecure patterns. The dismissing group was rated the highest on rejection and on having difficulty remembering while showing the highest levels of idealization of parents. The preoccupied group was the least coherent in the description of attachment experiences. As rated by a friend, the free-to-evaluate adolescents were found to be more ego resilient or higher on the ability to constructively regulate negative feelings in problem solving and social contexts. In addition, the preoccupied adolescents rated themselves as the least socially competent.

Research has also shown that the three patterns of working models are related to adolescent-mother, problem-solving interactions (Kobak, Cole, Ferenz-Gillies, Fleming, & Gamble, 1993). When observed during a discussion of a topic on which mother and teen disagree, free-to-evaluate adolescents were found to be the best at balancing assertiveness with acknowledgment of the parent's point of view. These adolescents showed the healthiest individuation pattern of seeking support for their viewpoint as well as being able to challenge their parent's opinion. They were also able to regulate negative emotions more effectively, which facilitated focus on problem solving.

This work on adolescents' working models of attachment and self-functioning makes it clear that representations of attachment relationships and experiences with parents are related to self-functioning, especially in regard to social competence and judgments of self-worth. The attachment interview provides an extremely rich source of data on the nature of working models for both cognitive and emotional processes of self-regulation (Kobak & Cole, 1994). However, the analyses of the interview make it difficult to differentiate the contribution of each parent to self-functioning because the individual's "state of mind" is rated in regard to both parents. From work in childhood, we know that the concordance between attachment quality with parents is far from perfect (e.g., Belsky, Garduque, & Hrncir, 1984; Belsky & Rovine, 1987; Fox, Kimmerly, & Schafer, 1991; Main & Weston, 1981). We might, therefore, expect that the representation of the self-with-mother would be different than the other-with-father, particularly when the relationship with one parent is secure and the other insecure. How and whether differences in these relationships affect the adolescent's model of attachment relationships and self-development is an issue in need of attention (Lewis, 1994).

The attachment interview also tends to focus attention on the nature of the relationship with parents and does not as clearly reveal how the self is represented in regard to each parent. For attachment theorists there exists a general working model of close relationships, a state of mind that operates across all relationships and which is derived from early parent-child relationships. In contrast, we believe that individuals have distinct self-with-other representations for each relationship. These representations are influenced by past and current experiences in the parent-child relationship, but representations are not identical as they are predominantly influenced by experiences with a particular person (see Furman & Wehner, 1994, for a similar view). It would be of interest to examine how self-with-family-member representations, assessed using the methodology employed by Ogilvie and Ashmore (1991), are related to descriptions of relationship models derived from the attachment interview. This would help clarify how specific self characteristics from self-with-family-member representations are related to the cognitive and emotional regulation of attachment models. For example, would describing the self as lovable and loving with mother or father be related to a coherent model of attachment relationships with parents and to what extent would each of these representations and models relate to self-functioning in other relationships?

In addition to the studies using the attachment interview, some research has examined attachment in relation to adolescent self-development and esteem using self-report questionnaire data (e.g., Greenberg, Siegel, & Leitch, 1983; Kamptner, 1988; Kroger & Haslett, 1988; Lamborn &

Steinberg, 1993; Morgolin, Blyth, & Carbone, 1988; Ryan & Lynch, 1989; Steinberg & Silverberg, 1986). This work has generally shown that self-development is related to emotional support from parents. Some of these studies are of particular interest as they highlight differences in the relation between self-functioning and the relationship with mother compared with father. For example, some findings indicate that perceived acceptance from mother and support for independence from both parents are particularly important for self-ratings of self-esteem and lovability (Ryan & Lynch, 1989).

Based on observed family interaction, the work of Grotevant and Cooper (1985, 1986; Cooper, Grotevant, & Condon, 1983) illuminates how individuality and connectedness in family relationships are associated with adolescent identity formation. Individuality is operationalized in terms of two dimensions: self-assertion and separateness. Self-assertion involves awareness of one's own point of view and being able to express it clearly, while separateness entails the ability to recognize and articulate differences between the self and others. Connectedness also is indexed using two dimensions: mutuality and permeability. Permeability involves the degree to which an individual is open to the ideas of others. Mutuality pertains to respect and sensitivity to the feelings and thoughts of others. Identity formation is examined in regard to the concept of identity exploration, which considers the extent to which the adolescent has actively appraised a variety of options in the realms of occupational choice, politics, religion, sex roles, dating, and friendship (Marcia, 1966). In general, the results of this work indicate that adolescent identity exploration is facilitated by a combination of connectedness, which enables adolescents to feel supported in their identity explorations outside the family, and separateness, which gives the adolescent the encouragement to explore personal positions. In contrast, the lowest levels of identity exploration were found in adolescents from families that avoided disagreements and blurred boundaries between members.

Of special interest from a systems point of view are the differential findings for particular family subsystems. For males, it is only the father-son subsystem that is important. Mutuality from father to adolescent and reciprocated separateness between adolescent and father are related to higher levels of identity exploration. For females, interactions in both parent and sibling subsystems are related to identity exploration. Separateness in the father-daughter and adolescent-sibling subsystems are positively associated with identity exploration. Mutuality from daughter to mother is negatively related to identity exploration, perhaps suggesting that such mutuality is related to the likelihood of accepting the traditional female role. The marital relationship also is associated with identity exploration. Females with higher identity exploration are from families where fathers express more separateness and less mutuality to their wives. Consequently, for females, there is a more complex configuration of separateness and mutuality with family members directly (parent-adolescent, sibling-adolescent) and indirectly (mother-father) in regard to identity formation.

Taken together, these findings have several implications for the importance, content, and structure of self-with-family-member representations. First, they suggest that such representations should be important for identity formation. For boys, representation of self-with-father may be particularly important; whereas for girls, representations with both parents and siblings are salient. Thus, for girls there may be a greater complexity in the relation between general construction of the self-identity and self-with-family-member representations. Several theorists have suggested that social relations are more central to the self-definition of females (Archer, 1985; Gilligan, 1982). One possible index of this phenomenon would be the importance of self-with-family-member representation for identity formation or other global self-definitions and evaluations.

The content of adolescent self-with-family representation may be useful to explore in terms of the four dimensions of mutuality, permeability, separateness, and self-assertion. Each of these dimensions could be thought of in regard to how it defines the self and others in a particular family relationship. Assertion would involve the extent to which I see myself as able to express my viewpoint (e.g., I am assertive, dominating, dominated). Permeability would concern the extent to which I see myself as understanding (e.g., I am understanding, discounting, discounted). Mutuality would involve the extent to which I see myself as open-minded (e.g., I am flexible, rigid). Separateness would concern the extent to which I see myself as different from or similar to a particular family member. Examination of family interactions that index individuality and connectedness and the self-with-family-member representations that are related to the relationships reflected in these interactions would help us gain a clearer understanding about the link between interactions, self-representations, and individual competence.

An emphasis on the family interactions on which individuation and identity formation are based can also be found in the work of Hauser and his colleagues (Hauser et al., 1984; Hauser, Powers, & Noam, 1991; Powers, Hauser, & Kilner, 1989). The family interactions of concern are those that define the processes of enabling and constraining. Enabling refers to interactions that facilitate the development of the self, such as acceptance and empathy (affective enabling), as well as problem solving and explaining (cognitive enabling). Constraining involves interactions that inhibit the development of the self, such as judging and devaluing (affective constraining) as well as distracting and indifference (cognitive constraining). Self-development is studied in regard to ego development in which there is a progression from preconformist (concretist, demanding) to conformist (awareness of inner states, moral judgments) to postconformist (high degree of self-perception, cognitive complexity, and acceptance of individual differences). The results from this work indicate the particular importance of affective enabling between mother, father, and adolescent in facilitating higher levels of the adolescent's ego development. From a systems perspective, there appear to be mutual influences between parent and adolescent concerning reiterated cycles of acceptance and understanding that may function to encourage the adolescent to value complexity in interpersonal relations and acceptance of his or her own ideas. These findings suggest that self-with-parent representations that involve the feelings and thoughts of "I am understood/accepted by my parent" and "I accept/understand my parent" may be positively related to ego development.

In summary, adolescence is a developmental period during which self-with-parent representations should undergo a series of transformations as individuation processes unfold and self-identities are developed. Compared with children, adolescents' cognitive capacities make them more easily accessed informants in regard to their self-with-family-member representations. The available literature on individuation and attachment in adolescence provides a good understanding about what family processes and interactions and representations of parents enhance the development of the self. What is needed is a better understanding of how self-with-family-member representations may mediate the relation between family interactions and relationships and the development of general positive self-functioning (e.g., self-esteem, social competence, ego resilience). Also needed, but clearly costly to obtain, is developmental data on the intraindividual transformations of self-with-family-member representations, family interactions, and relationships across several functions, including, but not limited to, the attachment system.

The Sibling-Child Subsystem

It is quite clear that sibling interaction and relationships are independent sources of variance in child development (e.g., Cicirelli, 1982; Dunn & Kendrick, 1982; Stocker, Dunn, & Plomin, 1989; Sutton-Smith, 1982; Zajonc, 1976), and sibling effects are frequently examined within the context of the parent-child-sibling subsystem or the entire family system. Just as fathers are rarely considered without mothers, sibling studies often go beyond parent-child or sibling-sibling relationships to include the interdependence of these subsystems. The majority of past attempts to understand sibling relationships have examined the influence of family structure variables, such as birth order and the age differences between siblings (e.g., Abramovitch, Pepler, & Corter, 1982; Cicirelli, 1982; Koch, 1960; Sutton-Smith & Rosenberg, 1970). Most of the results from these studies are inconsistent and have yielded few insights into the processes that characterize sibling relationships.

More recent work has focused on the influence of parental behavior, in most cases the mother's (e.g., Bryant & Crockenberg, 1980; Dunn & Kendrick, 1982; Howe, 1986; Stewart, Mobley, Van Tuyl, & Salvador,

1987; Stocker et al., 1989) and to a lesser extent the father's (Volling & Belsky, 1992), and the marital dyad's (Furman & Giberson, 1995), on the relationship between siblings. In general, maternal behavior toward first-born children has been shown to correlate with the qualities of the sibling relationship. Differential maternal treatment of the siblings within a family, whereby mothers are differentially affectionate, responsive, or controlling toward their children, has been associated with less friendly and more conflictual sibling relationships. For fathers, the meager evidence that exists suggests that their differential behavior is related to the extent of prosocial behavior between siblings. Taken together, these findings suggest how family interactions might influence self-with-sibling representations in regard to conflict and nurturance.

Perhaps one of the most striking qualities of sibling relationships is their dual nature of positive and negative attributes. It has been argued that sibling relationships are among the most volatile of human relationships as they are rooted in ambivalence (Pfouts, 1976). On the one hand, sibling rivalry is seen as the basis for most of the negative aspects of sibling relationships such as emotional struggles involving issues of sibling anger, identity, and competition for recognition and approval from parents. On the other hand, there are the positive features of closeness, supportive caregiving, and companionship. Self-with-sibling representations would thus be expected to be characterized by the qualities of both competition and support.

Interviews and questionnaire responses of children, adolescents, and young adults indicate support for the idea that sibling relationships have a good deal of both positive and negative qualities (Buhrmester & Furman, 1987; Furman & Buhrmester, 1985; Furman & Buhrmester, 1992). Siblings were found to characterize sibling relationships in terms of such attributes as intimacy, companionship, quarreling, and competition. Four factors appeared to capture individuals' perceptions of their sibling relationships: relative status/power, warmth closeness, conflict, and rivalry. We would expect the nature of self-with-sibling representations to be related to these factors.

Some studies suggest that the individual's status as younger or older sibling in a particular sibling subsystem is of particular importance for the development of self-with-sibling representations. Older siblings are more likely to perceive themselves as nurturant and dominating, while younger siblings are more likely to report being nurtured and dominated (Buhrmester & Furman, 1987). Brody and colleagues (Brody, Stoneman, MacKinnon, & MacKinnon, 1985; Stoneman, Brody, & MacKinnon, 1984) distinguish a coherent set of roles that children use when interacting with their siblings: helper, helpee, teacher, learner, manager, managee, and observer. Not surprisingly, the older sibling was more likely to assume the roles of teacher, helper, and manager. A similar set of roles in siblings has also been identified across early to late childhood (Vandell, Minnett, &

Santrock, 1987). Although these roles may become less extreme with age, there is evidence that they can continue to characterize sibling subsystems into adolescence and adulthood (Furman & Buhrmester, 1992; Searcy & Eisenberg, 1992).

It has been argued that because sibling relationships are more intense in childhood than adolescence, such relationships should have their greatest effects on personality and adjustment in childhood (Buhrmester & Furman, 1990). Thus, we might expect self-with-sibling representations in childhood to be more related to global self-representations compared with later developmental periods. On the other hand, individual differences exist in sibling relationships within and across developmental periods especially in regard to dominance and nurturance. For some individuals, self-with-sibling representations may remain highly salient for their identity and functioning. There is a dearth of information on when or whether this is the case.

Although there is some indication that models of the self in regard to parents are related to behavior with adults and peers outside the family, little is known about how self-with-sibling representations might be related to self-with-peer representations, interactions, or relationships. Yet it is thought to be the case that skills used with siblings are carried over into those used with peers at least in early childhood. Of particular interest is the notion of social comparison; siblings may be more likely to judge themselves in regard to a sibling (a child who is more like me) than a parent (an adult who is less like me). Siblings may be viewed as primary targets for social comparison not only within the family system but in the larger social network as well (Bryant, 1982).

A psychoanalytic formulation of social comparison within the family system suggests the entire family system must be considered as an influence on self-with-sibling representations (Schachter, 1982, 1985; Schachter, Gilutz, Shore, & Adler, 1978; Schachter & Stone, 1985). It is argued that siblings come to perceive themselves as different from one another and that this deidentification is a means of diluting the negative emotions associated with intense competition. Furthermore, a primary means for viewing oneself as different from one's sibling is through split-parent identification. This process involves each sibling in a pair identifying with a different parent. Unlike same-sex parent, split-parent identification implies that the entire family system, not simply the parent-child or sibling-sibling subsystems, must be considered in determining the salience of particular self-with-family-member representations for self-development. Research with young adults based on this formulation indicates that it is especially applicable to same-sex siblings who are the first two children (Schachter, 1982). It may be that these types of dyads are ones for which self-with-sibling representations are particularly salient from childhood onward.

In summary, although we probably know the least about the nature of self-with-sibling representations and their influence on the development of the global self and social competence, there is every reason to believe this would be a fruitful area of study. This may especially be so in sibling relationships characterized by intense competition or dominance in childhood.

Self-with-Family Representations

Family systems theorists emphasize that the family is a complex system that cannot be fully understood by studying isolated individuals or dyadic interactions. A central issue of interest has been understanding the different roles and behaviors individuals express within their family. A great deal of work has focused on deviant families and elucidating the function of an individual's behavior within the family system (e.g., Barnes & Olson, 1985; Beavers, 1982; Belsky & Pensky, 1988; Caspi & Elder, 1988; Christensen & Margolin, 1988; Constantine, 1986; Olson, Sprenkle, & Russell, 1979; Patterson & Dishion, 1988; Watzlawick, 1984). For example, in the service of family maintenance, children from alcoholic families have been described as taking certain roles, including "parental child," "caretaker," "peacemaker," and "scapegoat" (e.g., Minuchin, 1974). However, empirical support for these prototypic roles characterizing children of alcoholics as a group is limited with the exception of the acting-out or scapegoat role, which has been shown to be more prevalent among this population (Sher, 1991). Research does indicate that children of alcoholics do show lower self-esteem in childhood, adolescence, and young adulthood (Bennett, Wolin, Reiss, 1988; Berkowitz & Perkins, 1988; Clair & Genest, 1987; Roosa, Sandler, Beals, & Short, 1988; Sher, Walitzer, Wood, & Brent, 1991). Although no empirical work exists, there may be a connection between children of alcoholics' representation of themselves within the family (their role), and their general self-functioning. We believe that examining the self-with-family representations would provide a conceptually clearer link between family environment and individual self-conceptions in the offspring of alcoholic families.

Another body of family literature exists that assesses the influence of changes in family structure on children's adaptation (Allison & Furstenberg, 1989; Baumrind, 1989; Bohannon, 1975; Bray, 1988; Guidubaldi, 1988; Hetherington, 1989; Hetherington, Cox, & Cox, 1985; Perry & Pfuhl, 1963; Rosenberg, 1965; Touliatos & Lindholm, 1980; Wallerstein & Kelly, 1980; Zill, 1988). In particular, literature on children's coping with marital transitions has been concerned with how different family subsystems, including the marital relationship, parenting relationship, and sibling relationship, are related to children's adjustment (Hetherington & Clingempeel, 1992; Johnston, 1990; Kurdek, 1986; Portes, Howell, Brown, Eichenberger, & Mas, 1992). An important finding from this work is that family structure alone is not sufficient for predicting variations in children's adjustment. Divorce and remarriage involve a series of changes that can affect all aspects of family functioning, requiring mutual adaptation in the marital, parental, and sibling relationships (Hetherington, 1988; MacKinnon, 1989). Regardless of family structure, the quality of the marital relationship appears related to the quality of each parent's relationship with his or her children (Anderson, Linder, & Bennion, 1992). Authoritative parenting, that is parenting characterized by warmth, involvement, support, and monitoring, is consistently associated with high levels of social and scholastic competence in children from nondivorced, divorced, and remarried families. In addition, the quality of sibling relationships is consistently associated with children's adjustment across all family types, with perhaps a more significant role in remarried families. Thus, it is the marital relationship's influence on parenting in combination with sibling relationships that affects the child's adjustment.

An important addition to this work could be provided by asking children how they view themselves in regard to each of these subsystems (marital, parental, and sibling) and then to determine how such representations might affect general esteem and competence. Such an approach would provide a more specific understanding of how particular family subsystems are related to the child's evolving sense of self during times of family transition. The focus, however, would still be on subsystems rather than the entire family system. In fact, most of the research from a systems perspective has assessed the functioning of dyads and triads and has not captured the functioning of the system as a whole. A notable exception to this is the work of Reiss and Oliveri (Oliveri & Reiss, 1981a, 1981b; Reiss, 1981; Reiss & Oliveri, 1983a, 1983b, 1984).

According to these investigators, every family has a family paradigm to provide a stable, shared orientation that guides the family's perceptions and behavior in novel situations. This paradigm is a system of constructs that serve as a point around which the family organizes. Thus, one way of describing an entire family system is by describing the shared beliefs, assumptions, and orientations of the family system. Shared family constructs pertain to three orthogonal dimensions of family functioning: configuration, coordination, and closure. Configuration refers to a sense of mastery in the family. Families high on this dimension believe they can gain control in a novel or challenging environment through investigation; that, as a family, through their efforts they can master the situation. Coordination concerns solidarity in family organization and refers to the degree to which each member dovetails his or her efforts with others in the family. Families high in coordination define problems as involving the whole family. Consequently, information concerning events are shared and efforts to respond are coordinated among family members. Closure refers to the role of the past in the family's attempt to cope with the present. For families high in closure, current experience is the major influence on what they believe and how they act. Families low on closure are oriented toward their past; family traditions and perspectives play an important role in their efforts to interpret the here and now. The conceptualization and validation of these dimensions was originally based on the verbal and nonverbal behavior of families in a laboratory setting but has been extended to include the nature of daily routines in families and their social network patterns (Reiss & Oliveri, 1983a, 1984).

The importance of this body of work is that it gives us a measure of entire family functioning which is not adding across dyadic and triadic relationships within the family. What remains unknown, however, is the extent to which these shared family concepts are related to specific self-representations in regard to the entire family, and then to what extent the self-representations are related to general self-functioning. Building on the methodology developed by Reiss and Oliveri, one could ask individual members of the family how they see themselves in relation to their family after completion of the laboratory problem-solving task. This approach could yield information that would be beyond the level of dyadic and triadic self-representations. Of particular interest would be the extent to which self-representations with specific family members are similar to or different from self-with-entire-family representations and how these representations are related to family dimensions of configuration, closure, and coordination as well as individual self-concepts and evaluations. It would also be of interest to examine the interface between different family members' representations of themselves-with-the-family.

THE FAMILY SELF-CONCEPT MODEL

Throughout this chapter, we have tried to specify issues of interest and the relevant literature for examining the meaning of the term "family self-concept." Past work has provided a rich foundation for suggesting the importance, development, and function of family self-concepts, but very limited work exists that specifically addresses the idea of self-with-family representations as a conceptual link between interactions and self-functioning. Figure 8.1 presents a heuristic model for describing the factors important for understanding the significance of the family self-concept within, as well as across, particular developmental periods.

On the far left side, the general components of the model for the self in relation to a family member are given. The use of self in the model is meant to designate the focal family member whose representations are being studied, whether infant, child, adolescent, or adult. In the illustration of specific cells and in our discussion of the model, we use the mother and the attachment function to highlight some of the model's characteristics. However, it should be kept in mind that the model can be used to apply to any family member and particular function. The model comprises four components most immediately relevant to our concern with family

	Infancy	Childhood	Adolescence	Adulthood
Self/Family-Member Interaction	Separation protest / Affectionate contact on reunion / Mother responsive to infant distress	Affectionate contact on reunion / Engage in responsive, positive conversation	Affectionate contact on reunion / Tolerance for differences / Responsive, positive conversation	Affectionate contact on reunion / Tolerance for differences / Responsive, positive conversation
Self/Family-Member Relationship	Warm / Comfortable / Reliable	Warm / Comfortable / Reliable	Warm / Comfortable / Reliable	Warm / Comfortable / Reliable
Self-with-Family-Member Representation	Not measurable	I am loved / I am valued / I am accepted	Loved/loving / Valued/valuing / Accepted/accepting	Loved/loving / Valued/valuing / Accepted/accepting
Global Self-Evaluation/Concept	Not measurable	Secure model of self / Self-worth / Autonomy	Secure model of self / Self-worth / Autonomy	Secure model of self / Self-worth / Autonomy

Figure 8.1 The Family Self-Concept model illustrated using the attachment function.

functioning and self-representations: self/family-member interactions, self/family-member relationship, self-with-family-member representations, and global self-evaluations or conceptions. These elements can be considered as they relate to each other at a given time point as well as across time points within a developmental period. Time points can also be within as well as across developmental periods such as childhood, adolescence, and adulthood. Although the model obviously indicates an interest in the development of the self-with-family-member representation, we believe that examination of concurrent relations are of equal interest and importance in demonstrating a link between family interactions, relationships, and internal representations of the self.

Beginning with the interactions that are used to define a particular function, age-appropriate behaviors must be studied for the child as well as the interaction partner. The behavior of both partners must be examined to index how the dyad's pattern may define relationships. For example, data reported by Waters et al. (1990) indicate that attachment behaviors, such as seeking proximity or verbal signaling are not merely learned but taught. Just as the child may seek proximity to the mother or monitor her availability in more sophisticated ways, the mother can, to varying degrees, monitor the child's exploration of the environment. As mentioned in the section on the parent-child subsystem, both parent and adolescent behaviors facilitate individuation.

One form of interaction that has been understudied but that should have direct relevance to self-with-family-member representations is autobiographical material constructed by parents with children. Snow (1990) offers some exciting suggestions for areas to explore concerning the ways in which parents contribute to the development of self in children. She delineates how parents help children construct narratives about personal events in their lives. For example, reviewing family photographs provides the opportunity to discuss how the child is alike or different from family members in physical as well as psychological attributes or interpersonal behaviors. Photographs also provide physical reminders of important events in the child's life that can elicit a telling or retelling of what the child and other family members did, said, or felt.

Important events, such as birthday parties, or more everyday occurrences, such as mealtime conversations, provide the interpersonal arena for the discussion and construction of self-narratives. With very young children, 2 to 4 years of age, the parent leads the discussion of the autobiographical events prompting the child to remember by focusing on important behavior and interpreting its meaning. Although young children show interest in and access to recalled events, the responsibility for remembering and narrating most of the incident being retold resides with the parent (Engel, 1986; Snow, 1990). With age, children take more initiative in remembering specific events and interpreting the meaning of these events in their autobiography (Eder, Gerlach, & Perlmutter, 1987).

There is considerable evidence that children's memories of events are partial and inaccurate and are influenced by current relationships and circumstances (e.g., Lewis & Feiring, in press; Rudy & Goodman, 1991; Saywitz, Goodman, Nicholas, & Moan, 1991; Yarrow, Campbell, & Burton, 1970). One study examined mothers and elementary school student's recollections of their relationship in preschool (Yarrow et al., 1970). The "real history" comparison data were derived from researchers' preschool observations, ratings, and assessment. Results indicated that there was little overall association between the children's recollection of their relationship with their mother in preschool and the research record of the relationship. The association between mothers' recollections and the research record was no better than their children's. Recollection was, however, associated with the current status of the relationship. In general, the extent to which the current relationship was positive was the extent to which the past was recalled in positive terms.

Another study examined adolescents' recollections of their childhood and how they were related to observations of mother-child attachment in infancy (Lewis & Feiring, in press). The adolescents' recollections of childhood were not related to past ratings of security of attachment. In particular, those adolescents who, as infants, were classified as insecure were not more likely than those rated as secure to describe their childhood as unhappy or insecure. However, adolescents with negative recollections of their childhood rated themselves as more poorly adjusted than adolescents with positive recollections of their childhood. Although one could argue that these recollections do not measure the unconscious working models of the mother-child relationship, the results of this study nevertheless suggest that self-development can be viewed, at least in part, as a reconstruction of past events based on current functioning.

These examples have focused on the affective and attachment nature of the mother-child relationship, but we want to emphasize the generality of the notion that there is much insight to be gained from examining current constructions of autobiographical narratives relevant for other functions. Recent work on parental attributions concerning children's successes and failures in learning tasks indicates how the interpretation of self-achievement events by the parent can influence self-evaluations pertaining to intelligence and feelings of self-worth with family members and with teachers (Alessandri & Lewis, 1993; Dweck & Gillard, 1975).

The preceding findings suggest that the interaction component of our model must consider, in addition to observations of interactive behavior, the verbalized interpretation of the behavior by the parent and child. This could be for ongoing events or for discussion of past events. Examining the relation between the parent's and child's construction of the child's autobiographical stories and the self-with-parent representations would give us a clearer understanding of the foundation of such representations. We suspect that the coconstructed narratives and attributions made by the parent about the child's behavior in the family are equally, if not more, important than the actual behavior itself.

The second component in our model is the relationship between the child and the family member. Here we believe it is important that the relationship be defined in regard to a specific function and that the relationship be considered from each partner's point of view when possible. Consequently, if we are interested in attachment, then the relationship qualities of security-insecurity and the extent to which the attachment relationship is activated or deactivated are important to assess (Kobak & Sceery, 1988). Examination of other functions would require the specification of essential relationship qualities. For example, companionship or intimacy might involve indexing the qualities of enjoyment and reciprocity. As we discussed previously, it is not always easy to disentangle the observation of interactions from the specification of relationships and this is especially so with young children. With older children and adults, the qualities of relationships can be assessed through verbal report, although there may remain the problems of how to reconcile discrepancies in each partner's view of the relationship and how to index views that may not be accessible to consciousness (Cook & Goldstein, 1993).

The third component of the model has been the focus of this chapter, the family self-concept. In the preverbal child, it is not possible to directly measure the self-with-other representations, but by 3 to 4 years of age, self-with-other statements can probably be elicited using adaptations of the puppet-play methodology described by Cassidy (1988). For older children, the dialogue methodology developed by Reid, Landesman-Ramey, and Burchinal (1990) could be modified to assess self-with-specific-family-member representations. "Dialogues about Families" was designed to tap children's perceptions about themselves and their families in a developmentally sensitive way. Parallel methodology is available for adolescents and adults. The dialogues involve children's ratings of behavioral qualities in themselves and other family members, perceptions of and satisfaction with different types of social support, and understanding of family goals and different family members' priorities. The particular dialogue, "What I'm like and what others in my family are like," is of particular interest. The first part of this dialogue elicits children's self-ratings on a set of behavioral dimensions that were previously determined to be highly valued by parents of children aged 5 to 14 years. These dimensions include cooperative, creative, emotionally stable, happy, honest, independent, eager to learn, loving, responsible, self-confident, and caring. The second part of the dialogue obtains children's ratings of each family member on the same dimensions. Some results from the use of this methodology indicate that children's perceptions of themselves are highly associated with their perceptions of both mother and father. Furthermore, perceptions of emotional support from both parents are associated with more positive self-appraisals.

In its current form, the dialogues do not focus on the self in relationships, but rather the self in general. It would, therefore, be important in our view to assess self-with-other representations perhaps simply by asking children to make ratings after imagining themselves with a particular family member. There is also the problem of providing dimensions for rating, rather than allowing self-generated descriptions. We would prefer the more idiographic approach of using self-derived descriptions that could also be examined for common themes. Nevertheless, we believe that "Dialogues about Families" provides a good strategy for obtaining children's viewpoints about themselves and their families.

For adolescents and adults, Ogilvie and Ashmore (1991) have developed a method that involves consideration of the entire network of significant others. Subjects are asked to form images of themselves in interaction with family members, close friends, and other important people, including enemies, and then to rate how they experience themselves in the context of each important relationship. Obtaining descriptive information on the nature of self-with-family-member representations in childhood, adolescence, and adulthood would be a major contribution to our understanding of the importance of the family in self-development. It would also enable us to examine the extent to which the self-with-other-family-member representations contribute to overall evaluations of the self.

This brings us to the fourth component of the model, the global self-concepts and evaluations. We wish to indicate here the global self in reference to a particular function but not a particular person. Thus, for the attachment function, it would be important to examine the relation between self-with-mother representation and global feelings of self-worth, social acceptance, and autonomy. Alternatively, global self-concepts of academic competence or behavioral conduct could be related to the function of information exchange and self-with-family-member representations that pertain to this function.

As we consider all the components of the model together, several questions arise. First, are there contemporaneous relations between interactions with family members and relationships with them (the external interactables) and the self-with-family-member representations and global self-concepts (the internal representables)? For the attachment function, the theory would postulate a strong relation among all four components in early childhood. The data indicate, on the other hand, that the external interactables are only modestly interrelated while the internal representables are inconsistently related (Cassidy, 1988). Another question that arises from the model is the extent to which the relations between the components remain the same across different time points. For example, theory would suggest much stronger associations between self-with-parent representations in childhood than in adolescence or adulthood. Research on children's ratings of the importance of different network members indicates that parents are perceived as the most important companions until adolescence, when friends become more important. However, parents remain a central source for meeting intimacy needs into adolescence (Buhrmester & Furman, 1987). The social networks of adolescents are more extensive in their membership and alternative sources for self-with-other representations increase as relationships with friends become more salient (Blyth, Hill, & Thiel, 1982; Feiring & Lewis, 1991; Grotevant & Cooper, 1985). Nevertheless, there is clear evidence that the centrality of parents is often transformed and not diminished in the adolescent's social world (Lamborn & Steinberg, 1993; Ryan & Lynch, 1989). How these changes in the child's relationship with the parents may be related to changes in the child's self-representation with parents and the extent to which these representations contribute to global self-assessments have gone unaddressed in theory and research.

Another important issue concerns the examination of continuity for each component of the model. Regarding the self-with-family-member component, the extent to which continuity in such representations is due to the stability in child-with-family-member relationships would require longitudinal data and regression analyses that would provide estimates of the contribution of relationships to representations across time. Of course, the converse of the preceding statement would have to be considered whereby continuity in the child-with-family-member relationship is related to the representation of the particular relationship. This pathway is the one favored by some attachment theorists (e.g., Main et al., 1985; Sroufe & Fleeson, 1986).

Before concluding our discussion of Figure 8.1, we must highlight its limitations. First, the model only provides for the examination of relationships and representations at the dyadic level. It would obviously be important to consider interactions between relationships and representations of the self-with-the-entire-family system. Although the perception of one's relationship to the family has been assessed (Feiring & Lewis, 1987; Landesman, Jaccard, & Gunderson, 1991; Lewis & Feiring, 1982; Reiss & Oliveri, 1984), measurement of the entire system is a complex task posing significant procedural and interpretive difficulties.

Perhaps the most significant limitation of the model is the absence of components that indicate the influence of factors exogenous to the immediate family. To determine the relative importance of particular self-with-family-member representations to global conceptions requires comparison with the importance of self-with-non-family-member representations. A recent study by Harter and Monsour (1992) indicates that from the child's point of view, the ability to make such comparisons probably emerges in adolescence and increases across this developmental period. These researchers examined 7th, 9th, and 11th graders' self-generated descriptions for self with parents, with friends, with romantic partners, and in the classroom. There was a systematic and significant linear decrease in the proportion of overlapping attributes across grade level for the three role-related comparisons of self with parent versus self with friends, self with parents versus self in the classroom, and self with friends versus self in the classroom. However, some anecdotal data suggested that the most central self-with-parent representations were described in terms of caring and understanding, while central self-with-friend representations were characterized as happy and outgoing.

CONCLUSION

We began this chapter by noting the undefined meaning of the term "family self-concept." Using the idea of self-with-other representation, we have tried to specify how individuals' representations of themselves with particular family members and within the context of particular family subsystems may provide a better understanding about the links between family relationships and self-functioning from early childhood into adulthood. Whereas our knowledge of family functioning and its impact on self-development has clearly moved beyond a singular focus on the mother-child dyad, it is nevertheless still true that the preponderance of work continues to emphasize the attachment function and the centrality of the parents' roles. In delineating the meaning of the family self-concept, we have attempted to go beyond this parent-child attachment focus to provide a family systems perspective that highlights multiple relationships and functions among family members. In our struggle to construct meaningful ways of conceptualizing the family self-concept, we have relied on a rich and extensive body of theory and research about child and family functioning that was not, in most cases, originally intended to address issues of self-with-family-member representations. We hope that the ideas set forth here on the meaning and significance of the family self-concept as extrapolated from the work of others will provide a useful set of guidelines for future thought and investigation.

REFERENCES

Abramovitch, R., Pepler, D., & Corter, C. (1982). Patterns of sibling interaction among preschool-age children. In M. E. Lamb & B. Sutton-Smith (Eds.), *Sibling relationships: Their nature and significance across the lifespan* (pp. 61–86). Hillsdale, NJ: Erlbaum.

Achenbach, T. M. (1979). The child behavior profile: An empirically based system for assessing children's behavioral problems and competencies. *International Journal of Mental Health, 7,* 24–42.

Ainsworth, M. D. S., Blehar, M. C., Waters, E., & Wall, S. (1978). *Patterns of attachment: A psychological study of the strange situation.* Hillsdale, NJ: Erlbaum.

Alessandri, S. M., & Lewis, M. (1993). Parental evaluation and its relation to shame and pride in young children. *Sex Roles, 29*(5/6), 335–343.

Allen, J. P., Hauser, S. T., Bell, K. L., & O'Connor, T. G. (1994). Longitudinal assessment of autonomy and relatedness in adolescent-family interactions as predictors of adolescent ego development and self-esteem. *Child Development, 65,* 179–194.

Allison, P. D., & Furstenberg, F. F. (1989). How marital dissolution affects children: Variations by age and sex. *Developmental Psychology, 25,* 540–549.

Anderson, E. R., Lindner, M. S., & Bennion, L. D. (1992). The effect of family relationships on adolescent development during family reorganization. In E. M. Hetherington & W. G. Clingempeel (Eds.), Growing points of attachment theory and research. *Monographs of the Society for Research in Child Development, 57* (2-3, Serial No. 227), 178–199.

Archer, S. L. (1985). Identity and choice of social roles. In A. S. Waterman (Ed.), *Identity in adolescence: Processes and contents* (pp. 79–100). San Francisco, CA: Jossey-Bass.

Arend, R., Gove, F. L., & Sroufe, L. A. (1979). Continuity of individual adaptation from infancy to kindergarten: A predictive study of ego-resiliency and curiosity in preschoolers. *Child Development, 50,* 950–959.

Bailey, W. T. (1982, April). *Affinity: An ethological theory of the infant-father relationship.* Paper presented at the Third International Conference on Infant Studies, Austin, TX.

Barnes, H., & Olson, D. (1985). Parent-adolescent communication and the Circumplex Model. *Child Development, 56,* 438–447.

Baumrind, D. (1989, April). *Sex-differentiated socialization effects in childhood and adolescence in divorced and intact families.* Paper presented at the meeting of the Society for Research in Child Development, Kansas City, MO.

Beavers, W. (1982). Health, midrange and severely dysfunctional families. In F. Walsh (Ed.), *Normal family processes.* New York: Guilford.

Belsky, J., Garduque, L., & Hrncir, E. (1984). Assessing performance, competence and executive capacity in infant play: Relations to home environment and security of attachment. *Developmental Psychology, 20,* 406–417.

Belsky, J., Gilstrap, B., & Rovine, M. (1984). The Pennsylvania infant and family development project: 1. Stability and change in mother-infant and father-infant interaction in a family setting at one, three, and nine months. *Child Development, 55,* 692–705.

Belsky, J., & Pensky, E. (1988). Developmental history, personality, and family relationships: Toward an emergent family system. In R. A. Hinde & J. Stevenson-Hinde (Eds.), *Relationships within families: Mutual influences* (pp. 193–217). Oxford, England: Clarendon Press.

Belsky, J., & Rovine, M. (1987). Temperament and attachment security in the strange situation: An empirical rapprochement. *Child Development, 58,* 787–795.

Bennett, L. A., Wolin, S. J., & Reiss, D. (1988). Cognitive, behavioral and emotional problems among school-age children of alcoholic parents. *American Journal of Psychiatry, 145,* 185–190.

Berger, P. (1966). Identity as a problem in the sociology of knowledge. *Archives Europeennes de Sociologie, 7,* 105–115.

Berkowitz, A., & Perkins, H. W. (1988). Personality characteristics of children of alcoholics. *Journal of Consulting and Clinical Psychology, 56,* 206–209.

Block, J. H., & Block, J. (1980). The role of ego-control and ego-resiliency in the organization of behavior. In W. A. Collins (Ed.), *Minnesota Symposia on Child Psychology* (Vol. 13, pp. 39–101). Hillsdale, NJ: Erlbaum.

Blyth, D. A., Hill, J. P., & Thiel, K. S. (1982). Early adolescents' significant others: Grade and gender differences with familial and non-familial adults and young people. *Journal of Youth and Adolescence, 11,* 425–450.

Bohannon, P. (1975). *Stepfathers and the mental health of their children* (Final report). La Jolla, CA: Western Behavioral Science Institute.

Bowlby, J. (1969). *Attachment and loss: Vol. 1. Attachment.* New York: Basic Books.

Bowlby, J. (1973). *Attachment and loss: Vol. 2. Separation.* New York: Basic Books.

Bowlby, J. (1980). *Attachment and loss: Vol. 3. Loss, sadness and depression.* New York: Basic Books.

Bracken, B. A., & Crain, R. M. (1994). Children's and adolescents' interpersonal relations: Do age, race, and gender define normalcy? *Journal of Psychoeducational Assessment, 12,* 14–32.

Bray, J. H. (1988). Children's development during early remarriage. In E. M. Hetherington & J. D. Arasteh (Eds.), *Impact of divorce, single parenting and stepparenting on children* (pp. 279–298). Hillsdale, NJ: Erlbaum.

Bretherton, I. (1987). New perspectives on attachment relations: Security, communication, and internal working models. In J. D. Osofsky (Ed.), *Handbook of Infant Development* (2nd ed., pp. 1061–1100). New York: Wiley.

Bretherton, I. (1990). Open communication and internal working models: Their role in the development of attachment relationships. In R. A. Thompson (Ed.), *Nebraska Symposium on Motivation: Socioemotional Development* (pp. 57–113). Lincoln: University of Nebraska Press.

Bridges, L. J., Connell, J. P., & Belsky, J. (1988). Similarities and differences in infant-mother and infant-father interaction in the strange situation: A component process analysis. *Developmental Psychology, 24*(1), 92–100.

Brody, G. H., Stoneman, Z., MacKinnon, C. E., & MacKinnon, R. (1985). Role relationships and behavior between preschool-aged and school-aged sibling pairs. *Developmental Psychology, 21,* 124–129.

Bronfenbrenner, U. (1986). Ecology of the family as a context for human development. *Developmental Psychology, 22,* 723–742.

Bronfenbrenner, U., & Crouter, A. C. (1983). The evolution of environmental models in developmental research. In W. Kessen & P. H. Mussen (Eds.), *History, theory, and methods: Handbook of child psychology* (Vol. 1, pp. 357–414). New York: Wiley.

Bronstein, P. (1984). Differences in mothers' and fathers' behaviors toward children: A cross-cultural comparison. *Developmental Psychology, 20,* 995–1003.

Bryant, B. K. (1982). Sibling relationships in middle childhood. In M. E. Lamb & B. Sutton-Smith (Eds.), *Sibling relationships: Their nature and significance across the lifespan* (pp. 87–121). Hillsdale, NJ: Erlbaum.

Bryant, B. K., & Crockenberg, S. B. (1980). Correlates and dimensions of prosocial behavior: A study of female siblings with their mothers. *Child Development, 51,* 529–544.

Buhrmester, D., Comparo, L., Christensen, A., Shapiro Gonzalez, L., & Hinshaw, S. P. (1992). Mother and fathers interacting in dyads and triads with normal and hyperactive sons. *Developmental Psychology, 28,* 500–509.

Buhrmester, D., & Furman, W. (1987). The development of companionship and intimacy. *Child Development, 58,* 1101–1113.

Buhrmester, D., & Furman, W. (1990). Perceptions of sibling relationships during middle childhood and adolescence. *Child Development, 61*(5), 1387–1398.

Caldwell, B. M., & Bradley, R. H. (1984). *Home observation for measurement of the environment.* Little Rock: University of Arkansas.

Caspi, A., & Elder, G. H., Jr. (1988). Emergent family patterns: The intergenerational construction of problem behaviour and relationships. In R. A. Hinde & J. Stevenson-Hinde (Eds.), *Relationships within families: Mutual influences* (pp. 218–240). Oxford, England: Clarendon Press.

Cassidy, J. (1988). Child-mother attachment and the self in six-year-olds. *Child Development, 59,* 121–134.

Christensen, A., & Margolin, G. (1988). Conflict and alliance in distressed and nondistressed families. In R. A. Hinde & J. Stevenson-Hinde (Eds.), *Relationships within families: Mutual influences* (pp. 263–282). Oxford, England: Clarendon Press.

Cicirelli, V. C. (1982). Sibling influence throughout the lifespan. In M. E. Lamb & B. Sutton-Smith (Eds.), *Sibling relationships: Their nature and significance across the lifespan* (pp. 267–284). Hillsdale, NJ: Erlbaum.

Clair, D., & Genest, M. (1987). Variables associated with the adjustment of offspring of alcoholic fathers. *Journal of Studies on Alcohol, 48,* 345–355.

Clarke-Stewart, K. A. (1978). And daddy makes three: The father's impact on mother and young child. *Child Development, 49*(2), 466–478.

Clarke-Stewart, K. A. (1980). The father's contribution to children's cognitive and social development in early childhood. In F. A. Pedersen (Ed.), *The father-infant relationship: Observational studies in the family setting* (pp. 111–146). New York: Praeger Special Studies.

Cochran, M. M., & Brassard, J. A. (1979). Child development and personal social networks. *Child Development, 50,* 601–616.

Constantine, L. (1986). *Family paradigms: The practice of theory in family therapy.* New York: Guilford.

Cook, W. L., & Goldstein, M. J. (1993). Multiple perspectives on family relationships: A latent variables model. *Child Development, 64*(5), 1377–1388.

Cooley, C. H. (1902). *Human nature and the social order.* New York: Scribner's.

Cooper, C. R., Grotevant, H. D., & Condon, S. M. (1983). Individuality and connectedness in the family as a context for adolescent identity formation and role taking skill. In H. D. Grotevant & C. R. Cooper (Eds.), *Adolescent development in the family: New directions for child development* (pp. 43–59). San Francisco, CA: Jossey-Bass.

Damon, W. (1983). *Social and personality development: Infancy through adolescence.* New York: Norton.

Deaux, K. (1991). Social identities: Thoughts on structure and change. In R. C. Curtis (Ed.), *The relational self: Theoretical convergences in psychoanalysis and social psychology* (pp. 77–93). New York: Guilford.

Dickstein, E. (1977). Self and self-esteem: Theoretical foundations and their implications for research. *Human Development, 20,* 129–140.

Dozier, M., & Kobak, R. R. (1992). Psychophysiology in attachment interviews: Converging evidence for deactivating strategies. *Child Development, 63,* 1473–1480.

Dunn, J., & Kendrick, C. (1982). Siblings and their mothers: Developing relationships within the family. In M. E. Lamb & B. Sutton-Smith (Eds.), *Sibling relationships: Their nature and significance across the lifespan* (pp. 153–165). Hillsdale, NJ: Erlbaum.

Dweck, C. S., & Gillard, D. (1975). Expectancy statements as determinants of reaction to failure: Sex differences in persistence and expectancy change. *Journal of Personality and Social Psychology, 25,* 109–116.

Eder, R. A., Gerlach, S. G., & Perlmutter, M. (1987). In search of children's selves: Development of the specific and general components of the self-concept. *Child Development, 58*(4), 1044–1050.

Elicker, J., Englund, M., & Sroufe, L. A. (1992). Predicting peer competence and peer relationships in childhood from early parent-child relationships. In R. Parke & G. Ladd (Eds.), *Family-peer relationships: Modes of linkage* (pp. 77–106). Hillsdale, NJ: Erlbaum.

Engel, S. (1986). *Learning to reminisce: A developmental study of how young children talk about the past.* Unpublished doctoral dissertation, City University of New York.

Epstein, S. (1991). Cognitive-experiential self-theory: An integrative theory of personality. In R. Curtis (Ed.), *The relational self* (pp. 111–137). New York: Guilford.

Feiring, C., & Coates, D. L. (1987). Social networks and gender differences in the life space of opportunity: Introduction. *Sex Roles, 17*(11/12), 611–620.

Feiring, C., & Lewis, M. (1987). The ecology of some middle class families at dinner. *International Journal of Behavioral Development, 10*(3), 377–390.

Feiring, C., & Lewis, M. (1991). The transition from middle childhood to early adolescence: Sex differences in the social network and perceived self-competence. *Sex Roles, 24*(7/8), 489–509.

Fonagy, P., Steele, M., Steele, H., Moran, G. S., & Higgitt, A. C. (1991). The capacity for understanding mental states: The reflective self in parent and child and its significance for security of attachment. *Infant Mental Health Journal, 12*(3), 201–218.

Fox, N. A., Kimmerly, N., & Schafer, W. (1991). Attachment to mother/attachment to father: A meta-analysis. *Child Development, 62,* 210–225.

Freud, S. (1959). Instincts and their vicissitudes. In *Collected papers*. New York, NY: Basic Books. (Original work published 1915)

Furman, W. (1987, March). *Social support, stress, and adjustment in adolescence*. Paper presented at the meeting of the Society for Research in Child Development, Baltimore, MD.

Furman, W., & Buhrmester, D. (1985). Children's perceptions of the personal relationships in their social networks. *Developmental Psychology, 21*, 1014–1024.

Furman, W., & Buhrmester, D. (1992). Age and sex differences in perceptions of networks of personal relationships. *Child Development, 63*, 103–115.

Furman, W., & Giberson, R. S. (1995). Identifying the links between parents and their children's sibling relationships. In S. Shulman (Ed.), *Close relationship in social-emotional development*. Norwood, NJ: Abex.

Furman, W., & Wehner, E. A. (1994). Romantic views: Toward a theory of adolescent romantic relationships. In R. Montemayor, G. R. Adams, T. P. Gullota (Eds.), *Advances in adolescent development: Vol. 3. Personal Relationships during adolescence* (pp. 168–195). Thousand Oaks, CA: Sage.

George, C., Kaplan, N., & Main, M. (1985). *The attachment interview for adults*. Unpublished manuscript, University of California, Berkeley, Department of Psychology.

Gergen, K. J. (1968). Personal consistency and the presentation of self. In C. Gordon & K. J. Gergen (Eds.), *The self in social interaction* (pp. 299–308). New York: Wiley.

Gilligan, C. (1982). *In a different voice: Psychological theory and women's development*. Cambridge, MA: Harvard University Press.

Greenberg, M. T., Siegel, J. M., & Leitch, C. J. (1983). The nature and importance of attachment relationships to parents and peers during adolescence. *Journal of Youth and Adolescence, 12*, 373–386.

Grotevant, H. D., & Cooper, C. R. (1985). Patterns of interaction in family relationships and the development of identity exploration in adolescence. *Child Development, 56*, 415–428.

Grotevant, H. D., & Cooper, C. R. (1986). Individuation in family relationships: A perspective on individual differences in the development of identity and role-taking skill in adolescence. *Human Development, 29*, 82–100.

Guidubaldi, J. (1988). Differences in children's divorce adjustment across grade level and gender: A report from the N.A.S.P.-Kent State Nationwide Project. In S. A. Wolchick & P. Karoly (Eds.), *Children of divorce: Empirical perspectives on adjustment* (pp. 185–231). New York: Gardner Press.

Harter, S. (1986). Processes underlying the construction, maintenance, and enhancement of the self-concept in children. In J. Suls & A. Greenwald (Eds.), *Psychological perspectives on the self* (Vol. 3, pp. 137–181). Hillsdale, NJ: Erlbaum.

Harter, S. (1990). Causes, correlates, and the functional role of global self-worth: A life-span perspective. In R. J. Sternberg & J. Kolligian, Jr. (Eds.), *Competence considered* (pp. 67–97). New Haven, CT: Yale University Press.

Harter, S., & Monsour, A. (1992). Developmental analysis of conflict caused by opposing attributes in the adolescent self-portrait. *Developmental Psychology, 28*(2), 251–260.

Harter, S., & Pike, R. (1984). The pictorial scale of perceived competence and social acceptance for young children. *Child Development, 55,* 1969–1982.

Hauser, S. T., Powers, S. I., & Noam, G. G. (1991). *Adolescents and their families.* New York: Free Press.

Hauser, S. T., Powers, S. I., Noam, G. G., Jacobson, A. M., Weiss, B., & Follansbee, D. J. (1984). Familial contexts of adolescent ego development. *Child Development, 55,* 195–213.

Hetherington, E. M. (1988). Parents, children and siblings six years after divorce. In R. Hinde & J. Stevenson-Hinde (Eds.), *Relationships within families* (pp. 311–331). Cambridge: Cambridge University Press.

Hetherington, E. M. (1989). Coping with family transitions: Winners, losers, and survivors. *Child Development, 60,* 1–14.

Hetherington, E. M., & Clingempeel, W. G. (1992). Coping with marital transitions: A family systems perspective. *Monographs of the Society for Research in Child Development, 57*(2–3, Serial No. 227).

Hetherington, E. M., Cox, M. J., & Cox, R. (1985). Long-term effects of divorce and remarriage on the adjustment of children. *Journal of the American Academy of Psychiatry, 24,* 518–530.

Hill, J. P., & Holmbeck, G. N. (1986). Attachment and autonomy during adolescence. In G. J. Whitehurst (Ed.), *Annals of child development* (Vol. 3, pp. 145–189). Greenwich, CT: JAI Press.

Hinde, R. A. (1976). Interactions, relationships, and social structure. *Man, 11,* 1–17.

Hinde, R. A. (1979). *Towards understanding relationships.* London: Academic Press.

Hinde, R. A. (1988). Introduction. In R. A. Hinde & J. Stevenson-Hinde (Eds.), *Relationships within families: Mutual influences* (pp. 1–4). Oxford, England: Clarendon Press.

Howe, N. (1986). *Socialization, social cognitive factors and the development of the sibling relationship.* Unpublished doctoral dissertation, University of Waterloo, Waterloo, Canada.

Huston, T. L., & Robins, E. (1982). Conceptual and methodological issues in studying close relationships. *Journal of Marriage and the Family, 44,* 901–925.

James, W. (1890). *The principles of psychology.* New York: Holt.

Johnston, J. R. (1990). Role diffusion and role reversal: Structural variations in divorced families and children's functioning. *Family Relations, 39,* 405–413.

Kamptner, N. L. (1988). Identity development in late adolescence: Causal modeling of social and familial influences. *Journal of Youth and Adolescence, 17,* 493–514.

Kobak, R. R., & Cole, H. E. (1994). Attachment and meta-monitoring: Implications for adolescent autonomy and psychopathology. In D. Cicchetti (Ed.), *Rochester Symposium on Developmental Psychopathology: Vol. 5. The self and its disorders.* Rochester, NY: Rochester University Press.

Kobak, R. R., Cole, H. E., Ferenz-Gillies, R., Fleming, W. S., & Gamble, W. (1993). Attachment and emotion regulation during mother-teen problem-solving: A control theory analysis. *Child Development, 64*(1), 231–245.

Kobak, R. R., & Sceery, A. (1988). Attachment in late adolescence: Working models, affect regulation, and representations of self and others. *Child Development, 59,* 135–146.

Koch, H. L. (1960). The relation of certain formal attributes of siblings to attitudes held toward each other and toward their parents. *Monographs of the Society for Research in Child Development, 25*(1–124, Serial No. 78).

Kotelchuck, M. (1976). The infant's relationship to the father: Experimental evidence. In M. E. Lamb (Ed.), *The role of the father in child development* (pp. 329–344). New York: Wiley.

Kroger, J., & Haslett, S. (1988). Separation/individuation and ego identity status in late adolescence: A two year longitudinal study. *Journal of Youth and Adolescence, 17,* 59–79.

Kurdek, L. A. (1986). Children's reasoning about parental divorce. In R. D. Ashmore & D. M. Brodzinsky (Eds.), *Thinking about the family: Views of parents and children* (pp. 233–276). Hillsdale, NJ: Erlbaum.

LaFreniere, P. J., & Sroufe, L. A. (1985). Profiles of peer competence in the preschool: Interrelations between measures, influence of social ecology, and relation to attachment history. *Developmental Psychology, 21,* 56–69.

Lamb, M. E. (1976). Interactions between 8-month-old children and their fathers and mothers. In M. E. Lamb (Ed.), *The role of the father in child development* (pp. 307–327). New York: Wiley.

Lamb, M. E. (1977). Father-infant and mother-infant interaction in the first year of life. *Child Development, 48,* 167–181.

Lamb, M. E. (Ed.). (1981). *The role of the father in child development* (2nd ed.). New York: Wiley.

Lamb, M. E. (1982). The father-child relationship: A synthesis of biological, evolutionary and social perspectives. In L. W. Hoffman, R. Gandelman, & H. R. Schoffman (Eds.), *Parenting: Its causes and consequences* (pp. 55–73). Hillsdale, NJ: Erlbaum.

Lamb, M. E., Thompson, R., Gardner, W., & Charnov, E. (1985). *Infant-mother attachment: The origins and developmental significance of individual differences in strange situation behavior.* Hillsdale, NJ: Erlbaum.

Lamborn, S. D., & Steinberg, L. (1993). Emotional autonomy redux: Revisiting Ryan and Lynch. *Child Development, 64*(2), 483–499.

Landesman, S., Jaccard, J., & Gunderson, V. (1991). The family environment: The combined influence of family behavior, goals, strategies, resources, and individual experiences. In M. Lewis & S. Feinman (Eds.), *Social influences and socialization in infancy: Genesis of behavior* (Vol. 6, pp. 63–96). New York: Plenum.

Lessing, D. (1964). *Martha quest.* New York: New American Library.

Lewis, M. (1982). The social network systems model: Toward a theory of social development. In T. Field, A. Huston, H. C. Quay, L. Troll, & G. E. Finley (Eds.), *Review of human development* (pp. 180–214). New York: Wiley.

Lewis, M. (1987). Social development in infancy and early childhood. In J. Osofsky (Ed.), *Handbook of infancy, Second edition* (pp. 419–493). New York: Wiley.

Lewis, M. (1994). Does attachment imply *a* relationship or *multiple* relationships? *Psychological Inquiry, 5,* 47–51.

Lewis, M. & Brooks-Gunn, J. (1979). *Social cognition and the acquisition of self.* New York: Plenum.

Lewis, M., & Feiring, C. (1978). The child's social world. In R. M. Lerner & G. B. Spanier (Eds.), *Child influences on marital and family interaction: A life-span perspective.* New York: Academic Press.

Lewis, M., & Feiring, C. (1979). The child's social network: Social object, social functions and their relationship. In M. Lewis & L. Rosenblum (Eds.), *The child and its family: The genesis of behavior* (Vol. 2, pp. 9–27). New York: Plenum.

Lewis, M., & Feiring, C. (1982). Some American families at dinner. In L. Laosa & I. Sigel (Eds.), *Families as learning environments for children* (pp. 115–145). New York: Plenum.

Lewis, M., & Feiring, C. (1991). Attachment as personal characteristic or a measure of the environment. In J. Gewirtz & B. Kurtines (Eds.), *Intersections with attachment* (pp. 1–21). Hillsdale, NJ: Erlbaum.

Lewis, M., & Feiring, C. (in press). Developmental outcomes as history. *Journal of Developmental Psychopathology.*

Lewis, M., & Weinraub, M. (1976). The father's role in the infant's social network. In M. E. Lamb (Ed.), *The role of the father in child development.* New York: Wiley.

Lytton, H. (1980). *Parent-child interaction: The socialization process observed in twin and singleton families.* New York: Plenum.

MacDonald, K., & Parke, R. D. (1984). Bridging the gap: Parent-child play interaction and peer interactive competence. *Child Development, 55,* 1265–1277.

Mackey, W. C. (1985). *Fathering behaviors: The dynamics of the man-child bond.* New York: Plenum.

MacKinnon, C. E. (1989). An observational investigation of sibling interactions in married and divorced families. *Developmental Psychology, 25,* 36–44.

Mahler, M. S., Pine, F., & Bergman, A. (1975). *The psychological birth of the infant.* New York: Basic Books.

Main, M., & Cassidy, J. (1985). *Assessments of child-parent attachment at six years of age.* Unpublished scoring manual.

Main, M., & Cassidy, J. (1988). Categories of response to reunion with the parent at age six: Predictable from infant attachment classifications and stable over a one-month period. *Developmental Psychology, 24,* 415–426.

Main, M., & Goldwyn, R. (1985). Adult attachment classification system. Unpublished manuscript, University of California, Berkeley, Department of Psychology.

Main, M., Kaplan, N., & Cassidy, J. (1985). Security in infancy, childhood, and adulthood: A move to the level of representation. In I. Bretherton & E. Waters (Eds.), Growing points of attachment theory and research. *Monographs of the Society for Research in Child Development, 50*(1–2, Serial No. 209), 66–104.

Main, M., & Weston, D. R. (1981). The quality of the toddler's relationship to mother and to father: Related to conflict behavior and the readiness to establish new relationships. *Child Development, 52,* 932–940.

Marcia, J. E. (1966). Development and validation of ego identity status. *Journal of Personality and Social Psychology, 3,* 551–558.

Margolin, L., Blyth, D., & Carbone, D. (1988). The family as a looking glass: Interpreting family influences on adolescent self esteem for a symbolic interaction perspective. *Journal of Early Adolescence, 8,* 211–224.

Markus, H., & Sentis, K. (1982). The self in social information processing. In J. Suls (Ed.), *Social psychological perspectives on the self* (Vol. 1, pp. 41–70). Hillsdale, NJ: Erlbaum.

Markus, H., & Wurf, E. (1987). The dynamic self-concept: A social psychological perspective. *Annual Review of Psychology, 38,* 299–337.

Matas, L., Arend, R. A., & Sroufe, L. A. (1978). Continuity of adaptation in the second year: The relationship between quality of attachment and later competence. *Child Development, 49,* 547–556.

McGuire, W. J., & McGuire, C. V. (1982). Significant others in self-space: Sex differences and developmental trends in the self. In J. Suls (Ed.), *Social psychological perspectives on the self* (Vol. 1, pp. 71–96). Hillsdale, NJ: Erlbaum.

McGuire, W. J., & McGuire, C. V. (1988). Content and process in the experience of self. In L. Berkowitz (Ed.), *Advances in experimental social psychology* (Vol. 21, pp. 97–141). New York: Academic Press.

McGuire, W. J., McGuire, C. V., & Cheever, J. (1986). The self in society: Effects of social contexts on the sense of self. *British Journal of Social Psychology, 25,* 259–270.

Mead, G. H. (1934). *Mind, self and society: From the standpoint of a social behaviorist.* Chicago: University of Chicago Press.

Memmi, A. (1984). *Dependence.* Boston, MA: Beacon.

Minuchin, P. (1988). Relationships within the family: A systems perspective on development. In R. A. Hinde & J. Stevenson-Hinde (Eds.), *Relationships within families: Mutual influences* (pp. 7–26). Oxford, England: Clarendon Press.

Minuchin, S. (1974). *Families and family therapy.* Cambridge, MA: Harvard University Press.

Monane, J. H. (1967). *A sociology of human systems.* New York: Appleton-Century-Crofts.

Moos, R. H. & Moos, B. S. (1976). A typology of family social environments. *Family Process, 15*(4), 357–371.

Nair, D., & Jason, L. A., (1985). An investigation and analysis of social networks among children. *Special Services in the Schools, 14,* 43–52.

Ogilvie, D. M., & Ashmore, R. D. (1991). Self-with-other representation as a unit of analysis in self-concept research. In R. C. Curtis (Ed.), *The relational self: Theoretical convergences in psychoanalysis and social psychology* (pp. 282–314). New York: Guilford.

Oliveri, M. E., & Reiss, D. (1981a). The structure of families' ties to their kin: The shaping role of social constructions. *Journal of Marriage and the Family, 43,* 391–407.

Oliveri, M. E., & Reiss, D. (1981b). A theory-based empirical classification of family problem-solving behavior. *Family Process, 20,* 409–418.

Oliveri, M. E., & Reiss, D. (1987). Social networks of family members: Distinctive roles of mothers and fathers. *Sex Roles, 17*(11/12), 719–736.

Olson, D. H., Sprenkle, D. H., & Russell, C. S. (1979). Circumplex model of marital and family systems: I. Cohesion and adaptability dimensions, family types, and clinical applications. *Family Process, 18,* 3–28.

Parke, R. D., MacDonald, K. B., Beitel, A., & Bhavnagri, N. (1988). The role of the family in the development of peer relationships. In R. DeV. Peters & R. J. McMahon (Eds.), *Social learning and systems approaches to marriage and the family* (pp. 17–44). New York: Brunner/Mazel.

Parsons, T., & Bales, R. F. (1955). *Family socialization and interaction process.* Glencoe, IL: Free Press.

Patterson, G. R., & Dishion, T. J. (1988). Multilevel family process models: Traits, interactions, and relationships. In R. A. Hinde & J. Stevenson-Hinde (Eds.), *Relationships within families: Mutual influences* (pp. 283–310). Oxford, England: Clarendon Press.

Pedersen, F. A., & Robson, K. S. (1969). Father participation in infancy. *American Journal of Orthopsychiatry, 39,* 466–472.

Perry, J. B., & Pfuhl, E. H. (1963). Adjustment of children in "solo" and "remarriage" homes. *Marriage and Family Living, 25,* 221–223.

Pfouts, J. H. (1976). The sibling relationship: A forgotten dimension. *Social Work, 21,* 200–204.

Phares, V., & Compas, B. E. (1992). The role of fathers in child and adolescent psychopathology: Make room for daddy. *Psychological Bulletin, 111,* 387–412.

Pleck, J. H. (1985). *Working wives/working husbands.* Beverly Hills, CA: Sage.

Portes, P. R., Howell, S. C., Brown, J. H., Eichenberger, S., & Mas, C. A. (1992). Family functions and children's postdivorce adjustment. *American Journal of Orthopsychiatry, 62,* 613–617.

Powers, S. I., Hauser, S. T., & Kilner, L. A. (1989). Adolescent mental health. *American Psychologist, 44*(2), 200–208.

Radin, N., & Russell, G. (1983). Increased father participation and child development outcomes. In M. E. Lamb & A. Sagi (Eds.), *Fatherhood and family policy* (pp. 191–218). Hillsdale, NJ: Erlbaum.

Reid, M., Landesman-Ramey, S., & Burchinal, M. (1990). Dialogues with children about their families. In W. Damon (Series Ed.), *New directions for child development;* I. Bretherton & M. W. Watson (Eds.), *Children's perspectives on the family* (Vol. 48, pp. 1–28). San Francisco, CA: Jossey-Bass.

Reiss, D. (1981). *The family's construction of reality.* Cambridge, MA: Harvard University Press.

Reiss, D., & Oliveri, M. E. (1983a). The family's construction of social reality and its ties to its kin network: An exploration of causal direction. *Journal of Marriage and the Family, 45,* 81–91.

Reiss, D., & Oliveri, M. E. (1983b). Sensory experience and family process: Perceptual styles tend to run in but not necessarily run families. *Family Process, 22,* 289–308.

Riess, D. & Oliveri, M. E. (1984). Family paradigm and family coping: A proposal for linking the family's intrinsic adaptive capacities to its responsiveness to stress. In B. N. Adams & J. L. Campbell (Eds.), *Framing the family: Contemporary portraits*. Prospect Heights, IL: Waveland Press.

Richters, J. E., & Waters, E. (1991). Attachment and socialization: The positive side of social influence. In M. Lewis & S. Feinman (Eds.), *Social Influences and socialization in infancy: Genesis of behavior* (Vol. 6, pp. 185–213). New York: Plenum.

Roosa, M. S., Sandler, I. N., Beals, J., & Short, J. L. (1988). Risk status of adolescent children of problem drinking parents. *American Journal of Community Psychology, 16*, 225–239.

Rosenberg, M. (1965). *Society and the adolescent self-image*. Princeton, NJ: Princeton University Press.

Rosenberg, M. (1979). *Conceiving the self.* New York: Basic Books.

Rudy, L., & Goodman, G. S. (1991). Effects of participation on children's reports: Implications for children's testimony. *Developmental Psychology, 27*, 527–538.

Russell, G., & Russell, A. (1987). Mother-child and father-child relationships in middle childhood. *Child Development, 58*, 1573–1585.

Ryan, R., & Lynch, J. (1989). Emotional autonomy versus detachment: Revisiting the vicissitudes of adolescence and young adulthood. *Child Development, 60*, 340–356.

Sandler, I. N., Wolchik, S. A., & Braver, S. L. (1985). Social support and children of divorce. In I. G. Sarason & B. R. Sarason (Eds.), *Social support: Theory, research and applications* (pp. 371–389). Dordrecht, Netherlands: Martinus Nijhoff Publishers.

Saywitz, K. D., Goodman, G. S., Nicholas, E., & Moan, S. F. (1991). Children's memories of a physical examination involving genital touch: Implications for report of child sexual abuse. *Journal of Consulting and Clinical Psychology, 59*, 682–691.

Schachter, F. F. (1982). Sibling deidentification and split-parent identification: A family tetrad. In M. E. Lamb & B. Sutton-Smith (Eds.), *Sibling relationships: Their nature and significance across the lifespan* (pp. 123–151). Hillsdale, NJ: Erlbaum.

Schachter, F. F. (1985). Sibling deidentification in the clinic: Devil vs. angel. *Family Process, 24*(3), 415–427.

Schachter, F. F., Gilutz, G., Shore, E., & Adler, M. (1978). Sibling deidentification judged by mothers: Cross-validation and developmental studies. *Child Development, 49*, 543–546.

Schachter, F. F., & Stone, R. K. (1985). Difficult sibling, easy sibling: Temperament and the within-family environment. *Child Development, 56*(5), 1335–1344.

Schafer, R. B., & Keith, P. M. (1985). A causal model approach to the symbolic interactionist view of the self-concept. *Journal of Personality and Social Psychology, 48*, 963–969.

Searcy, E., & Eisenberg, N. (1992). Defensiveness in response to aid from a sibling. *Journal of Personality and Social Psychology, 62*(3), 422–433.

Selman, R. (1980). *The growth of interpersonal understanding.* New York: Academic Press.

Sher, K. J. (1991). *Children of alcoholics: A critical appraisal of theory and research.* Chicago: University of Chicago Press.

Sher, K. J., Walitzer, K. S., Wood, P., & Brent, E. E. (1991). Characteristics of children of alcoholics: Putative risk factors, substance use and abuse, and psychopathology. *Journal of Abnormal Psychology.*

Snow, C. E. (1990). Building memories: The ontogeny of autobiography. In D. Cicchetti & M. Beeghly (Eds.), *The self in transition: Infancy to childhood* (pp. 213–242). Chicago, IL: University of Chicago Press.

Sroufe, L. A. (1979). Socioemotional development. In J. D. Osofsky (Ed.), *Handbook of infant development* (pp. 462–516). New York: Wiley.

Sroufe, L. A. (1983). Infant-caregiver attachment and patterns of adaptation in preschool: The roots of maladaption and competence. In M. Perlmutter (Ed.), *Development and policy concerning children with special needs: The Minnesota Symposia on Child Psychology* (Vol. 16, pp. 41–83). Hillsdale, NJ: Erlbaum.

Sroufe, L. A. (1990). An organizational perspective on the self. In D. Cicchetti & M. Beeghly (Eds.), *The self in transition: Infancy to childhood* (pp. 281–307). Chicago, IL: University of Chicago Press.

Sroufe, L. A., Egeland, B., & Kreutzer, T. (1990). The fate of early experience following developmental change: Longitudinal approaches to individual adaptation in childhood. *Child Development, 61,* 1363–1373.

Sroufe, L. A., & Fleeson, J. (1986). Attachment and the construction of relationships. In W. Hartup & Z. Rubin (Eds.), *Relationships and development* (pp. 51–71). Hillsdale, NJ: Erlbaum.

Steinberg, L., & Silverberg, S. B. (1986). The vicissitudes of autonomy in early adolescence. *Child Development, 57,* 841–851.

Stern, D. N. (1985). *The interpersonal world of the infant: A view from psychoanalysis and developmental psychology.* New York: Basic Books.

Stewart, R. B., Mobley, L. A., Van Tuyl, S. S., & Salvador, M. A. (1987). The firstborn's adjustment to the birth of a sibling: A longitudinal assessment. *Child Development, 58,* 341–355.

Stocker, C., Dunn, J., & Plomin, R. (1989). Sibling relationships: Links with child temperament, maternal behavior, and family structure. *Child Development, 60,* 715–727.

Stoneman, Z., Brody, G. H., & MacKinnon, C. (1984). Naturalistic observations of children's activities and roles while playing with their siblings and friends. *Child Development, 55,* 617–627.

Stryker, S. (1987). Identity theory: Developments and extensions. In K. Yardley & T. Honess (Eds.), *Self and identity: Psychological perspectives* (pp. 89–103). Chichester, England: Wiley.

Sullivan, H. S. (1953). *The interpersonal theory of psychiatry.* New York: Norton.

Sutton-Smith, B. (1982). Birth order and sibling status effects. In M. E. Lamb & B. Sutton-Smith (Eds.), *Sibling relationships: Their nature and significance across the lifespan* (pp. 153–165). Hillsdale, NJ: Erlbaum.

Sutton-Smith, B., & Rosenberg, B. G. (1970). *The sibling.* New York: Holt, Rinehart & Winston.

Tajfel, H. (1981). *Human groups and social categories.* Cambridge, England: Cambridge University Press.

Tomkins, S. S. (1987). Script theory. In J. Aronoff, A. I. Rabin, & R. A. Zucker (Eds.), *The emergence of personality* (pp. 147–216). New York: Springer.

Touliatos, J., & Lindholm, B. W. (1980). Teachers' perceptions of behavior problems in children from intact, single-parent and stepparent families. *Psychology in the Schools, 17,* 264–269.

Troll, L. E. (1987). Gender differences in cross-generation networks. *Sex Roles, 17*(11/12), 751–766.

Vandell, D. L., Minnett, A. M., & Santrock, J. W. (1987). Age differences in sibling relationships during middle childhood. *Journal of Applied Developmental Psychology, 8,* 247–257.

Volling, B. L., & Belsky, J. (1992). The contribution of mother-child and father-child relationships to the quality of sibling interaction: A longitudinal study. *Child Development, 63,* 1209–1222.

Von Bertalanffy, L. (1967). *Robots, men, and minds: Psychology in the modern world.* New York: Braziller.

Wallerstein, J. S., & Kelly, J. B. (1980). *Surviving the breakup: How children and parents cope with divorce.* New York: Basic.

Waters, E., Kondo-Ikemura, K., Posada, G., & Richters, J. E., III (1990). Learning to love: Mechanisms and milestones. In M. Gunnar & L. A. Sroufe (Eds.), *Minnesota Symposia on Child Psychology* (Vol. 23, pp. 217–255). Hillsdale, NJ: Erlbaum.

Waters, E., Wippman, J., & Sroufe, L. A. (1979). Attachment, positive affect, and competence in the peer group: Two studies in construct validation. *Child Development, 50,* 821–829.

Watzlawick, P. (Ed.). (1984). *The invented reality.* New York: Norton.

Weiss, R. S. (1974). The provisions of social relationships. In Z. Rubin (Ed.), *Doing unto others: Joining, molding, conforming, helping, loving* (pp. 17–26). Englewood Cliffs, NJ: Prentice-Hall.

Yarrow, M. R., Campbell, J. D., & Burton, R. V. (1970). Recollections of childhood: A study of the retrospective method. *Monographs of the Society for Research in Child Development, 35*(5, Serial No. 138).

Youniss, J., & Smollar, J. (1985). *Adolescent relations with mothers, fathers, and friends.* Chicago, IL: University of Chicago Press.

Zajonc, R. B. (1976). Family configuration and intelligence. *Science, 192,* 227–236.

Zelkowitz, P. (1989). Parents and children as informants concerning children's social networks. In D. Belle (Ed.), *Children's social networks and social supports* (pp. 221–237). New York: Wiley.

Zill, N. (1988). Behavior, achievement, and health problems among children in stepfamilies: Findings from a national survey of child health. In E. M. Hetherington & J. D. Arasteh (Eds.), *Impact of divorce, single parenting and stepparenting on children* (pp. 325–368). Hillsdale, NJ: Erlbaum.

CHAPTER 9

Physical Self-Concept

RISA J. STEIN

The contribution of the physical self to global self-concept is observed frequently in the literature (e.g., Thornton & Ryckman, 1991). Attractive adults and those with greater physical prowess often attain greater popularity, preferential treatment, and positive attributes than nonattractive individuals (Hatfield & Sprecher, 1986). Because of the differences in how more and less attractive people are treated by society, investigators might theorize that differences in self-concept would also develop. Indeed, studies have shown that physical attractiveness is positively correlated with self-concept (Adams, 1977; Lerner & Karabenick, 1974; Lerner, Karabenick, & Stuart, 1973; Lerner, Orlos, & Knapp, 1976; Mathes & Kahn, 1975; Simmons & Rosenberg, 1975). In general, individuals possessing a more positive sense of their physical abilities tend also to have higher self-esteems (Lerner et al., 1973, 1976; Ryckman, Robbins, Thornton, & Cantrell, 1982).

Lerner and colleagues (1976) hypothesize about the breakdown of the physical attractiveness/performance contributions to global self-concept by gender:

> The adolescent female's (self-concept) should relate more to her attitudes about her body as an instrument of individual effectiveness. Conversely, the adolescent male's self-concept should be more highly related to physical effectiveness attitudes than to physical attractiveness attitudes. (p. 314)

Contrary to this hypothesis, Thornton and Ryckman (1991), in a more recent study found that physical effectiveness is no less important to the adolescent female's self-concept than it is for the adolescent male. The authors attribute the lack of differences between the sexes primarily to changing social roles for women.

Rosenberg (1965) and McGuire and Padawer-Singer (1976) have each suggested that various components of self-concept hold varying levels of importance for the individual. Components of global self-concept that have received considerable attention include physical, social, competence, affect, academic, and family self-concepts (Bracken, 1992). Bracken, Bunch, Keith, and Keith (1992) suggest:

> Researchers should consider the theoretical linkages between each of the six dimensions of self-concept and the other variables in question. For example, rather than studying the effects of athletic ability on "self-concept," it would make sense to study the effects of athletic ability specifically on physical or competence self concepts. (p. 10)

Moreover, Bracken et al. (1992) also state that intervention studies often fail to increase self-concept because global self-concept is insufficiently sensitive to specific treatments. The various components of self-concept are, however, more sensitive to specific interventions and are often more appropriate measures than global self-concept.

Of interest in this chapter is the "physical self-concept" of children. This concept may require clarification so as not to be confused with frequently related terms. Fleming and Courtney (1984) consider self-concept to be a general term that subsumes the construct of self-esteem. These authors go on to state that "self-concept . . . includes pure self-descriptions, which are distinguishable from self-esteem, because such descriptions do not necessarily imply judgement" (p. 406). Shavelson, Hubner, and Stanton (1976), on the other hand, argue that the distinction between self-concept and self-esteem has not been demonstrated empirically and is conceptually unclear. Bracken and colleagues (1992) also failed to find a distinction between self-concept and self-esteem measures in a multiple instrument factor analysis. For the purposes of this chapter, physical self-concept will be defined as children's perceptions and/or estimations of their physical performance and physical appearance.

Physical self-concept should not be confused with the construct of body image. Body image pertains more directly to affect-bound evaluations of physical appearance (Birtchnell, Dolan, & Lacey, 1987; Wardle & Foley, 1989). Hence, the distinction between these two terms may reflect that individuals may report that they perceive themselves as being overweight (relating to physical self-concept) and then report that being overweight distresses them greatly (pertaining to body image). However, there is not necessarily a positive relationship between the two variables. Many individuals report that they are overweight, but feel content with their body size and shape. Moreover, neither physical self-concept or body image necessarily relate positively to objective data pertaining to weight status (Markus, Hamill, & Sentis, 1987). For instance, a woman may report that she perceives and estimates herself to be overweight. She may also be distraught by this perception. However, her body mass index and relative weight norms may classify her well within or even below the average weight range for her peers.

A relationship similar to that found between physical self-concept and weight status is evident between physical self-concept and actual physical performance. A number of studies (e.g., Haywood, 1980; Heaps, 1978; Sonstroem, 1974, 1976; Tucker, 1975) have found that an individual's physical self-concept is not necessarily linked to actual physical perform- ance. Riley (1983) reported that *observed* physical performance assessed using several activities (e.g., standing broad jump, pull-ups, timed run/ walk) was not related to physical self-concept, whereas *estimation* of phys- ical performance was related to physical self-concept. This difference be- tween perception and reality may be due to varying levels of comfort with one's own body or unrealistic and idealistic notions of attractiveness and performance.

As previously mentioned, physical self-concept is also related to overall or global self-concept in that it constitutes one facet of multidimensional self-concept. For children in particular, physical self-concept may be an es- pecially important component of global self-concept. For instance, Fisher and Cleveland (1968) noted that children's dissatisfaction with their bod- ies, in general, had adverse effects on their global self-concepts. Moreover, Klesges, Haddock, Stein, Klesges, Eck, and Hanson (1992) studying 3- to 5-year-old children and Keller, Ford, and Meacham (1978), studying 5- to 8-year-old children both suggested that perhaps one component of global self-concept in children is a physical dimension—physical performance.

Factor analysis has provided support for the multidimensionality of physical self-concept, which was found to comprise physical appearance, physical performance, and weight-control behaviors (Franzoi & Shields, 1984). Marsh and colleagues (Marsh, 1986; Marsh & Jackson, 1986; Marsh & Peart, 1988) argue for the separation of physical appearance and physical performance in the assessment of physical self-concept, suggest- ing that the combination of the two subdomains may not yield a second- order factor. Although the presently available measures all assess at least one of these three subdomains, only one of the existent measures of physi- cal self-concept addresses all three (the Children's Physical Self-Concept Scale).

In contrast to data supporting the multidimensional nature of physical self-concept, Bracken presents additional evidence suggesting that physi- cal self-concept is a unitary dimension. Bracken and colleagues (1992), in their factor analysis of five independent measures of self-concept found only one factor for physical self-concept. Moreover, in his 1992 manual on the Multidimensional Self-Concept Scale (MSCS), Bracken reports that the physical abilities and physical appearance subscales of Marsh's SDQ measures both correlated in the high .70s with his MSCS Physical sub- scale, suggesting unity of the physical self-concept construct.

Compared with the literature on older adolescents and adults, relatively few reviews have focused specifically on the physical self-concepts of young children. In an attempt to shed some light on the physical self-concepts of this younger age group, this chapter will focus specifically on children and young adolescents. It will first address the available instruments for assessing physical self-concept in children and adolescents. Next, an overview of physical self-concept in preadolescent and adolescent populations is presented. Third, a review of physical self-concept in special populations will be offered. This review will be followed by a discussion of the relationship between physical self-concept and eating disorders. Finally, future directions for this area will be highlighted.

PHYSICAL SELF-CONCEPT ASSESSMENT DEVICES

Although the data pertaining to the multidimensionality of physical self-concept are inconclusive, the components of physical self-concept assessed by each available measure will be reported so that future research may further investigate this issue. Most of the available measures include an assessment of one or more of the components of physical self-concept (e.g., physical appearance, physical performance, weight control). In addition, projective measures (e.g., Draw-A-Person test, Homonym test) have been used in the past to assess body image and/or physical self-concept (e.g., Olgas, 1974). Because these instruments are general personality tests not designed specifically to assess self-concept and since they therefore do not assess unique subdomains of physical self-concept, such tests will be excluded from this discussion. The review will begin with global self-esteem measures including subscales that purport to assess one or more subdomains of physical self-concept. Next, measures designed to assess physical self-concept will be reviewed. Finally, additional types of measures and body size estimation tests will be discussed.

Global Self-Concept Measures

Multidimensional Self Concept Scale (MSCS)

The MSCS (Bracken, 1992) has received considerable psychometric support as a multidimensional measure of global self-concept in children. The MSCS includes a 25-item physical subscale that assesses physical appearance and physical performance in combination. MSCS Physical subscale alpha coefficients range from .91 to .93 for Grades 5 through 12. In addition, the 4-week test-retest correlation for the MSCS Physical subscale is .81. Moreover, evidence of concurrent validity for the physical subscale is supported by a .83 correlation between it and the Piers-Harris Appearance and Attributes subscale with 65 fifth- and sixth-grade children. Correlations between the MSCS Physical subscale and the Physical Appearance subscales of the Self-Description Questionnaires (SDQI and SDQII) with fifth- and sixth-grade students resulted in coefficients of .62 and .74, respectively.

Piers-Harris Children's Self-Concept Scale

One of the most widely used self-concept instruments for children is the Piers-Harris Children's Self-Concept Scale (Piers & Harris, 1969). This measure includes a Physical Appearance and Attributes subscale consisting of 12 items. However, the authors report that they constructed the test as a measure of global self-concept and did not intend for the subscales to be used independently. The Piers-Harris was standardized on children in Grades 4 through 12 from a small town in Pennsylvania.

Little psychometric data have been presented on the Piers-Harris Physical Appearance and Attributes subscale. Unfortunately, although there is a dearth of available psychometric data, this subscale has been used frequently as a criterion measure in the concurrent validation of other instruments (Bracken, 1992; Mendelson & White, 1982).

The Self-Description Questionnaire, I (SDQI)

The SDQI, developed by Marsh (1986), includes physical abilities and physical appearance subscales for children. Each subscale comprises eight positively phrased items to which the examinee responds. The authors report that factor analysis was used extensively during the early versions of the SDQI in an attempt to increase the likelihood of finding a reliable and interpretable set of factors. Using the standardization sample of children in Grades 2 through 5, Marsh reported an alpha coefficient of .83 for the Physical Abilities subscale and .90 for the Physical Appearance subscale of the SDQI. Norms were created using the standardization sample, but stability and validity estimates pertaining to the SDQI are not reported in the test manual. In addition, the author does not report the criteria used to select or discard items.

Tennessee Self-Concept Scale (TSCS)

Developed originally by Fitts in 1965, the TSCS was standardized on individuals between the ages of 12 and 68. The TSCS includes an 18-item subscale, Physical Self-Concept, which was developed to assess state of health, physical appearance, physical skills, and sexuality. An alpha coefficient of .64 was reported for the Physical Self-Concept subscale of the TSCS using the WPS Test Report sample of 122 adolescents (Roid & Fitts, 1989). Also, using this sample, a 2-week test-retest correlation of .87 was obtained.

Scales Assessing Physical Self-Concept

Body-Esteem Scale (BES)

The BES (Mendelson & White, 1982) is a 24-item self-report instrument developed by the authors to "investigate the relation between body-esteem and self-esteem in children" (p. 900). Mendelson and White state that the 24 dichotomously answered (yes/no) test items "reflect how a person values his appearance and body . . . or how a person believes he is being evaluated by others" (p. 900). The standardization sample for the BES consisted of 36 boys and girls from 7.5 to 12 years of age enrolled in a Hebrew school in a middle-class section of Montreal, Quebec. Odd/even split-half reliability for this sample was .85. Additionally, the authors suggested that the measure was suitable for second-grade readers (Mendelson & White, 1982, p. 900) and evidenced face validity. In an effort to assess concurrent validity, the BES was correlated with the Physical Appearance and Attributes subscale of the Piers-Harris, which resulted in a correlation of .67.

Children's Eating Attitude Test-26 (ChEAT)

The Eating Attitudes Test (EAT; Garner, Olmsted, Bohr, & Garfinkle, 1982) is one of the most frequently used measures to assess eating attitudes in adults and older adolescents (Berland, Thompson, & Linton, 1986). Maloney and colleagues (Maloney, McGuire, & Daniels, 1988) administered the EAT-26 to trial subjects in the third and fourth grades. Test items that were difficult for the trial subjects to understand were modified with the use of simpler synonyms. The authors also modified items labeled by three consulting developmental specialists as too difficult for third- or fourth-grade children to understand. The children's version of the EAT-26 (ChEAT) employs the modified 26 self-report items. The ChEAT was normed on a group of 318 boys and girls from third through sixth grades in two schools in middle- to upper-class sections of Cincinnati. Total sample test-retest reliability for the ChEAT, with a 3-week time interval was .81, with a range from .75 to .88 for individual grade levels. Alpha was reported at .76 with a range of .68 to .70 for individual grades. Maloney and colleagues claim that the ChEAT evidences face validity. The ChEAT is also one of the few measures to assess weight-control behaviors in children.

The Children's Physical Self-Concept Scale (CPSS)

The CPSS (Stein, Bracken, Shadish, Haddock, 1995) is the only multidimensional measure of physical self-concept for children. This measure assesses overall physical self-concept as well as the subdomains of Physical Appearance, Physical Performance, and Weight Control Behaviors. The subscales each contain nine items and are answered using a specialized answer form presenting four glasses with varying amounts of water for each test item. Children respond to item stems using this graphic format in terms of frequency (e.g., "I never . . ." to "I always . . .") or quality (e.g., "I really . . ." to "I really don't . . ."). The scale can be administered by reading it aloud to a group, or it can be given on an individual basis. Because of this unique administration format and because item content is suitable for children in the primary grades, this measure is useful for child populations as young as first grade. The internal consistency for the overall measure for the entire sample is .77, and the three subdomains range from .60 to .81. Two-week test-retest reliability is .88 for the overall measure and ranges from .80 to .84 for the subdomains.

The CPSS has been shown to distinguish groups of overweight, diabetic, and normal children using global scores as well as subdomain scores. As part of a contrasted groups analysis, 20 children classified as 75% or above of relative weight (overweight), 20 children with diabetes, and 20 normal children were matched according to sex and grade and their scores on the CPSS compared. Results indicated that both normal and diabetic children obtained higher CPSS global scores and Physical Appearance subscale scores than did overweight children. In addition, although no differences between groups were obtained for the Physical Performance subscale, normal children scored higher on the Weight Control subscale than did overweight children.

Self-Perception Profile for Children (SPPC)

The SPPC (Harter, 1985) includes subdomains of Athletic Competence and Physical Appearance. Due to the requirement of a basic reading level, the scale is restricted to children above the age of 8 years. Alpha coefficients for the Athletic Competence and Physical Appearance subscales are .75 and .82, respectively. Factor analysis provides support for the six domains of self-concept assessed by the SPPC. Each subscale consists of six items, for a total of 36 items. The item format requires children first to select from two depictions of an individual the one they feel most resembles them. Then the examinees must decide whether that depiction is "sort of true" or "really true" of them.

Body Estimation Tasks

Children's perceptions of their body shapes and sizes may not necessarily reflect reality. One method of assessing children's perceptions of their body size and/or shape is to have them view pictures of a male or female in progressively thinning (or fattening) form such as those produced by Stunkard, Sorenson, and Schulsinger (1983) for adults. Collins (1991) used seven pictures of male and female children and adults created to illustrate body weight ranging from very thin to obese. This method of assessment would appear to be a suitable alternative to pencil-and-paper measures for preliterate children because the only requirement of the children performing this task is to select a figure in response to specific questions.

Collins (1991) developed drawings that depict child figures to illustrate weight ranging from very thin to obese. The figure drawings and five accompanying questions were pilot tested and administered to 159 first-, second-, and third-grade students. Collins asked her child sample five questions based on the illustrations:

1. "Which picture looks the most like you?"
2. "Which picture shows the way you want to look?"
3. "Which picture shows the way you think is best for girls/boys to look [opposite gender picture]?"
4. "Which picture shows the way you want to look when you grow up?"
5. "Which picture shows the way you think is best for grown-up women/men to look [opposite sex picture]?"

Collins also asked children to respond to two additional items. The first item was "I think I am: fat, skinny, in-between." The second item asked whether the children would like to lose weight, gain weight, or stay the same. Collins reported that the task was cognitively difficult for first graders and that younger children found particular amusement in selecting opposite-sex figures. The 3-day stability coefficient ranged from .38 to .71 for Collins' five test items. However, due to the younger children not taking the test seriously, particularly when selecting opposite-sex figures, validity may have been compromised.

Cash and Brown (1987) divided other body estimation tasks into two categories of body sites and whole body estimation procedures. Body sites estimation requires an individual to match the width of the distance between two points to closely approximate the width of a specific body site or region. The whole body estimation procedures involve presenting an individual with a whole body image (e.g., via distorted mirrors, videotape, overhead projection) that they can then modify to make smaller or larger to match their estimation of their own body width. With regard to specific body sites, Kreitler and Kreitler (1988) had 240 individuals, aged 4 through 30, close their eyes and spread their arms apart to represent their perceived width. In addition, light beams have been used that an individual can control and move closer or farther apart so as to estimate the width of a particular body region (Ruff & Barrios, 1986). Kreitler and Kreitler (1988) presented internal consistency coefficients of .75 to .88 for factors involving the body and .79 to .82 for factors involving the face using the hand separation method of body width estimation. They also presented 2-week test-retest correlations of .93 to .97. These novel assessment techniques appear promising, particularly for preliterate children. Additional investigative efforts should determine the usefulness of these types of measures with a child population and should further validate the psychometric properties of such devices.

Although a variety of measures have been designed to assess physical aspects of self-concept, limitations of the available instruments must also be noted. Crandall (1973) wrote the following regarding self-concept measures:

> Except for items written specifically for unique research populations, the casual generation of new scales is professionally irresponsible. The same careful attention researchers give to their basic experimental designs should be invested in their choice of the scale they will use. (p. 52)

Undoubtedly there are many measures for assessing physical self-concept; however, the psychometric properties of the better known measures are, in most cases, weak or nonexistent. Hence, the discussion of little-known measures would unlikely contribute much more to the discussion of physical self-concept assessment.

The majority of the measures designed to assess self-concept in children have been developed for use with children with at least a third-grade reading equivalence. Since a poor physical self-concept may begin to affect global self-concept and dietary habits at a very early age (Staffieri, 1967), the assessment of children prior to third grade is important. The assessment of young children is also important to determine the earliest possible developmental trends in physical self-concept and is a prerequisite for early intervention for eating disorders.

In addition to not being developed for use with very young children, some of the measures of physical self-concept used normative samples unrepresentative of the child population in the United States (SDQI, BES). In addition, some of the measures were standardized almost 30 years ago and thus may not reflect current trends and influences on children. For those interested in studying the physical self-concept, especially as a multi-dimensional construct, of young American children, very few measures are available.

PREADOLESCENT AND ADOLESCENT POPULATIONS

Adolescence has long been considered a tumultuous time of life. A primary factor contributing to the level of difficulty during this time is physical change (Pomerantz, 1979). Because of the changes in physique and the development of secondary sexual characteristics, adolescents become painfully aware of their physical appearance. Evidence of this hyperawareness is provided by Clifford (1971) who suggested that although adolescents are positive about their appearance in general, they seem concerned particularly about weight, height, and physique. In addition, the emphasis on physical appearance by children approaching adolescence is supported by Newcomb and Bukowski (1983) who report that older children more highly value personal appearance and athletic skills over academic skills when selecting friends. Moreover, although weak or nonsignificant relationships for preadolescents have been revealed between physical performance and self-concept (Heaps, 1978; Sonstroem, 1974, 1976), stronger and significant relationships have been found between physical estimations and self-concept.

Due to the emphasis on physical appearance and performance in adolescence, activities that focus on strengthening physical performance and emphasizing physical appearance may be thought to facilitate the development of a more positive physical self-concept. Hence, it may seem intuitive that an activity such as dance would benefit an adolescent in this regard. Bakker (1988) found just the opposite. In his study of female adolescent dance students, Bakker found that the physical self-concepts of the dancers were lower than those of female nondancers, based on physical appearance and physical performance. He speculated that this finding may be due to an attitude in the school environment that is critical of body appearance and physical abilities. The competitive environment and critical evaluations of others are then incorporated into the adolescents' own physical self-concepts.

Perhaps Bakker's counterintuitive finding is the result of adolescents focused on a competitive environment that produces self-critical physical self-concept. Adolescents with primary focuses unrelated to aspects of physical self-concept would serve as an interesting comparison group to assess the impact of primarily physical training versus primarily intellectual training on the development of physical self-concept. Cornell and colleagues (1990), assessed a group of gifted adolescents in Grades 5 through 11 who were attending a summer enrichment program. These researchers found that students' perceptions of physical performance were significantly related to peer status for boys but not for girls. Cornell et al. also found that perceptions of physical appearance were significantly related to peer status for boys but not for girls, whereas academic self-concept was significantly related to classroom peer status only for older girls.

Cornell et al.'s investigation of intellectually gifted female students revealed that they were less concerned about physical appearance than were their male counterparts. Hence, the literature suggests some variability among female adolescents with regard to their concerns about physical appearance. Additional data pertaining to potential physical self-concept mediating variables may facilitate understanding broader issues such as the development of physical self-concept among adolescents.

Typically, the literature suggests that girls are more concerned with their physical-self concepts than are boys, particularly with regard to physical appearance and weight control (Collins, 1991; Garner et al., 1980). Preliminary studies of children with particular physical and nonphysical inclinations (e.g., dancers vs. gifted students), however, suggest that additional emphasis on physical performance and physical appearance may be a potential mediating variable affecting adolescents' physical self-concepts.

PHYSICALLY HANDICAPPED POPULATIONS

Estimates in the United States reveal that approximately 9.5 million of the total 84 million American children are considered physically handicapped (Resnick, 1986). Because the appearance and functioning of one's body parts are important aspects of physical self-concept, it is reasonable to hypothesize that defects in either of these areas would affect a child's physical self-concept (Harvey & Greenway, 1984). In fact, evidence provided from researchers investigating diverse handicapping conditions supports this hypothesis. For instance, Hopper (1988) found that for an adolescent hearing-impaired sample, physical appearance was the domain most related to global self-concept.

During the first two years of life, the primary mode of learning is through action (Cohen, 1977). For this reason, further examination of the impact of physically handicapping conditions on the development of physical self-concept in children is essential. As Klesges et al. (1992) and Keller et al. (1978) have found, physical performance is a primary component of overall physical self-concept in children aged 3 through 8. Thus, if a child's physical functioning is limited, this limitation may negatively affect the child's physical self-concept and, in turn, diminish the child's global self-concept proportionately.

Clinical practice has documented the high incidence of depression and poor self-image in orthopedically handicapped children (Schecter, 1961) and children with cystic fibrosis (Lawler, Nakierlrey, & Wright, 1966), congenital heart defects (Glaser, Harrison, & Lynn, 1964), and spina bifida (Kolin, Scherzer, New, & Garfield, 1971). Moreover, Kinn (1964) found that 72 physically handicapped children had fewer close personal relationships and fewer opportunities for social participation than their nonhandicapped counterparts, which suggests that physical limitations might also affect a child's social development and self-concept.

Researchers have argued the plight of individuals with virtually every handicapping condition. For instance, it has been suggested that societal attitudes toward the visually impaired are frequently negative (Centers & Centers, 1963; Siller, Ferguson, Vann, & Holland, 1968; Wright, 1960). Others argue that because of societal importance of the face and skin, the cosmetically or facially disfigured may have lower physical self-concepts than others with bodily afflictions (Hill-Beuf & Porter, 1984). These authors suggest that both children and adults rank facial disfigurements among the least desirable handicaps (Goodman, Richardson, Dornbusch, & Hastorf, 1963; Richardson, Goodman, Hastorf, Dornbusch, 1961). Still others purport cerebral palsy to be the least desirable of all physical disabilities due to the negative attitudes associated with the typically extreme physical disability (Horn, 1975; Shears & Jensoma, 1969; McDaniel, 1976). It is difficult to dispute that the physical self-concepts of handicapped children are likely to suffer due to negative social attitudes and discrimination as well as impaired ability and lack of social contacts (Harvey & Greenway, 1984). Which handicapping condition is most devastating, however, may be a moot point.

Beyond the suggestion that their physical conditions may affect their self-concepts, the developing physical self-concepts of the handicapped and/or disfigured have received surprisingly little attention. The few studies investigating gender differences in the physical self-concepts of handicapped children are equivocal. For instance, in a descriptive report of children with vitiligo, a condition involving the depigmentation of the skin, Hill-Beuf and Porter (1984) suggest that there were no gender differences found in their population of 3- to 18-year-old children; both sexes were equally disturbed by this condition. In a study of 22 adolescents with cerebral palsy (CP), Magill and Hurlbut (1986) found that adolescents with CP were very similar to nondisabled controls on measures of self-concept. These authors also found, however, that female adolescents with CP scored significantly lower on the self-concept measures than males with CP or nondisabled children of either gender. Hopper (1988) revealed a reverse finding suggesting that hearing-impaired girls saw themselves as significantly more athletically competent, socially accepted, and physically more attractive than hearing-impaired boys. There may be a differential impact on physical self-concept for handicapped boys and girls due to the type of handicapping condition and differing societal standards of performance and appearance for the sexes.

Using the Self-Description Questionnaire, II (SDQII; Marsh, Parker, & Barnes, 1985) with preadolescents, Marsh and Peart (1988) reported that a physical training program had a significantly positive effect on perceptions and estimations of physical performance and physical appearance in preadolescent girls. Physical education has also been suggested by several researchers as a potential mediating variable between handicapping conditions and physical self-concept. Resnick (1986) in a study of sixty 12- to 20-year-olds with CP found that participation at the time of their investigation was not related to social psychological measures. However, those individuals who had participated in sports as children were found to be happier and less self-conscious than those who had no involvement with sports as children.

Sherrill, Hinson, Gench, Kennedy, and Low (1990) studied groups of disabled youth athletes, aged 9 to 18 years, with blindness, cerebral palsy, and dwarfism. Their results revealed that all groups scored within the average range on athletic and appearance scales from Harter's (1988) What Am I Like scale. Despite positive associations between physical education and physical self-concept, Garrison and Tesch (1978) suggest that underachievement in physical education may be very common for hearing-impaired children. The implications of this finding suggest that hearing-impaired children may begin with a low physical self-concept that only serves to maintain and further erode self-concept through lack of motor experiences over time.

An initial report suggests that physically handicapped children may benefit from special educational programs as well as programs stressing physical education. Harvey and Greenway (1984) indicate that children with congenital nonprogressive physical handicaps who attend special schools score higher on measures of physical appearance than their counterparts in regular schools.

Beyond the reports that children with physical handicaps often have poorer physical self-concepts, very little additional information has been presented regarding the physical self-concepts of handicapped and/or disfigured populations. Additional research is needed to determine more explicitly the interactions between age and gender with handicapping conditions. Also, future investigations should strive to identify and assess the properties of physical and special education programs that seem to benefit handicapped children. These beneficial properties could then be further developed and offered to this special population to facilitate their development of healthy positive physical self-concepts.

RELATIONSHIP BETWEEN PHYSICAL SELF-CONCEPT AND EATING DISORDERS

The literature pertaining to the relationship between eating disorders and physical self-concept is relatively strong. Research suggests that children's estimates and perceptions of physical appearance, self-reported dieting behaviors, and overall physical self-concept are more closely related to eating disorders than is the affective component, body image (Abraham & Beaumont, 1982; Loro & Orleans, 1981; Pyle, Mitchell, & Lokert, 1981). Recent studies reveal that older adolescents with eating disorders report initiating unhealthy dieting practices as very young children. Fairburn, Peveler, Jones, Hope, and Doll (1993) using a cognitive therapy approach to treat an adult population of female bulimics revealed that pretreatment concerns about body shape and weight and the pretreatment level of self-esteem were the only significant predictors of outcome.

Collins (1991) used human figure drawings with a population of first- through third-grade children and noted that, although many children selected middle-range illustrations as representative of themselves, many also selected different body sizes for ideal self. Collins reports that 42% and 14% of her female sample selected ideal representations thinner or heavier, respectively, than the present self-representation. In addition, 30% and 23% of the male sample selected ideal figures thinner or heavier, respectively, than the present self-representation. She suggested that children's selections of thinner figures for ideal self-representations than present self-representations occurred across all weight levels, races, ages, and school/community settings for females.

Mellin (1988) questioned 9-year-old normal-weight and obese girls about their attitudes and behaviors pertaining to dieting and found that approximately one-third of the total sample reported restrained eating, fear of fat, binge eating, and purging. Maloney and colleagues (1988) revealed that nearly 7% of their third- through sixth-grade sample scored in the anorexia nervosa range on the ChEAT. Stein et al. (1994) also found similar results based on a population of children from first through fifth grades. These authors found that 41% of their young sample desired to change their body size or shape. Although the direction of change was not investigated, it was revealing that such a high percentage of young children desired to change their physical appearance. In addition, these authors found that 25% of children in the first and second grades reported that they actively attempt to change their weight, as compared with only 13% of the fourth- and fifth-grade students. The large percentages of young children who report increased/restrained eating behaviors is indicative of the need for greater research efforts to concentrate on the dieting behaviors and attitudes of young children.

The surprisingly large percentage of children who score in the anorexia nervosa range on the ChEAT combined with the finding that a quarter of children in the first and second grades report weight-control behaviors should alert researchers that more investigative effort must be aimed at determining the relationship between physical self-concept and eating disorders. Maloney's group also stated that although performance on instruments such as the ChEAT is not sufficient to render formal eating disorder diagnoses, it may be useful to assess food preoccupation, eating attitudes, and dieting patterns in children. Moreover, measures such as the CPSS may be useful for determining the earliest age at which children initiate dieting practices. Future studies along those lines may offer insights into which groups of children are most prone to develop eating disorders. Such research could potentially aid in the development of successful intervention strategies.

Little has been written about eating disorders in very young children. The only study uncovered that involved disturbed eating behaviors in very young children was one of several case studies. In this article, Jaffe and Singer (1989) reported that the most common clinical manifestations of disordered eating in children include "slow eating, refusal to eat, ritualistic eating behaviors, and poor nutritional status" (p. 579). All other reports involve eating disorders with physiological etiology (e.g., pica, Prader-Willi syndrome). Stein and colleagues (1994) and Maloney and colleagues (1988), however, revealed that sizable numbers of young children are modifying their diets to effect a change in their body shape or size. Moreover, regardless of the direction of desired weight change, unhealthy dieting practices, including restricted or excessive intake, yo-yo dieting, and excessive exercise practices in very young children deserve additional attention. These weight-control behaviors may have serious health complications and may ultimately result in eating disorders or obesity.

Despite the surprising findings in this area and the fact that adolescents report unhealthy dieting practices beginning at an early age, very little research has been aimed at identifying what influences young children to initiate unhealthy dieting behaviors. In addition, because children as early as first and second grade are cognizant of their body shapes and sizes and actively attempt to modify them, investigations into the earliest age at which children become aware of societal preferences toward thinness and attempt to control their body shape and size may offer insights into early diagnosis of eating disorders and strategies for curtailing eating disorders and obesity.

CONCLUSION

The literature about physical self-concept is, for the most part, dated. A large proportion of the literature cited in this chapter was produced in the 1960s and 1970s. This is troubling because societal pressures and influences change over time. Investigators must only look so far as the pages of popular fashion magazines to witness the great extent to which the ideal figure, particularly for females, has changed in the past 30 years. Garner, Garfinkel, Schwartz, and Thompson (1980) surveyed *Playboy* centerfolds and Miss America pageant contestants from 1960 to 1978. For this 18-year time frame, the authors came to the overwhelming conclusion that as "the prevailing female role models have been getting thinner, the average women of a similar age have become heavier" (p. 490). Moreover, Bruch (1978) has indicated that the notions established by the fashion industry that weight control, equivalent to self-control, can result in beauty may particularly affect vulnerable adolescents. Younger children are not oblivious to these societal influences, either. In fact, Feldman, Feldman, and Goodman (1988) suggested that children are influenced by societal ideals of attractiveness before adolescence and that prepubertal girls find thinness desirable. The degree to which societal pressures to achieve an ideal body shape and size influence very young children to undertake unhealthy and potentially dangerous dieting practices should receive additional attention.

The assessment devices available to measure physical self-concept in young children are also lacking. Two of the most popular measures, the TSCS and the Pier-Harris were both developed in the 1960s. They are also part of another difficulty in assessing this area. Along with the majority of assessment devices, they were not intended to assess physical self-concept. The physical self-concept subdomains assessed by these instruments are simply part of the larger scale and were not intended for use independent of the overall scale. These subsets of physical self-concept items have not received adequate attention as to their psychometric properties to warrant their independent use. In some instances, these item sets have proven to possess inadequate psychometric properties and should not be used independently of the overall scale. In addition to these psychometric weaknesses, only one measure, the CPSS, is appropriate for use with children with less than a third-grade reading level.

Perhaps the most glaring controversy in the literature pertains to the issue of the multidimensional nature of the construct physical self-concept. Support for the multidimensional nature of the construct of physical self-concept comes from Franzoi and Shields (1984) and Marsh (1986) who suggest three and two factors, respectively. However, Bracken and colleagues (1992) found only a single factor for physical self-concept in their factor analysis of five multidimensional self-concept instruments. In addition, Bracken (1992) revealed high correlations between Marsh's SDQ physical self-concept subscales and the physical subscale of the MSCS. More attention should be paid to this issue to ensure the development of interventions appropriately based on specific physical self-concept needs.

Because very few instruments assess the extent to which children attempt to modify their body size and shape, prior factor analyses of the physical self-concepts of children have not included the hypothesized subscale of weight control. This area should receive additional attention as both a possible additional subscale of physical self-concept and an important indicator of the development of potentially negative dieting behaviors in children.

Future research may also endeavor to examine the relationship between physical self-concept and global self-concept over time. If physical self-concept is one of the primary building blocks for global self-concept among children, as has been suggested, then researchers should not exclude the development of children's physical self-concepts from consideration. Research on physical self-concept may enable practitioners to intervene before a child's poor physical self-image can negatively affect his or her developing global self-concept. Longitudinal physical self-concept investigations may also offer insights into which children are most vulnerable for eating disorders and obesity. Moreover, longitudinal investigations of handicapped children may be useful to determine whether physical self-concept has the same effect on global self-concept in this population as in the nonhandicapped population. Finally, physical and special education programs developed for handicapped children could be assessed over time to determine the impact of such programs on the physical self-concepts of children in these populations.

REFERENCES

Abraham, S. F., & Beaumont, P. J. (1982). How patients describe bulimia or binge-eating. *Psychological Medicine, 12,* 625–635.

Adams, G. R. (1977). Physical attractiveness, personality, and social reactions to peer pressure. *Journal of Psychology, 96,* 287–296.

Bakker, F. C. (1988). Personality differences between young dancers and non-dancers. *Personality and Individual Differences, 9,* 121–131.

Berland, N. W., Thompson, J. K., & Linton, P. H. (1986). Correlation between the EAT-26 and the EAT-40, the Eating Disorders Inventory, and the Restrained Eating Inventory. *International Journal of Eating Disorders, 5,* 569–574.

Birtchnell, S. A., Dolan, B. M., & Lacey, H. J. (1987). Body image distortion in noneating disordered women. *International Journal of Eating Disorders, 6,* 385–391.

Bracken, B. A. (1992). *Multidimensional Self Concept Scale.* Austin, TX: Pro-Ed

Bracken, B. A., Bunch, S., Keith, T. Z., & Keith, P. B. (1992). *Multidimensional self-concept: A five instrument factor analysis.* Paper presented at the 100th annual conference of the American Psychological Association, Washington, DC.

Bruch, H. (1978). *The golden cage.* Cambridge: Harvard University Press.

Cash, T. F., & Brown, T. A. (1987). Body-image in anorexia nervosa and bulemia nervosa: A review of the literature. *Behavior Modification, 11,* 487–521.

Centers, L., & Centers, R. (1963). Peer group attitudes toward the amputic child. *Journal of Social Psychology, 23,* 33–39.

Clifford, E. (1971). Body satisfaction in adolescence. *Perceptual and Motor Skills, 33,* 119–125.

Cohen, S. (1977). *Special people.* Englewood Cliffs, NJ: Prentice-Hall.

Collins, M. E. (1991). Body figure perceptions and preferences among preadolescent children. *International Journal of Eating Disorders, 10,* 199–208.

Cornell, D. G., Pelton, G. M., Bassin, L. E., Landrum, M., Ramsay, S. G., Cooley, M. R., Lynch, K. A., & Hamrick, E. (1990). Self-concept and peer status among gifted program youth. *Journal of Educational Psychology, 82,* 456–463.

Crandall, R. (1973). The measurement of self-esteem and related constructs. In J. P. Robinson & P. R. Shaver (Eds.), *Measures of social psychological attitudes* (2nd ed.). Ann Arbor, MI: Institute for Social Research.

Fairburn, C. G., Peveler, R. C., Jones, R., Hope, R. A., & Doll, H. A. (1993). Predictors of 12-month outcome in bulemia nervosa and the influence of attitudes to shape and weight. *Journal of Consulting and Clinical Psychology, 61,* 696–698.

Feldman, W., Feldman, E., & Goodman, J. T. (1988). Culture versus biology: Children's attitudes toward thinness and fatness. *Pediatrics, 81,* 190–194.

Fisher, S., & Cleveland, S. E. (1968). *Body image and personality.* (rev. ed.). New York: Dover Publications.

Fitts, W. H. (1965). *Tennessee Self-Concept Scale Manual.* Nashville, TN: Counselor Recordings and Tests.

Fleming, J. S., & Courtney, B. E. (1984). The dimensionality of self-esteem: II. Heirarchical facet model for revised measurement scales. *Journal of Personality and Social Psychology, 46,* 404–421.

Franzoi, S. L., & Shields, S. A. (1984). The Body Esteem Scale: Multidimensional structure and sex differences in a college population. *Journal of Personality Assessment, 48,* 173–178.

Garner, D. M., Garfinkel, P. E., Schwartz, D., & Thompson, M. (1980). Cultural expectations of thinness in women. *Psychological Reports, 47,* 483–491.

Garner, D. M., Olmsted, M. P., Bohr, Y., & Garfinkle, P. E. (1982). The Eating Attitudes Test: Psychometric features and clinical correlates. *Psychological Medicine, 12,* 871–878.

Garrison, W. M., & Tesch, S. C. (1978). Self-concept and deafness: A review of research literature. *Volta Review, 80,* 457–466.

Glaser, H. H., Harrison, G. S., & Lynn, D. B. (1964). Emotional implications of congenital heart disease in children. *Pediatrics, 33,* 367–379.

Goodman, H., Richardson, S., Dornbusch, S., & Hastorf, A. (1963). Variant reactions to physical disabilities. *American Sociological Review, 28,* 249.

Harter, S. (1985). *Manual for the Self-Perception Profile for Children.* Denver, CO: University of Denver.

Harter, S. (1988). *Manual for the Self-Perception Profile for Adolescents.* Denver, CO: Author.

Harvey, D. H. P., & Greenway, A. P. (1984). The self-concept of physically handicapped children and their nonhandicapped siblings: An empirical investigation. *Journal of Child Psychology and Psychiatry, 25,* 273–284.

Hatfield, E., & Sprecher, S. (1986). *Mirror, mirror . . . The importance of looks in everyday life.* Albany, NY: State University of New York Press.

Haywood, J. T. (1980). *The relationship of self-concept and attitudes toward physical education of freshman students in a private church-related university.* Unpublished doctoral dissertation, University of Alabama.

Heaps, R. A. (1978). Relating physical and psychological fitness: A psychological point of view. *Journal of Sports Medicine and Physical Fitness, 18,* 399–408.

Hill-Beuf, A., & Porter, J. D. R. (1984). Children coping with impaired appearance: Social and psychological influences. *General Hospital Psychiatry, 6,* 294–301.

Hopper, C. (1988). Self-concept and motor performance of hearing impaired boys and girls. *Adapted Physical Activity Quarterly, 5,* 293–304.

Horn, J. (1975). Reactions to the handicapped—Sweaty palms and saccharine words. *Psychology Today, 9,* 122–124.

Jaffe, A. C., & Singer, L. T. (1989). Atypical eating disorders in children. *International Journal of Eating Disorders, 8,* 575–582.

Keller, A., Ford, L. H., & Meacham, J. A. (1978). Dimensions of self-concept in preschool children. *Developmental Psychology, 14,* 483–489.

Kinn, W. T. (1964). Self-concept of the physically handicapped and nonhandicapped children. *Dissertation Abstracts, 24,* 5196–5197.

Klesges, R. C., Haddock, C. K. Stein, R. S., Klesges, L. M., Eck, L. H., & Hanson, C. L. (1992). Relationship between psychosocial functioning and body fat in preschool children: A longitudinal investigation. *Journal of Consulting and Clinical Psychology, 60,* 793–796.

Kolin, I., Scherzer, A., New, B., & Garfield, M. (1971). Studies of the school age child with meningomyelocele: Social and emotional adaptation. *Journal of Pediatrics, 78,* 1013–1019.

Kreitler, S., & Kreitler, H. (1988). Body-image: The dimension of size. *Genetic, Social, and General Psychology Monographs, 114,* 7–32.

Lawler, R. H., Nahiulrey, W., & Wright, N. (1966). Psychological implications of cystic fibrosis. *Canadian Medical Association Journal, 94,* 1043–1046.

Lerner, R. M., & Karabenick, S. A. (1974). Physical attractiveness, body attitudes, and self-concept in late adolescents. *Journal of Youth and Adolescence, 3,* 307–316.

Lerner, R. M., Karabenick, S. A., & Stuart, J. L. (1973). Relations among physical attractiveness, body attitudes, and self-concept in male and female college students. *Journal of Psychology, 85,* 119–129.

Lerner, R. M., Orlos, J. B., & Knapp, J. R. (1976). Physical attractiveness, physical effectiveness, and self-concept on late adolescents. *Adolescence, 11,* 313–326.

Loro, A. D., & Orleans, C. S. (1981). Binge eating in obesity: Preliminary findings and guidelines for behavioral analysis and treatment. *Addictive Behaviors, 6,* 155–166.

Magill, J., & Hurlbut, N. (1986). The self-esteem of adolescents with cerebral palsy. *American Journal of Occupational Therapy, 40,* 402–407.

Maloney, M. J., McGuire, J. B., & Daniels, S. R. (1988). Reliability testing of a children's version of the Eating Attitude Test. *Journal of the American Academy of Child and Adolescent Psychiatry, 27,* 541–543.

Markus, H., Hamill, R., & Sentis, K. P. (1987). Thinking fat: Self-schemas for body weight and the processing of weight relevant information. *Journal of Applied Social Psychology, 17,* 50–71.

Marsh, H. W. (1986). *The Self-Description Questionnaire (SDQ): A theoretical and empirical basis for the measurement of multiple dimensions of preadolescent self-concept: A test manual and a research monograph.* Faculty of Education, University of Sydney, NSW Australia.

Marsh, H. W., & Jackson, S. A. (1986). Multidimensional self-concepts, masculinity, and femininity as a function of women's involvement in athletics. *Sex Roles, 15,* 391–415.

Marsh, H. W., Parker, J., & Barnes, J. (1985). Multidimensional adolescent self-concepts: Their relationship to age, sex, and academic measures. *American Educational Research Journal, 22,* 422–444.

Marsh, H. W., & Peart, N. D. (1988). Competitive and cooperative physical fitness training for girls: Effects on physical fitness and multidimensional self-concepts. *Journal of Sports and Exercise Psychology, 10,* 390–407.

Mathes, E. W., & Kahn, A. (1975). Physical attractiveness, happiness, neuroticism, and self-esteem. *Journal of Psychology, 90,* 27–30.

McDaniel, J. W. (1976). *Physical disability and human behavior* (2nd ed.). Don Mills, Ontario: Pergamon.

McGuire, W. J., & Padaiver-Singer, A. (1976). Trait salience in the spontaneous self-concept. *Journal of Personality and Social Psychology, 33,* 743–754.

Mellin, L. M. (1988). Responding to disordered eating in children and adolescents. *Nutrition News, 51,* 5–7.

Mendelson, B. K., & White, D. R. (1982). Relation between body-esteem and self-esteem of obese and normal children. *Perceptual and Motor Skills, 54,* 899–905.

Newcomb, A. F., & Bukowski, W. M. (1983). Social impact and social preference as determinants of children's peer group status. *Developmental Psychology, 19,* 856–867.

Olgas, M. (1974). The relationship between parents' health status and body image of their children. *Nursing Research, 23,* 319–323.

Piers, E. V., & Harris, D. B. (1969). *The Piers-Harris Children's Self-Concept Scale.* Los Angeles: Western Psychological Services.

Pomerantz, S. C. (1979). Sex differences in the relative importance of self-esteem, physical self-satisfaction, and identity in predicting adolescent satisfaction. *Journal of Youth and Adolescence, 8,* 51–61.

Pyle, R. L., Mitchell, J. E., & Lokert, E. D. (1981). Bulimia: A report of 34 cases. *Journal of Clinical Psychiatry, 42,* 60–64.

Resnick, M. D. (1986). The social construction of disability. In R. W. Blum (Ed.), *Chronic illness and disabilities in childhood and adolescence.* Orlando, FL: Grune and Stratton.

Riley, J. H. (1983). The relationship of self-concept with physical estimation and physical performance for preadolescent boys and girls. *Journal of Early Adolescences, 3,* 327–333.

Roid, G. H., & Fitts, W. H. (1989). *Tennessee Self-Concept Scale, Revised manual.* Los Angeles: Western Psychological Services.

Rosenberg, M. (1965). *Society and the adolescent child.* Princeton, NJ: Princeton University Press.

Ruff, G. A., & Barrios, B. A. (1986). Realistic assessment of body image. *Behavioral Assessment, 8,* 237–252.

Ryckman, R. M., Robbins, M. A., Thornton, B., & Cantrell, P. (1982). Development and validation of a physical self-efficacy scale. *Journal of Personality and Social Psychology, 42,* 891–900.

Schecter, M. D. (1961). The orthopaedically handicapped child: Emotional reactions. *Archives of General Psychiatry, 4,* 247–253.

Shavelson, R. J., Hubner, J. J., & Stanton, G. C. (1976). Self-concept: Validation of construct interpretation. *Review of Educational Research, 46,* 407–441.

Shears, L. M., & Jensoma, C. J. (1969). Social acceptability of anomalous persons. *Exceptional Children, 36,* 91–96.

Sherrill, C., Hinson, M., Gench, B., Kennedy, S. O., & Low, L. (1990). Self-concepts of disabled youth athletes. *Perceptual and Motor Skills, 70,* 1093–1098.

Siller, J., Ferguson, L., Vann, D., & Holland, B. (1968). Structure of attitudes toward the physically disabled: The disability factor scale: Amputation, blindness, cosmetic conditions. *Proceedings of the 76th Annual Convention of the American Psychological Association,* 651–652.

Simmons, R. G., & Rosenberg, F. (1975). Sex, sex-roles, and self-image. *Journal of Youth and Adolescence, 4,* 229–258.

Sonstroem, R. J. (1974). Attitude testing examining certain psychological correlates of physical activity. *Research Quarterly, 45,* 93–103.

Sonstroem, R. J. (1976). The validity of self-perceptions regarding physical and athletic ability. *Medicine and Science in Sports, 8,* 126–132.

Staffieri, J. R. (1967). A study of social stereotype of body-image in children. *Journal of Personality and Social Psychology, 7,* 101–104.

Stein, R. J., Bracken, B. A., Shadish, W., & Haddock, C. K. (1995). *The development of the Children's Physical Self-Concept Scale.* Manuscript submitted for publication.

Stunkard, A. J., Sorenson, T., & Schulsinger, F. (1983). Use of the Danish adoption register for the study of obesity and thinness. In S. Kety, L. P. Rowland, R. L. Sidman, & S. N. Matthysse (Eds.), *The genetics of neurological and psychiatric disorders.* New York: Raven Press.

Thornton, B., & Ryckman, R. M. (1991). Relationship between physical attractiveness, physical effectiveness, and self-esteem: A cross-sectional analysis among adolescents. *Journal of Adolescence, 14,* 85–98.

Tucker, R. C. (1975). *Self-concept and physical achievement: Boys in an abilities grouped versus a traditional physical education program.* Unpublished Doctoral dissertation, University of Oregon.

Wardle, J., & Foley, E. (1989). Body image: Stability and sensitivity of body satisfaction and body size estimation. *International Journal of Eating Disorders, 8,* 55–62.

Wright, B. (1960). *Physical disability: A psychological approach.* New York: Harper & Row.

CHAPTER 10

The Influence of Age, Race, and Gender on Child and Adolescent Multidimensional Self-Concept

R. MICHELLE CRAIN

With the advent of increasingly sophisticated theoretical conceptualizations of self-concept and the more psychometrically sound instruments stemming from them (e.g., Bracken, 1992; Harter, 1982; Marsh, 1988; Shavelson, Hubner, & Stanton, 1976), researchers interested in the self-concepts of children and adolescents are in an excellent position to clarify and perhaps lay to rest some of the fundamental issues involved in understanding the nature of children's beliefs about themselves and their behaviors.

Three such issues are the extent to which children's global and multidimensional self-concepts are influenced by their age, gender, and racial/ethnic characteristics. Traditionally, there have been reasons to suggest that self-concept might vary as a function of these most basic human characteristics. Because certain important constructs such as social cognition (Shantz, 1983), moral development (Kohlberg, 1969), and conservation ability (Piaget, 1936/1952) are at least in part dependent on cognitive maturation, we might expect cognitive maturation also to influence self-concept development (e.g., moving from a concrete to an abstract description of the self, experiencing new contexts as one ages). Additionally, because psychosocial traits associated with males (e.g., leadership) have traditionally been viewed as more socially desirable than traits associated with females (e.g., nurturance) (Rosenkrantz, Vogel, Bee, Broverman, & Broverman, 1968), it might be hypothesized that females in general would have lower self-concepts than males (Hanes, Prawat, & Grissom, 1979). The individual's membership in racial or ethnic groups might also be expected to affect self-concept, because members of minorities may not compare their attributes automatically to the Anglo majority but rather to others who have similar cultural expectations and living experiences (see Hughes & Demo, 1989; Porter & Washington, 1979).

395

Previous research has tended to examine these three variables incidentally (or not at all), because the relationship between self-concept and other constructs (e.g., intelligence, achievement) or conditions (e.g., disabilities, giftedness, peer rejection) has typically been paramount in the literature (Osborne & LeGette, 1982). Moreover, many of the studies that *have* specifically examined demographic variables relative to self-concept have suffered from numerous conceptual and methodological flaws (see Wylie, 1979, 1989).

The assertion in this chapter, however, is that age, race, and gender influences on child and adolescent self-concept should be primary rather than incidental concerns among investigators. There is both a theoretical and a practical basis for this assertion. The theoretical basis concerns the equivalence of the self-concept construct across various groups of students with differing characteristics that can be construed as either *constitutional* or *acquired.* Constitutional characteristics are those that are fixed, such as the person's age or membership in a particular gender or ethnic group; as used in this chapter, constitutional characteristics refer specifically to these three status variables. Acquired characteristics, on the other hand, refer to any number of descriptors or exceptional groups to which a student may belong. This term includes referents that are commonly used to describe groups of children such as learning-disabled, peer-rejected, gifted, delinquent, emotionally disturbed, and so on.

An individual is typically described as having certain "foundational" qualities—what age he or she is, the fact that the individual *is* a he or a she, and sometimes the racial group to which the person belongs—before being described in other, less basic, terms. For example, you are likely to identify a child as male and Hispanic before identifying him as emotionally disturbed or gifted. Constitutional characteristics, then, are those that provide "starting points" for describing a particular person or groups of people (e.g., males, African Americans, 12-year-olds). Acquired characteristics are those that extend *across* the constitutional characteristics of age, race, and gender (e.g., 14-year-old Native American females who are "gifted").

This conceptualization of an individual's characteristics as either constitutional or acquired has important implications for the study of self-concept. First, it suggests that it may be beneficial to investigate self-concept in a hierarchical fashion, beginning with constitutional characteristics, followed by the interaction between constitutional and acquired characteristics. That is, status characteristics (alone as well as in combination), because of their foundational and fixed nature, should be subjected *first* to investigators' scrutiny. The equivalence of the self-concept construct among children and adolescents of different developmental levels, ethnic backgrounds, and genders must be understood before other, less foundational variables are studied. Once a better understanding is gained as to how the constitutional characteristics and their interactions are related to children's self-concepts, investigators can then use this knowledge as a "starting point" when studying the self-concepts of children with various acquired characteristics.

The second implication of the constitutional-acquired conceptualization, aside from its contribution to a better understanding of the self-concept construct, is its contribution to the efficacy of clinical and educational interventions. Because a major goal of education is to enhance and maintain positive self-concepts, it becomes important to discern how students' self-concepts might differ as a function of constitutional characteristics. If systematic differences exist across one or more of these characteristics, then assessment and intervention approaches can subsequently be modified or redesigned to be more responsive to students' needs.

Another practical reason for the assertion that age, race, and gender should be of primary interest among self-concept researchers is related to the development of an instrument's normative standards. Test authors must determine whether their instruments produce systematic age, race, and/or gender differences based on examinees' responses. If such differences exist, it then becomes imperative for validity purposes that separate norms be developed for the various student subgroups. If no such differences exist, a single collective normative group is most appropriate.

Although studying the effects of status is important, it is critical to determine how these variables interact with each other and with acquired characteristics and life experiences to influence both general and domain-specific self-concept. Should repeated investigations with psychometrically sound instruments find consistent and replicable status differences, researchers can then focus on what *aspects* of development associated with that status (e.g., school experiences, puberty, parent-adolescent conflict, transitions, expectations of significant others) are related to differences in self-concept. If age, race, and gender per se have little influence on child and adolescent self-concept, then investigators can delve more deeply into the competence, social, affective, academic, family, and physical aspects (see Chapter 12 for a discussion of the multifaceted nature of self-concept) of children's and adolescents' environments that govern self-concept development.

FOCUS OF THIS CHAPTER

This chapter will focus on the extant literature regarding differences in self-concept that may be attributed to the age, race, and gender groups to which children and adolescents belong. This chapter is not meant to be an exhaustive review of the many thousands of studies on self-concept (or self-esteem) that appear in the literature; several comprehensive reviews in this regard already exist (see Meece, Parsons, Kaczala, Goff, & Futterman, 1982; Porter & Washington, 1979; Wylie, 1979). The intent here is to highlight some of the representative studies focusing on age, race, and gender differences in self-concept that have appeared in the literature since Wylie's seminal work of 1979. The majority of the studies reviewed have emphasized global self-concept or self-esteem rather than context-dependent dimensions (e.g., family, physical, social). Although the preoccupation with global self-concept has given way in recent years to a multidimensional conceptualization, the generalizability of findings based on global self-concept to more specific facets has not yet been adequately tested (Marsh, 1991). The reader also should be aware that the terms *self-concept* and *self-esteem,* though treated by some investigators as conceptually and empirically distinct (e.g., Fleming & Courtney, 1984), are used interchangeably in this chapter as there appear to be no valid differences between the two terms (see Bracken, Bunch, Keith, & Keith, 1992; Shavelson, Hubner, & Stanton, 1976). Finally, the conclusion of this chapter will synthesize some of the most consistent and replicated findings regarding age, race, and gender differences in children's and adolescents' global and multidimensional self-concepts.

AGE DIFFERENCES IN SELF-CONCEPT

Do children's self-concepts change markedly as children themselves age, grow, change, and experience the world? Do adolescents enter a period of "storm and stress" whereby self-concept plummets and remains unstable for a number of years? These questions have been of great interest to investigators and to laypersons alike, although the focus here is not on the processes involved in self-concept development and maintenance but whether there are consistent, observable *differences* in children's self-concepts solely as a function of age. Hundreds of studies conducted prior to 1978 were reviewed by Wylie (1979), who concluded that there was no convincing evidence for any age-related effect, positive or negative, in global self-concept between the ages of 6 and 50 years. She concluded that virtually no systematic age effects existed when well known and good-quality self-concept instruments were used; whereas results were approximately equally divided between those showing increases, decreases, or stability in self-concept as a function of age when less well-known or poorly constructed instruments were used. Wylie also noted that investigations into specific self-concept domains (e.g., social, academic) were too inconsistent to warrant generalization. Fourteen years later, there is still relatively little research on specific facets of self-concept. Marsh and his colleagues as well as Harter and her colleagues are among those who have focused on both domain-specific and global self-concept, and some of their work will be reviewed here.

However, there *is* now much evidence that individuals ". . . do not typically go through a crisis, rebel against their elders, go through storm and stress, or have a torrid time . . ." during adolescence (Hattie, 1992, p. 132). Rather, researchers using more sophisticated theoretical models and more psychometrically sound instruments have concluded that age per se accounts for a very small proportion (less than 1%) of the variance in self-concept responses (Bracken, 1992; Marsh, Parker, & Barnes, 1985). Marsh (1991) does posit, however, that there is relatively strong support for a curvilinear age effect in global self-concept such that there is a decline during preadolescence, a reversal of this decline sometime during early or middle adolescence, and an increase in self-concept during late adolescence and early adulthood (Dusek & Flaherty, 1981; Marsh et al., 1985; Marsh, Smith, Marsh, & Owens, 1988; O'Malley & Bachman, 1983; Piers & Harris, 1964; Simmons, Rosenberg, & Rosenberg, 1973). He noted that although empirical support for this curvilinear effect was mixed, no study has found an *increase* in self-concept during preadolescence. Rosenberg (1985) also has argued cogently that disturbance of the self-image is most acute during early adolescence (although levels of general self-esteem do not decline as a function of age), a finding consistent with the preceding conclusions.

Marsh (1989, 1991) appropriately qualified his conclusions regarding the curvilinear effects of age on self-concept by noting that the studies he reviewed considered only a narrow range of ages within the preadolescent to early-adult period, or sampled only a few ages within this range. Furthermore, few of the considered studies met the stringent methodological criteria specified by Wylie (1979), and finally, he noted that it is not possible to generalize findings regarding overall self-concept to specific facets or dimensions of self-concept. Much more work is needed to determine whether such a curvilinear age effect really exists when psychometrically sound, multidimensional self-concept instruments are used, and if so, whether the purported "dip" in self-concept scores during early adolescence is meaningful in terms of educational efforts to enhance students' self-concepts.

In our own large-scale cross-sectional study (Crain & Bracken, 1994) of over 2,500 American students with the Multidimensional Self Concept Scale (MSCS; Bracken, 1992), we found statistically significant mean differences in global self-concept across the 9- to 19-year age range, such that 10- and 11-year-olds' (preadolescents as inferred from Marsh et al.'s work) global self-concepts were significantly *higher* than those of 16-year-olds. Also, 10-year-olds' global self-concepts were significantly higher than those of 15-year-olds. However, we questioned whether these differences were qualitatively meaningful, as the largest score difference for these four age groups (that of 10- vs. 16-year-olds) was less than one-half of their average standard deviation.

For the six domain-specific areas of self-concept measured by the MSCS, age had no significant effect. As a further test of the strength of the relationship between chronological age and level of self-concept, we calculated Pearson product moment correlations (Crain & Bracken, 1994). The age-raw score correlations for the MSCS scales were Social, .07; Competence, −.03; Affect, −.04; Academic, −.11; Family, −.11; Physical, −.07; and Total Scale, −.06. These essentially zero-level correlations further suggested that very little developmental progression or regression in self-concept occurs as a function of age, and that the differences that do exist appear to be more a result of chance variation (Bracken, 1992).

Marsh and colleagues have investigated age differences in a somewhat younger sample in their cross-sectional research with the Self-Description Questionnaire, I (SDQI; Marsh, 1988) (e.g., Marsh, 1984, 1989; Marsh, Barnes, Cairns, & Tidman, 1984; Marsh et al., 1985; Marsh et al., 1988) that suggests a steady linear decline in global and context-specific self-concepts between Grades 2 and 5. Marsh et al. (1984) reported a drop in six of the seven SDQI scales (Physical Appearance, Physical Ability, Peer Relationships, Parent Relationships, Reading, Mathematics, General School) and in all three global scores (Academic, Nonacademic, and General Self) across this age range. The Parent Relationships scale showed no effects of age, and for Peer Relationships there was a nonlinear effect in which self-concepts decreased from Grade 2 to Grade 4, but increased in Grade 5. However, the declines found in this study were only moderate and represented a drop of about one-third standard deviation (Marsh et al., 1984). It is unclear whether such differences can be ascribed to American students without further research, as virtually all the research conducted with the SDQ series of instruments has been conducted with Australian students; differences between Australian and American students may very well exist in terms of cultural traditions and educational contexts (e.g., many Australian students leave school after 10th grade, whereas American students generally attend school for two more years).

Dusek and Flaherty (1981), utilizing a sophisticated longitudinal-sequential design with a large sample ($N = 1,632$), found little longitudinal evidence for age effects in multiple dimensions of self-concept from Grades 5 through 12. The instrument of choice was a semantic-differential scale developed by Monge (1975) that was posited to consist of four factors: adjustment; masculinity/femininity; achievement/leadership; and congeniality/sociability. All four factors were stable across the age span studied. The age effects found in their cross-sectional analyses were significant but tended to be small and inconsistent across the three age cohorts they considered. Dusek and Flaherty concluded that self-concept during adolescence develops in a stable and continuous manner, with changes occurring slowly, gradually, and only at the individual student level. This study has many fine methodological qualities, although the instrument used could be considered problematic (see Wylie, 1979); the major contribution of this study was its portrayal of multidimensional adolescent self-concept as a stable, robust construct.

O'Malley and Bachman (1983) have directed their research efforts to discovering what happens to self-concept (they use the term *self-esteem*) during late adolescence and early adulthood (see also Bachman & O'Malley, 1977). Using large, national samples of students ranging in age from 13 to 23, they report longitudinal data that show a definite increase in general self-esteem (measured by some items of Rosenberg's (1965) scale) in the late adolescent years. However, this "definite increase" in self-esteem was a marginal change at best, accounting for an average increase of $\frac{1}{10}$ to $\frac{1}{12}$ standard deviation each year in the first four years after high school. The authors reviewed other research that supported their claim (e.g., McCarthy & Hoge, 1982; National Opinion Research Center, 1980) as well. The question becomes, what does this amount of change signify? Is it meaningful in practice? To suggest that the "burden of proof . . . has shifted to those who would deny the reality of that rise" (p. 257) seems somewhat overstated in light of these small differences. Moreover, Marsh and Shavelson (1985) and Marsh, Byrne, and Shavelson (1988) have argued that self-concept cannot be adequately understood if its multidimensionality is ignored, as was the case in the O'Malley and Bachman (1983) study.

In an effort to cover the entire period from preadolescence to early adulthood, Marsh (1989) summarized data from 12,266 Australian students who composed the normative groups for the SDQI (preadolescence), SDQII (early and middle adolescence), and SDQIII (late adolescence and early adulthood) instruments. For preadolescent (Grades 2–9) responses to the SDQI, there was a linear decline in self-concept with age for all scales and for the total score that occurred for both boys and girls.

For the early and middle adolescent responses to the SDQII (Grades 7–11), there was a reasonably consistent quadratic effect such that self-concept was relatively higher in Grade 7, declined in Grades 8 and 9 (after the transition to high school in Grade 7 for Australian students), and then increased in Grades 10 and 11. The effect was significant for 8 of the 11 scales and for the total score, and occurred for both boys and girls. However, the linear effects were not as consistent as were the quadratic effects: The former were positive for some scales (e.g., Physical Appearance) and negative for others (e.g., Physical Abilities, Parents), and the total score effect was not linear. Furthermore, the variance explained by age in the SDQII data was reportedly much smaller than in either the SDQI or SDQIII data (Marsh, 1989). In late adolescence and early adulthood (SDQIII), there was a reasonably consistent increase in self-concepts with age as measured by 11 of the 13 SDQIII scales (with positive effects for 9 of these scales and for the total score).

Although the work of Marsh and his colleagues spans a broad age range and is derived from a rich database, it is notable that age-raw score correlations are not reported in their studies. Age trends not only can be measured by mean score comparisons of responses to multidimensional self-concept instruments but also can be determined even more foundationally by the computation of age-raw score correlations (Bracken, 1992). It is somewhat surprising that Marsh and colleagues do not give equal weight to this method of data analysis in their investigations.

Drawing on his conclusions from the age-related findings presented earlier, Marsh (1989) pointed out that the presumed decline in self-concept occurring during preadolescence and early adolescence should not necessarily be construed as "bad" or be blamed on society or the educational system. Indeed, it may be that very young children have unrealistically high self-concepts, and that the decline in scores found during preadolescence may merely suggest a more realistic, objective view of self that occurs as a result of cognitive maturation and additional life experience. Supporting this hypothesis are Stipek's (1981) findings that children's self-perceptions of their "smartness" dropped between kindergarten and third grade; she concluded that children are merely more objective in their ratings as they get older because they have learned to incorporate external feedback into their self-perceptions.

In a recent effort to clarify the structure of multidimensional self-concept in young children (a group typically underrepresented in self-concept research), Marsh, Craven, and Debus (1991) used a modified version of the SDQI with children between the ages of 5 and 8 years. One of the major purposes of the study was to test Harter's (1983) claim that general or global self-concept does not exist before the age of 8. Another purpose was to determine how the factor structure of self-concept varies in the age range of 5 to 8 years (do the same factors appear that have been found with older children?). Marsh et al. (1991) also examined age and gender differences in self-concept for these young children.

Several interesting and important findings emerged from this study, paramount of which was that all eight factors of the SDQI (Physical Ability, Physical Appearance, Peer Relationships, Parent Relationships, Reading, Mathematics, General School, and General Self) were present among this young sample, even the kindergarteners. Age was significantly related to three of the scales: Physical Appearance, Peer Relations, and General School. Only the linear effect of age was significant and was such that self-concept declined from kindergarten to third grade. However, it is notable that none of the age effects (alone or in combination with other variables) accounted for more than 2% of the variance in responses, rendering age a modest moderator variable at best. Additionally, as Stipek (1981) noted, there may be no "decline" in self-concept at all, but rather a sharpening of cognitive skills that lead to more accurate self-perception.

Marsh et al. (1991) concluded that their findings cast doubt on previous assumptions that context-specific self-concept factors are not well defined in early childhood (e.g., Harter & Pike, 1984), and that a general self-concept factor does not exist in children younger than 8 years of age

(Harter, 1983; Harter & Pike, 1984; Silon & Harter, 1985). Certainly, further examination of very young children's multidimensional self-concepts is a fruitful topic for future investigators.

EFFECTS OF AGE ON SELF-CONCEPT: SUMMARY AND IMPLICATIONS

There is as yet no coherent picture of age effects in multidimensional self-concepts of children and adolescents. One major reason for the ambiguity has been the almost exclusive focus on global rather than domain-specific self-concept. Much more intriguing than age differences in global self-concept is the notion that specific domains of self-concept may differ as a function of age. For example, age seems to have no bearing on children's and adolescents' self-concepts of their relationships with their parents (Crain & Bracken, 1994; Marsh, 1989; Walker & Greene, 1986), although children's ratings of the *quality* of their parent-child relationships definitely take a turn for the worse with the advent of midadolescence (Bracken & Crain, 1994; Furman & Buhrmester, 1992). However, these seemingly contradictory findings are not difficult to reconcile. For example, although adolescents may have occasionally volatile conflicts with their parents and tend to turn more toward peers for support/companionship (contributing to the lower ratings of the *interpersonal quality* of the parent-child relationship), most maintain positive self-perceptions regarding their own valuable roles within their families (contributing to the stability of adolescents' *self-concept* of the parent-child relationship).

In other self-concept domains, age may very well play a minor role. For example, age appears to affect children's perceptions of their *abilities* as they progress to higher grade levels, although the general conclusion has been that it is not being a particular age that causes the decline but rather cognitive maturation that allows children access to external feedback to evaluate their performance in different areas (Marsh, 1989; Stipek, 1981). Additionally, although there may be a small statistical increase in global self-concept (or "self-esteem") from late adolescence to early adulthood (e.g., Marsh, 1989; O'Malley & Bachman, 1983), authors have been hard put to explain the broader meaningfulness of what appears to be a very slight change. Zero-order correlations between students' ages and their raw scores on self-concept instruments, such as those found in the Crain and Bracken (1994) study, further support the hypothesis that there is negligible developmental progression or regression of multidimensional self-concept. Longitudinal research may well uncover clinically meaningful age-related differences in children's views of themselves, but for now, it seems warranted to say that age is essentially a weak moderator of domain-specific self-concepts at best.

RACE DIFFERENCES IN SELF-CONCEPT

The idea that persons of racial/ethnic minority status may differ from the white majority in levels of self-concept has received a great deal of attention over the past 50 years (see Porter & Washington, 1979; Wylie, 1979). By far, the most extensively studied groups have been whites and blacks, with only a minute proportion of research devoted to investigation of self-concept among other ethnic minority groups. Fortunately, corresponding to the rapidly changing demographics of the U.S. student population, interest in this line of research appears to be increasing. As with age differences, studies of race differences in children's self-concepts have focused almost exclusively on global self-concept. Because self-concept has been demonstrated again and again to be multidimensional, it is imperative for researchers to address domain-specific self-concepts of students with varying racial/ethnic characteristics, as well as to consider the personal and social processes that may underlie their development and maintenance.

Early investigations into racial differences in self-concept were plagued by a host of methodological problems, not the least of which was the technical quality of the self-concept instruments used (a problem that persists in self-concept research to this day). Many researchers claimed that white students had higher self-concepts than black students (Osborne & LeGette, 1982; Stenner & Katzenmeyer, 1976; Trowbridge, 1972), while just as many others claimed that black students' self-concepts were not low but were actually *higher* than those of whites (Lay & Wakstein, 1985; Powers et al., 1971). Still others found no differences between student groups (e.g., Hirsch & Rapkin, 1987; Zirkel & Moses, 1971). Early findings, based as they were on students' responses to psychometrically inadequate instruments, generated considerable debate on what societal processes were responsible for one group's self-concept being higher than another's. Psychological research on black-white self-concept has in fact been criticized for not successfully addressing the complex social contexts in which self-concept develops (Porter & Washington, 1979). For example, in most early research, socioeconomic status (SES) was seldom viewed as a mediating variable. Now, however, as many studies have shown that racial differences in self-concept are confounded when SES is not taken into consideration, it is critical to include it in present-day research (see Grant & Sleeter, 1986). In fact, a number of investigators have suggested that social class is a more powerful predictor of self-concept than race itself (Gordon, 1969; Kohr, Coldiron, Skiffington, Masters, & Blust, 1988; Samuels, 1973; Yancey, Rigsby, & McCarthy, 1972).

Although early findings were inconsistent in direction and magnitude, the bulk of research in this area now appears to support the position that black individuals do not report lower levels of global self-concept than do whites when the effects of SES are controlled (see Porter & Washington, 1979). There does remain some difference of opinion whether blacks report self-concept at a level equal to or higher than that of whites. As stated earlier, however, most studies in this regard have concentrated on global or overall self-concept, and scant attention has been paid to how students of differing racial and ethnic characteristics might respond to instruments utilizing domain-specific scales.

In our own study (Crain & Bracken, 1994), we found that black students reported significantly higher global self-concepts than did white or Hispanic students on the Multidimensional Self Concept Scale (Bracken, 1992). However, as the largest score difference between these three groups (i.e., black vs. Hispanic students) was less than one-third standard deviation, we surmised that belonging to a particular racial group had no great bearing on students' overall self-concept. In the subscale analysis, the only significant difference among racial groups was in physical self-concept. On this subscale of the MSCS, black students rated their physical self-concepts higher than did white or Hispanic students, albeit by less than one-third standard deviation. Thus, in this large-scale study, both global and domain-specific self-concepts appear to be relatively impervious to differences among students' ethnic backgrounds.

Other researchers have reported differences between black and white students on domain-specific scales. For example, Osborne and LeGette (1982) found that black adolescents reported lower academic self-concepts than did white adolescents on three different instruments, the Coopersmith Self-Esteem Inventory (SEI; Coopersmith, 1967), the Piers-Harris Children's Self-Concept Scale (Piers, 1969), and the Self-Concept of Ability Scale-General (SCA; Brookover, Paterson, & Thomas, 1962). Race differences also were found for the SEI global score and for the SEI Social Self score, with white students reporting higher self-concepts in these areas than did black students. However, these findings are questionable due to the small, geographically restricted sample as well as to the known psychometric weaknesses of the SEI (Wylie, 1989).

Oanh and Michael (1977) studied children of six ethnic groups (including Vietnamese, Asian [non-Vietnamese], and a group of children of mixed ethnicity) and found that black students scored higher than all other groups on the Piers-Harris Physical Appearance and Attributes scale. Vietnamese children tended to have the lowest domain-specific and global self-concepts, and black children tended to have the highest.

Mboya (1994) based the development of his own multidimensional self-concept scale, the Self-Description Inventory (SDI; Mboya, 1993), on the theoretical orientation espoused by Shavelson et al. (1976). The SDI has 8 scales (Relations with Family, General School, Physical Abilities, Physical Appearance, Emotional Stability, Music Ability, Relations with Peers, and Health) and has adequate psychometric properties. In his large cross-cultural study with black and white adolescents living in South Africa (ages 13–20 years), Mboya (1994) found that black adolescents reported higher self-concepts than whites in global self-concept, General School,

Physical Appearance, and Music Ability. White adolescents scored higher on Physical Abilities and Emotional Stability scales than did black adolescents. For the other three scales (Relations with Family, Relations with Peers, and Health), the effect of race was not statistically significant.

Although Mboya asserted that these differences were interpretable on racial bases, it was noted that the student samples were drawn from markedly different areas in terms of socioeconomic status. Specifically, the 814 black adolescents were from high schools that represented mostly poor and economically deprived working-class communities, whereas the 314 white adolescents were from high schools that served mostly middle-class communities. Mboya did not use SES as an independent variable; therefore, the racial effects may have been confounded by very real differences in social and economic characteristics of the two student groups. However, this study obviously is a welcome addition to investigations of multidimensional self-concept among children from varying racial/ethnic groups.

Although research with children from other racial/ethnic groups is quite rare, several studies have been conducted with Native American children. Long and Hamlin (1988) found that white children had higher overall self-concept scores on the Piers-Harris than did Native American children. Additionally, the P-H factor scores of behavior and school/intellectual status were higher for white than for Native American children. The authors hypothesized that Native American children's lower scores in these areas reflected an internalization of negative feedback from significant adults, including teachers, the majority of whom are white. However, they presented no empirical evidence to support this claim. Long and Hamlin also found that white and Native American children's self-concept scores were more similar within each school (they sampled four) than across schools by ethnic group, and suggested that responses to the P-H reflected the child's view of self within a given social context rather than one specifically determined by ethnicity.

Rotenberg and Cranwell (1989) believe that the lower scores of Native American children that have been found on conventional tests of self-esteem/self-concept (e.g., Halpin, Halpin, & Whiddon, 1981) are misleading because the attributes assessed by conventional instruments are important to the self-concepts of white children but not to the self-concepts of children from other cultures. In their study, they used an open self-description measure ("20 statements" test; Kuhn & McPartland, 1954) and a transformational measure of self-concept (Mohr, 1978) with Native American and white children in grades 3 through 6. (It should be noted for methodological purposes that the Native American children lived and attended school on their reservation, while the white children attended a public school.) The authors found that Native American children referred more frequently to kinship roles, traditional customs, beliefs, and moral worth in their open self-descriptions than did white children. Native American children also showed greater external orientation (i.e., physical ability) on both measures, which the authors hypothesized was due to the importance of nature and its mastery in Native American culture, causing the children to emphasize such external attributes as physical prowess in their self-concepts.

Some research has been conducted with Asian and Pacific American (APA) children with attention to global self-concept and to racial and physical self-concept (e.g., Fox & Jordan, 1973; Oanh & Michael, 1977). This and other research has shown that, in general, APA children's physical and racial self-concepts (i.e., racial identification and preference) appear to be more negative than those of white children and occasionally those of children in other ethnic groups, such as blacks (Chang, 1975). The physical self-concept of minority children may be crucial in that physical attributes of certain minority peoples are visibly distinctive from those of the white majority. Distinguishing features may include skin color, eye shape, hair color, facial configuration, and height—even when other features such as dress and speech are indistinguishable from those of the white majority.

In such a study, Pang, Mizokawa, Morishima, and Olstad (1989) used the Piers-Harris with 29 Japanese American children and 47 white children in Grades 4 through 6. The authors added nine items to the instrument that addressed issues of particular physical salience for APA children, including skin color, eye shape, hair color, and stature. Analyses revealed no significant differences on total P-H scores between the two groups, but on both the P-H Physical Appearance and Attributes scale and the authors' modified physical scale (as well as on the combination of both scales), Japanese American students scored significantly lower than did white students. However, according to the P-H manual (Piers, 1984), the white students' corresponding mean T-score as reported in this study was in the "slightly above average" range while the Japanese-American students' mean T-score was solidly within the "average" range. Thus, the significantly lower scores of the Japanese-American students should perhaps not be looked on as necessarily "bad" or as meaning that they have a "poor" physical self-concept. Although Pang et al. (1989) did not make this conclusion clear, they do emphasize that most self-concept research with ethnic minorities has focused on global profiles and may be "missing the point" by not distinguishing between important multiple domains of self-concept. The authors justifiably see the need for increased attention to multidimensional self-concepts of racial/ethnic minority children.

EFFECTS OF RACE/ETHNICITY ON SELF-CONCEPT: SUMMARY AND IMPLICATIONS

Most studies that have focused on racial/ethnic differences in self-concept have emphasized global profiles, and have primarily used black and white children as subjects. Early evidence was contradictory in nature as to differences between groups; the consensus now appears to be that black children have global self-concepts that are at least equal to and possibly better than those of their white counterparts.

Interesting differences between groups have emerged from multidimensional investigations. One finding that seems to appear repeatedly in more recent literature is the relative salience of physical self-concept (particularly appearance self-concept) when considering race/ethnicity. Most of the multidimensional studies reviewed here report differences between levels of physical self-concept for students from racially/ethnically diverse groups. Black students tend to report higher physical self-concepts than any other group, whereas children from Asian descent tend to report lower self-concepts in this area.

These intriguing findings perhaps reflect societal and/or cultural standards and norms about what characteristics constitute physical attractiveness and prowess. If this were the case, however, white children would be more likely to report higher physical self-concepts than would other children because of whites' majority status in this country and subsequently greater input into "societal standards." Alternatively (and more likely), values and standards placed on physical appearance and ability may vary from culture to culture, and may be much more salient in one group than in another. Physical self-concept is probably the most "external" domain typically measured with multidimensional instruments, in that people "are" their physical bodies and constantly receive direct and indirect feedback about their own and others' physical condition (Bracken, 1992). Because it is so easily "seen" and responded to by the individual and by others, and because the major racial groups in this country each have distinguishable physical characteristics, physical self-concept (at least in terms of appearance) may accrue differential weighting in terms of importance for children and adolescents as a function of race.

The finding that physical self-concept may be particularly salient to racial/ethnic groups provokes two recommendations and one cautionary statement. First, we should carefully define what is meant by physical self-concept. Can one scale capture both physical *appearance* as well as physical *ability* at games, sports, and other physical activities, or do these two aspects of self require independent scales? Marsh (1990) has demonstrated empirical support for the a priori separation of these two physical traits, and includes two separate physical scales on the SDQ series of instruments. Other multidimensional instruments, such as the Pier-Harris, Harter's Perceived Competence Scale, and the Multidimensional Self Concept Scale, have one physical scale that combines item stems referring both to appearance and ability. A recent factor analysis of five well-known self-concept/self-esteem instruments (Bracken et al., 1992), four of which had items or scales pertaining to the physical realm, revealed only one physical factor rather than two. Further research is necessary to determine whether physical self-concept scales do indeed need to be independent in terms of appearance and ability in this country, especially as the studies utilizing the SDQ series of instruments are based primarily on responses from Australian students.

If the two traits are independent, it then becomes imperative to learn how much each contributes to the self-concepts of children from different racial/ethnic groups. Perhaps greater value is placed on physical ability in some groups, whereas appearance may be paramount to physical self-concept in other groups. Health also may play a role in determining a child's perception of physical self, as Mboya's (1994) study illustrates, and also deserves further investigation.

As a final note, the cautionary statement is this: Just because one group scores "lower" than another does not necessarily mean that group has a *poor* self-concept. In fact, most raw score differences on self-concept instruments among groups of students are small indeed when the standard deviation is taken into consideration; that is, there generally is more variability within groups than across groups. Also, it is common knowledge that responses to self-concept instruments are negatively skewed. As always, it is good to remember that "statistically significant" differences do not always mean clinically significant or meaningful differences.

GENDER DIFFERENCES IN SELF-CONCEPT

Although assessing the relationship between self-concept and gender is common, conclusions should be made pertaining to both sexes unless it can be consistently demonstrated that gender contributes sufficient variance to the assessment of self-concept (Hattie, 1992). There have been many opinions as to the basis of the differences between male and female self-concepts. Hattie (1992) noted:

> . . . Arguments for differences in self concept between the sexes are that females are in a minority group status, females fulfill societal expected roles, females have more role conflict than males, females are more socially and economically dependent, and cultural ideology calls for women to be regarded as inferior. These arguments . . . are post-hoc justifications. Moreover, it is not obvious that these reasons necessarily will translate into females having lower self concepts. (p. 177)

Although many theorists have used these arguments to explain observed differences in self-concept, there is little (if any) empirical evidence to support these arguments. Indeed, much of the literature on differences between boys' and girls' self-concepts is ambiguous, inconsistent, and methodologically inadequate.

Wylie (1979) concluded that there was no convincing evidence that boys and girls differ in their global self-concept at any age level. She suggested, however, that differences in domain-specific self-concepts might well have been veiled because of past reliance on unidimensional measures. Most of the research to date suggests that boys have only slightly higher global self-concept and "esteem" scores (as measured by variations of the 10-item Rosenberg scale) than do girls (e.g., O'Malley & Bachman, 1979). However, because research since the mid-1980s has tended to utilize multi-dimensional instruments to assess self-concept, more recent conclusions can be drawn regarding gender differences, and these will be the focus of this review.

Piers (1984) has concluded that an accumulating body of evidence suggests that there are gender differences in domain-specific self-concepts. For example, she reported that boys systematically report less anxiety and more problematic behavior than girls on the Piers-Harris Children's Self-Concept Scale (Piers, 1969, 1984). Although Piers found no gender differences in total self-concept using the cluster scales' normative sample ($N = 485$), consistent with Wylie's (1979) conclusion, she found significant gender differences on 33 of the 80 items that appeared consistent with sex stereotypes. Applying Cohen's (1969) conventions for magnitudes of small, medium, and large effect sizes, however, she reported that none of the P-H items indicated a large difference (effect sizes greater than .8) between genders, and only 5 of the 33 items indicated medium effects (effect sizes greater than .5). For example, the items "I have pretty eyes" (yes) was endorsed more frequently by girls, and "I cry easily" (no) was more often endorsed by boys (see Piers, 1984, for further information).

Marsh and colleagues, using the SDQ series of instruments and encompassing the age range from preadolescence to late adolescence, have found consistent gender differences in domain-specific self-concepts of Australian students, although the direction of the differences varies by domain (and although the factor structure for boys and girls is relatively invariant across the age range; see Byrne & Shavelson, 1987; Marsh, 1987a). Most notably, these studies have revealed that preadolescent boys (Grades 2–5) have higher self-concepts than girls in the areas of math, general self, physical appearance, and physical abilities, whereas girls have higher self-concepts in the areas of reading and general school (Marsh et al., 1984; Marsh, Relich, & Smith, 1983).

During the adolescent years (Grades 6–10), girls tend to score higher than boys in the SDQII domains of Verbal, Honesty-Trustworthiness, and Same-Sex Relations, whereas boys tend to have higher scores in Physical Abilities, Physical Appearance, and Math. Smaller differences have been found in General School and Academic scales (favoring girls), and General Self and Emotional Stability scales (favoring boys) (Byrne & Shavelson, 1986; Marsh, 1987b; Marsh et al., 1985; Marsh, Byrne, & Shavelson, 1988; Marsh, Smith et al., 1988). Additional evidence supporting the hypothesis that adolescent girls have lower math and higher reading self-concepts than boys comes from Meece et al. (1982) and from Stevenson and Newman

(1986). Interestingly, these studies showed no differences between boys and girls in math and reading self-concepts during the primary school years, suggesting that expectations of significant others (e.g., parents, teachers) in addition to subtly transmitted gender stereotypes (e.g., through various forms of media) may reach an apex during the adolescent years that contributes to the beginning of the divergence between girls and boys on these measures of self-concept.

Because self-perceptions of young girls and boys tend to run along traditional sex stereotype lines, we may be tempted to believe that gender is a major moderator of self-concept responses among children. Again, however, a cautious view of this hypothesis is necessary. Marsh (1985) noted that, for responses of 3,562 Australian students who made up the normative sample of the SDQI, observed gender effects were very small and accounted for only 0.66% of the variance in Total self-concept scores and for less than 2% of the variance of any one subscale score that showed gender differences. Only the sex effect in Physical Abilities accounted for more than 3% of the variance. Similar percentages were reported in Marsh et al. (1984) (also utilizing the SDQI) and in Marsh et al. (1985), a study that utilized the SDQII with adolescents.

The limited meaningfulness of gender as a moderating variable in self-concept also was illustrated in our study using the Multidimensional Self Concept Scale (Crain & Bracken, 1994). Boys and girls did not differ in their Total self-concept or on any of the domain-specific subscales except for the Physical scale. Here, as in other studies, boys rated their Physical self-concepts significantly higher than did girls, albeit by about one-third standard deviation (4 raw score points). This small difference indicates only minor clinical significance and may reflect the large sample size.

Other studies have found gender effects in domain-specific self-concepts. Osborne and LeGette (1982), using the Piers-Harris, the Self-Concept of Ability Scale, and the Coopersmith SEI, found that adolescent boys and girls did not differ in global self-concept. However, boys had significantly higher domain-specific self-concepts on the Piers-Harris clusters of physical appearance and attributes and anxiety (higher scores indicating lower anxiety), whereas girls had better self-concepts in the behavior and social domains than did boys (consistent with conclusions made in Piers & Harris, 1964 and Piers, 1984). These differences occurred across grade levels (Grades 7, 9, 11), racial/ethnic characteristics (white and African American), and social class characteristics.

Mboya (1994), using the Self-Description Inventory (Mboya, 1993), found that adolescent boys had higher self-concepts than girls in the domains of family, physical abilities, physical appearance, music ability, and health, while girls had higher self-concepts than boys in general school and emotional stability domains. Boys also reported higher levels of global self-concept than did girls. Again, these differences occurred irrespective of age and ethnic characteristics of the sample.

Gender differences in young children's domain-specific self-concepts also have been examined. Marsh et al. (1991), using an individually administered version of the SDQI with children between the ages of 5 and 8 years, found results strikingly similar to those Marsh and colleagues have obtained with older children. Young girls had substantially lower self-concepts of physical ability, and modestly higher self-concepts in physical appearance and reading than did boys. There was also an Age × Sex interaction for physical ability. Whereas boys had higher self-concepts in this domain at all three ages, the sizes of the gender differences increased with age. Marsh et al. (1991) noted that only this difference accounted for more than 2% of the variance in any of the individually administered SDQI scores. Interestingly, it appears from this study that young girls have a slight advantage over young boys in the physical appearance realm that seems to disappear as children get older.

EFFECTS OF GENDER ON SELF-CONCEPT: SUMMARY AND IMPLICATIONS

Many studies, some previously noted, have found differences in domain-specific self-concepts of boys and girls that tend to run along gender-stereotype lines. The physical abilities domain appears to reflect the largest difference between the sexes; this is perhaps not surprising in view of the much greater emphasis on boys' participation in sports and games (and the greater variety of sports activities available to boys) during the school years. Physical appearance also is an area in which boys tend to have higher self-concepts than girls, albeit beginning only during early adolescence. Harter (1990) has suggested that girls consider physical attractiveness to be more important than do boys, yet girls become more dissatisfied with their appearance during adolescence than do boys. She concludes that there is a group of related perceptions among girls that contribute to their lower self-concept in this area, including a less favorable body image, greater self-consciousness, feelings of unattractiveness, more negative attitudes toward their own gender, and recognition of the value society places on appearance. Harter noted that the relationship between perceived appearance and self-concept is not confined to adolescence but is extremely robust across the life span, a finding corroborated by Pliner, Chaiken, and Flett (1990) in their life-span study of gender differences in concern with body weight and physical appearance. In this study, females across the entire age span from 10 to 79 years were much more concerned than were males about eating, body weight, and physical appearance and thus had lower appearance self-concepts.

It is important to remember, however, that the divergence between boys and girls in these self-concept domains is not very great and thus, has limited clinical significance. It does not appear warranted, for example, that educational settings should embark immediately on developing programs to improve adolescent girls' physical appearance and ability self-concepts in an effort to bring them more "up to par" with boys' perceptions in these domains. It appears from the literature that, by and large, boys and girls are clinically more similar than different on measures of domain-specific self-concept. The small differences that exist tend to be consistent with gender stereotypes.

Gender historically has been lauded as one of the most important contributors to the variance in children's and adolescents' self-concepts, and undoubtedly will continue to be examined (as well it should be) in future research. However, gender as a moderator of multidimensional self-concept should perhaps receive less emphasis than other variables such as effects of pubertal changes or societal attitudes that contribute to gender differences. As female members of our society continue to experience expanded roles and success in the workplace and in the recreation/sports arena, we may see interesting changes over time in the self-concept formation of young girls.

CONCLUSION

This chapter has reviewed some of the most current research investigating age, race, and gender differences in children's and adolescents' multi-dimensional self-concepts. What general conclusions can be made given the multitude of methodological approaches, definitions of self-concept, and instruments that have been used? There seem to be several recurring findings regarding the effects of age, race, and gender variables on domain-specific self-concept.

For age, the most robust finding is that overall or general self-concept may increase slightly during late adolescence. Research with this age group has typically used variations of the Rosenberg scale rather than multi-dimensional instruments (e.g., O'Malley & Bachman, 1983). Several studies report a curvilinear age effect in multidimensional self-concept such that some domains decline during preadolescence, rebound sometime during early or middle adolescence, and increase during late adolescence and early adulthood (e.g., Marsh, 1991). Interestingly, not all self-concept domains show this decline across age; Family self-concept is a good example (Crain & Bracken, 1994; Marsh, 1991). However, it is too early to completely accept the preceding conclusions until more longitudinal studies are conducted. Researchers also need to consider other methods of examining age/self-concept relationships in addition to mean score comparisons. For example, zero-order correlations (e.g., Crain & Bracken, 1994) have shown little relationship between chronological age and domain-specific raw scores. It does not appear that "age" per se has much to do systematically with whatever changes may take place during this time; more likely, what changes there are almost undoubtedly result from the different educational, social, and physical contexts that preadolescents begin to experience (e.g., junior high/middle school, puberty, increased importance of the peer group).

Investigations of racial/ethnic differences in domain-specific self-concept have quite consistently shown variations in physical appearance self-concept, although there are scant differences between groups in overall self-concept and in other domain-specific areas. In general, Asian children tend to have the lowest physical appearance self-concepts and black children the highest, with white children somewhere in between. However, the magnitude of these score differences always should be taken into account; children's perceptions of their physical appearance do not appear to be excessively divergent. Thus, available evidence does not support the notion that one racial/ethnic group of children suffers unduly from negative physical appearance self-concepts relative to other groups.

For gender, the largest and most consistently found difference is the divergence between boys' and girls' perceptions of their physical ability self-concept. Boys consistently report higher self-concepts in this area across all age groups. Physical appearance self-concept, when it is measured separately, presents a somewhat more complex phenomenon. Boys and girls tend not to differ in their physical appearance self-concepts during the primary school years; however, boys consistently rate themselves more positively than girls in this area with the advent of adolescence. A number of possible explanations exist, with the most likely being different societal expectations placed on male and female appearance of which children do not become completely cognizant until the advent of adolescence (concurrent with pubertal changes and the beginning of opposite-sex relationships). For example, both men and women tend to view physical attractiveness as more important for women as a means of attracting a mate, but focus on other qualities such as financial status for men (Pliner et al., 1990). Again, however, the magnitude of the differences in boys' and girls' self-perceptions in these areas do not necessitate a call for action on the part of educational and clinical personnel. Boys and girls tend to be much more similar than different when it comes to multidimensional self-concept.

In summary, there will likely never be a complete consensus of opinion regarding the effects of these constitutional student characteristics on self-concept because of the hodgepodge of studies using different methodological approaches and self-concept instruments (a condition not likely to go away). Researchers' attitudes and beliefs about the broader meaningfulness of age, race, and gender also will continue to contribute to the divergence of opinion regarding self-concept differences.

My argument is not that there are absolutely no differences in children's and adolescents' multidimensional self-concepts as a function of age, race, and gender; it is simply that the differences found in the extant literature are not large enough to be clinically relevant. What I have done is presented evidence related to points raised at the beginning of this chapter. The first was the theoretical basis for examining age, race, and gender in relation to multidimensional self-concept. The point made was that the equivalence of the self-concept construct should be determined to be generally invariant across groups of students with differing constitutional characteristics— which it is, at least according to Marsh and colleagues, who have done most of the factor-analytic work in this area. Although the chapter did not focus specifically on factor equivalence across groups, most of the available research has shown that self-concept factors are essentially the same across groups of children of different ages and of both genders. Preliminary work with children of different racial/ethnic characteristics (e.g., Mboya, 1994) has shown likewise that the factor structure of self-concept is largely invariant regardless of the child's race. Taken together, these findings reveal the multidimensional self-concept to be an extremely robust construct that is meaningful and similarly defined among children and adolescents who differ in all sorts of ways (age, race, and gender status). Therefore, investigations that *combine* students' constitutional and acquired characteristics (e.g., disability conditions, achievement levels, family variables) should be conducted to determine their cumulative influences on self-concept rather than continuing to focus solely on age, race, and gender as moderating variables.

We can claim to know more about the self-concept construct now that we know that its structure is largely invariant across age, race, and gender. The question then becomes related to the second point made at the beginning of the chapter: Given this knowledge, does anything need to be done to ensure that self-concept intervention programs in schools are specific to the types of children they are serving (different programs for different groups of students)? The answer right now appears to be a resounding "no." The only way self-concept intervention programs need to be individualized is through the specific area or domain targeted for improvement. For example, an intervention designed to improve academic self-concept should create increased opportunities for academic success for entire groups of students; techniques need not differ just because a student is black or white, a boy or a girl, a 13-year-old or a 17-year-old. The empirical evidence reviewed in this chapter does not support individualized self-concept interventions based on students' constitutional characteristics.

The last point made in the beginning of this chapter was that age, race, and gender should be examined systematically to determine whether single collective normative groups are most appropriate for self-concept instruments. While the practice of examining such variables during the construction of a new instrument should of course continue, developers of new instruments will undoubtedly find that collapsing their data into a single normative group is the most valid approach. Raw score differences among children of various age, race, and gender groups on multidimensional self-concept instruments are simply not that large statistically. In fact, if a test developer discovers large score discrepancies among groups of children with varying constitutional characteristics, he or she would be well advised to take a very close look at the construction of the instrument itself and at the items of which it consists.

Researchers using multidimensional self-concept instruments should always conduct preliminary analyses to determine whether data show systematic age, race, or gender differences. These three variables are so foundational that *not* to examine them would be gravely remiss. However, researchers can now justifiably focus on children's and adolescents' acquired characteristics as opposed to constitutional ones such as age, race, and gender in order to further advance our understanding of one of the most pervasive and meaningful psychological constructs of our time.

REFERENCES

Bachman, J. G., & O'Malley, P. M. (1977). Self-esteem in young men: A longitudinal analysis of the impact of educational and occupational attainment. *Journal of Personality and Social Psychology, 35,* 365–380.

Bracken, B. A. (1992). *Examiner's manual for the Multidimensional Self Concept Scale.* Austin, TX: Pro-Ed.

Bracken, B. A., Bunch, S., Keith, T. Z., & Keith, P. B. (1992, August). *Multidimensional self concept: A five instrument factor analysis.* Paper presented at the annual conference of the American Psychological Association, Washington, DC.

Bracken, B. A., & Crain, R. M. (1994). Children's and adolescents' interpersonal relations: Do age, race, and gender define normalcy? *Journal of Psychoeducational Assessment, 12,* 14–32.

Brookover, W. B., Paterson, A., & Thomas, S. (1962). *Self-concept of ability and school achievement.* East Lansing, MI: Educational Publication Services.

Byrne, B. M., & Shavelson, R. J. (1986). On the structure of adolescent self-concept. *Journal of Educational Psychology, 78,* 474–481.

Byrne, B. M., & Shavelson, R. J. (1987). Adolescent self-concept: Testing the assumption of equivalence across gender. *American Educational Research Journal, 24,* 365–385.

Chang, T. S. (1975). The self-concept of children in ethnic groups: Black American and Korean American. *Elementary School Journal, 76,* 52–58.

Cohen, J. (1969). *Statistical power analysis for the behavioral sciences.* New York: Academic Press.

Coopersmith, S. A. (1967). *Coopersmith Self-Esteem Inventory.* Palo Alto, CA: Consulting Psychologist Press.

Crain, R. M., & Bracken, B. A. (1994). Age, race, and gender differences in child and adolescent self concept: Evidence from a behavioral-acquisition, context-dependent model. *School Psychology Review, 23,* 496–511.

Dusek, J. B., & Flaherty, J. F. (1981). The development of the self-concept during the adolescent years. *Monographs of the Society for Research in Child Development, 46*(4, Serial No. 191).

Fleming, J. S., & Courtney, B. E. (1984). The dimensionality of self-esteem: II. Hierarchical facet model for revised measurement scales. *Journal of Personality and Social Psychology, 46,* 404–421.

Fox, D., & Jordan, V. (1973). Racial preference and identification of American Chinese, Black and White children. *Genetic Psychology Monographs, 88,* 139–143.

Furman, W., & Buhrmester, D. (1992). Age and sex differences in perceptions of networks of personal relationships. *Child Development, 63,* 103–115.

Gordon, C. (1969). *Looking ahead: Self-conception, race, and family factors as determinants of adolescent achievement orientation.* Washington, DC: American Sociological Association Arnold and Caroline Rose Monograph Series.

Grant, C. A., & Sleeter, C. E. (1986). Race, class, and gender in education research: An argument for integrative analysis. *Review of Educational Research, 56,* 195–211.

Halpin, G., Halpin, G., & Whiddon, T. (1981). Locus of control and self-esteem among Indians and whites: A cross-cultural comparison. *Psychological Reports, 48,* 91–98.

Hanes, B., Prawat, R., & Grissom, S. (1979). Sex-role perceptions during adolescence. *Journal of Educational Psychology, 71,* 850–855.

Harter, S. (1982). The Perceived Competence Scale for Children. *Child Development, 53,* 87–97.

Harter, S. (1983). Developmental perspectives on the self-system. In P. H. Mussen (Ed.) & E. M. Hetherington (Series Ed.), *Handbook of child psychology: Vol. 4. Socialization, personality and social development* (pp. 275–385). New York: Wiley.

Harter, S. (1990). Self and identity development. In S. S. Feldman & G. R. Elliott (Eds.), *At the threshold: The developing adolescent* (pp. 352–387). Cambridge, MA: Harvard University Press.

Harter, S., & Pike, R. (1984). The pictorial scale of perceived competence and social acceptance for young children. *Child Development, 55,* 1969–1982.

Hattie, J. B. (1992). *Self-concept.* Hillsdale, NJ: Erlbaum.

Hirsch, B. J., & Rapkin, B. D. (1987). The transition to junior high school: A longitudinal study of self-esteem, psychological symptomatology, school life, and social support. *Child Development, 58,* 1235–1243.

Hughes, M., & Demo, D. H. (1989). Self-perceptions of Black Americans: Self-esteem and personal efficacy. *American Journal of Sociology, 95,* 132–159.

Kohlberg, L. (1969). Stage and sequence: The cognitive-developmental approach to socialization. In D. A. Goslin (Ed.), *Handbook of socialization theory and research* (pp. 347–480). Chicago: Rand McNally.

Kohr, R. L., Coldiron, J. R., Skiffington, E. W., Masters, J. R., & Blust, R. S. (1988). The influence of race, class, and gender on self-esteem for fifth, eighth, and eleventh grade students in Pennsylvania schools. *Journal of Negro Education, 57,* 467–481.

Kuhn, M. H., & McPartland, T. C. (1954). An empirical investigation of self-attitudes. *American Sociological Review, 19,* 68–76.

Lay, R., & Wakstein, J. (1985). Race, academic achievement, and self-concept of ability. *Research in Higher Education, 22,* 43–64.

Long, K. A., & Hamlin, C. M. (1988). Use of the Piers-Harris Self-Concept Scale with Indian children: Cultural considerations. *Nursing Research, 37,* 42–46.

Marsh, H. W. (1984). *Age and sex effects in multiple dimensions of preadolescent self-concept.* (ERIC Document Reproduction Service No. ED 252 600)

Marsh, H. W. (1985). Age and sex effects in multiple dimensions of preadolescent self-concept: A replication and extension. *Australian Journal of Psychology, 37,* 197–204.

Marsh, H. W. (1987a). The factorial invariance of responses by males and females to a multidimensional self-concept instrument: Substantive and methodological issues. *Multivariate Behavioral Research, 22,* 457–480.

Marsh, H. W. (1987b). Masculinity, femininity, and androgyny: Their relations to multiple dimensions of self-concept. *Multivariate Behavioral Research, 22,* 91–118.

Marsh, H. W. (1988). *Self-Description Questionnaire, I: Manual and research monograph.* San Antonio, TX: Psychological Corp.

Marsh, H. W. (1989). Age and sex effects in multiple dimensions of self-concept: Preadolescence to early adulthood. *Journal of Educational Psychology, 81,* 417–430.

Marsh, H. W. (1990). Confirmatory factor analysis of multitrait-multimethod data: The construct validation of multidimensional self-concept responses. *Journal of Personality, 58,* 661–692.

Marsh, H. W. (1991). *Self-Description Questionnaire, II: Manual and research monograph.* San Antonio, TX: Psychological Corp.

Marsh, H. W., Barnes, J., Cairns, L., & Tidman, M. (1984). The Self-Description Questionnaire (SDQ): Age effects in the structure and level of self-concept for preadolescent children. *Journal of Educational Psychology, 75,* 940–956.

Marsh, H. W., Byrne, B. M., & Shavelson, R. J. (1988). A multifaceted academic self-concept: Its hierarchical structure and its relation to academic achievement. *Journal of Educational Psychology, 80,* 366–380.

Marsh, H. W., Craven, R. G., & Debus, R. (1991). Self-concepts of young children 5 to 8 years of age: Measurement and multidimensional structure. *Journal of Educational Psychology, 83,* 377–392.

Marsh, H. W., Parker, J., & Barnes, J. (1985). Multidimensional adolescent self-concepts: Their relationship to age, sex, and academic measures. *American Educational Research Journal, 22,* 422–444.

Marsh, H. W., Relich, J. D., & Smith, I. D. (1983). Self-concept: The construct validity of interpretations based upon the SDQ. *Journal of Personality and Social Psychology, 45,* 173–187.

Marsh, H. W., & Shavelson, R. J. (1985). Self-concept: Its multifaceted, hierarchical structure. *Educational Psychologist, 20,* 107–125.

Marsh, H. W., Smith, I. D., Marsh, M. R., & Owens, L. (1988). The transition from single-sex to coeducational high schools: Effects on multiple dimensions of self-concept and on academic achievement. *American Educational Research Journal, 25,* 237–269.

Mboya, M. M. (1993). Development and construct validity of a self-description inventory for African adolescents. *Psychological Reports, 72,* 183–191.

Mboya, M. M. (1994). Cross-cultural study of the structure and level of multi-dimensional self-concepts in secondary school students. *School Psychology International, 15,* 163–171.

McCarthy, J. D., & Hoge, D. R. (1982). Analysis of age effects in longitudinal studies of adolescent self-esteem. *Developmental Psychology, 18,* 372–379.

Meece, J. L., Parsons, J. E., Kaczala, C. M., Goff, S. B., & Futterman, R. (1982). Sex differences in math achievement: Toward a model of academic choice. *Psychological Bulletin, 91,* 324–348.

Mohr, D. M. (1978). Development of attributes of personal identity. *Developmental Psychology, 14,* 427–428.

Monge, R. H. (1975). Structure of the self-concept from adolescence through old age. *Experimental Aging Research, 1,* 281–291.

National Opinion Research Center. (1980). *High school and beyond: A national longitudinal study for the 1980s.* Chicago: Author.

Oanh, N. T., & Michael, W. B. (1977). The predictive validity of each of ten measures of self-concept relative to teachers' ratings of achievement in mathematics and reading of Vietnamese children and of those from five other ethnic groups. *Educational and Psychological Measurement, 37,* 1005–1016.

O'Malley, P. M., & Bachman, J. G. (1979). Self-esteem and education: Sex and cohort comparisons among high school seniors. *Journal of Personality and Social Psychology, 37,* 1153–1159.

O'Malley, P. M., & Bachman, J. G. (1983). Self-esteem: Change and stability between ages 13 and 23. *Developmental Psychology, 19,* 257–268.

Osborne, W. L., & LeGette, H. R. (1982). Sex, race, grade level, and social class differences in self-concept. *Measurement and Evaluation in Guidance, 14,* 195–201.

Pang, V. O., Mizokawa, D. T., Morishima, J. K., & Olstad, R. G. (1989). Self-concepts of Japanese-American children. *Journal of Cross-Cultural Psychology, 20,* 99–109.

Piaget, J. (1952). *The origins of intelligence in children.* New York: International Universities Press. (Original work published 1936)

Piers, E. V. (1969). *Manual for the Piers-Harris Children's Self-Concept Scale.* Nashville, TN: Counselor Recordings and Tests.

Piers, E. V. (1984). *Piers-Harris Children's Self-Concept Scale: Revised manual.* Los Angeles, CA: Western Psychological Services.

Piers, E. V., & Harris, D. B. (1964). Age and other correlates of self-concept in children. *Journal of Educational Psychology, 55,* 91–95.

Pliner, P., Chaiken, S., & Flett, G. L. (1990). Gender differences in concern with body weight and physical appearance over the life span. *Personality and Social Psychology Bulletin, 16,* 263–273.

Porter, J. R., & Washington, R. E. (1979). Black identity and self-esteem: A review of studies of black self-concept, 1968–1978. In A. Inkeles, J. Coleman, & R. H. Turner (Eds.), *Annual Review of Sociology, 5,* 53–74. Palo Alto, CA: Annual Reviews.

Powers, J. M., Drane, H. T., Close, B. L., Noonan, M. P., Wines, A. M., & Marshall, J. C. (1971). A research note on the self-perception of youth. *American Educational Research Journal, 8,* 665–670.

Rosenberg, M. (1965). *Society and the adolescent self-image.* Princeton, NJ: Princeton University Press.

Rosenberg, M. (1985). Self-concept and psychological well-being in adolescence. In R. L. Leahy (Ed.), *The development of self* (pp. 55–121). Orlando, FL: Academic Press.

Rosenkrantz, P., Vogel, W., Bee, H., Broverman, I., & Broverman, D. (1968). Sex role stereotypes and self-conceptions in college students. *Journal of Consulting and Clinical Psychology, 32,* 287–295.

Rotenberg, K. J., & Cranwell, F. R. (1989). Self-concept in American Indian and White children. *Journal of Cross-Cultural Psychology, 20,* 39–53.

Samuels, S. C. (1973). An investigation into the self-concepts of lower- and middle-class black and white kindergarten children. *Journal of Negro Education, 42,* 467–472.

Shantz, C. U. (1983). Social cognition. In J. H. Flavell & E. M. Markman (Eds.), *Handbook of child psychology: Vol. 3. Cognitive development* (4th ed., pp. 495–555). New York: Wiley.

Shavelson, R. J., Hubner, J. J., & Stanton, G. C. (1976). Self-concept: Validation of construct interpretations. *Review of Educational Research, 46,* 407–441.

Silon, E. L., & Harter, S. (1985). Assessment of perceived competence, motivational orientation, and anxiety in segregated and mainstreamed educable mentally retarded children. *Journal of Educational Psychology, 77,* 217–230.

Simmons, R. G., Rosenberg, F., & Rosenberg, M. (1973). Disturbance in the self-image at adolescence. *American Sociological Review, 38,* 553–568.

Stenner, A. J., & Katzenmeyer, W. G. (1976). Self-concept, ability, and achievement in a sample of sixth grade students. *Journal of Educational Research, 69,* 270–273.

Stevenson, H. W., & Newman, R. S. (1986). Long-term prediction of achievement and attitudes in mathematics and reading. *Child Development, 57,* 646–659.

Stipek, D. J. (1981). Children's perceptions of their own and their classmates' ability. *Journal of Educational Psychology, 73,* 404–410.

Trowbridge, N. (1972). Self-concept and socio-economic status in elementary school children. *American Educational Research Journal, 9,* 525–537.

Walker, L. S., & Greene, J. W. (1986). The social context of adolescent self-esteem. *Journal of Youth and Adolescence, 15,* 315–323.

Wylie, R. C. (1979). *The self-concept: Vol. 2. Theory and research on selected topics* (rev. ed.). Lincoln: University of Nebraska Press.

Wylie, R. C. (1989). *Measures of self-concept.* Lincoln: University of Nebraska Press.

Yancey, W. L., Rigsby, L., & McCarthy, J. D. (1972). Social position and self-evaluation: The relative importance of race. *American Journal of Sociology, 78,* 338–359.

Zirkel, P. A., & Moses, E. G. (1971). Self-concept and ethnic group membership among public school students. *American Educational Research Journal, 8,* 253–265.

CHAPTER 11

Future Directions in Self-Concept Research

JOHN HATTIE and HERBERT W. MARSH

The most dramatic improvement in self-concept research from 1985 to 1995 relates to the evolution of more clearly articulated models. This is a most pleasing direction given the trend evident in the 1960s and 1970s of using self-concept as a "throw it in and see what happens" variable. Much of the credit for this development can be traced to Shavelson, Hubner, and Stanton's (1976) article. Many of their conjectures have now become basic knowledge, and the chapters in this book have again demonstrated the acceptance of the multidimensional notion of self-concept. Although there will continue to be minor disagreements as to which conceptualization of the multidimensional model of self-concept is more defensible, this debate will continue to drive studies with rich implications for research across many domains such as education, psychotherapy, and well-being.

We identify five issues as the most important future research issues that need to be tackled during the next decade. By debating these issues, we can further the usefulness of our research and will encounter the most critical issues that are blocking our path to understanding. The first issue relates to the hierarchical nature of self-concept. The nature and importance of this hierarchy is outlined leading to a discussion as to how the literature from cognitive processing can help our understanding. This leads to the suggestion that because individuals use many strategies to maintain or protect their conceptions of self, there are critical questions about the motivations to develop a sense of self. The second issue is concerned with the effects of self-concept on people's lives. There is an unresolved debate about how critical self-concept is in our lives and two areas are discussed as examples of this debate: the nature of the relationship between self-concept and achievement and the effectiveness of programs to enhance self-concept. The third issue relates to the impact of social and cultural effects on self-concept and is illustrated through gender studies and developmental issues. The fourth issue is a perennial one, the sorting out of the terminology confusion in this area; future studies are needed to provide clarification and discrimination between the many terms in this area. The fifth issue (briefly mentioned as it is discussed in a previous chapter) reinforces the concern about the efficacy of the instruments to measure self-concept.

THE HIERARCHICAL NATURE OF SELF-CONCEPT

This book has demonstrated that we have an enormous depth and breadth of understanding about the various dimensions of self-concept. We suggest that the future direction in self-concept research will relate more to the hierarchical aspects than the multidimensional aspects. A reader who merely scans the chapter headings of this book could regard self-concept as such a collection of multiple self-concepts. Future research needs to be devoted to understanding the mechanisms linking these lower-order conceptions of self-concepts into a higher-order notions of self.

Although Shavelson et al. (1976) claimed that the self was a hierarchical notion, the research on this claim has been fleeting. There are many possible ways that the lower-order dimensions of self-concept can be integrated to form a high-order notion. For example, the information from the separate dimensions may be integrated prior to the individual making a decision, or a decision may be made about information on each dimension and then integrated to make a response (see Massaro & Friedman, 1990; Shaw, 1982). It may be that individuals do not use simple weighted additive models when integrating information about the self, but use other combination rules such as noncompensatory, partially compensatory, or compensatory models (Coombs, 1954; Hattie, Krakowski, Rogers & Swaminathan, in press); the use of probabilities as per the Bayes theorem to form conceptions about the self; a criterion rule whereby information is integrated such that when a criterion is surpassed a decision is made; a relative goodness-of-fit rule whereby information is integrated until a relative goodness of fit with predictable outcomes for the individual is met and then a decision is made; or a fuzzy set model whereby continuous valued features are mapped against prototype descriptions in memory and a decision is made on the basis of the relative goodness of fit with this relative prototype.

It may be that individuals have higher-order executive or planning capabilities to meld the various self-concepts. This notion parallels the research by Das (1980; Das & Jarman, 1991; Das, Kirby, & Jarman, 1979), based on Luria's (1973) model of simultaneous and successive processing. That is, there may be different modes of integrating information that lead to the same manifestations of self-concept. One method is the simultaneous method, or the synthesis of separate elements into a whole with no necessary dependence on the position of each in the whole. The other method is the successive method, which refers to the processing of information in serial order. As well, there is an executive or planning component that uses the information integrated by the two methods. It may be similarly, that there are various methods for integrating concepts of self and an executive or planning component that attends to this information.

Some researchers have questioned whether integration is critical and prefer to emphasize "working, on-line, or accessible self-concepts" (Markus & Nurius, 1986; Oyserman & Markus, 1993; Rhodewalt, 1986; Rhodewalt & Agustsdottir, 1986). The contention is that not all conceptions of self will be accessible at any one time. Self-concept is continually active, and some conceptions are "tentative, fleeting and peripheral, others are highly elaborated and function as enduring, meaning-making, or interpretative structures that help individuals lend coherence to their own life experiences" (Oyserman & Markus, 1993, p. 191). These working selves, claimed Oyserman and Markus, can be conceived as packages of self-knowledge, and form coordinates of the individual's experiential world. Although it may seem convenient to incorporate the sociocultural influences of gender and so on, the notion of "working selves" makes the individual sound almost chameleon, without a central purpose, sense of agency, or an identity. It emphasizes the specific aspects of the self rather than the manner in which the individual processes these various working selves, and assimilates and accommodates information into prior beliefs about the self.

The notion of working selves has a parallel in the intelligence literature. There has been a negative reaction to the presence of g or general factor underlying intelligence, and some have posited models which do not include g. Gardner (1985), for example, developed his theory of multiple intelligences, whereby he identified eight separate intelligences that are unrelated. Thus, a person could have a high social intelligence, but such knowledge would not necessarily lead to predictions about that person's musical intelligence. As with the subsequent discussion of models such as Gardner's, there will be increased attention on the cognitive processes and social contexts involved in developing conceptions of self. There will be more concern about the tacit enfolding of the self as each of us come to have a view of "our" world and how we are shaped by this world. These views may be static at any one moment only when our snapshot is fast enough that we can "stop" the flying arrow, and it is most important that we understand the contexts and the direction in which the arrow is flying.

The place of general self-concept will remain a controversial issue. The issues relate to whether individuals somehow integrate lower-order dimensions, or whether they have a general self-concept which mediates these dimensions. The general self-concept may have a critical role in mediating the information about aspects of self (see Brown, 1993). Most current research considers the higher-order conceptions of self-concept as some kind of amalgam of the lower-order concepts, whereas the converse may be the case. It may be that there are critical information-processing competencies that bias, select, and retain information and affectations about self, and these may be different depending on the level of self-concept and on the sources of developing these biases (e.g., cultural and social sources). This is not claiming that individuals distort reality to maintain their self-images of being positive and effective people, as claimed by many (Dunning, Meyerowitz, & Holzberg, 1989; Taylor & Brown, 1988). The individual's perception of reality is a "reality," and the greater concern is the various ways in which individuals select, bias and retain information.

A key to unraveling this issue may be a closer study of the development of self-concept. Hattie (1992) argued that for most young children the self is unlikely to be hierarchical particularly as the capability to "think" hierarchically (or synthesize/integrate) only begins to emerge at about 11 to 13 years (Luria, 1966, 1973). With respect to self-concept, as opposed say to intelligence (see Piaget, 1977), this is a conjecture that needs more research. Marsh (1990c), for example, has provided some evidence that children as young as 5 or 6 have a "general" self-concept and that the structure of self may be multidimensional (see also Harter, 1983 for contrasting discussions on this development).

It is probable that there are individual differences in the degree and complexity of any hierarchy relating to self-concept. In a study by Boundy (1990), an independent measure of complexity or the capability of integrating information was used to classify adolescents into those who were able and those unable to synthesize. A hierarchical model of self-concept provided the best fit for those who could synthesize information and a nonhierarchical model provided best fit for those who could not synthesize.

Linville (1982) has demonstrated the importance of complexity in predicting self-concept. She argued that "self-representations may differ in terms of both the number of self-aspects and the degree to which distinctions are made among self-aspects" (p. 664). Her use of a measure of dimensionality based on information theory assesses the minimal number of independent binary attributes underlying a person's sorting of beliefs about the self. This method of determining self-complexity relates more to the hierarchical than the multifaceted notion of self, although it incorporates both. Linville (1987) proposed that greater self-complexity is a protective factor for people under stress, primarily because greater self-complexity involves having self-aspects that are more distinct from one another; thus when there is stress, those high in self-complexity are more likely to constrain their thoughts and feelings provided by events to immediately salient self-aspects, and have a greater number of self-aspects unaffected. Thus a complex cognitive representation of the self may serve to moderate the adverse physical and mental health effects of stressful events.

A different approach to understanding how individuals synthesize the various dimensions of self-concept has been proposed by Markus and Sentis (1982). They proposed a distinction between schematics, those individuals assumed to have a schema in a particular domain, and aschematics, those assumed to be without such a structure in that domain. These two groups differed in processing time for decisions and in confidence for these decisions and this suggested that for the schematics "information about the self is organized in such a way that it can be readily accessed for efficient processing, . . . (and) in such a way that it is not necessary to search through all the confirming evidence before making judgments about the self" (p. 55). This is compatible with the notion that the self can be "seen as a system of substructures, as a hierarchy or universal, particularistic, and idiosyncratic knowledge structures about the self that are embedded within each other. These structures will be activated as processing units depending on the nature or goal of the processing act or task and the nature of the external stimuli" (p. 58).

Another conception of self other than as hierarchical and multifaceted was proposed by Greenwald and Pratkanis (1984). They contrasted various views of self based more on the manner that information about the self is processed: self as schema that views the self as a system of schemata in memory (Markus, 1977; Markus & Sentis, 1982); self as hierarchical category structure (Rogers, 1981); self as multidimensional space defined by a general evaluative dimension and an intellectual good/bad dimension (Breckler & Greenwald, 1982); self as prototype whereby individuals have a prototype with which to compare novel stimuli (Kuiper, 1981); and self as associative network wherein propositions about the self are stored in the form of propositions that relate the self and specific episodes and generic information about the self (Bower & Gilligan, 1979).

Brown (1993) dispensed with the notion of a hierarchy altogether. He contended that high self-esteem "involves a generic, global liking for oneself that is not dependent on the belief that one possesses specific attributes, but that is nevertheless accompanied by the general and fluid perception that one is good at a great many things" (p. 27). This is a very top-down model that emphasizes the general component as the guiding aspect of the conception of self. Brown proposed that there were domain-specific self-concepts, but claimed that they differed from the general self in that they were narrower and less encompassing, and that they were cognitively rather than affectively based. He disagreed with models such as those of Shavelson et al. (1976), Rosenberg (1979), and Coopersmith (1967), which proposed that the global self was some amalgam of the specific self-concepts. Instead, he claimed that global self-concept was the major mediator in beliefs about specific attributes of the self. "The indiscriminate and mutable nature of these beliefs (about specific self) may not provide the stable foundation for self-esteem" (p. 28).

Brown argued that if a person's self-esteem is founded on the belief that he or she is competent only in some circumscribed set of domains, then the self would be fragile and vulnerable to attack. Rather, depending on earlier models of self-consistency, Brown contended that persons are primarily concerned with preserving a global sense of worthiness and adequacy, and they seek to "alter and modify their particular beliefs about the self in an attempt to attain this goal" (p. 33). People with low self-esteem modify specific beliefs about the self to enhance their feelings of personal worth and are unlike their high self-esteem peers who engage in "forms of self-enhancement that directly implicate the self" (p. 48). Such models typically depend on promoting the notion that there is but one major motivation or process for retaining a positive conception of self. This seems unnecessarily restrictive, particularly given the number of processes promoted by many cognitive psychologists.

These concerns, however, about the degree to which the self may be hierarchical lead to questions about fundamental notions of many models of self-concept and measures of "general" self-concept (Marsh, 1986a, 1987b, 1990c; Marsh & Hocevar, 1985; Marsh & McDonald-Holmes, 1990; Marsh & Smith, 1987). Knowledge of the general self-concept may not be informative, may predict little, and may be moderated by so many contextual concerns as to be meaningless. Working at the "general" level may not be beneficial or worthwhile if the aim is to enhance self-concept—it just may be too difficult to change at this level. As indicated in Chapter 2 of this volume, there has been a noted lack of success in determining the weightings that individuals use to form a general conception of self, probably because there are so many social and cultural influences on the self, at any particular time, such that the general self is more fluid and dynamic than generalized weighting models can capture (Marsh, 1987b).

From this discussion of the hierarchical nature of self-concept, we have identified many unresolved questions that are in need of future research. The fundamental question relates to *how,* or *if,* the various conceptions of self are integrated or synthesized into higher-order notions of self-concept. The two aspects of most interest are the weighting of the lower-order dimensions of self-concept, and the planning or executive component that processes the dimensions. Then the place, nature, and importance of the general self-concept (or other higher-order dimensions) would become more apparent. It may be that there are key development transitions, or individual differences, or it may be that there is no "top-down" notion.

An Emphasis on Cognition

To address the question as to how individuals synthesize information to form conceptions of self, it is probable that we will need to turn to the rich literature in cognitive processing. To demonstrate the value of this literature, we may need to develop models that place more attention on the individual as a processor of information. For example, Hattie (1992) provided a facet analysis or a series of reduction sentences of a model of self-concept that highlights the importance of cognitive processing: Our self-concepts or conceptions of our self are cognitive appraisals, expressed in terms of descriptions, expectations, and/or prescriptions, integrated across various dimensions that we attribute to ourselves. The integration is conducted primarily through self-testing or self-status quo tendencies. These attributes may be consistent or inconsistent depending on the type or amount of confirmation or disconfirmation our appraisals received from ourselves or from others.

The claim that conceptions of our self are cognitive appraisals places much emphasis on the individual as an appraiser. This does not mean there is a rational faculty embedded in each person that dictates all behavior and thoughts. It only states that our conceptions of our self relate to our beliefs and/or knowledge, particularly to the interrelationships between these beliefs. The term *appraisal* is used to further clarify the cognitions that we have about ourselves. Appraisals involve values; our thoughts about our selves relate to value statements and these may be good or bad, rational or irrational, frustrating or not frustrating, adaptive or maladaptive, appropriate or inappropriate, reasonable or unreasonable, justified or unjustified. A related interpretation is that appraisals refer to the way a person construes the significance of an encounter for his or her well-being. These encounters may be irrelevant, benign, harmful, or threatening (see Arnold, 1960; Lazarus, 1982; Lazarus, Averill, & Opton, 1970; Lazarus & DeLongis, 1983).

It is critical to note, however, that as James (1890) remarked, we are less involved with making explanations and more often involved in making choices.

> People can be viewed as continually attempting to impose some sort of order and coherence on the events in which they find themselves immersed. In order to survive we must extract some meaning from our experiences so that we can understand, anticipate, and, thus, exercise some control over life's experiences. We do this by making choices—choices about how to interpret events, choices among alternative courses of actions, (and) choices among evaluations of our actions. (James, 1890, p. 56)

These arguments place much emphasis on choice, decision making, and interpretation of the environments we find ourselves in and project ourselves into. The manner in which we do this, while maintaining or enhancing a conception of self, needs much more research.

The preceding analysis places much attention on the person as an appraiser who makes decisions and choices on the basis of beliefs about his or her self. Using the vast literature in cognitive processing, it is most likely that individuals select, bias, and retain information, and do so differently from others. It is certain that many cognitive processes are involved in making such choices and decisions (to select, retain, and bias information).

Swann and colleagues have provided much evidence for there being two major tendencies that individuals adopt to perform this biasing, which they termed self-enhancement and self-verification, respectively (Sherman, Judd, & Park, 1989; Skov & Sherman, 1986; Snyder & Swann, 1978; Swann, 1985; Swann, Pelham, & Chidester, 1988; Swann, Pelham & Krull, 1989; Swann & Read, 1981). They use self-enhancement as seeking positive or self-enhancing feedback, and self-verification as seeking accurate or self-verifying feedback. It is likely, however, that individuals can "self-enhance" even if they seek information that appears negative in that they may seek such information that confirms their beliefs about their status quo; and thus there are fewer risks of failure, inconsistency, or necessity for changing beliefs that have worked for them up to now. We also suggest that those who seek to test their belief systems may accommodate inaccurate information and often grow as a consequence of accommodating those views that may be inconsistent with their prior beliefs (see Hattie, 1992; Laing, 1969, 1971; Weber & Crocker, 1983).

The two tendencies can be in conflict, such as when new knowledge is to be learned. When such conflict occurs, self-verification is preferred by those who can tolerate ambiguities, whereas self-enhancement is preferred by those seeking consistency (Swann, Hixon, Stein-Seroussi, & Gilbert, 1990). Swann et al. argued that self-enhancement requires nothing more than characterizing the self-relevant stimulus, whereas self-verification requires more cognitive resources. Those who use many self-verification tendencies are more likely to have internal locus of control or attempt to change the world to fit their needs and wants, whereas those who use many self-enhancement tendencies are more likely to have external locus of control or fit in with the real, seemingly unchangeable, necessities of the world.

Some researchers have begun to assess the conditions under which these tendencies are used, although little is agreed at this stage. For example, Strube and Roemmele (1985) found that all individuals preferred self-verification but low self-esteem subjects had a greater tendency to self-enhance. Trope and colleagues (Trope, 1982, 1983; Trope & Ben-Yair, 1982; Trope & Brickman, 1975) claimed that there was a single underlying motivation to seek realistic self-assessment even at the expense of appearing inconsistent and ineffective. Future research profitably could identify the conditions that mediate the use of self-verification and self-enhancement.

The argument is not that individuals use one or the other tendency, but that all individuals use these tendencies, more or less, and may engage in different strategies to protect the self-enhancement. Brown, Collins, and Schmidt (1988), for example, suggested that those with high self-esteem tend to engage in direct forms of self-enhancement (esteem-enhancing biases that explicitly center around the self) whereas those with low self-esteem tend to bolster self-worth indirectly (using biases that involve others).

Swann, Pelham, and Krull (1989) argued that "all people are simultaneously motivated to self-enhance and self-verify and that they will work to satisfy both motives when possible" (p. 783), and they later added that neither self-enhancement nor self-verification theory alone can adequately explain people's feedback-seeking activities. People with inaccurate self-views do indeed desire praise, but their self-verification strivings override this desire when they recognize that praise disconfirms their self-concepts

(Swann, 1990; Swann, Wenzlaff, & Tafarodi, 1992). "The plight of depressed persons is surely an unenviable one, as they are trapped between a desire for praise and a conviction that they do not deserve it" (Swann, 1990, p. 317). A further example is to consider "a man who perceived himself as dullwitted. If his wife remarks that she thinks he is brilliant, he will probably be disturbed because her comment challenges a long-standing self-conception and implies that he may not know himself after all. And, if he does not know himself, what does he know" (Swann, Stein-Seroussi, & Giesler, 1992, p. 393; see also Swann & Hill, 1982). If the wife recognizes his limitations, he will be confident that their interrelationships will proceed smoothly and harmoniously. This is probably, as we would argue, because the wife provides predictability about her reactions, comments, and criticisms.

Swann and Pelham (1988; Pelham & Swann, 1989) found that individuals were inclined to keep roommates whose appraisals of them were congruent with their self-views and drop roommates whose appraisals were not congruent with their self-views. After similar demonstrations across a variety of situations, Swann and Brown (1990) suggested that "by carefully choosing self-congruent interaction partners and by evoking self-confirmatory reactions from others, people may bring others to see them as they see themselves. In so doing, people theoretically create interpersonal environments that help stabilize their self-conceptions" (p. 158)—even if the self-views are inaccurate. An advantage of this strategy is that as individuals become more insulated against self-discrepant feedback, it increases the likelihood of receiving positive confirmation, and it allows for a sense of stability when processing information about the self.

Not only do people seek and benefit from feedback that confirms their self-concepts, but those with positive self-concepts are more likely to seek positive feedback, and those with negative self-concepts to seek unfavorable feedback, although both groups *prefer* favorable feedback and have adverse stress reactions to negative feedback (Swann, Griffin, Predmore, & Gaines, 1987). Thus, claimed Swann, those with negative self-concepts are trapped between seeking negative or self-enhancing feedback because they prefer positive feedback and it bolsters their sense of self-control. The easiest way to resolve this seeming paradox for these individuals is that they try to avoid seeking negative information altogether and seek only positive information.

These arguments about the importance of feedback underline the importance of others in defining self-concept. When we are with those whom we regard as similar to us (such as our family, class, or sports team), then we are more likely to receive predictable information and we are more aware of reactions expected from us. Not only are we known by the company we keep, "people know themselves by the company they keep as well" (Brown, Novick, Lord, & Richards, 1992, p. 726). Thus, people do not necessarily seek positive information if it is inconsistent with their self-views but prefer relationships and information with individuals who see them as they see themselves, even if this means seeking relationships with people who think poorly of them (Swann, Hixon, Stein-Seroussi, & Gilbert, 1989). We become adept at soliciting feedback that confirms our self-views (Coyne, 1976; Curtis & Miller, 1986) and seek out information about others that fits with our own beliefs about our self (e.g., extroverts learn about others by asking questions about issues related to extroversion, whereas introverts ask about introversion; Fong & Markus, 1982). Such notions underline the remarkable consistency of self-concept and the difficulties in changing conceptions of self. As Sherman (1989) has noted, these tendencies imply that the self has inertia: "As self-relevant information is attended to and interpreted in the light of current self-beliefs, the self is likely to remain unchanged" (p. 306).

It is not clear whether self-enhancement must necessarily involve doing whatever it takes to feel *good* about oneself, as it is more likely that individuals are preserving the status quo. That is, they are doing whatever it takes to preserve a concept of self that has so far worked for them in the sense they know how to cope with threats to the self. We thus suggest that self-enhancement and self-verification may be more appropriately labeled, respectively, (a) *Self-status quo tendencies,* which refer to the wish to be viewed as one believes one is; to do whatever it takes to preserve this concept of self either by maximizing positive self-evaluations or by minimizing negative self-evaluations; and (b) *Self-testing tendencies,* which refer to the seeking of confirmation and/or disconfirmation about conceptions of self, being achieved through hypothesis-confirming tendencies and the use of strategies that allow for the best opportunities for self-expression.

Whatever the best terminology, the future research agenda is clear. The role of cognitive processing in the formation of concepts about self, and in making choices that are mediated by self-concepts needs more clarification. It may be that the ways we select, bias, and retain information is a function of our beliefs about ourselves, and the research by Swann and colleagues is most profitable in pointing to areas for further research, particularly with respect to the conditions under which this biasing occurs.

Strategies to Maintain, Protect, and/or Enhance Self-Concept

An exciting research area relates to the many strategies that are used to maintain a concept of self, to enhance self-esteem, and to maintain self-respect—using either or both of the preceding tendencies. There is already much research demonstrating how individuals attribute success and failure to either their own efforts or other factors. There is a long history of reviews demonstrating that we attribute success to ourselves for positive outcomes and blame others for negative outcomes (Bradely, 1978; Zuckerman, 1979). Snyder, Gangestad, and Simpson (1983) have discussed extensively the manner in which self-esteem can distort information-processing cognitions associated with the attribution of causality, and how we tend toward self-protective attributions especially when these performances are scrutinized by others.

It would be most useful to conduct further research on the various strategies that individuals use to cope with their environment. Such strategies have been referred to by a variety of generic labels: self-serving biases (Marsh, 1986b; Riess, Rosenfield, Melburg, & Tedeschi, 1981); need for approval (Crowne & Marlowe, 1964); self-monitoring (Snyder, 1974, 1979, 1987); and self-deception (Sackheim, 1983; Sackheim & Gur, 1978). At least six major strategies have so far been identified.

Self-Handicapping

This involves providing a *handicap* that can be used as an explanation for maintaining beliefs, and accounting for success or failure that is inconsistent with prior beliefs (Jones & Berglas, 1978). For example, a student could claim he scored 100% on an examination because the items were too easy rather than because of ability or effort in learning. Self-handicapping occurs when individuals are typically uncertain about their abilities and competencies and when there is high salience of an evaluative task; it happens more often in public versus private performance situations (Rhodewalt & Agustsdottir, 1986). Self-handicapping is less likely to occur when there are positive extrinsic incentives for good performance (Greenberg & Pyszczynski, 1985), when environmental handicaps preexist, and when there is high public salience of the excuse value of the handicapping behavior (Smith et al., 1982). It can derive from "an abnormal investment in the question of self-worth" (Jones & Berglas, 1978, p. 205), and the person must believe that his or her handicap will be viewed by others as a legitimate reason for potential failure. It is critical to note that self-handicapping is not unique to low self-esteem persons. It is used by both high and low self-esteem individuals: high self-esteem people—to enhance success; low self-esteem people—to protect themselves against the threat of failure (Tice, 1991).

Discounting

A related strategy is *discounting,* whereby praise, punishment, or feedback is "dismissed" as being information that is not valuable, accurate, or worthwhile for the individual. For example, when a teacher tells a child that he or she is doing a great job, the child's reaction is to discount this by claiming, "She always says that," "She's only trying to make me feel good," or "It's only because it is neat, not correct."

Distortion

Another strategy is *distortion,* whereby individual events, dispositions, or beliefs can be distorted, usually retrospectively, to maintain the status quo. Baumeister and Covington (1985) found that high self-esteem individuals sought to conceal their reactions to persuasive messages by retrospectively expressing greater premessage agreement (distorting their initial attitudes) than those with low self-esteem. Thus, as Baumeister, Tice, and Hutton (1989) have claimed, "yielding to persuasion is a self-protective strategy, whereas rejection of influence is an individuating and self-enhancing strategy" (p. 569). McFarland and Ross (1987) asked subjects to rate themselves, their dating partners, and their relationships on a number of dimensions. Two months later, subjects made current evaluations and were asked to recall their previous ratings. Recall was greatly distorted toward current beliefs (see also Ross & Conway, 1986).

Social Comparison

A further powerful strategy is *social comparison*. Low self-esteem individuals constantly monitor other peers' behavior for cues and attributions to explain/enhance their conceptions of self. They compare themselves with others, and social comparison sets standards or frames of reference. Individuals can choose the points of reference and make salient those activities they wish to excel in or set as a challenge (Campbell & Fairey, 1985; Campbell, Fairey & Fehr, 1986; Campbell & Fehr, 1990). For example, very successful mathematics students might have a high math self-concept in an average math class, but after being sent to a gifted mathematics class, their self-concept could plummet as they now compare themselves with this new cohort. These comparisons are usually private, as low self-esteem people are less likely to make public comparisons (see Baumeister, Tice, & Hutton, 1989; Tesser, Campbell, & Smith, 1984). "Unable to convince themselves privately that they possess favorable qualities, these individuals may instead attempt to feel better about themselves by engaging in behaviors, observable to themselves and others, that suggest that they are capable, likable, intelligent, and so forth" (Baumgardner, Kaufman, & Levy, 1989, p. 919). Baumgardner et al. further suggested that low self-esteem people adopt a coping style that may initially intend to disconfirm negative feedback but, over time, actually confirms a negative self-view. This spiral is often noted in psychotherapy. High self-esteem individuals appear to have more cues as to when it is not socially desirable to berate the source of negative feedback (Baumgardner, Kaufman, & Levy, 1989).

Low self-esteem individuals often compare themselves to those less fortunate than themselves (Wood, 1989), and often attempt to present themselves as more confident to impress others and maybe even themselves (Baumgardner, 1990). Public boasting, however, can create an impression of competence and engender interpersonal antipathy, particularly when the audience is aware of a person's prior poor performance (Baumeister, 1982; Schlenker & Leary, 1982).

Goal Setting

A further strategy that has emerged primarily out of the management literature is *goal setting* (Locke & Latham, 1992). To attain goals, individuals must exert effort, persist over time, pay attention to what they are doing, monitor their plans'and actions, evaluate their progress, and have commitment to their goals regardless of whether they are self-set, participatively set, or assigned. The finding that specific and challenging goals lead to better performance than vague or do-your-best goals has become one of the fundamental premises of goal-setting theory (Chidester & Grigsby, 1984; Hunter & Schmidt, 1983; Locke, 1987; Mento, Steel, & Karren, 1987; Tubbs, 1986; Wood & Locke, 1987; Wood, Mento, & Locke, 1987). Setting difficult goals is most effective at promoting attainment because it directs the individual's attention to relevant behaviors or outcomes, it conveys normative information to individuals by suggesting or specifying what level of performance they could be expected to attain, it energizes task performance by motivating individuals to exert effort in line with the difficulty or demands of the goal, and it commands persistence and students work longer and are more tenacious than with easy goals. Dweck and Leggett (1988) differentiated between performance goals, in which individuals are concerned with gaining favorable judgments of their competence, and learning goals in which individuals are concerned with increasing their competence. This is similar to the difference between self-status quo and self-testing, and like Dweck and Leggett, we propose that different goals can lead to different response patterns.

Self-Monitoring

Individuals actively plan, enact, and guide their behavioral choices in social situations through the process of *self-monitoring* (Snyder & Cantor, 1980). High self-monitors make their behavioral choices on the basis of situational information. Thus, high self-monitors are more dictated to by the external environment and by social comparison.

The Effects of the Strategies

These six strategies explain how individuals can bias, select, and retain information that affect their self-concepts. It is likely that we all use the strategies to varying extents to provide predictability in our lives. For example, the various seemingly irrational beliefs that individuals hold allow them extra predictability as to what to do or how to react in new situations. This effect highlights the enormous difficulties in devising programs to change self-esteem. Daly and Burton (1983) reported high correlations between many irrational beliefs and low self-esteem, particularly problem avoidance, helplessness, high self-expectations, and demand for approval. They noted that individuals with irrational beliefs have a high need to be approved by others, a need to excel in all endeavors to feel worthwhile as a person, obsessive anxiety about possible calamities in the future, and the idea that it is better to avoid problems than to face them. It must be noted, however, that "irrationality" is a culturally bound term and many have noted its value-laden connotations; what is irrational for one person may be rational for another (Derrida, 1976; Laing, 1969, 1971).

Future research may identify other strategies that individuals use to protect, maintain, and/or enhance their conceptions of self. A better understanding of these strategies may become pivotal in understanding how we process the information that feeds our self-concepts, and may have profound implications for programs to enhance self-concept. They also suggest that there may be more critical underlying motivations that cause us to bias, select, and retain information.

The Importance of Control

Much of the impetus for using these strategies derives from a desire to have a cognitive sense of control over situations and selves (White, 1959). By having such a sense of control, individuals can maintain a sense of worth and identity, can represent themselves to others with an internal sense of consistency, and can strive to verify their self-conceptions by acquiring self-confirmatory feedback.

Hattie (1992) argued that further investigation of control may lead to much richer understandings of self-concept and may even provide the basis of alternative theories of self-concept. The notion of control does not necessarily refer to explicit intentional control, but more to a desire to exert some order and control over the mass of sometimes confusing and conflicting data individuals need to process about themselves and their perceptions of their world. It is too simple, however, to consider control as a single phenomenon. Bandura and Wood (1989) made a distinction between two aspects of control. The first concerned the level of personal efficacy to effect changes by creative uses of capabilities and enlistment of effort. The second concerned the changeableness or controllability of the environment. They regarded individuals who were low in personal self-efficacy as likely to effect limited change even in environments that provide many opportunities (Seligman, 1975, termed this notion learned helplessness). The stronger the perceived self-efficacy, the higher the goals individuals set for themselves, and the firmer their commitment to them. For school principals, Bandura and Wood demonstrated that viewing an organization as controllable increases perceived self-efficacy to manage it. In their study, the principals began with equally high ambitious goals, but those who viewed the organization as influenceable set themselves rising goals, whereas those who regarded the organization as difficult to change continued to lower their sights.

Rothbaum, Weisz, and Snyder (1982) distinguished between primary and secondary control. Primary control refers to an individual's attempt to bring the environment into line with his or her beliefs and wishes, whereas secondary control relates to individuals bringing themselves into line with their perceived environment. Both forms of control allow people to exert some influence over future events, which Langer (1975, 1989) called the "illusion of control." Primary control requires a higher self-efficacy, that is the degree of confidence that a person has about influencing future events, whereas secondary control relates more to learned helplessness. This distinction between primary and secondary control may be culturally bound as many Confucian-based societies promote the idea of the individual accommodating to the environment rather than exerting influence over it; yet at the same time, these students believe very much in effort, which is controllable, as the means to achievement.

We can also distinguish between control over process and control over product (Hattie, Jones, & Hosenni, 1991). A student can have the perception of control by understanding and seeking products, and/or can have control by understanding and enjoying processes. Those individuals who tend to seek control over products concentrate more on the goals of a task and are more likely to attribute success and failure to their ability and other factors controlled by them. Those who seek control over process concentrate more on the actual methods of performing the task and are more likely to attribute success or failure to environmental conditions or to other people such as teachers. In our Western school system, it seems that dwelling on control over process seems to be counterproductive in enhancing achievement.

These notions of control over product and process, and personal efficacy and changeability relate to our expectations or what "we back ourselves to do" (James, 1890). Reasonably accurate appraisal of our own capabilities and appropriate expectations are of considerable value in successful functioning. Large misjudgments of personal efficacy in either direction can mitigate against success. Judgments of efficacy can also determine how much effort people will expend and how long they will persist in the face of obstacles or aversive experiences. Weisz (1986) traced the development of control and suggested that individuals may seek a sense of control using two broad processes: (a) attempting to change existing realities to bring them in line with their wishes, and (b) attempting to accommodate to existing realities to effect a more satisfying fit with those realities. There is already much research to demonstrate that individuals prefer to have a sense of control in the sense of added predictability and it is likely that this predictability will remain a critical research issue in self-concept (Arkin & Baumgardner, 1985; Baumgardner, Kaufman, & Levy, 1989; McFarlin & Blascovich, 1981). It would be most profitable to further the research on the role of control in the formation of self-concepts, and the importance that our conceptions of self play in providing predictability for future interactions and interpretations.

THE EFFECTS OF SELF-CONCEPT ON PEOPLE'S LIVES

There has been little research demonstrating the importance of self-concept for predicting behaviors. Most research has considered self-concept as a post hoc explanation of behavior or as a correlate of behavior. It may be valuable to ascertain when self-esteem is a predictor, when it is an outcome, and when it is not involved at all. We engage in many activities besides having conceptions of self, and for some, self-concept may be very low in the maintenance and value hierarchy. It is thus not surprising that self-concept can be a poor predictor of behavior for some, maybe many, people. Although some closely monitor their self (Markus, 1977), most do not go around uttering saliences about their self and then act. In this section, we review two major areas wherein self-concept may play a major role.

Self and Academic Achievement

An important area where self-concept may play a major role is academic achievement. This topic has been addressed in Chapter 7 in this book, and thus only brief mention is given here.

The relationships between self and academic achievement are low. The earlier meta-analysis by Hansford and Hattie (1982) found an *overall* .20 correlation; the more recent meta-analyses by Muller, Gullung, and Bocci (1988) reported an average of .18; and Holden, Moncher, and Schinke (1990) found .13. Thus about 4% of the variance is in common. Such a correlation makes it very difficult to tease out causal directions, so it is not surprising that there are as many studies reporting that changes in self lead to changes in achievement as there are for the opposite directional argument.

Particular dimensions of self-concept have stronger correlations with achievement. For example, the components of academic self-concept would be expected to, and do have, higher correlations than the preceding averages (Marsh, 1986b, 1988a, 1989b; Marsh, Byrne, & Shavelson, 1988). For example, Marsh (1988a) reported a median correlation of .39 between reading self-concept and verbal achievement indicators, and a median of .33 between math self-concept and mathematics achievement. Moreover, Marsh (1986b, 1988a, 1989b, 1990b) found that whereas mathematics and verbal achievements were substantially correlated, mathematics and verbal self-concepts were nearly uncorrelated. He posited the internal/external frame of reference (I/E) model to explain this phenomenon (Marsh & Parker, 1984). The I/E model states that self-concepts are formed in relation to both internal and external processes or frames of reference. According to the external process, students compare their own mathematics and verbal skills with those of other students in their frame of reference and use this external, relativistic comparison as one basis of their academic self-concept in each of the two areas. According to the internal process, students compare their self-perceived mathematics skills with their self-perceived verbal skills and use this internal, relativistic comparison as a second basis of their academic self-concept in each of the two areas. This is a variant of the compensatory model discussed in Chapter 2 of this book. For example, consider students who accurately perceive their mathematics and verbal skills to be below average but whose mathematics skills are better than their verbal skills. These students have mathematics skills that are below average relative to other students (an external comparison) but that are above average relative to their verbal skills (an internal comparison). Depending on how these two components are weighted, these students may have average or even an above-average mathematics self-concept despite their poor mathematics skills (see also Marsh, 1989b, 1990a; Marsh, Byrne, & Shavelson, 1988).

Given the correlations between academic self-concepts and academic achievement, it is possible to investigate causal relationships. Calsyn and Kenny (1977) contrasted what they termed self-enhancement and skill-development models of the self-concept and achievement relation. According to the self-enhancement model, self-concept is a primary determinant of academic achievement. Support for this model would provide a strong justification for self-concept enhancement interventions explicit or implicit in many educational programs. In contrast, the skill development model implies that academic self-concept emerges principally as a consequence of academic achievement. According to this model, the best way to enhance academic self-concept is to develop stronger academic skills.

Future research could well attend to the nature of the causal mechanisms that relate self and achievement. For example, following Baumeister, Tice, and Hutton (1989; see also Baumeister & Tice, 1985), we would argue that different goals and different systems of primary control are associated with different levels of self-esteem. Both high and low self-esteem individuals prefer to succeed, but people with high self-esteem *expect* to succeed more than those with low self-esteem (McFarlin & Blascovich, 1981). Primary control is activated with high self-esteem individuals after initial success as this signifies a talent or potential ability, whereas for the low self-esteem individuals this confirms a deficiency that needs to be remedied. Thus, different goals and different systems of primary control are associated with different levels of self-esteem.

Baumeister and Tice (1985) further argued that low self-esteem people aimed to transform a deficient feature into a passing one and they reacted more favorably to positive (success) evaluations, even if unexpected, and less favorably to negative (failure) evaluations, even if expected (see also McFarlin & Blascovich, 1981). Low self-esteem individuals indicate, however, that unfavorable feedback is more self-descriptive than favorable feedback. They tolerate little deviation from equilibrium. Baumeister, Tice, and Hutton (1989) have argued that low self-esteem people show moderately high persistence at the task after failure, consistent with the view that they are interested in remedying their deficiencies to reach a passable level of performance, which would afford them protection against humiliating failure. Further, they tend to avoid tasks following initial success because such success signifies that they have already reached an adequate level of performance, and further tests merely run the risk of disconfirming the favorable outcome.

Intervention Studies

It would appear from much of the literature that it is easy to enhance self-esteem as there are so many programs, and so many "nice feelings" are generated as a consequence of these programs. The evidence, however, of the success of these programs is to the contrary.

There is a need for some benchmarks to evaluate the success of various programs. A first source for determining such a benchmark is from a meta-analysis of programs to enhance self-concept primarily conducted by psychotherapists. J. C. Hattie (1992) was interested in whether programs that were more cognitively based (e.g., based on cognitive behavioral programs) were different in their effectiveness from more affectively based programs (e.g., phenomenological approaches and existentialism). This distinction does not imply that the cognitively oriented programs ignore emotions or affect but that these phenomena are more related to or modified by concentrating on cognitive states such as thoughts, conceptions, or processes.

Hattie synthesized the results from 89 coded articles, and 485 effect-sizes. The average effect-size was .37 ($SD = .12$), indicating that 10% of those who had some intervention had enhanced conceptions of self compared with those who received no treatment. Programs at the more cognitive end of the continuum were more effective (Mean = .48) compared with the programs at the more affective end (Mean = .12). Adults are much more malleable in terms of self-concept than are children, and individuals in the preadolescent period experienced the greatest difficulty in change. For young children, cognitive skills are still very concrete, whereas for adults cognitive skills are more abstract and complex. The adolescent is more likely to be moving into the more complex arena of synthesizing across many dimensions of self.

Many cognitive therapies aim to integrate the individual's thoughts about him- or herself and replace maladaptive thoughts with more realistic thoughts (confirmable by self and others). These aims are achieved by providing much feedback, which helps individuals create situations where they learn more control, and eliminate conflicting thoughts that detract from the perceptions of the self. Persons high in control perceive that they have the ability to cope with aversive events, and because they believe they can minimize the effects of unpleasant events, they have fewer reasons to be stressed, or fear outcomes. Those who believe they are low in control or self-efficacy expect more aversive events (and that these events may be intermittent), and thus have higher levels of anxiety or arousal.

As a consequence of these analyses, appropriate goals can be set for the programs. For example, some goals of a whole school program to enhance self-esteem could include:

1. To enable students to identify and recognize appropriate and inappropriate coping strategies used to preserve existing self-esteem.
2. To enable students to identify and recognize appropriate and inappropriate coping strategies to enhance self-esteem.
3. To enable staff to enhance the quality and reception of feedback through an awareness of the manner in which information is used or ignored by individuals.
4. To provide opportunities for students to adopt, use, and practice more functional strategies for the development of a healthy self-esteem.

A second source of information to establish some benchmarks is a synthesis of meta-analyses. Over the past few years Hattie (1987, 1990) has published a series of studies synthesizing many meta-analyses to answer two major questions: Can we devise a measurement procedure to address the question as to whether schools have an effect on student outcomes? and What are the salient features of schooling that affect student outcomes? (Hattie, 1987, 1992). Briefly, a unidimensional continuum has been devised on which the various effects of schooling can be located. This continuum, calibrated in standard deviation units or effect-sizes, provides the measurement basis to address the question of the effects of schooling. It is possible to statistically synthesize the results of a large number of studies, and thus ascertain the typical effects of schooling, and identify the innovations or changes that improve achievement in a systematically positive manner. Over 130 meta-analyses that related some facet of school learning to achievement outcomes for regular students were synthesized. Altogether, 22,155 effect-sizes from 7,827 studies were computed, representing approximately 5 to 15 million students, and covering almost all methods of innovation. With respect to achievement, the typical effect is .40 ($SE = .02$), the typical effect for attitude outcomes is .28 ($SE = .02$), and specifically for self-esteem effects (across 1,399 effect-sizes) is .19 ($SE = .04$).

These are the benchmark figures, and they provide a standard from which to judge effects. This continuum provides a method for measuring the effects of various programs on attitudinal and affective outcomes. Table 11.1 presents some comparisons for the outcomes of self-esteem programs.

The effects of most educational interventions are much smaller than effects derived from psychotherapy and out-of-classroom settings. It would be difficult to derive information from these effects to form the basis of a successful intervention, except for the consistently negative effects of retaining students a grade. The synthesis of meta-analyses on achievement outcomes pointed to the power of feedback, setting difficult goals, and the importance of the qualities of teachers, and it is expected that these factors

TABLE 11.1   Effect-Sizes from Various Meta-Analyses Relating to Self-Esteem

	No. Effects	Mean	SE
In psychotherapy settings	387	.37	.10
Cognitive oriented programs	186	.47	.80
Affectively oriented programs	68	.12	.73
In classroom settings			
Overall self-esteem effects	1,399	.19	.04
In other contexts			
Goals and self-efficacy	20	1.04	.02
Outward Bound and self-esteem	217	.26	.02
Comparisons			
Overall achievement	165,258	.40	.02
All affective variables	24,780	.28	.02

would also be critical in developing self-esteem (see Hattie, 1992). At least, when promoting programs to enhance self-esteem, the typical effect from previous studies is .19 of a standard deviation increase, and this is the magnitude that can at least be expected when evaluating new programs (relative to the costs).

An example of using these benchmarks is provided by an evaluation of the Australian Outward Bound program (Marsh & Richards, 1988; Marsh, Richards, & Barnes, 1986). It is argued elsewhere (Hattie, 1992; Richards, 1977) that the Outward Bound experience is effective in enhancing self-esteem because it sets difficult goals and tasks are structured so that students attain these goals; increases the amount and quality of feedback that is vital to learning and controlling the learning process; and demands that individuals reassess their coping strategies. A meta-analysis based on the Australian Outward Bound program indicated that the overall mean effect was .38, and for self-esteem changes was .32. This effect exceeded the typical value obtained from most school-based programs, equaled that from intensive psychotherapy, and was greater than the effect from other Outward Bound programs (overall mean effect-size = .29, mean for self-esteem = .11). Thus, using the benchmarks of .19 from all programs to enhance self-esteem, it can be confidently concluded that the Australian Outward Bound program is most effective in enhancing self-esteem.

There are many directions for future research with respect to the effects of self-concept on people's lives. The causal mechanisms that connect self-concept to achievement are desperately needed, and such research must go beyond simply relating the two attributes. Similarly, more attention to the key determinants that lead to changes in intervention programs would be most profitable. Setting clear goals for the intervention programs, and comparing the outcomes to competing effect-sizes would allow evaluators to more appropriately assess the value of self-concept interventions.

THE IMPACT OF SOCIAL AND CULTURAL EFFECTS ON SELF-CONCEPT

Reverting to our earlier analogy with intelligence, a recent trend in this literature is to move beyond the view that intelligence is something some have more of than others and to consider intelligence as something related to the interrelationship among ideas, behavioral contexts, and outcomes (Kinceloe & Steinberg, 1993; Walkerdine, 1984). Such thinking is based on the notion that individuals operate simultaneously at different cognitive stages, that development is always interactive with the environment, and always in the process of being reshaped and reformed. This conception is based on Foucault (1984) who argued that social forces shape our understanding of what constitutes knowledge and thus shape our conceptions of self. As a consequence, postformal thinking places more emphasis on enfolding sequences or the process of becoming (as per Allport, 1937, 1955; Sartre, 1943/1957; 1965). Sartre claimed that people *make* definitions and therefore can never be ultimately reduced to the definitions. The history of words attests to the way people make and change definitions and how they invent new words. To define is to hold static, to make a thing of a human. I may be defined as a psychologist but I am not just a psychologist. I am both being and not being. "Being is. Being is in itself. Being is what it is" (Sartre, 1943/1957, p. 29). Individuals continually make themselves and they are that toward which they project themselves but which they are not yet. Consequently, Sartre denied the existence of a self-substance. When he spoke of our pursuit of a self, he meant that we cannot say that a particular "self" *is* something any more than we can say that at any given instant the flying arrow *is* at the point C on the designated path A–Z. The nature of the self is that it is continually choosing to project itself toward future possibilities. This self is a process rather than an entity. Sartre, however, does not deny the existence of an active, organizing, individual consciousness but sees it as a relation between the subject and him- or herself. The self is "in a perpetually unstable equilibrium between identity as absolute cohesion without a trace of diversity and unity as a synthesis of multiplicity" (Sartre, 1955, p. 124). This process of becoming or enfolding is often not easily categorized or generalized, as it is tacit and gradual and depends very much on the contexts or settings in which we develop.

Exploration of these arguments by Sartre and, more recently, by poststructuralists will require different measurement models than those used today. There will be more emphasis on individuals' conceptions of their social world, and a concentrated effort to understand the ways in which the contexts and interactions with the environment affect the views an individual possesses about the self (as in Bracken's 1992 context-dependent behavioral model of self). Self-concept will come to be regarded as more fluid, interactive with the environment, and simultaneously operating at different stages. Given that our knowledge of the "structure" of self-concept is now well advanced, as indicated by the chapters in this book, it may be a worthwhile direction to pursue the more "dynamic" aspects of self-concept, assess the causal mechanisms of change, and ask questions about the many influences of the environment and differing conceptions of context on the formation of the self.

We know too little about some of the more recent social and cultural effects on the development of self-esteem, such as unemployment, wars, poverty, advertising, and racism. Too often, previous research efforts in these areas have been based on measures of self-esteem normed on people located in middle-class comfortable situations. These sociocultural influences are becoming more critical in understanding the development of self-concept, and more attention is being placed on how self-concept relates to social and cultural contexts such as ethnicity, gender, social class, religion, and nationality (Triandis, 1989). Much of the earlier work on these topics regarded these social and cultural influences as a correlate of self-concept, but future research will need to assess how these influences weave a major influence in developing self-concept, and particularly how they lead to differing ways that individuals integrate the various conceptions of self into a sense of identity and person.

A related and exciting development is the research on the effects of cultural differences in self-concept. Triandis (1989) has argued that the private self, that is cognitions that involve traits, states or behaviors, is emphasized more in individualistic cultures, whereas the collective self, that is cognitions about group membership, is emphasized more in collective societies (see also Marsella, DeVos, & Hsu, 1985; Shweder & Miller, 1985). Gergen (1982, 1990) has documented the commitment in Western societies toward the private self and individualization of the other. "That is, others tend to be characterized in terms of individual units, and to be understood as viewing each other in the same terms" (1990, p. 574). If, claimed Gergen, we abandon the notion that the locus of knowledge of the self lies within the minds of individuals, we can turn to the relationships among persons and consider "intersubjective meanings" and the complex system of relationships that these serve as a basis for individuals when interpreting their concepts of self.

We nominate two major "cultural" areas that could profit from more research: the effects of gender on self-concept, and developmental issues.

Gender Studies

With the increased attention to cultural and social interpretations, more research on the influence of gender should be forthcoming. One example is the work on the effects of gender as a context and cultural influence on the ways an individual views his or her world. Eagly (1987) argued that the central core of the stereotypes of males and females was the idea that males are more "agentic" (self-assertive and motivated to master) and females are more "communal" (selfless and concerned with others). The social roles associated with these traits (homemakers and child rearers vs. breadwinners) are still predominantly occupied by females and this can reinforce the stereotypes of these roles. Hoffman and Hurst (1990) argued, however, that the stereotyped views of males and females are largely attempts to rationalize, justify, or explain the sexual division of labor, and the "most powerful rationale imaginable is probably the simple assumption that there are inherent differences between males and females that make each sex better suited for its role" (p. 199). Regardless of the supposed causes of the differences, any continual reinforcement of the stereotypes could lead to further differences in the treatment of males and females.

Crocker and Major (1989) argued that there was little evidence for claiming gender differences in self-esteem, and they suggested that this does not necessarily mean that females have similar scores to males. Rather females could engage in a variety of strategies of self-protection such as attributing negative feedback to prejudice against females; selectively comparing their outcomes with those of other females; and selectively devaluing those attributes on which their female peers typically fare poorly and valuing those attributes on which their female peers excel. Oyserman and Markus (1993) claimed that for men, self-esteem is connected with "an individuation process in which personal, distinguishing achievements are emphasized. In contrast, women's self-esteem can be linked to a process in which connections and attachments to others are emphasized" (p. 198).

Hattie and McInman (1991) used a meta-analysis based on over 400 effect-sizes and reported differences in mean self-concept scores for males and females on only a few dimensions. The specific dimensions favoring males were mathematics and physical ability self-concepts, and dimensions favoring females were verbal self-concept. More important, there appear to be differences in the manner that males and females integrate these conceptions across various dimensions. These differences do not necessarily translate into differences on global self-concept or self-esteem.

Extending the claims by Crocker and Major (1989), cited earlier, there may be different strategies for integrating self-concepts between males and females. There is evidence, albeit limited, that females are more likely to use self-testing tendencies and males are more likely to use self-status quo tendencies. For example, Roberts and Nolen-Hoeksema (1989) found that males consistently demonstrated a self-status quo perception of their levels of productivity compared with objective criteria, whereas females were more reactive to the valence of feedback and underestimated actual productivity:

> Females more readily than the men, considered the external information, whether positive or negative, to have self-evaluative meaning . . . (and) despite their greater incorporation of evaluative feedback into their own self-evaluations of their competence, do not actually perform any differently

than men. . . . women truly do incorporate others' opinions of their competence into their own, but are not necessarily daunted in terms of their performance by these opinions. In other words, women may accept a negative evaluation of a past performance as accurate, but not interpret this to mean that they are incapable of improving their performance on future tasks.(p. 741)

Thus, Roberts and Nolen-Hoeksema (1989) found that males showed clear evidence for a self-status quo defensiveness against negative competence feedback, whereas females considered these evaluations to be more informative about and verifying of their abilities. The self-status quo defensive processes used by males included selective responding, and they allowed positive feedback to influence them more than negative feedback in a manner that was maximally protective of self-esteem (see also Elliott, 1986, 1988).

Roberts and Nolen-Hoeksema (1989) also noted that when there is no feedback, males showed generally higher expectations for performance and tended to judge their own performance more favorably than females. When females were provided with clear feedback about their abilities, they did not think less of their own performance than males. When feedback was more subjective, there was evidence that females' self-evaluations were more negative in general. This is particularly manifest given that males receive far more evaluative attention in the classroom than females (Berk & Lewis, 1977). Nolen-Hoeksema (1987) found that male overestimations were greater in a negative feedback condition than in a positive feedback condition, and than females' overestimations in the negative condition, which suggests a greater defensiveness on the part of males against negative feedback in particular.

These processing differences relate to the differing attributions placed on performance. Deaux and Farris (1977) found that males not only evaluated their performance more positively than did females, but also males viewed skill rather than luck as more responsible for their performance. Thus, "men expect to do better, assume they have done better, predict a higher level of performance for themselves, evaluate their completed performance more favorably, and use causal explanations which are consistent with this self-enhancing pattern. These differences were marked only on the tasks labeled masculine" (p. 64).

These arguments suggest that males tend to have more self-status quo tendencies and thus tend to overestimate some facets of their self-concepts in reaction to positive information and devalue or not recognize negative information, whereas females tend to be more self-testing and are more able to tolerate negative information. These differences begin to emerge during the adolescent years and are most marked among adults. These differences are not necessarily a function of actual differences of ability or achievement, but probably are manifest because of the amount of ability information contained in the evaluations they receive from others, differences in attributions placed on performance, and social pressures on young adolescent males and females. This highlights the importance of the early adolescent years in developing processes for integrating conceptions of self (Hattie, 1992).

If there are differences in the manner in which males and females integrate conceptions of self, again the place of "general" or "global" self-concept becomes important. Rosenberg argued that we need to go beyond global esteem and consider the conceptions on which the esteem is based. There are differences on some first-order dimensions of self-concept, such as self-confidence, physical ability, mathematics, reading, or verbal dimensions of self-concept. And there are differences in the manner in which these first-order dimensions are integrated to form overall self-esteem. It thus becomes important not to add together scores on various first-order dimensions to infer overall self-esteem. Differences occur particularly when a scale requests individuals to attribute only positive concerns to themselves (as males more readily do) rather than to attribute positive and negative concerns to themselves (as females more readily attribute negative attributes).

From the preceding, it can be seen that there is much support for a diverse integration model: Females appear more willing to recognize, and are more responsive to, negative attributes (they tend to be self-verifiers), whereas males prefer to attribute positive attributes (they tend to be self-enhancers). These differences in integration are particularly noted among adults. Further research on the processes of integrating conceptions of self is likely to further enlighten the relationships between gender and self-esteem as there may be other critical differences between males and females in their methods of integrating conceptions of self to form self-esteem.

Developmental Issues

Too little is known about how self-esteem develops and there are few longitudinal studies of self-concept change (but see Conley, 1985). The person is not born with a multifaceted, hierarchical self-concept but is born into a world of expectations (see Harrè, 1979). How these expectations, which are culturally bound, transform into low and high self-esteem is not understood. The development throughout adulthood is also unknown, and too often, researchers recollect James's (1890) claim that self-concept is set in plaster by age 30. Others have argued for earlier ages where development of self-concept stops. Rosenberg (1979) claimed that "people who have developed self-pictures early in life frequently continue to hold these self-views long after the actual self has changed radically" (p. 58). Anderson (1952) argued that the first year is the most important for developing self-concept and that "each succeeding year becomes of lesser importance, until the image is essentially completed before adolescence" (p. 224).

Others have described stages for the growth of self-concept (Dickstein, 1977; Erikson, 1963; Jacobson, 1964; Mead, 1934), but there are numerous arguments against "stage" models, particularly those that involve invariant stages (see McCall, 1977; Wohlwill, 1973). The objectors claim that certain features of a stage model can be assimilated earlier than predicted or in a different sequence. There are probably not stages that a person must go through, nor must they go through each phase in order, nor experience all aspects; rather it is most probable that there are loose associations between various events in the development of self-concept and age. The development of self is more a process of parallel developments. Hattie (1992) argued that there were seven such parallel developments: As we learn to distinguish between the self and others (Kelly, 1955; Laing, 1969); as we learn to distinguish the self from the environment (Lafitte, 1957; Lewis & Brooks-Gunn, 1979); as major reference groups change, which in turn leads to changes in expectations (Mischel, 1977); as the individual changes the source of personal causation (de Charms, 1968); as we change in cognitive processing, particularly with the development of formal operations (Piaget, 1977); as we change and/or realize cultural values; and as we change the manner in which we receive confirmation and disconfirmation (Laing, 1971).

Self-concept is generally much more stable in adult life than in younger age groups (see McCrae & Costa, 1982; Mortimer, Finch, & Kumka, 1982) although we know too little about the development of self during adulthood and we do know that it is easier to change or enhance adults' self-concept. Some researchers have argued that there are major reassessments of the value of life and self at the beginning of middle age (Butler, 1974; Greenleigh, 1970; Marmor, 1968; Neugarten & Datan, 1974); and the earlier claims as to the critical influence of life stresses are being revised. Life stresses do not seem to be as important as once claimed (Costa & McCrae, 1978, 1980). Levinson (1978) contended that there were four polarities that must be redefined and integrated during adulthood: (a) young and old, (b) creation and destruction, (c) masculine and feminine, and (d) attachment and separation. Costa and McCrae (1980) have contended that it may be more profitable to look for the means by which stability is maintained.

There are probably changes associated with old age but the research is limited (cf. Suls & Mullen, 1982, p. 115). Perhaps it is more accurate to associate these changes in self-concept not so much with old *age* as with the latter periods in one's life when stress and coping are major considerations (see Eisdorfer, 1983; Lazarus & DeLongis, 1983).

THE TERMINOLOGY CONFUSION

There are many related self-terms, and their proliferation leads to murky understandings and confusion. Some have regarded self-esteem and self-concept as part of the *self system* and seem to revert to Allport's notion of becoming, of Kernberg's (1975) notion of the self as part of a greater affective-cognitive structure that consists of self-representations and their related affect dispositions. Others have regarded self-concept as but one kind of self-knowledge. Neisser (1988) identified four other kinds of self-knowledge: the ecological self as that self as perceived with respect to the physical environment; the interpersonal self; the extended self based primarily on our personal memories and anticipations; and the private self relating to those conscious experiences that are not available to anyone else.

Future research needs to concentrate on formulating how the various aspects of the self-system converge and discriminant. Such clarification would greatly assist in assessing the dependability of measurement of the various topics. Although appropriate multitrait and multimethod convergence and discrimination are minimum conditions for the dependability of tests of self-esteem, self-concept, or self-whatever, such discrimination must commence from a clear theoretical set of explications about the nature of the differences (Marsh, 1989a).

For example, there is much overlap between self-esteem and self-concept, and it has not been possible to find studies where the distinction has been operationalized such that differential conclusions arise from studies based on self-concept or self-esteem. This should not be interpreted, however, as implying that the distinction is not important and it is suggested that providing meaningful distinctions will continue to be a future issue in the self literature.

Another term often used as a synonym for self-concept and self-esteem is *self-efficacy.* This latter term, promoted by Bandura (1977, p. 31), relates to "people's judgments of their capabilities to organize and execute courses of action required to attain designated types of performances." Bandura proposed that self-efficacy varies on three dimensions: level or the number of tasks a person can do; strength or how resolutely a person believes in an ability to perform a task; and generality or the extent to which the expectancy generalizes across situations (see Bandura, 1986). Given the situational specificity of self-efficacy, individuals thus have a range of both low and high self-efficacy expectancies. Self-efficacy can influence the behaviors a person chooses, the degree of effort and persistence, and the level of arousal.

We suggest that there are differences in emphasis rather than differences in underlying notions between self-esteem, self-concept, and self-efficacy. The self system critically involves descriptions, prescriptions, and expectations and these appraisals are related, usually hierarchically, and depend very much on knowledge or belief claims. We are not merely a collection of rational faculties; we also have commitment. It is with respect to our differing perceptions of commitment that we can conceive self-esteem. Our conceptions of our self or self-concepts are relative to what we consider *important,* not necessarily to our capabilities and/or knowledge. Only if I regard certain aspects of my self-concept as important will there be effects on my beliefs about self-esteem. Self-esteem relates to the conviction that aspects of my behavior or self that I desire to be esteemed are worthwhile. We place importance on certain aspects, and we want to believe we are worthwhile in these areas. Thus self-esteem is relative to what we "back ourselves" to be and to do and, claimed James (1890), to give up pretensions is as blessed a relief as to get them gratified.

Thus, it is suggested that self-esteem relates to the salience of dimensions and is entwined with our sense of worth. An individual's sense of worth may be in a variety of areas: the body (beautiful) is of the highest importance to some, but for others it may be more important to be academically able, to have a happy family life, to gain respect from others, or to have a desirable personality. It is probable that only a resurgence of interest in idiographic methods will lead to the discovery of the role of commitment and salience across the many dimensions (see Higgins, 1987; Roche & Marsh, 1993).

THE EFFICACY OF THE INSTRUMENTS TO MEASURE SELF-CONCEPT

Although this topic has been covered in Chapter 3 of this volume, we would be remiss not to cite this topic as a major area needing further research. Despite there being almost as many tests of self-concept and self-esteem as there are researchers, what is surprising is that most lack any sort of credibility, are based on no theoretical explication of self-concept, randomly use the terms self-esteem and self-concept, appear to relate little to behavior, and rarely survive beyond the author's article. Moreover, many of the tests are identified by different terms, but it has been most difficult to demonstrate a distinction between these terms (such as between self-concept and self-esteem).

The number of self-concept tests is still increasing, and the following are proposed as a first litmus test that, if passed, should improve the minimum quality of scales:

1. Does the test derive from a clearly articulated and defensible theoretical model?
2. Is there evidence of reasonable unidimensionality of scales?
3. Is there information about how the user should interpret the test scores (see Messick, 1991)?
4. Is the test interpretation aimed at screening (a lesser requirement of rigor) or diagnosis (a greater requirement of rigor)?
5. Is there evidence from multitrait-multimethod analyses of the convergent and divergent validity of the test?
6. Is there information on the standardization of the test?

It is likely that more than 90% of self-concept tests could not pass these simple litmus tests, and some more widely known tests would also fail. There are few well-established and recognized tests of self-concept and few resources contrasting the performance of these tests (Marsh, 1988b; Wylie, 1989).

Most important for future research is the need to assess how individuals weight the various dimensions of self-concept to form an overall self-esteem. As argued earlier, this may vary for males and females, across various ages, and across and within cultures. Moreover, a major disappointment that future researchers could remedy is the lack of measures to differentiate self-concept and self-esteem.

CONCLUSION

This research agenda has pointed to a rich foundation of studies on which future researchers can build conceptualizations about self-concept and self-esteem. Many past achievements have furthered our understandings, and it is an easy prediction to contend that there will be many more such developments. We have identified the processes by which individuals integrate the various concepts of self into a general or global self-concept as a major theme of future studies. We do not wake each morning to reconceptualize our self from the many dimensions; we are not chameleons, at least usually not to ourselves. So how do we synthesize the many parts of the self and how do we process information that we constantly transmit and receive? This increased attention to the dynamic rather than structural aspects of self-concept is much needed, but it can only become central once the multidimensional nature of self-concept is agreed upon. Because we select, bias, and retain only certain information, we need more research to determine how we cognitively process information about the self that allows us to protect, maintain and/or enhance our concept of self. Then, we can consider the underlying motivations for the self-concept, which we have suggested may begin from a desire to bring more predictability to our past, present, and future. Many strategies have been suggested that allow us to maintain our self-concept, and more research could detail how the strategies interrelate and whether there are others of more importance. Such research may be critical for developing programs to change self-concept.

There seems to be an unstated assumption underlying the very large amount of literature on self-concept that knowing more about self-concept will affect people's lives. To the contrary, for many people knowing about their self-concept has little effect on their lives and leads others to have little understanding of their behaviors. We need to highlight this assumption and ask about the relationship between self-concept and other facets of our lives. A good example is the assumption that self-concept has something to do with academic achievement. There would be few schools or teachers who have not used "low self-esteem" to explain why some students have difficulty learning, or vice versa—although the research supporting this belief is most equivocal. There is already too much research merely reporting correlations between self-concept and achievement (or some other worthwhile variable), whereas what is desperately needed are more longitudinal studies relating to the mechanisms by which self-concept relates to achievement and vice versa. A most exciting future direction relates to understanding the causal mechanisms explaining the link between self-concept and achievement. There is merit in replacing the question: "What is the relationship between self-concept and achievement?" with "What is the relationship between self-concept and learning?" There are more dynamic and direct links between how students learn and their conceptions of self, whereas the links between the achievement outcomes and self-concept are not so direct.

We have noted the difficulties for those aiming to enhance self-concept. The exciting news is that most of the effects are positive but these effects are typically quite small. The suggestion is that enhancement programs based on identifying the individuals' coping strategies that allow maintenance of the status quo of their self-concept is a prerequisite to change, and replacing these strategies with others that encourage self-testing is more likely to lead to change. There is much need for research to ascertain the most appropriate coping strategies and then to relate these to self-concept change. The present research by Swann and colleagues (e.g., Swann, 1985, 1990; Swann & Brown, 1990; Swann & Pelham, 1988) is exciting in pointing to directions for future research. Clarification of such fundamental issues as the underlying processes (e.g., self-enhancement, self-verification), the usefulness of these processes, and their applicability to change, learning, and adaptation promises to offer many solutions to the most important issues in self-concept research.

For too long, self-concept research has been conducted in a social vacuum. We know much about the self-concepts of middle-class Western people in developed countries. As the poststructuralists are demonstrating, the importance of the culture too often has been underestimated. Factors such as gender and ethnicity are not correlates, but may be the fundamental underpinnings for explaining self-concept and its development (see Bracken, 1992). We may need to be much more idiographic in our measurement methods to begin to understand these pervasive influences of social and cultural factors.

Throughout this chapter, there has been a inclination to use the terms self-concept and self-esteem interchangeably. This is because, so far, while we can make clear philosophical differences between the terms, it has not been possible to operationalize these differences. The major differences relate to salience and commitment of the various conceptions of self, and this suggests that the fundamental measurement issue relates to how we weight the various lower-order concepts of self. There is much need for major breakthroughs in this area, and it may come through a closer investigation of the cognitive-behavioral processes that are used to form more general self-concepts than by exploring differential weighting through psychometrics.

Perhaps the safest prediction as to future research is that much attention will be placed on measurement instruments. As always, we need to be vigilant that any instrument, particularly those used for diagnostic and placement decisions more than those used for screening and research purposes, meets appropriately rigorous psychometric standards. There are far too many self-concept instruments that would not pass the barest minimum criteria. The self-concept literature has been too handicapped by poor measurement tools and only when we have purged some of these tests can we begin to investigate the more underlying dynamic as well as structural issues that are so critical for future research.

As noted at the beginning of this chapter, the topic of self-concept has occupied the minds of many researchers and the product of this occupation has filled much journal space. We see no diminution in this attention and trust that the research agendas we have suggested can help concentrate the task on advancing our understanding and improve our own self-efficacy in promoting the topic as worthy of academic study.

REFERENCES

Allport, G. W. (1937). *Personality: A psychological interpretation.* New York: Holt.

Allport, G. W. (1955). *Becoming.* New Haven, CT: Yale University Press.

Anderson, C. M. (1952). The self-image: A theory of dynamics of behavior. *Mental Hygiene, 36,* 227–244.

Arkin, R. M., & Baumgardner, A. H. (1985). Self-handicapping. In J. H. Harvey & G. Weary (Eds.), *Attribution, basic issues and applications* (pp. 169–202). London: Academic Press.

Arnold, M. B. (1960). *Emotion and personality* (Vols. 1 & 2). New York: Columbia University Press.

Bandura, A. (1977). Self-efficacy: Toward a unifying theory of behavioral change. *Psychological Review, 84,* 191–215.

Bandura, A. (1986). *Social foundations of thought and action: A social cognitive theory.* Englewood Cliffs, NJ: Prentice-Hall.

Bandura, A., & Wood, R. (1989). Effects of perceived controllability and performance standards on self-regulation of complex decision making. *Journal of Personality and Social Psychology, 56,* 805–814.

Baumeister, R. F. (1982). A self-presentational view of social phenomena. *Psychological Bulletin, 91,* 3–16.

Baumeister, R. F., & Covington, M. V. (1985). Self-esteem, persuasion, and retrospective distortion of initial attitudes. *Electronic Social Psychology, 1,* 1–22.

Baumeister, R. F., & Tice, D. M. (1985). Self-esteem and responses to success and failure: Subsequent performance and intrinsic motivation. *Journal of Personality, 53,* 450–467.

Baumeister, R. F., Tice, D. M., & Hutton, D. G. (1989). Self-presentation, motivation and personality differences in self-esteem. *Journal of Personality, 57,* 547–579.

Baumgardner, A. H. (1990). To know oneself is to like oneself: Self-certainty and self-affect. *Journal of Personality and Social Psychology, 58,* 1062–1072.

Baumgardner, A. H., Kaufman, C. M., & Levy, P. E. (1989). Regulating affect interpersonally: When low esteem leads to greater enhancement. *Journal of Personality and Social Psychology, 56,* 907–921.

Berk, L. E., & Lewis, N. G. (1977). Sex role and social behavior in four school environments. *Elementary School Journal, 77,* 205–217.

Boundy, N. (1990). *Self-concept: A pilot study to test whether some same-age adolescents' self-conceptions can best fit a unifactorial model and others a hierarchical model.* Unpublished master's thesis, University of Western Australia, Perth, Australia.

Bower, G. H., & Gilligan, S. G. (1979). Remembering information relating to one's self. *Journal of Research in Personality, 13,* 420–432.

Bracken, B. A. (1992). *Multidimensional self concept scale.* Austin, TX: Pro-Ed.

Bradely, G. W. (1978). Self-serving biases in the attribution process: A re-examination of the fact or fiction question. *Journal of Personality and Social Psychology, 36,* 56–71.

Breckler, S. J., & Greenwald, A. G. (1982). *Charting coordinates for the self-concept in multidimensional trait space.* Paper presented at the Annual Conference of the American Psychological Association, Washington, DC.

Brown, J. D. (1993). Self-esteem and self-evaluation: Feeling is believing. In J. Suls (Ed.), *Psychological perspectives on the self* (Vol. 4, pp. 27–58). Hillsdale, NJ: Erlbaum.

Brown, J. D., Collins, R. L., & Schmidt, G. W. (1988). Self-esteem and direct versus indirect forms of self-enhancement. *Journal of Personality and Social Psychology, 55,* 445–453.

Brown, J. D., Novick, N. J., Lord, K. A., & Richards, J. M. (1992). When Gulliver travels: Social context, psychological closeness, and self-appraisals. *Journal of Personality and Social Psychology, 60,* 717–727.

Butler, R. N. (1974). Psychiatry and psychology of the middle aged. In A. Freedman, H. Kaplan, & J. Sadock (Eds.), *Comprehensive textbook of psychiatry* (pp. 60–71). Baltimore, MD: Williams & Wilkins.

Calsyn, R. J., & Kenny, D. A. (1977). Self-concept of ability and perceived evaluation of others: Cause or effect of academic achievement. *Journal of Educational Psychology, 69,* 136–145.

Campbell, J. D., & Fairey, P. J. (1985). Effects of self-esteem, hypothetical explanations, and verbalization of expectancies on future performance. *Journal of Personality and Social Psychology, 48,* 1097–1111.

Campbell, J. D., Fairey, P. J., & Fehr, B. (1986). Better than me or better than thee? Reactions to intrapersonal and interpersonal performance feedback. *Journal of Personality, 54,* 122–133.

Campbell, J. D., & Fehr, B. (1990). Self-esteem and perceptions of conveyed impressions: Is negative affectivity associated with greater realism? *Journal of Personality and Social Psychology, 58,* 479–493.

Chidester, T. R., & Grigsby, W. C. (1984). A meta-analysis of the goal setting performance literature. *Academy of Management Proceedings,* 202–206.

Conley, J. J. (1985). Longitudinal stability of personality traits: A multitrait-multimethod-multioccasion analysis. *Journal of Personality and Social Psychology, 49,* 1266–1282.

Coombs, C. H. (1954). *A theory of data.* New York: Wiley.

Coopersmith, S. (1967). *The antecedents of self-esteem.* San Francisco: Freeman.

Costa, P. T., Jr., & McCrae, R. R. (1978). Objective personality assessment. In M. Storardt, I. C. Siegler, & M. F. Elias (Eds.), *The clinical psychology of aging* (pp. 119–144). New York: Plenum.

Costa, P. T., Jr., & McCrae, R. R. (1980). Still stable after all these years: Personality as a key to some issues in adulthood and old age. In P. B. Baltes & O. G. Brim, Jr., (Eds.), *Life-span development and behavior* (Vol. 3, pp. 65–102). New York: Academic Press.

Coyne, J. C. (1976). Toward an interactional description of depression. *Psychiatry, 39,* 28–40.

Crocker, J., & Major, B. (1989). Social stigma and self-esteem: The self-protective properties of stigma. *Psychological Review, 96,* 608–630.

Crowne, D., & Marlowe, D. (1964). *The approval motive.* New York: Wiley.

Curtis, R. C., & Miller, K. (1986). Believing another likes or dislikes you: Behavior making the beliefs come true. *Journal of Personality and Social Psychology, 51,* 284–290.

Daly, M. J., & Burton, R. C. (1983). Self-esteem and irrational beliefs: An exploratory investigation with implications for counseling. *Journal of Counseling Psychology, 30,* 361–366.

Das, J. P. (1980). Planning: Theoretical considerations and empirical evidence. *Psychological Research, 541,* 141–151.

Das, J. P., & Jarman, R. F. (1991). Cognitive integration: Alternative model for intelligence. In H. A. H. Rowe (Ed.), *Intelligence: Reconceptualization and measurement* (pp. 163–182). Hillsdale, NJ: Erlbaum.

Das, J. P., Kirby, J., & Jarman, R. F. (1979). *Simultaneous and successive cognitive processes.* New York: Academic Press.

Deaux, K., & Farris, E. (1977). Attributing causes for one's own performance: The effects of sex, norms, and outcome. *Journal of Research in Personality, 11,* 59–72.

de Charms, R. (1968). *Personal causation: The internal affective determinants of behavior.* New York: Academic Press.

Derrida, J. (1976). *Of grammatology.* Baltimore, MD: Johns Hopkins University Press.

Dickstein, E. (1977). Self and self-esteem: Theoretical foundations and their implications for research. *Human Development, 20,* 129–140.

Dunning, D., Meyerowitz, J. A., & Holzberg, A. D. (1989). Ambiguity and self-evaluation: The role of idiosyncratic definitions in self-serving assessments of ability. *Journal of Personality and Social Psychology, 57,* 1082–1090.

Dweck, C. S., & Leggett, E. L. (1988). A social-cognitive approach to motivation and personality. *Psychological Review, 95,* 256–273.

Eagly, A. H. (1987). *Sex differences in social behavior: A social-role interpretation.* Hillsdale, NJ: Erlbaum.

Eisdorfer, C. (1983). Conceptual models of aging: The challenge of a new frontier. *American Psychologist, 38,* 197–202.

Elliott, G. C. (1986). Self-esteem and self-consistency: A theoretical and empirical link between two primary motivations. *Social Psychology Quarterly, 49,* 207–218.

Elliott, G. C. (1988). Gender differences in self-consistency: Evidence from an investigation of self-concept structure. *Journal of Youth and Adolescence, 17,* 41–57.

Erikson, E. H. (1963). *Childhood and society* (2nd ed.). New York: Norton.

Fong, G. T., & Markus, H. (1982). Self-schemas and judgements about others. *Social Cognition, 4,* 191–204.

Foucault, M. (1984). *The Foucault reader.* New York: Pantheon.

Gardner, H. (1985). *Frames of mind.* London: Paladin.

Gergen, K. J. (1982). Toward transformation in social knowledge. New York: Springer-Verlag.

Gergen, K. J. (1990). Social understanding and the inscription of self. In J. W. Stigler, R. A. Shweder, & G. Herdt (Eds.), *Cultural psychology: Essays on comparative human development* (pp. 569–606). Cambridge, MA: Cambridge University Press.

Greenberg, A. G., & Pyszczynski, T. (1985). Compensatory self-inflation: A response to the threat to self-regard of public failure. *Journal of Personality and Social Psychology, 49,* 273–280.

Greenleigh, L. (1970). Facing the challenge of change in middle age. *Geriatrics, 29,* 61–66.

Greenwald, A. G., & Pratkanis, A. R. (1984). The self. In R. S. Wyer & J. K. Srull (Eds.), *Handbook of social cognition* (Vol. 3, pp. 129–178). Hillsdale, NJ: Erlbaum.

Hansford, B. C., & Hattie, J. A. (1982). The relationship between self and achievement/performance measures. *Review of Educational Research, 52,* 123–142.

Harrè, R. O. M. (1979). *Social being: A theory for social psychology.* Totowa, NJ: Rowman & Littlefield.

Harter, S. (1983). Developmental perspectives on the self-system. In P. H. Mussen (Ed.), *Handbook of child psychology* (4th ed., Vol. 4, pp. 275–285). New York: Wiley.

Hattie, J. A. (1987). Identifying the salient facets of a model of student learning: A synthesis of meta-analyses. *International Journal of Educational Research, 11*, 187–212.

Hattie, J. A. (1990). Measuring the effects of schooling. *Australian Journal of Education, 36*, 5–13.

Hattie, J. A. (1992). *Self-concept.* Hillsdale, NJ: Erlbaum.

Hattie, J. A., Jones, R., & Hosenni, D. (1991). *Student control over learning.* Manuscript submitted for publication.

Hattie, J. A., Krakowski, K., Rogers, H. J., & Swaminathan, H. (in press). An assessment of Stout's index of essential dimensionality. *Applied Psychological Measurement.*

Hattie, J. A., & McInman, A. (1991). *Gender differences in self-concept.* Manuscript submitted for publication.

Hattie, J. C. (1992). Enhancing self-concept. In J. A. Hattie (Ed.). *Self-concept* (pp. 221–240). Hillsdale, NJ: Erlbaum.

Higgins, E. T. (1987). Self-discrepancy: A theory relating self and affect. *Psychological Review, 94*, 319–340.

Hoffman, C., & Hurst, N. (1990). Gender stereotypes: Perception or rationalization? *Journal of Personality and Social Psychology, 58*, 197–208.

Holden, G. W., Moncher, M. S., & Schinke, S. P. (1990). Self-efficacy of children and adolescents: A meta-analysis. *Psychological Reports, 70*, 1044–1046.

Hunter, J. E., & Schmidt, F. L. (1983). Quantifying the effects of psychological interventions on employee job performance and work force productivity. *American Psychologist, 38*, 473–478.

Jacobson, E. (1964). *The self and the object world.* New York: International Universities Press.

James, W. (1890). *Principles of psychology* (2 vols.). Chicago: Encyclopedia Britannica.

Jones, E. E., & Berglas, S. (1978). Control of attribution's about the self through self-handicapping strategies: The appeal of alcohol and the role of underachievement. *Personality and Social Psychology Bulletin, 4*, 200–206.

Kelly, G. A. (1955). *The psychology of personal constructs.* New York: Norton.

Kernberg, O. F. (1975). *Borderline conditions and pathological narcissism.* New York: Aronson.

Kinceloe, J. L., & Steinberg, S. R. (1993). A tentative description of post-formal thinking: The critical confrontation with cognitive theory. *Harvard Educational Review, 63*, 296–320.

Kuiper, N. A. (1981). Convergent evidence for the self as a prototype: The "inverted U RT" effect for self and other judgements. *Personality and Social Psychological Bulletin, 7*, 438–443.

Lafitte, P. (1957). *The person in psychology: Reality or abstraction.* London: Routledge & Kegan Paul.

Laing, R. D. (1969). *The self and others.* New York: Pantheon.

Laing, R. D. (1971). *The politics of the family and other essays.* New York: Pantheon.

Langer, E. (1975). The illusion of control. *Journal of Personality and Social Psychology, 32,* 311–329.

Langer, E. (1989). *Mindfulness.* Reading, MA: Addison-Wesley.

Lazarus, R. S. (1982). Thoughts on the relations between emotion and cognition. *American Psychologist, 37,* 1019–1024.

Lazarus, R. S., Averill, J. R., & Opton, E. M. (1970). Toward a cognitive theory of emotion. In M. Arnold (Ed.), *Feelings and emotions: The Loyola Symposium* (pp. 207–232). New York: Academic.

Lazarus, R. S., & DeLongis, A. (1983). Psychological stress and coping in aging. *American Psychologist, 8,* 245–254.

Levinson, D. J. (1978). *The seasons of a man's life.* New York: Ballantine Books.

Lewis, M., & Brooks-Gunn, J. (1979). *Social cognition and the acquisition of self.* New York: Plenum.

Linville, P. W. (1982). Affective consequences of complexity regarding the self and others. In M. S. Clark & S. T. Fiske (Eds.), *Affect and cognition: The seventeenth annual Carnegie Symposium on Cognition* (pp. 79–109). Hillsdale, NJ: Erlbaum.

Linville, P. W. (1987). Self-complexity as a cognitive buffer against stress-related illness and depression. *Journal of Personality and Social Psychology, 52,* 663–676.

Locke, E. A. (1987). How to motivate employees. *State Legislature, 13,* 30–31.

Locke, E. A., & Latham, G. P. (1992). *A theory of goal setting and task performance.* Englewood Cliffs, NJ: Prentice-Hall.

Luria, A. R. (1966). *Higher cortical functions in man.* New York: Basic Books.

Luria, A. R. (1973). *The working brain: An introduction to neuropsychology.* London: Penguin.

Markus, H. (1977). Self-schemata and processing information about the self. *Journal of Personality and Social Psychology, 35,* 63–78.

Markus, H., & Nurius, P. (1986). Possible selves. *American Psychologist, 41,* 954–969.

Markus, H., & Sentis, K. (1982). The self in social information processing. In J. Suls (Ed.), *Psychological perspectives on the self* (Vol. 1, pp. 41–70). Hillsdale, NJ: Erlbaum.

Marmor, J. (1968). The crisis of middle age. *Psychiatric Digest, 29,* 18.

Marsella, A. J., DeVos, G., & Hsu, F. L. K. (1985). *Culture and self: Asian and Western perspectives.* New York: Tavistock Publications.

Marsh, H. W. (1986a). Global self-esteem: Its relation to weighted averages of specific facets of self-concept and their importance. *Journal of Personality and Social Psychology, 51,* 1224–1236.

Marsh, H. W. (1986b). Verbal and math self-concepts: An internal/external frame of reference model. *American Educational Research Journal, 23,* 129–149.

Marsh, H. W. (1987a). The big-fish-little-pond effect on academic self-concept. *Journal of Educational Psychology, 79,* 280–295.

Marsh, H. W. (1987b). The hierarchical structure of self-concept and the application of hierarchical confirmatory factor analysis. *Journal of Educational Measurement, 24,* 17–19.

Marsh, H. W. (1988a). The content specificity of math and English anxieties: The high school and beyond study. *Anxiety Research, 1,* 137–149.

Marsh, H. W. (1988b). *The Self Description Questionnaire (SDQ): A theoretical and empirical basis for the measurement of multiple dimensions of preadolescent self-concept: A test manual and a research monograph.* San Antonio: Psychological Corp.

Marsh, H. W. (1989a). Confirmatory factor analysis of multitrait-multimethod data: Many problems and a few solutions. *Applied Psychological Measurement, 13,* 335–361.

Marsh, H. W. (1989b). Sex differences in the development of verbal and mathematics constructs: The high school and beyond study. *American Educational Research Journal, 26,* 191–225.

Marsh, H. W. (1990a). Causal ordering of academic self-concept and academic achievement: A multiwave, longitudinal panel analysis. *Journal of Educational Psychology, 82,* 646–656.

Marsh, H. W. (1990b). The influence of internal and external frames of reference on the formation of math and English self-concepts. *Journal of Educational Psychology, 82,* 107–116.

Marsh, H. W. (1990c). The structure of academic self-concept: The Marsh/Shavelson model. *Journal of Educational Psychology, 82,* 623–636.

Marsh, H. W., Byrne, B., & Shavelson, R. (1988). A multifaceted academic self-concept: Its hierarchical structure and its relation to academic achievement. *Journal of Educational Psychology, 80,* 366–380.

Marsh, H. W., & Hocevar, D. (1985). The application of confirmatory factor analysis to the study of self concept: First and higher order factor structures and their invariance across groups. *Psychological Bulletin, 97,* 565–582.

Marsh, H. W., & McDonald-Holmes, I. Q. (1990). Multidimensional self-concept: Construct validation of responses by children. *American Education Research Journal, 27,* 89–117.

Marsh, H. W., & Parker, J. W. (1984). Determinants of student self-concept: Is it better to be a relatively large fish in a small pond even if you don't learn to swim as well? *Journal of Personality and Social Psychology, 47,* 213–231.

Marsh, H. W., & Richards, G. (1988). The Outward Bound bridging course for low-achieving high school males: Effect on academic achievement and multidimensional self-concepts. *Australian Journal of Psychology, 40,* 281–298.

Marsh, H. W., Richards, G. E., & Barnes, J. (1986). Multidimensional self-concepts: The effect of participation in an Outward Bound program. *Journal of Personality and Social Psychology, 50,* 195–204.

Marsh, H. W., & Smith, I. D. (1987). A cross-national study of the structure and level of multidimensional self-concepts: An application of confirmatory factor analysis. *Australian Journal of Psychology, 39,* 61–77.

Massaro, D. W., & Friedman, D. (1990). Models of integration given multiple sources of information. *Psychological Bulletin, 97,* 225–252.

McCall, R. (1977). Challenges to a science of developmental psychology. *Child Development, 48,* 333–344.

McCrae, R. R., & Costa, P. T. (1982). Self-concept and the stability of personality: Cross-sectional comparisons of self-reports and ratings. *Journal of Personality and Social Psychology, 43,* 1282–1292.

McFarland, C., & Ross, M. (1987). The relation between current impressions and memories of self and dating partners. *Personality and Social Psychology Bulletin, 13,* 228–238.

McFarlin, D. B., & Blascovich, J. (1981). Effects of self-esteem and performance feedback on future affective preferences and cognitive expectations. *Journal of Personality and Social Psychology, 40,* 521–531.

Mead, G. H. (1934). *Mind, self and society.* Chicago: University of Chicago Press.

Mento, A. J., Steel, R. P., & Karren, R. J. (1987). A meta-analytic study of the effects of goal setting on task performance: 1966–1984. *Organizational Behavior and Human Decision Processes, 39,* 52–83.

Messick, S. (1991). Validity. In R. L. Linn (Ed.), *Educational measurement* (3rd ed., pp. 13–103). New York: American Council on Education and Macmillan.

Mischel, T. (Ed.). (1977). *The self: Psychological and philosophical issues.* Oxford, England: Basil Blackwell.

Mortimer, J. T., Finch, M. D., & Kumka, D. (1982). Persistence and change in development: The multidimensional self-concept. In P. B. Baltes & O. G. Brim, Jr. (Eds.), *Life-span development and behavior* (Vol. 4, pp. 263–313). New York: Academic Press.

Muller, J. C., Gullung, P., & Bocci, V. (1988). Concept de soi et performance scolaire: Une meta-analyse [Self-concept and academic achievement: A meta-analysis]. *Orientation Scolaire et Professionnelle, 17,* 53–69.

Neisser, U. (1988). Five kinds of self-knowledge. *Philosophical Psychology, 1,* 35–59.

Neugarten, B. L., & Datan, N. (1974). The middle years. In S. Arieti (Ed.), *American handbook of psychiatry: The foundations of psychiatry* (Vol. 1). New York: Basic Books.

Nolen-Hoeksema, S. (1987). Sex differences in unipolar depression: Evidence and theory. *Psychological Bulletin, 101,* 259–282.

Oyserman, D., & Markus, H. R. (1993). The sociocultural self. In J. Suls (Ed.), *Psychological perspectives on the self* (Vol. 4, pp. 187–220). Hillsdale, NJ: Erlbaum.

Pelham, B. W., & Swann, W. B. (1989). From self-conceptions to self-worth: On the sources and structure of global self-esteem. *Journal of Personality and Social Psychology, 57,* 672–680.

Piaget, J. (1977). *The development of thought: Equilibration of cognitive structures.* New York: Viking.

Rhodewalt, F. (1986). Self-presentation and the phenomenal self: On the stability and malleability of self-conceptions. In R. Baumeister (Ed.), *Private and public selves.* New York: Springer-Verlag.

Rhodewalt, F., & Agustsdottir, S. (1986). Effects of personality. *Journal of Personality and Social Psychology, 50,* 47–55.

Richards, G. E. (1977). *Some educational implications and contributions of Outward Bound.* Sydney, Australia: Outward Bound Foundation.

Riess, M., Rosenfield, P., Melburg, B., & Tedeschi, J. T. (1981). Self-serving attributions: Biased private perceptions and distorted public descriptions. *Journal of Personality and Social Psychology, 41,* 224–231.

Roberts, T., & Nolen-Hoeksema, S. (1989). Sex differences in reactions to evaluative feedback. *Sex Roles, 21,* 725–747.

Roche, L. A., & Marsh, H. W. (1993, December). *The comparison on nonthetic (highly structured) and idiographic (open-ended) measures of multifaceted self-concepts.* Paper presented at the Australian Association for Research in Education Conference, Fremantle, WA.

Rogers, T. B. (1981). A model of the self as an aspect of the human information processing system. In N. Cantor & J. F. Kihlstrom (Eds.), *Personality, cognition, and social interaction* (pp. 193–214). Hillsdale, NJ: Erlbaum.

Rosenberg, M. (1979). *Conceiving the self.* New York: Basic Books.

Ross, M., & Conway, M. (1986). Remembering one's own past: The construction of personal histories. In R. M. Sorrentino & E. T. Higgins (Eds.), *Handbook of motivation and cognition: Foundations of social behavior* (pp. 122–144). New York: Guilford.

Rothbaum, F., Weisz, J. R., & Snyder, S. S. (1982). Changing the world and changing the self: A two-process model of perceived control. *Journal of Personality and Social Psychology, 42,* 5–37.

Sackheim, H. A. (1983). Self-deception, self-esteem, and depression: The adaptive value of lying to oneself. In J. Masling (Ed.), *Empirical studies in emotional disorder and psychotherapy* (pp. 51–83). New York: Plenum.

Sackheim, H. A., & Gur, R. C. (1978). Self-deception, self-confrontation, and consciousness. In G. E. Schwartz & D. Shapiro (Eds.), *Consciousness and self-regulation: Advances in research* (Vol. 2). New York: Plenum.

Sartre, J. P. (1955). *Literary and philosophical essays.* London: Richer.

Sartre, J. P. (1957). *Being and nothingness.* (H. E. Barnes, Trans.). New York: Philosophical Library. (Original work published in 1943)

Sartre, J. P. (1965). *The philosophy of J. P. Sartre.* New York: Random House.

Schlenker, B. R., & Leary, M. R. (1982). Social anxiety and self-presentation: A conceptualisation and model. *Psychological Bulletin, 92,* 641–669.

Seligman, M. E. P. (1975). *Helplessness: On depression, development, and death.* San Francisco: Freeman.

Shavelson, R. J., Hubner, J. J., & Stanton, G. C. (1976). Self-concept: Validation of construct interpretations. *Review of Educational Research, 46,* 407–441.

Shaw, M. L. (1982). Attending to multiple sources of information: I. The integration of information in decision making. *Cognitive Psychology, 14,* 252–409.

Sherman, S. J. (1989). Social cognition. *Annual Review of Psychology, 40,* 281–326.

Sherman, S. J., Judd, C. M., & Park, B. (1989). Social cognition. *Annual Review of Psychology, 40,* 281–326.

Shweder, R. A., & Miller, J. G. (1985). The social construction of the person: How is it possible? In K. J. Gergen & K. E. Davis (Eds.), *The social construction of the person.* New York: Springer-Verlag.

Skov, R. B., & Sherman, S. J. (1986). Information gathering processes: Diagnosticity, hypothesis confirmatory strategies and perceived hypothesis confirmation. *Journal of Experimental Social Psychology, 22,* 93–121.

Smith, T. W., Snyder, C. R., & Handelsman, M. M. (1982). On the self-serving function of an academic wooden leg: Test anxiety as a self-handicapping strategy. *Journal of Personality and Social Psychology, 42,* 787–797.

Snyder, M. (1974). Self-monitoring of expressive behavior. *Journal of Personality and Social Psychology, 30,* 526–537.

Snyder, M. (1979). Self-monitoring processes. In L. Berkowitz (Ed.), *Advances in experimental social psychology* (Vol. 12, pp. 85–128). New York: Academic Press.

Snyder, M. (1987). *Public appearances/private realities.* New York: Freeman.

Snyder, M., & Cantor, N. (1980). Thinking about ourselves and others: Self-monitoring and social knowledge. *Journal of Personality and Social Psychology, 39,* 222–234.

Snyder, M., Gangestad, S., & Simpson, J. A. (1983). Choosing friends as activity partners: The role of self-monitoring. *Journal of Personality and Social Psychology, 45,* 1061–1072.

Snyder, M., & Swann, W. B., Jr. (1978). Behavioral confirmation in social interaction: From social perception to social reality. *Journal of Experimental Social Psychology, 14,* 148–162.

Strube, M. J., & Roemmele, L. P. (1985). Self-enhancement, self-assessment, and self-evaluative task choice. *Journal of Personality and Social Psychology, 49,* 981–993.

Suls, J., & Mullen, B. (1982). From the cradle to the grave: Comparison and self-evaluation across the life-span. In J. Suls (Ed.), *Psychological perspectives on the self* (Vol. 1, pp. 97–128). Hillsdale, NJ: Erlbaum.

Swann, W. B. (1985). The self as architect of social reality. In B. Schlenker (Ed.), *The self and social life* (pp. 100–125). New York: McGraw-Hill.

Swann, W. B. (1990). To be adored or to be known: The interplay of self-enhancement and self-verification. In R. M. Sorretino & E. T. Higgins (Eds.), *Motivation and cognition* (Vol 2, pp. 408–448). New York: Guildford.

Swann, W. B., & Brown, J. D. (1990). From self to health: Self-verification and identity disruption. In B. R. Sarason, I. G. Sarason, & G. R. Pierce (Eds.), *Social support: An interactional review.* New York: Wiley.

Swann, W. B., Griffin, J. J., Predmore, S. C., & Gaines, B. (1987). The cognitive-affective crossfire: When self-consistency confronts self-enhancement. *Journal of Personality and Social Psychology, 52,* 882–889.

Swann, W. B., & Hill, C. A. (1982). When our identities are mistaken: Reaffirming self-conceptions through social interaction. *Journal of Personality and Social Psychology, 43,* 59–66.

Swann, W. B., Hixon, J. G., Stein-Seroussi, A., & Gilbert, D. J. (1990). The fleeting gleam of praise: Cognitive processes underlying behavioral reactions to self-relevant feedback. *Journal of Personality and Social Psychology, 59,* 17–26.

Swann, W. B., Pelham, B. W., & Chidester, T. (1988). Change through paradox: Using self-verification to alter beliefs. *Journal of Personality and Social Psychology, 54,* 268–273.

Swann, W. B., Pelham, B. W., & Krull, D. S. (1989). Agreeable fancy or disagreeable truth? Reconciling self-enhancement and self-verification. *Journal of Personality and Social Psychology, 57,* 782–791.

Swann, W. B., & Read, S. J. (1981). Self-verification processes: How we sustain our self-conceptions. *Journal of Experimental Social Psychology, 17,* 351–373.

Swann, W. B., Stein-Seroussi, A., & Giesler, R. B. (1992). Why people self-verify. *Journal of Personality and Social Psychology, 62,* 392–401.

Swann, W. B., Wenzlaff, R. M., & Tafarodi, R. W. (1992). Depression and the search for negative evaluations: More evidence of the role of self-verification strivings. *Journal of Abnormal Psychology, 101,* 314–317.

Taylor, S. E., & Brown, J. D. (1988). Illusion and well-being: A social psychological perspective on mental health. *Psychological Bulletin, 103,* 193–210.

Tesser, A., Campbell, J., & Smith, M. (1984). Friendship choice and performance: Self-evaluation maintenance in children. *Journal of Personality and Social Psychology, 46,* 561–574.

Tice, D. M. (1991). Esteem protection or enhancement? Self-handicapping motives and attribution's differ by trait self-esteem. *Journal of Personality and Social Psychology, 60,* 711–725.

Triandis, H. C. (1989). The self and social behavior in differing cultural contexts. *Psychological Review, 96,* 506–521.

Trope, Y. (1982). Self-assessment and task performance. *Journal of Experimental and Social Psychology, 18,* 201–215.

Trope, Y. (1983). Self-assessment and task performance. *Journal of Experimental Social Psychology, 18,* 201–215.

Trope, Y., & Ben-Yair, E. (1982). Task construction and persistence as means for self-assessment of abilities. *Journal of Personality and Social Psychology, 42,* 637–645.

Trope, Y., & Brickman, P. (1975). Difficulty and diagnosticity as determinants of choice among tasks. *Journal of Personality and Social Psychology, 31,* 918–925.

Tubbs, M. E. (1986). Goal-setting: A meta-analytic examination of the empirical evidence. *Journal of Applied Psychology, 71,* 474–488.

Walkerdine, V. (1984). Developmental psychology and the child-centered pedagogy: The insertion of Piaget into early education. In J. Henriques, W. Holloway, C. Urwin, C. Venn, & V. Walkerdine (Eds.), *Changing the subject* (pp. 153–202). New York: Methuen.

Weber, R., & Crocker, J. (1983). Cognitive processes in the revision of stereotype beliefs. *Journal of Personality and Social Psychology, 45,* 961–977.

Weisz, J. R. (1986). Understanding the developing understanding of control. In M. Perlmutter (Ed.), *Cognitive perspectives on children's social and behavioral development* (pp. 219–278). Hillsdale, NJ: Erlbaum.

White, R. (1959). Motivation reconsidered: The concept of competence. *Psychological Review, 66,* 297–323.

Wohlwill, J. (1973). *The study of behavioral development.* New York: Academic Press.

Wood, J. V. (1989). Theory and research concerning social comparisons of personal attributes. *Psychological Bulletin, 106,* 231–248.

Wood, R. E., & Locke, E. A. (1987). The relation of self-efficacy and grade goals to academic performance. *Educational and Psychological Measurement, 47,* 1013–1024.

Wood, R. E., Mento, A. J., & Locke, E. A. (1987). Task complexity as a moderator of goal effects: A meta-analysis. *Journal of Applied Psychology, 72,* 416–425.

Wylie, R. C. (1989). *Measures of self-concept.* Lincoln: University of Nebraska Press.

Zuckerman, M. (1979). Attribution of success and failure revisited, or: The motivational bias is alive and well in attribution theory. *Journal of Personality, 47,* 245–287.

CHAPTER 12

Clinical Applications of a Context-Dependent, Multidimensional Model of Self-Concept

BRUCE A. BRACKEN

Self-concept has been treated abundantly as a dependent or independent measure in research, with over 11,000 studies cited in the American Psychological Association's PsychINFO 1974–1992 database. Although self-concept has received widespread research attention, it seems to have fallen short of its potential as a useful construct in the clinical practice of psychology. The focus of this chapter will be to describe a model of self-concept that appears to have utility for both research and clinical practice, and that underpins a new self-concept instrument, the *Multidimensional Self Concept Scale* (MSCS; Bracken, 1992). The MSCS is founded on a multidimensional, context-dependent theoretical model that emphasizes the importance of children's and adolescents' differential adjustment in the various contexts in which they operate. As such, the model emphasizes an assessment approach that evaluates children's and adolescents' adjustment within the multiple primary contexts in which they find themselves operating on a daily basis; contexts that are each identified frequently in the self-concept literature and instrumentation (e.g., Bannister & Agnew, 1977; Cauce, 1987; Coopersmith, 1967, 1984; Epstein, 1973; Franzoi & Shields, 1984; Harter, 1978, 1982a, 1982b; Keller, Ford, & Meacham, 1978; L'Ecuyer, 1981; Marsh & Holmes, 1990; Minton, 1979; Piers, 1984; Roid & Fitts, 1988; Rosenberg, 1979; Shavelson, Hubner, & Stanton, 1976). The chapter will first describe the MSCS theoretical model, and then it will elaborate on the clinical applications of the multidimensional model of self-concept.

A MULTIDIMENSIONAL, CONTEXT-DEPENDENT MODEL OF SELF-CONCEPT

Shavelson et al. (1976) in their seminal article lamented that there was no agreed-on definition of self-concept. They stated: "The lack of empirically demonstrated equivalence among self-concept measurements makes it impossible to generalize across studies using different (self-concept) instruments" (p. 409). In an effort to provide a foundation for a consensus in the definition of self-concept, Shavelson and his colleagues proposed seven definitional characteristics that they believed underpinned the construct. They proposed that a definition of self-concept should consider the construct's (a) theoretical organization, (b) multifaceted nature, (c) hierarchical structure, (d) stability, (e) developmental nature, (f) evaluative underpinnings, and (g) differentiality from other constructs.

These definitional characteristics have largely dominated psychologists' perceptions of self-concept since the 1976 article, and have resulted in a number of scales that have adopted the definitional characteristics, at least in part. One of these instruments, addressed in considerable detail in Chapter 2, is the Australian-based *Self-Description Questionnaires* (SDQI, SDQII) developed by Marsh (1988, 1990). Another instrument that reflects the Shavelson et al. criteria is the *Multidimensional Self Concept Scale* (MSCS; Bracken, 1992), which was developed and normed in the United States. Although these instruments share several foundational features, they also differ in some important respects. Marsh and Hattie describe various self-concept theoretical models and the SDQ model in considerable detail in Chapter 2. The focus of this chapter will be to describe the manner in which the MSCS model coincides with the Shavelson definitional characteristics and to discuss how a multidimensional model of self-concept can be useful in clinical practice.

Cognitive versus Behavioral "Self" Debate

Efforts to describe the essence of an individual have produced a heated debate between behaviorists and cognitivists that is as old as the profession of modern psychology. Despite the recent death of behaviorism's most ardent defender, B. F. Skinner, the cognitive/behavioral polemics will likely continue for many years. One area of debate that continues unabated is whether the "self" is an actual internal system as viewed by cognitivists (e.g., Kernberg, 1975) or whether the self is better defined from a behavioral perspective as a recognizable pattern of behavior that is so unique to an individual that it constitutes that person's "self" (e.g., Bracken, 1992). As the first person to propose a theory of self-concept, William James (1890/1983) would not be considered a behaviorist, but he is credited for emphasizing the importance of an individual's behavioral accomplishments, as depicted in his formula (Self-Esteem = Success/Pretensions).

Approaching self-concept more from a cognitive orientation, Harter (1983) has provided a masterful historical description of, and developmental model for, a cognitive self system that includes self-concept or self-esteem. Her description of the developing self includes such attributes as self-actualization, self-control, self-confidence, self-esteem, self-regard, self-regulation, self-respect, self-reward, and so on. The heart of this system appears to be an entity, a proposed structure, within the individual called the "self." In the cognitive model, self is hyphenated because it is related to, and has control over, various self-functions (e.g., *self*-designated rewards; *self*-originated control; a *self* that has reached a level of accomplishment that is identified as "actualized"). Hyphenated self-terminology has become widely accepted in both lay and professional literature. The "self" has become widely recognized in cognitive and lay circles as the essence of an individual; from this perspective, the self appears to be considered the sensing, feeling, monitoring, and regulating part of the individual.

In contrast to a cognitive approach to psychology, Skinner devoted his professional career to convincing psychologists that behavior is the most important unit of study, rather than mentalistic or cognitive phenomena. Because the self is not an observable phenomenon, one can only make inferences about self-related constructs by observing and making inferences about an individual's behavior. Foundational behavioral tenets suggest that past behavior predicts future behavior; past experiences and reinforcements predict the probability of future responses; past behavior within given environments predicts future behaviors in similar environments or contexts; and behavior that is observed can be acquired through learning and imitation (Bandura, 1977, 1986). In his last publication before his death, Skinner (1990) made a final valiant effort to convince psychologists that behavior, not the self, should be studied. He concluded:

> In face-to-face contact with another person, references to an initiating self are unavoidable. There is a "you," and there is an "I," I see what "you" do and hear what "you" say and you see what "I" do and hear what "I" say. We do not see the histories of selection responsible for what is done and therefore infer an internal origination, but the successful use of the vernacular in the practice of psychology offers no support for its use in a science. In a scientific analysis, histories of variation and selection play the role of initiator. There is no place in a scientific analysis of behavior for a mind or self. (p. 1209)

According to Skinner (1990), the behavior of an organism is the product of three types of variation and selection: biological evolution of the species, operant conditioning and imitation, and cultural evolution. Biological evolution of the species sets the limits for what members of that species can and cannot do (e.g., humans can talk, but they cannot fly). Biological evolution also prepares a species for survival in environments that are similar to the one in which the species evolved. Operant conditioning increases the likelihood of certain behaviors through reinforcement of those behaviors. It is through operant conditioning and imitation that much of human behavior is shaped and acquired. The third contributor to human behavior is evolution of culture. Cultures prepare groups only for the kinds of worlds in which the group evolved. In combination, these three influences shape the behavior of an individual within specific and general environmental contexts, and set the parameters for predicting the future behaviors of that individual within similar contexts.

From a behavioral perspective, people's self-concepts are inferred from their unique patterns of behavior—their professed fears, likes, and dislikes; their actions within various contexts; their responses to various stimuli. In a self-report format, individuals make descriptive and evaluative 'self-efficacy' personal statements that reflect their past behaviors and predict their future behaviors (Bandura, 1986). A person who strongly endorses the statement, "I feel uncomfortable when I am with people I don't know" is reporting a history of discomfort when in social situations and is allowing the prediction of future discomfort in social contexts. Such discomfort continues to be predictable until the individual's social behaviors are differentially reinforced or the environment becomes more conducive to relaxed, less stressful social interactions.

The use of self-report or third-party statements to better understand a person's past experiences has a long history in behavioral assessment (e.g., behavior rating scales, self-report inventories). Such self-reports are behaviors elicited by sentence stems that serve as discriminating stimuli. A person's response to such stimuli reflects that individual's behavioral history and facilitates the prediction of that individual's future behaviors.

Organizational Structure

This author agrees with Shavelson et al. (1976) that self-concept develops in an organized fashion; however, the nature of the organization is what separates the behaviorally oriented MSCS model from other cognitive approaches to self-concept. In the MSCS model, self-concept is viewed as being acquired according to behavioral principles. As children act on and within their environments, their behaviors are shaped incrementally according to their successes and failures, how others react to them and their actions, and how others model behaviors and communicate expectations. Cooley (1902) coined the term "looking-glass self" to reflect the importance that other people's reactions have on our own developing self-perceptions. With direct and indirect environmental feedback of this sort, children learn specific and generalized evaluative response patterns that incorporate, and are consistent with, their past experiences.

Self-concept is typically assessed in a self-report fashion by requiring examinees to indicate the degree to which they agree with statements about themselves as agents who act on their environments within a variety of context domains. Thus, in a behavioral conceptualization of self-concept, the construct represents individuals' *learned* evaluations and judgments of themselves based on their successes and failures, reinforcement histories, and the ways in which others react to them and interact with them.

Multifaceted Nature

Rather than having a single unidimensional self-concept, children develop as many self-concepts as the unique environmental contexts in which they find themselves operating as either passive or active agents. Though the number and range of specific contexts available to children are vast, the typical child spends most of his or her time acting on or within the following six primary environmental contexts: *social, competence, affect, academic, family,* and *physical.* The existence of these six primary dimensions of adjustment is not only supported empirically but is also reflected in the self-concept literature and, to some lesser or greater degree, in the many existing self-concept scales.

These six primary context-dependent domains are not mutually exclusive; in fact, primary contexts overlap considerably and create more specific or secondary contexts for consideration. For example, children experience social successes and failures in primary social settings (e.g., dances, playgrounds), as well as in secondary social settings (e.g., family or academic contexts). The overlap among primary contexts is extensive and includes all the domains.

Though the six contexts identified in the MSCS model are considered primary and unique, they are moderately intercorrelated (Bracken, 1992). Because of the interrelated nature of these important life-contexts and the generalizability of children's behaviors across primary contexts, it is understandable that early self-concept researchers treated the construct as unidimensional (e.g., Rosenberg, 1979).

Six Primary Contexts

Social

As mentioned in the previous examples, children interact socially in many different settings. The other people who influence children's social self-concepts include everyone with whom the children have social contact; however, friends, classmates, family members, teachers, and neighbors (adults and age peers) tend to make up the majority of individuals with whom most children interact on a regular basis and in a meaningful fashion.

Children's social self-concepts are affected by the reactions of other people, the extent to which they are accepted or approached in positive ways, and their ability to achieve goals and objectives through successful social interactions (Cooley, 1902). As social agents within primary social contexts (e.g., playgrounds, social outings, dances) and across other secondary social contexts (e.g., school, church) children learn how accepted they are by other people and how effective they are at meeting their own personal needs through social intercourse. This acquired knowledge is the basis for their self-evaluations and social self-concepts (see Chapter 4 for a detailed description of social self-concept and its correlates).

Though this domain is represented in the MSCS by the Social Scale, many other self-concept instruments assess a similar construct under other related subscale names. As examples of the prevalence of the Social domain in extant self-concept scales, the Coopersmith Self-Esteem Inventory (Coopersmith, 1984) includes a Social Self-Peers subscale; the Piers-Harris Self-Concept Scale (Piers, 1984) includes a Popularity subscale; and the Self-Esteem Index (SEI; Brown & Alexander, 1990) assesses a Peer Popularity subscale. Related to social self-concept, Marsh assesses Peer Relations on the Self-Description Questionnaire, I (SDQI, 1988) and Same-Sex Relations and Opposite-Sex Relations on the Self-Description Questionnaire, II (SDQII, 1990); however, Bracken (1993) makes a distinction between children's interpersonal relations and their social self-concepts. The *Assessment of Interpersonal Relations* (Bracken, 1993) assesses children's same-sex and opposite-sex interpersonal relations in its Male Peers and Female Peers subscales, which are theoretically focused more on elements of social support (e.g., instrumental support, emotional support, informational support) than social acceptance.

Competence

As agents who act on their environments, from birth on children succeed or fail in their attempts to solve problems, attain goals, bring about desired outcomes, and function effectively. Infants cry when they are hungry or wet, and the extent to which caregivers meet these needs reinforces the infants' sense of competence. As children increase in age, they succeed or fail in countless endeavors, and others react to their successes and failings; as a result, children evaluate their actions and make generalizations about their competence within and across a variety of settings. Children vary in their levels of competence across the six primary contexts, and whereas one child might excel in physical competence, another child might excel in social or academic competence. Across domains, children acquire a generalized sense of competence; within individual domains children gain a sense of competence that is unique and separate from their impressions of global competence.

The existence of a competence self-concept domain as assessed by other self-concept scales is less evident than the social domain; however, competence as an element of self-evaluation underlies most existing self-concept scales. For example, in a five instrument factor analyses, a competence factor emerged, with each of the instruments producing factor loadings at a level between .29 and .52 on the competence factor (Bracken, Bunch, Keith, & Keith, 1992). Susan Harter's work (e.g., Harter, 1982b) addresses the competence dimension as a central element of self-concept. (For a detailed description of competence self-concept and related concepts, see Chapter 5, in this volume.)

Affect

Children respond affectively according to the extent to which their behaviors are differentially reinforced, extinguished, punished, or as they react to personal and environmental evaluations of their behavior. When children succeed at an activity, achieve, or are accepted or praised by others, the accomplishment is typically accompanied by a positive affective response; likewise, failure, frustration, or rejection are often followed by negative affective responses, such as anger or sadness. As children's affective behavioral patterns develop and become more consistent, children begin to recognize, evaluate, monitor, describe, and discuss their affective states. Affective behaviors may occur in anticipation of, simultaneously with, or in response to situations in which the child is involved. Much like the social domain, the affect domain is assessed by a number of existing self-concept scales, including the satisfaction subscale of the Tennessee Self-Concept Scale (TSCS); the SEI Personal Security subscale; the Piers-Harris Happiness-Satisfaction subscale; and the Emotional Stability subscale of the SDQII. The Prouts, (Chapter 6, this volume), discuss the relationship between self-concept and affective, behavioral, and physical conditions and disorders among children and adolescents.

Academic

During much of the calendar year, children spend a significant portion of each weekday attending school and participating in school-related activities. From early in the morning, children prepare to go to school; during the day they attend and participate in a variety of activities at school; and after school, they complete homework assignments, discuss their current school day with parents and family members, participate in extracurricular school activities, and plan for their next school day.

Within the academic context, children evaluate, or others evaluate, their academic performance in and across a variety of academic subject areas. Also, children interact with others, share ideas, express thoughts, respond to teachers' questions and task demands, and are judged by their peers and teachers according to how well they perform all these school-related experiences.

Academic self-concept is a widely assessed construct, as evidenced by its ubiquitous nature among existing self-concept scales. Academic self-concept is assessed as a general academic domain by many instruments (e.g., Coopersmith, School-Academic; Piers-Harris, Intellectual/School; SEI, Academic Competence) and as specific academic subject areas by other instruments (e.g., SDQI, SDQII).

Family

The typical child spends more time within the family context than in any other setting, except possibly school. The family constellation, for most children, also constitutes the context within which they have interacted for the longest period of time. Children's family self-concepts need not be considered as developing only within the biological unit to which the child was born; rather "family" should be considered more generically, and should refer to those individuals with whom the child lives or on whom the child is dependent for care, security, and nurturance. A child's "family" might consist of a traditional natural family unit (biological mother, father, and siblings); however, almost as common are various forms of reconstituted or substituted family units, such as stepfamilies, foster families, extended families, surrogate families, single-parent families with or without siblings, or any other familial living arrangement (U.S. Bureau of the Census, 1980).

Family self-concept is also widely assessed by existing self-concept scales. As with social self-concept, the SDQI and SDQII questionably assess family self-concept from a relationship orientation with the Parent Relations scales, much as the *Assessment of Interpersonal Relations* (AIR; Bracken, 1993) assesses family (Mother and Father scales) and extrafamily relationships (Male Peers, Female Peers, and Teacher scales). Other self-concept scales clearly identify a family-oriented self-concept domain (e.g., TSCS, Family subscale; SEI, Familial Acceptance scale; Coopersmith, Home-Parents scale). Chapter 8, in this volume, describes family self-concept and its correlates.

Physical

Because people *are* their physical bodies, the physical domain is an important area of psychosocial adjustment. Children constantly receive direct and indirect feedback about their physical condition, attractiveness, physical prowess, dress, height, weight, health, and so on. Children's physical attributes, including physical abilities and attractiveness, constitute the physical domain. The reactions of others to the child's physical attributes, as well as the comparisons a child makes of his or her physical attributes relative to the physical attributes of others, contribute to the child's physical self-concept.

Physical self-concept and its relationship to such conditions as weight control and eating disorders, disease and other health related factors, and physical handicapping conditions is considered in detail in Chapter 9. Physical self-concept also is commonly assessed by existing self-concept scales. The Piers-Harris Self-Concept Scale, for example, includes a Physical Appearance/Attributes subscale; the Tennessee Self-Concept Scale includes a Physical subscale; and the SDQI and SDQII include both Physical Abilities and Physical Appearance subscales.

The six MSCS context-dependent domains are represented regularly in the vast number of existing self-concept scales and the self-concept and psychosocial adjustment literature (see Bracken & Mills, 1994; Hattie, 1992; Keith & Bracken, this volume; Wylie, 1979, 1989 for descriptions and reviews of extant scales). No other primary self-concept domains are identified as regularly in the literature as these six domains; the domains are also frequently assessed by the full range of available psychoeducational assessment tests and scales. The Appendix at the end of this chapter further attests to the ubiquitous nature of these primary contexts. The Appendix lists over 70 commonly used psychological and educational tests and scales, all of which assess one or more of the six context-dependent domains.

Hierarchical Dimensionality

Shavelson et al. (1976) proposed that self-concept is hierarchically arranged in a multiple-tiered fashion. Shavelson and his colleagues proposed that self-concept, like intelligence, can be conceptualized as a large general dimension, which is underpinned by several primary self-concept domains, and underpinned further by even more specified subdomains of self-concept (see Chapter 2, this volume, for a discussion and graphical representation).

The theoretical model of the MSCS is based on a hierarchical structure similar to that proposed by Shavelson et al.; however, the MSCS model is depicted in a slightly different format from the linear vertical and horizontal arrangement presented by Shavelson et al. (See Figure 12.1). With each of the six primary self-concept domains overlapping to a moderate degree, it is presumed that at the heart of the self-concept dimensions is a supraordinate generalized self-concept—similar to Spearman's conceptualization of general intelligence, g. The six MSCS primary self-concept domains also are similar in nature to Thurstone's (1938) conceptualization of primary intellectual abilities. Vernon's (1950) conceptualization of intelligence merges Spearman's and Thurstone's earlier theoretical and empirical efforts. Like Vernon's assumptions about intelligence, the MSCS scales are moderately intercorrelated (Bracken, 1992) and produce a supraordinate g factor and separate primary factors in both single-instrument (Keith, 1994; Keith & Bracken, 1995) and multiple-instrument factor analyses (Bracken, Bunch, Keith, & Keith, 1992).

Though global self-concept is represented in the Venn diagram where the six self-concept dimensions overlap collectively, it should be noted that each scale also is shown to overlap individually with two adjacent self-concept domains. In this sense, the Venn diagram is limited in its representation of the MSCS model because it depicts only contiguous domains as overlapping. Despite this graphical limitation, the model proposes that *all* self-concept domains overlap with each other (something

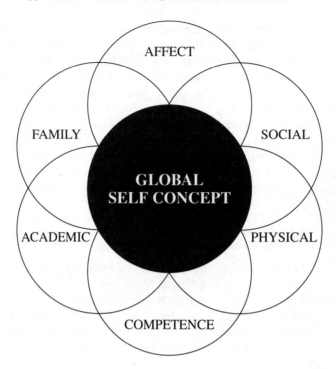

Figure 12.1   Multidimensional Self Concept Scale. From *Multidimensional Self Concept Scale* by B. A. Bracken, 1992. Copyright 1992 Pro-Ed. Used with permission.

that is not easily depicted in a two-dimensional diagram) (Bracken, 1992). This two-dimensional limitation also is present in the figure that depicts the Shavelson et al. model (see Figures 2.1f and 2.2, Chapter 2). The lack of physical overlap among the primary domains depicted in the Shavelson model would suggest that the domains are independent and are presumed to share no variance with any of the other scales, a position that apparently was not intended by the authors.

The MSCS self-concept model assumes that the various primary self-concept dimensions are of the same approximate importance in their contribution to global self-concept, though it is recognized that individual dimensions may be more or less important than other dimensions for individual children. Operationally, however, the MSCS is designed such that each subscale contributes equally to the MSCS total self-concept score (global self-concept); the instrument was developed with an equal number of items (25) per subscale. This balanced operationalization and weighting represents the position that until demonstrated empirically to be otherwise, the six dimensions should be treated as approximately equal in importance.

At the next hierarchical level, the MSCS Venn diagram shows that where each primary domain overlaps individually with another domain, a blended subdomain of self-concept is created. For example, where the social domain overlaps with academic self-concept, the interaction represents the *social* events in a child's life that occur in or in relation to an *academic* setting (school). Just as children interact in primary social settings on the neighborhood playgrounds, at dances, and so on, children also have significant amounts of social interactions on school property. Also, just as the social domain overlaps with each of the other domains, children experience social interactions in each of these other primary contexts. For example, children's social acceptance can be affected by their social skills and competence. Additionally, children's social interactions may lead to related affective responses, and their social acceptance and desirability can be affected and determined in part by their physical attractiveness and prowess. Also, the child's social functioning occurs at times within the home setting and is therefore influenced by family expectations and pressures.

The overlap of the MSCS domains is demonstrated not only through a logical rationale approach, but empirically. The MSCS domains all have squared multiple correlations that range from .37 to .70, which demonstrate considerable shared variance among the six domains (Bracken, 1992) and support an underlying general self-concept. Concomitantly, to demonstrate the uniqueness of the MSCS subscales, MSCS subscale specificities have been computed. In addition to demonstrating considerable shared variance, each subscale possesses sizable portions of specific variance (range = .17 to .60). Each subscale's specificity meets Kaufman's (1979) suggested criteria for deciding whether a subscale possesses sufficient specificity to treat psychometrically and clinically as a unique construct. According to Kaufman's (1979) recommended criteria, each of the MSCS subscales appear to contribute substantially to both *g* and specific aspects of self-concept.

Stability

Because self-concept is viewed by this author as a learned behavioral response pattern, it is reasonable to expect self-concept to be a stable construct. In fact, the self-concept literature consistently has shown that self-concept, especially global self-concept, is a stable trait (e.g., Wylie, 1979). As a stable construct, self-concept changes only gradually, in an incremental way, as children's environments change, as they change within or adapt to their environments, or as they no longer function within certain environments (e.g., graduate or drop out of school).

Global self-concept, as measured by the MSCS, is a more stable construct than the individual self-concepts assessed by the six MSCS subscales (Bracken, 1992). The MSCS Total Scale score evidenced a 4-week short-term stability coefficient of .90, whereas the six domains' stability coefficients ranged from .73 to .81. It makes sense intuitively that the more global the construct, the less it would be affected by individual day-to-day influences. Conversely, the more specific the domain or area of adjustment, the

more malleable or modifiable would be self-perceptions within that domain. For example, a child may have an average global self-concept, but
the same child's academic self-concept might be diminished because of a
history of detrimental experiences within academic settings. Should the
child become successful academically, her day-to-day improvement
would be expected to influence her academic self-concept more than her
global self-concept. Her global self-concept would be expected to improve only incrementally and in direct proportion to the contribution of
academic self-concept to global self-concept. The child's academic self-
concept would be expected to reflect more directly than global self-
concept the successes and gains she has recently experienced in the
academic setting.

Developmental Characteristics

Self-concept is developmental in the sense that, like many acquired
human characteristics (e.g., intelligence; Burt, 1954; Piaget, 1969), it appears to become increasingly defined, recognizable, and differentiated
with age. Newborns, with a very limited history of experiences and environmental exposures, would be expected to exhibit a fairly undifferentiated, self-awareness. However, as they gain experiences, act on different
environments, and differentially evaluate experiences and actions, their
self-concepts would be expected to become successively less diffuse.

Because young children live relatively protected lives, they are only exposed gradually to new environments and people. Therefore, initially children's self-concepts may be shaped more by the influences of their
families than other domains. As children grow older and begin to interact
more independently with a broader spectrum of people and environments,
they are exposed to new experiences that allow them to evaluate themselves within a continually increasing number of new settings. Children
gradually experience somewhat consistent outcomes *within* similar environmental contexts and somewhat inconsistent outcomes *across* different
environmental contexts, and these differential learning experiences lead to
more clearly differentiated domain-specific self-concepts. A proposed sequence in which dimensions of self-concept unfold and become differentiated would be based only on conjecture at this point; however, typical early
childhood experiences would suggest that family, competence, and social
domains probably develop earlier than other domains, especially academic
and physical.

Evaluative Underpinnings

The MSCS model of self-concept acquisition posits that individuals evaluate their actions and behavioral outcomes as they interact with their environments. Self-concept is not only a personal self-description but also

connotes an underlying evaluation. The MSCS model proposes that children acquire their self-concepts as a result of an evaluative process based on information gained from two perspectives *(personal* and *other)* and four standards *(absolute, ipsative, comparative,* and *ideal).*

Perspectives

Children gain information directly from their personal experiences *(personal perspective)* and indirectly or vicariously from others *(other perspective).* These two perspectives allow children to gauge their abilities from their own personal observations, as well as from the reactions and behaviors of others.

Personal Perspective. A personal perspective is the process whereby information is gained through an individual's direct interaction with his environment. As an agent acting on the environment, the individual will sometimes succeed and sometimes fail at attempts to attain goals, influence, or alter the environment. Those direct experiences and observations of successes and failures create the basis for the personal perspective.

Other Perspective. A person's view of his or her own behavior can be acquired directly through the evaluation of self-actions, as in the personal perspective; or it can be acquired indirectly by viewing, considering, and adopting another individual's evaluation. This latter process of observation and adopted evaluation provides the basis of the "other" perspective, and is similar to Cooley's (1902) concept of the looking-glass self.

Standards

Individuals evaluate their behaviors according to whether they clearly succeed or fail at activities *(absolute standard),* how well they perform in one activity or domain relative to how well they perform overall *(ipsative standard),* how well they perform in a domain relative to the performance of other people within that same domain *(comparative standard),* and how well they or others believe they should be able to perform in individual domains *(ideal standard).*

Absolute Standard. An absolute standard is similar to the application of minimal criteria in a criterion-referenced assessment. With this standard, children evaluate whether their current level of performance is minimally acceptable or adequate—similar to a "Pass/Fail" or criterion-based grading system. A child who tries to leap across a mud puddle and falls short knows without having to be told or without comparing his effort to anyone else's, that his effort to clear the puddle was not successful.

Ipsative Standard. As a child gains an estimation of what her *overall* abilities are like, she evaluates her successes and failures within *specific* areas of functioning by comparing her performance in those unique dimensions to her *overall* ability. A child who has exceptional musical talent relative to her overall abilities will recognize her relative area of strength. Whether she appreciates her relative strength may depend on the extent to which she or others appreciate her relatively well-developed musical abilities. If her musical talent is appreciated, then this relative "gift" might very well enhance her specific and global self-concepts. The use of an ipsative evaluation standard is similar to Marx and Winne's (1980) compensatory model of self-concept, whereby individuals highlight their perceived areas of strength to compensate for their self-perceived areas of weakness.

Any child may demonstrate ipsative strengths and/or weaknesses regardless of where in the normative range the child's scores may fall. Children with exceptionally positive self-regard in all domains may still have one or more domains that are significantly lower than the others. Similarly, children with overall low self-regard across domains may still exhibit significantly better adjustment in one or more of the remaining domains.

Comparative Standard. The comparative standard in children's self-evaluations is similar to the use of normative data in norm-referenced assessment. Comparative evaluative standards are essentially norms that result from observing the performance of other individuals, and then evaluating the self against that normative standard. The comparative standard may be applied appropriately (e.g., when the child's performance is compared with the abilities of children of a similar age) or inappropriately (e.g., when the child's abilities are compared with the abilities of an adult or an older child). In the latter instance, the comparative referent would be too high a standard to permit a fair and reasonable comparison.

Ideal Standard.   Idealistic evaluations are based on the expectation of how well a child should be able to perform a task, given an ideal and often unrealistic standard. As such, the ideal standard is similar to criterion-referenced assessment where the performance criterion has been set at a very high level. Typically an ideal standard is set beyond the range of the child's current level of performance, and as a result very few individuals perform at an ideal level. Idealistic expectations might reflect a child's self-imposed personal standards or the standards imposed by other people, either directly or indirectly.

A number of theorists and therapists have recognized the potentially detrimental effects of the irrational adoption or imposition of ideal standards. For example, Dinkmeyer, Pew, and Dinkmeyer (1979) describe the unhealthy and self-defeating behaviors associated with "mistaken goals." Adlerian psychologists (e.g., Adler, 1970; Mosak, 1979; Shulman, 1973) recognize the guilt-riddled behaviors associated with adopting unreasonable "shoulds" and "oughts." Also, Rogers and Dymond (1954) emphasized the potential negative effects of ideal standards and posited that the magnitude of disparity between a person's real and ideal self serves as an index of that individual's social-emotional adjustment.

There is nothing wrong with realistically seeking ideal goals or desiring the satisfaction and feeling of glory when one succeeds. However, when an ideal goal turns into self-defeating, irrational, or obsessive behavior, then it is detrimental to the individual. Behaviors that are detrimental tend to reduce children's feelings of competence and success, and negatively affect their developing self-concepts.

Perspectives and Standards in Combination

Given two perspectives and four evaluative standards, children may employ any of eight combinations of perspectives and standards (and likely use all eight combinations from time to time) while acquiring their self-concepts. It might be anticipated that children who attribute their successes or failures to others also would be most affected by evaluative information provided by other people (the other perspective); whereas, individuals who are more internally controlled may rely more heavily on their own self-evaluations *(personal perspective)* (Weiner, 1972; Weiner & Graham, 1983). Similarly, some individuals may be exposed more often to one evaluative standard more than any of the other standards. For example, parents who regularly compare their children with other children (e.g., peers, siblings) might create an increased salience for the comparative standard of evaluation for their children. On the other hand, parents or children who value the attainment of idealistic goals may be more sensitive to ideal evaluative standards. And, parents or children who are more laissez-faire by nature may be affected more by the natural consequences of absolute evaluative standards than comparative or ideal standards (Glasser, 1972). Individuals likely employ each of the four standards and two perspectives in the development and maintenance of their self-concepts; the extent to which individuals emphasize either perspective or any of the four standards in their self-evaluations is unique to the individual and may vary considerably across individuals. It is the clinician's role to determine which perspectives and standards are most salient for their clients when assessing and attempting to improve their clients' self-concepts.

Absolute Standard—Personal Perspective

An absolute personal perspective occurs when children act on the environment and judge for themselves *(personal perspective)* whether their performance was either effective or ineffective in absolute terms. The perspective taken is personal because the child judges the success of his or her own actions and efforts. The standard is absolute because it is based on a minimal level of effective functioning. For example, individuals attempt to read materials of differing difficulty levels (e.g., newspapers, magazines, textbooks), and they determine *(personal perspective)* whether their current reading abilities are sufficient to comprehend what they are attempting to read *(absolute standard)*. In this case, individuals experience a personal observation of their own reading efficiency and judge their abilities on an absolute scale.

Ipsative Standard—Personal Perspective

An ipsative personal perspective occurs when children become aware of their overall level of ability or competence *(personal perspective)*, and contrast their individual actions with their overall abilities or skills *(ipsative standard)*. For example, a boy might be moderately successful at most things, but through his participation in physical education and organized sports he has observed that he is not a very good athlete. He is not especially adept physically and is painfully aware that he cannot run, throw, jump, play basketball, football, or baseball as well as he can do most other things. Given his personal knowledge of his abilities, he contrasts his limited athletic performance with his performance in other areas of life and judges that his physical abilities are personally *(ipsatively)* substandard.

Comparative Standard—Personal Perspective

A comparative personal perspective occurs when children act on their environment and are more or less successful in their efforts than are other people. In this combination of standard and perspective, children observe and evaluate their own level of performance *(personal perspective)*, and compare that performance to how well other individuals perform similar actions *(comparative standard)*. Even young children are acutely aware when their peers receive more invitations to social outings than they do. The child who recognizes that others receive more social attention and are more accepted and comfortable in social settings, is applying the comparative standard through the personal perspective.

Ideal Standard—Personal Perspective

An ideal personal perspective is employed when children evaluate their behaviors based on an imposed or adopted "ideal" standard. When their level of performance is discrepant from the ideal, their self-concept may be affected. A young girl with self-recognized marginal musical skill *(personal perspective)* might have a strong idealized desire to be a member of the school's symphony orchestra *(ideal standard)*. In this instance, the student's competence self-concept may be affected in either direction depending on whether she attains her ideal goal.

Absolute Standard—Other Perspective

An absolute standard evaluated through an other perspective occurs when an individual attempts actions that are then evaluated by other individuals.

For example, when a young child attempts to climb a tree, his parents may tell him to stop because they fear *(personal perspective)* that he will fall and get hurt *(absolute standard)*. The message communicated to the child in part is that his parents do not trust his ability to climb trees safely. The child observes (hears), considers, and adopts (or rejects) the parents' perspective that he is not a minimally competent tree climber, which may in turn contribute to or detract from his physical and/or competence self-concepts.

Ipsative Standard—Other Perspective

An ipsative standard considered from an other perspective occurs when someone evaluates a child's ability in a specific area and contrasts that ability with the child's overall abilities. For example, a boy's parents might be aware *(other perspective)* that their son has no special talents, except his well-developed artistic skills *(ipsative standard)*. Because the boy does most things only moderately well, his artistic abilities are considered to be very well developed relative to his overall skills and abilities. The parents' reactions, either positive or negative, to their son's singular talent will have some effect on his developing self-concept.

Comparative Standard—Other Perspective

A comparative standard adopted from an other perspective exists when someone evaluates a child's performance against the normative standard of a reference group. For example, a parent who tells his child that he should make grades like his sister's, is communicating *(other perspective)* that the child's level of academic performance is substandard relative to his sister's level of performance *(comparative standard)*. Competitive sports, judged activities (e.g., forensics, band competitions), or the process of selecting individuals for competitive positions or awards are all instances in which children are judged by others in a comparative fashion.

Ideal Standard—Other Perspective

An ideal standard taken from an other perspective exists when others compare a child's performance against some "ideal" level of performance. In such instances, the ideal performance that is set as the standard is determined by the individual who is doing the evaluation. In such a scenario, the child might learn to strive to accomplish another's ideals, or the child might experience frustration and a diminished self-concept on learning that the other individual's ideal is too far beyond the child's current or soon-to-be acquired level of ability. It is through the ideal standard that we sometimes impose unreasonable oughts and shoulds on our children and ourselves (e.g., "You *should* be able to do that by now"; "You *ought* to run (and be elected) for class office").

THE ENVIRONMENTAL-BEHAVIORAL INTERACTIVE ASPECT OF THE MSCS MODEL

The MSCS is founded on the assumption that children's self-concepts are learned behavioral patterns that have come under the stimulus control of context-specific environments. It is presumed that children respond in fairly predictable fashions when in specific settings (stimulus and response generalizations), thus demonstrating relatively stable self-concepts in each respective context-specific domain. Additionally, children's developed self-concepts in the various domains allow for the prediction of future behavior in each respective domain. Hence, self-concept is an interaction between environmental contexts and the child's behavioral response to the environment.

As children act on their environments, respond to the stimuli within the environments, and have histories of reinforcement within each of these environments, their behaviors are shaped over time. As children act within various environments, they also evaluate the effectiveness of their actions in each environmental context. Over time the child's and other individual's evaluative behaviors become fairly consistent within each specific context, and this consistency in self and other evaluation is a reflection of the child's context-specific self-concept. Context and its influences are essential considerations when evaluating children's differential domain-specific self-concepts (see Chapter 11, this volume). Finally, the various context-specific self-concepts, in combination, are represented in a generalized response pattern that occurs across many environmental domains or contexts. This generalized response pattern constitutes global self-concept.

Construct Differentiality

The MSCS model assumes that self-concept is related to other constructs (e.g., intelligence, achievement, social skills), but it is also discernible. As a construct, self-concept is not a "real" entity; it is not a physical condition within the individual. It is a behavior pattern that is acquired as individuals interact with and act on different environments. Although *academic self-concept* is not the same as *academic ability*, it is part of a behavioral pattern that the individual acquires through the evaluation of successes and failures in academic settings and activities. It is manifested in an evaluative statement or action that stems from previous academic experiences, and it is predictive of future academic performance. Just as academic behaviors are an indication of what the person can do academically, academic self-concept is a personal evaluation of how well he or she does *perform* in an academic environment, and it also leads to a prediction of how well that individual *will likely do* in future academic settings. Bloom (1976) posited, ". . . for most practical purposes, academic self-concept is the strongest of the affect measures in predicting school achievement" (p. 95). Similarly,

Hansford and Hattie (1982) in a meta-analysis that examined the relationship between self-concept and academic achievement concluded that the relationship between the two variables is stronger when academic self-concept is the predictor variable rather than global self-concept.

Definition

Given the seven definitional characteristics of self-concept as reflected in the MSCS adaptation of the Shavelson et al. (1976) model, self-concept is defined as "a multidimensional and context-dependent learned behavioral pattern that reflects an individual's evaluation of past behaviors and experiences, influences an individual's current behaviors, and predicts an individual's future behaviors" (Bracken, 1992, p. 10). Such a definition of self-concept is useful in clinical practice because psychoeducational assessments enable the diagnosis of the child's current areas of strength and weakness or adjustment and maladjustment. Further, assessments allow for prognostic statements to be made about the child's future adjustment, with and without interventions, and they can lead to theoretically defensible interventions to address clients' adjustment difficulties.

CONTEXT-DEPENDENT SELF-CONCEPT SCALE INTERPRETATION

Levels of Interpretation

The interpretation of any test should follow the guidelines provided in the examiner's manual of the instrument (American Psychological Association, 1985). However, most current self-concept scales provide little if any guidance as to how best interpret and use the results in clinical practice (Bracken & Mills, 1994; Hattie & Marsh, Chapter 11, this volume; Keith & Bracken, Chapter 3, this volume; Wylie, 1979, 1989). In fact, many of the existing instruments do not even identify in their respective examiner's manuals the intended uses for the scale, suggesting that clinical applications may not have been intended or may not be warranted. The remainder of this chapter addresses the clinical use of the MSCS, which was intended to be employed as a research tool and clinical assessment device.

When considering the use of self-concept scales in clinical practice, an issue of utmost importance is whether individual subscales or the instrument's total scale score should take interpretive precedence. Though clinical use of the SDQII is not identified by its author, Marsh (1990) suggests that SDQII subscales should take interpretive precedence over the total scale score. Other authors place more value on the total scale score, in part because of weak support for subscales (e.g., Coopersmith Self-Esteem Inventory, Coopersmith, 1984).

Before deciding the level at which to begin scale interpretation, it is important for investigators to determine the contexts to which they desire to make diagnostic or predictive statements. They must decide whether they are interested foremost in making global diagnostic statements and behavioral predictions or statements and predictions that are specific to one or more of the individual primary contexts. The decision of which score takes precedence in interpretation should stem from the intended use and psychometric qualities of each scale. Psychologists interested in making global statements about a child's affectivity or adjustment would be advised to begin interpretation at the instrument's most global and psychometrically strongest level (the total scale score).

Self-concept, like intelligence, produces a large single, global factor during factor analysis, prior to any rotation of the matrix. With intelligence tests, the principal factor is typically characterized as *g,* or general intellectual abilities (after Spearman, 1927); similarly, the single unrotated factor produced by the MSCS, and other self-concept scales, is best characterized as psychometric *g,* or *general affectivity* (Bracken, Bunch, Keith, & Keith, 1992; Keith, 1994; Keith & Bracken, 1995). General affectivity can be thought of as a global representation of an individual's affective nature—an overall depiction of the individual's adjustment or affective state or essence. (For a review of the relationship between global self-concept and a wide variety of psychological conditions or disorders, see Chapter 6, this volume. Also, see the *Diagnostic and Statistical Manual of Mental Disorders,* Fourth Edition, American Psychiatric Association, 1994, for a thorough consideration of the many psychiatric disorders that include diminished self-concept as a diagnostic criterion or comorbid condition.)

As an instrument's best measure of general affectivity, the total scale score is the best predictor of an individual's behavior across various primary environmental contexts. The predictive power of the total scale score is enhanced, as compared with the predictive ability of subscales, because of its stronger psychometric qualities and more inclusive content sampling. For example, the internal consistency of the MSCS Total Scale score for the entire standardization sample of 2,501 subjects is .98; reliability of the six individual MSCS subscales ranges from .87 to .97, with a median coefficient of .915. The MSCS Total Scale score is also the instrument's most stable measure ($r = .90$ over a 4-week interval, compared with subscale stability coefficients that range from .73 to .81). And, the coverage of relevant content is more comprehensive when all 150 items are considered, rather than any set of 25 items representing the respective subscales. Thus, the MSCS Total Scale score produces the most reliable and stable scores, and it represents the broadest possible sample of affective content. And, as argued by Jensen (1984, 1987) about the importance of the intellectual *g* factor, the self-concept *g* factor also explains the largest portion of the instrument's variance. As such, the Total Scale score should be the point at which investigators begin interpretation of the MSCS when making important diagnostic decisions or statements of a global nature. Although some instruments (e.g., the SDQII) produce acceptable levels of subscale reliability with as few as 8 to 10 items, a serious consideration is whether so few items adequately sample the universe of content relevant to the domain. If a reliable score is all the examiner desires, 8 to 10 items may well suffice; however, if a reliable score and representative, meaningful item content for clinical analysis are desired, then more items are likely necessary.

Although the MSCS Total Scale score is the best representation of a child's general affectivity, individual MSCS scales provide a clearer reflection of the child's affectivity within specific contexts (social, affect, academic, competence, family, and physical). These specific context-dependent domains are primary areas of affective functioning for children and adolescents. Because the MSCS scales correspond to context domains of primary importance, they tend to be more sensitive than global self-concept to the student's affective functioning within the respective context domains (e.g., Jackson, 1994; Montgomery, 1994). For example, if the examiner is interested in determining a child's affectivity or adjustment within the academic setting or predicting a child's future academic achievement, then academic self-concept would provide a better estimate or predictor than other subscales or the Total Scale score (Bloom, 1976; Hansford & Hattie, 1982; Schicke & Fagan, 1994).

Wylie (1979), among others, lamented that efforts to improve children's self-concepts tend to end in failure (also see Kohn, 1994, for a discussion related to the failures of self-concept intervention programs). These failures are attributed in part to poorly developed and atheoretical intervention strategies and the insensitivity of global self-concept to the influences of focused intervention strategies. Unidimensional self-concept scales generally comprise a disparate collection of items, combined in some unevenly weighted scheme that is intended to reflect global self-concept (Shavelson et al., 1976). When used in clinical practice, global self-concept scores can be overly sensitive or insensitive to specific areas of adjustment. Whereas we might expect a focused intervention (e.g., social skills training) to affect change within a specific self-concept domain (e.g., social domain), such a focused intervention is much less likely to influence global self-concept or separate dimensions of self-concept that are unrelated to the intervention focus (e.g., academic, family, physical, competence). Therefore, if self-concept assessment is implemented for the purposes of remediating specific self-concept deficiencies, both the assessment and the intervention strategies should be focused uniquely on the specific self-concept domain of interest. Also, the intervention should be planned according to recognized theories of self-concept acquisition, rather than provide merely a series of "feel good" exercises.

After interpreting the most reliable data sources available (total scale score, subscale scores), the examiner should consider the child's responses to clusters of items that assess an area of similar content. Although MSCS items in the physical domain produce a single "physical" factor (Bracken, Bunch, Keith, & Keith, 1992), physical items seem to cluster informally such that they relate to specific physical attributes. Content sampling of items in the physical domain might identify such specific attributes as physical abilities/prowess (e.g., I am good at sports; I am strong), physical appearance/attractiveness (e.g., I like the way I look; Others think I am attractive), or physical health/condition (e.g., I hardly ever get sick; I tire too quickly). By considering the examinees' responses to clusters of items with common content, examiners can generate hypotheses about the examinees' feelings about specific areas of adjustment that may be identified within (e.g., prowess, health, appearance) and across primary domains (e.g., general competence, social competence, academic competence, physical competence).

In addition to considering children's responses to clusters of items with common content, examiners should consider responses to individual items, especially when individual responses differ markedly from the examinee's typical mode of response within a domain. Although a child might demonstrate a generally positive family self-concept, for example, a strong negative response to a single item (e.g., My parents care about my education) might identify intense feelings about an important aspect of the family milieu. Given a strong negative response to such an item, the examiner would want to consider the child's responses to items throughout the Academic Scale for additional information. Though this particular child may feel loved and cared for by his or her family overall, such a strong response to this item and related items on the Academic Scale may warrant a follow-up clinical interview to investigate the perceived causes and possible ramifications of the child's perceptions. By using this single item as a springboard, the examiner could provide closer scrutiny to the responses made to other related items, conduct a focused clinical interview, and "triangulate" these sources of information to fully investigate the child's feelings and perceptions.

It should be noted that these latter two levels of scale interpretation are the least reliable and most subjective; however, interpretation at these levels can provide meaningful clues and provide a segue into the exploration of examinees' feelings, beliefs, or concerns about specific events, actions, or aspects of their lives. Item interpretation of this sort is less reliable because the emphasis is placed on single items or small clusters of items. Item interpretation is more subjective because areas that the examiner believes are important may ultimately be irrelevant to the examinee; likewise, areas discounted by the examiner, in reality, may be important to the examinee. In contrast, examiners all too often merely report test scores without examining the student's pattern of response to sets of items. Such an overreliance on test scores fails to address the important information provided at the item level. Wise analysis of self-concept scales can extend their utility well beyond traditional quantitative analysis into a richer form of qualitative analysis of the child's adjustment.

Forms of Interpretation: Norm-Referenced versus Ipsative Approaches

Norm-Referenced Scale Interpretation

Of central importance in test interpretation is the norm to which an examinee's performance should be compared. Nearly all the existing self-concept scales allow for norm-referenced test interpretation; that is, the examinee's raw scores are compared with the distribution of scores that make up the normative sample to obtain standard scores and percentile ranks. Standard scores employed by most self-concept scales are either of the deviation IQ metric (Mean = 100; $SD = 15$) or the T Score (Mean = 50; $SD = 10$), both of which originate from the Z Score and therefore can be transformed into any desired form of standard score for the comparison of children's performances across instruments.

The use of norm-referenced tests assumes that the test's norms apply to and are appropriate for the child who has been assessed. A serious problem common among existing self-concept scales is that normative samples are frequently not representative of the population for which the scales are intended to be used, thus limiting their applicability and generalizability. The *Piers-Harris Children's Self-Concept Scale* (Piers, 1984), for example, was normed in a small town in Pennsylvania; the Coopersmith Self-Esteem Inventory (Coopersmith, 1984) was normed in central Connecticut; and, the Self Description Questionnaires, I and II (Marsh, 1988, 1990) were both normed in Australia. The assumption that the norms are suitable for or applicable to the examinee is violated for each of these instruments, and for many others (see Bracken & Mills, 1994; Keith & Bracken, Chapter 3, this volume).

When deciding whether to adopt and use one scale or another, examiners should question this important variable: Does the normative sample include children who are similar to the children who are being assessed? If the examiner works primarily with African American children from the rural southern United States, or Native American children from Oklahoma, or Hispanic children from the southwestern United States, or Asian American children living on the West Coast, or even sons or daughters of white factory workers from the midwestern United States, how applicable or appropriate would the Piers-Harris, Coopersmith, or SDQ norms be? Norms gathered in another country or even select regions of the United States would not be representative of the children who live in the various regions of the United States mentioned previously, especially if the scales are being used for norm-referenced clinical comparisons. The best that could be said about any particular child's performance on these instruments is that compared with children from Connecticut, Pennsylvania, or Sydney, Australia, the examinee scored at a given level. For obvious legal and ethical reasons, such a limited generalization severely curtails the potential use of scales in clinical practice with such limited, nonrepresentative normative samples.

When making norm-referenced comparisons, clinicians should ensure that the instruments they use provide a wide variety of descriptors of the child's performance (e.g., standard scores, percentile ranks, confidence intervals, self-concept classifications) (American Psychological Association, 1985). Standard scores provide a *quantitative* description of the child's performance based on where the child's obtained score falls along the distribution of scores in the norm sample. Similarly, percentiles permit the ranking of a child's performance such that the examiner can indicate the percentage of children in the normative sample who scored at or below the child's obtained score (e.g., Rachel's Academic self-concept score was ranked at the 85th percentile as compared with her peers in the normative sample). Given an instrument's Standard Error of Measurement (SEM), examiners can develop confidence intervals around an examinee's obtained score to identify the range of scores that would include the child's hypothetical "true score" with some predetermined level of confidence. For example, given Rachel's percentile rank, her corresponding MSCS Total Scale standard score would be 116. With a Standard Error of Measurement of 2.2 for the MSCS Total Scale Score, the examiner can state that with 68% confidence Rachel's "true score" would lie in a range of scores between 113.8 to 118.2 (116 ± 2.2). Along with such quantitative descriptors, the MSCS self-concept classification also provides a *qualitative* description of the child's current self-concept (e.g., Average Self-Concept; Moderately Negative Self-Concept). In combination, the quantitative and qualitative descriptors applied to the Total Scale and the six MSCS scales present to parents, teachers, and other professionals a portrait of the child's current levels of global and domain-specific self-concepts relative to the children who compose the normative sample.

Ipsative Scale Interpretation

In contrast to norm-referenced assessment, sometimes it is more important clinically to conduct intrachild analyses to determine whether a child demonstrates strengths or weaknesses within individual self-concept domains as compared with his or her own *overall* self-concept. Intrachild analysis of this sort is known as ipsative profile analysis and is based on the processes of comparing an examinee's individual subtest or scale scores with the examinee's average subtest or scale score. Though Cattell (1944) coined the concept of ipsative test interpretation and Davis (1959) is known for developing the working formula for its implementation,

Kaufman (1979) made ipsative profile analysis popular in psychoeducational assessment with the Wechsler Intelligence Scale for Children—Revised (Wechsler, 1974). There are far too few self-concept scales that reflect sufficient psychometric sophistication to allow for ipsative subscale analysis, which is another reason why many self-concept scales are not suitable for clinical applications.

The ipsative form of profile analysis is used to identify domains of self-concept that stand out as the examinee's "personal problem areas" or "areas of personal strength." The process is especially useful when all the examinee's scores cluster normatively within the same general range (e.g., subaverage, average, above average). Even within a fairly constricted range of scores one or more self-concept domains may deviate significantly from the child's average self-concept score; such ipsative deviation can suggest to clinicians specific areas of concern or support for the child.

As an example of how norm-referenced and ipsative interpretations can be meaningfully employed, consider the following case. Jessica, a 13-year-old female, was assessed on the MSCS. Jessica had the following scores for each of the respective MSCS scales: Social, 108; Competence, 123; Affect, 117; Academic, 127; Family, 126; and, Physical, 120. In each self-concept domain, Jessica scored normatively in the Average range or above, and her associated percentile ranks ranged from the 71st percentile (Social Scale) to the 96th percentile (Academic Scale). It would seem from a norm-referenced perspective, overall Jessica appears to be a well-adjusted child, projecting no reasons for concern.

To conduct an ipsative analysis, the examiner summed Jessica's MSCS scale scores and divided by the number of scales (i.e., 6) and found that her average scale score was 120 (rounded). By subtracting Jessica's average scale score from each of the obtained scale scores, we find resulting difference scores of -12, Social; $+3$, Competence; -3 Affect; $+7$, Academic; $+6$, Family; and, 0, Physical. The ipsative analysis of Jessica's MSCS profile shows that her overall positive self-concept is lowered somewhat by her ipsatively less positive Social and Affect domains. By entering Table 3.3 in the MSCS manual (Bracken, 1992; p. 28), the examiner will find that none of Jessica's scores deviate significantly from her average scale score in the positive direction—that is, she has no ipsative self-concept strengths. However, with a 12-point negative deviation from her average scale score ($p < .05$), Jessica's Social Scale is identified as a relative weakness. Though her Family score is greater than her average scale score by 6 points, it does not deviate significantly from average (a 7-point difference is required at the .05 level of significance).

Given this particular profile of scores, Jessica demonstrated normatively average to above-average self-concepts in each of the six MSCS domains. However, in contrast to her norm-referenced performance, Jessica is identified as having a weakness in the Social domain relative to her overall level of adjustment. An astute clinician would follow up on

Jessica's responses to individual items within and across all domains, and especially within the Social domain, in an effort to identify Jessica's specific areas of concern. After developing hypotheses about potential areas of concern, the clinician could then conduct an exploratory clinical interview using the MSCS items and Jessica's responses as a guide to conduct a more extensive personality assessment.

The sensitivity of the MSCS ipsative profile analysis, as compared with norm-referenced analysis, makes possible and encourages the systematic examination of otherwise less detectable areas of adjustment difficulty. Ipsative profile analysis is especially sensitive because it is a relative standard of comparison that employs the child's own overall level of adjustment as the point of comparison as opposed to the normative sample's overall level of adjustment.

SELF-CONCEPT AS PART OF A LARGER ASSESSMENT BATTERY

As good measures of affectivity, both general and domain-specific self-concept scales can contribute meaningfully to school-based or clinic-based psychoeducational assessment of children's and adolescents' affectivity and adjustment. Self-concept scales have been used in only a limited fashion in psychoeducational assessments for a variety of reasons (e.g., limited technical adequacy, poor normative samples, lack of comparability of scores across instruments). However, self-concept scales also have enjoyed limited clinical use because there has not been an existing "umbrella" interpretive scheme that permits the integration of self-concept scales with tests assessing other important constructs (e.g., intellectual, achievement, adaptive behavior).

Bracken (1992) proposed the multidimensional, context-dependent model of assessment as a systematic process for interpreting and integrating test results across a wide variety of psychoeducational instruments. The Appendix at the end of this chapter identifies over 70 instruments that assess children's functioning in one or more of the MSCS six context-domains. Using the information presented in the Appendix, clinicians can identify or create batteries of instruments according to the multidimensional, context-dependent model, or the model can be superimposed on clinicians' existing batteries. The function of the proposed model is to provide a comprehensive interpretive format by which clinicians can analyze, integrate, and synthesize data across instruments and domains; a scheme which also provides a meaningful integrative format for writing psychological reports and planning psychoeducational interventions.

Application of the multidimensional, context-dependent assessment model not only permits the integration of information across instruments and domains, but, importantly, across various reporting sources.

All participating members of an assessment team can apply whatever technologies they typically employ, whether formal or informal (e.g., observations, tests, interviews, third-party reports), to gather information about the child's adjustment and/or abilities within each of the context-domains. A multiple-source, multiple-instrument, multiple-setting assessment paradigm provides a comprehensive evaluation of the child and allows for the triangulation and verification of information. Such multi-member, team-oriented assessments are common and are mandated for school-based psychoeducational assessments throughout the United States (e.g., Public Law 94-142; Public Law 99-457).

Comparison of information gained through multiple sources, about multiple constructs, and through the administration of multiple instruments is fairly easily performed. To synthesize such a seemingly disparate collection of information, the examiner must separate and sort scales, subscales, and subtests into each of their respective context-domains. Once similar scales are combined within segregated domains, the examiner can then examine the child's scores within and across domains for consistency. To determine whether scores differ meaningfully from one another within and across domains, examiners can compute and employ the *Standard Error of the Difference* (Anastasi, 1988) as a criterion of significance. Or, the examiner can use a more casual one standard deviation difference "rule of thumb" criterion, which works well when scales are sufficiently reliable. This criterion is appropriate when any two scales have reliabilities equal to or greater than .85; that is, at this level of reliability difference scores of no more than one standard deviation would be considered significant at the .05 alpha level. The rule of thumb is best applied when only two scores are being contrasted because of the alpha slippage that occurs when making multiple contrasts (Silverstein, 1976); however, because this process is used only for generating hypotheses about the child, it is sufficiently conservative for such exploratory work even when making multiple contrasts.

By either applying the *Standard Error of the Difference* or the rule of thumb criterion, the examiner can easily consider the consistency of examinees' scores across instruments to identify specific areas of strength or weakness. Such multiple-instrument analyses improve examiners' judgment and decision-making reliability due to the increased number of scores contributing to the respective domains. For example, if an examiner employs several measures of social adjustment and the scores from each these respective measures are fairly consistent (do not vary significantly), the examiner's judgment about the child's social adjustment will likely be more accurate and reliable than if decisions were based on a single instrument or scale. Also, when considering scores within a battery that reflect both the child's abilities and affectivity, the examiner can identify whether the child's level of affectivity is commensurate with his or her assessed abilities within specific domains (e.g., whether the child's academic self-concept is comparable to his or her academic achievement).

The following case study combines a number of instruments that collectively reflect the MSCS multidimensional model. The instruments include objective and projective personality measures, as well as tests of intelligence and achievement. A brief description of the examinee will be presented, followed by a normative and ipsative interpretation of her performance on the MSCS. Finally, an integration of her assessment results across a variety of instruments will be provided.

CASE STUDY: SAMANTHA, AGE 11

Background

Samantha and her brother Kenny live with their mother (Karen) and their mother's boyfriend, David. Samantha's parents are divorced and Samantha's father (Steven) only irregularly takes advantage of his weekend visitation rights. Samantha and Kenny stay home alone for extended periods due to Karen's and David's work schedules, and Samantha is responsible for Kenny's care in her mother's absence. Samantha is expected to perform many of the domestic chores around the house, such as laundry, cleaning, and dishwashing. Samantha's father believes that she is burdened with too many domestic responsibilities for her age. Samantha's mother recognizes that Samantha resents her many responsibilities, and she believes that Samantha is especially unhappy over the loss of peer interactions as a result of having to stay home to care for Kenny. Samantha is often moody, sad, and withdrawn when at home; however, sometimes she is manipulative and at times she expresses anger.

Samantha is believed by her mother and teachers to be a very competent individual. She is bright and socially precocious. Though her grades have fallen considerably during the past year, her teachers believe she is capable of a much higher academic performance. They have voiced concern about the discrepancy between Samantha's abilities and current level of achievement.

Academically, Samantha earns mostly Bs and Cs, and she completes homework without reminders. Generally, she receives good conduct grades, and she enjoys reading as a recreational activity. Because of her home responsibilities, Samantha is unable to participate in after-school events or sports.

Socially, Samantha is described by her mother as comfortable with people of all ages. She has several close friends her own age, and she makes friends easily. Her good verbal skills and physical attractiveness have facilitated her social acceptance. Her only limitation socially is that she is not allowed to have friends over to the house when her mother is not home, and she may not leave the house during her mother's absence. Though Kenny is allowed to go to neighbors' houses when his mother is not at home, Samantha must remain at home so that Kenny will not have to return to an empty house. Depending on his work schedule and days off, sometimes David is home with Samantha and Kenny while their mother is at work.

Physically, Samantha is in good health and is developed beyond age expectancy. She is aware that she is considered physically attractive, and her career aspiration is to be a model.

Tests Administered

- Woodcock-Johnson Psychoeducational Battery-Revised—Tests of Cognitive Ability and Tests of Achievement (Woodcock & Johnson, 1989).
- Multidimensional Self Concept Scale (Bracken, 1992).
- Assessment of Interpersonal Relations (Bracken, 1993).
- Memphis State Sentence Completion Blank.
- Human Figure Drawing: Koppitz Scoring System (Koppitz, 1968).
- Roberts Apperception Test for Children (McArthur & Roberts, 1982).

MSCS Normative and Ipsative Results

As can be seen from Figure 12.2, Samantha's Total Scale Self-Concept Score on the MSCS is 108, which is classified as Average and ranked at the 71st percentile as compared with her peers. With 90% confidence, Samantha's "true" MSCS Total Scale Score would be included in a range of scores between 104 and 112. Consistent with her Total Scale Score, each of the six self-concept domains are in the Average range, except the Physical

	Raw Score	Standard Score	Confidence Interval 90%	Classification	%ile Rank	Standard Score	Difference Score	.05/.01 Classification
Social	81	108	110–116	Avg	71	108	+1	Avg
Competence	74	99	90–108	Avg	48	99	−8	Avg
Affect	83	110	103–117	Avg	74	110	+3	Avg
Academic	80	109	102–116	Avg	73	109	+2	Avg
Family	79	93	89–97	Avg	33	93	−14	Weakness
Physical	92	123	116–130	Very Pos	94	123	+16	Strength
TOTAL SCALE	489	108	104–112	Avg	71	—	—	—

Figure 12.2 Samantha's MSCS Norm-Referenced and Ipsative Interpretation. From *Multidimensional Self Concept Scale* by B. A. Bracken, 1992. Copyright 1992 Pro-Ed. Used with permission.

Scale which is normatively and ipsatively a strength (standard score = 123, 92nd percentile). Samantha's Family self-concept is 14 points lower than her average scale score of 107, and is identified as an ipsative weakness. Although her normatively average Competence Scale is only one point below the normative mean of 100, it is approaching significance as an ipsative weakness when compared with her average scale score (i.e., -8 points). Because of the contradiction between Samantha's mother's perception of her daughter as a very competent individual and Samantha's nonsignificant trend toward an ipsatively weak Competence Scale, each of the measures in the battery will be examined to explore the domain more thoroughly.

Overall, it appears that Samantha has average global and domain-specific self-concepts, with the exception of a Very Positive Physical self-concept. Exploration of her responses to clusters of items and single items within each scale will be reserved for the following section, which will combine the MSCS data with the information provided by a full compliment of instruments in the psychoeducational battery.

Summary of Test Results by Domain

Within the Competence domain, Samantha demonstrated Above Average cognitive abilities as evidenced by her Woodcock-Johnson Broad Cognitive Ability Score of 118, which is ranked at the 88th Percentile. With 68% confidence, Samantha's "true" Cognitive Ability Score would be expected in the range from 114 to 122. Although Samantha's MSCS Competence Scale standard score of 99 is significantly lower than her WJ-R Cognitive Ability Score, she strongly endorsed items on the scale that were of a cognitive nature (e.g., "I lack common sense," Strongly Disagree; "I am not very smart," Strongly Disagree; "I can do most things pretty well," Agree). Samantha demonstrated poorer Competence Self-Concept, however, in areas related to motivation and personal actions (e.g., "I frequently put off doing important things until it is too late," Strongly Agree; "I waste money foolishly," Strongly Agree).

Samantha's Human Figure Drawing was a large drawing of a very shapely, well-dressed, and made-up female whom she identified as herself. The drawing suggests social and physical confidence and possibly too much self-awareness and narcissistic appreciation. Relatedly, Samantha's responses to competence-oriented sentence completion blanks were of a social nature. For example, she indicated, "When I try . . . *to talk to people, they listen*" and "I know a lot about . . . *music, money, and friends.*" Overall, Samantha appears to be a cognitively and socially competent individual, and her scores on the respective Competence measures are consistently in the average to above-average range. Issues of concern to Samantha in the Competence domain appear to be related to self-control and motivation.

Within the Academic Domain, Samantha's current academic achievement was assessed to be in the above-average to the superior range. Consistent with her self-report of enjoying reading, Samantha earned a WJ-R Broad Reading score of 135. She also earned Broad Math and Broad Knowledge scores of 119 and 113, respectively. Relative to such a high level of academic achievement, Samantha's standard score of 85 on the Teachers relations scale of the *Assessment of Interpersonal Relations* (AIR; Bracken, 1993) suggests that she may have relationship difficulties with her teachers at school. Her Average Academic self-concept score (SS = 109) on the MSCS reflects the difference between her high academic achievement and her problematic teacher relations.

By considering Samantha's responses to specific items on the MSCS, it appears that motivational and self-control issues again surface as areas that are problematic for her in the academic domain (e.g., "I frequently feel unprepared for class," Strongly Agree; "I have poor study habits," Agree; "My teachers like my classroom behavior," Disagree). And though she believes she is skilled in the content areas of reading (Strongly Agree) and science (Agree) and agrees that in general "Most subjects are pretty easy" (Strongly Agree), she identifies mathematics as a subject that is difficult for her (e.g., "I am good at mathematics," Strongly Disagree).

Consistent with her sense of social competence, Samantha strongly agrees that "Classmates usually like my ideas" and that "Most people would rather work with me than someone else." Also consistent with the low score on the AIR Teachers Scale, Samantha's responses to sentence completion blanks indicate that for her school is largely a social event, and that she does not particularly care for her teachers (e.g., "I wish my teacher would . . . *kiss a bug!*") an unexplained response to a sentence completion blank that is both clinically revealing and is additional cause for concern is her claim, "Teachers usually . . . *fear for me.*"

Socially, Samantha has consistently demonstrated competence, acceptance, and enjoyment. Her Social Scale score on the MSCS (SS = 108) and her high scores on the AIR Male Peers and Female Peers scores of 118 and 127, respectively, provide further support for her overall social comfort and peer acceptance. Though she endorsed most MSCS items positively on the Social Scale, she agreed with the statement that "People tell lies about me" and "I often feel like I am left out of things." Being left out of activities is a natural consequence of Samantha's home responsibilities, and the perception that people tell lies about her is not in itself unusual for an 11-year-old. However, increasing evidence develops in Samantha's portfolio that proves more troubling—for example, Samantha's responses to the following sentence completion stems: "When I am with adults . . . *I act like one*" and "Girls are . . . *jealous of me,*" and finally, "Boys tell me . . . *I am beautiful.*" Such responses, combined with her teachers' "fears" suggest the possibility of precocious attention to and concern about male/female relations for an 11-year-old.

Although thus far in the interpretive process Samantha has demonstrated some normative strengths (scores that exceed one standard deviation above the normative mean—a score of 115 and above), she has not demonstrated any ipsative strengths or weaknesses. Within the Physical domain, Samantha's MSCS Physical Scale score of 123 is classified normatively as Very Positive and is also an ipsative strength. On the Physical scale, Samantha endorsed all the items positively, regardless of content (i.e., attractiveness, abilities, health). Her self-perception of being physically attractive was evidenced in her "glamorous" self-drawing on the Human Figure Drawing. Most revealing, however, are her responses to the sentence completion blanks: "Others think I look . . . *very good in just about everything I wear*"; "My face . . . *is very beautiful*"; "My body . . . *has a very nice figure*"; "When I wear . . . *a swimsuit, I get a lot of stares*"; and, "I think I look . . . *Gorgeous.*"

Within the family domain, Samantha's Family Scale score of 93 is a normatively average, but ipsatively weak. Additionally, she reports very poor interpersonal relations with her mother (AIR Mother Scale score = 78) and normatively average, but ipsatively weak father relations (AIR Father Scale score = 94). On the MSCS Samantha strongly agreed that "My parents don't trust me." On the AIR Mother Scale, Samantha cites a lack of being understood, being treated unfairly, the lack of maternal acceptance, difficulty being honest with her mother, and the inability to tell secrets to her mother as areas with which she strongly agreed. On the Family-oriented sentence completion blanks, she used words such as "weird" and "unreal" to describe her family. Finally, on the Roberts Apperception Test for Children, Samantha told stories about family scenarios that involved considerable conflict, which resulted in significant T scores on the Unresolved Conflict Scale ($T = 85$) and Rejection Scale ($T = 65$).

Consistent with Samantha's Average score on the MSCS Affect Scale ($SS = 110$) and subaverage scores on the clinical subscales of the Roberts Apperception Test ($T = 40$, Depression; $T = 35$, Anxiety), her overall demeanor was positive, yet controlled and aloof. However, examination of specific MSCS items suggested that Samantha has conflicting affective self-perceptions. For example, Samantha agreed with the MSCS statements "My life is unstable" and "I am frequently confused about my feelings." In addition, her completion of affect-oriented sentence completion blanks included "I hate . . . *when my mother says I am lying*"; "My greatest fear . . . *is that I will get fat and wrinkly*"; and, "I am afraid . . . *of getting old and ugly.*" Such concerns are atypical for an 11-year-old child, and given the expressed conflict with her mother as indicated on the AIR, the Roberts, and the sentence completion blank, it appears that Samantha has more affective concerns than are evident in the scores of the various instruments. These qualitatively discerned concerns appear to be related paradoxically to her otherwise positive interpersonal relations and physical attractiveness, possibly giving her good reason for being "confused."

With all the information provided by the instruments included in this battery, the examiner conducted a follow-up clinical interview. Samantha's responses to the various MSCS, AIR, and sentence completion blanks suggested more than typical preoccupation with beauty and social relations. Of particular concern were items that indicated that her teachers feared for her, that her mother disbelieved and distrusted her, that when she is with adults she acts like an adult, and that she often experiences feelings of confusion. The interview addressed these issues directly, seeking clarification of the origin and implications of her feelings. What was revealed with surprisingly little hesitation was that Samantha was being sexually abused by David, her mother's boyfriend. Being physically well developed beyond her years, left alone with her mother's boyfriend in the evenings while her mother worked, and being susceptible to an adult male's flattery and attention, Samantha was vulnerable to opportunistic sexual abuse. Though Samantha had initially told her mother of David's early advances, her mother varied between disbelieving and accusing her daughter—but, she neither intervened nor confronted David. As a result of this evaluation, the Department of Human Services was called and the sexual abuse was reported. The Department of Human Services intervened immediately.

The instruments in this battery collectively painted a portrait of Samantha's abilities and adjustment across the six primary context-domains. By attending to her normative and ipsative patterns of scores on the MSCS and AIR and her responses to individual items, important clues were revealed that otherwise might not have been forthcoming. Although detailing the normative and ipsative analyses of the instruments and revealing specific item content were not possible due to space, the reader can gain a sense of Samantha's abilities and adjustment within and across the various domains. The findings that Samantha is a competent (socially, physically, and academically) but confused and conflicted individual is apparent. That she was experiencing relationship stress with her mother and teachers, and that she is preoccupied with her physical beauty and sexuality were gleaned because information was systematically synthesized by domain across instruments. Information came to light both within and across domains that guided a follow-up clinical interview. And, as a result of the structure provided by the MSCS context-dependent, multidimensional model, the examiner was able to develop hypotheses about Samantha that revealed her sexual abuse. Further, the MSCS model permitted the analysis, synthesis, and expression of detailed information into a structured psychological report in a concise and cogent fashion.

Clinical Improvement of Children's Self-Concepts

This chapter has defined a model of self-concept that has both theoretical and practical implications for the clinical practice of psychology. Not only is the model useful for the understanding of children's and adolescents'

496   Clinical Applications of a Context-Dependent, Multidimensional Model

adjustment, but it can be applied equally well in research settings where self-concept or adjustment within one or more of the primary context-domains is of interest. Either as a clinical tool or research instrument, the multidimensional, context-dependent model may provide an avenue for the systematic consideration of the construct of self-concept, in its multiple dimensions and as a reflection of general affectivity. This model also has direct implications for improving children's and adolescents' self-images.

By understanding the manner in which children and adolescents acquire their self-concepts and appreciating the importance of the six primary self-concept domains, clinicians can work systematically toward improving the way children and adolescents feel about themselves within and across context-domains. However, an understanding of the principles of self-concept acquisition also acknowledges that the foremost goal of self-concept enhancement should be to help the individual acquire the competencies, skills, and abilities that will bring about increased success and foster positive self-evaluations in a natural fashion. Direct instruction to improve the child's competencies (e.g., tutoring, social-skills training, self-care, and hygiene) should lead to improved self-efficacy and concomitant improved self-concept. Also, modeling and reinforcement of appropriate behaviors through successive approximations permit gradual skill building in naturalistic settings.

In some instances, it is important to recognize that the environment simply may not be conducive to the development of positive self-concepts (e.g., the setting is too taxing for the child's abilities), and a change of environment might be necessary before self-concept improvements are likely. A child who attends a highly competitive high school might be unable to meet the intellectual and academic demands of such a competitive school. In such an instance, the child might benefit from transferring to another less competitive school, rather than face continual defeat and failure in his or her current placement. Alternatively, the child might benefit from a modified academic schedule that includes some competitive courses with some less challenging courses, thus allowing more time to concentrate on academically challenging work. Sometimes a more sensitive or more accepting environment will enable a child to stay in his or her current placement.

The second important acknowledgment that must be made is that all people sometimes employ faulty self-perceptions based on irrational or non-reality-based beliefs and expectations. In such instances, clinicians need to help their clients recognize their unreasonable self-expectations and possibly seek more reasonable standards of self-acceptance (it is also important that others in the child's environment adopt reasonable expectations of the child). To alter clients' perceptions and adopt more reasonable goals or expectations, clinicians should help their clients reframe self-perceptions by learning to highlight and appreciate positive rather than negative self-attributes, behaviors, or outcomes. Also, reframing helps the client see that problems and mistakes are not as catastrophic as they may first appear, and that life's normal failings happen to everyone. Helping the client put things into their proper perspective is of utmost importance in reframing.

This chapter provided a theoretical foundation for a multidimensional and context-dependent model of self-concept acquisition. The model provides a rationale for how children adopt self-perceptions based on information provided by two perspectives and evaluated against four standards. Children's acquired self-concepts reflect past experiences and allow for the prediction of future behaviors. General affectivity and global behavior are best predicted by the self-concept total scale score, whereas domain-specific self-concepts are better predictors of domain-specific behaviors. The use of a multidimensional, context-dependent model of social-emotional adjustment allows for the combination of multiple sources of information, multiple respondents, and multiple constructs in the clinical assessment of children and adolescents. Such theory-based psychoeducational assessment provides a direct linkage between assessment results and focused, context-dependent intervention strategies.

REFERENCES

Achenbach, T. M., & Edelbrock, C. S. (1983). *Manual for the Child Behavior Checklist and Revised Child Behavior Profile.* Burlington, VT: University of Vermont.

Achenbach, T. M., & Edelbrock, C. S. (1986). *Manual for the teacher's report form and teacher version of the Child Behavior Checklist and Revised Child Behavior Profile.* Burlington, VT: University of Vermont.

Achenbach, T. M., & Edelbrock, C. S. (1987). *Manual for the Youth Self-Report and Profile.* Burlington, VT: University of Vermont.

Adams, G. L. (1984a). *Comprehensive Test of Adaptive Behavior.* San Antonio, TX: Psychological Corp.

Adams, G. L. (1984b). *Normative Adaptive Behavior Checklist.* San Antonio, TX: Psychological Corp.

Adler, A. (1970). Superiority. In H. L. Ansbacher & R. R. Ansbacher (Eds.), *Superiority and social interest* (pp. 45–82). Itasca, IL: Peacock.

APA. (1985). *Standards for educational and psychological testing.* Washington, DC: American Psychological Association.

American Psychiatric Association. (1994). *Diagnostic and statistical manual of mental disorders* (4th ed.). Washington, DC: Author.

Anastasi, A. (1988). *Psychological testing.* New York: Macmillan.

Bandura, A. (1977). *Social learning theory.* Englewood Cliffs, NJ: Prentice-Hall.

Bandura, A. (1986). *Social foundations of thought and action: A social-cognitive theory.* Englewood Cliffs, NJ: Prentice-Hall.

Bannister, D., & Agnew, J. (1977). The child's construing of self. In J. Cole (Ed.), *Nebraska Symposium on Motivation.* Lincoln: University of Nebraska Press.

Beck, A. T. (1987a). *Beck Depression Inventory.* San Antonio, TX: Psychological Corp.

Beck, A. T. (1987b). *Beck Hopelessness Scale.* San Antonio, TX: Psychological Corp.

Birleson, P. (1980). The validity of depressive disorder in childhood and the development of a self-rating scale: A research report. *Journal of Child Psychology and Psychiatry, 22,* 73–87.

Bloom, B. S. (1976). *Human characteristics and school learning.* New York: McGraw-Hill.

Bracken, B. A. (1987). Limitations of preschool instruments and standards for minimal levels of technical adequacy. *Journal of Psychoeducational Assessment, 5,* 313–326.

Bracken, B. A. (1988). Ten psychometric reasons why similar tests produce dissimilar results. *Journal of School Psychology, 26,* 155–166.

Bracken, B. A. (1992). *Multidimensional Self Concept Scale.* Austin, TX: Pro-Ed.

Bracken, B. A. (1993). *Assessment of interpersonal relations.* Austin, TX: Pro-Ed.

Bracken, B. A., Bunch, S., Keith, T. Z., & Keith, P. B. (1992, August). *Multidimensional self concept: A five instrument factor analysis.* Paper presented at the American Psychological Association's annual conference, Washington, DC.

Bracken, B. A., & Mills, B. C. (1994). School counselors' assessment of self-concept: A comprehensive review of 10 instruments. *The School Counselor, 42,* 14–31.

Brookover, W. B., Thomas, S., & Paterson, A. (1964). Self concept of ability and school achievement. *Sociology of Education, 37,* 271–278.

Brown, L., & Alexander, J. (1990). *Self-Esteem Index.* Austin, TX: Pro-Ed.

Brown, L., & Hammill, D. (1990). *Behavior Rating Profile-2.* Austin, TX: Pro-Ed.

Brown, L., & Leigh, J. E. (1986). *Adaptive Behavior Inventory.* Austin, TX: Pro-Ed.

Bruininks, R. H. (1978). *Bruininks-Oseretsky Test of Motor Proficiency.* Circle Pines, MN: American Guidance Service.

Burks, H. (1968). *Manual for Burks' Behavior Rating Scales.* El Monte, CA: Arden Press.

Burt, C. (1954). The differentiation of intellectual abilities. *British Journal of Educational Psychology, 24,* 76–90.

Cattell, R. B. (1944). Psychological measurement: Normative, ipsative, and interactive. *Psychological Bulletin, 51,* 91–97.

Cattell, R. B., Cattell, M. D., & Johns, E. (1984). *High School Personality Questionnaire.* Champaign, IL: Institute for Personality and Ability Testing.

Cattell, R. B., & IPAT Staff. (1986). *Sixteen Personality Factor Questionnaire.* Champaign, IL: Institute for Personality and Ability Testing.

Cattell, R. B., Scheier, I. H., & IPAT Staff. (1976). *IPAT Anxiety Scale.* Champaign, IL: Institute for Personality and Ability Testing.

Cauce, A. M. (1987). School and peer competence in early adolescence: Test of domain-specific self-perceived competence. *Developmental Psychology, 23,* 287–291.

Conners, C. K. (1989). *Conner's Rating Scales.* Austin, TX: Pro-Ed.

Connolly, A. J. (1988). *Key math revised: A diagnostic inventory of essential mathematics.* Circle Pines, MN: American Guidance Service.

Cooley, C. H. (1902). *Human nature and the social order.* New York: Scribner's.

Coopersmith, S. (1967). *The antecedents of self-esteem.* San Francisco: Freeman.

Coopersmith, S. (1984). *Coopersmith Self-Esteem Inventory.* Palo Alto, CA: Consulting Psychologist Press.

Davis, F. B. (1959). Interpretation of differences among averages and individual test scores. *Journal of Educational Psychology, 50,* 162–170.

Dinkmeyer, D. C., Pew, W. L., & Dinkmeyer, D. C., Jr. (1979). *Adlerian Counseling and Psychotherapy.* Monterey, CA: Brooks/Cole.

Edwards, A. L. (1959). *Edwards Personal Preference Schedule.* San Antonio, TX: Psychological Corp.

Elliott, C. D. (1990). *Differential Ability Scales.* San Antonio, TX: Psychological Corp.

Epstein, S. (1973). The self-concept revisited or a theory of a theory. *American Psychologist, 28,* 405-416.

Franzoi, S. L., & Shields, S. A. (1984). The Body Esteem Scale: Multidimensional structure and sex differences in a college population. *Journal of Personality Assessment, 48,* 173–178.

Glaser, W. (1972). *The identity society.* New York: Harper & Row.

Gordon, L. V. (1978). *Gordon Personal Profile-Inventory.* San Antonio, TX: Psychological Corp.

Gough, H. G. (1987). *California Psychological Inventory—Revised.* Palo Alto, CA: Consulting Psychologist Press.

Gresham, F., & Elliott, S. (1990). *Social Skills Rating System.* Circle Pines, MN: American Guidance Service.

Hansford, B. C., & Hattie, J. A. (1982). The relationship between self and achievement/performance measures. *Review of Educational Research, 52,* 123–142.

Harter, S. (1978). Effectance motivation reconsidered: Toward a developmental model. *Human Development, 1,* 34–64.

Harter, S. (1982a). Children's understanding of multiple emotions: A cognitive-developmental approach. In W. F. Overton (Ed.), *The relationship between social and cognitive development.* Hillsdale, NJ: Erlbaum.

Harter, S. (1982b). The Perceived Competence Scale for Children. *Child Development, 53,* 87–97.

Harter, S. (1983). Developmental perspectives on the self-system. In P. H. Mussen (Ed.), *Handbook of child psychology* (Vol. 4, 4th ed., pp. 275–385). New York: Wiley.

Hathaway, S. R., & Monachesi, E. D. (1963). *Adolescent personality and behavior: MMPI patterns of normal, delinquent, dropout, and other outcomes.* Minneapolis: University of Minnesota Press.

Hattie, J. A. (1992). *Self-concept*. Hillsdale, NJ: Erlbaum.

Hutton, J. B., & Roberts, T. G. (1986). *Social-Emotional Dimension scale: A measure of school behavior*. Austin, TX: Pro-Ed.

Jackson, L. D. (1994). *The relationship between children's self-concepts and social acceptance*. Unpublished master's thesis, University of Memphis, Memphis, TN.

James, W. (1983). *Principles of Psychology* (Vol. 1). Cambridge, MA: Harvard University Press. (original work published 1890)

Jensen, A. R. (1984). Test validity: g versus the specificity doctrine. *Journal of Social and Biological Structures, 7,* 93–118.

Jensen, A. R. (1987). The g beyond factor analysis. In R. R. Ronning, J. C. Conoley, J. A. Gover, & J. C. Witt (Eds.), *The influence of cognitive psychology on testing* (pp. 87–142). Hillsdale, NJ: Erlbaum.

Kaufman, A. S. (1979). *Intelligent testing with the WISC-R*. New York: Wiley.

Kazdin, A. E., French, N. H., Unis, A. S., Esveldt-Dawson, K., & Sheuck, R. B. (1983). Hopelessness, depression, and suicidal intent among psychiatrically disturbed inpatient children. *Journal of Consulting and Clinical Psychology, 51,* 504–510.

Keith, L. C. (1994). *Self-concept or self-concepts: A factor analytic study of a multidimensional model*. Unpublished master's thesis, University of Memphis, Memphis, TN.

Keith, L. C., & Bracken, B. A. (1995, March). *Confirmatory factor analysis of a multidimensional model of self-concept: An examination of construct validity*. Paper presented at the National Association of School Psychologists' annual conference, Chicago, IL.

Keller, A., Ford, L. H., & Meacham, J. A. (1978). Dimensions of self-concept in preschool children. *Developmental Psychology, 14,* 483–489.

Kernberg, O. F. (1975). *Borderline conditions and pathological narcissism*. New York: Aronson.

Kohn, A. (1994). The truth about self-esteem. *Phi Delta Kappan, 76,* 272–283.

Koppitz, E. M. (1968). *Psychological evaluation of children's human figure drawings*. Needham Heights, MA: Allyn & Bacon.

Kovacs, M. (1983). *The Children's Depression Inventory: A self-rated depression scale for school-aged youngsters*. Unpublished manuscript.

L'Ecuyer, R. (1981). The development of the self-concept through the life-span. In M. D. Lynch, A. A. Norem-Hebeisen, & K. Gergen (Eds.), *Self concept: Advances in theory and research*. Cambridge, MA: Ballinger.

Markwardt, F. C. (1989). *Peabody Individual Achievement Test—Revised*. Circle Pines, MN: American Guidance Service.

Marsh, H. W. (1988). *Self-Description Questionnaire, I*. San Antonio, TX: Psychological Corp.

Marsh, H. W. (1990). *Self-Description Questionnaire, II*. San Antonio, TX: Psychological Corp.

Marsh, H. W., & Holmes, I. W. (1990). Multidimensional self-concepts: Construct validation of responses by children. *American Educational Research Journal, 27,* 89–117.

Marx, R. W., & Winne, P. H. (1980). Self-concept validation research: Some current complexities. *Measurement and Evaluation in Guidance, 13,* 72–82.

Matson, J. L., Rotatori, A. F., & Helsel, W. J. (1983). Development of a rating scale to measure social skills in children: The Matson Evaluation of Social Skills with Youngsters (MESSY). *Behavior Research and Therapy, 21,* 335–340.

McArthur, D. S., & Roberts, G. E. (1982). *Roberts Apperception Test for Children.* Los Angeles: Western Psychological Services.

McCarney, S. B., & Leigh, J. E. (1990). *Behavior Evaluation Scale—2.* Austin, TX: Pro-Ed.

Mercer, J. R., & Lewis, J. F. (1978). *Adaptive Behavior Inventory for Children.* San Antonio, TX: Psychological Corp.

Miller, L. C. (1981). *School Behavior Checklist.* Los Angeles: Western Psychological Services.

Millon, T., Green, C. J., & Meagher, R. B. (1982). *Millon Adolescent Personality Inventory Manual.* Minneapolis: National Computer Systems, Inc.

Minton, B. (1979). *Dimensions of information underlying children's judgments of their competence.* Unpublished master's thesis, University of Denver, Denver, CO.

Montgomery, M. S. (1994). Self-concept and children with learning disabilities: Observer-child concordance across six context-dependent domains. *Journal of Learning Disabilities, 27,* 254–262.

Mooney, R. L., & Gordon, L. V. (1950). *Mooney Problem Check Lists.* San Antonio, TX: Psychological Corp.

Moos, R. H., & Moos, B. S. (1986). *Family Environment Scale Manual* (Rev. ed.). Palo Alto, CA: Consulting Psychologist Press.

Mosak, H. H. (1979). Adlerian psychotherapy. In R. K. Corsini (Ed.), *Current psychotherapies* (2nd ed., pp. 35–84). Itasca, IL: Peacock.

Neeper, R., Lahey, B. B., & Frick, P. J. (1990). *Comprehensive Behavior Rating Scale for Children.* San Antonio, TX: Psychological Corp.

Olson, D. H., & Barnes, H. (1982). *The Quality of Life Inventory.* (Available from Family Social Science, University of Minnesota, St. Paul, MN 55108.)

Olson, D. H., McCubbin, H. I., Barnes, H., Larsen, A., Muxen, M., & Wilson, M. (1982a). *The Family Coping Strategies Inventory.* (Available from Family Social Science, University of Minnesota, St. Paul, MN 55108)

Olson, D. H., McCubbin, H. I., Barnes, H., Larsen, A., Muxen, M., & Wilson, M. (1982b). *The Parent-Adolescent Communication Scale.* (Available from Family Social Science, University of Minnesota, St. Paul, MN 55108)

Olson, D., Portner, J., & Lavee, Y. (1985). *FACES III.* (Available from Family Social Science, University of Minnesota, St. Paul, MN 55108)

Olson, D. H., & Wilson, M. (1982). *The Family Satisfaction Inventory.* (Available from Family Social Science, University of Minnesota, St. Paul, MN 55108)

Owen, S. V., & Baum, S. M. (1985). *Development of an academic self-efficacy scale for upper elementary school children.* Unpublished manuscript, University of Connecticut, Storrs, CN.

Pease, D., Clark, S. G., & Crase, S. J. (1982). *Iowa social competence scales.* Ames: Iowa State University.

Perosa, L. M. (1986). *The revision of the Structural Family Interaction Scale.* Unpublished manuscript.

Piaget, J. (1969). *The origins of intellect: Piaget's theory.* San Francisco: Freeman.

Piers, E. V. (1984). *Piers-Harris children's self-concept scale: Revised manual.* Los Angeles: Western Psychological Services.

Pino, C. J., Simons, N., & Slawinowski, M. J. (1984). *Children's Version/Family Environment Scale.* Palo Alto, CA: Consulting Psychologist Press.

Porter, R. B., & Cattell, R. B. (1982). *Children's Personality Questionnaire.* Champaign, IL: Institute for Personality and Ability Testing.

Reynolds, C. R., & Richmond, B. O. (1985). *Revised Children's Manifest Anxiety Scale (RCMAS).* Los Angeles: Western Psychological Services.

Reynolds, W. M. (1987). *Reynolds Adolescent Depression Scale.* Odessa, FL: Psychological Assessment Resources.

Rogers, C., & Dymond, R. (1954). *Psychotherapy and personality change.* Chicago: University of Chicago Press.

Rohner, R. P. (1984). *Handbook for the study of parental acceptance and rejection* (Rev. ed.). Storrs: University of Connecticut, Center for the Study of Parental Acceptance and Rejection.

Roid, G. H., & Fitts, W. H. (1988). *Tennessee Self-Concept Scale, Revised manual.* Los Angeles, CA: Western Psychological Services.

Rosenberg, M. (1979). *Conceiving the self.* New York: Basic Books.

Sarason, S. B., Davidson, K. S., Lighthall, F. F., Waite, R. R., & Ruebush, B. (1960). *Anxiety in elementary school children.* New York: Wiley.

Schicke, M. C., & Fagan, T. K. (1994). Contributions of self-concept and intelligence to the prediction of academic achievement among grade 4, 6, and 8 students. *Canadian Journal of School Psychology, 10,* 62–69.

Schinka, J. A. (1985a). *Children's Problems Checklist.* Odessa, FL: Psychological Assessment Resources.

Schinka, J. A. (1985b). *Personal Problems Checklist—Adolescent.* Odessa, FL: Psychological Assessment Resources.

Shavelson, R. J., Hubner, J. J., & Stanton, G. C. (1976). Validation of construct interpretations. *Review of Educational Research, 46,* 407–441.

Shulman, B. H. (1973). *Contributions to individual psychology.* Chicago: Alfred Adler Institute.

Silverstein, A. B. (1976). Variance components in the subtests of the WISC-R. *Psychological Reports, 39,* 1109–1110.

Skinner, B. F. (1990). Can psychology be a science of mind. *American Psychologist, 45,* 1206–1210.

Skinner, H. A., Steinhauer, P. D., & Santa-Barbara, J. (1984). *The Family Assessment Measure: Administration and interpretation guide.* (Available from Addiction Research Foundation, Toronto, Ontario, Canada)

Sparrow, S. S., Balla, D. A., & Cicchetti, D. V. (1984). *Vineland Adaptive Behavior Scales.* Circle Pines, MN: American Guidance Service.

Spearman, C. E. (1927). *The abilities of man.* New York: Macmillan.

Spielberger, C. D. (1973). *Manual for the State-Trait Anxiety Inventory for Children.* Palo Alto, CA: Consulting Psychologist Press.

Spielberger, C. D. (1983). *Manual for the State-Trait Anxiety Inventory* (Rev. ed.). Palo Alto, CA: Consulting Psychologist Press.

Thorndike, R. L., Hagen, E. P., & Sattler, J. M. (1986). *Stanford-Binet Intelligence Scale* (4th ed.). Chicago: Riverside.

Thurstone, L. (1938). *Primary mental abilities* (Psychometric Monographs No. 1). Chicago: University of Chicago Press.

Ulrich, D. A. (1985). *Test of Gross Motor Development.* Austin, TX: Pro-Ed.

U.S. Bureau of the Census. (1980). *Statistical abstract of the United States.* Washington, DC: Author.

Vernon, P. E. (1950). *The structure of human abilities.* London: Methuen.

Waksman, S. A. (1984). *Waksman Social Skills Rating Scale.* Portland, OR: ASIEP Education Co.

Walker, H. M. (1983). *Walker Problem Behavior Identification Checklist.* Los Angeles: Western Psychological Services.

Wechsler, D. (1974). *Wechsler Intelligence Scale for Children—Revised.* San Antonio, TX: Psychological Corp.

Wechsler, D. (1981). *Wechsler Adult Intelligence Scale—Revised.* San Antonio, TX: Psychological Corp.

Wechsler, D. (1993). *Wechsler Intelligence Scale for Children—III.* San Antonio, TX: Psychological Corp.

Weiner, B. (1972). *Theories of motivation.* Chicago: Markham.

Weiner, B., & Graham, S. (1983). An attributional approach to emotional development. In Izard, Kagan, & Zajonc (Eds.), *Emotion, cognition and behavior.* Hillsdale, NJ: Erlbaum.

Weissman, M., Orvaschel, H., & Padian, N. (1980). Children's symptom and social functioning: Self reports scales. *Journal of Nervous and Mental Disease, 168,* 736–740.

Wheeler, V. A., & Ladd, G. W. (1982). Assessment of children's self-efficacy for social interactions with peers. *Developmental Psychology, 18,* 795–805.

Wirt, R. D., Lachar, D., Klinedinst, J. K., & Seat, P. D. (1984). *Multidimensional description of child personality: A manual for the Personality Inventory for Children, Revised.* Los Angeles: Western Psychological Services.

Woodcock, R. W. (1987). *Woodcock Reading Mastery Tests—Revised.* Circle Pines, MN: American Guidance Service.

Woodcock, R. W., & Johnson, M. B. (1989). *Woodcock-Johnson Psychoeducational Battery.* Allen, TX: DLM Teaching Resources.

Wylie, R. C. (1974). *The self-concept: A review of methodological considerations and measuring instruments* (2nd ed., Vol. 1). Lincoln: University of Nebraska Press.

Wylie, R. C. (1979). *The self-concept: The theory and research on selected topics* (Vol. 2). Lincoln: University of Nebraska Press.

Wylie, R. C. (1989). *Measures of self-concept.* Lincoln: University of Nebraska Press.

APPENDIX

Common Psychoeducational Instruments That Assess the Six MSCS Dimensions

Scales	Social	Competence	Affect	Academic	Family	Physical
Adaptive Behavior Inventory (Brown & Leigh, 1986)	X	X		X		
Adaptive Behavior Inventory for Children (Mercer & Lewis, 1978)	X	X		X	X	
Assessment of Interpersonal Relations (Bracken, 1993)	X			X	X	
Beck Depression Inventory (Beck, 1987a)			X			
Beck Hopelessness Scale (Beck, 1987b)			X			
Behavior Evaluation Scale—2 (McCarney & Leigh, 1990)	X		X	X		X
Behavior Rating Profile—2 (Brown & Hammill, 1990)						
Student Form	X			X	X	
Parent Form				X	X	
Teacher Form				X		
Bruininks-Oseretsky Test of Motor Proficiency (Bruininks, 1978)						X
Burks' Behavior Rating Scales (Burks, 1968)	X	X	X	X		X
California Psychological Inventory—Revised (Gough, 1987)	X	X	X	X		
Center for Epidemiological Studies Depression Scale for Children (Weissman, Orvaschel, & Padian, 1980)			X			
Child Behavior Checklist for Ages 4–16 (Achenbach & Edelbrock, 1983)	X	X				
Teacher's Report Form (Achenbach & Edelbrock, 1986)	X	X		X		

	1	2	3	4	5	6
Youth Self-Report (Achenbach & Edelbrock, 1987)	X	X				
Children's Depression Inventory (Kovacs, 1983)				X		
Children's Personality Questionnaire (Porter & Cattell, 1982)		X		X		
Children's Problems Checklist (Schinka, 1985a)		X		X		X
Children's Self-Efficacy for Peer Interaction Scale (Wheeler & Ladd, 1982)	X					
Comprehensive Behavior Rating Scale for Children (Neeper, Lahey, & Frick, 1990)	X	X		X		X
Comprehensive Test of Adaptive Behavior (Adams, 1984a)	X	X		X		X
Conner's Rating Scales (Conners, 1989)						
Teacher 28	X			X		
Teacher 39				X		
Parent 48	X			X		X
Parent 93				X		X
Depression Self-Rating Scale (Birleson, 1980)				X		
Differential Ability Scales (Elliott, 1990)		X				
Edwards Personal Preference Schedule (Edwards, 1959)	X	X		X		
Family Adaptability and Cohesion Evaluation Scales, III (Olson, Portner, & Lavee, 1985)					X	

(Continued)

Scales	Social	Competence	Affect	Academic	Family	Physical
Family Assessment Measure, III (Skinner, Steinhauer, & Santa-Barbara, 1984)					X	
Family Coping Strategies Inventory (Olson, McCubbin, Barnes, Larsen, Muxen, & Wilson, 1982a)					X	
Family Environment Scale (Moos & Moos, 1986) Children's version (Pino, Simons, & Slawinowski, 1984)					X	
Family Satisfaction Inventory (Olson & Wilson, 1982)					X	
Generalized Anxiety Scale for Children (Sarason, Davidson, Lighthall, Waite, & Ruebush, 1960)			X			
Gordon Personal Profile-Inventory (Gordon, 1978)	X	X	X			
High School Personality Questionnaire (Cattell, Cattell, & Johns, 1984)	X	X	X			X
Hopelessness Scale (Kazdin, French, Unis, Esveldt-Dawson, & Sherick, 1983)			X			
IPAT Anxiety Scale (Cattell, Scheier, & IPAT Staff, 1976)			X			
Iowa Social Competence Scales (Pease, Clark, & Crase, 1982)	X		X		X	
KeyMath Revised: A Diagnostic Inventory of Essential Mathematics (Connolly, 1988)				X		
Matson Evaluation of Social Skills with Youngsters (Matson, Rotatori, & Helsel, 1983)	X					X

Instrument				
Millon Adolescent Personality Inventory (Millon, Green, & Meagher, 1982)		X		
Minnesota Multiphasic Personality Inventory, Adolescent Norms (Hathaway & Monachesi, 1963)	X	X		X
Mooney Problem Checklists (Mooney & Gordon, 1950)	X		X	X
Normative Adaptive Behavior Checklist (Adams, 1984b)	X	X	X	X
Parent Acceptance-Rejection Questionnaire (Rohner, 1984)			X	X
Parent-Adolescent Communication Scale (Olson, McCubbin, Barnes, Larsen, Muxen, & Wilson, 1982b)		X		X
Peabody Individual Achievement Test-Revised (Markwardt, 1989)			X	
Personal Problems Checklist—Adolescent (Schinka, 1985b)	X	X	X	X
Personality Inventory for Children (Wirt, Lachar, Klinedinst, & Seat, 1984)	X	X	X	X
Piers-Harris Children's Self-Concept Scale (Piers, 1984)	X	X	X	X
Quality of Life Inventory (Olson & Barnes, 1982)	X	X	X	X
Revised Children's Manifest Anxiety Scale (Reynolds & Richmond, 1985)		X		
Reynolds Adolescent Depression Scale (Reynolds, 1987)		X		
Roberts Apperception Test for Children (McArthur & Roberts, 1982)	X	X	X	X

(Continued)

Scales	Social	Competence	Affect	Academic	Family	Physical
School Behavior Checklist (Miller, 1981)	X	X	X	X		
Self-Concept of Academic Ability (Brookover, Thomas, & Paterson, 1964)				X		
Self-Description Questionnaire, I (Marsh, 1988)	X			X	X	X
Self-Description Questionnaire, II (Marsh, 1990)	X		X	X	X	X
Self-Efficacy for Academic Tasks (Owen & Baum, 1985)				X		
Self-Esteem Index (Brown & Alexander, 1990)	X	X		X	X	X
Self-Esteem Inventory (Coopersmith, 1984)	X			X	X	
Self-Perception Profile for Children (Harter, 1982b)	X	X		X		X
Sixteen Personality Factor Questionnaire (Cattell & IPAT Staff, 1986)	X	X	X			
Social Skills Rating System (Gresham & Elliott, 1990)	X	X				
Social-Emotional Dimension Scale (Hutton & Roberts, 1986)	X		X	X		X
Stanford-Binet Intelligence Scale, 4th Edition (Thorndike, Hagen, & Sattler, 1986)		X				
State-Trait Anxiety Inventory for Children (Spielberger, 1973)			X			
State-Trait Anxiety Inventory (Spielberger, 1983)			X			

Structural Family Interaction Scale-Revised
(Form A)
  (Perosa, 1986)   X

Tennessee Self-Concept Scale
  (Roid & Fitts, 1988)   X   X   X

Test of Gross Motor Development
  (Ulrich, 1985)   X   X

Vineland Adaptive Behavior Scales
  (Sparrow, Balla, & Cicchetti, 1984)   X   X   X

Waksman Social Skills Rating Scale
  (Waksman, 1984)   X

Walker Problem Behavior Identification Checklist
  (Walker, 1983)   X

Wechsler Adult Intelligence Scale—Revised
  (Wechsler, 1981)   X

Wechsler Intelligence Scale for Children—III
  (Wechsler, 1993)   X

Woodcock-Johnson Psychoeducational
Battery-Revised: Achievement
  (Woodcock & Johnson, 1989)   X

Woodcock-Johnson Psychoeducational
Battery—Revised: Cognitive
  (Woodcock & Johnson, 1989)   X

Woodcock Reading Mastery Tests—Revised
  (Woodcock, 1987)   X

Source: From *Multidimensional Self Concept Scale* by B. A. Bracken, 1992, Austin, TX: Pro-Ed. Copyright 1992 by Pro-Ed. Used with permission.

Author Index

Abbott, D. A., 178
Abraham, S. F., 386
Abramovitch, R., 348
Abramson, L. Y., 29, 210, 224–225
Achenbach, T. M., 338, 506–507
Ackerman, J. J., 264
Adams, G. L., 507, 509
Adams, G. R., 374
Adams, J. A., 271
Adams, N. E., 221
Adler, A., 476
Adler, M., 210, 350
Agnew, J., 463
Agustsdottir, S., 423, 431
Ainsworth, M. D. S., 242, 323, 331, 333
Akamatsu, T. J., 192
Alessandri, S. M., 356
Alexander, J., 138, 295, 468, 510
Alfon, M. C. A., 290
Allen, D. M., 277
Allen, J. E., 196
Allen, J. P., 341
Allesandri, A., 178
Allison, P. D., 351
Alloy, T., 29
Allport, G. W., 24, 441, 447
Als, H., 230
Amato, G., 235–237, 241
Amerikaner, M., 204
Ames, C., 215
Anastasi, A., 489
Anderson, C. M., 445
Anderson, E. R., 352
Andrews, D., 274
Archer, S. L., 347
Arellano, O. R., 297

Arend, R. A., 331, 334
Arkin, R. M., 435
Arnold, M. B., 427
Asher, S. R., 191–192, 194, 200
Ashmore, C., 319, 321–322, 345, 358
Astilla, E., 303
Atkinson, J. W., 214, 216
Averill, J. R., 427

Bachman, J. G., 304, 399, 401, 403, 410, 413
Bailey, W. T., 340
Bakker, F. C., 383
Bales, R. F., 339
Balk, D. E., 277
Balla, D. A., 13, 264, 269, 511
Bandura, A., 30, 210–211, 218–224, 238, 248, 434, 447, 465–466
Bannister, D., 463
Barabas, G., 271
Bardos, A. N., 153
Barnes, H., 351, 508–509
Barnes, J., 62, 68, 72, 91, 180, 182, 186, 188, 291, 385, 399–400, 440
Barrett, K. C., 226–228
Barrios, B. A., 381
Bartlett, F. C., 8
Battle, J., 29, 91
Baum, S. M., 510
Baumeister, R. F., 26, 29, 431–432, 437
Baumgardner, A. H., 432, 435
Baumrind, D., 237–238, 351
Beals, J., 351
Bear, G. G., 201
Beaumont, P. J., 386
Beavers, W., 351

513

Subject Index